HARDY RHODODENDRON SPECIES

HARDY RHODODENDRON SPECIES

A Guide to Identification

JAMES CULLEN

With photographs by
DEBBIE WHITE AND FRIEDA CHRISTIE

Published in association with the
Royal Botanic Garden Edinburgh

TIMBER PRESS

Published in 2005 by
Timber Press, Inc.
The Haseltine Building
133 S.W. Second Avenue, Suite 450
Portland, Oregon 97204-3527, U.S.A.
www.timberpress.com
For contact information for editorial, marketing, sales, and distribution in the United Kingdom, see www.timberpress.com/uk.

Printed in China

Library of Congress Cataloging-in-Publication Data

Cullen, J. (James)
Hardy rhododendron species : a guide to identification / James Cullen ; with photographs by Debbie White and Frieda Christie.
p. cm.
"Published in association with the Royal Botanic Garden Edinburgh."
Includes bibliographical references and index.
ISBN 0-88192-723-6 (hardback)
1. Rhododendrons—Identification. I. Royal Botanic Garden, Edinburgh. II. Title.
QK495.E68C85 2005
635.9'3366—dc22

2005002199

A catalog record for this book is also available from the British Library.

In memory of Richard L. Shaw,

curator of living collections,
first at the Royal Botanic Gardens, Kew,
later at the Royal Botanic Garden Edinburgh

Contents

Preface

THE AIM of this volume is to provide an accurate means of identification for those species of the genus *Rhododendron* that are cultivated in Britain, western Europe, and parts of North America. The stress is very much on the species: this is not a manual for the identification of hybrids. The knowledgeable rhododendron grower looking at this statement might well think, "What's the good of that? A very large proportion of the rhododendrons cultivated in the areas mentioned are, in fact, hybrids, and what's really needed is some means of accurate identification for these."

The assertion that many of the rhododendrons cultivated in these areas are hybrids is, indeed, correct (except for the contents of a few botanic gardens), and it is also true that an accurate means of identifying them would be extremely useful. However, well over 30,000 hybrids and cultivars have been developed during the last 250 years, many of them deliberately and knowingly, others accidentally; and, being long-lived woody plants, many of them, even the older ones, are still in existence. In order to understand, identify, and name these hybrids, it is necessary first to understand the species (and subspecies, varieties, and, indeed, the overall classification of the genus) which occur in the wild. This cannot be overstressed: the wild species form the foundation on which the hybrids are raised, and if they are not understood, the hybrids cannot be understood. While this book does touch on some significant features of the hybrids, their identification is a matter of considerable difficulty which will ultimately require a very large, separate reference. The production of a reliable list of hybrids and their parents is an ongoing process; reference should be made to Fletcher (1952) and the supplements to it published annually since 1952 by the Royal Horticultural Society.

In this book, the accurate identification of the species (and the groups—subgenera, sections, and subsections—between the genus and the species) is made possible through standard taxonomic forms: keys and descriptions. The layout of these follows normal practice, though the descriptions are broken down into individual characteristics so as to make comparison of one with another as easy as possible. In addition to the standard dichotomous keys, 2 other identification tools are provided: identification tables and character lists. I hope these will help gardeners to identify species accurately while soothing any fears about using scientific keys.

This book does not, of course, include the many new species of *Rhododendron* which have been described in recent years but which have not yet found their way into cultivation in Europe. For illustrations of many of these, see *Flora of China Illustrations,* volume 14 (Raven et al. 2005; Science Press, Beijing).

Acknowledgements

This book represents the fruit of many years' work on the genus, which I first became interested in while working in the early 1960s at Ness Botanic Gardens (University of Liverpool). This interest continued when I returned to the Royal Botanic Garden Edinburgh in the 1970s. So many people have helped me to an understanding of the genus that it is impossible to list them all—I hope they will accept this general thanks for the assistance they have given me. In particular, though, I must thank the staff of the Royal Botanic Garden Edinburgh, especially those in charge of the living collections, herbarium, and library. The photographs in this book are of plants growing in the Edinburgh garden, and I am extremely grateful to Debbie White and Frieda Christie for taking so much trouble to get exactly the pictures I wanted. Also I must thank Ida Maspero for her help in dealing with the publication of the book. Anna Mumford and Mindy Fitch of Timber Press have been constantly helpful and extremely patient in waiting for the completed typescript. The online library catalogue of the Royal Botanic Gardens, Kew, has made the job of searching the literature much easier, and I am very grateful for its existence, though I can't acknowledge, because I don't know, those who did all the work to make it possible.

Introduction to Classification and Identification

THE CLASSIFICATION of plants is a process rather than an object. It exists in history and is constantly modified as new discoveries are made or new interpretations of old facts are accepted. The process is entirely open: anyone with the interest or knowledge can make a contribution by publishing a paper which has classificatory content, and this content then becomes available for acceptance or rejection. Of course, to be published in a reputable scientific journal, such a contribution would have to be peer reviewed; any efforts that are not serious or properly informed would be cut out. Furthermore, even after publication there is no official stamp of approval which states that the work is accepted. It remains there, in publication, for others to pick up and use as they think fit. Thus, at any moment, classification is like a snapshot of what taxonomists currently accept; it is a changing, unmoderated consensus. Contributions may lie fallow for 10, 20, 30 years or more and then be picked up and incorporated into the current consensus, while others which have been accepted as important for years may be dropped. The fact that this process is entirely unmoderated (I am not thinking here of nomenclature, which is governed by regularly altered [improved?] international rules) comes as a great surprise to most gardeners, who tend to think there is some authority which rules that "this plant belongs to species A, which is distinguished from species B, C, D, and so forth in particular ways, and which belongs to genus X and family Y"—and that's what is accepted. The realisation that this is not the case is often a shock at first, though most find it ultimately liberating.

The History of Classification

In order to have a working understanding of the classification of a group of plants, it is necessary to have some idea of the way the current situation has come about. The history of the classification is based on other histories: the history of exploration and the finding of new taxa, the history of taxonomic thought, and, with plants like rhododendrons, which are important to gardeners, the history of their introduction into horticulture and their propagation thereafter. (The history of rhododendrons in gardens is dealt with in considerable detail in Cynthia Postan's *The Rhododendron Story,* published by the Royal Horticultural Society in 1996.)

The history of the exploration of the world and the discovery and introduction of new plants, including *Rhododendron* species and other taxa, is well documented and has often been related (see especially Philipson and Philipson 1974, 1996). It is useful to note how history directly affects the slowly changing taxonomic consensus.

Though rhododendrons of some kind have been known to Western gardeners since early historic times, the present discussion finds a convenient starting point in the publication, in 1753, of *Species Plantarum* by Carolus Linnaeus (Carl von Linné). *Species Plantarum,* which is used as the starting point for the binomial system of plant nomenclature, was probably the first conscious scientific attempt to record and distinguish *all* plants known at the time. It includes information on about 10,000 species, of which only 9 fall into what today would be considered *Rhododendron.* Linnaeus treats these 9 species under 2 generic names: *Azalea* (including what are now known as *R. indicum, R. ponticum, R. luteum, R. viscosum,* and *R. lapponicum,* as well as the plant currently known as *Loiseleuria procumbens*), and *Rhododendron* (including *R. ferrugineum, R. dauricum, R. hirsutum,* and *R. maximum,* as well as *Rhodothamnus chamaecistus*).

The distinction Linnaeus made between the 2 genera was based on his breaking down of the whole of the flowering plants into groups based on the number of stamens and the number of ovary units in the flower. Thus, *Azalea* belongs in the Pentandria Monogyna (plants in which the flowers have 5 stamens and a unitary ovary), whereas *Rhododendron* belongs in Decandria Monogyna (plants with 10 stamens in the flower and a unitary ovary). Linnaeus clearly got quite a lot of his counting wrong, as *R. ponticum* and *R. lapponicum* generally have 10 stamens rather than 5.

The separation into 2 genera, which has bedevilled the classification ever since 1753 (one of the most frequently asked questions at gatherings where rhododendrons are discussed is "What exactly is an azalea, anyway?"), illustrates a very common phenomenon seen in the early stages of classification, before most of the units to be included in it have been discovered: because of the paucity of material available, distinctions between supposed units can be made which later are found to have little or no significance.

The 9 species known to Linnaeus in 1753 (less than 1⁄100 of the total known today) are, with the exception of *R. indicum,* from marginal areas of the distribution of the genus: Turkey, eastern United States, Scandinavia, the Alps, and eastern Russia (Dauria). At the time, nothing was known of the riches of the Himalaya, western China, or Papua New Guinea (this last for section *Vireya,* which is not covered in this book.) Towards the end of the 18th century, rhododendrons were being grown in gardens, and gardeners were looking for new kinds. The first rhododendron to be illustrated in *Curtis's Botanical Magazine* (first published in 1787 and continuously published since then under various titles—a fine barometer of which new species are fashionable at any particular time) was *R. canadense* (plate 474, published in 1800). This species was unknown to Linnaeus in 1753, although it is also from one of the marginal areas.

As plant exploration continued and expanded during the early part of the 19th century, the number of species known to science and available to gardeners slowly expanded. Many tropical and subtropical species (section *Vireya*) were discovered and introduced from Southeast Asia by the Dutch, and several more hardy species were discovered in North America. The earliest introductions from the Himalaya (*R. arboreum*, *R. campanulatum*) came in the late 1820s, and these plants were prized by gardeners for their "exotic" qualities. Towards the middle of the century it became clear that it was relatively easy to hybridise rhododendrons. This immediately led to attempts to combine particular qualities of the slightly tender *R. arboreum*, such as plant size and exotic flower shape and colour, with smaller, hardier species. For example, *R.* ×*russellianum*, raised in 1831, is a hybrid between the Himalayan *R. arboreum* and the eastern North American *R. catawbiense*. This was an attempt to combine the great hardiness and moderate size of *catawbiense* with the striking flower trusses and leaf indumentum of *arboreum*, and it illustrates the point that the possibility of crossing species from widely different geographical areas was already understood.

Similarly, in the 1840s, Pierre Mortier, the baker of Ghent, Belgium, began to hybridise various deciduous species still thought to belong to the genus *Azalea*. Most of these species were North American, though it is possible he made use of the Chinese *R. molle* as well. The result of Mortier's crosses was a group of hybrids now known as Ghent azaleas. Mortier was particularly careful not to reveal the species he had used to produce these hybrids, and the secret died with him (though much can be inferred from the nature of the plants of the group which still exist). His hybrids were further developed in the United Kingdom in the late 19th and early 20th centuries (Knaphill and Exbury azaleas).

The next major step in *Rhododendron* study and introduction came with Joseph Hooker's collecting expedition to Sikkim (eastern India, adjacent to western Xizang [Tibet]) which took place from 1848 to 1850. Hooker collected plants of all kinds, not just rhododendrons, and collected a large number of herbarium specimens (for the herbarium of the Royal Botanic Gardens, Kew, where his father, William Hooker, was Director) as well as seed for introduction to horticulture. His work on the identification and classification of the rhododendrons he discovered was handsomely published in 2 volumes as *Rhododendrons of the Sikkim Himalaya* (1849, 1851), which includes very precise descriptions and notes on 43 species (many of them new) and 33 beautiful hand-coloured paintings done by Hooker himself (some of them of the plants *in situ*) and engraved by W. H. Fitch. At 49 × 33 cm, these painting are very grand, and they initiated a tradition of the publication of books of paintings of rhododendrons, which continues to this day.

Hooker realised that the climatic conditions in which he collected his rhododendrons (mostly in forests at more than 3000 m in altitude) suggested that the plants could be successfully grown in parts of Britain. The seed he collected was distributed to many notable gardens, and many of the plants were raised to flowering size. Several plants which are thought, with some confidence, to be Hooker rhododendrons, still survive in British gardens—for example, at Castle Kennedy in Dumfriesshire. For more detail about Hooker's travels and publication, and the existence today of plants introduced by him, see Forrest (1996).

The publication of Hooker's work, and the expansion of British interests in "British India" (which eventually included Burma [Myanmar]) led to a trickle of new species in the 3rd quarter of the 19th century. The striking nature of many of these Himalayan plants produced a further wave of hybridisation, as these new species were crossed both among themselves and with American and European species already in cultivation (notably *R. ponticum* and its allies), giving rise to what are now termed Old Hardy Hybrids, very tough plants, many of which are still to be found in parks and gardens of 19th-century origin.

In the 1870s and 1880s, French Jesuit missionaries were allowed for the first time into various parts of China. Many of them had botanical interests (and, as far as can be judged, plenty of time on their hands) and collected both herbarium specimens and seed, which they sent back to the Muséum National d'Histoire Naturelle and the Jardin des Plantes in Paris. Their collections, particularly those of Pére Armand David and Pére Jean Marie Delavay, who collected mainly in southwestern China, showed for the first time that this area, especially the part of it adjacent to the eastern end of the Himalayan chain, where deep river valleys cut through mountain ranges more than 7000 m in altitude, had an astonishingly rich flora, including many species of *Rhododendron*. The herbarium specimens they collected were worked over by Adrien Franchet of the Muséum National d'Histoire Naturelle, the great unsung hero of *Rhododendron* classification. He published descriptions and fine illustrations of many species in *Plantae Davidianae*, published in 2 parts (1883, 1889), and *Plantae Delavayanae*, published in 3 parts (1889–1890). Franchet was an excellent taxonomist: most of the species he described as new have persisted and been recognised right through to the present day. More detail on the French missionary collectors is provided in Lennon (1985).

The seeds collected by the missionaries were sent back to the Jardin des Plantes for raising and growing on, though it seems none survived as living plants for very long. According to rumour they were given a highly inappropriate stove treatment, something unsuitable for these plants, even if practical for the more tropical species of section *Vireya* which were being grown by the Dutch.

The accuracy of this rumour is uncertain, but regardless, the publication of

Franchet's work and the rumours of what was happening in the Jardin des Plantes alerted several botanists and gardeners in Britain to the potential riches of southwestern China. This led to many discussions and ultimately to the sending of George Forrest on the first of his expeditions to the area. Forrest, who had been a herbarium assistant at the Royal Botanic Garden Edinburgh for some years, was supported by a group of keen growers, headed at first by A. K. Bulley of Ness near Chester, founder of Bees' Seeds and a very enthusiastic rhododendron grower (see McLean 1997), and supported by Sir Isaac Bayley Balfour, Regius Keeper at Edinburgh from 1888 to 1922, who had recommended Forrest as the right man in the first instance.

Forrest was the ideal plant collector. His outstanding herbarium material, including more than 2000 collections of rhododendrons, is now in the herbarium of the Royal Botanic Garden Edinburgh, with duplicate (partial) sets in other herbaria, including that in Beijing. As far as *Rhododendron* is concerned (though it applies really across the board), he collected very carefully and made well-dried, well-presented specimens with detailed notes on their localities, habitats, and altitudes, and on various characteristics of the plants themselves, such as flower colour. He labelled plants from which he collected specimens in flower so they could be revisited in autumn for the collection of seed, and he did this either by himself or with the help of native Chinese collectors he had personally trained. Thus, for most of his seed introductions to gardens, we have not only the living plants but also the herbarium specimens of the original wild plants in flower and in fruit. The existence of such series of specimens, all with cross-referenced numbers, allows us to determine whether the living plants that we have under these numbers belong to the same species (subspecies, variety) as the material he originally collected. (If they don't, of course, then the Forrest number on the living plant is incorrect and must be dropped.)

Forrest made 9 expeditions to western China (parts of Yunnan, Sichuan, and Xizang), with occasional diversions into adjacent Burma. Many of the expeditions lasted more than a year, allowing him to revisit areas at different times. Forrest died on his final expedition in 1931. He had made almost 30,000 gatherings (herbarium specimens), of which more than 2000 were rhododendrons. A high proportion of these were also collected as seed, and many are available today as living plants. The seed was sent back to a consortium of growers and gardeners in Britain and distributed among them for growing on. The main set, however, and the herbarium specimens were sent to Edinburgh, where Balfour and his co-workers and successors worked on their classification.

Much detail about Forrest and his collections is available in Brenda McLean's "George Forrest" (2004a), a digest of which has also been published (2004b). Earlier relevant publications include Cooper, Curle, and Fair (1935) and Cowan (1952).

Another important collector working in the same broad area and at the same time (and later) was Frank Kingdon-Ward. Kingdon-Ward was the son of Marshall Ward, Professor of Botany at Cambridge from 1895 to 1906, but was himself more of a geographer than a botanist. However, he made numerous expeditions to eastern Asia, which he subsidised by collecting plants and seeds. He covered a wider area than Forrest, collecting in eastern India, western Xizang, and subtropical Burma as well as in southwestern China. He collected a considerable number of rhododendrons, both as herbarium specimens and as seed. His collections are not so well organised as Forrest's: for many seed numbers there is no equivalent herbarium specimen (either in flower or in fruit), so it is not possible to compare living plants with his original material. Nonetheless, Kingdon-Ward visited areas not touched by other collectors, and his plants are extremely important. He made his last expedition (to Burma) in 1953. He wrote many books on his travels, and these were extremely popular. They contain much helpful information on the rhododendrons he collected. For further details of Kingdon-Ward's life and expeditions, see Schweinfurth and Schweinfurth-Marby (1975).

The 3rd really important rhododendron collector operating in southwestern China in the first half of the 20th century was Joseph Rock. Rock was an American of Viennese origin, a polymath whose interests included botany, zoology, anthropology, languages, and photography. He collected a large number of artefacts of all kinds, as well as botanical and zoological specimens. For a considerable period he had a house in Lijiang in Yunnan, and collected widely in Yunnan, Sichuan, and further north in Hubei. Like Forrest, Rock tried to collect suites of specimens (seed, herbarium specimens in flower and in fruit) linked by cross-referenced numbers, but he was not as consistent as Forrest in this. In 1949 Rock had to leave Yunnan for Burma, travelling ahead of Mao Tse-tung's Red Army; while retreating, he continued to collect specimens and seed. His herbarium specimens, at least of *Rhododendron,* ended up in Edinburgh, and the seed he collected was distributed mainly by the U.S. Department of Agriculture; much of it arrived in Britain and was grown on.

The only Chinese collector of rhododendrons well known in Britain was T. T. Yü. Yü made extensive collections of rhododendrons in Yunnan, Sichuan, and Xizang in the 1930s; in order to identify them he had to bring them to Edinburgh to compare them with the material being worked on by Balfour's successors (particularly Sir William Wright Smith). At the outbreak of the Second World War, Yü had to return to China, but a duplicate set of his collections was left in Edinburgh for further study. This included some seed, which was, of course, grown on.

Forrest, Kingdon-Ward, Rock, and Yü were the main collectors of what is now thought of as the classic period of rhododendron collection in China, but there were others who collected in areas more marginal to the extremely rich Yunnan-Sichuan area. Such areas clearly had fewer species, but those that were found were usually different from those from Yunnan and Sichuan. Notable among these collectors are E. H. Wilson, who collected in northern Sichuan and Hubei (see Wilson 1913), and Reginald Farrer, who collected in Burma and in areas of Hubei and Gansu (see Cox 1933). Also of minor importance for rhododendrons were the German collectors Heinrich Handel-Mazzetti and Camillo Karl Schneider, both of whom did some co-collecting with Forrest.

Lists of field notes from the classic collections were published privately during the 1930s, and lists of collectors' numbers continued to be published in the various editions of *The Rhododendron Handbook* (1947 and later).

During the classic period in China, collecting also continued in the Himalaya and western Xizang. Most notable among these collectors were Frank Ludlow and Charles Sherriff, as well as their co-collectors, George Taylor, H. Elliott, and G. H. Hicks. Between 1933 and 1949 they collected in Bhutan, southwestern Xizang, Kashmir, and Sikkim. They again collected both seed and herbarium specimens, but not in the highly coordinated suites of Forrest's collections. Their herbarium specimens were returned to the Natural History Museum in London, where Ludlow was a staff member, with a duplicate set to Edinburgh; seed was sent directly to Edinburgh and was distributed from there to other gardens. More information on these collectors and their collections can be found in Fletcher (1975). Other collectors working in the Himalayan area were R. E. Cooper, Curator at the Edinburgh garden between 1934 and 1950, and G. E. Cave of the Calcutta Botanic Garden.

Because of the activities of all these collectors, an enormous amount of new rhododendron material arrived in Edinburgh, mainly in the form of herbarium specimens but also as seed which grew into living plants. The job of classifying and describing all this new material fell to Isaac Bayley Balfour, who, as previously mentioned, was Regius Keeper at Edinburgh. With this new material, Balfour and his co-workers, including Forrest, Kingdon-Ward, and Farrer, as well as other herbarium staff members at Edinburgh such as William Wright Smith (who succeeded Balfour as Regius Keeper), H. F. Tagg, and W. E. Evans, were presented with a number of problems. What of it represented new species, hitherto unknown? What of it was already known and described? How should the species, once described, be grouped so that new ones could be quickly placed with those they most resembled? It was necessary that these problems be dealt with quickly, as botanists and gardeners (particularly those interested in hybridisation) were anxious to have names and descriptions for all the plants. Most of the taxonomic work was done on the basis of the herbarium specimens accumulated at Edinburgh and elsewhere. For more on the importance of such specimens, see Cullen (1996).

In an amazing series of papers, published between 1916 and 1921, Balfour described 320 new species of *Rhododendron*. The amount of work and study behind this publication (which amounts to 460 pages) is truly phenomenal and shows Balfour's ability to understand and synthesise a vast amount of information, which of course includes consideration of not only the new species but also those found to be already known. It seems that Balfour developed 2 rules of thumb to help him get through the vast amount of material: 1) no species occurred in both India (specifically the Himalaya) and China, and 2) if a specimen seemed different enough from the others it should be described as a new species so that attention could be drawn to it (if eventually it turned out not to be new, at least it wouldn't be overlooked).

The grouping of the species occupied Balfour from an early stage, and notes on groupings occur in various places in his long first paper, published in 1916. He began to group the species into "series." These were defined by choosing well-known and clearly defined species as the centres of each series, and then grouping around them the species that seemed most similar. Each series was named after the central species (for example, *Thomsonii* series), adding around this the species that seemed most similar. Among the first fruits of this process was Balfour's publication of a review of the species in what he then called the "Irroratum" series (1917), to be followed shortly by a revision of the "Maddenii" series by J. B. Hutchinson (1919) of the Royal Botanic Gardens, Kew. Later some of the series were divided into 2 or more subseries.

The subsequent development of the "series" classification, which was acknowledged by its author as a temporary expedient to cope with the vast numbers of new species, can be followed in the pages of the *Rhododendron Society Notes,* of which the first issue was published in 1917, the last in 1931.

This system was brought to a position of stability in 1930 with the publication by the Rhododendron Society of *The Species of Rhododendron* (a 2nd "edition" was produced almost immediately by the publication of individual pages which could easily be placed in the original publication in the correct place in the alphabetical sequence). The book was edited by J. B. Stevenson of Tower Court, a notable rhododendron grower and a founding member of the Rhododendron Society. The actual writing was done by H. F. Tagg, who dealt with the elepidote species; J. B. Hutchinson, who handled the lepidote species; and Alfred Rehder of the Arnold Arboretum, near Boston, Massachusetts, who contributed the text of the *Azalea* series, following the publication, 9 years earlier, of his and E. H. Wilson's monograph of the group (1921). Leaving aside the subtropical species of section *Vireya* (the names of the species of this group were merely listed) and including the additions which formed the 2nd edition, the book includes descriptions of 685 species arranged in 42 series, some of them subdivided into subseries, making a total of 75 supraspecific units. Within each series or subseries, the species are alphabetically arranged, the subseries are alphabetically ordered within the series, and the series themselves form a single alphabetical sequence. One page is dedicated to each species, hence the ease of production and inclusion of additional pages. Under each series and subseries is a key to the species included within it, though there is no key to the series themselves. The objectives of the book were cogently set out by the editor:

> The aim of those responsible for the issue of the present handbook has been to provide a single-page description of each species and to attempt to group the species into series so as to facilitate understanding and recognition. The first half of this task, though extensive, has been accomplished with a degree of completeness, but the second part is admittedly tentative and will no doubt require adjustment. There are many difficulties. The number of species is in itself somewhat overwhelming; many are inadequately known; sometimes only imperfect dried specimens are available; lines of demarcation between one series and another are sometimes definite, but in other cases very difficult to draw; observations on living material are often not forthcoming, as many species are not yet in cultivation; the original specimens on which the descriptions are based—what are known as *types*—are to be found some in one herbarium and some in another, scattered throughout the botanical institutions of the world.
>
> It is therefore with no idea of finality that the present book appears. Though one may assume that the majority of the species of the genus are known, there are many still to be found, for the geographical area of the genus is as yet inadequately explored.

Though much has changed and improved, these views still have force.

Work along lines deriving from the publication of *The Species of Rhododendron* continued at the Royal Botanic Garden Edinburgh by J. M. Cowan and H. H. Davidian, involving the publications of revisions of various series (mainly in the Royal Horticultural Society's *Rhododendron Yearbook*). This process led ultimately to the publication of Davidian's *Rhododendron Species* in 4 volumes (1982–1995).

Meanwhile, other taxonomists were working on the subtropical species of section *Vireya*. This work culminated in the publication of the account of the genus in the Dutch-organised *Flora Malesiana* (1968), written over a long period by Herman Sleumer, a very experienced Berlin-trained taxonomist. Sleumer was well aware of the "series" classification developed at Edinburgh and knew it did not conform to the way supraspecific classification was dealt with in the rest of the flowering plants under the *International Code of Botanical Nomenclature*. In "Ein System der Gattung *Rhododendron*" (1949), Sleumer made a first attempt at correcting this situation, bringing the series and subseries into the standard taxonomic hierarchy (subgenera, sections, subsections); most of the series reappear in Sleumer's classification, mainly at the level of subsection, though some are at the sectional or subgeneric level. This classification conformed to normal taxonomic practice and was accepted almost everywhere in the world except Britain and the United States, where the gardeners' classification remained in use.

Following the closure of China and the publication of Sleumer's revision (both in 1949), a certain amount of retrenchment took place, as the flood of potential new species more or less dried up. On the purely taxonomic side, J. M. Cowan and H. H. Davidian continued with work in the Edinburgh tradition but also stimulated work in other areas, notably the anatomy of the leaves, leading to 2 important publications: Hayes, Keenan, and Cowan's study of the leaf anatomy (1951) and Cowan's *The Rhododendron Leaf: A Study of the Epidermal Appendages* (1950), which, as the title implies, concentrates on the hairs and scales of the leaf surfaces. Both publications were concerned with the use of anatomical characters in the classification of the genus.

Since 1950 much work has been carried out using other techniques to improve the classification. Of these projects, the most important has been the study of secondary chemical products (Harborne and Williams 1969; Harborne 1980; Evans, Knights, and Math 1975; Evans, Knights, Math, and Ritchie 1975; Evans et al. 1980), as well as further, more detailed studies of other structures, such as hairs (Seithe 1960, 1980), seeds (Hedegaard 1980), and the ovary and fruit (Palser et al. 1985).

In 1972 the Royal Botanic Garden Edinburgh decided that its taxonomic work should concentrate on the family Ericaceae, with special emphasis on the genus *Rhododendron* (the garden holds the largest collection of both herbarium and living specimens of *Rhododendron* in the world). D. F. Chamberlain and I took on the study of the genus, revisiting all the results of former Edinburgh workers. All herbarium specimens were restudied in great detail, living specimens in the Edinburgh and other gardens were revised, and the whole was compared with the overall revision of the genus produced by Sleumer. All this work, which later involved Melva and Bill Philipson, who had revised the "Lapponicum" series independently in 1975, and Walter S. Judd and Kathleen Kron, who worked on various "azalea" groups, was published as a series of papers in *Notes from the Royal Botanic Garden Edinburgh*. This work forms the basis of the study of the genus today, and of this book.

Name Changes

Gardeners are often confounded and annoyed by the changes in the names of species (and higher groups) when these changes seem to be pulled out of a hat for no obvious reason by taxonomic botanists. Rhododendron growers are no different in this respect, and it seems worthwhile to illustrate some of the reasons why plant names do change and what the genuine advantages are of the taxonomic process.

The almost frenzied exploration of new areas and description of new species that characterised the first 40 years of the 20th century produced a complex situation in which some species were described more than once, giving rise to 2 or more names for the same species. The *International Code of Botanical Nomenclature* provides a means for deciding which of several competing names (synonyms) is the one that should be used; generally the selected name is the oldest one conforming to the rules. Of course, the decision as to what the actual species are is separate, and based on the taxonomist's judgement.

The existence of synonyms, for species or other taxonomic units, arises from several sources: older, formerly overlooked names can be found again; widely used names can be judged illegitimate under the rules; and, of course, the same unit can be described and named more than once. The main cause for this is that the variability of the species (or higher groups) is not fully appreciated. This was particularly true in the early days of exploration, when the number of specimens representing each "species" was relatively small.

All plant species are variable in almost all their features, including the features used in making distinctions between them. A collector, coming across a population of plants for the first time, may well collect a few specimens from it. These specimens may be adjudged to be a new species, which is then described and named. Let us say this population occurs in China and has flowers with corollas 2.8–3.2 cm long. Later, in the Himalaya, another population is found of plants very similar to the first ones but with corollas 1.5–2.5 cm long. Because of the clear distinction in corolla length, it is decided that this 2nd, Chinese population represents a new species, allied to the first one but differing, *inter alia*, in corolla size. In the early days these species are represented in herbaria and gardens by a small number of specimens. Later, collections in both areas produce more specimens from different populations, and study of the corolla sizes reveals that all is not as clear-cut as had been thought: in the Himalayan populations, corollas are found up to 2.7 cm long, and in the Chinese populations, corollas are 2.4–3.7 cm long. Thus the clear distinction in size is obscured, and the total range of corolla length is 1.5–3.7. It is found that most of the Himalayan plants have corollas 1.5–2.5 cm long, with just a few plants with corollas longer than this; the Chinese plants mostly have corollas 2.6–3.7 cm long, with just a small number with corollas as small as 2.4 cm. In both instances the exceptional plants are concentrated in the border zone between the 2 clusters of "normal" plants. In this case, what were originally considered separate species would be treated as subspecies of the one species. (The case illustrated concerns *R. virgatum* from the Himalaya and *R. oleifolium* from China, which ended up as 2 subspecies; *R. virgatum* is the older name, so these plants are now known as *R. virgatum* subsp. *virgatum* and *R. virgatum* subsp. *oleifolium*.) This illustrates the point that taxonomists deal with what material is available at the time they are working. The earlier treatment as 2 species was not wrong: it was appropriate for the time and the material known.

A similar case might be that, as further collections were made, all distinctions between the former species blurred, so that it could not be said there were clusters of "normal" plants with exceptional ones geographically in between. In this case the 2 species would be merged into one, the name being provided by the one with the older name, the other becoming a synonym. This is the case, for instance, with *R. edgeworthii* (Himalaya) and *R. bullatum* (China). Again, if it were found later that a distinction like that between subspecies could be made, but that there were no geographical or ecological distinctions between the 2 former species, they would become varieties (*varietates*) of one species. Equally, if the "exceptional" specimens turned out to be very few in relation to the numbers of "normal" specimens, the 2 species would continue to be recognised, with the intermediates treated as putative hybrids between them.

It should be stressed that this example is necessarily oversimplified, being based on one characteristic (corolla length) and only 2 species. In nature the situation is generally more complex, involving several independent morphological features and several original "species."

This reduction of names to synonyms can have some unfortunate results in terms of finding information about a particular species—and the purpose of giving plants names is so that such information is readily available. In 1886, Adrien Franchet described a small rhododendron with purplish flowers and a very short calyx not fringed with hairs, naming it *R. polycladum*. This plant was collected by Pére Jean Marie Delavay in Yunnan in western China but was not, as such, introduced to cultivation. In 1913, in an area of China not too far from where *R. polycladum* had been collected, George Forrest found a similar plant of which he collected both seed and herbarium specimens. When Isaac Bayley Balfour and William Wright Smith looked at this Forrest collection in 1915 and 1916, they regarded it as a new species (they had not seen any material of Franchet's *R. polycladum* at that time), comparing it to 2 other known species, *R. fastigiatum* and *R. impeditum*, and naming it *R. scintillans*. Under this name it was introduced into cultivation, and, being small and relatively easy to grow and propagate, it became a popular plant with gardeners. Much information about it (the best growing techniques, propagation methods, pests and diseases, and so forth) was accumulated and published, all under the name *R. scintillans*. In 1975, in their revision of the Lapponicum Group of rhododendrons, Melva and Bill Philipson decided that there were no significant differences between the plants called *R. polycladum* and those called *R. scintillans*, and that they should be placed in the same species, which, because of the rule of priority, would have to be called *R. polycladum*, with *R. scintillans* as a synonym. Unfortunately, all that is known about the plant before 1975 is to be found in the literature under the name *scintillans*; a search for *polycladum* reveals very little. Nonetheless, because of the rules of nomenclature, the plant has to be called *R. polycladum;* however, if you want to find out about the plant, you need to know that it was, for a long time, called *R. scintillans.*

The Current Classification

All this activity has produced the classification in use today. This classification is based on much information, most of it structural and morphological, some of it anatomical, chemical, or physiological. The genus *Rhododendron* is divided above the species level into 8 subgenera, each of which may be divided into sections and subsections.

The following list outlines this classification. Names in square brackets are groups not included in this book. Names in bold typeface can be considered equivalent to the old Balfourian "series" and may be used on their own, without the superstructure of subgenera and sections, when talking about a particular group; thus it is possible to refer to Lapponica rhododendrons or the Lapponica Group, or to Pontica rhododendrons (which means only subsection *Pontica*) or the Ponticum Group.

Rhododendron
- Subgenus *Hymenanthes*
  - Section *Pontica*
    - Subsection ***Fortunea***
    - Subsection ***Auriculata***
    - Subsection ***Grandia***
    - Subsection ***Falconera***
    - Subsection ***Williamsiana***
    - Subsection ***Campylocarpa***
    - Subsection ***Maculifera***
    - Subsection ***Selensia***
    - Subsection ***Glischra***
    - Subsection ***Venatora***
    - Subsection ***Irrorata***
    - Subsection ***Pontica***
    - Subsection ***Argyrophylla***
    - Subsection ***Arborea***
    - Subsection ***Taliensia***
    - Subsection ***Fulva***
    - Subsection ***Lanata***
    - Subsection ***Campanulata***
    - Subsection ***Griersoniana***
    - Subsection ***Parishia***
    - Subsection ***Barbata***
    - Subsection ***Neriiflora***
    - Subsection ***Fulgensia***
    - Subsection ***Thomsonia***
- Subgenus *Tsutsusi*
  - Section ***Tsutsusi***
  - Section ***Brachycalyx***
- Subgenus *Pentanthera*
  - Section ***Rhodora***
  - Section ***Sciadorhodion***
  - Section ***Viscidula***
  - Section ***Pentanthera***
- Subgenus **Therorhodion**
- Subgenus *Azaleastrum*
  - Section ***Azaleastrum***
  - Section ***Choniastrum***
- Subgenus ***Candidastrum***
- Subgenus ***Mumeazalea***

Subgenus *Rhododendron*
Section *Rhododendron*
Subsection ***Edgeworthia***
Subsection ***Maddenia***
Subsection ***Moupinensia***
Subsection ***Monantha***
Subsection ***Triflora***
Subsection ***Scabrifolia***
Subsection ***Heliolepida***
Subsection ***Caroliniana***
Subsection ***Lapponica***
Subsection ***Rhododendron***
Subsection ***Rhodorastra***
Subsection ***Saluenensia***
[Subsection ***Fragariflora***]
Subsection ***Uniflora***
Subsection ***Cinnabarina***
Subsection ***Tephropepla***
Subsection ***Virgata***
Subsection ***Micrantha***
Subsection ***Boothia***
Subsection ***Camelliiflora***
Subsection ***Glauca***
Subsection ***Campylogyna***
Subsection ***Genestieriana***
Subsection ***Lepidota***
Subsection ***Baileya***
Subsection ***Trichoclada***
Subsection ***Afghanica***
Section ***Pogonanthum***
[Subgenus/section *Vireya*]

Rhododendron Structure

Familiarity with certain structures is essential when making practical identifications. Most of these structures are visible to the naked eye, but a lens magnifying between 10× and 20× is necessary for a clear understanding of hair and scale types.

Habit. All rhododendrons are woody plants. Most are medium shrubs (1–8 m), but a few are taller trees, and yet a few others are subshrubs, forming low mounds or mats, with the woody, persistent parts small and insignificant. In all rhododendrons the branches, like the leaves, are spirally arranged, but because of the way the plants grow (with the leaves and branches tending to be borne close together, forming false whorls which are separated by rather long leafless or branchless shoots), they take on a very distinctive architecture. In most shrubby species the form is rather rounded and the leaves develop as a relatively thin covering over the network of falsely whorled, essentially bare branches. Some shrubby species are epiphytic, growing on the branches of other plants, or chasmophytic, growing on cliffs or rocky ledges. By suppression of many branches in the false whorls, such plants tend to be of rather straggly habit, with long bare branches bearing clusters of smaller branches at their ends. However, the basic structure of these and the tree-like forms is similar to that of the normal shrubs.

New shoots are produced from buds in the axils of the leaves. Mostly these expand following flowering, and if conditions are good, the stem portion of the new shoot extends rapidly, bearing the leaves in a condensed spiral at the top, the whole being terminated by a bud which may produce an inflorescence or may continue extension growth in the following year. In a few groups the new growth is produced from the same bud as that which produces the inflorescence. Details of the various arrangements of shoots and inflorescences in the buds have some identificatory significance (see Philipson 1985).

Older shoots develop a distinct bark, which is sometimes helpful in identification. The most common type is greyish brown and striate, with lines of paler colour, but not splitting into flakes or segments. Other types include a bark which peels in sheets; such bark is often coppery and very smooth, and the young bark underneath is greenish copper. Occasionally the bark shreds in long, string-like segments. Not enough is known about rhododendron barks for this character to be used in a major way in identification; nevertheless, information about bark is provided in "*Rhododendron:* Keys and Descriptions."

The shoots bear lenticels and may also be covered with hairs or scales (see *indumentum*).

Leaves. The leaves provide many characters of importance in identification. See *indumentum,* for example, for information on hairs and scales.

a) Position. The leaves are borne in a spiral on the shoot, though this is not always immediately obvious, and the internodes tend to be rather short, so that the leaves are generally condensed into false whorls at the ends of the shoots. In some species the number of leaves in the pseudowhorl is important.

b) Duration. The leaves of most species are evergreen, meaning they last 2 or more winters; as is common with evergreen leaves, they are usually thick and leathery. In some groups the leaves are deciduous, opening in spring and falling in late autumn (sometimes with conspicuous autumn colour). Such leaves are thinner and of a parchment-like texture, much more flexible than evergreen leaves. There is generally little difficulty in deciding whether a particular plant has evergreen or deciduous leaves. A few species have semi-evergreen leaves, meaning only some leaves fall each autumn. In subgenus *Tsutsusi* there tends to be a leaf dimorphism: leaves produced during summer are small and persist through to the following summer, whereas leaves opening in spring tend to be larger and more or less deciduous.

c) Shape. Generally the leaves are narrow in relation to their length, tapering both to the base and the apex. There is some variation in overall shape, but this is not great. The base of the blade may be tapering, cordate (heart-shaped), or auriculate (having small, backwardly pointing projections at the point where it joins the stalk). The apex is generally tapered and usually bears a mucro (small swelling). In some species the mature leaves are revolute (having their margins rolled downwards). The size of the leaves varies enormously from species to species; the length varies from a few millimetres to almost a metre.

d) Young leaves in the bud. The young leaves are packed into the vegetative bud in 2 distinct ways. In all species but one of subgenus *Rhododendron* the leaves are flat or slightly curved, overlapping each other; similar young leaves occur in subgenus *Therorhodion.* In all the other subgenera, and in *R. pendulum,* which belongs to subgenus *Rhododendron,* the young leaves are revolute; as they expand from the bud, the margins unroll and the leaf generally becomes more or less flat. This feature, which was first examined by Sinclair (1937), is best seen just as the bud is opening, or by taking a cross section of a nearly mature bud. It is not the case that leaves that are revolute when mature have been revolute in the bud; the revolute margins of mature leaves are generally a later development. In a very few species, the scales of the vegetative buds (perulae) persist on the stems for a longer or shorter period.

e) Leaf stalk (petiole). The leaves of most species are stalked (petiolate), though the stalk itself is sometimes rather short. It is generally rather thick and is usually more or less circular in section (terete), though in a few species it may be distinctly flattened. In a few of the small, creeping, lepidote species, the upper leaves, especially those just beneath the inflorescence, are scarcely stalked at all, the blade extending down to the point of attachment with the stem.

Indumentum. Many parts of the plant, especially the leaves, stems, flower stalks, calyces, corollas, and ovary, may bear emergences (hairs or scales) of various types, giving a characteristic appearance to the organs in question. In general terms, those on the lower surface of the leaves are the most important in general identification, although those in other places are sometimes significant. Some species, or individual plant parts, are glabrous, meaning they are without emergences of any kind.

The emergences have been studied in great detail—see, for example, Cowan (1950) and Seithe (1960, 1980). They fall into 2 classes: hairs and lepidote scales. Though both begin development in a similar way, they are very different in their final forms, and there is generally no difficulty in deciding whether a particular plant has hairs or scales. Any particular species can have hairs of 2 or more kinds, or scales and hairs of 2 or more kinds. Scales are generally very obvious on the lower surface of the leaf, and their presence defines subgenus *Rhododendron;* species of the other subgenera do not have scales. This distinction is of enormous classificatory and identificatory importance, and it is clearly also important in the biology of the plants, as is shown by the fact that, in general terms, it is relatively easy to hybridise a scaly species with another scaly species, or a nonscaly species with another nonscaly species, while it is much more difficult (though not impossible) to hybridise a scaly species with a nonscaly species.

Cowan and Seithe have identified many types of hairs and scales in the genus. Because hairs and scales of different types can occur on the same plant, it is necessary to examine material very carefully in deciding what types are present. Hair and scale types are illustrated in figures 1 (pp. 28 and 29) and 2 (p. 30).

a) Simple, unicellular hairs. These are generally very short hairs made up of single cells. They are found rather rarely, mainly in subgenus *Rhododendron*. When they are very short, essentially forming projections from each cell of the lower leaf epidermis, they are known as papillae. The presence of such papillae imparts a greenish white colour to the lower leaf surface, as with the leaves of *R. zaleucum* and *R. neriiflorum*.

b) Larger, multicellular hairs. In such hairs the cells are arranged in a single series; that is, the hair consists of several cells borne one above the other. Such hairs are the loriform bristles found in many species of subgenus *Rhododendron*, such as on the leaf margins of *R. yunnanense*. Similar hairs are often also found on the inflorescence bud scales.

c) Setose hairs. Figures 1a and 1b. These are tough and bristle-like, made up of many cells arranged in several series, so that the base of the hair (the broadest part) is several cells wide, while the body of the hair itself is fewer cells in width, the number of cells diminishing upwards as the hair narrows. The apex of the bristle may be pointed, as in the leaf stalk bristles of *R. barbatum*, or may bear a sticky, glandular head, as in the setose glands of *R. griersonianum*. Flattened bristles (figure 1c) are found in most species of subgenus *Tsutsusi*.

d) Glandular hairs. Figures 1b and 1d. Glands have a long or short stalk bearing a multicellular head, generally sticky and glistening, and reddish brown or yellow when fresh. In a few cases the stalk is very reduced and the glands are borne on the leaf surface itself.

e) Radiate hairs. Figures 1e and 1f. These are shortly stalked or stalkless rosettes of cells of varying shape; sometimes the cells are spherical, in other cases bottle-shaped.

f) Rosulate hairs. Figures 1g and 1h. These are similar to radiate hairs, but the cells are much longer than broad, usually narrowly cylindric; the stalk may be long or short.

g) Vesicular hairs. Figure 1i. These are rather strange-looking hairs, with a short, multicellular stalk bearing several bladder-like, multicellular projections at the top. These are found only in *R. vesiculiferum* of subsection *Glischra*, which is not cultivated.

h) Stellate hairs. Figures 1j and 1k. These have quite a long, multicellular stalk with rigid, spreading branches at the top.

i) Folioliferous hairs. Figure 1l. These hairs have a long stalk with spreading arms at the top. The cells forming the arms are relatively broad and tapered, appearing superficially like leaves (hence the name).

j) Fasciculate hairs. Figure 1m. These hairs have a broad stalk made up of many small cells, and spreading, cylindric arms made up of several cells arranged end to end.

k) Capitellate hairs. Figure 1n. These are similar to fasciculate hairs but with a very short stalk.

l) Flagellate hairs. Figure 1o. With these hairs, the stalk is relatively long and made up of several cells arranged parallel to each other. The free branches at the top are scarcely spreading.

m) Ramiform hairs. Figure 1p. These hairs have a short stalk with many branched arms at the top.

n) Cup-shaped hairs. Figures 1q and 1r. These have a short, multicellular stalk on top of which is borne a wide or narrow cup-shaped structure made of many individual cells joined together. Such hairs only occur in the species of subsection *Falconera*.

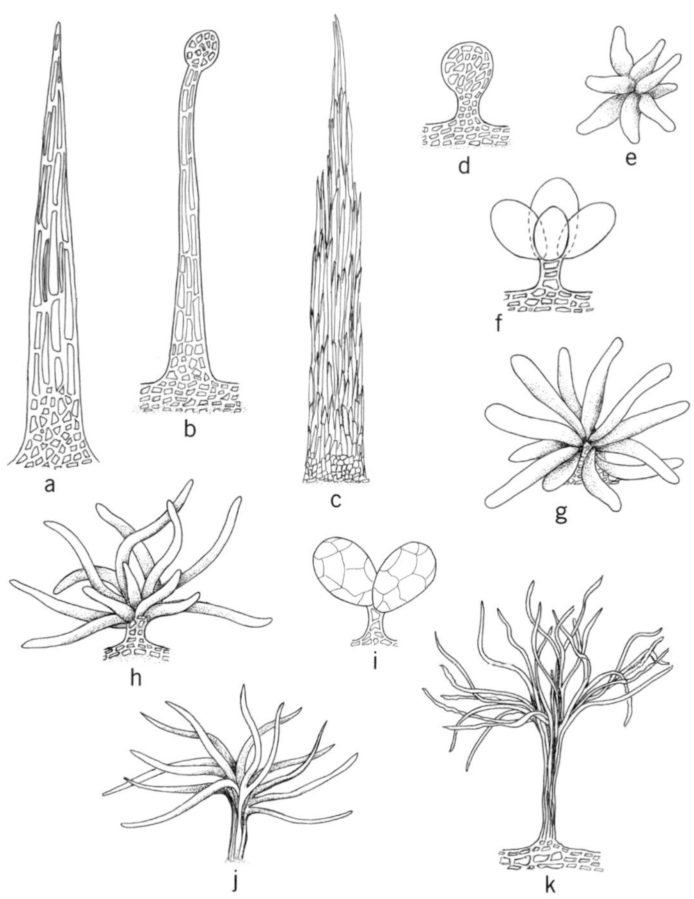

Figure 1. Hair types: a) large, multicellular, setose; b) setose, glandular; c) flattened; d) glandular; e–f) radiate; g–h) rosulate; i) vesicular; j–k) stellate;

o) "Normal" lepidote scales. Figures 2a and 2e (for example, see *R. yunnanense, R. rubiginosum,* and *R. lepidotum* leaf surfaces, pp. 294, 317, and 391). These scales have a short, multicellular stalk and a flattened, mushroom-like cap. The cap has a rather dense centre made up of several small cells which may be somewhat domed, and an entire, circular rim made up of cells which are elongated along the radii. The relative sizes of the centre and the rim vary. The stalk is sometimes sunk into a depression in the surface of the leaf, so that the scale appears to lie on the leaf surface; in other cases the scales may be in several tiers, with longer and shorter stalks, or the rims may be angled upwards, making for a funnel-shaped scale.

p) Lacerate scales. Figure 2b (for example, see *R. anthopogon* var. *hypenanthum* leaf surface, p. 405). The rim is jaggedly toothed to a short distance from the margin. Such scales tend to have stalks of varying lengths, forming tiers on the leaf surface.

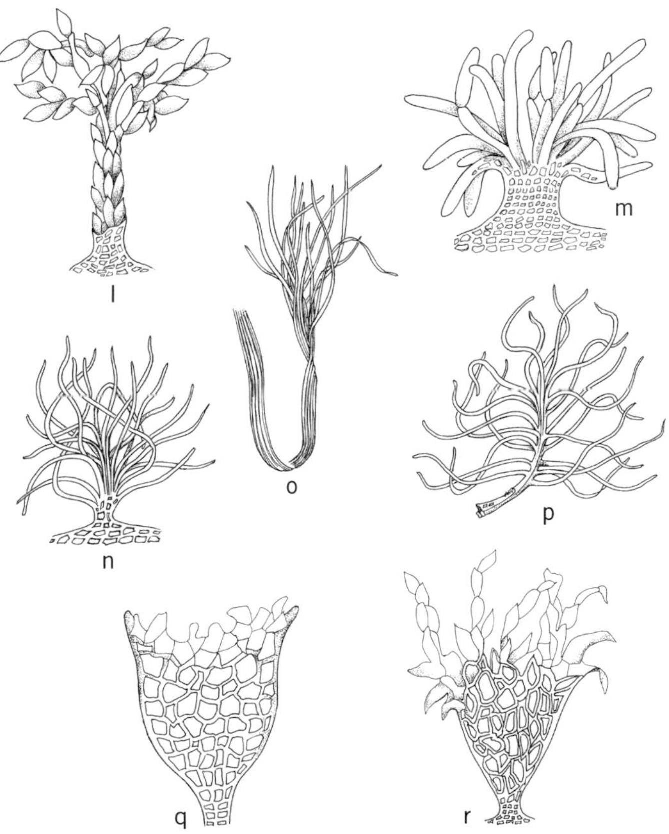

l) folioliferous; m) fasciculate; n) capitellate; o) flagellate; p) ramiform; and q–r) cup-shaped.
ILLUSTRATION BY RODELLA PURVES, COURTESY OF ROYAL BOTANIC GARDEN EDINBURGH

q) Stellate scales. Figure 2d. These are rather like lacerate scales but with the cap divided into several narrowly triangular arms arranged in a star-like manner.

r) Undulate scales. Figure 2f (for example, see *R. russatum* leaf surface, p. 336). These are like normal scales, but the rim, rather than being circular and entire, has a wavy margin, producing an irregular shape.

s) Vesicular scales. Figures 2c and 2i (for example, see *R. mekongense* var. *mekongense* leaf surface, p. 398). In scales of this type the rim is scarcely developed, and the centre forms a very domed or almost spherical structure.

t) Crenulate scales. Figure 2h (for example, see *R. saluenense* subsp. *saluenense* and *R. baileyi* leaf surfaces, pp. 351 and 394). The margin of the rim is slightly scolloped. Like lacerate scales, these tend to occur in tiers.

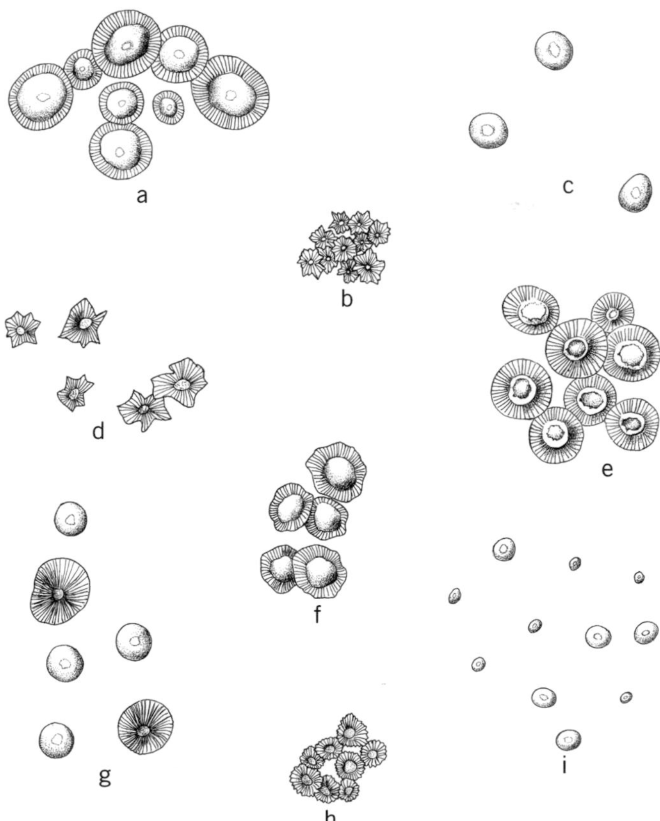

Figure 2. Scale types: a) lepidote, in 3 size groups; b) lacerate; c) very distant, vesicular; d) stellate; e) lepidote, overlapping; f) undulate; g) of more than one form and size; h) crenulate; and i) vesicular, in 2 size groups. ILLUSTRATION BY RODELLA PURVES, COURTESY OF ROYAL BOTANIC GARDEN EDINBURGH

The scales occur in various colours, though yellow-brown is most common. Pink scales occur in *R. intricatum* and several other species, and dark red to almost black scales occur in *R. mekongense*. In a few species, some or all of the scales have a whitish, milky appearance. Scales of more than one form and size can occur together on a single leaf surface, as in figure 2g.

Inflorescences. In most species the inflorescences terminate the shoot, being found at the centre of a false whorl of leaves. A few groups have inflorescences that are axillary, meaning they are lateral and borne in the axil of one of the leaves. The inflorescences may contain 1–30 flowers. When there are 2 or more flowers, they are arranged in a raceme. The raceme may have a long or short rachis, and the flower stalks (pedicels) themselves may also be long or short; they are usually ascending. When the inflorescences are one-flowered and axillary, secondary false racemes may be built up, as occurs in *R. virgatum*. Rhododendron inflorescences are traditionally referred to as "trusses."

a) Inflorescence buds. Because of their 3-dimensional structure and their short life as fully formed organs, these are not well known (they are generally not available in herbarium specimens, having fallen apart in the drying process, and are watched mainly with impatience in living plants). In most species the inflorescence buds are laid down (that is, their development begins) between late summer and autumn, soon after the flush of new leaves is over. They remain in a dormant state over winter until, at the appropriate time, they rapidly grow and open, revealing the flowers. The buds consist of a protective covering of overlapping scales (bud scales, or bracts), which are often hairy or sticky with resinous material. The inflorescence is surrounded by bracts; the inner bracts have flowers in the axils. On each flower stalk are borne 2 thread-like organs; these are bracteoles. In almost all species, the bracts and bracteoles fall as the bud opens and so are not generally available in herbarium specimens.

The nearly mature buds may be spherical, ovoid, or somewhat cylindrical. They are usually greenish or brownish but may occasionally be yellow, red, or almost white. The bud scales, where they are not overlapped by others, are generally hairy or scaly or both, and the scales are often margined with hairs. In the species of subgenus *Rhododendron* section *Pogonanthum*, these hairs are branched—an unusual feature which immediately distinguishes this section within the subgenus.

Very little information is available about the inflorescence buds, but this information is included in "*Rhododendron:* Keys and Descriptions." It should be noted, however, that the features of the buds are not greatly used as diagnostics.

The relationships between vegetative and inflorescence buds are discussed in Philipson (1980).

b) Mature inflorescences. As previously mentioned, the inflorescence may contain one or more flowers. Each flower is stalked, and the stalks may all arise from more or less the same point on the axis, giving rise to an umbellate raceme, or the rachis of the inflorescence may be elongate, producing a pyramidal raceme. In subgenus *Hymenanthes* subsection *Pontica* the rachis is quite long in flower, and it elongates in fruit, giving rise to characteristically pyramidal fruiting racemes. The flower stalks diverge at various angles, though they are usually ascending, and the flower is borne at the top of the stalk with a usually conspicuous angle between them, the flower tending to nod. The main exception to this rule is in subgenus *Rhododendron* subsection *Lapponica,* where the flower stalk and the axis of the flower (through the centre of the ovary and continuing along the style) form a single line. In most cases the flowers nod, but in a few species, notably *R. spinuliferum,* the flower is fully erect.

The flower stalk may be glabrous, hairy, or lepidote, depending on the species. In several subshrubby species which form mounds or mats near the ground surface, the flower stalks become elongate, hardened, and erect in fruit, holding the capsules well above the leaves and other vegetation.

Calyx. In most plants the calyx functions to protect the more delicate parts of the flower (corolla, stamens, ovary) while in bud. In *Rhododendron* this function has largely been taken over by the inflorescence bud scales, so the calyx is often reduced, sometimes being little more than a ridge below the insertion of the corolla. In other cases this ridge can be obscurely lobed, and in yet others the calyx is clearly present and lobed. A few species have large, well-developed calyces; these, however, tend to be coloured like the petals and really variable in shape and size, sometimes forming a cup. When present, the calyx may be glabrous, hairy, or scaly.

Corolla. This is the most striking part of the flower, and its features are among the best observed in the genus. It is sympetalous, that is, made up of a long or short basal tubular part which is lobed to a varying degree towards the top. Mostly the corolla is 5-lobed, but 4-lobed corollas occur in *R. tschonoskii,* and corollas with up to 10 lobes also occur. The lobes may be shorter, about as long, or longer than the tube. The size of the corolla, measured from its base to the tip of the longest lobe, varies from about 6 mm to 20 cm. It is variably bilaterally symmetric (zygomorphic).

The corolla may be entirely glabrous outside, or somewhat scaly or hairy, especially towards the base of the tube. In *R. lutescens* the corolla has backwardly pointing hairs all over its outer surface, and in several species of section *Pentameter* and subsections *Rhodorastra* and *Saluenensia* the whole of the corolla is densely hairy with short hairs; in section *Pentanthera* these are usually glandular, rendering the outside of the corolla sticky to the touch. In most species there is a zone of hairs (which corresponds in position more or less with the tufts of hairs often found on the filaments of the stamens) in the corolla tube near but not at the base.

In many species of subgenus *Hymenanthes,* nectar sacs are developed at the base of the corolla tube. There are as many of these as there are corolla lobes, and each is a small dark-coloured hollow in which nectar collects. In cultivation many flowers with such nectar sacs are attacked from the back by insects, which create a hole in the corolla tube that allows them to get at the nectar. The nectary itself is generally a small ring of glandular tissue at the base of the ovary (see Philipson 1985). In the majority of species the nectar is sticky and not great in volume, but in some species, notably those with nectar sacs in the corolla, *R. cinnabarinum* and its allies, and *R. spinuliferum,* the nectar is copious and more watery. In *R. cinnabarinum* it collects as 5 clear drops in the base of the corolla tube, while in *R. spinuliferum* it fills most of the erect tube.

The shape of the corolla, as seen from the side, is particularly variable, and there is a considerable degree of terminology associated with this. Corolla shapes are illustrated in figure 3 (p. 34).

a) Campanulate. Figures 3a–3c. Here the corolla is bell-shaped, having a rather rounded base, a longer or shorter, almost parallel-sided tube, and spreading lobes. Very widely campanulate corollas (for example, those of *R. souliei*) are described as openly campanulate or even bowl-shaped or saucer-shaped (figure 3d). Corollas with a short campanulate tube and short, slightly spreading lobes are described as ventricose-campanulate (figure 3 o).

b) Funnel-shaped. Figure 3m. In corollas of this type, the tube, seen from the side, flares from the narrow, acute base to the apex of the lobes, which are scarcely reflexed. Depending on the exact degree of flaring of the tube and spreading of the lobes, the corolla may be described as openly funnel-shaped or very openly funnel-shaped.

c) Tubular. Figure 3n. These corollas have a rounded base, a long, parallel-sided tube, and scarcely spreading lobes. There is some degree of variation in the amount of spreading of the lobes and the sides of the tube. In section *Pogonanthum* the corollas have relatively long, parallel-sided tubes and a 5-lobed limb which spreads more or less at right angles to the tube; a corolla of this type is described as hypocrateriform or salver-shaped.

These are the main categories of corolla shape. However, it is important to note that many species have corollas which are intermediate in shape between those described above; these may be described as tubular-campanulate (figures e–g) or funnel-campanulate (figures h–j).

Most species have a corolla tube which is round in section towards the base, but in many species of subsection *Maddenia* (among others), the tube is fluted, with as many channels as corolla lobes.

The colour of the corolla is extremely variable throughout the genus. Almost every shade is present except for a pure blue (magenta-tinged blues occur in *R. augustinii* and in some species of subsection *Lapponica*). Usually there is a blotch of contrasting (usually darker) colour on the upper side of the tube, and spots of a similar colour are often found further up the tube and on the bases of the upper lobes. Such blotches and spots, which presumably help guide visiting insects towards the nectar, are absent in species of section *Vireya*.

The flowers of the species in several groups—notably those which are moth-pollinated, such as subsections *Fortunea* and *Maddenia*—are fragrant, especially in the evenings. This feature is of importance in pollination. There are clearly differences in the fragrances observed (for instance, most species of subsection *Fortunea* have a scent not present in other groups, ranging from a cucumber-like undernote to a sweet aroma), but the fragrances are so difficult to describe that little information is available about them.

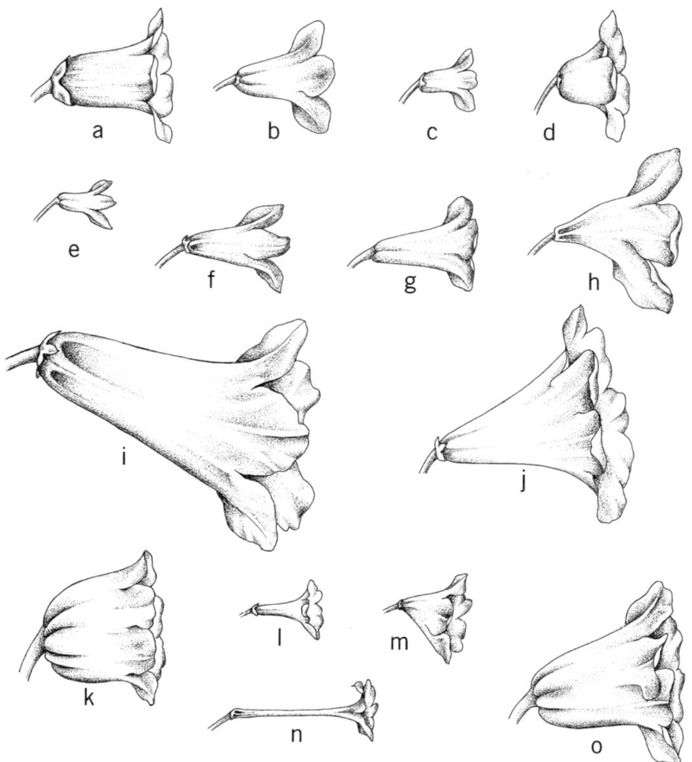

Figure 3. Corolla shapes: a–c) campanulate; d) openly campanulate; e–g) tubular-campanulate; h–j) funnel-campanulate; k) obliquely campanulate; l) with parallel-sided tube and spreading limb; m) openly funnel-shaped; n) with long, parallel-sided tube and small, spreading limb; and o) ventricose-campanulate. ILLUSTRATION BY RODELLA PURVES, COURTESY OF ROYAL BOTANIC GARDEN EDINBURGH

Stamens. The stamens in rhododendrons are generally 10 in number, but any number between 4 and 27 is possible; the number of stamens is quite an important diagnostic in recognising the groups above the species level. Each stamen has a characteristically long filament, which often bears a tuft of hairs towards but just above the base and an anther which opens at the apparent apex by 2 pores (the apex is "apparent" because, during development, the anthers, like those of most genera in the family Ericaceae, invert, so that the pores are actually in the morphological base of the anther). There is quite a range of variation in the colour of the anthers, from near white to yellow, brown, red, purple, dark brown, and black, but little is known of the taxonomic importance of this character.

In almost all species the stamens are declinate, meaning they are curved downwards from their origin, arching up to some extent towards their apices. However, in many species of section *Rhododendron* this is not the case; the stamens of these species have straight filaments of different lengths (the shorter ones towards the upper side of the flower) and are arranged symmetrically around the ovary.

The pollen of rhododendrons is not powdery like that of most plants; the individual grains (actually tetrads of grains) are held in a sticky, stringy, almost indestructible material known as viscin. All the pollen from a single anther sac (of which there are 2 to each anther, each with a pore) tends to cohere in a string. In rhododendron gardens these strings are most easily seen trailing from flying bees on warm days during the peak flowering season.

Ovary. The ovary is in the centre of the flower and is generally cylindric-conical or rounded and cylindric, bearing the single style at the top. There are generally 5 cells in the ovary, but some species have ovaries with up to 10 cells. Each cell contains numerous ovules attached to the central column (axile placentation). The ovary is variously hairy or scaly or both; only rarely is it entirely glabrous. The structure of the ovary is described in detail by Palser, Philipson, and Philipson (1985).

The style is usually declinate like the stamens, and longer than them. In some species the style is straight and shorter than the stamens, and sometimes club-shaped (clavate) above. In those scaly species which have nondeclinate stamens, the style is rather thick and sharply bent downwards from its insertion on top of the ovary, turning up just above the apex, so that the stigma faces in the same direction as the flower as a whole. In rare cases the ovary tapers smoothly into the style; more commonly the style is inserted into a shouldered depression on top of the ovary. The style may be hairy, glandular, or scaly, especially towards the base, or it may be glabrous. The stigma, borne at the apex of the style, consists of a sheath containing as many rounded, sticky lobes as there are cells in the ovary.

Capsule. The capsule of most hardy species is a hard, woody structure. It may be conical or cylindrical, straight or variously curved. The capsule eventually opens by means of small, apical splits into the cells (loculicidal dehiscence), which allows the small seeds to escape. There are as many cells in the capsule as there are in the ovary from which it develops. The body of the capsule may be hairy, scaly, or glabrous.

Seeds. The seeds of rhododendrons, though relatively small, can be placed in 4 main categories. In the first category the seed is rounded and broadly winged all around, with prominent appendages at each end. In the 2nd, the seed is more elongate, with a narrow wing and large appendages at each end. In the 3rd, the seed is elongate and more or less unwinged, with the appendages at each end very small to minute. In the 4th, the seed is elongate, without wings, and with a tail-like appendage at each end. These different kinds of seed are important in the classification of the genus and the identification of the species. They were first studied by Kingdon-Ward (1935), who recognised only 3 types: a "forest" type, including the first 2 categories; an "alpine" type (the 3rd category); and an "epiphytic" type (the 4th category). Kingdon-Ward's study has been vastly extended by Hedegaard (1980), who provides numerous illustrations of the seeds and points out that some of them, such as *R. canadense,* are quite unique in the flowering plants.

Practical Identification

The first phase of the process of identification consists of matching an unknown plant to a description. This book describes 295 commonly cultivated species and 76 uncommonly cultivated species; clearly it is necessary to narrow down the possibilities for a match. (It is possible, of course, though very inefficient, to start reading the description of species 1 and continue with 2, 3, 4, and so on, until you find a match, but this would be confusing and is not recommended.) Three tools are presented for this purpose: standard, dichotomous, bracketed keys, identification tables, and character lists. These aids essentially present the same information in different formats, thus stressing that keys and similar tools are really only typographic layouts designed to make identification easier and more efficient. Gardeners are often suspicious of such tools, but this suspicion is misplaced: the proper use of any of these tools, or any combination of them, should lead to an accurate match, provided one understands the jargon.

Rhododendron: Keys and Descriptions

BRACKETED, dichotomous keys are the standard identificatory tools used in most taxonomic works, and with which most gardeners are at least familiar, if not comfortable. They present information about the plants as pairs (couplets) of propositions (leads), with the members of each pair containing alternative and usually mutually exclusive facts about the plants concerned. Each couplet is numbered, and each lead is lettered *a* or *b*, so the key consists of information numbered *1a, 1b, 2a, 2b, 3a, 3b,* and so forth. At the right-hand margin of each lead is either the name of a taxon or a number which leads you to the next relevant couplet.

The best way to learn how to use a key is by example, and so an example is included here. This particular sample is taken from the key to subgenera and sections which begins on p. 42; however, the same principles apply to all the other bracketed, dichotomous keys in this book. Though quite short, this key illustrates the process very neatly.

Begin with the first pair of propositions:

1 a Plant bearing lepidote scales on at least the lower leaf surface, usually also on some or all of the following: young shoots, flower stalks, calyx, corolla, leaf upper surface; leaves curved or more or less flat in bud (exception: *R. pendulum*) 2

b Plant without such scales on any part; leaves revolute in bud (exception: *R. camtschaticum*) 4

This couplet is fairly straightforward; it simply asks whether the plant has lepidote scales. Scales are generally easy to see on at least some part of the plant, so a decision as to their absence or presence should be unproblematic. In addition to this, each lead asks about the leaves in bud. If the plant has scales, the leaves in bud will be flat or curved (with the one exception noted); if scales are absent, the leaves will be revolute in bud (again, with one exception). It is worth noting that in most cases this 2nd clause of each lead is redundant, since, if the unknown specimen is flowering, it is extremely unlikely to have young leaves with it. This does not matter, however, as the presence or absence of scales is completely diagnostic; the leaf character is just there as confirmation.

If the unknown plant clearly has scales, follow the cue of the "2" at the end of the first lead and move on to couplet 2. This couplet is more complicated than couplet 1 but follows the same general form:

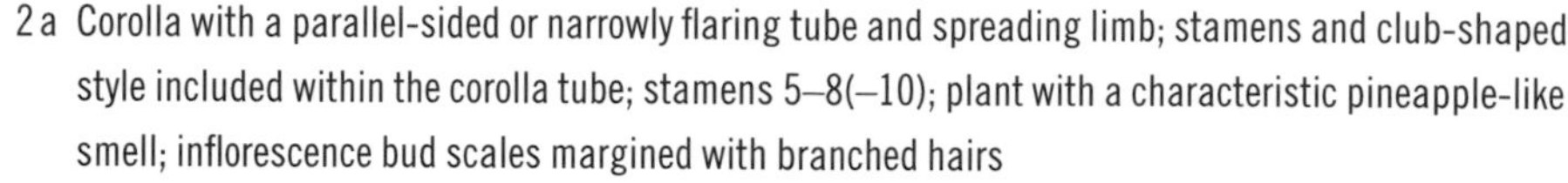

2a Corolla with a parallel-sided or narrowly flaring tube and spreading limb; stamens and club-shaped style included within the corolla tube; stamens 5–8(–10); plant with a characteristic pineapple-like smell; inflorescence bud scales margined with branched hairs
. . . . Subgenus ***Rhododendron*** section ***Pogonanthum*** (p. 402)

b Corolla rarely shaped as above; stamens and style usually projecting from the corolla tube; style never club-shaped; stamens usually 10; plants variously aromatic but not as above; inflorescence bud scales either without hairs or margined with simple hairs
. . . . .Subgenus ***Rhododendron*** section ***Rhododendron*** (p. 261)

This couplet distinguishes between the 2 sections of subgenus *Rhododendron* included in the book. The details of each lead need to be read and understood completely before an attempt is made to compare either lead with an unknown plant. If the plant has a corolla with a parallel-sided or narrowly flaring tube and spreading limb, the probability is high that it will agree with 2a, but this is only a probability. Note how 2b begins: "Corolla rarely shaped as above." This means that in most cases in which the plant agrees with 2b, the corolla is not shaped as described in 2a, but there are exceptions. Thus this particular character is significant but not conclusive (though, of course, if the corolla is not shaped as described in 2a, it can be concluded that the plant will agree with 2b).

In the light of this uncertainty it is necessary to look at further characters mentioned in the couplets. The next part of 2a indicates "stamens and club-shaped style included within the corolla tube," while 2b suggests "stamens and style usually projecting from the corolla tube; style never club-shaped." Two separate issues are dealt with here: the projection of the style and stamens from the corolla tube, and the shape of the style. If the stamens and style project from the corolla tube, the plant agrees with 2b, and this is conclusive. If, however, the stamens and style are included in the corolla tube, the probability is that the plant agrees with 2a, but this is not conclusive, since the use of the word "usually" in 2b indicates that there are exceptions. As for the shape of the style, if it is club-shaped it agrees definitely with 2a, and if it is not club-shaped it agrees definitely with 2b. This character is conclusive because all members of section *Pogonanthum* have club-shaped styles, and no members of section *Rhododendron* do.

The next proposition concerns the stamens. In 2a, "stamens 5–8(–10)" means that to match 2a, the number of stamens can be any number between 5 and 10, but that 5, 6, 7, or 8 are most common. In 2b, "stamens usually 10" means that in most of the plants falling under this group, the stamens are 10, but some have more or fewer. If more than 10 stamens are present, the plant clearly belongs with 2b; if there are fewer, then, again, the character is inconclusive.

There are 2 other characters in the propositions, one concerning aroma, the other concerning the type of hairs (if any) on the bud scales. These are both conclusive characters, but, with any individual unknown plant, it may not be possible to determine either of them. Thus, you have to take the balance of probabilities in each case. If this is done carefully, there will be no difficulty in deciding whether the unknown plant matches 2a or 2b.

Each lead of couplet 2 produces a named group and the page number on which that group can be found; turning to this page number, you will find a description of the group and a new key from which to begin. The keys continue on in this way, ultimately leading to the name of an individual, numbered species.

Because the classification is hierarchical, there are several opportunities to check whether the identification is proceeding correctly. Thus, each subgenus is briefly described, followed by each section and subsection, and then the species. Having reached the name of one of any of these groups in a key, check that the plant matches the description of that group and, if so, proceed to the next stage, or, if not, return to the original keys, making sure to use them correctly.

The plant descriptions in this book follow the same basic form. Each organ or structure forms a heading, followed by a precise description. For example:

LEAVES oblong-elliptic or oblong or obovate, 2.5–7 cm, hairy above when young, hairless beneath except for long, adpressed hairs on the midrib

This way of laying out descriptions, which is adapted from *The Species of Rhododendron* and so should be familiar to many rhododendron lovers, allows for easy comparison between taxa. This is especially important where an identification is somewhat doubtful, making it necessary to compare descriptions of various species to achieve a definite result. Because all the taxa are listed in a systematic way, rather than alphabetically, taxa which are similar to each other occur close together in the text, thus rendering their comparison particularly easy. You must read through the whole of each description and compare it with the unknown plant before coming to any reasonably confident conclusion about identification. Finally, once the species of the plant has been determined, it can be compared with good-quality illustrations of named plants, and ultimately with reliably named herbarium specimens or living material in a garden.

Some headings included in the plant descriptions of this chapter are not actually descriptive but provide additional information likely to be useful in identification. Synonyms, if there are any, follow the main species name. This is followed by a list of published illustrations of the particular species; these lists do not pretend to be comprehensive but provide access to the most easily available accurate illustrations in the taxonomic literature. Additional headings follow the plant description, providing information on, for example, distribution (that is, the wild distribution of the species) and flowering period (using very general seasonal terms).

Hardiness information is based on the hardiness zones developed by the U.S. Department of Agriculture in collaboration with the American Horticultural Society, as far as they can be applied to western Europe. A detailed explanation of how these zones, which are based essentially on temperature ranges, can be applied to Europe is given in Krüssmann (1984, vol. 1: 42–46). Because of their very nature, such zones are imprecise, and the variability of the plants themselves means that such indications should be taken as mere guidance. *Rhododendron maddenii,* for instance, includes plants which occur in wild locations in the Himalaya as low as 2000 m, and others which occur at altitudes of more than 3400 m. Plants from the first location are not hardy anywhere in Britain, whereas those from the 2nd location will grow out of doors in Edinburgh. Giving a single hardiness zone can only be a compromise.

Following each species description, there is often a note as to what classic wild-origin material is available in cultivation. This is based on 25 years' knowledge of such collections. "Classic wild-origin material" refers to the collections of Forrest, Kingdon-Ward, Rock, Farrer, Wilson, Ludlow, Sherriff, and so forth; these materials are identified by the collector's name and the number for the particular collection (*Wilson 1232,* for example). For more recently collected, often not fully identified material, less detail is provided.

Those species most likely to be found in cultivation are keyed and numbered. In addition to these, brief diagnostic descriptions of less commonly cultivated species are included at the ends of appropriate groups; these are not keyed but are linked to a numbered species, to which they will, in general, key out.

Genus *Rhododendron* Linnaeus

HABIT trees or large or small to very small shrubs, often hairy or with lepidote scales

LEAVES usually evergreen but deciduous in some groups, alternate but often condensed into false whorls near the ends of the branches, mostly entire (rarely margins finely scolloped), often revolute; flat or revolute in bud

VEGETATIVE BUDS terminal or axillary; bud scales usually quickly deciduous, occasionally persistent

INFLORESCENCES usually terminal (sometimes axillary), usually with umbel-like racemes (occasionally reduced to one or 2 flowers), at first enclosed in inflorescence buds covered by deciduous, hairy and/or scaly bud scales (bracts), which generally fall as the flowers open; bracteoles usually present, 2 borne on each flower stalk, similar to the bracts but narrower and usually quickly deciduous

CALYX 5- or more-lobed or very reduced and rim-like (sometimes large and petal-like)

COROLLA weakly to strongly bilaterally symmetric, tubular, campanulate, funnel-shaped, or almost flat, rarely with a parallel-sided tube and spreading lobes, usually 5-lobed but occasionally up to 7- or 8-lobed, the lobes shorter to longer than the tube, variously coloured, often with contrasting spots or blotches on the upper part of the tube or the upper lobes, sometimes with distinct dark blotches or nectar sacs at the base of the tube

NECTARY around the base of the ovary; nectar usually a sticky smear but sometimes watery or collected into 5 or more droplets, or held in the nectar sacs of the corolla

STAMENS usually 10, more rarely (4–)5–9 or up to 27, radially arranged or declinate; filaments hairy or not; anthers white, bluish grey, yellow, or brown to almost black, each opening by 2 distinct pores at the apex

POLLEN released as sticky, thread-forming masses

OVARY usually 5-celled, occasionally to 12-celled; ovules numerous

STYLE straight, declinate, or sharply deflexed from the top of the ovary, sometimes continuing the line of the flower stalk but more often at an angle to it, hairy or scaly or not, sometimes the ovary tapering into the style but more often the style borne in a shouldered depression on top of the ovary

STIGMA capitate, often large, consisting of as many receptive lobes as there are ovary cells surrounded by a sheath

FRUIT a loculicidal capsule, often woody when opening only near the apex, or softer and opening along most of its length

Seeds numerous, sometimes winged, or with long tail-like appendages at one or both ends

Distribution with major centres in western China (Yunnan) and Papua New Guinea, but extending south to northern Australia and north to Japan, eastern China, and eastern Russia, the Himalaya as far west as eastern Afghanistan and Pakistan, the Caucasus and the Black Sea coast of Turkey, eastern and central Europe, Spain, eastern and western North America

There are about a thousand species over the whole range of the genus. Many of these have been introduced into cultivation over the last 160 years; many have persisted, but many others have been lost. Numerous man-made hybrids are cultivated in gardens.

There is a complex hierarchy of subgenera, sections, and subsections.

1a Plant bearing lepidote scales on at least the lower leaf surface, usually also on some or all of the following: young shoots, flower stalks, calyx, corolla, leaf upper surface; leaves curved or more or less flat in bud (exception: *R. pendulum*) 2

b Plant without such scales on any part; leaves revolute in bud (exception: *R. camtschaticum*) 4

2a Corolla with a parallel-sided or narrowly flaring tube and spreading limb; stamens and club-shaped style included within the corolla tube; stamens 5–8(–10); plant with a characteristic pineapple-like smell; inflorescence bud scales margined with branched hairs . . . . Subgenus ***Rhododendron*** section ***Pogonanthum*** (p. 402)

b Corolla rarely shaped as above; stamens and style usually projecting from the corolla tube; style never club-shaped; stamens usually 10; plants variously aromatic but not as above; inflorescence bud scales either without hairs or margined with simple hairs 3

3a Capsule hard and woody, the valves opening only slightly, not curling back; seeds various but without tail-like appendages at each end (exception: *R. virgatum*); corolla often with spots of a contrasting colour; scales not lacerate . . . Subgenus ***Rhododendron*** section ***Rhododendron*** (p. 261)

b Capsule softer, the valves curling back and twisted; seeds usually with tail-like appendages at both ends; corolla unspotted; scales often lacerate . . . . Subgenus ***Rhododendron*** section ***Vireya*** (not covered in this book)

4a Inflorescences and inflorescence buds terminal on the shoots; new vegetative growth from buds below the inflorescence, or from the inflorescence bud itself 5

b Inflorescences and inflorescence buds lateral on the shoots; new vegetative growth continuing the shoot above the inflorescence 12

5a At least some of the leaves evergreen (or, if all deciduous, none longer than 1 cm) 6

b All leaves deciduous, at least some longer than 1 cm 7

6 a Leaves generally dimorphic (spring and summer leaves), the summer leaves evergreen (more rarely leaves monomorphic and deciduous but only up to 1 cm long); new shoots from the same terminal bud as the inflorescences; flattened bristles present . . . Subgenus ***Tsutsusi*** section ***Tsutsusi*** (p. 206)

b Leaves not dimorphic, always evergreen, and longer than 1 cm; new shoots from separate buds below the inflorescence bud; hairs absent or various but not flattened . . . . .Subgenus ***Hymenanthes*** section ***Pontica*** (p. 48)

7 a Plant low and creeping; corolla very deeply split between the 2 lower lobes; bracts green and leaf-like, though differing in size from the foliage leaves . . . . .Subgenus ***Therorhodion*** (p. 247)

b Plant not low and creeping, usually an upright shrub; corolla not split as above; bracts usually not leaf-like in colour, shape, or size 8

8 a Flattened bristles present; leaves usually in false whorls of 3 at the tips of the shoots . . . . .Subgenus ***Tsutsusi*** section ***Brachycalyx*** (p. 220)

b Flattened bristles absent, though hairs of other kinds often present; leaves not obviously in false whorls, or, if so, in false whorls of 5 9

9 a Corolla hairy outside; stamens 5 . . . . Subgenus ***Pentanthera*** section ***Pentanthera*** (p. 236)

b Corolla hairless outside; stamens 7–10 10

10 a Corolla more or less regular, white, unspotted, tubular-campanulate . . . . .Subgenus ***Pentanthera*** section ***Viscidula*** (p. 234)

b Corolla bilaterally symmetric, variously coloured, usually spotted in a contrasting colour; rotate, campanulate, or funnel-shaped 11

11 a Corolla 2-lipped, the upper 3 lobes fused higher than the lower 2, hairless inside . . . . Subgenus ***Pentanthera*** section ***Rhodora*** (p. 227)

b Corolla not 2-lipped, hairy inside . . . . Subgenus ***Pentanthera*** section ***Sciadorhodion*** (p. 230)

12 a Leaves evergreen 13

b Leaves deciduous 14

13 a Stamens 5 . . . . Subgenus ***Azaleastrum*** section ***Azaleastrum*** (p. 250)

b Stamens 10 . . . . Subgenus ***Azaleastrum*** section ***Choniastrum*** (p. 253)

14 a Stamens 5 . . . . Subgenus ***Mumeazalea*** (p. 258)

b Stamens 10 . . . . Subgenus ***Candidastrum*** (p. 256)

Subgenus *Hymenanthes* (Blume) K. Koch

HABIT without lepidote scales on any part
YOUNG LEAVES revolute

A subgenus containing a single large section.

Subgenus *Hymenanthes*

Section *Pontica* G. Don

HABIT scales absent
LEAVES evergreen
RACEME always terminal

This section is made up of 24 subsections, most of which include species which are common in cultivation.

1a Stamens more than 10; corolla lobes usually more than 5 2
b Stamens 10; corolla lobes 5 9
2a Young shoots and petioles stipitate-glandular-bristly, the bristles conspicuous . . . . Subsection ***Auriculata*** (p. 61)
b Young shoots and petioles hairy or glabrous but not conspicuously stipitate-glandular 3
3a Leaf indumentum composed, at least in part, of cup-shaped hairs . . . Subsection ***Falconera*** (p. 72)
b Leaf indumentum not containing cup-shaped hairs, or totally absent 4
4a Mature leaves glabrous beneath, occasionally with persistent hair bases or sparse hairs near the midrib 5
b Mature leaves conspicuously hairy beneath 6
5a Corolla with obvious, dark nectar sacs . . . . Subsection ***Irrorata*** (p. 108)
b Corolla without dark nectar sacs . . . . Subsection ***Fortunea*** (p. 48)
6a Corolla lobes 5 . . . . Subsection ***Argyrophylla*** (p. 126)
b Corolla lobes 6 or more 7
7a Inflorescence more or less spherical, dense; rachis very short or absent . . Subsection ***Grandia*** (p. 63)
b Inflorescence more or less pyramidal; rachis 1–2 cm 8
8a Leaf indumentum beneath whitish to buff, 2-layered; ovary glabrous . . Subsection ***Taliensia*** (p. 139)
b Leaf indumentum beneath one-layered, grey to fawn; ovary white-tomentose . . . . Subsection ***Pontica*** (p. 115)
9a Corolla with conspicuous black, dark red, or purple nectar sacs at the base, often tubular-campanulate and red 10
b Corolla without nectar sacs, never tubular-campanulate, rarely red 26
10a Mature leaves more or less glabrous beneath, occasionally with hair bases or a few scattered hairs or glands near the midrib 11
b Mature leaves obviously hairy beneath over most of the surface 18
11a Style glandular or glandular-hairy over most of its length 12
b Style neither glandular nor hairy 14

12 a Young shoots and petioles hairy or not, but not stipitate-glandular . . Subsection ***Thomsonia*** (p. 196)
b Young shoots (and often petioles) stipitate-glandular 13
13 a Ovary tomentose and with glandular hairs . . . . Subsection ***Parishia*** (p. 167)
b Ovary with glandular hairs only, not tomentose . . . . Subsection ***Irrorata*** (p. 108)
14 a Calyx obsolete or to 3 mm, if obvious then disc-like or rarely weakly 5-lobed 15
b Calyx 3 mm or more, obviously 5-lobed or cupular and coloured 16
15 a Petioles absent or up to 5 mm; inflorescence dense, spherical; corolla red . . . . Subsection ***Barbata*** (p. 170)
b Petioles more than 5 mm; inflorescence loose, not spherical; corolla usually not red . . . . Subsection ***Irrorata*** (p. 108)
16 a Ovary glabrous or stipitate-glandular, not tomentose . . . . Subsection ***Thomsonia*** (p. 196)
b Ovary tomentose, sometimes also stipitate-glandular 17
17 a Young shoots and petioles with glandular bristles . . . . Subsection ***Venatora*** (p. 106)
b Young shoots and petioles without glandular bristles . . . . Subsection ***Neriiflora*** (p. 174)
18 a Young shoots and petioles bristly, the bristles sometimes glandular 19
b Young shoots and petioles not bristly 22
19 a Rachis of inflorescence to 4 cm; style glandular in the lower half . . . . . .Subsection ***Parishia*** (p. 167)
b Rachis of inflorescence at most 1 cm; style not glandular, or glandular only at the base 20
20 a Inflorescence dense, spherical; petioles usually with dense, eglandular bristles . . . . Subsection ***Barbata*** (p. 170)
b Inflorescence loose, not spherical; petioles usually with glandular bristles 21
21 a Leaves with crisped, glandular bristles beneath . . . . Subsection ***Maculifera*** (p. 88)
b Leaves with a dense, 2-layered, nonglandular indumentum beneath . .Subsection ***Neriiflora*** (p. 174)
22 a Corolla purplish to violet . . . . Subsection ***Argyrophylla*** (p. 126)
b Corolla not purplish to violet 23
23 a Leaves densely hairy beneath; ovary glabrous . . . . Subsection ***Fulgensia*** (p. 193)
b Combination of characters not as above 24
24 a Calyx 1–2 mm . . . . Subsection ***Arborea*** (p. 133)
b Calyx 3 mm or more 25
25 a Ovary glabrous or stipitate-glandular only . . . . Subsection ***Thomsonia*** (p. 196)
b Ovary tomentose, sometimes also stipitate-glandular . . . . Subsection ***Neriiflora*** (p. 174)
26 a Young shoots and usually petioles with a covering of often glandular bristles 27
b Young shoots and petioles without bristles 30
27 a Corolla densely hairy outside . . . . Subsection ***Griersoniana*** (p. 165)
b Corolla not densely hairy outside 28
28 a Calyx indistinct, rim-like, to 1 mm at most . . . . Subsection ***Williamsiana*** (p. 80)
b Calyx more than 1 mm, often 5-lobed 29

29 a Leaves bristly beneath . . . . Subsection ***Glischra*** (p. 100)

b Leaves variously hairy or glabrous but not bristly beneath . . . . Subsection ***Selensia*** (p. 95)

30 a Inflorescence usually many-flowered, pyramidal; rachis usually well developed, to 6 cm; corolla lobes as long as or longer than the tube . . . . Subsection ***Pontica*** (p. 115)

b Combination of characters not as above 31

31 a Mature leaf lamina glabrous beneath; midrib hairy or not 32

b Mature leaf lamina hairy beneath, usually densely so 35

32 a Midrib of leaf persistently hairy beneath with folioliferous hairs . . . . . Subsection ***Maculifera*** (p. 88)

b Midrib of leaf glabrous beneath or with very sparse hairs near its base 33

33 a Leaves relatively broad; bases rounded to cordate . . . . Subsection ***Campylocarpa*** (p. 82)

b Leaves relatively narrow; bases tapering 34

34 a Corolla 5–6 cm . . . . Subsection ***Fortunea*** (p. 48)

b Corolla 2.5–4 cm . . . . Subsection ***Irrorata*** (p. 108)

35 a Leaf indumentum beneath white to fawn 36

b Leaf indumentum beneath reddish to brown 39

36 a Ovary tomentose 37

b Ovary glabrous 38

37 a Hairs radiate . . . . Subsection ***Taliensia*** (p. 139)

b Hairs rosulate to ramiform . . . . Subsection ***Argyrophylla*** (p. 126)

38 a Longest leaves 14 cm or more; corolla with a purplish blotch . . . . Subsection ***Fulva*** (p. 157)

b Longest leaves up to 14 cm; corolla without a purplish blotch . . . . Subsection ***Taliensia*** (p. 139)

39 a Leaf indumentum 2-layered; lower layer compacted and whitish, obscured by the reddish brown upper layer 40

b Leaf indumentum one-layered, lacking the whitish lower layer 41

40 a Upper layer of indumentum woolly; hairs ramiform . . . . .Subsection ***Taliensia*** (p. 139)

b Upper layer of indumentum granular; hairs capitellate . . . . Subsection ***Fulva*** (p. 157)

41 a Leaf hairs dendroid and crisped . . . . Subsection ***Lanata*** (p. 160)

b Leaf hairs not dendroid and crisped 42

42 a Leaf indumentum compacted, composed of radiate or long-rayed hairs (if hairs ramiform, then indumentum splitting and becoming patchy) . . . . Subsection ***Taliensia*** (p. 139)

b Leaf indumentum loose, composed of fasciculate, capitellate, or very rarely ramiform hairs . . . . Subsection ***Campanulata*** (p. 162)

Subgenus *Hymenanthes*

Section ***Pontica***

Subsection ***Fortunea*** Sleumer (*Fortunei* series)

HABIT shrubs or small trees; young shoots at first with a thin whitish or grey fluffy indumentum, soon more or less hairless

LEAVES with more or less persistent fluffy indumentum on the midrib, or with a sparse indumentum of stellate hairs

RACEME 5- to 30-flowered, loose; rachis 3–70 mm

CALYX minute to well developed

COROLLA 5- to 8-lobed, funnel-campanulate to openly campanulate; nectar sacs usually absent

STAMENS 10–16

OVARY with shortly stalked glands or hairless

STYLE glandular throughout or hairless

SEEDS not much longer than broad, conspicuously winged and with large appendages at each end (especially in *R. griffithianum*)

A group of about 18 species, generally rather large shrubs or trees, and rather tender and susceptible to frost damage, so not often seen outside major collections. Most species belonging to the group have a corolla with more than 5 lobes, and there are often more than 10 stamens. Several species have fragrant flowers.

Their leaf anatomy is reasonably uniform. They have a 2-layered upper epidermis, the cells more or less equal in size, the cuticle half as deep to as deep as the epidermal cells; thin-walled cells (water tissue) are well developed, and the cells of the lower epidermis have either no papillae or the papillae are very small. Sclereids are present in the leaf tissue of some of the species.

1a Style glandular throughout 2
b Style hairless or with a few glands at the base 6
2a Calyx 1.5–2 cm . . . . . **8. *R. griffithianum***
b Calyx 1–10 mm 3
3a Rachis of inflorescence 5–10 mm; glands on style usually red . . . . . **4. *R. vernicosum***
b Rachis of inflorescence 1.5–6 cm; glands on style white 4
4a Leaf base cordate . . . . . **7. *R. hemsleyanum***
b Leaf base rounded 5
5a Filaments hairless . . . . . **6. *R. fortunei***
b Filaments hairy below the middle . . . . . **5. *R. decorum***

6a Leaves circular to ovate-circular, 1.2–1.5 × as long as broad .... **9. *R. orbiculare***
b Leaves ovate to oblanceolate, 1.7–6 × as long as broad 7
7a Stigma a flattened disc; racemes 5- to 30-flowered .... **3. *R. calophytum***
b Stigma capitate; racemes 5- to 12-flowered 8
8a Corolla 2.5–4 cm; leaves 6–14 cm .... **10. *R. oreodoxa***
b Corolla 4–7 cm; leaves 9.5–25 cm 9
9a Corolla with a basal blotch; leaves completely hairless beneath .... **2. *R. praevernum***
b Corolla without a basal blotch; leaves with a more or less persistent indumentum along the midrib beneath .... **1. *R. sutchuenense***

1. ***Rhododendron sutchuenense*** Franchet

ILLUSTRATION Millais, *Rhododendrons*, t. 16 (1917); *Iconographia Cormophytorum Sinicorum* 3, t. 4179 (1974); Cox and Cox, *The Encyclopedia of Rhododendron Species*, 61 (1997)

HABIT shrub to 5 m; bark brownish, scaling in quite large, oblong flakes

LEAVES oblong-lanceolate, 11–25 cm, 3.3–4.2 × as long as broad; upper surface hairless; lower surface with a fluffy, more or less persistent indumentum along the midrib

INFLORESCENCE BUDS fusiform, mostly green; scales yellowish green to brown, some notched with dark brown apices, the outer scales slightly hairy with brown hairs, the inner densely white-hairy and cuspidate

CALYX 1–2 mm, hairless

COROLLA 5- to 6-lobed, widely campanulate, 5–7.5 cm, pink with darker spots but no basal blotch

STAMENS 12–15; filaments hairy towards the base; anthers reddish brown

OVARY AND STYLE hairless

CAPSULE 4.5–5 cm, slightly curved

DISTRIBUTION western China (northern Sichuan, Shaanxi, Hubei, Guizhou, Guangxi)

FLOWERING spring

HARDINESS ZONE 6

Classic wild-collected material is available under *Wilson 1232*. More recent nonauthenticated material is available from Sichuan.

A large, long-lived shrub suitable only for the largest gardens. It is a parent of several hybrids, notably 'Lady Linlithgow' (× *R. thomsonii*). Also found in some collections is *R.* ×*geraldii* (Hutchinson) Ivens (*R. sutchuenense* × *R. praevernum*), illustrated in Davidian, *The Rhododendron Species* 2, pl. 49 (1992); and Cox and Cox, *The Encyclopedia of Rhododendron Species*, 61 (1997).

2. *Rhododendron praevernum* Hutchinson

ILLUSTRATION *Garden* 84: 115 (1920); *Iconographia Cormophytorum Sinicorum* 3, t. 4172 (1974); Davidian, *The Rhododendron Species* 2, pl. 48 (1992); Cox and Cox, *The Encyclopedia of Rhododendron Species,* 60 (1997); Feng, *Rhododendrons of China,* pl. 9: 1–3 (1999)

HABIT shrub to 2 m or more; bark brownish grey, finely ridged

LEAVES elliptic-oblanceolate, 10–18 cm, 3–4 × as long as broad, entirely hairless

INFLORESCENCE BUDS spherical, mostly green; scales completely hairless, the outer with a brown notch at the tip, the inner pointed

CALYX 1–2 mm, hairless

COROLLA 5–lobed, campanulate, 5–6 cm, white (occasionally suffused with pink) and with a purple blotch and spots, hairless outside, puberulent within towards the base

STAMENS 10; filaments shortly hairy towards the base; anthers brown

OVARY AND STYLE hairless

CAPSULE to 3 cm

DISTRIBUTION China (southeastern Sichuan, Hubei)

FLOWERING spring

HARDINESS ZONE 6

A relatively uncommon species in gardens and collections.

3. *Rhododendron calophytum* Franchet

HABIT tree to 12 m

LEAVES oblong-oblanceolate, 14–30 cm, 3.5–6 × as long as broad, completely hairless when mature or rarely with vestiges of juvenile indumentum persisting along the midrib beneath

CALYX 1 mm, hairless

COROLLA 5- to 7-lobed, openly campanulate, 4–6 cm, hairless, pinkish white with purple spots and a basal blotch

STAMENS 15–20

OVARY AND STYLE hairless

CAPSULE 2.5–3 cm

DISTRIBUTION China (northeastern Yunnan, central and eastern Sichuan)

FLOWERING spring

HARDINESS ZONE 6

Two varieties are found in the wild.

R. *calophytum* var. ***calophytum***

ILLUSTRATION *Curtis's Botanical Magazine,* 9173 (1927), reprinted in Halliday, *The Illustrated Rhododendron,* pl. 58 (2001); *Iconographia Cormophytorum Sinicorum* 3, t. 4173 (1974); Fang, *Sichuan Rhododendron of China,* 38, 39 (1986); Davidian, *The Rhododendron Species* 2, pl. 42 (1992); Feng, *Rhododendrons of China* 2, pl. 1: 1–7 (1992); Cox and Cox, *The Encyclopedia of Rhododendron Species,* 50, 51 (1997)

LEAVES 18–30 cm long, with acuminate apices

RACEME 15- to 30-flowered

Classic wild-collected material is available under *Wilson 1367, 4279.* More recent non-authenticated material from Sichuan is also in cultivation.

R. *calophytum* var. ***openshawianum*** (Rehder and Wilson) Chamberlain

ILLUSTRATION *Iconographia Cormophytorum Sinicorum* 3, t. 4174 (1974); Cox and Cox, *The Encyclopedia of Rhododendron Species,* 51 (1997)

LEAVES shorter and cuspidate at the apex

RACEME 5- to 10-flowered

4. *Rhododendron vernicosum* Franchet

SYNONYM *R. rhantum* Balfour and W. W. Smith

ILLUSTRATION *Curtis's Botanical Magazine,* 8834 (1920) and 8904–8905 (1921); Millais, *Rhododendrons,* t. 28 (1924); *Iconographia Cormophytorum Sinicorum* 3, t. 4162 (1974); Fang, *Sichuan Rhododendron of China,* 11, 13, 15, 16 (1986); Feng, *Rhododendrons of China* 1, pl. 19: 1–2 (1988); Davidian, *The Rhododendron Species* 2, pl. 50–51 (1992); Cox and Cox, *The Encyclopedia of Rhododendron Species,* 62 (1997)

HABIT shrub or small tree to 8 m

LEAVES elliptic or ovate-elliptic to obovate-elliptic, 5–10 cm, 1.5–2.2 × as long as broad, hairless except for the presence of punctate hair bases on the lower surface

CALYX to 2 mm, with rounded, stipitate-glandular lobes

COROLLA broadly funnel-campanulate, 6- to 7-lobed, pale pink to pinkish purple with crimson spots

STAMENS usually 14; filaments hairless

OVARY AND STYLE with shortly stalked, red glands

CAPSULE 1.7–3 cm, curved

DISTRIBUTION western China (northern Yunnan, southwestern Sichuan)

FLOWERING spring

HARDINESS ZONE 7

Classic wild-collected material is available under *Forrest 5881, 10075, 15606, McLaren P71, Rock 4012, 4021, 11331, 11404, 11408, 18139,* and *Yü 13809, 13961, 14694.* More recent nonauthenticated material from Sichuan and Yunnan is also in cultivation.

5. *Rhododendron decorum* Franchet

HABIT shrub or small tree to 6 m; bark brown, cracking

LEAVES oblanceolate to elliptic, 6–20 cm, 2–3 × as long as broad, hairless when mature except for punctate hair bases on the lower surface

INFLORESCENCE BUDS narrowly ovoid, pinkish green, bloomed; scales with a few brown-headed glands on the back, and with a fine marginal fringe

CALYX 1–3 mm; lobes rounded, with shortly stalked glands

COROLLA 6- to 7-lobed, funnel-campanulate, 4.5–11 cm, usually sparsely glandular outside, often more densely so within, white to pale pink, with or without green or crimson spots

STAMENS 14–16; filaments hairy; anthers pale yellow

OVARY AND STYLE with shortly stalked, whitish glands

CAPSULE 2–3 cm

DISTRIBUTION western China (Yunnan, Sichuan, Guizhou), northeastern Myanmar, Laos

FLOWERING spring

HARDINESS ZONE 7

R. decorum subsp. *decorum*

ILLUSTRATION *Curtis's Botanical Magazine,* 8659 (1916); *Iconographia Cormophytorum Sinicorum* 3, t. 4155 (1974); Fang, *Sichuan Rhododendron of China,* 24, 25 (1986); Feng, *Rhododendrons of China* 1, pl. 18: 1–3 (1988); Moser, *Rhododendron: Wildarten und Hybriden,* 160 (1991); Kneller, *The Book of Rhododendrons,* 25 (1995); Cox and Cox, *The Encyclopedia of Rhododendron Species,* 52 (1997)

LEAVES to 12 cm

COROLLA 4–6.5 cm

Classic wild-collected material is available under *Forrest 30887.* Material is also grown under *Forrest 21,* but this is not a genuine collecting number. Material grown as *Yü 10958* is probably *R. decorum.* Recent nonauthenticated material from Yunnan and Sichuan is also cultivated.

R. decorum subsp. *decorum* flower and leaf

R. decorum subsp. *decorum* detail

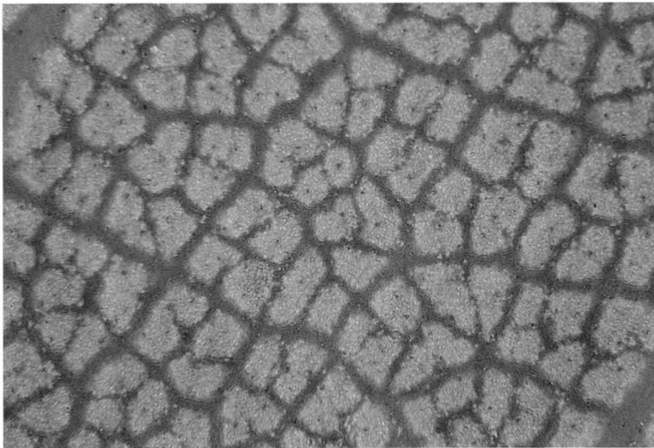

R. decorum subsp. *decorum* leaf surface

R. *decorum* subsp. ***diaprepes*** (Balfour and W. W. Smith) T. L. Ming

SYNONYM *R. diaprepes* Balfour and W. W. Smith

ILLUSTRATION *Curtis's Botanical Magazine,* 9524 (1938), reprinted in Halliday, *The Illustrated Rhododendron,* pl. 59 (2001); *Iconographia Cormophytorum Sinicorum* 3, t. 4156 (1974); Cox and Cox, *The Encyclopedia of Rhododendron Species,* 53 (1997)

LEAVES longer than 12 cm

COROLLA longer than 6.5 cm

Classic wild-collected material is available under *Forrest 27727.* Recent nonauthenticated material from Yunnan is also cultivated.

Subspecies *diaprepes* is a parent of the widely grown, late-flowering 'Polar Bear' (× *R. auriculatum*).

6. *Rhododendron fortunei* Lindley

HABIT shrub or tree to 10 m

LEAVES broadly oblanceolate to obovate, 8–18 cm, 1.7–4 × as long as broad, hairless when mature except for persistent hair bases beneath

CALYX 1–5 mm; lobes minute, rounded, hairless or with shortly stalked glands

COROLLA 7-lobed, openly campanulate or funnel-campanulate, 5.5–7 cm, pale pink to almost pure white, glandular or hairless outside

STAMENS 14–16; filaments hairless

CAPSULE 2.5–4 cm, straight or curved

DISTRIBUTION China (widespread)

FLOWERING spring

HARDINESS ZONE 6

R. *fortunei* subsp. ***fortunei***

ILLUSTRATION *Curtis's Botanical Magazine,* 5696 (1866), reprinted in Halliday, *The Illustrated Rhododendron,* pl. 60 (2001); *Journal of the Royal Horticultural Society* 42: 41 (1916); *Iconographia Cormophytorum Sinicorum* 3, t. 4158 (1974); Moser, *Rhododendron: Wildarten und Hybriden,* 170 (1991); Davidian, *The Rhododendron Species* 2, pl. 44 (1992); Feng, *Rhododendrons of China* 2, pl. 2: 1–4 (1992); Cox and Cox, *The Encyclopedia of Rhododendron Species,* 53 (1997)

LEAVES obovate, 1.8–2.5 × as long as broad

A parent of numerous hybrids, in particular 'Loderi' (× *R. griffithianum*).

R. fortunei subsp. ***discolor*** (Franchet) Chamberlain

SYNONYMS *R. discolor* Franchet; *R. houlstonii* Hemsley and Wilson

ILLUSTRATION *Curtis's Botanical Magazine,* 8696 (1917); Fang, *Icones Plantarum Omeiensium,* t. 29 (1942); *Iconographia Cormophytorum Sinicorum* 3, t. 4161 (1974); *Kew Magazine* 3, pl. 55 (1986), reprinted in Halliday, *The Illustrated Rhododendron,* pl. 61 (2001)

LEAVES oblanceolate, 2.8–4 × as long as broad

A parent of many hybrids, including 'Argosy' (× *R. auriculatum*), 'A. Gilbert' (× *R. campylocarpum*), 'Goldsworth Orange' (× *R. dichroanthum*), and 'Albatross' (× *R.* 'Loderi').

7. *Rhododendron hemsleyanum* Wilson

ILLUSTRATION Fang, *Icones Plantarum Omeiensium,* t. 30 (1942); *Iconographia Cormophytorum Sinicorum* 3, t. 4160 (1974); Fang, *Sichuan Rhododendron of China,* 20, 21 (1986); Cox and Cox, *The Encyclopedia of Rhododendron Species,* 56 (1997); Feng, *Rhododendrons of China* 3, pl. 4 (1999)

HABIT shrub or small tree to 8 m

LEAVES ovate to ovate-elliptic, 10–20 cm, 1.7–2.5 × as long as broad, hairless except for a few punctate hair bases on the lower surface and a few shortly stalked glands towards the base

CALYX to 1 mm, hairless or with shortly stalked glands

COROLLA 6- to 7-lobed, campanulate, 4.5–6 cm, hairless or somewhat glandular outside, pure white

STAMENS usually 14; filaments hairless

OVARY AND STYLE glandular throughout

CAPSULE to 3 cm

DISTRIBUTION western China (Sichuan)

FLOWERING spring

HARDINESS ZONE 8

Recent nonauthenticated material from Sichuan (Emei Shan) is in cultivation.

8. *Rhododendron griffithianum* Wight

SYNONYMS *R. aucklandii* Hooker; *R. griffithianum* var. *aucklandii* (Hooker) Hooker

ILLUSTRATION Hooker, *Rhododendrons of the Sikkim Himalaya,* t. 11 (1851); *Curtis's Botanical Magazine,* 5065 (1858); *Gartenflora* 15, t. 517 (1866); *Garden* 20: 328 (1881); Millais, *Rhododendrons,* 8 (1917); *Rhododendron and Camellia Yearbook* 41: f. 4 (1986); Davidian, *The Rhododendron Species* 2, pl. 45 (1992)

HABIT shrub or tree to 10 m
LEAVES oblong, 10–30 cm, 2.6–3.8 × as long as broad, hairless throughout
CALYX 1.5–2 cm, cup-like, with rounded lobes, hairless
COROLLA 5-lobed, openly campanulate, 4.5–8 cm, pale pink at first, soon fading to white, hairless
STAMENS 12–18; filaments hairless
OVARY AND STYLE glandular throughout
CAPSULE 2.2–4 cm
DISTRIBUTION Himalaya
FLOWERING late spring
HARDINESS ZONE 8

Recent nonauthenticated material from India (West Bengal, Sikkim) and Bhutan is in cultivation.

Only marginally hardy in most of Europe, this species has contributed to many spectacular and hardier hybrids, notably *R.* 'Loderi' (*R.* ×*loderi* Hort.), which is *R. griffithianum* × *R. fortunei* subsp. *fortunei*, and of which there are numerous selections, such as 'Loderi King George' and 'Loderi Sir Joseph Hooker'.

9. *Rhododendron orbiculare* Decaisne
HABIT shrub or tree to 15 m, usually much less; bark pale brown, flaking
LEAVES circular to ovate-circular, 7–12.5 cm, 1.2–1.5 × as long as broad; base cordate, entirely hairless
INFLORESCENCE BUDS ovoid, pointed, reddish, somewhat bloomed; scales finely pointed, glabrous except for a few fine marginal hairs
CALYX minute, with rounded, hairless lobes
COROLLA 7-lobed, campanulate, 3.5–4 cm, rose-pink, unspotted
STAMENS 14; filaments hairless
OVARY with shortly stalked glands
CAPSULE 1.5–2 cm, straight to hooked
DISTRIBUTION western China (central and southern Sichuan, Guangxi)
FLOWERING spring
HARDINESS ZONE 6

R. *orbiculare* subsp. ***orbiculare***

ILLUSTRATION *Curtis's Botanical Magazine,* 8775 (1918); Stevenson, *The Species of Rhododendron,* 279 (1930); *Iconographia Cormophytorum Sinicorum* 3, t. 4163 (1974); Fang, *Sichuan Rhododendron of China,* 26–28 (1986); Davidian, *The Rhododendron Species* 2, pl. 52 (1992); Cox and Cox, *The Encyclopedia of Rhododendron Species,* 57–58 (1997); Feng, *Rhododendrons of China* 3, pl. 8: 1–4 (1999)

LEAVES 7–9.5 cm, about 1.2 × as long as broad

Recent nonauthenticated material from Sichuan is in cultivation.

A parent of the widely grown 'Temple Belle' (× *R. williamsianum*).

R. *orbiculare* subsp. ***cardiobasis*** (Sleumer) Chamberlain

SYNONYM *R. cardiobasis* Sleumer

ILLUSTRATION *Iconographia Cormophytorum Sinicorum* 3, t. 4164 (1974); Cox and Cox, *The Encyclopedia of Rhododendron Species,* 58 (1997)

LEAVES to 12.5 cm, about 1.5 × as long as broad

10. *Rhododendron oreodoxa* Franchet

HABIT shrub or small tree to 5 m; bark brownish grey, reddish towards the base, ridged

LEAVES obovate-elliptic to elliptic, 6–8.5 cm, 2–3.2 × as long as broad, hairless when mature except for punctate hair bases on the lower surface

INFLORESCENCE BUDS more or less spherical but slightly pointed, often shiny; scales mostly brown (sometimes the inner greenish), densely silky-hairy all over

CALYX small, hairless

COROLLA usually 7-lobed, rarely 5- to 6-lobed, campanulate, 3.5–4 cm, deep pink, hairless or somewhat hairy within

STAMENS 10–14; filaments hairless or shortly downy; anthers pale brown to very dark brown or almost black

OVARY hairless or with shortly stalked glands

STYLE hairless

CAPSULE 2–2.5 cm, curved

DISTRIBUTION western China (northwestern Yunnan, Sichuan, Gansu, Shaanxi, Hubei)

FLOWERING late spring

HARDINESS ZONE 6

A variable species divided into 3 varieties, 2 of which are cultivated.

R. *oreodoxa* var. ***oreodoxa***

SYNONYM *R. haematocheilum* Craib

ILLUSTRATION *Curtis's Botanical Magazine,* 8518 (1913); *Gartenflora* 84: 133 (1935); *Iconographia Cormophytorum Sinicorum* 3, t. 4165 (1974); Fang, *Sichuan Rhododendron of China,* 29–31 (1986); Feng, *Rhododendrons of China* 2, pl. 4: 1–2 (1992); Cox and Cox, *The Encyclopedia of Rhododendron Species,* 59 (1997)

OVARY hairless

Classic wild-collected material is available under *Wilson 4245, 4247.*

R. *oreodoxa* var. ***fargesii*** (Franchet) Chamberlain

SYNONYMS *R. fargesii* Franchet; *R. erubescens* Hutchinson

ILLUSTRATION *Curtis's Botanical Magazine,* 8643 (1916) and 8736 (1917); Stevenson, *The Species of Rhododendron,* 284 (1930); *Iconographia Cormophytorum Sinicorum* 3, t. 4167 (1974); Fang, *Sichuan Rhododendron of China,* 32–33 (1986); Davidian, *The Rhododendron Species* 2, pl. 43 (1992); Feng, *Rhododendrons of China* 2, pl. 5: 1–7 (1992); Cox and Cox, *The Encyclopedia of Rhododendron Species,* 59 (1997)

OVARY with shortly stalked glands

Wild-origin material is available under *Sino-American Botanical Expedition 942.* Recent nonauthenticated material from Sichuan is in cultivation.

Variety *shensiense* Chamberlain, with its flower stalks sparsely hairy and its corolla apparently always 5-lobed, is not in cultivation.

Rhododendron planetum Balfour is a name applied to a chance (garden) hybrid of an unknown species of subsection *Fortunea,* though much material in cultivation under this name is a variant of *R. oreodoxa. Rhododendron planetum* is illustrated in *Iconographia Cormophytorum Sinicorum* 3, t. 4171 (1974); and Cox and Cox, *The Encyclopedia of Rhododendron Species,* 61 (1997).

Less commonly cultivated are:

Rhododendron faithae Chun

ILLUSTRATION *Iconographia Cormophytorum Sinicorum* 3, t. 4159 (1974)

Similar to *R. fortunei* and keying out to it.

LEAVES generally larger, 16–22.5 cm

COROLLA larger, 7.5–9 cm

DISTRIBUTION western China (Guangdong, Guangxi)

R. oreodoxa var. *oreodoxa* flower and leaf

R. oreodoxa var. *oreodoxa* detail

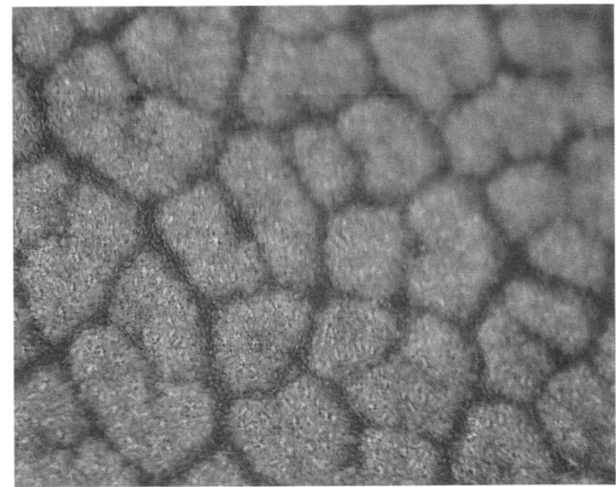

R. oreodoxa var. *oreodoxa* leaf surface

Rhododendron praeteritium Hutchinson
Keying out near *R. oreodoxa.*
COROLLA 5-lobed, with conspicuous nectar sacs
DISTRIBUTION China (western Hubei)

Described from a cultivated plant raised from seed collected by E. H. Wilson, it may well be a hybrid of *R. oreodoxa.*

Rhododendron serotinum Hutchinson
ILLUSTRATION *Iconographia Cormophytorum Sinicorum* 3, t. 4157 (1974)
Apparently similar to *R. decorum.*
DISTRIBUTION possibly western China (southern Yunnan)
FLOWERING from late summer to autumn (August–October)

Also described from a cultivated plant, this is probably unknown in the wild. Its status is uncertain.

Subgenus *Hymenanthes*

Section *Pontica*

Subsection *Auriculata* Sleumer (*Auriculatum* series)

HABIT trees to 6 m; young shoots densely glandular-bristly; vegetative buds long, fusiform, with very long, narrow bud scales
LEAVES margins fringed with glands or small bristles; lower surface with scattered hairs
RACEME 6- to 15-flowered
CALYX minute
COROLLA 7-lobed, funnel-shaped
STAMENS 14–15
OVARY with shortly stalked glands, tapering into the style
STYLE glandular throughout
SEEDS longer than broad, narrowly winged and with appendages at each end

A group of 2 species, very similar to subsection *Fortunea* but differing in the bristly shoots, long, fusiform vegetative buds, and tapering ovary. *Rhododendron auriculatum* is the only cultivated species. It has leaves with a 2-layered upper epidermis, the cells of both layers of approximately the same size, the cuticle about half as thick as the epidermal cells are deep; some water tissue is present, and the cells of the lower epidermis are without papillae. Sclereids have not been reported from the leaves of *R. auriculatum*.

11. *Rhododendron auriculatum* Hemsley
ILLUSTRATION *Curtis's Botanical Magazine,* 8786 (1919), reprinted in Halliday, *The Illustrated Rhododendron,* pl. 62 (2001); *Journal of the Royal Horticultural Society* 28: f. 25 (1903); *Iconographia Cormophytorum Sinicorum* 3, t. 4117 (1974); Kneller, *The Book of Rhododendrons,* 15 (1995); Cox and Cox, *The Encyclopedia of Rhododendron Species,* 24 (1997); Feng, *Rhododendrons of China* 3, pl. 11 (1999)
HABIT shrub or tree to 6 m; young shoots glandular-bristly
LEAVES oblong to oblong-oblanceolate, 15–30 cm, 2.5–3.5 × as long as broad; base auriculate; margin fringed with small glands; lower surface velvety especially on midrib and veins, also glandular; stalks glandular-bristly
CALYX 2 mm, with minute, glandular lobes
COROLLA fragrant, 7-lobed, 8–11 cm, funnel-shaped, white or cream to pink, greenish at the base
STAMENS 14; anthers pinkish white

Ovary and style glandular
Capsule 2–3.5 cm
Distribution China (Sichuan, Hubei, Guizhou)
Flowering late spring
Hardiness zone 6

A parent of 'Polar Bear' (× *R. decorum* subsp. *diaprepes*) and other hybrids.

R. auriculatum flower and leaf. PHOTO BY RAY COX

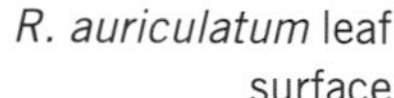

R. auriculatum leaf surface

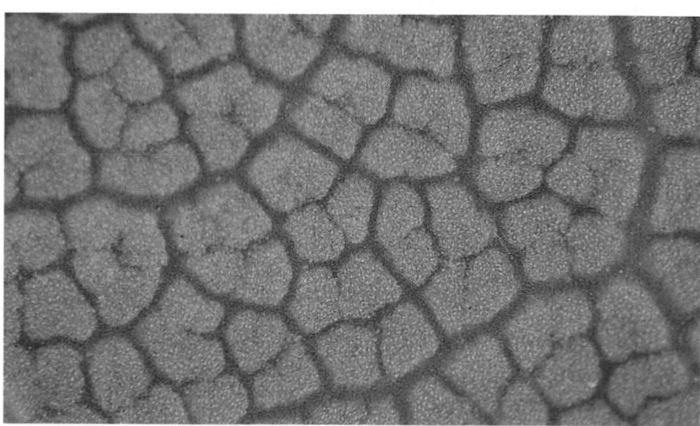

Subgenus *Hymenanthes*

Section *Pontica*

Subsection *Grandia* Sleumer (*Grande* series)

Habit large shrubs or trees to 30 m; young shoots hairless or shortly hairy

Leaves large, to 70 cm; lower surface with a one- or 2-layered indumentum, silvery or buff, usually compacted, the upper layer (when present) composed of rosulate or dendroid hairs

Raceme 12- to 30-flowered, dense; rachis 2–6 cm

Calyx minute

Corolla fleshy, 6- to 10-lobed, tubular-campanulate, funnel-campanulate or ventricose-campanulate; nectar sacs usually absent

Stamens 12–18

Ovary shortly hairy and glandular, rarely hairless

Style hairless

Seeds not much longer than broad and with conspicuous wings and appendages at each end

A group of 11 species of large shrubs or trees, characteristically with tubular-campanulate, funnel-campanulate, or ventricose-campanulate corollas and more than 10 stamens. The leaves have a 2- or 3-layered upper epidermis, the cells all approximately the same size, the cuticle thin to about half as deep as the epidermal cells; little water tissue is present, and the cells of the lower epidermis are without papillae. Sclereids are present in the leaf tissue of all species.

1a Ovary hairless; leaf stalks to 5 mm . . . . **20. *R. watsonii***
 b Ovary shortly hairy; leaf stalks at least 10 mm 2
2a Leaf stalks strongly flattened and winged . . . . **16. *R. praestans***
 b Leaf stalks terete, at most only slightly winged 3
3a Corolla ventricose-campanulate or obliquely campanulate; leaf indumentum silvery, compacted, one-layered 4
 b Corolla tubular-campanulate to funnel-campanulate; leaf indumentum absent or silvery to buff, not compacted, sometimes 2-layered 6
4a Ovary and flower stalks glandular . . . . **13. *R. grande***
 b Ovary and flower stalks eglandular 5
5a Leaves 8–28 cm wide, 2.2–2.8 × as long as broad; corolla pale cream-white . . . . . **14. *R. sinogrande***
 b Leaves 4–10 cm wide (rarely more), 3–5 × as long as broad; corolla pink . . . . **15. *R. montroseanum***

6a Corolla lemon-yellow; leaf indumentum 2-layered, the upper layer woolly . . . . . . **19. *R. macabeanum***
b Corolla pink to rosy purple; leaf indumentum one- or 2-layered but never woolly 7
7a Flower stalks 2–2.5 cm; leaf indumentum buff, sometimes restricted to the margins, or absent . . . . **17. *R. protistum***
b Flower stalks 8–15 mm; leaf indumentum whitish, felted or cobwebby 8
8a Raceme with about 15 flowers; leaves 11–16 cm . . . . **12. *R. wattii***
b Raceme with about 30 flowers; leaves 20–32 cm . . . . **18. *R. magnificum***

12. *Rhododendron wattii* Cowan

HABIT shrub or small tree to 7 m
LEAVES obovate to oblong, 11–16 cm, 2–2.3 × as long as broad, hairless above, with a sparse, whitish, felted indumentum beneath
CALYX 1–2 mm, glandular
COROLLA tubular-campanulate, 6-lobed, 3.5–5.5 cm, pink with darker spots and purplish basal patches (which may be nectar sacs)
OVARY densely woolly, brownish
STYLE hairless
DISTRIBUTION northeastern India (Manipur)
FLOWERING spring
HARDINESS ZONE 9

A rather obscure species which may have had a hybrid origin.

13. *Rhododendron grande* Wight

SYNONYM *R. argenteum* Hooker
ILLUSTRATION *Curtis's Botanical Magazine*, 5054 (1858), reprinted in Halliday, *The Illustrated Rhododendron*, pl. 63 (2001) and 6948 (1887); *Garden* 48: 102 (1895), 59: 342 (1901); *Gartenflora* 60, t. 1588–1589 (1911); *Iconographia Cormophytorum Sinicorum* 3, t. 4216 (1974); *Rhododendron and Camellia Yearbook* 40: f. 12 (1987); Davidian, *The Rhododendron Species* 2, pl. 61 (1992); Cox and Cox, *The Encyclopedia of Rhododendron Species*, 76 (1997); Feng, *Rhododendrons of China* 3, pl. 13 (1999)
HABIT tree to 12 m; bark reddish brown, scaling
LEAVES elliptic to oblanceolate, 15–27 cm, 2.4–3.3 × as long as broad, hairless above, with a thin, silvery, compacted indumentum beneath
INFLORESCENCE BUDS ovoid-fusiform, reddish green; inner scales cuspidate, sticky, densely white-hairy on the surface, brown-hairy towards the tip
CALYX to 1 mm, glandular

COROLLA 8-lobed, ventricose-campanulate, 5–7 cm, pale yellow, rarely with a purplish tinge, with purple nectar sacs
STAMENS 15–16
OVARY densely covered with shortly stalked glands, sometimes also with a dense, pale brown hair covering
STYLE hairless
CAPSULE 3–4.5 cm
DISTRIBUTION Himalaya, western China (southern Xizang)
FLOWERING spring
HARDINESS ZONE 8

Recent nonauthenticated material from India (Sikkim), Nepal, and Bhutan is in cultivation.

14. *Rhododendron sinogrande* Balfour and W. W. Smith
ILLUSTRATION *Curtis's Botanical Magazine,* 8973 (1922); Stevenson, *The Species of Rhododendron,* 317 (1930); *Iconographia Cormophytorum Sinicorum* 3, t. 4217 (1974); Feng, *Rhododendrons of China* 1, pl. 43: 1–3 (1988); Davidian, *The Rhododendron Species* 2, pl. 67 (1992)—leaves only; Kneller, *The Book of Rhododendrons,* 35 (1995); Cox and Cox, *The Encyclopedia of Rhododendron Species,* 84 (1997)
HABIT tree to 10 m; young shoots with sparse grey hairs; bark greyish, breaking into large flakes
LEAVES oblong-oblanceolate to oblong-elliptic, 20–70(–100) cm, hairless and wrinkled above when mature, with a silvery or fawn indumentum beneath
INFLORESCENCE BUDS fusiform, yellowish; scales brown at the apex, glabrous
CALYX to 2 mm, with indications of 8–10 lobes, hairy
COROLLA ventricose-campanulate, 8- to 10-lobed, 4–6 cm, pale cream with a crimson blotch at the base
STAMENS 18–20; anthers pale brown
OVARY with dense, reddish hairs
CAPSULE 4–7 cm, slightly curved
DISTRIBUTION western China (southeastern Xizang, western Yunnan), northeastern Myanmar
FLOWERING spring
HARDINESS ZONE 8

Classic wild-origin material is available under *Forrest 20387* and *Kingdon-Ward 21111.* Recent nonauthenticated material from Yunnan is also in cultivation.

15. *Rhododendron montroseanum* Davidian

SYNONYM *R. mollyanum* Cowan and Davidian

ILLUSTRATION *Rhododendron and Camellia Yearbook* 18, t. 1–2 (1963); *The Garden* 110: 268 (1985); Davidian, *The Rhododendron Species* 2, pl. 64 (1992); Cox and Cox, *The Encyclopedia of Rhododendron Species,* 79–80 (1997); Feng, *Rhododendrons of China* 3, pl. 14: 1–2 (1999)

HABIT tree to 15 m; bark brown, flaking

LEAVES oblanceolate, 2–3 cm (rarely more), 3–3.5 × as long as broad, hairless above, with a thin, silvery, compacted indumentum beneath

VEGETATIVE BUD SCALES deciduous, falling early

INFLORESCENCE BUDS ovoid-spherical, brownish; outer scales with a dense covering of ginger-brown hairs; inner scales with whitish hairs

CALYX to 1 mm, hairy

COROLLA ventricose-campanulate, 8-lobed, to 5 cm, pink with a crimson blotch at the base

STAMENS 16; anthers purple-brown

OVARY densely reddish-hairy

DISTRIBUTION western China (southern Xizang), northeastern Myanmar

FLOWERING spring

HARDINESS ZONE 8

16. *Rhododendron praestans* Balfour and W. W. Smith

SYNONYMS *R. coryphaeum* Balfour and Forrest; *R. semnum* Balfour and Forrest

ILLUSTRATION Stevenson, *The Species of Rhododendron,* 307 (1930); *Iconographia Cormophytorum Sinicorum* 3, t. 4218 (1974); Feng, *Rhododendrons of China* 1, pl. 40: 1–2 (1988); Davidian, *The Rhododendron Species* 2, pl. 65 (1992); Cox and Cox, *The Encyclopedia of Rhododendron Species,* 80–81 (1997)

HABIT shrub or small tree to 10 m; bark grey-brown, flaking

LEAVES oblong-obovate to oblanceolate, mostly 20–30 cm (occasionally less or more), 2.2–3 × as long as broad, hairless above, with a compacted, silvery indumentum beneath

INFLORESCENCE BUDS large, fusiform; lower scales bright green, brownish, and cuspidate at the apex, not very hairy, the inner densely white-hairy and less cuspidate

CALYX 1–2 mm, hairy

COROLLA 7- to 8-lobed, obliquely campanulate, 3.5–5 cm, pale yellow or white flushed with pink, with a crimson basal blotch and spots

STAMENS usually about 16; anthers very pale brown
OVARY densely hairy with buff hairs
CAPSULE 3–4 cm, usually curved
DISTRIBUTION western China (southeastern Xizang, northwestern Yunnan)
FLOWERING spring
HARDINESS ZONE 7

Classic wild-collected material is available under *Forrest 18914, 25717, Kingdon-Ward 13369,* and *Rock 103, 153, 10913.* Recent nonauthenticated material from Yunnan is also in cultivation.

17. *Rhododendron protistum* Balfour and Forrest
HABIT tree to 30 m in the wild
LEAVES 20–40 cm (rarely less), 2.2–3 × as long as broad, hairless above, hairless beneath when young, though sometimes developing a buff, continuous, adpressed indumentum, at least along a marginal band, as the leaf matures
CALYX to 2 mm, hairy, with broadly triangular lobes
COROLLA funnel-campanulate, 8-lobed, 5–7.5 cm, pink or sometimes whitish at the base, with a dark basal blotch and nectar sacs
STAMENS 16
OVARY densely reddish-hairy
CAPSULE 4–5 cm
DISTRIBUTION western China (western Yunnan), northeastern Myanmar
FLOWERING spring
HARDINESS ZONE 9

R. protistum var. ***protistum***
ILLUSTRATION Cox and Cox, *The Encyclopedia of Rhododendron Species,* 82 (1997)
MATURE LEAVES with the indumentum on the lower surface sparse and discontinuous, or forming a marginal band

Classic wild-origin material is available under *Kingdon-Ward 8069.*

R. protistum var. ***giganteum*** (Tagg) Chamberlain
SYNONYM *R. giganteum* Tagg
ILLUSTRATION *Curtis's Botanical Magazine,* n.s., 253 (1955), reprinted in Halliday, *The Illustrated Rhododendron,* pl. 64 (2001); *Iconographia Cormophytorum Sinicorum* 3, t.

4215 (1974); Feng, *Rhododendrons of China* 1, pl. 39: 1–2 (1988); Cox and Cox, *The Encyclopedia of Rhododendron Species,* 81–82 (1997)

MATURE LEAVES with continuous indumentum on the lower surface

Classic wild-origin material is available under *Kingdon-Ward 21498.*

This may be merely a juvenile phase of var. *protistum.*

18. *Rhododendron magnificum* Kingdon-Ward

ILLUSTRATION *Rhododendron Yearbook* 5: f. 38 (1950)

HABIT tree to 18 m

LEAVES broadly obovate, 20–32 cm, 1.7–2.3 × as long as broad; upper surface hairless; lower surface with a thin, continuous but apparently 2-layered indumentum, the lower layer compacted, the upper fluffy

CALYX to 1 mm, with triangular lobes, reddish-hairy

COROLLA funnel-campanulate, 8-lobed, 4.5–6 cm, pinkish purple with dark nectar sacs

STAMENS usually 16

OVARY densely reddish-hairy

DISTRIBUTION western China (western Yunnan), northeastern Myanmar

FLOWERING spring

HARDINESS ZONE 9

19. *Rhododendron macabeanum* Balfour

ILLUSTRATION *Curtis's Botanical Magazine,* n.s., 187 (1952), reprinted in Halliday, *The Illustrated Rhododendron,* pl. 65 (2001); *Rhododendrons with Camellias and Magnolias* 10: f. 25 (1955) and 44: 149 (1992); Davidian, *The Rhododendron Species* 2, pl. 62 (1992); Cox and Cox, *The Encyclopedia of Rhododendron Species,* 77–78 (1997)

HABIT tree to 15 m; bark brownish, breaking into oblong flakes; underbark rather cinnamon-brown

LEAVES broadly ovate to broadly elliptic, 14–25 cm, 1.3–1.8 × as long as broad, hairless above when mature, with a dense, 2-layered indumentum beneath, the lower layer compacted and whitish, the upper woolly and composed largely of rosulate hairs, though with some ramiform hairs as well

INFLORESCENCE BUDS large, almost spherical though slightly tapered at both ends; lower scales green tipped with brown, usually split at the tips and hairless, the median whitish with cuspidate or shouldered brown tip and with silky white hairs, the inner whitish with pale brown tips and with silky white or white and brown hairs

Calyx to 1 mm, hairy, with shortly triangular lobes
Corolla tubular-campanulate to narrowly funnel-campanulate, to 5 cm, lemon-yellow with a purple blotch at the base
Stamens 16
Ovary densely reddish-hairy
Capsule 2–4 cm, curved
Distribution northeastern India (Nagaland, Manipur)
Flowering spring
Hardiness zone 8

Classic wild-origin material is available under *Kingdon-Ward 7724*.

R. macabeanum flower and leaf

R. macabeanum detail

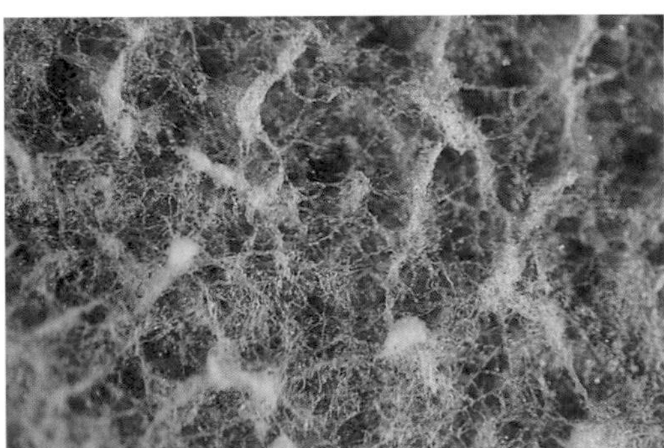

R. macabeanum leaf surface

20. *Rhododendron watsonii* Hemsley and Wilson

ILLUSTRATION *Iconographia Cormophytorum Sinicorum* 3, t. 4220 (1974); Davidian, *The Rhododendron Species* 2, pl. 68 (1992); Feng, *Rhododendrons of China* 2, pl. 6: 1–6 (1992); Cox and Cox, *The Encyclopedia of Rhododendron Species*, 85 (1997)

HABIT shrub or small tree to 6 m; bark brown, striate

LEAVES 10–20 cm, 2–2.3 × as long as broad, hairless above, with a thin, whitish, compacted indumentum beneath

INFLORESCENCE BUDS more or less spherical though slightly tapered to the apex, greenish; scales sparsely hairy except around the margins and at the tip

CALYX to 2 mm, with broadly triangular, fleshy lobes

COROLLA campanulate, 7-lobed, 3.5–4 cm, white with a crimson basal blotch

STAMENS 14

OVARY hairless

CAPSULE 3–3.5 cm

DISTRIBUTION western China (central and northern Sichuan, Gansu)

FLOWERING spring

HARDINESS ZONE 9

Recent nonauthenticated material from Sichuan and Gansu is in cultivation.

Less commonly cultivated are:

Rhododendron kesangiae Long and Rushforth

Similar to *R. grande*, but:

LEAVES broadly elliptic to obovate, 20–30 × c. 10 cm; lateral veins 12–15 pairs per side; indumentum without cup-shaped hairs

COROLLA rose

CAPSULE narrower, 3.5–4 cm × 9–10 mm

DISTRIBUTION Bhutan

Recently described and introduced, not yet widely spread in gardens.

Rhododendron pudorosum Cowan

ILLUSTRATION *The Rhododendron Handbook,* f. 1 (1997); Davidian, *The Rhododendron Species* 2, pl. 66 (1992)

Keying out to *R. montroseanum,* but:

VEGETATIVE BUD SCALES persistent

DISTRIBUTION western China (Xizang)

Rare in cultivation.

Rhododendron sidereum Balfour

Keying out to *R. montroseanum* but also similar to *R. grande* and *R. sinogrande.*

ILLUSTRATION *Curtis's Botanical Magazine,* n.s., 638 (1973)

LEAVES narrower, 9–16 × 4–6.5 cm

COROLLA yellow

DISTRIBUTION China (Yunnan), northeastern Upper Burma (Myanmar)

Subgenus *Hymenanthes*

Section *Pontica*

Subsection *Falconera* Sleumer (*Falconeri* series)

HABIT large shrubs or trees to 12 m; young shoots hairless to fluffy-hairy
LEAVES large (to 40 cm); lower surface with a dense whitish to rusty red indumentum composed of cup-shaped hairs, sometimes also with a compacted lower layer
RACEME dense, 10- to 25-flowered; rachis 1–6 cm
CALYX 1–3 mm
COROLLA usually 7- to 10-lobed; funnel-campanulate, obliquely campanulate, or ventricose-campanulate; nectar sacs absent
STAMENS usually 14–18
OVARY shortly hairy, glandular, or hairless; style hairless
SEEDS not much longer than broad, usually with conspicuous wings and appendages (wings rarely somewhat narrow)

There are 10 species of large shrubs, characterised by the presence of cup-shaped hairs on the lower surface of the leaves. Anatomically the leaves are very similar to those of subsection *Grandia*. They have a 2- or 3-layered upper epidermis, the cells more or less equal in size, the cuticle half as thick as to thicker than the cells; the cells of the lower epidermis are without papillae, but water tissue is better developed than in the species of subsection *Grandia*. Sclereids are present in the leaf tissue of all species.

1a Leaf stalks flattened, winged .... **21. *R. basilicum***
 b Leaf stalks terete, not flattened 2
2a Ovary and flower stalks glandular .... **26. *R. falconeri***
 b Ovary and flower stalks eglandular 3
3a Ovary hairless .... **23. *R. galactinum***
 b Ovary densely hairy 4
4a Leaves 1.5–2.5 × as long as broad, the upper surface more or less wrinkled; corolla pale yellow .... **22. *R. rex***
 b Leaves 2.4–4 × as long as broad, the upper surface more or less smooth; indumentum silvery buff to rusty; corolla white to rose-purple 5
5a Corolla intense pink or rose-purple, without spots .... **25. *R. hodgsonii***
 b Corolla white or pale pink, usually spotted 6
6a Leaves 4.8–6.2 cm wide; indumentum whitish to fawn, more rarely pale cinnamon-brown .... **24. *R. coriaceum***
 b Leaves 5–13.5 cm wide; indumentum fawn to rusty brown .... **22. *R. rex***

21. *Rhododendron basilicum* Balfour and W. W. Smith

ILLUSTRATION *Iconographia Cormophytorum Sinicorum* 3, t. 4214 (1974); Davidian, *The Rhododendron Species* 2, pl. 33–34 (1992); Cox and Cox, *The Encyclopedia of Rhododendron Species*, 38–39 (1997); Feng, *Rhododendrons of China* 3, pl. 15 (1999)

HABIT shrub or tree to 10 m; bark grey-brown, flaking

LEAVES obovate to oblanceolate, 17–25 cm, 1.8–2.4 × as long as broad, hairless above with deeply impressed veins, with a 2-layered indumentum beneath, the lower layer compacted, the upper thick, at first greyish, later reddish brown, composed of broadly cup-shaped, scarcely fimbriate hairs; leaf stalk flattened and winged

CALYX about 2 mm, with rounded lobes, tomentose

COROLLA fleshy, 8-lobed, obliquely campanulate, 3.5–5 cm, pale yellow with a crimson blotch

STAMENS 16; anthers brown

OVARY densely reddish-hairy

CAPSULE 2–3 cm, straight or curved

DISTRIBUTION western China (western Yunnan), northeastern Myanmar

FLOWERING spring

HARDINESS ZONE 8

Classic wild-origin material is available under *Forrest 16002, 24139,* and *Rock 25393.*

22. *Rhododendron rex* Léveillé

HABIT large shrubs or small trees to 12 m; bark striate (grey-brown) or not (brown) and coming off in large flakes; underbark smooth, cinnamon-brown

LEAVES obovate to oblanceolate, 10–37 cm, 1.5–3.8 × as long as broad; upper surface more or less hairless, smooth or finely wrinkled; lower surface with a dense fawn to reddish indumentum composed of slightly to strongly fimbriate, cup-shaped hairs

INFLORESCENCE BUDS almost spherical, sometimes slightly sticky, the outer scales sometimes with prominent midribs, pale green; scales white- or brown-hairy

CALYX 1–2 mm, usually shortly hairy

COROLLA obliquely campanulate or campanulate, 7- to 8-lobed, white, pale yellow, or pink, with a crimson basal blotch and spots

STAMENS 14–16; anthers pale brown or dark purple

OVARY with a dense covering of brown hairs

CAPSULE 2.5–3.5 cm, curved

DISTRIBUTION western China (northwestern, western, and northeastern Yunnan, southeastern Xizang, southern Sichuan), northeastern Myanmar

FLOWERING spring
HARDINESS ZONE 7

A variable species. Three intergrading subspecies are recognised in the wild, and all are in cultivation.

R. *rex* subsp. ***rex***

ILLUSTRATION *Rhododendron and Camellia Yearbook* 10: f. 25 (1955); *Iconographia Cormophytorum Sinicorum* 3, t. 4211 (1974); Fang, *Sichuan Rhododendron of China,* 61–63 (1986); Feng, *Rhododendrons of China* 1, pl. 7: 1–4 (1988); Cox and Cox, *The Encyclopedia of Rhododendron Species,* 46 (1997)
LEAVES 2.4–3.1 × as long as broad, with a fawn indumentum of slightly fimbriate, cup-shaped hairs
COROLLA white flushed with pink
DISTRIBUTION western China (southern Sichuan, northeastern Yunnan)

Classic wild-origin material is available under *Rock 18234.*

R. *rex* subsp. ***fictolacteum*** (Balfour) Chamberlain

SYNONYM *R. fictolacteum* Balfour
ILLUSTRATION *Journal of the Royal Horticultural Society* 42: f. 11 (1916); Millais, *Rhododendrons,* 164 (1917); *Rhododendron Yearbook* 4, f. 36 (1948); *Iconographia Cormophytorum Sinicorum* 3, t. 4209 (1974); Cox, *The Larger Species of Rhododendron,* t. 4 (1979); Feng, *Rhododendrons of China* 1, pl. 37: 1–4 (1992); Davidian, *The Rhododendron Species* 2, pl. 38 (1992); Cox and Cox, *The Encyclopedia of Rhododendron Species,* 46–47 (1997)
LEAVES 2–3.8 × as long as broad, with a brown indumentum of moderately fimbriate cup-shaped hairs
COROLLA white or pink
ANTHERS pinkish brown
DISTRIBUTION western China (western Yunnan, southeastern Xizang), northeastern Myanmar

Classic wild-collected material is available under *Forrest 22020, 25512, 25719, Kingdon-Ward 4509,* and *Rock 193, 11378, 25444.* Recent nonauthenticated material from Yunnan is also in cultivation.

R. rex subsp. *fictolacteum* flower and leaf

R. rex subsp. *fictolacteum* detail

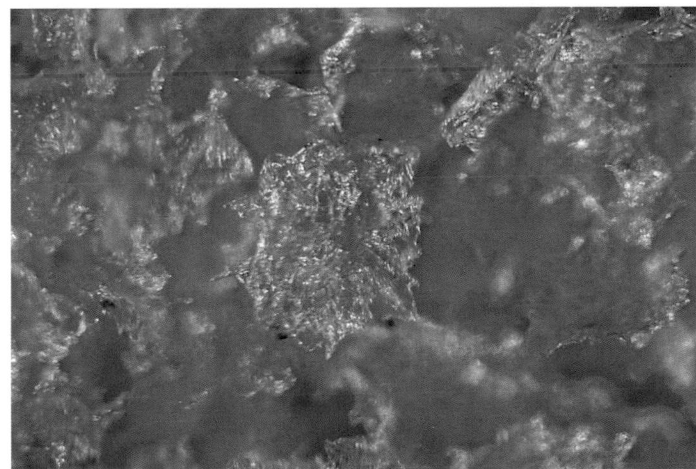

R. rex subsp. *fictolacteum* leaf surface

R. rex subsp. ***arizelum*** (Balfour and Forrest) Chamberlain

SYNONYM *R. arizelum* Balfour and Forrest

ILLUSTRATION *Iconographia Cormophytorum Sinicorum* 3, t. 4208 (1974); Feng, *Rhododendrons of China* 1, pl. 35: 1–3 (1988); Davidian, *The Rhododendron Species* 2, pl. 31–32 (1992); Cox and Cox, *The Encyclopedia of Rhododendron Species,* 37–38 (1997)

Similar to subsp. *fictolacteum,* but:

LEAVES 1.5–2 × as long as broad, with strongly fimbriate hairs

COROLLA yellow

DISTRIBUTION western China (western Yunnan), northeastern Myanmar

Classic wild-origin material is available under *Farrer 863, Forrest 21862, 21866, 25608, 25627, 27108, Kingdon-Ward 5877, 8163, 9544,* and *Rock 16, 25, 51A, 97, 11207, 18337.* Material grown as *Rock 22106* from China (Yunnan) is doubtful.

23. *Rhododendron galactinum* Tagg

ILLUSTRATION *Curtis's Botanical Magazine,* n.s., 231 (1954); *Iconographia Cormophytorum Sinicorum* 3, t. 4213 (1974); Fang, *Sichuan Rhododendron of China,* 57–60 (1986); Feng, *Rhododendrons of China* 2, pl. 8: 1–2 (1992); Cox and Cox, *The Encyclopedia of Rhododendron Species,* 42 (1997)

HABIT tree to 8 m; bark orange-brown, flaking

LEAVES ovate-lanceolate, 14–20 cm, 2.6–3.3 × as long as broad, hairless and smooth above, with a 2-layered indumentum beneath, the lower layer whitish and compacted, the upper dense, cinnamon-brown, composed of strongly fimbriate, narrowly cup-shaped hairs

INFLORESCENCE BUDS elongate-spherical, greenish; scales densely hairy, mealy, with white fasciculate hairs (hairs at the tips of the scales sometimes brown); outer scales with prominent midrib

CALYX to 1 mm, shortly hairy, with triangular teeth

COROLLA 7-lobed, campanulate, 3–5 cm, pale pink with a crimson basal blotch

STAMENS 14

OVARY hairless or with a few reddish hairs

DISTRIBUTION western China (central Sichuan)

FLOWERING spring

HARDINESS ZONE 5

Classic wild-collected material is available under *Wilson 4254.* Recent nonauthenticated material from Sichuan is in cultivation.

24. *Rhododendron coriaceum* Franchet

ILLUSTRATION *Curtis's Botanical Magazine*, n.s., 462 (1965); *Iconographia Cormophytorum Sinicorum* 3, t. 4212 (1974); *Rhododendron and Camellia Yearbook* 37, opposite 48 (1983); Feng, *Rhododendrons of China* 1, pl. 36: 1–2 (1988); Davidian, *The Rhododendron Species* 2, pl. 35 (1992); Cox and Cox, *The Encyclopedia of Rhododendron Species*, 39 (1997)

HABIT shrub or small tree to 7.5 m

LEAVES oblanceolate, 12–25 cm, 2.5–4 × as long as broad, becoming hairless above, with a dense, 2-layered indumentum beneath, the lower layer compacted, the upper whitish or brown, composed of broadly cup-shaped hairs

CALYX to 1 mm; lobes minute

COROLLA funnel-campanulate, 3.5–4 cm, white sometimes flushed with pink and with a red basal blotch, occasionally also spotted red

STAMENS 10–14

OVARY densely reddish-hairy

CAPSULE 1.8–2.5 cm, curved or straight

DISTRIBUTION western China (northwestern Yunnan, southeastern Xizang)

FLOWERING spring

HARDINESS ZONE 9

Classic wild-collected material is available under *Forrest 16364, 21843, 25622, 25872*, and *Rock 120, 140*.

25. *Rhododendron hodgsonii* Hooker

ILLUSTRATION Hooker, *Rhododendrons of the Sikkim Himalaya*, t. 15 (1851); *Revue Horticole*, ser. 4, 4: 421 (1855) and 191 (1866); *Curtis's Botanical Magazine*, 5552 (1866), reprinted in Halliday, *The Illustrated Rhododendron*, pl. 66 (2001); *Iconographia Cormophytorum Sinicorum* 3, t. 4210 (1974); Davidian, *The Rhododendron Species* 2, pl. 39 (1992); Cox and Cox, *The Encyclopedia of Rhododendron Species*, 43 (1997)

HABIT shrub or small tree to 11 m; bark scaling in large flakes; underbark smooth, purple-brown

LEAVES obovate to oblanceolate or elliptic, 17–24 cm, 2.4–3.2 × as long as broad; upper surface becoming hairless, not strongly wrinkled; lower surface with a dense, 2-layered, silvery to cinnamon-brown indumentum, the lower layer compacted, the upper of slightly fimbriate, broadly cup-shaped hairs

CALYX 2–3 mm, sparsely hairy

COROLLA fleshy, 7- to 8-lobed, rarely to 10-lobed, tubular-campanulate, 3–5 cm, pink to magenta or purple, with a darker basal blotch

STAMENS 15–18; anthers brown
OVARY hairy
CAPSULE 3–4 cm, curved
DISTRIBUTION Himalaya, western China (southern Xizang)
FLOWERING spring
HARDINESS ZONE 9

Classic wild-origin material is available under *Ludlow, Sherriff, and Hicks 21296* and *Spring-Smythe 9, 42A*. Recent nonauthenticated material from India (West Bengal, Sikkim), Bhutan, and Nepal is also in cultivation.

26. *Rhododendron falconeri* Hooker
HABIT tree to 12 m; bark brown, scaling in large flakes; underbark smooth, cinnamon-brown
LEAVES broadly elliptic to obovate, 18–35 cm, 1.4–2.3 × as long as broad; upper surface hairless or scurfy, wrinkled; lower surface with a 2-layered indumentum, the lower layer white and compacted, the upper dense, reddish, composed of cup-shaped, fimbriate hairs
CALYX to 2 mm, glandular-sticky
COROLLA fleshy, obliquely campanulate, 4–5 cm, whitish to pink or pale cream with darker tips, with a purplish basal blotch
STAMENS 12–16
OVARY densely glandular-sticky
CAPSULE to 4 cm, straight
DISTRIBUTION Himalaya
FLOWERING spring
HARDINESS ZONE 9

R. falconeri subsp. ***falconeri***
ILLUSTRATION Hooker, *Rhododendrons of the Sikkim Himalaya*, t. 10 (1849); *Flore des Serres*, ser. 1, 5: t. 477–480 (1849), ser. 2, 1: t. 1166–1167 (1856); *Curtis's Botanical Magazine*, 4924 (1856), reprinted in Halliday, *The Illustrated Rhododendron*, 67 (2001); Davidian, *The Rhododendron Species* 2, pl. 36–37 (1992); Kneller, *The Book of Rhododendrons*, 23 (1995); Cox and Cox, *The Encyclopedia of Rhododendron Species*, 40–41 (1997)
LEAVES hairless above at maturity
COROLLA white to cream

Wild-origin material is available under *Cave 6712* and *Sinclair and Long 5695.* Recent nonauthenticated material from Nepal and Bhutan is also in cultivation.

R. falconeri subsp. ***eximium*** (Nuttall) Chamberlain
SYNONYM *R. eximium* Nuttall
ILLUSTRATION *Curtis's Botanical Magazine,* 7317 (1893)
LEAVES scurfy above
COROLLA pink with darker tips

Recent nonauthenticated material from Bhutan is in cultivation.

Less commonly cultivated are:

Rhododendron rothschildii Davidian
Keying out to *R. basilicum,* but:
LEAVES indumentum 2-layered and agglutinated, the upper layer patchy
DISTRIBUTION western China (northwestern Yunnan)

Rhododendron semnoides Tagg and Forrest
ILLUSTRATION *Iconographia Cormophytorum Sinicorum* 3, t. 4219 (1974)
Keying out to *R. basilicum,* but:
LEAVES indumentum composed of strongly fimbriate, narrowly cup-shaped hairs
COROLLA pink or white
DISTRIBUTION western China (southeastern Xizang, northwestern Yunnan)

Rhododendron preptum Balfour and Forrest
Keying out to *R. rex,* but:
LEAVES about 2.5 × as long as broad, with a buff to light brown indumentum beneath
DISTRIBUTION northeastern Upper Burma (Myanmar)

Rhododendron sino-falconeri Balfour
Probably keying out to *R. rex.*
LEAVES about 2.5 × as long as broad, with a buff to light brown indumentum
DISTRIBUTION western China (southeastern Yunnan), Vietnam

Subgenus *Hymenanthes*

Section ***Pontica***

Subsection ***Williamsiana*** Chamberlain (*Thomsonii* series *Williamsianum* subseries)

HABIT dwarf shrubs; young shoots glandular-bristly; bark smooth
LEAVES mostly hairless at maturity
RACEME loose, 2- to 5-flowered; rachis to 5 mm
CALYX 1–3 mm
COROLLA 5-lobed, campanulate, without nectar sacs
STAMENS 10; filaments hairless
OVARY with shortly stalked glands
STYLE glandular throughout

A group of 2 species, of which only *R. williamsianum* is cultivated. It is apparently related to subsection *Campylocarpa*. The leaves have a 2-layered upper epidermis, the cells of each layer more or less equal, the cuticle about half as thick as the cells are deep; water tissue is absent, and the cells of the lower epidermis are prolonged as papillae. Sclereids occur occasionally.

27. *Rhododendron williamsianum* Rehder and Wilson
ILLUSTRATION *Curtis's Botanical Magazine,* 8935 (1922), reprinted in Halliday, *The Illustrated Rhododendron,* pl. 68 (2001); *Gardeners' Chronicle* 93, t. 1 (1935); *Iconographia Cormophytorum Sinicorum* 3, t. 4178 (1974); Fang, *Sichuan Rhododendron of China,* 65–66 (1986); Moser, *Rhododendron: Wildarten und Hybriden,* 252 (1991); Davidian, *The Rhododendron Species* 3, pl. 105–106 (1992); Kneller, *The Book of Rhododendrons,* 57 (1995); Cox and Cox, *The Encyclopedia of Rhododendron Species,* 202–203 (1997)
HABIT dwarf shrub to 1.5 m; young shoots glandular-bristly; bark grey-brown, shredding
LEAVES ovate-circular, 2–4.5 cm, about 1.3 × as long as broad, mostly hairless but with some stalkless, reddish glands beneath
INFLORESCENCE BUDS elongate-ovoid, dark red towards the base, pale and yellowish above; outer scales glabrous; inner scales with dense white hairs on the surface and forming a fringe
CALYX to 1 mm, glandular-ciliate
COROLLA campanulate, 3–4 cm, pale pink with darker spots
STAMENS filaments hairless; anthers brown

Ovary glandular
Style glandular to the apex
Capsule 1.5–1.8 cm
Distribution western China (central Sichuan)
Flowering spring
Hardiness zone 7

Recent nonauthenticated material from Sichuan is in cultivation.

A parent of many hybrids, including 'Temple Belle' (× *R. orbiculare* subsp. *orbiculare*).

R. williamsianum flower and leaf

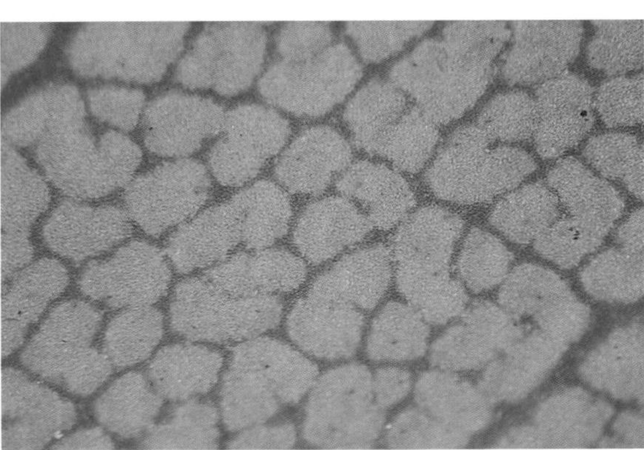

R. williamsianum leaf surface

Subgenus *Hymenanthes*

Section *Pontica*

Subsection *Campylocarpa* Sleumer (*Campylocarpum* series; *Souliei* series)

HABIT shrubs or small trees to 6 m; young shoots with shortly stalked glands or hairless

LEAVES hairless on both surfaces when mature

RACEME 4- to 15-flowered, loose; rachis c. 5 mm

CALYX minute to well developed and cup-like

COROLLA campanulate to saucer-shaped, 5-lobed, without nectar sacs

STAMENS 10

OVARY with shortly stalked glands

STYLE hairless or glandular throughout

SEEDS longer than broad, winged (occasionally narrowly) and with appendages at each end

There are 4 species, forming a group distantly related to *R. oreodoxa* in subsection *Fortunea*, characterised by their openly campanulate to bowl-shaped corollas. The leaves have a 2-layered upper epidermis, the cells of both layers approximately equal, the cuticle thin to about half as thick as the cells are deep; water tissue is absent, and the cells of the lower epidermis are generally prolonged as papillae, though these are sometimes very small.

1 a Style hairless; corolla campanulate to funnel-campanulate; calyx 1–5 mm 2
b Style glandular throughout; corolla saucer-shaped; calyx 3–15 mm 3
2 a Corolla whitish to pink .... **28. *R. callimorphum***
b Corolla pale to sulphur-yellow .... **29. *R. campylocarpum***
3 a Corolla purplish pink .... **31. *R. souliei***
b Corolla white to yellow .... **30. *R. wardii***

28. *Rhododendron callimorphum* Balfour and W. W. Smith

HABIT to 2 m (rarely more); young shoots with shortly stalked glands

LEAVES broadly ovate to circular, 3.5–7 cm, 1–1.5 × as long as broad, cordate at the base; upper surface hairless; lower surface glaucous with minute, red, stalkless glands and sometimes also some shortly stalked glands

CALYX to 2 mm, with shortly stalked glands

COROLLA campanulate, 3–4 cm, white to rose-pink, sometimes with purple spots and a faint basal blotch

OVARY with stalked glands

STYLE hairless or with a few glands at the base
CAPSULE 1.5–2 cm, curved
DISTRIBUTION western China (western Yunnan)
FLOWERING spring
HARDINESS ZONE 7

R. *callimorphum* var. ***callimorphum***
SYNONYM *R. cyclium* Balfour and Forrest
ILLUSTRATION *Curtis's Botanical Magazine*, 8789 (1919); *Iconographia Cormophytorum Sinicorum* 3, t. 4181 (1974); Davidian, *The Rhododendron Species* 3, pl. 91–93 (1992); Feng, *Rhododendrons of China* 2, pl. 10 (1992)
COROLLA pink

Classic wild-origin material is available under *Forrest 27389*.

R. *callimorphum* var. ***myiagrum*** (Balfour and Forrest) Chamberlain
SYNONYM *R. myiagrum* Balfour and Forrest
COROLLA white

Classic wild-origin material is available under *Kingdon-Ward 6962*.

29. *Rhododendron campylocarpum* Hooker
HABIT shrub or small tree to 5 m; young shoots with a few shortly stalked glands; bark greyish brown, finely striate
LEAVES circular to elliptic, 3–10 cm, 1–2.5 × as long as broad, hairless or rarely with a few reddish glands near the base on the lower surface
INFLORESCENCE BUDS mostly brownish, reddish above, green towards the base; scales with brown and white hairs, the inner cuspidate
CALYX 3–5 mm, with rounded lobes bearing shortly stalked glands
COROLLA campanulate, 2.5–4 cm, pale sulphur-yellow, sometimes tinged with red in bud, with or without a basal blotch
STAMENS anthers dark brown
OVARY densely covered with glands
STYLE hairless or glandular
CAPSULE 1.3–2 cm, curved
DISTRIBUTION Himalaya, western China (Xizang, Yunnan), northeastern Myanmar
FLOWERING spring
HARDINESS ZONE 6

R. *campylocarpum* subsp. ***campylocarpum***

ILLUSTRATION Hooker, *Rhododendrons of the Sikkim Himalaya*, t. 30 (1851); *Curtis's Botanical Magazine*, 4968 (1857), reprinted in Halliday, *The Illustrated Rhododendron*, pl. 69 (2001); *Garden* 18: 277 (1880), 28: 319 (1885), 54: 182 (1898), 58: 45 (1900), 78: 573 (1914), 83: 276 (1919); *Iconographia Cormophytorum Sinicorum* 3, t. 4180 (1974); Feng, *Rhododendrons of China* 1, pl. 5: 2 (1992); Davidian, *The Rhododendron Species* 3, pl. 95–96 (1992); Cox and Cox, *The Encyclopedia of Rhododendron Species*, 33–34 (1997); Feng, *Rhododendrons of China* 3, pl. 16: 1–6 (1999)

LEAVES elliptic, 1.6–2.5 × as long as broad

DISTRIBUTION Himalaya and western China (Xizang)

Wild-origin material is available under *Spring-Smythe 12, 13, 32A*. Recent nonauthenticated material from Bhutan and China is also in cultivation.

Widely used as a parent in hybridisation.

R. *campylocarpum* subsp. ***caloxanthum*** (Balfour and Farrer) Chamberlain

SYNONYMS *R. caloxanthum* Balfour and Farrer; *R. telopeum* Balfour and Forrest

ILLUSTRATION Cox, *The Plant Introductions of Reginald Farrer*, 76 (1930); Davidian, *The Rhododendron Species* 3, pl. 94 (1992)

LEAVES circular, 1–1.5 × as long as broad

DISTRIBUTION western China (Xizang, western Yunnan), northeastern Myanmar

Classic wild-origin material is available under *Farrer 937, Forrest 21875, 26985, 27123, 27125,* and *Rock 1, 18373, 18383.*

30. *Rhododendron wardii* W. W. Smith

HABIT shrub or small tree to 8 m; young shoots sparsely glandular or hairless; bark grey-brown, striate

LEAVES narrowly obovate to broadly ovate, 6–11 cm, 1.5–2.5 × as long as broad, entirely hairless, somewhat glaucous beneath; leaf stalks sometimes with shortly stalked glands

INFLORESCENCE BUDS ovoid, fusiform, or almost spherical but pointed, purplish, and bloomed; glabrous

CALYX 5–15 mm, cup-like when well developed; lobes rounded, glandular-ciliate

COROLLA saucer-shaped, 2.5–4 cm, white to pale yellow, with or without a purplish basal blotch

OVARY with shortly stalked glands

STYLE glandular to the apex
CAPSULE 2–2.5 cm, straight or curved
DISTRIBUTION western China (southeastern Xizang, northwestern Yunnan, southwestern Sichuan)
FLOWERING spring
HARDINESS ZONE 7

R. wardii var. **wardii**
SYNONYMS *R. astrocalyx* Balfour and Forrest; *R. croceum* Balfour and W. W. Smith; *R. litiense* Balfour and Forrest
ILLUSTRATION *Curtis's Botanical Magazine*, n.s., 587 (1972), reprinted in Halliday, *The Illustrated Rhododendron*, pl. 70 (2001); *Iconographia Cormophytorum Sinicorum* 3, t. 4176 (1974); *Rhododendrons with Camellias and Magnolias* 44: 49 (1992); Fang,

R. wardii var. *wardii* flower and leaf

R. wardii var. *wardii* detail

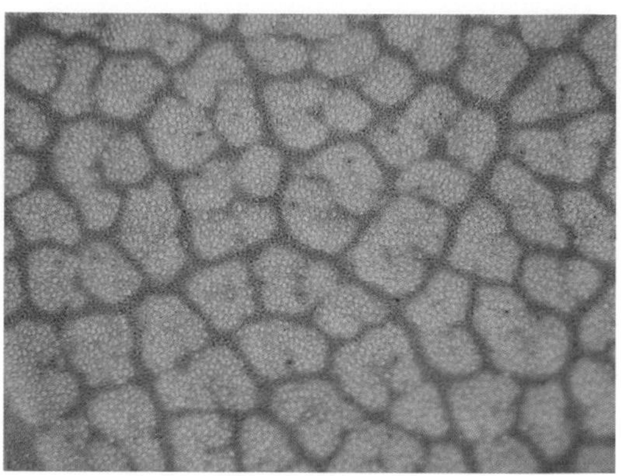

R. wardii var. *wardii* leaf surface

Sichuan Rhododendron of China, 68–71 (1986); Feng, *Rhododendrons of China* 1, pl. 8: 1–4 (1988); Davidian, *The Rhododendron Species* 3, pl. 100–102 (1992); Cox and Cox, *The Encyclopedia of Rhododendron Species,* 36 (1997)

COROLLA yellow

Classic wild-collected material is available under *Forrest 21017, 21551, 25534, Kingdon-Ward 4170, 4410, 5736, Ludlow, Sherriff, and Elliott 15764, Ludlow, Sherriff, and Taylor 5679, 6586,* and *Rock 18333, 23314, 24339, 25391.* Recent nonauthenticated material from Yunnan is also in cultivation.

Very widely used in hybridisation, and a parent of the frequently grown 'Cowslip' (× *R. williamsianum*).

R. wardii var. **puralbum** (Balfour and W. W. Smith) Chamberlain

SYNONYM *R. puralbum* Balfour and W. W. Smith

ILLUSTRATION Davidian, *The Rhododendron Species* 3, pl. 104 (1992); Cox and Cox, *The Encyclopedia of Rhododendron Species,* 36–37 (1997)

COROLLA white

Classic wild-origin material is available under *Forrest 10616* and *Yü 14757.*

31. *Rhododendron souliei* Franchet

ILLUSTRATION *Curtis's Botanical Magazine,* 8622 (1915); Stevenson, *The Species of Rhododendron,* 731 (1930); *Iconographia Cormophytorum Sinicorum* 3, t. 4177 (1974); Davidian, *The Rhododendron Species* 3, pl. 103 (1992); Kneller, *The Book of Rhododendrons,* 21 (1995); Cox and Cox, *The Encyclopedia of Rhododendron Species,* 35 (1997)

HABIT shrub to 5 m; young shoots hairless or glandular

LEAVES broadly ovate, 5.5–8 cm, 1.4–2 × as long as broad, hairless; leaf stalks sometimes with shortly stalked glands

CALYX 3–8 mm; lobes rounded, glandular-ciliate

COROLLA openly saucer-shaped, 2.5–4 cm, pale purplish pink

OVARY densely covered with shortly stalked glands

STYLE glandular to the apex

CAPSULE 1.8–2.2 cm, slightly curved

DISTRIBUTION western China (Sichuan)

FLOWERING spring

HARDINESS ZONE 6

Recent nonauthenticated material from Sichuan is in cultivation.

Subgenus *Hymenanthes*

Section *Pontica*

Subsection ***Maculifera*** Sleumer (*Barbatum* series *Maculiferum* subseries)

HABIT large shrubs or small trees; young shoots shortly hairy or glandular-bristly
LEAVES lower surface with a more or less persistent indumentum composed of flagellate, folioliferous, long-rayed or stellate hairs
RACEME loose or dense, 5- to 20-flowered; rachis 2–20 mm
CALYX usually minute
COROLLA 5-lobed, narrowly to widely campanulate and without nectar sacs, or tubular-campanulate and with nectar sacs
STAMENS 10
OVARY hairy or with shortly stalked glands, very rarely hairless
SEEDS elongate, narrowly winged and with (sometimes very large) appendages at each end

A group of 9 species. Each species is only loosely related, making the group rather variable, especially in hair type and corolla shape. The leaves have a 2- or 3-layered upper epidermis, the cells of each layer approximately equal, the cuticle generally as thick as the cells are deep; water tissue is usually present, and the cells of the lower epidermis are not prolonged as papillae.

1a Corolla tubular-campanulate, usually with depressed nectar sacs, dark red, rarely white; young shoots with shortly stalked glands or glandular bristles .... **33. *R. strigillosum***
b Corolla narrowly to widely campanulate; nectar sacs absent; young shoots with matted hairs 2
2a Leaf base more or less tapering; leaf stalks and midrib beneath densely rusty-hairy; calyx 6–10 mm .... **32. *R. longesquamatum***
b Leaf base rounded; leaf stalks and midrib beneath with sparse, evanescent or persistent, greyish or brownish indumentum; calyx 1–2 mm 3
3a Leaves 10–15 cm 4
b Leaves 3–10 cm 5
4a Flower stalks, ovary, and style base with at least a few glands or hairs ....**36. *R. morii***
b Flower stalks and ovary without glands; style base hairless .... **34. *R. pachytrichum***
5a Flower stalks 2.5–3 cm .... **37. *R. pseudochrysanthum***
b Flower stalks 1.3–2 cm .... **35. *R. maculiferum***

32. *Rhododendron longesquamatum* Schneider

ILLUSTRATION *Curtis's Botanical Magazine,* 9430 (1936), reprinted in Halliday, *The Illustrated Rhododendron,* pl. 71 (2001); *Iconographia Cormophytorum Sinicorum* 3, t. 4126 (1974); Fang, *Sichuan Rhododendron of China,* 86–87 (1986); Davidian, *The Rhododendron Species* 2, pl. 19 (1992); Feng, *Rhododendrons of China* 2, pl. 11: 1–5 (1992); Cox and Cox, *The Encyclopedia of Rhododendron Species,* 100 (1997)

HABIT shrub to 3 m or more; young shoots densely red-hairy

LEAVES elliptic to oblanceolate, 6–11 cm, about 3 × as long as broad; upper surface with shortly stalked glands and reddish-hairy (hairs flagellate) when young, the hairs confined to the midrib when mature; lower surface of blade hairless, though midrib reddish-hairy

CALYX 6–10 mm; lobes tongue-shaped, with shortly stalked glands

COROLLA openly campanulate, 4–4.5 cm, rose-pink

OVARY AND THE LOWER HALF OF THE STYLE with shortly stalked glands

DISTRIBUTION western China (Sichuan)

FLOWERING spring

HARDINESS ZONE 5

Recent nonauthenticated material from Sichuan is in cultivation.

33. *Rhododendron strigillosum* Franchet

ILLUSTRATION Millais, *Rhododendrons,* t. 152 (1924); Fang, *Icones Plantarum Omeiensium,* t. 23 (1942); *Iconographia Cormophytorum Sinicorum* 3, t. 4122 (1974); Davidian, *The Rhododendron Species* 2, pl. 24 (1992); Feng, *Rhododendrons of China* 2, pl. 16: 1–7 (1992); Cox and Cox, *The Encyclopedia of Rhododendron Species,* 107 (1997)

HABIT shrub to 2.5 m; young shoots with a dense covering of shortly stalked glands; bark brown, striate

LEAVES elliptic to oblanceolate, 7.5–14 cm, 2.7–3.7 × as long as broad; margins sometimes ciliate; upper surface more or less hairless; lower surface with varying quantities of usually persistent, crisped bristles with glandular or branched tips, grading into larger bristles on the midrib

INFLORESCENCE BUDS fusiform, dark reddish; scales cuspidate, densely whitish- or greyish-hairy

CALYX to 1 mm

COROLLA tubular-campanulate, 4–6 cm, deep red, with deep, darker nectar sacs

STAMENS anthers very dark, almost black

OVARY with long, weak, glandular hairs

STYLE hairless

Capsule 1.5–2 cm
Distribution western China (Sichuan, northeastern Yunnan)
Flowering spring
Hardiness zone 8

Classic wild-origin material is available under *Wilson 1341*. Recent nonauthenticated material from Sichuan is also in cultivation.

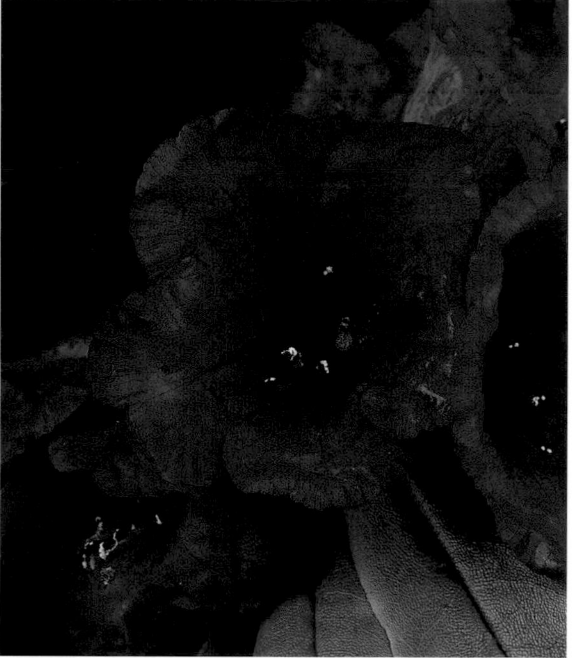

R. strigillosum flower

R. strigillosum detail

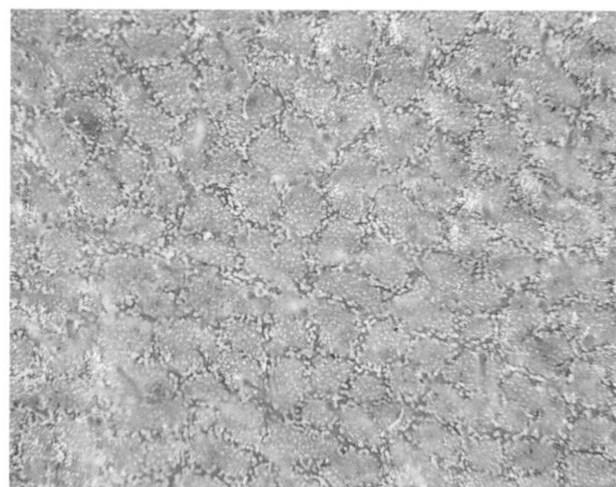

R. strigillosum leaf surface

34. *Rhododendron pachytrichum* Franchet

SYNONYM *R. monosematum* Hutchinson

ILLUSTRATION Fang, *Icones Plantarum Omeiensium*, t. 22 (1942); *Iconographia Cormophytorum Sinicorum* 3, t. 4123 and 4128 (1974); Fang, *Sichuan Rhododendron of China*, 88–91 (1986); Davidian, *The Rhododendron Species* 2, pl. 20 (1992); Feng, *Rhododendrons of China* 2, pl. 14: 1–2 (1992); Cox and Cox, *The Encyclopedia of Rhododendron Species*, 103–104 (1997)

HABIT shrub or small tree to 6 m; young shoots hairy; bark brownish or brownish grey, splitting into oblong flakes

LEAVES elliptic to obovate, 9–15 cm, 2.7–4.5 × as long as broad, hairless on both surfaces except for a few folioliferous hairs towards the midrib beneath

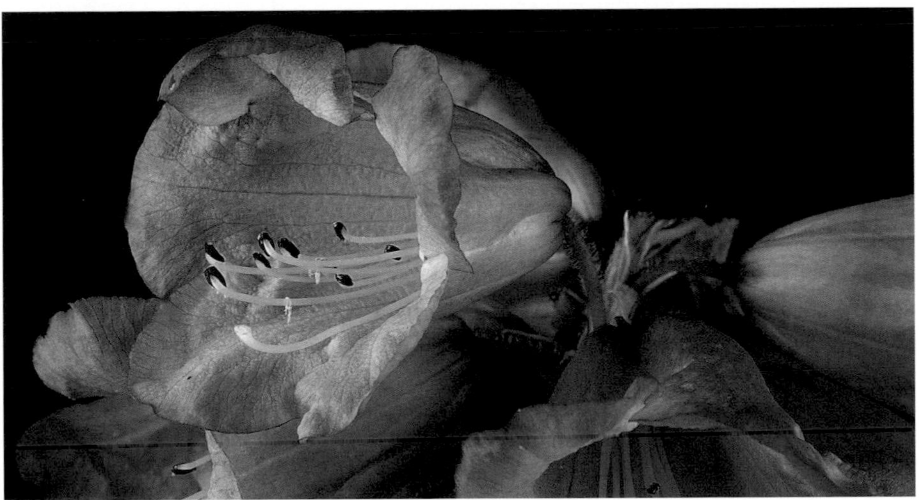

R. pachytrichum flower

R. pachytrichum detail

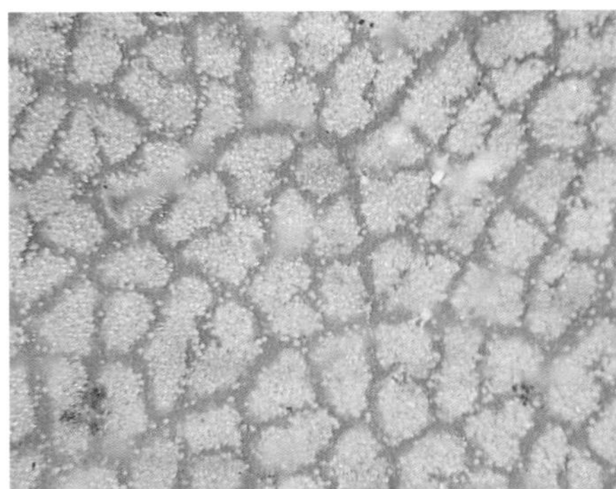

R. pachytrichum leaf surface

INFLORESCENCE BUDS ovoid to fusiform and pointed; outer scales brown or green and hairless; inner scales cuspidate, with white and brown hairs

CALYX to 1.5 mm, with rounded, ciliate lobes

COROLLA narrowly campanulate, 3.5–4 cm, white suffused with pink, with a purple basal blotch and spots

OVARY densely hairy, not glandular

STYLE hairless or glandular at the base

CAPSULE to 2 cm

DISTRIBUTION western China (northeastern Yunnan, Sichuan)

FLOWERING spring

HARDINESS ZONE 6

Classic wild-origin material is available under *Wilson 1203, 1435 1522.* Recent nonauthenticated material from Sichuan is also in cultivation.

35. ***Rhododendron maculiferum*** Franchet

HABIT shrub or small tree to 10 m; young shoots with a fine indumentum at first

LEAVES elliptic or oblong to obovate, 5–10 cm, 1.5–3 × as long as broad, hairless at maturity except for a thick indumentum of folioliferous hairs on the midrib beneath

CALYX to 1 mm; lobes rounded, hairless to shortly hairy

COROLLA openly campanulate, 2.5–3 cm, white suffused with pale pink, with a purple blotch at the base and a few spots; nectar sacs absent

OVARY densely reddish-hairy to hairless

CAPSULE to 2 cm, curved

DISTRIBUTION China (Anhui, Gansu, Guangxi, Guizhou, Hubei, Jiangxi, Shaanxi, Sichuan, Zhejiang)

FLOWERING spring

HARDINESS ZONE 9

R. *maculiferum* subsp. ***maculiferum***

ILLUSTRATION Millais, *Rhododendrons,* 24 (1917); *Iconographia Cormophytorum Sinicorum* 3, t. 4129 (1974); Cox and Cox, *The Encyclopedia of Rhododendron Species,* 101 (1997)

FLOWER STALKS, CALYX, AND OVARY shortly hairy

Recent nonauthenticated material from Guizhou and Hubei is in cultivation.

R. maculiferum subsp. **anwheiense** (Wilson) Chamberlain

SYNONYM *R. anwheiense* Wilson

ILLUSTRATION *Iconographia Cormophytorum Sinicorum* 3, t. 4127 (1974); Cox and Cox, *The Encyclopedia of Rhododendron Species,* 99 (1997); Feng, *Rhododendrons of China* 3, pl. 17: 1–3 (1999)

FLOWER STALKS, OVARY, AND CALYX hairless

36. *Rhododendron morii* Hayata

ILLUSTRATION *Curtis's Botanical Magazine,* n.s., 517 (1968), reprinted in Halliday, *The Illustrated Rhododendron,* pl. 72 (2001); *Rhododendron and Camellia Yearbook* 40: f. 6 (1987); Feng, *Rhododendrons of China* 2, pl. 12: 1–3 (1992); Cox and Cox, *The Encyclopedia of Rhododendron Species,* 101 (1997)

HABIT shrub or small tree to 8 m; young shoots with a dense, blackish indumentum which soon falls; bark grey-brown, breaking into oblong plates

LEAVES lanceolate to elliptic, 7–14 cm, about 4 × as long as broad, hairless above, hairless beneath except for a fluffy indumentum of folioliferous hairs on the midrib

INFLORESCENCE BUDS fusiform; scales mostly pale green, with brown, acuminate (or almost cuspidate) tips, only the inner hairy on the surface, but all with a tuft of hairs at the brown apex

CALYX to 2 mm, with broad, rounded, glandular-ciliate lobes

COROLLA widely campanulate, 3–5 cm, white sometimes tinged with pink, usually with a red basal blotch and some spots, without nectar sacs

STAMENS anthers cream with a brown ring around each pore

OVARY densely hairy and with a few shortly stalked glands

STYLE hairy at the base only

CAPSULE 1.3–1.7 cm

DISTRIBUTION Taiwan

FLOWERING late spring

HARDINESS ZONE 7

Wild-collected material is available under *Patrick* (without number), *Rhododendron Venture (Taiwan) 9834,* and *Wilson 10955.*

37. *Rhododendron pseudochrysanthum* Hayata

ILLUSTRATION *Curtis's Botanical Magazine*, n.s., 284 (1956); *Rhododendron and Camellia Yearbook* 11: f. 23 (1956); Davidian, *The Rhododendron Species* 3, pl. 20–21 (1992); Feng, *Rhododendrons of China* 2, pl. 15: 1–4 (1992); Kneller, *The Book of Rhododendrons*, 41 (1995); Cox and Cox, *The Encyclopedia of Rhododendron Species*, 104–105 (1997)

HABIT shrub to 3 m; young shoots with a reddish or grey indumentum

LEAVES ovate to elliptic, 3–8 cm, 2–3 × as long as broad, hairless above when mature, with a soon-falling fluffy indumentum beneath, of which only remains persist into maturity, except for mixed folioliferous hairs and glands along the midrib

CALYX to 2 mm, glandular-ciliate, with rounded lobes

COROLLA campanulate, 3–4 cm, pink, with deeper lines outside and spots within

OVARY with dense, shortly stalked glands

STYLE hairless

CAPSULE to 1 cm

DISTRIBUTION Taiwan

FLOWERING spring

HARDINESS ZONE 8

Wild-origin material is available under *Rhododendron Venture (Taiwan) 72/003* and *Wilson 10928*.

Less commonly cultivated are:

Rhododendron sikangense Fang

SYNONYM *R. cookeanum* Davidian

ILLUSTRATION *Iconographia Cormophytorum Sinicorum* 3, t. 4185 (1974)

Keying out to *R. morii* or *R. pachytrichum*, but:

LEAVES 2–2.5 × as long as broad, with stellate hairs (mixed with glands), as in subsection *Parishia* but with flowers more like those of subsection *Maculifera*

DISTRIBUTION western China (southwestern Sichuan)

Rhododendron pachysanthum Hayata

Similar to *R. pseudochrysanthum*, but:

LEAVES indumentum persisting and containing ramiform hairs

DISTRIBUTION Taiwan

Subgenus *Hymenanthes*

Section ***Pontica***

Subsection ***Selensia*** Sleumer (*Thomsonii* series *Selense* and *Martinianum* subseries)

HABIT shrubs or small trees; young shoots with shortly stalked glands or small glandular bristles, sometimes also with sparse dendroid hairs
LEAVES hairless beneath or with a thin indumentum of dendroid hairs
RACEME one- to 10-flowered, loose; rachis very short
CALYX 1–10 mm
COROLLA 5-lobed, funnel-campanulate to campanulate, without nectar sacs
STAMENS 10
OVARY with shortly stalked glands, sometimes also with dendroid hairs
STYLE hairless
SEEDS elongate, narrowly winged and with appendages at each end

There are 7 species, characterised by the presence of ramiform hairs on the lower surface of the leaves (sometimes persisting only on or near the midrib). The leaves have a 2-layered upper epidermis, the cells of both layers generally similar in size (in R. *bainbridgeanum* the cells of the lower layer are deeper than those of the upper layer), the cuticle thin or up to half as thick as the cells are deep; water tissue is generally absent, and the cells of the lower epidermis are not prolonged into papillae, or such papillae are very small. Sclereids are few or absent.

1 a Young shoots and leaf stalks with glandular bristles 2
b Young shoots and leaf stalks with shortly stalked glands or more or less hairless 4
2 a Leaves with a more or less continuous indumentum beneath, 2.3–3.2 × as long as broad . . . . **38. *R. bainbridgeanum***
b Leaves glabrous or with very sparse indumentum beneath, 1.5–2.5 × as long as broad 3
3 a Leaves broadly obovate, 3.5–6 cm wide; corolla campanulate . . . . **41. *R. hirtipes***
b Leaves obovate to elliptic, 1.8–4 cm wide; corolla funnel-campanulate . . . . **39. *R. selense***
4 a Leaves 4.5–5 cm; racemes one- to 4-flowered . . . . **40. *R. martinianum***
b Leaves 5–12 cm; racemes 3- to 10-flowered . . . . **39. *R. selense***

38. *Rhododendron bainbridgeanum* Tagg and Forrest
ILLUSTRATION Cox and Cox, *The Encyclopedia of Rhododendron Species,* 150–151 (1997)
HABIT to 2 m; young shoots with glandular bristles; bark brown, cracking into oblong plates

LEAVES obovate to elliptic, 8–12 cm, 2.3–3.2 × as long as broad, hairless above and with a continuous, felted, dark brown indumentum which contains glands (especially towards the base of the midrib) beneath

INFLORESCENCE BUDS fusiform; scales broad, brownish green, and slightly cuspidate, the inner especially so, as well as white-hairy

CALYX 3–6 mm, with shortly stalked glands; lobes unequal, rounded

COROLLA campanulate, 3–3.5 cm, white to cream-yellow, usually flushed with pink

OVARY densely glandular

STYLE usually glandular at the base

CAPSULE 1.5–2 cm

DISTRIBUTION western China (Xizang, Yunnan), northeastern Myanmar

FLOWERING spring

HARDINESS ZONE 8

Classic wild-origin material is available under *Forrest 21821*.

39. *Rhododendron selense* Franchet

HABIT shrub or small tree to 5 m; young shoots with gland-tipped bristles or shortly stalked glands; bark brown or yellowish brown, striate or breaking into small oblong plates

LEAVES ovate to obovate or elliptic, 3.5–9 cm; upper surface hairless; lower surface often with a few hairs towards the base near the midrib when mature, or with sparse brown hairs

INFLORESCENCE BUDS fusiform; scales cuspidate and at least the innermost densely white-hairy, sometimes with brown-headed glands on the surface; outer scales brown or purplish brown; inner scales pale brown to green

CALYX 1–8 mm; lobes ovate, rounded, or tongue-shaped, with shortly stalked glands

COROLLA funnel-campanulate, 2.5–4 cm, white or cream to deep pink, with or without purple spots

STAMENS 10; anthers brown or whitish

OVARY with shortly stalked glands

STYLE hairless

CAPSULE 1.2–3.5 cm, curved

DISTRIBUTION western China (southeastern Xizang, northwestern and western Yunnan, southwestern Sichuan)

FLOWERING spring

HARDINESS ZONE 8

A variable species, divided into 4 subspecies in the wild, 2 of which are cultivated.

R. selense subsp. **selense**

SYNONYM *R. probum* Balfour and Forrest

ILLUSTRATION *Iconographia Cormophytorum Sinicorum* 3, t. 4175 (1974); Davidian, *The Rhododendron Species* 3, pl. 97 (1992); Feng, *Rhododendrons of China* 2, pl. 7 (1992); Cox and Cox, *The Encyclopedia of Rhododendron Species,* 154 (1997)

HABIT young shoots with shortly stalked glands

CALYX longest lobe 2 mm (rarely to 5 mm)

ANTHERS often whitish

DISTRIBUTION western China (northwestern Yunnan, southeastern Xizang)

Classic wild-collected material is available under *Forrest 16318* and *Yü 7867*. Recent nonauthenticated material from Yunnan is also in cultivation.

R. selense subsp. *selense* flower

R. selense subsp. *selense* detail

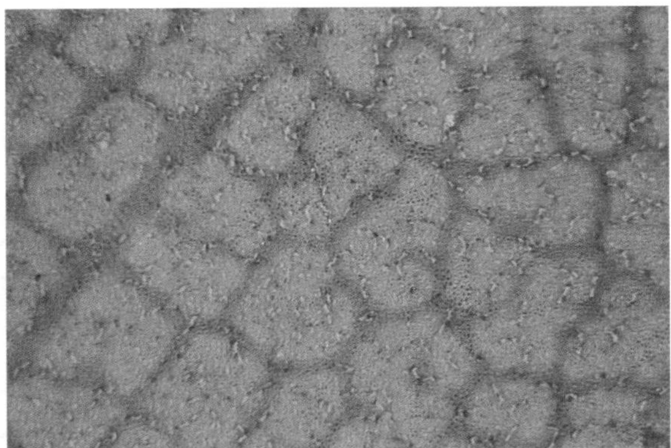

R. selense subsp. *selense* leaf surface

R. selense subsp. ***dasycladum*** (Balfour and W. W. Smith) Chamberlain

SYNONYM *R. dasycladum* Balfour and W. W. Smith

ILLUSTRATION Cox and Cox, *The Encyclopedia of Rhododendron Species,* 154–155 (1997); Feng, *Rhododendrons of China* 3, pl. 20 (1999); Halliday, *The Illustrated Rhododendron,* pl. 73 (2001)

HABIT young shoots with gland-tipped bristles; bark brown, breaking into very small oblong plates

INFLORESCENCE BUDS more or less fusiform; scales cuspidate, the innermost densely white-hairy; outer scales brown; inner scales pale brown to green

CALYX longest lobe 2–8 mm

STAMENS anthers brown

DISTRIBUTION western China (western Yunnan, southwestern Sichuan)

Classic wild-collected material is available under *Forrest 11312* and *Rock 11289, 25426.*

There are 2 other subspecies: *setiferum* (Balfour and Forrest) Chamberlain, with a persistent leaf indumentum, and *jucundum* (Balfour and W. W. Smith) Chamberlain, which is similar to subsp. *dasycladum* but with a glaucous bloom on the undersides of its leaves and its longest calyx lobes generally 4–6 mm. Neither of these subspecies is in general cultivation, though subsp. *setiferum* is illustrated in Davidian, *The Rhododendron Species* 3, pl. 99 [1992]; and subsp. *jucundum* is illustrated in Kneller, *The Book of Rhododendrons,* 49 (1995), and Cox and Cox, *The Encyclopedia of Rhododendron Species,* 155 (1997).

40. *Rhododendron martinianum* Balfour and Forrest

ILLUSTRATION Cox and Cox, *The Encyclopedia of Rhododendron Species,* 153 (1997)

HABIT shrub to 2 m; young shoots with shortly stalked glands or glandular bristles, rarely hairless

LEAVES elliptic to obovate, 4.5–5 cm, 2–2.3 × as long as broad, hairless throughout except for punctate hair bases on the lower surface

CALYX 1–3 mm; lobes rounded, with shortly stalked glands

COROLLA funnel-campanulate, to 3 cm, pale yellow or white flushed with pink, more rarely entirely pink, though usually dark pink in bud, spotted or not

OVARY AND THE BASE OF THE STYLE densely covered with shortly stalked glands

CAPSULE 2–2.5 cm, curved

DISTRIBUTION western China (northeastern Yunnan, southeastern Xizang), northeastern Myanmar

FLOWERING spring
HARDINESS ZONE 7

Classic wild-origin material is available under *Kingdon-Ward 21557*.

41. *Rhododendron hirtipes* Tagg

ILLUSTRATION *The Rhododendron Handbook*, f. 25 (1997); Cox and Cox, *The Encyclopedia of Rhododendron Species*, 152 (1997)

HABIT low shrub to small tree to 8 m; young shoots with glandular bristles; bark greyish brown, coarsely striate

LEAVES broadly ovate, 5–11 cm, 1.6–2.2 × as long as broad, hairless above, with scattered shortly stalked glands and a sparse fluffy indumentum beneath; midrib with glandular bristles near the base; margins sometimes ciliate towards the base

INFLORESCENCE BUDS ovoid; scales greenish or yellowish, sticky, somewhat hairy, scarcely cuspidate

CALYX 4–10 mm, with shortly stalked glands; lobes rounded

COROLLA campanulate, to 4 cm, white to pink, usually with a few purple spots, darker in bud

STAMENS 10; anthers pale brown

OVARY AND THE BASE OF THE STYLE densely covered with shortly stalked glands

CAPSULE to 2 cm, straight or curved

DISTRIBUTION western China (southeastern Xizang)

FLOWERING spring

HARDINESS ZONE 6

Classic wild-collected material is available under *Kingdon-Ward 5659* and *Ludlow, Sherriff, and Taylor 3624*.

Subgenus *Hymenanthes*

Section *Pontica*

Subsection *Glischra* (Tagg) Chamberlain (*Barbatum* series *Glischrum* subseries)

HABIT small shrubs to small trees; young shoots densely glandular-bristly; bud scales often persistent for several years

LEAVES sometimes with persistent bristles above and shortly stalked glands or bristles beneath, or with a dense indumentum of ramiform hairs

RACEME loose, 6- to 14-flowered; rachis 5–15 mm

CALYX well developed

COROLLA 5-lobed, campanulate to funnel-campanulate, without nectar sacs

STAMENS 10

OVARY densely glandular or glandular-bristly

STYLE hairless or glandular at the base

SEEDS elongate, narrowly winged and with appendages (sometimes rather small) at each end

A group of 6 species characterised by the presence of long bristles on the leaves and petioles. The leaves have a 2-layered upper epidermis, the cells of the lower layer considerably larger than those of the upper layer, the cuticle half as thick to as thick as the cells of the upper layer are deep; water tissue is generally present, and the cells of the lower epidermis are generally not prolonged into papillae. Sclereids are present in the leaf tissue of all species.

1a Lower surface of leaves with a dense covering of loosely matted hairs 2
 b Lower surface of leaves with or without a thin, persistent hair covering, often bristly 3
2a Leaves 7–17 × 2.3–4.2 cm; apex cuspidate; large shrubs to 5 m . . . . **45. *R. crinigerum***
 b Leaves 3–7 × 1–2 cm; apex blunt; dwarf shrubs to 1.5 m . . . . **46. *R. recurvoides***
3a Leaves 1.8–2.4 × as long as broad . . . . **43. *R. habrotrichum***
 b Leaves 2.4–4.2 × as long as broad 4
4a Calyx fleshy, cup-like, 8–20 mm; corolla rose-crimson . . . . **44. *R. diphrocalyx***
 b Calyx neither fleshy nor cup-like, deeply lobed, 7–10 mm; corolla white to pale pink . .**42. *R. glischrum***

42. *Rhododendron glischrum* Balfour and W. W. Smith

HABIT shrub or small tree to 8 m; young shoots densely glandular-bristly; bark pale greenish brown, cracking

LEAVES obovate to elliptic, 11.5–30 cm, 2–4 × as long as broad; margins ciliate; upper surface smooth to wrinkled, with some glandular bristles on the midrib near the base (rarely sparsely all over the surface); lower surface with a dense covering of bristles, especially on the midrib and veins, sometimes also with a thin brown covering of hairs

INFLORESCENCE BUDS ovoid, green; scales with white hairs and bristles; outer scales narrow and with well-developed midribs

CALYX 5–10 mm; lobes tongue-shaped, ciliate

COROLLA campanulate, 3–5 cm, pink to scarlet or occasionally white flushed with pink, with purple spots and usually also a basal blotch

OVARY densely covered with shortly stalked glands

STYLE hairless or glandular at the base

CAPSULE 1.5–2 cm

DISTRIBUTION western China (southern Xizang, northwestern Yunnan), northeastern Myanmar

FLOWERING spring

HARDINESS ZONE 8

R. *glischrum* subsp. ***glischrum***

ILLUSTRATION *Iconographia Cormophytorum Sinicorum* 3, t. 4121 (1974); Davidian, *The Rhododendron Species* 2, pl. 17 (1992); Feng, *Rhododendrons of China* 2, pl. 4: 1–2 (1992); Cox and Cox, *The Encyclopedia of Rhododendron Species,* 71 (1997)

LEAVES upper surface mostly smooth and hairless; lower surface without short hairs

Classic wild-collected material is available under *Forrest 25645.*

R. *glischrum* subsp. ***glischroides*** (Tagg and Forrest) Chamberlain

ILLUSTRATION Kneller, *The Book of Rhododendrons,* 33 (1995); Cox and Cox, *The Encyclopedia of Rhododendron Species,* 69–70 (1997)

SYNONYM *R. glischroides* Tagg and Forrest

LEAVES upper surface wrinkled; lower surface with veins thinly covered with short hairs

R. *glischrum* subsp. ***rude*** (Tagg and Forrest) Chamberlain

SYNONYM *R. rude* Tagg and Forrest

ILLUSTRATION *Rhododendron and Camellia Yearbook* 41: f. 8 (1988); *The Rhododendron Handbook,* f. 18 (1997); Davidian, *The Rhododendron Species* 2, pl. 23 (1992); Cox and Cox, *The Encyclopedia of Rhododendron Species,* 71–72 (1997)

LEAVES upper surface with a sparse covering of bristles

43. *Rhododendron habrotrichum* Balfour and W. W. Smith

ILLUSTRATION Millais, *Rhododendrons,* 152 (1924); Davidian, *The Rhododendron Species* 2, pl. 18 (1992); Cox and Cox, *The Encyclopedia of Rhododendron Species,* 72 (1997); Halliday, *The Illustrated Rhododendron,* pl. 74 (2001)

HABIT shrub to 4 m; young shoots densely glandular-bristly

LEAVES ovate to obovate, 7–16 cm, 1.8–2.4 × as long as broad; margins bristly-ciliate; upper surface smooth, hairless; lower surface hairless except for gland-tipped bristles on the midrib and main veins

CALYX 1–1.5 cm, with rounded lobes, red, glandular

COROLLA campanulate, 4–5 cm, white flushed with pink, with or without purple spots and a basal blotch

OVARY densely glandular-bristly

CAPSULE to 2 cm

DISTRIBUTION western China (western Yunnan), northeastern Myanmar

FLOWERING spring

HARDINESS ZONE 8

Classic wild-collected material is available under *Forrest 15778.*

44. *Rhododendron diphrocalyx* Balfour

ILLUSTRATION Millais, *Rhododendrons,* 152 (1924)

HABIT shrub to 5 m; young shoots bristly

LEAVES elliptic to obovate, 9–14 cm, 2.4–2.8 × as long as broad, hairless except for a few bristles at the base of the midrib beneath

CALYX 8–20 mm, fleshy, reddish, with unequal, rounded, ciliate lobes

COROLLA funnel-campanulate, 3–4 cm, pale to deep crimson, without spots; nectar sacs obscure

OVARY AND THE BASE OF THE STYLE densely reddish-hairy, with a few shortly stalked glands

CAPSULE to 2.5 cm

DISTRIBUTION unknown, perhaps of garden origin

FLOWERING spring

HARDINESS ZONE 8

Classic wild-collected material is available under *Forrest 15665.*

It has been suggested that this is perhaps a hybrid between *R. habrotrichum* and *R. neriiflorum* or one of its allies.

45. *Rhododendron crinigerum* Franchet

SYNONYM *R. ixeuticum* Balfour and W. W. Smith

ILLUSTRATION *Curtis's Botanical Magazine*, 9464 (1936), reprinted in Halliday, *The Illustrated Rhododendron*, pl. 75 (2001); *Iconographia Cormophytorum Sinicorum* 3, t. 4120 (1974); Davidian, *The Rhododendron Species* 2, pl. 16 (1992); Feng, *Rhododendrons of China* 2, pl. 3 (1992); Cox and Cox, *The Encyclopedia of Rhododendron Species*, 68–69 (1997)

HABIT shrub or small tree to 5 m; young shoots sparsely covered with shortly stalked glands; bark brown, striate

R. crinigerum flower and leaf

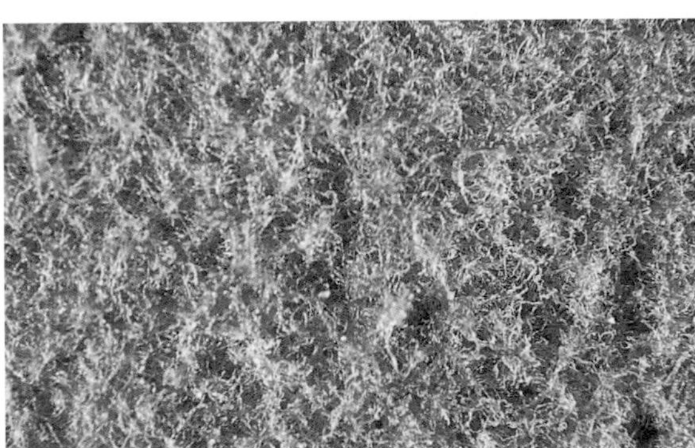

R. crinigerum leaf surface

LEAVES obovate to oblanceolate, 7–17 cm, 3–4 × as long as broad; upper surface hairless when mature; lower surface with a usually dense indumentum of matted, fawn to red-brown, ramiform hairs intermixed with a few glands
INFLORESCENCE BUDS ovoid, purplish brown; scales long-pointed, with simple or branched white hairs, the tips of the scales pointing outwards and upwards
CALYX 5–10 mm, densely covered with shortly stalked glands; lobes irregular, rounded
COROLLA campanulate, 3–4 cm, white flushed with pink, with a purple basal blotch and usually some spots
STAMENS anthers pale or yellowish brown
OVARY with shortly stalked glands
STYLE hairless or glandular at the base
CAPSULE to 1.5 cm
DISTRIBUTION western China (northwestern Yunnan, southeastern Xizang), northeastern Myanmar
FLOWERING spring
HARDINESS ZONE 7

Classic wild-collected material is available under *Rock 2, 38, 100, 10983.*

The information above refers to var. *crinigerum;* var. *euadenium* Tagg and Forrest, which is rarely cultivated, has leaves more densely glandular beneath.

46. *Rhododendron recurvoides* Tagg and Kingdon-Ward

ILLUSTRATION *Quarterly Bulletin of the American Rhododendron Society* 32: 171 (1978); Cox and Cox, *The Encyclopedia of Rhododendron Species,* 73 (1997)
HABIT shrub to 1.5 m; young shoots glandular-bristly; bark brownish to ginger, hairy when young, with the remains of old bud scales
LEAVES lanceolate to oblanceolate, 3–7 cm, 3–3.5 × as long as broad; upper surface rough from the persistent bases of small glandular bristles; lower surface with a dense cinnamon-brown indumentum of ramiform hairs
INFLORESCENCE BUDS ovoid, mostly brown but inner scales pale green to almost white; scales pointed and with brown hairs
CALYX 8–10 mm, with rounded lobes, glandular
COROLLA campanulate, to 3 cm, white flushed with pink, spotted with crimson, though without a basal blotch
STAMENS anthers pale brown
OVARY densely glandular-bristly
STYLE hairless

DISTRIBUTION northeastern Myanmar
FLOWERING spring
HARDINESS ZONE 9

Classic wild-collected material is available under *Kingdon-Ward 7184* (the type collection).

Less commonly cultivated are:

Rhododendron adenosum Davidian
Probably keying out to *R. glischrum,* but:
LEAVES 7.5–10 cm long, with cartilaginous, papillose margins
DISTRIBUTION western China (southwestern Sichuan)

The leaves of this species are unique within the subsection.

Rhododendron spilotum Balfour and Farrer

Based on material collected by Farrer in Upper Burma (Myanmar), this may be a hybrid of a species of subsection *Glischra;* material in cultivation under this name is usually incorrectly identified.

Subgenus *Hymenanthes*

Section *Pontica*

Subsection *Venatora* Chamberlain

HABIT straggling shrub to 3 m; young shoots glandular-bristly and fluffy-hairy
LEAVES hairless at maturity except for a thin indumentum on the midrib beneath, which contains folioliferous hairs
RACEME 7- to 10-flowered; rachis short
CALYX 5-lobed
COROLLA 5-lobed, fleshy, tubular-campanulate, with nectar sacs
STAMENS 10; filaments hairless
OVARY shortly hairy, with shortly stalked glands
STYLE hairless
SEEDS elongate, narrowly winged and with appendages at each end

Rhododendron venator is the only species. The leaves have a 2-layered upper epidermis, the cells of each layer more or less equal in size, the cuticle as thick as the cells are deep; water tissue is present, and the cells of the lower epidermis are not prolonged into papillae.

47. *Rhododendron venator* Tagg
ILLUSTRATION *The Garden* 110: 267 (1987); *The Rhododendron Handbook*, f. 24 (1997); Davidian, *The Rhododendron Species* 3, pl. 37 (1992); Kneller, *The Book of Rhododendrons*, 55 (1995); Cox and Cox, *The Encyclopedia of Rhododendron Species*, 201–202 (1997); Halliday, *The Illustrated Rhododendron*, pl. 76 (2001)
HABIT shrub to 3 m; young shoots glandular-bristly and shortly hairy
LEAVES elliptic to lanceolate, 8.5–14 cm, 3.5–4 × as long as broad, hairless except for the presence of mixed stellate and folioliferous hairs on the midrib beneath
CALYX 3–5 mm, shortly hairy and glandular, glandular-ciliate
COROLLA fleshy, tubular-campanulate, 3–3.5 cm, crimson with darker nectar sacs
OVARY tomentose, with shortly stalked glands
CAPSULE to 2 cm, curved
DISTRIBUTION western China (southeastern Xizang)
FLOWERING spring
HARDINESS ZONE 8

Classic wild-collected material is available under *Kingdon-Ward 6285* (the type collection).

R. venator flower and leaf

R. venator detail

R. venator leaf surface

Subgenus *Hymenanthes*

Section *Pontica*

Subsection *Irrorata* Sleumer (*Irroratum* series *Irroratum* subseries)

HABIT shrubs or small trees; young shoots with a covering of shortly stalked glands and sometimes eglandular hairs

LEAVES usually hairless when mature, but with punctate, reddish hair bases or with a thin covering of dendroid hairs embedded in a surface film

RACEME loose or dense, 4- to 20-flowered; rachis usually 5–10 mm (sometimes more)

CALYX minute or cup-like

COROLLA 5- to 7-lobed, tubular-campanulate to openly campanulate, with or without nectar sacs

STAMENS 10–14

OVARY hairless, shortly hairy, or with shortly stalked glands

STYLE hairless or glandular throughout

SEEDS elongate, winged and with appendages at each end

A group of about 18 species characterised in part by the persistence of red, punctate hair bases on the lower surface of the leaves; the corollas of several of the species are conspicuously spotted. The leaves have a 2-layered upper epidermis, the cells of each layer more or less equal in size, the cuticle half as thick to as thick as the cells are deep; water tissue is generally present, and the cells of the lower epidermis are not prolonged into papillae. Sclereids are present in the leaf tissue of all species.

1a Leaves with a continuous, persistent indumentum beneath .... **52. *R. tanastylum***
  b Leaves hairless or with a few scattered hairs beneath 2
2a Leaves 3–6 cm .... **48. *R. aberconwayi***
  b Leaves 6.5–15 cm 3
3a Corolla openly campanulate; leaf stalks hairless .... **49. *R. annae***
  b Corolla tubular-campanulate to funnel-campanulate; leaf stalks hairy or glandular, at least at first 4
4a Flower stalks, ovary, and leaf stalks with shortly stalked glands; corolla yellow, white, pink, or red .... **51. *R. irroratum***
  b Flower stalks, ovary, and leaf stalks either not glandular or with glandular bristles; corolla crimson to purple 5
5a Corolla 6- to 7-lobed .... **53. *R. anthosphaerum***
  b Corolla 5-lobed 6
6a Corolla 2.8–3.5 cm, white flushed with pink .... **50. *R. araiophyllum***
  b Corolla 4 cm or more, crimson .... **52. *R. tanastylum***

48. *Rhododendron aberconwayi* Cowan

ILLUSTRATION Davidian, *The Rhododendron Species* 2, pl. 69 (1992); Cox and Cox, *The Encyclopedia of Rhododendron Species,* 87 (1997); Feng, *Rhododendrons of China* 3, pl. 21: 1–7 (1999)

HABIT to 2 m; bark brown, striate

LEAVES thick, elliptic, 3–6 cm, about 3 × as long as broad, hairless when mature but with punctate hair bases beneath

INFLORESCENCE BUDS ovoid, pinkish green; scales with mixed brown and white hairs; margins conspicuously fringed with white hairs

CALYX c. 1 mm

COROLLA white to pale rose with purple spots, 2.8–3.5 cm, openly campanulate, without nectar sacs

OVARY AND STYLE glandular

CAPSULE 1.8–2 cm

DISTRIBUTION western China (northeastern Yunnan)

FLOWERING spring

HARDINESS ZONE 7

Classic wild-collected material is available under *McLaren U35A.*

49. *Rhododendron annae* Franchet

SYNONYM *R. laxiflorum* Balfour and Forrest

ILLUSTRATION *Iconographia Cormophytorum Sinicorum* 3, t. 4184 (1974); *Curtis's Botanical Magazine,* n.s., 385 (1962); Feng, *Rhododendrons of China* 2, pl. 18: 1–4 and pl. 19: 1–2 (1992); Cox and Cox, *The Encyclopedia of Rhododendron Species,* 88 (1997)

HABIT to 6 m; bark grey-brown, striate

LEAVES elliptic to oblanceolate, 6–15 cm, 3.5–4.5 × as long as broad, hairless when mature but with punctate hair bases over the veins beneath

CALYX 1–2 mm; lobes gland-fringed

COROLLA openly campanulate, 2.5–4 cm, without nectar sacs, white with a red flush, sometimes with purple spots

OVARY AND STYLE glandular

CAPSULE 1.3–2.5 cm

DISTRIBUTION western China (western Yunnan, Guizhou), northeastern Myanmar

FLOWERING spring

HARDINESS ZONE 7

Classic wild-collected material is available under *Forrest 15954, 27706.*

50. *Rhododendron araiophyllum* Balfour and W. W. Smith

ILLUSTRATION Feng, *Rhododendrons of China* 1, pl. 22 (1988); Cox and Cox, *The Encyclopedia of Rhododendron Species,* 90 (1997); Halliday, *The Illustrated Rhododendron,* pl. 77 (2001)

Similar to *R. annae,* but:

HABIT shrub or tree to 6.5 m; bark grey-brown, cracking into oblong plates

LEAVES without punctate hair bases

INFLORESCENCE BUDS fusiform; scales slightly hairy and a little sticky; lower scales dark mahogany-brown, cuspidate, the inner yellowish with reddish brown tips

STAMENS anthers brown

STYLE hairless

DISTRIBUTION western China (western Yunnan), northeastern Myanmar

FLOWERING spring

HARDINESS ZONE 8

51. *Rhododendron irroratum* Franchet

Illustrations *Curtis's Botanical Magazine,* 7361 (1894); Stevenson, *The Species of Rhododendron,* 345 (1930); *Iconographia Cormophytorum Sinicorum* 3, t. 4182 (1974); Fang, *Sichuan Rhododendron of China,* 93–96 (1986); Feng, *Rhododendrons of China* 1, pl. 25: 1–5 (1988); Davidian, *The Rhododendron Species* 2, pl. 70 (1992); Kneller, *The Book of Rhododendrons,* 37 (1995); Cox and Cox, *The Encyclopedia of Rhododendron Species,* 90–91 (1997).

HABIT shrub or small tree to 9 m; bark brown to greyish brown, striate or cracking into oblong plates

LEAVES oblanceolate to elliptic, 7–14 cm, 3–4 × as long as broad, hairless when mature but with red, punctate hair bases on the veins beneath

INFLORESCENCE BUDS ovoid or obovoid, mostly brown or the upper pinkish brown, broad, cuspidate, hairy at least near the tips, sometimes slightly sticky

CALYX to 2 mm, densely glandular, sometimes also with dendroid hairs

COROLLA campanulate to tubular-campanulate, 3.5–5 cm, downy within near the base, with nectar sacs, white or cream to violet-pink, with greenish or purple spots

STAMENS 10; anthers brown

OVARY with shortly stalked glands, often also with some dendroid hairs

STYLE glandular throughout

CAPSULE 1–2.5 cm, curved

DISTRIBUTION western China (Yunnan, Sichuan), Vietnam, Indonesia (Sumatra)
FLOWERING spring
HARDINESS ZONE 7

Represented in cultivation by the following classic collections: *Forrest 5851, 15097,* and *Rock 192.* Recent nonauthenticated material from Yunnan is also in cultivation.

A variable species, divided into 3 subspecies in the wild; only subsp. *irroratum* (Yunnan, Sichuan only) is in cultivation.

52. *Rhododendron tanastylum* Balfour and Kingdon-Ward
ILLUSTRATION Feng, *Rhododendrons of China* 3, pl. 26: 1–5 (1999)
HABIT shrub or small tree to 4 m (rarely more)
LEAVES elliptic to oblanceolate, 7.5–15 cm, 2.5–5 × as long as broad, hairless throughout or with a thin indumentum and punctate hair bases beneath
CALYX to 2 mm, glandular, sometimes also shortly hairy
COROLLA tubular-campanulate, 4.5–5.5 cm, deep pink to deep crimson, with black nectar sacs and few to many spots
OVARY hairless or with reddish hairs and glands
STYLE hairless
CAPSULE 1.1–2.3 cm
DISTRIBUTION northeastern India (Arunachal Pradesh), western China (western Yunnan), northeastern Myanmar
FLOWERING spring
HARDINESS ZONE 9

There are 2 varieties known in the wild, but only var. *tanastylum,* described above, is in cultivation.

53. *Rhododendron anthosphaerum* Diels
SYNONYM *R. eritimum* Balfour and W. W. Smith
ILLUSTRATION *Curtis's Botanical Magazine,* 9083 (1926), reprinted in Halliday, *The Illustrated Rhododendron,* pl. 79 (2001); *Iconographia Cormophytorum Sinicorum* 3, t. 4186 (1974); Feng, *Rhododendrons of China* 1, pl. 21: 1–3 (1988); Cox and Cox, *The Encyclopedia of Rhododendron Species,* 89 (1997)
HABIT shrub or tree to 12 m; bark brown, reddish brown, or greyish, cracking into oblong plates
LEAVES elliptic-obovate to oblong, 6–16 cm, 3–4 × as long as broad, hairless at maturity but with punctate hair bases beneath

R. anthosphaerum flower and leaf

R. anthosphaerum detail

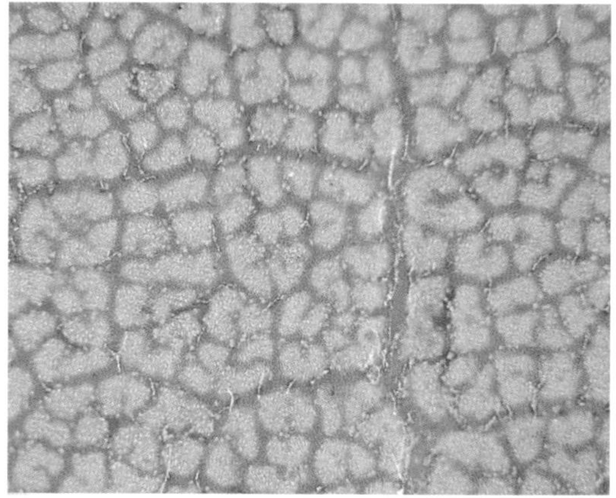

R. anthosphaerum leaf surface

INFLORESCENCE BUDS spherical to ovoid, green or brown; scales cuspidate and hairy, especially near the tips; outer scales broad
CALYX 1–2 mm, hairless or glandular
COROLLA 6- to 7-lobed, tubular-campanulate, with nectar sacs, 3–4.5 cm, pink, crimson, magenta, or rarely peach, sometimes with darker spots and a basal blotch
STAMENS 10; anthers mid to dark brown
OVARY AND STYLE hairless, rarely ovary with a few reddish hairs
CAPSULE 2–2.5 cm
DISTRIBUTION western China (Yunnan, southeastern Xizang), northeastern Myanmar
FLOWERING spring
HARDINESS ZONE 8

Classic wild-collected material is available under *Forrest 5848, 10651, 18168, 21686, 24600, 25984, Kingdon-Ward 5458,* and *Rock 121, 163, 11354.* Recent nonauthenticated material from Yunnan is also in cultivation.

A variable species, some of whose variants have been named in the past. Of these, that formerly known as *R. eritimum,* with a crimson to magenta corolla 3.5–4.5 cm long, is most likely to be found in gardens.

Less commonly cultivated are:

Rhododendron kendrickii Nuttall
ILLUSTRATION *Curtis's Botanical Magazine,* 5129 (1859), reprinted in Halliday, *The Illustrated Rhododendron,* pl. 78 (2001)
Keying out to *R. tanastylum,* but:
LEAVES 4–6 × as long as broad, almost completely hairless beneath
INFLORESCENCES 10- to 20-flowered
COROLLA scarlet to crimson
DISTRIBUTION northeastern India (Arunachal Pradesh), Bhutan, western China (southern Xizang)

Rhododendron leptopeplum Balfour and Forrest

Keying out to *R. tanastylum,* but:

LEAVES persistently hairy beneath

CALYX 4–6 mm

OVARY with glandular hairs only

DISTRIBUTION western China (northwestern Yunnan)

Rhododendron lukiangense Franchet

Similar to *R. tanastylum* and keying out to it.

LEAVES almost completely hairless beneath

INFLORESCENCES 6- to 15-flowered

COROLLA 4–4.5 cm, rose

CAPSULE 5–7 × as long as broad

DISTRIBUTION western China (northwestern Yunnan, southwestern Sichuan, southeastern Xizang)

Rhododendron ramsdenianum Cowan

Very similar to *R. kendrickii,* but:

LEAVES 2.8–3.5 × as long as broad

DISTRIBUTION western China (southeastern Xizang), perhaps also Bhutan

Subgenus *Hymenanthes*

Section *Pontica*

Subsection *Pontica* Sleumer (*Ponticum* series)

HABIT shrubs or small trees; young shoots hairless to densely hairy and with shortly stalked glands

LEAVES hairless beneath but sometimes with persistent, punctate hair bases or an indumentum of dendroid hairs

INFLORESCENCES loose or dense, 5- to 20-flowered; rachis usually elongate

CALYX 1–9 mm

COROLLA 5- or rarely 7-lobed for about half its length, campanulate to funnel-campanulate, without nectar sacs, usually with brownish, greenish, or yellowish spots

STAMENS 10

OVARY hairless, glandular, or hairy

STYLE hairless

SEEDS elongate, narrowly winged and with (sometimes large) appendages at each end

A group of 12 species, mostly found in areas outside of the main Chinese centre of the genus. They are characterised by the elongate, raceme-like inflorescence with many flowers, and a tendency for the corolla to be very deeply lobed. Anatomically the leaves of these species are rather variable. Mostly they have a 2-layered upper epidermis, the cells of each layer similar in size (cells of the lower layer larger in *R. ponticum;* epidermis one-layered in *R. catawbiense* and some subspecies of *R. degronianum*), the cuticle thin to as thick as the cells are deep; water tissue is generally absent, and the cells of the lower epidermis are generally not prolonged into papillae. Sclereids are few or absent.

1a Lower surface of leaves with reddish, punctate hair bases (sometimes also with scattered dendroid hairs) . . . . **54. *R. hyperythrum***

b Lower surface of leaves hairless and without punctate hair bases, or densely hairy 2

2a Leaves hairless beneath or with a thin, sparse indumentum at maturity 3

b Leaves persistently hairy beneath with a continuous, adpressed or woolly indumentum 8

3a Corolla yellow; dwarf shrub, 20–100 cm . . . . **61. *R. aureum***

b Corolla whitish to lilac-purple; shrub, usually more than 1 m 4

4a Ovary hairless . . . . **62. *R. ponticum***

b Ovary glandular and/or hairy 5

5a Leaves 3.5–4 × as long as broad; ovary and flower stalks glandular; calyx 3–5 mm . . . . **64. *R. maximum***

b Leaves to 3 × as long as broad; ovary and flower stalks eglandular; calyx 1–2 mm 6

6 a Corolla lilac-purple; leaves 1.8–2.3 × as long as broad .... **63. *R. catawbiense***
b Corolla white flushed with pink, to pink; leaves more than 2.3 × as long as broad 7
7 a Leaf apex acute; base cuneate; corolla 3–4 cm .... **65. *R. macrophyllum***
b Leaf apex and base rounded; corolla to 2.5 cm .... **55. *R. brachycarpum***
8 a Dwarf shrub to 1 m; leaves with a compacted indumentum beneath; corolla yellow or creamy white .... **60. *R. caucasicum***
b Taller shrub, more than 1 m; leaves with compacted to woolly indumentum beneath; corolla white to pink, rarely yellowish 9
9 a Leaves to 2.5 × as long as broad; corolla to 2.5 cm; leaf indumentum compacted, thin .... **55. *R. brachycarpum***
b Leaves more than 2.5 × as long as broad; corolla longer than 2.5 cm; leaf indumentum usually thick, compacted to woolly 10
10 a Leaf indumentum very thick, covering the midribs beneath; similar indumentum present on the one-year-old shoots .... **57. *R. yakushimanum***
b Leaf indumentum thick, but not covering the midribs beneath; one-year-old shoots sparsely hairy 11
11 a Young shoots eglandular; inflorescence rachis 2–20 mm .... **56. *R. degronianum***
b Young shoots with at least some glands; inflorescence rachis 2.5 cm or more 12
12 a Ovary and leaf stalks with shortly stalked glands; leaves 11–21 cm; calyx 5–9 mm . . **58. *R. ungernii***
b Ovary and leaf stalks eglandular; leaves to 11 cm; calyx 2–3 mm .... **59. *R. smirnowii***

54. ***Rhododendron hyperythrum*** Hayata

ILLUSTRATION *Curtis's Botanical Magazine*, n.s., 109 (1950); Feng, *Rhododendrons of China* 2, pl. 23: 1–3 (1992); Cox and Cox, *The Encyclopedia of Rhododendron Species*, 144 (1997)

HABIT shrub; young shoots hairless; bark chestnut-brown, shredding into long strips and oblong plates

LEAVES elliptic, 8–12 cm, 3.2–3.4 × as long as broad, hairless throughout when mature except for some punctate hair bases beneath and at times some persistent dendroid hairs towards the base and on the midrib

INFLORESCENCE BUDS very narrowly fusiform, conspicuously long, with many scales; scales long-tapered; lower scales brown, sometimes notched; upper scales green, with white and pale brown hairs

CALYX to 3 mm, sparsely hairy

COROLLA funnel-campanulate, 3.5–4.5 cm, white with reddish spots

STAMENS 10; anthers very pale brown

OVARY densely glandular; style glandular in the lower part

DISTRIBUTION Taiwan
FLOWERING late spring
HARDINESS ZONE 8

Wild-collected material is in cultivation under *Patrick* (without number).

55. *Rhododendron brachycarpum* G. Don
HABIT to 3 m; young shoots hairy, mature shoots hairless
LEAVES oblong to obovate, 7–11 cm, 2.3–2.5 × as long as broad; upper surface hairless; lower surface hairless or with a compacted, greyish to fawn indumentum
CALYX 2 mm; tube hairy; lobes hairless
COROLLA broadly funnel-campanulate, to 2.5 cm, white to pale pink, with greenish spots
OVARY densely hairy
STYLE hairless
CAPSULE 2–3 cm
DISTRIBUTION Japan, Korea
FLOWERING spring
HARDINESS ZONE 6

R. *brachycarpum* subsp. ***brachycarpum***
ILLUSTRATION Cox and Cox, *The Encyclopedia of Rhododendron Species,* 137–138 (1997)
LEAVES lower surface with persistent indumentum

Wild-collected material is in cultivation under *Doleshy 13* and *Kwanak Arboretum, Seoul* (without number). Recent nonauthenticated material from Japan and Korea is also in cultivation.

R. *brachycarpum* subsp. ***fauriei*** (Franchet) Chamberlain
SYNONYM *R. fauriei* Franchet
ILLUSTRATION Nakai, *Flora Sylvatica Koreana* 8, t. 8 (1919); Cox and Cox, *The Encyclopedia of Rhododendron Species,* 138 (1997)
LEAVES hairless beneath when mature

Recent nonauthenticated material from Japan and South Korea is in cultivation.

56. *Rhododendron degronianum* Carrière

SYNONYM *R. japonicum* (Blume) Schneider

HABIT shrub to 2.5 m; young shoots sparsely to densely hairy, eglandular

LEAVES elliptic to oblanceolate, 8–14 cm, 3–4 × as long as broad, hairless above, with a dense, compacted, grey to fawn indumentum beneath, rarely the indumentum quickly falling

CALYX 2–3 mm; lobes rounded-triangular, hairless

COROLLA 5- to 7-lobed, 3–4.5 cm, widely funnel-campanulate, pink, with conspicuous darker spots

OVARY white-hairy

CAPSULE 2.2 cm or more

DISTRIBUTION Japan

FLOWERING late spring

HARDINESS ZONE 7

The classification of the Japanese species of subsection *Pontica* is complex and difficult. The account given here follows Chamberlain and Doleshy (1987).

R. degronianum subsp. ***degronianum***

SYNONYMS *R. metternichii* Siebold and Zuccarini var. *pentamerum* Maximowicz; *R. japonicum* (Blume) Schneider var. *pentamerum* (Maximowicz) Hutchinson

ILLUSTRATION Makino, *An Illustrated Flora of Japan*, 925 (1949); *Quarterly Bulletin of the American Rhododendron Society* 27: 35 (1973); Davidian, *The Rhododendron Species* 3, pl. 52 (1992); Cox and Cox, *The Encyclopedia of Rhododendron Species*, 141–142 (1997)

HABIT bark brown to greyish brown, striate, ultimately shredding in long strips

INDUMENTUM generally velvety, heavily felted, or spongy, but sparse or absent on the midribs of the leaves beneath and on the one-year-old shoots

INFLORESCENCE BUDS spherical and slightly pointed to fusiform; outer scales green or brown, narrow; inner scales brown, densely white-hairy

COROLLA funnel-shaped, 5-lobed

STAMENS anthers white or yellowish brown

DISTRIBUTION northern Japan

Recent nonauthenticated material from Japan is in cultivation.

R. degronianum subsp. ***heptamerum*** (Maximowicz) Hara

SYNONYMS *R. metternichii* Siebold and Zuccarini; *R. metternichii* var. *heptamerum* Maximowicz; *R. japonicum* (Blume) Schneider

ILLUSTRATION Davidian, *The Rhododendron Species* 3, pl. 51 (1992); Cox and Cox, *The Encyclopedia of Rhododendron Species,* 142 (1997)
LEAVES indumentum thin or thick
COROLLA funnel-shaped, 7-lobed
DISTRIBUTION central and southern Japan

Represented in cultivation by wild-collected material under *Doleshy* 5. Recent nonauthenticated material from Japan is also in cultivation.

Variable and divided by Hara into several varieties, of which only var. *heptamerum* is important in cultivation.

57. ***Rhododendron yakushimanum*** Nakai

SYNONYM *R. degronianum* subsp. *yakushimanum* (Nakai) Hara
Very similar to *R. degronianum,* but:
LEAVES indumentum very thick and dense, covering the midribs beneath as well as the rest of the surface
ONE-YEAR-OLD SHOOTS with similar indumentum to the leaves beneath
COROLLA 5-lobed, broadly based, campanulate
DISTRIBUTION Japan
FLOWERING late spring
HARDINESS ZONE 8

R. yakushimanum flower and leaf

R. yakushimanum detail

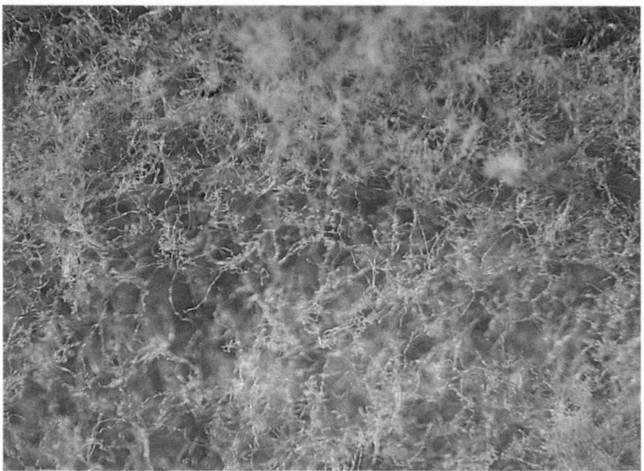

R. yakushimanum leaf surface

R. *yakushimanum* subsp. ***yakushimanum***

ILLUSTRATION *Curtis's Botanical Magazine,* n.s., 771 (1979), reprinted in Halliday, *The Illustrated Rhododendron,* pl. 80 (2001); Davidian, *The Rhododendron Species* 3, pl. 45–46 (1992); Kneller, *The Book of Rhododendrons,* 47 (1995); Cox and Cox, *The Encyclopedia of Rhododendron Species,* 143 (1997)

LEAVES 3–4 × as long as broad

CALYX 2–3 mm; lobes rounded, hairless

DISTRIBUTION southern Japan (Yaku Shima)

Recent nonauthenticated material from Japan is in cultivation.

This subspecies, found in most gardens and nurseries under the name *R. yakushimanum,* has been much used in recent hybridisation as a parent of a range of striking, very hardy hybrids.

R. *yakushimanum* subsp. ***makinoi*** (Tagg) Hara

ILLUSTRATION Davidian, *The Rhododendron Species* 3, pl. 39 (1992); Cox and Cox, *The Encyclopedia of Rhododendron Species,* 145–146 (1997)

LEAVES long and narrow, at least 7 × as long as broad

CALYX 5–7 mm; lobes with coarse hairs

DISTRIBUTION Japan

Recent nonauthenticated material from Japan is in cultivation.

58. *Rhododendron ungernii* Trautvetter

ILLUSTRATION *Gartenflora* 35, t. 1226 (1886); *Curtis's Botanical Magazine*, 8332 (1910); Cox and Cox, *The Encyclopedia of Rhododendron Species*, 149 (1997)

HABIT shrub or small tree to 7 m; young shoots densely white-woolly, with some stalked glands mixed in

LEAVES oblanceolate to obovate, hairless above when mature, with a dense, white or fawn, woolly indumentum beneath

CALYX 5–9 mm; lobes lanceolate, acute, with shortly stalked glands

COROLLA funnel-campanulate, to 3.5 cm, white, sometimes flushed with pink, with greenish spots

OVARY with brownish, stalked glands and white, longer, eglandular hairs

CAPSULE 1.2–1.5 cm

DISTRIBUTION northeastern Turkey, Georgia

FLOWERING spring

HARDINESS ZONE 5

Recent nonauthenticated material from Turkey is in cultivation.

59. *Rhododendron smirnowii* Trautvetter

ILLUSTRATION *Revue Horticole*, t. 500 (1899); Cox and Cox, *The Encyclopedia of Rhododendron Species*, 148–149 (1997)

HABIT shrub to 4 m; young shoots with dense, white, woolly hairs

LEAVES oblanceolate to elliptic, 7.5–14 cm, 2.8–4.5 × as long as broad; upper surface hairless when mature; lower surface with a dense, white to brown, woolly indumentum

CALYX 2–3 mm; lobes broadly triangular, with a sparse floccose indumentum and some shortly stalked glands

COROLLA funnel-campanulate, 3.5–4 cm, pink with yellowish spots

OVARY densely white-hairy, eglandular

CAPSULE to 1.5 cm

DISTRIBUTION northeastern Turkey and adjacent Georgia

FLOWERING late spring

HARDINESS ZONE 4

Wild-collected material is in cultivation under *Apold, Cox, and Hutchison 129A, 129B.*

60. *Rhododendron caucasicum* Pallas

ILLUSTRATION *Curtis's Botanical Magazine,* 1145 (1808) and 3422 (1835); Moser, *Rhododendron: Wildarten und Hybriden,* 19 (1991); Cox and Cox, *The Encyclopedia of Rhododendron Species,* 140 (1997)

HABIT small shrub to 1 m; young shoots sparsely hairy

LEAVES obovate to elliptic, 4–7.5 cm, 2.2–3 × as long as broad, hairless above, with a dense, compacted, fawn to brown indumentum beneath

CALYX 1–2 mm, hairy

COROLLA broadly campanulate, 3–3.5 cm, whitish to yellow, sometimes flushed with pink, with greenish spots

OVARY densely hairy with dendroid hairs

STYLE hairless

CAPSULE 1.5–2 cm

DISTRIBUTION Turkey, Caucasus

FLOWERING late spring

HARDINESS ZONE 6

Wild-collected material is in cultivation under *Cary Arboretum* (without number), *Cuba* (without number), and *Davis 20904.*

Widely hybridised with early introductions from the Himalaya, producing a range of hardy hybrids, such as *R.* ×*nobleanum* (× a pale variant of *R. arboreum*), 'Cunningham's White' (also perhaps × *R. arboreum*), and 'Goldsworth Yellow' (× *R. campylocarpum*).

61. *Rhododendron aureum* Georgi

SYNONYM *R. chrysanthum* Pallas

ILLUSTRATION Pallas, *Flora Rossica,* t. 30 (1784); Busch, *Flora Sibiriae et Orientis extremi* (Ericaceae), t. 63 (1915); *Curtis's Botanical Magazine,* 8882 (1921); Davidian, *The Rhododendron Species* 3, pl. 43–44 (1992); Cox and Cox, *The Encyclopedia of Rhododendron Species,* 136 (1997)

HABIT to 1 m; leaf bud scales persistent

LEAVES ovate to broadly elliptic, 2.5–15 cm, 2–2.5 × as long as broad, hairless when mature

RACEME rather loose, 5- to 8-flowered

CALYX 2–3 mm; lobes hairy, rounded-triangular

COROLLA widely campanulate, 2.5–3 cm, usually yellow, often spotted

OVARY with reddish hairs

STYLE hairless

CAPSULE 1 cm

DISTRIBUTION eastern Russia, Korea, Japan, northern China
FLOWERING spring
HARDINESS ZONE 2

Recent nonauthenticated material from the former Soviet Union, China, and Japan is in cultivation.

Variety *aureum* is described above; var. *hypopitys* (Pojarkova) Chamberlain, with deciduous bud scales and longer leaves (perhaps only a shade form of var. *aureum*) is not in cultivation.

62. *Rhododendron ponticum* Linnaeus

SYNONYM *R. baeticum* Boissier and Reuter
ILLUSTRATION *Curtis's Botanical Magazine,* 690 (1803); Cox and Cox, *The Encyclopedia of Rhododendron Species,* 147–148 (1997)
HABIT shrub to 8 m; young shoots hairless
LEAVES oblanceolate to broadly elliptic, 6–18 cm, 1.8–5 × as long as broad, entirely hairless when mature
CALYX 1–2 mm, hairless; lobes shallowly triangular
COROLLA campanulate, 3.5–5 cm, lilac-pink to purple, usually with greenish yellow spots
OVARY AND STYLE hairless
CAPSULE 1.5–2.5 cm
DISTRIBUTION western Mediterranean area (Spain, Portugal), eastern Mediterranean area (Bulgaria, northern Turkey, Caucasus, Lebanon), widely naturalised in many parts of Britain and Ireland
FLOWERING late spring
HARDINESS ZONE 6

Recent nonauthenticated material from Portugal and Turkey is in cultivation.

Often used as a grafting stock for material belonging to section *Pontica,* and widely hybridised with early Himalayan introductions. Much of the material introduced to and naturalised in Britain and other parts of Europe may well be of hybrid origin.

63. *Rhododendron catawbiense* Michaux

ILLUSTRATION *Curtis's Botanical Magazine,* 1671 (1814); Moser, *Rhododendron: Wildarten und Hybriden,* 33 (1991); Davidian, *The Rhododendron Species* 3, pl. 41 (1992); Cox and Cox, *The Encyclopedia of Rhododendron Species,* 139 (1997); Holmgren, *The Illustrated Companion to Gleason and Cronquist's Manual,* 184 (1998)

HABIT shrub to 3 m; young shoots hairy at first
LEAVES broadly elliptic to obovate, 6.5–11.5 cm, 1.9–2.3 × as long as broad, hairless when mature but with persistent hair bases beneath
CALYX to 1 mm, hairless
COROLLA funnel-campanulate, 3–4.5 cm, usually lilac-purple with faint spots
OVARY hairy with reddish hairs
STYLE hairless
CAPSULE to 2 cm
DISTRIBUTION eastern United States (Virginia, North Carolina)
FLOWERING late spring
HARDINESS ZONE 4

Wild-collected material is in cultivation under *Sandeman 161, Serbin* (without number), and *Wisley* (without number). Recent nonauthenticated material from the United States is in cultivation.

Very similar to *R. ponticum.*

64. *Rhododendron maximum* Linnaeus

ILLUSTRATION *Curtis's Botanical Magazine,* 951 (1806), reprinted in Halliday, *The Illustrated Rhododendron,* t. 81 (2001); Davidian, *The Rhododendron Species* 3, pl. 40 (1992); Cox and Cox, *The Encyclopedia of Rhododendron Species,* 146–147 (1997); Holmgren, *The Illustrated Companion to Gleason and Cronquist's Manual,* 184 (1998)
HABIT shrub or small tree to 3.5 m; young shoots hairy and with shortly stalked glands, soon hairless
LEAVES oblanceolate to elliptic, 10–16 cm, 3.3–4 × as long as broad; upper surface hairless; lower surface with a thin indumentum embedded in a thin film which persists towards the base near the midrib
CALYX 3–5 mm; lobes rounded, with shortly stalked glands
COROLLA campanulate, 2.5–3 cm, white to pinkish purple, with yellowish green spots
OVARY hairy, with shortly stalked glands
STYLE hairless
CAPSULE 1.7–2 cm
DISTRIBUTION eastern North America (from Nova Scotia to northern Georgia)
FLOWERING late spring
HARDINESS ZONE 3

Wild-collected material is in cultivation under *American Rhododendron Society* (without number) and *Serbin* (without number). Recent nonauthenticated material from the United States is also in cultivation.

65. *Rhododendron macrophyllum* G. Don

SYNONYM *R. californicum* Hooker

ILLUSTRATION *Curtis's Botanical Magazine,* 4863 (1855), reprinted in Halliday, *The Illustrated Rhododendron,* pl. 82 (2001); Abrams and Ferris, *Illustrated Flora of the Pacific Northwest* 3: f. 3676 (1944); Davidian, *The Rhododendron Species* 3, pl. 47–50 (1992); Cox and Cox, *The Encyclopedia of Rhododendron Species,* 144–145 (1997)

HABIT shrub to 4 m; young shoots soon hairless

LEAVES broadly elliptic, 6.5–17 cm, 2.5–2.8 × as long as broad, hairless throughout when mature

CALYX to 1 mm, hairless

COROLLA broadly campanulate, 3–4 cm, white to pink, with yellowish spots

OVARY densely reddish-hairy

STYLE hairless

CAPSULE to 2.5 cm

DISTRIBUTION western North America (from British Columbia to California)

FLOWERING spring

HARDINESS ZONE 6

Wild-collected material is in cultivation under *American Rock Garden Society* (without number) and *Vancouver Botanic Garden* (without number). Recent nonauthenticated material from Canada and the United States is also in cultivation.

Subgenus *Hymenanthes*

Section *Pontica*

Subsection *Argyrophylla* Sleumer (*Argyrophyllum* series; *Floribundum* series)

HABIT shrubs or small trees to 11 m; bark rough; young shoots with a thin indumentum

LEAVES with a thin and compacted indumentum on the lower surface, made up of rosulate hairs, or with a 2-layered indumentum, the upper layer woolly-hairy, of white or fawn (rarely yellowish) ramiform hairs

RACEME loose or dense, 4- to 30-flowered

CALYX usually minute

COROLLA 5-lobed, openly campanulate to funnel-campanulate; nectar sacs usually absent

STAMENS 10 in cultivated species, more than 10 in other species

OVARY hairless or with a thin, glandular or eglandular indumentum

STYLE hairless or glandular throughout

SEEDS elongate, winged and with usually large appendages at each end

A group of 13 species, generally similar to subsection *Pontica* but with less deeply lobed corollas, less elongate raceme axes, and a Chinese distribution. The leaves have a one- or 2-layered upper epidermis; when 2-layered, the cells are equal in size, the cuticle half as thick to as thick as the cells are deep. Water tissue is well developed, and the cells of the lower epidermis are generally prolonged into small papillae. Sclereids are present in the leaf tissue of all species.

1a Leaves with a 2-layered indumentum, the upper layer more or less woolly and loose; raceme with 4–12 flowers 2

b Leaves with a one-layered, compacted indumentum; racemes with 5–30 flowers 3

2a Inflorescence rachis 1–1.5 cm; leaves 4–4.5 × as long as broad . . . . **67. *R. hunnewellianum***

b Inflorescence rachis usually 3–7 mm; leaves 2.3–3.3 × as long as broad . . . . **66. *R. floribundum***

3a Inflorescence rachis 3–5 mm 4

b Inflorescence rachis 1–4 cm (rarely less) 5

4a Flower stalks 5–10 mm; leaf indumentum white; corolla purplish to violet, with nectar sacs . . . . **71. *R. rirei***

b Flower stalks 2–4 cm; leaf indumentum fawn, shining; corolla pink, without nectar sacs . . . . **70. *R. insigne***

5a Style glandular throughout . . . . **68. *R. thayerianum***

b Style hairless or with a few glands at the base . . . . **69. *R. argyrophyllum***

66. *Rhododendron floribundum* Franchet

ILLUSTRATION *Curtis's Botanical Magazine,* 9609 (1940); *Iconographia Cormophytorum Sinicorum* 3, t. 4240 (1974)

HABIT shrub or small tree to 5 m

LEAVES oblanceolate to elliptic, 10–18 cm, 3–3.3 × as long as broad; upper surface hairless when mature, with deeply impressed veins; lower surface with a 2-layered indumentum at least covering the veins, the lower layer adpressed and whitish, the upper loose and woolly, yellowish at first, becoming white or greyish, the hairs ramiform

CALYX to 1 mm

COROLLA broadly campanulate, to 4 cm, magenta-pink, with crimson spots and a basal blotch

OVARY densely hairy

STYLE hairless

CAPSULE 2–3 cm, sometimes curved

DISTRIBUTION western China (Sichuan)

FLOWERING spring

HARDINESS ZONE 8

Classic wild-collected material is available under *Wilson 4266.* Recent nonauthenticated material from Sichuan is also in cultivation.

67. *Rhododendron hunnewellianum* Rehder and Wilson

ILLUSTRATION Fang, *Sichuan Rhododendron of China,* 115–117 (1986)

HABIT shrub or small tree to 6 m; bark greyish brown, breaking into irregular, oblong plates

LEAVES narrowly oblanceolate, 7–15 cm, 4–4.5 × as long as broad, hairless above, with a 2-layered indumentum beneath, the lower layer compacted and whitish, the upper falling or persistent, white to yellow, consisting of ramiform hairs intermixed with scattered glands (especially on the midrib)

INFLORESCENCE BUDS ovoid to cylindric; scales mainly green, the lower with brown edges, all shortly pointed, densely covered with white, silky hairs

CALYX to 1 mm; lobes minute, glandular-ciliate

COROLLA widely campanulate, 4–5 cm, white to pink or purple, with purple spots

STAMENS 10; anthers reddish brown

OVARY densely yellowish-hairy

CAPSULE 2–2.5 cm

DISTRIBUTION western China (central Sichuan, Gansu)

FLOWERING spring
HARDINESS ZONE 9

Classic wild-collected material is available under *Wilson 1198*.

Variety *hunnewellianum* is described above; var. *rockii* (Wilson) Chamberlain, with shorter leaves whose upper indumentum layer turns yellow with age, is not in cultivation.

68. *Rhododendron thayerianum* Rehder and Wilson

ILLUSTRATION *Curtis's Botanical Magazine*, 8983 (1923), reprinted in Halliday, *The Illustrated Rhododendron*, pl. 84 (2001); *Iconographia Cormophytorum Sinicorum* 3, t. 4194 (1974); Davidian, *The Rhododendron Species* 2, pl. 11 (1992); Cox and Cox, *The Encyclopedia of Rhododendron Species*, 23 (1997)
HABIT shrub to 4 m; bud scales persistent, at least on young shoots
LEAVES narrowly oblanceolate, 8–13 cm, 3.5–5 × as long as broad, hairless above, with a dense, compacted, fawn indumentum beneath
CALYX 2–5 mm, with rounded, glandular lobes
COROLLA funnel-shaped, 2.5–3 cm, white tinged with pink, with reddish spots
OVARY with reddish, shortly stalked glands (sometimes some hairs eglandular)
STYLE glandular to the apex
CAPSULE to 2 cm
DISTRIBUTION western China (Sichuan)
FLOWERING late spring
HARDINESS ZONE 7

Classic wild-collected material is available under *Wilson 4273*.

69. *Rhododendron argyrophyllum* Franchet

HABIT to 12 m
LEAVES elliptic to oblanceolate, 1.8–6 cm, 2.7–3.6 × as long as broad, hairless above, with a thin, silvery to fawn, compacted indumentum beneath; pedicels 2–2.5 cm
CALYX 2 mm, with broadly triangular, hairy, sometimes glandular-ciliate lobes
COROLLA funnel-campanulate or open-campanulate, 3–5.5 cm, white to pale pink, with purple spots
OVARY with thin, white or rarely reddish hairs
STYLE hairless
CAPSULE 1–2.5 cm
DISTRIBUTION China (Yunnan, Sichuan, Shaanxi, Hubei)
FLOWERING spring
HARDINESS ZONE 6

R. argyrophyllum flower and leaf

R. argyrophyllum detail

R. argyrophyllum leaf surface

R. *argyrophyllum* subsp. ***argyrophyllum***

ILLUSTRATION Fang, *Icones Plantarum Omeiensium,* t. 19 (1942); *Iconographia Cormophytorum Sinicorum* 3, t. 4190 (1974); Fang, *Sichuan Rhododendron of China,* 103–105 (1986); Davidian, *The Rhododendron Species* 3, pl. 9 (1992); Feng, *Rhododendrons of China* 2, pl. 24: 1–3 (1992); Cox and Cox, *The Encyclopedia of Rhododendron Species,* 17 (1997)

FLOWER STALKS eglandular

OVARY eglandular

Classic wild-collected material is available under *Wilson 1210, 4275A*. Recent nonauthenticated material from Sichuan is also in cultivation.

R. *argyrophyllum* subsp. ***hypoglaucum*** (Hemsley) Chamberlain

SYNONYM *R. hypoglaucum* Hemsley

ILLUSTRATION *Curtis's Botanical Magazine,* 8469 (1916); Stevenson, *The Species of Rhododendron,* 30 (1930); *Iconographia Cormophytorum Sinicorum* 3, t. 4189 (1974)

FLOWER STALKS glandular

OVARY glandular

Classic wild-collected material is available under *Wilson 5137*. Recent nonauthenticated material from Sichuan and Hubei is also in cultivation.

A 3rd subspecies, *nankingense* (Cowan) Chamberlain, with longer leaves and larger corollas, and a 4th, *omeiense* (Rehder and Wilson) Chamberlain, with an eglandular ovary, are not currently in cultivation.

70. *Rhododendron insigne* Hemsley and Wilson

ILLUSTRATION Millais, *Rhododendrons,* t. 202 (1923); *Rhododendron and Camellia Yearbook* 24, t. 13 (1969); *Iconographia Cormophytorum Sinicorum* 3, t. 4193 (1974); Kneller, *The Book of Rhododendrons,* 13 (1995); Cox and Cox, *The Encyclopedia of Rhododendron Species,* 21 (1997)

HABIT shrub to 3.5 m

LEAVES elliptic, 7–13 cm, 3–3.5 × as long as broad; upper surface hairless; lower surface with a compacted fawn indumentum with a shiny surface film

CALYX 1–2 mm, with minute lobes, floccose

COROLLA widely campanulate, to 4 cm, pink with a darker median line on each lobe

OVARY densely white-hairy

STYLE hairless

CAPSULE to 2.5 cm

DISTRIBUTION western China (Sichuan)
FLOWERING spring
HARDINESS ZONE 6

71. *Rhododendron rirei* Hemsley and Wilson

ILLUSTRATION Fang, *Icones Plantarum Omeiensium*, t. 21 (1942); *Iconographia Cormophytorum Sinicorum* 3, t. 4192 (1974); Fang, *Sichuan Rhododendron of China*, 106–111 (1986); Cox and Cox, *The Encyclopedia of Rhododendron Species*, 22 (1997); Halliday, *The Illustrated Rhododendron*, pl. 83 (2001)

HABIT small tree, 3.5–16 m; bark greyish brown and striate, breaking into oblong plates

LEAVES elliptic to oblanceolate, 9.5–17 cm, 2.7–3.3 × as long as broad; upper surface hairless; lower surface with a thin, compacted, white indumentum embedded in a surface film

INFLORESCENCE BUDS scales greenish where exposed, reddish where covered, tapered but not cuspidate, densely white-hairy

CALYX 1–2 mm, with triangular lobes and a thin, whitish, mealy indumentum

COROLLA campanulate, 4–5 cm, purplish to violet, with darker nectar sacs

STAMENS 10; anthers mid brown

OVARY densely grey-hairy

STYLE hairless

CAPSULE to 2.5 cm

DISTRIBUTION western China (Sichuan, possibly Guizhou)

FLOWERING spring

HARDINESS ZONE 7

Classic wild-collected material is available under *Wilson 5139*. Recent nonauthenticated material from Sichuan and Guizhou is also in cultivation.

Less commonly cultivated are:

Rhododendron haofui Chun and Fang

ILLUSTRATION *Iconographia Cormophytorum Sinicorum* 3, t. 4196 (1974)

Probably keying out to *R. hunnewellianum*, but:

STAMENS 18–20

DISTRIBUTION China (Guizhou, Guangxi, Hunan)

The only species in the subsection with flowers with more than 10 stamens.

Rhododendron formosanum Hemsley

Similar to *R. argyrophyllum* and *R. thayerianum*, and perhaps keying out to either, but:

LEAVES 4.5–5.5 × as long as broad, with a fawn indumentum

STYLE glandless or glandular only at the base

DISTRIBUTION Taiwan

Rhododendron pingianum Fang

ILLUSTRATION *Iconographia Cormophytorum Sinicorum* 3, t. 4191 (1974)

Similar to and keying out to *R. argyrophyllum*, but:

PEDICELS 3–4 cm

OVARY with reddish hairs

DISTRIBUTION western China (central Sichuan)

Rhododendron simiarum Hance

ILLUSTRATION *Iconographia Cormophytorum Sinicorum* 3, t. 4199 (1974)

Similar to *R. argyrophyllum*, but:

LEAVES indumentum fawn to brown

OVARY glandular and tomentose

DISTRIBUTION southern and eastern China (from Sichuan to Zhejiang and Hong Kong)

Rhododendron adenopodum Franchet

ILLUSTRATION *Gardeners' Chronicle* 45, 291 (1909); Halliday, *The Illustrated Rhododendron*, pl. 83 (2001)

Probably keying out to either *R. rirei* or *R. insigne*, but:

LEAVES with long stalks (c. 3 cm)

CALYX 3–6 mm but sometimes as long as 15 mm

COROLLA 4.2–5 cm

DISTRIBUTION China (eastern Sichuan, Hubei)

Formerly placed in subsection *Pontica* but better accommodated here.

Subgenus *Hymenanthes*

Section *Pontica*

Subsection *Arborea* Sleumer (*Arboreum* series)

HABIT generally trees or large shrubs with rough bark; young shoots densely hairy
LEAVES lower surface covered with a dense, spongy to compacted, one- or 2-layered indumentum, usually of dendroid hairs
RACEME dense, 10- to 25-flowered
CALYX minute
COROLLA 5-lobed, campanulate or tubular-campanulate, with nectar sacs
STAMENS 10
OVARY densely hairy, sometimes also glandular
STYLE hairless
SEEDS elongate, narrowly winged to almost unwinged, with appendages at each end

A group of 3 species, characterised by corollas with pronounced nectar sacs, allied to *R. rirei* in subsection *Argyrophylla,* but sufficiently distinct. Anatomically the leaves are rather different. They consistently have a 3-layered upper epidermis, the cells in all the layers more or less equal in size, the cuticle half as thick to as thick as the cells are deep; water tissue is absent, and the cells of the lower epidermis are not prolonged into papillae. Sclereids are present in the leaf tissue of all species.

1a Leaves 16–22 cm, with a 2-layered indumentum beneath, the upper layer woolly-hairy .... **73. *R. lanigerum***
b Leaves 6.5–19 cm; if leaves more than 15 cm, indumentum one-layered and compacted 2
2a Corolla varying shades of rose-pink to deep carmine, rarely pure white; usually a tree with a well-defined trunk .... **72. *R. arboreum***
b Corolla lilac to deep magenta; usually a tree with several main branches arising from near the base .... **74. *R. niveum***

72. *Rhododendron arboreum* J. E. Smith

HABIT tree to 50 m in the wild though usually much less in gardens, usually with a well-defined trunk; bark pale brown, flaking
LEAVES variable, 6.5–19 cm, 2.2–6.5 × as long as broad; upper surface hairless and wrinkled; lower surface with a dense, compacted, spongy indumentum of dendroid hairs
CALYX 1–2 mm; lobes rounded, sparsely glandular or hairless

COROLLA tubular-campanulate, fleshy, 3–5 cm, pink to deep crimson or rarely white, often with dark spots and with dark nectar sacs
OVARY white-hairy, sometimes glandular
CAPSULE 1.5–3 cm
DISTRIBUTION from the Himalaya and China to Thailand, southern India, and Sri Lanka
FLOWERING spring
HARDINESS ZONE 7

R. arboreum subsp. **arboreum**
ILLUSTRATION *Edwards's Botanical Register* 11, t. 890 (1825); Hooker, *Exotic Flora* 3, t. 168 (1827); *Flore des Serres,* ser. 1, 9: t. 945 (1853–1854); *Iconographia Cormophytorum Sinicorum* 3, t. 4130 (1974); Halliday, *The Illustrated Rhododendron,* pl. 86a and 86b (2001)
LEAVES more or less flat, 8–19 cm, with a silvery or white indumentum beneath
DISTRIBUTION Himalaya

Wild-collected material is available under *Munich Botanic Garden* (without number).

R. arboreum subsp. **cinnamomeum** (Lindley) Tagg
LEAVES flat, 6.5–11 cm

R. arboreum subsp. **cinnamomeum** var. **cinnamomeum** Lindley
SYNONYMS *R. cinnamomeum* G. Don; *R. campbelliae* Hooker; *R. arboreum* subsp. *campbelliae* (Hooker) Tagg
ILLUSTRATION *Edwards's Botanical Register* 23, t. 1982 (1837)
LEAVES lower surface with a 2-layered indumentum, the lower layer compacted and whitish or fawn, the upper floccose and reddish
COROLLA pink to red or rarely white
DISTRIBUTION Himalaya

Wild-collected material is available under *Cave 6715.* Recent nonauthenticated material from Nepal and Bhutan is also in cultivation.

R. arboreum subsp. *cinnamomeum* flower and leaf

R. arboreum subsp. *cinnamomeum* detail

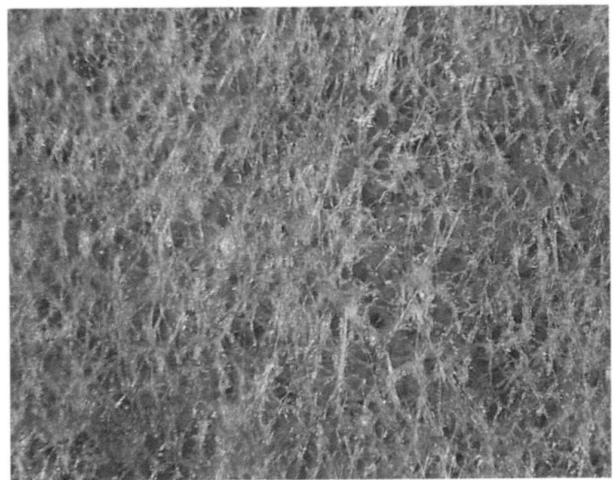

R. arboreum subsp. *cinnamomeum* leaf surface

R. arboreum subsp. ***cinnamomeum*** var. ***roseum*** Lindley

SYNONYM *R. album* Buchanan-Hamilton

ILLUSTRATION *Edwards's Botanical Register* 15, t. 1240 (1829); Feng, *Rhododendrons of China* 3, pl. 32: 1–3 (1999); Kneller, *The Book of Rhododendrons,* 11 (1999)

Similar to var. *cinnamomeum,* but:

LEAVES with a one-layered, fawn to whitish, compacted indumentum

COROLLA usually reddish

DISTRIBUTION Himalaya

Wild-collected material is available under *Bartholomew 151, Cave 6715* (see also subsp. arboreum), *Chamberlain* (without number), *Hruby 6, Ludlow and Sherriff 2893, Ludlow, Sherriff, and Taylor 6411, Milde Arboretum* (without number), and *Schilling 2649.*

R. arboreum subsp. ***delavayi*** (Franchet) Chamberlain

SYNONYM *R. delavayi* Franchet

ILLUSTRATION *Curtis's Botanical Magazine,* 8137 (1907); *Iconographia Cormophytorum Sinicorum* 3, t. 4131 (1974); Feng, *Rhododendrons of China* 1, pl. 1 (1988)

LEAVES 7–15.5 cm, with a one-layered, whitish to fawn, spongy indumentum beneath

COROLLA red

DISTRIBUTION eastern India, Myanmar, China to Thailand

Wild-collected material is available under *Kunming Botanic Garden* (without number). Recent nonauthenticated material from Bhutan, China (Yunnan), and Thailand is also in cultivation.

R. arboreum subsp. ***nilagiricum*** (Zenker) Tagg

SYNONYM *R. nilagiricum* Zenker

ILLUSTRATION *Curtis's Botanical Magazine,* 4381 (1848) and 9323 (1933); Wight, *Spicilegium Neilgherrense* 2, t. 131 (1851)

LEAF APEX rounded

DISTRIBUTION southern India

R. arboreum subsp. ***zeylanicum*** (Booth) Tagg

SYNONYM *R. zeylanicum* Booth

ILLUSTRATION Millais, *Rhododendrons,* t. 24 (1917)

LEAVES strongly concave; lower surface with a spongy, fawn indumentum

COROLLA red
DISTRIBUTION Sri Lanka

Wild-collected material is available under *Grierson* (without number).

Variants of *R. arboreum* have been widely used in hybridisation.

The following relatively recent collections belong to *R. arboreum*, but the subspecies and varieties that they represent have not yet been determined: *Bailey 5, Bluefield 12, Clark and Sinclair 1523, 1532, 1561, 1695, Dingle 1, 5, Kumar 698, 715, Milde Arboretum* (without number), *Rushforth 938, 966,* and *Spring-Smythe 26.*

73. ***Rhododendron lanigerum*** Tagg

SYNONYM *R. silvaticum* Cowan
ILLUSTRATION *The Rhododendron Handbook*, f. 2 (1997); Davidian, *The Rhododendron Species* 2, pl. 7–8 (1992); Feng, *Rhododendrons of China* 3, pl. 33: 1–2 (1999)
HABIT shrub or small tree to 7 m; bark smooth, brownish, ultimately cracking into oblong plates
LEAVES elliptic to oblanceolate, 16–22 cm, 3.3–4 × as long as broad; upper surface wrinkled and more or less hairless at maturity, though with traces of indumentum along the midrib; lower surface with a dense, whitish to fawn, woolly indumentum of dendroid hairs overlying a more compacted layer
INFLORESCENCE BUDS almost spherical though pointed at first, later oblong; lower scales green covered with brown hairs, pointed, the inner greenish, with prominent, shining, silvery white hairs
CALYX fleshy, hairless, with small teeth
COROLLA campanulate, to 3.5 cm, deep pink to pinkish purple, with darker nectar sacs
STAMENS 10; anthers pink or brownish
OVARY densely hairy
CAPSULE to 2 cm
DISTRIBUTION western China (southern Xizang) and adjacent northeastern India (Delei Valley)
FLOWERING spring
HARDINESS ZONE 7

Classic wild-collected material is available under *Kingdon-Ward 6258, 8251* (the type collection).

74. *Rhododendron niveum* Hooker

ILLUSTRATION *Curtis's Botanical Magazine,* 4730 (1853) and 6827 (1885), the latter reprinted in Halliday, *The Illustrated Rhododendron,* pl. 87 (2001); *Rhododendron and Camellia Yearbook* 37, opposite 48 (1983); Cox and Cox, *The Encyclopedia of Rhododendron Species,* 15 (1997)

HABIT tree to 6 m; bark greenish brown, finely striate

LEAVES oblanceolate-elliptic, 11–17 cm, 3–3.8 × as long as broad, hairless above, with a dense, compacted, fawn indumentum of dendroid hairs beneath

INFLORESCENCE BUDS spherical, greenish or brownish; scales with white hairs on the surface and brownish hairs on the margins

CALYX 1–2 mm, with obscure lobes

COROLLA tubular-campanulate, 3–3.5 cm, deep magenta to purple, with darker nectar sacs

OVARY with white or fawn hairs

CAPSULE to 2 cm

DISTRIBUTION Himalaya (Sikkim, Bhutan)

FLOWERING spring

HARDINESS ZONE 7

Wild-collected material is available under *Gould 22, Pradhan* (without number), and *Pradhan and Lachungpa 2, 21.*

Subgenus *Hymenanthes*

Section *Pontica*

Subsection *Taliensia* Sleumer (*Taliense* series; *Lacteum* series)

HABIT dwarf shrubs to small trees; young shoots hairless to densely hairy, sometimes also with shortly stalked glands

LEAVES usually with a dense, one- or 2-layered, woolly, felted or compacted indumentum beneath composed of radiate, ramiform, or fasciculate hairs (indumentum rarely sparse or absent)

RACEME usually dense, 5- to 20-flowered; rachis 3–25 mm

CALYX minute to 1.2 cm

COROLLA 5- to 7-lobed, campanulate to funnel-campanulate, without nectar sacs

STAMENS 10(–14)

OVARY hairless to densely hairy and/or glandular

STYLE usually hairless, occasionally glandular throughout

SEEDS elongate, narrowly winged to unwinged, usually with appendages at each end, but occasionally the appendages very small

The subsection contains about 40 species which are very difficult to identify. Anatomically the leaves are rather uniform. They consistently have a 2- or 3-layered upper epidermis, the cells of each layer more or less equal in size, the cuticle generally as thick as the cells are deep; water tissue is absent, and the cells of the lower epidermis are not prolonged into papillae. Sclereids are present in the leaf tissue of most species but are absent in *R. lacteum*, *R. beesianum*, and *R. wightii*.

1 a Calyx 5–15 mm; ovary hairy and/or glandular 2
b Calyx 0.5–5 mm; ovary hairless to hairy and/or glandular 4
2 a Leaf indumentum whitish to pale pink . . . . **77. *R. balfourianum***
b Leaf indumentum olive-brown to rusty brown or deep pink 3
3 a Leaf indumentum olive-brown, containing some glands . . . . **76. *R. adenogynum***
b Leaf indumentum deep pink to rusty brown, without glands . . . . **75. *R. bureavii***
4 a Mature leaf indumentum silvery, whitish, or fawn, occasionally becoming pale pink 5
b Mature leaf indumentum deep yellowish brown to rusty brown, sometimes evanescent or splitting and becoming patchy 6
5 a Corolla 4–5 cm, 7-lobed . . . . **86. *R. clementinae***
b Corolla 2.5–4 cm, 5-lobed . . . . **85. *R. aganniphum***
6 a Upper surface of leaf puckered, with deeply impressed veins . . . . **89. *R. wiltonii***
b Upper surface of leaf not as above 7

7 a Mature leaves hairless beneath except for a thin, fluffy indumentum that persists near the midrib, or with a thin, agglutinated indumentum, apparently 2-layered, that sometimes splits and becomes patchy 8
b Mature leaves with a continuous, one- or 2-layered, sometimes compacted though not agglutinated indumentum 11
8 a Young leaves with a whitish to yellowish indumentum that becomes deep brown and split at maturity; hairs ramiform . . . . . **85. *R. aganniphum***
b Young leaves with a brown indumentum of radiate hairs, sometimes becoming hairless at maturity 9
9 a Leaves hairless at maturity or with a discontinuous indumentum . . . . . **87. *R. przewalskii***
b Leaves with a more or less continuous though sometimes split indumentum at maturity, composed of felted or agglutinated radiate or almost ramiform hairs 10
10 a Ovary hairless or with a few scattered hairs . . . . . **83. *R. phaeochrysum***
b Ovary sparsely glandular and/or hairy . . . . . **82. *R. alutaceum***
11 a Ovary entirely hairless . . . . . **78. *R. taliense***
b Ovary hairy and/or glandular or minutely papillose, at least towards the apex 12
12 a Leaf indumentum one-layered, sparse or dense; corolla white or pink . . . . . **90. *R. wasonii***
b Leaf indumentum 2-layered, usually dense; corolla white, pink, purplish, or pale yellow 13
13 a Ovary densely hairy, sometimes also glandular 14
b Ovary hairless or with a few scattered hairs or minute papillae 17
14 a Pedicels hairless or sparsely hairy . . . . . **88. *R. rufum***
b Pedicels densely hairy, sometimes glandular 15
15 a Ovary and leaf stalks glandular and hairy . . . . . **79. *R. roxieanum***
b Ovary and leaf stalks hairy but eglandular 16
16 a Leaves 4–7 cm; corolla white flushed with reddish . . . . . **81. *R. bathyphyllum***
b Leaves 2–5 cm; corolla white or yellow . . . . . **80. *R. proteoides***
17 a Corolla yellow 18
b Corolla white, sometimes flushed with pink 19
18 a Corolla pure yellow, usually without spots; leaf indumentum of radiate hairs . . . . . **91. *R. lacteum***
b Corolla pale yellow, spotted; leaf indumentum of ramiform hairs . . . . . **93. *R. wightii***
19 a Inflorescence rachis at least 2 cm; ovary densely hairy . . . . . **92. *R. beesianum***
b Inflorescence rachis at most 1.5 cm; ovary usually hairless or sparsely hairy . . . . . **84. *R. traillianum***

75. ***Rhododendron bureavii*** Franchet

ILLUSTRATION Fang, *Sichuan Rhododendron of China,* 137–139 (1986); Moser, *Rhododendron: Wildarten und Hybriden,* 136 (1991); Davidian, *The Rhododendron Species* 3, pl. 56 (1992); Feng, *Rhododendrons of China* 2, pl. 30: 1–4 (1992); Kneller, *The Book of Rhododendrons,* 51 (1995); Cox and Cox, *The Encyclopedia of Rhododendron Species,* 163 (1997)

HABIT shrub to 3 or rarely to 6 m
LEAVES elliptic, 4.5–12 cm, 1.7–3 × as long as broad; lower surface with a dense, woolly, ramiform indumentum, pink when young, becoming rich rusty red; base tapering or rounded
CALYX 5–10 mm; lobes fleshy or membranous, densely hairy, glandular
COROLLA campanulate, 2.5–4 cm, white flushed with pink to pink, sometimes with purple spots
OVARY densely glandular, sometimes also with eglandular hairs
STYLE usually glandular at least towards the base
CAPSULE to 1.5 cm
DISTRIBUTION western China (western Yunnan)
FLOWERING spring
HARDINESS ZONE 6

Classic wild-collected material is available under *Forrest 15609, McLaren 106,* and *Rock 25436, 25439.* Recent nonauthenticated material from Sichuan is also in cultivation.

76. *Rhododendron adenogynum* Diels
SYNONYM *R. adenophorum* Balfour and W. W. Smith
ILLUSTRATION *Curtis's Botanical Magazine,* 9253 (1929); Stevenson, *The Species of Rhododendron,* 632 (1930); *Iconographia Cormophytorum Sinicorum* 3, t. 4234 (1974); Feng, *Rhododendrons of China* 1, pl. 46: 1–4 (1988); Davidian, *The Rhododendron Species* 3, pl. 53–55 (1992); Cox and Cox, *The Encyclopedia of Rhododendron Species,* 156 (1997)
HABIT shrub or small tree to 4 m
LEAVES elliptic or narrowly so, 6–11 cm, 2–2.5 × as long as broad; lower surface with a usually dense, spongy covering of ramiform hairs, yellowish at first, olive-brown when mature, containing some glands
CALYX (4–)8–15 mm, glandular; lobes unequal
COROLLA campanulate, 3–4.5 cm, white flushed with pink or pale pink
OVARY with shortly stalked glands
STYLE glandular in the lower third
DISTRIBUTION western China (southeastern Xizang, western Yunnan, southwestern Sichuan)
FLOWERING spring
HARDINESS ZONE 6

Classic wild-collected material is available under *Forrest 20444, Rock 25305,* and *Yü 14955.* Recent nonauthenticated material from Yunnan is also in cultivation.

77. *Rhododendron balfourianum* Diels

ILLUSTRATION *Curtis's Botanical Magazine*, n.s., 531 (1969); Feng, *Rhododendrons of China* 1, pl. 48: 1–5 (1988); Cox and Cox, *The Encyclopedia of Rhododendron Species*, 161 (1997)

HABIT to 4.5 m

LEAVES ovate-lanceolate to elliptic, 4.5–12 cm, 2–3 × as long as broad; lower surface with a dense, compacted, one-layered indumentum of ramiform hairs, silvery white when young, sometimes pinkish brown at maturity, usually shining and with a thin surface film

CALYX 6–10 mm, glandular; lobes rounded, glandular-ciliate

COROLLA campanulate, 3.5–4 cm, pale to deep pink, with purple spots

OVARY glandular

STYLE glandular in the lower third

CAPSULE 1–2 cm

DISTRIBUTION western China (Yunnan, southwestern Sichuan)

FLOWERING spring

HARDINESS ZONE 6

Classic wild-collected material is available under *Forrest 16316, 16811, 29256, 29263*. Recent nonauthenticated material from Yunnan is also in cultivation.

78. *Rhododendron taliense* Franchet

ILLUSTRATION *Iconographia Cormophytorum Sinicorum* 3, t. 4226 (1974); Feng, *Rhododendrons of China* 1, pl. 51: 1–2 (1988); Davidian, *The Rhododendron Species* 3, pl. 60–61 (1992); Cox and Cox, *The Encyclopedia of Rhododendron Species*, 180 (1997)

HABIT shrub to 4 m

LEAVES 5–11 cm, 2.2–3.5 × as long as broad; upper surface hairless; lower surface with a 2-layered indumentum, the lower layer compacted, the upper loose or felted, brownish, composed of ramiform hairs

CALYX to 2 mm, hairless

COROLLA campanulate, 3–3.5 cm, white or rarely yellow, sometimes flushed with pink, with crimson spots

OVARY AND STYLE hairless

CAPSULE 1.5–2 cm

DISTRIBUTION western China (western Yunnan)

FLOWERING spring

HARDINESS ZONE 6

Recent nonauthenticated material from Yunnan is in cultivation.

79. *Rhododendron roxieanum* Forrest

HABIT shrub, usually to 2.5 m (rarely more)

LEAVES linear to elliptic, 5–12 cm, 2.2–15 × as long as broad, hairless above, with a thick, 2-layered indumentum beneath, the lower layer compacted, with radiate hairs, the upper loose, woolly, reddish brown

CALYX 0.5–2 mm, hairy, glandular

COROLLA funnel-campanulate, 2–4 cm, white or rarely pale yellow, sometimes flushed with pink, with purple spots

OVARY reddish-hairy and glandular

CAPSULE 1–1.5 cm

DISTRIBUTION western China (southeastern Xizang, northwestern Yunnan, southwestern Sichuan)

FLOWERING spring

HARDINESS ZONE 7

R. roxieanum var. ***roxieanum***

ILLUSTRATION *Curtis's Botanical Magazine,* 9383 (1935); *Rhododendron and Camellia Yearbook* 19: f. 34 (1964); *Iconographia Cormophytorum Sinicorum* 3, t. 4239 (1974); Cox, *Dwarf Rhododendrons,* t. 5 (1973); *The Garden* 112: 274 (1987); Davidian, *The Rhododendron Species* 3, pl. 65–66 (1992); Feng, *Rhododendrons of China* 2, pl. 39: 1–2 and 40: 1–3 (1992); Cox and Cox, *The Encyclopedia of Rhododendron Species,* 177–178 (1997)

LEAVES more than 4 × as long as broad, with acute apices

Classic wild-collected material is available under *Rock 158, 11285, 25422.*

R. roxieanum var. ***cucullatum*** (Handel-Mazzetti) Chamberlain

SYNONYMS *R. cucullatum* Handel-Mazzetti; *R. globigerum* Balfour and Forrest

ILLUSTRATION Cox and Cox, *The Encyclopedia of Rhododendron Species,* 177–178 (1997); Feng, *Rhododendrons of China* 3, pl. 38 (1999)

LEAVES up to 4 × as long as broad, the apex acute or hooded

Classic wild-collected material is available under *Rock 10920.*

80. *Rhododendron proteoides* Balfour and W. W. Smith

ILLUSTRATION Cox and Cox, *The Encyclopedia of Rhododendron Species,* 174 (1997)

HABIT small shrub to 1 m

LEAVES elliptic, 2–4 cm, 3–4 × as long as broad, with a cucullate apex; upper surface hairless; lower surface with a 2-layered indumentum, the lower layer compacted and composed of radiate hairs, the upper loosely woolly, brown to reddish at first, bleaching with age, composed of ramiform hairs

CALYX very small, hairless

COROLLA campanulate, 2.5–3.5 cm, white to cream flushed with pink, with purple spots

OVARY reddish-hairy, eglandular

CAPSULE 6–7 mm

DISTRIBUTION western China (southeastern Xizang, northwestern Yunnan, southwestern Sichuan)

FLOWERING spring

HARDINESS ZONE 7

Classic wild-collected material is available under *Rock 151*.

81. *Rhododendron bathyphyllum* Balfour and Forrest

ILLUSTRATION Feng, *Rhododendrons of China* 2, pl. 29: 1–3 (1992)

HABIT to 1.5 m

LEAVES elliptic to oblong, 4–7 cm, 2.7–3.5 × as long as broad; apex cucullate; lower surface with a 2-layered indumentum, the lower layer compacted, the upper dark reddish brown and composed of close ramiform hairs

CALYX very small, hairless

COROLLA campanulate, 3–3.5 cm, white flushed with pink, with red spots

OVARY densely reddish-hairy

STYLE hairless

CAPSULE 1 cm

DISTRIBUTION western China (southeastern Xizang, northwestern Yunnan)

FLOWERING spring

HARDINESS ZONE 8

Classic wild-collected material is available under *Forrest 14718* (the type collection).

82. *Rhododendron alutaceum* Balfour and W. W. Smith

HABIT to 4.5 m; bark brown, cracking

LEAVES oblong to oblanceolate, 5–17 cm, 2–6 × as long as broad; lower surface with a 2-layered indumentum, the lower layer whitish and compacted, the upper ramiform-hairy, looser, sometimes falling, brown or reddish

INFLORESCENCE BUDS ovoid, brownish; scales narrow, pointed, the surface with sparse brown hairs, the margins densely fringed with brown hairs
CALYX 0.5–1 mm, hairy
COROLLA campanulate to funnel-campanulate, 3–4 cm, white to pink, with crimson spots, sometimes with a purple basal blotch
STAMENS anthers pale brown
OVARY sparsely hairy to hairless
STYLE hairless
CAPSULE 1.2–2 cm
DISTRIBUTION western China (southeastern Xizang, northwestern Yunnan, southwestern and central Sichuan)
FLOWERING spring
HARDINESS ZONE 7

Classic wild-collected material is available under *Rock 11100, 11123.*

Variable and including 3 varieties, only one of which (var. *alutaceum*) is cultivated generally.

83. *Rhododendron phaeochrysum* Balfour and W. W. Smith
HABIT shrub to 4.5 m; bark greyish brown, cracking into oblong plates
LEAVES elliptic to ovate-oblong, hairless above, with a dense, compacted or felted, brown indumentum beneath of radiate to almost ramiform hairs
INFLORESCENCE BUDS ovoid, green or yellowish; scales hairless except for a fringe of fine white hairs
CALYX to 1 mm, usually hairless
COROLLA funnel-campanulate, 2–5 cm, white flushed with pink, with crimson spots
OVARY hairless or with a few short hairs, especially at the apex
STYLE hairless
CAPSULE 1.3–2 cm
DISTRIBUTION western China (southern Xizang, northwestern Yunnan, southwestern and central Sichuan)
FLOWERING spring
HARDINESS ZONE 8

Three varieties exist in the wild, of which 2 are generally cultivated.

R. *phaeochrysum* var. ***phaeochrysum***

SYNONYM *R. dryophyllum* Balfour and Forrest

ILLUSTRATION *Rhododendron and Camellia Yearbook* 10: f. 45 (1955); *Iconographia Cormophytorum Sinicorum* 3, t. 4205 (1974); Fang, *Sichuan Rhododendron of China,* 155–157 (1986); Feng, *Rhododendrons of China* 1, pl. 32: 1–3 (1992); Davidian, *The Rhododendron Species* 2, pl. 73 and 75–76 (1992); Cox and Cox, *The Encyclopedia of Rhododendron Species,* 170 (1997)

LEAVES 8–14.5 cm

INFLORESCENCE BUDS almost spherical but slightly pointed; scales all brown, or the outer green towards the base, hairy all over the surface or only towards the edges

COROLLA 3.2—5 cm

STAMENS anthers very pale brown to almost white

Classic wild-collected material is available under *Forrest 10547, Ludlow, Sherriff, and Taylor 6612,* and *Rock 11333.* Recent nonauthenticated material from Yunnan is also in cultivation.

R. *phaeochrysum* var. ***levistratum*** (Balfour and Forrest) Chamberlain

SYNONYMS *R. levistratum* Balfour and Forrest; *R. sigillatum* Balfour and Forrest; *R. dryophyllum* misapplied

ILLUSTRATION Fang, *Sichuan Rhododendron of China,* 160–161 (1986); Cox and Cox, *The Encyclopedia of Rhododendron Species,* 170 (1997)

LEAVES 4–9 cm

INFLORESCENCE BUDS spherical to oblong-fusiform; scales broad, rounded and usually cuspidate, fringed with hairs or with inner scales hairy all over

COROLLA 2–3.5 cm

STAMENS anthers pale brown or yellowish

Classic wild-collected material is available under *Forrest 19574, Rock 11333,* and *H. Smith 13982.* Recent nonauthenticated material from Yunnan and Sichuan is also in cultivation.

There is a 3rd variety, *agglutinatum* (Balfour and Forrest) Chamberlain), characterised by the indumentum on the lower surface of the leaf being agglutinated and sometimes splitting; it is possibly of hybrid origin, with parents *R. phaeochrysum* and *R. aganniphum.* It is illustrated in Feng, *Rhododendrons of China* 1, pl. 33: 1–3 (1988–1999).

84. *Rhododendron traillianum* Forrest and W. W. Smith

ILLUSTRATION *Curtis's Botanical Magazine*, 8900 (1938); *Iconographia Cormophytorum Sinicorum* 3, t. 4204 (1974); Feng, *Rhododendrons of China* 1, pl. 34: 1–2 (1988); Davidian, *The Rhododendron Species* 2, pl. 77 (1992); Cox and Cox, *The Encyclopedia of Rhododendron Species*, 181–182 (1997); Feng, *Rhododendrons of China* 3, pl. 39: 1–2 (1999)

HABIT shrub or small tree to 8 m; bark cinnamon-brown, breaking into long strips

LEAVES obovate to elliptic, 7–13 cm, 2–3 × as long as broad, hairless above, with a dense, powdery, compacted indumentum beneath composed of reddish brown, short- or long-rayed radiate hairs

INFLORESCENCE BUDS fusiform; scales mostly green, cuspidate, margined with brown hairs and with sparse brown hairs on the surface

CALYX to 1 mm, hairless

COROLLA funnel-campanulate, 2.5–4.0 cm, white, sometimes flushed with pink, with crimson spots

OVARY hairless or with sparse, red-brown hairs

STAMENS anthers very pale brown to almost yellow

STYLE hairless

CAPSULE 1.5–2.5 cm, straight or curved

DISTRIBUTION western China (southeastern Xizang, northwestern and western Yunnan, southwestern Sichuan)

FLOWERING spring

HARDINESS ZONE 7

Classic wild-collected material is available under *Rock 11470, 18444*. Recent nonauthenticated material from Yunnan and Sichuan is also in cultivation. In the wild, 2 varieties occur: var. *traillianum*, described above, and var. *dictyotum* (Tagg) Chamberlain (*R. dictyotum* Tagg), which has leaves with hairs with long ribbon-like arms, and a corolla to 4.5 cm.

85. *Rhododendron aganniphum* Forrest and W. W. Smith

HABIT to 3 m; bark grey-brown, breaking into oblong plates

LEAVES elliptic to broadly ovate-lanceolate, 4–12 cm, 1.7–2.8 × as long as broad; lower surface with a dense covering of compacted, ramiform hairs, whitish or yellowish at first, becoming brown

INFLORESCENCE BUDS scales mostly brown, notched, hairy

CALYX 0.5–1 mm

COROLLA campanulate, 3–3.5 cm, white, often flushed with pink
ANTHERS mid brown
OVARY AND STYLE hairless
CAPSULE 1–2 cm
DISTRIBUTION western China (southeastern Xizang, northwestern Yunnan, southwestern Sichuan)
FLOWERING spring
HARDINESS ZONE 7

R. aganniphum var. ***aganniphum***
SYNONYM *R. glaucopeplum* Balfour and Forrest
ILLUSTRATION Fang, *Sichuan Rhododendron of China,* 127–129 (1986); Feng, *Rhododendrons of China* 1, pl. 47: 1–2 (1988); Davidian, *The Rhododendron Species* 3, pl. 62 (1992); Cox and Cox, *The Encyclopedia of Rhododendron Species,* 158 (1997)
LEAVES indumentum remaining pale and intact at maturity

Classic wild-collected material is available under *Forrest 16472, 25520,* and *Rock 23307.* Recent nonauthenticated material from Yunnan is also in cultivation.

R. aganniphum var. ***flavorufum*** (Balfour and Forrest) Chamberlain
SYNONYM *R. flavorufum* Balfour and Forrest
ILLUSTRATION Davidian, *The Rhododendron Species* 3, pl. 63–64 (1992); Feng, *Rhododendrons of China* 2, pl. 28: 1–2 (1992); Cox and Cox, *The Encyclopedia of Rhododendron Species,* 159 (1997)
LEAVES indumentum turning deep red-brown and becoming patchy

Classic wild-collected material is available under *Forrest 14368.* Recent nonauthenticated material from Yunnan is also in cultivation.

R. aganniphum var. *flavorufum* flower and leaf. PHOTO BY RAY COX

R. aganniphum var. *flavorufum* leaf surface

86. ***Rhododendron clementinae*** Forrest

ILLUSTRATION *Curtis's Botanical Magazine,* 9392 (1935); *Iconographia Cormophytorum Sinicorum* 3, t. 4229 (1974); Cox and Cox, *The Encyclopedia of Rhododendron Species,* 165 (1997); Feng, *Rhododendrons of China* 3, pl. 34: 1–4 (1999)

HABIT to 3 m; bark brownish, cracking

LEAVES ovate-lanceolate, 6.5–14 cm, 1.5–2 × as long as broad, hairless above, with a 2-layered whitish to buff indumentum beneath, the lower layer compacted, the upper looser and composed of ramiform hairs

INFLORESCENCE BUDS ovoid, green; scales hairless except for a fringe of minute white hairs

CALYX to 1 mm, with rounded lobes, hairless

COROLLA 7-lobed, campanulate, 4–5 cm, white to deep pink, with purple spots

STAMENS 12–14

OVARY AND STYLE hairless

CAPSULE to 2 cm

DISTRIBUTION western China (northwestern Yunnan, southwestern Sichuan)

FLOWERING spring

HARDINESS ZONE 6

Classic wild-collected material is available under *Forrest 25917* and *Rock 25401.*

87. ***Rhododendron przewalskii*** Maximowicz

ILLUSTRATION *Iconographia Cormophytorum Sinicorum* 3, t. 4206 (1974); Fang, *Sichuan Rhododendron of China,* 162–164 (1986); Feng, *Rhododendrons of China* 2, pl. 37: 1–5 (1992); Cox and Cox, *The Encyclopedia of Rhododendron Species,* 175 (1997)

HABIT shrub to 3 m

LEAVES broadly elliptic, 5–10 cm, 1.8–3 × as long as broad, hairless above, with a compacted, whitish to pale brown indumentum beneath composed of long-rayed hairs, the indumentum sometimes rather deciduous

CALYX minute, hairless

COROLLA campanulate, 2.5–3.5 cm, white to pale pink, with purple spots

OVARY AND STYLE hairless

CAPSULE to 2 cm

DISTRIBUTION China (Qinghai, Gansu, northern and central Sichuan)

FLOWERING spring

HARDINESS ZONE 6

Recent nonauthenticated material from Sichuan is in cultivation.

The name *Rhododendron purdomii* is misapplied to various hybrids involving species of subsection *Taliensia* in cultivation. Genuine *R. purdomii* Rehder and Wilson is not in cultivation but is illustrated in *Iconographia Cormophytorum Sinicorum* 3, t. 4227 (1974). It is allied to *R. przewalskii* and is known for certain from only one collection in China (Shaanxi).

88. ***Rhododendron rufum*** Batalin

ILLUSTRATION *Iconographia Cormophytorum Sinicorum* 3, t. 4233 (1974); Feng, *Rhododendrons of China* 2, pl. 41: 1–8 (1992); Cox and Cox, *The Encyclopedia of Rhododendron Species*, 178–179 (1997)

HABIT shrub to 4.5 m

LEAVES 6.5–11 cm, 2.2–3 × as long as broad, hairless above, with a dense, 2-layered indumentum beneath, the lower layer whitish, compacted, and embedded in a surface film, the upper reddish brown, with ramiform hairs

CALYX minute, hairy

COROLLA campanulate, 2–3.2 cm, white to pink, with crimson spots

OVARY densely reddish-hairy, with a few shortly stalked glands

CAPSULE 1.5–2.5 cm, curved

DISTRIBUTION western China (northern Sichuan, Gansu)

HARDINESS ZONE 7

Wild-collected material is available under *Hummel 31*. Recent nonauthenticated material from Sichuan is also in cultivation.

89. ***Rhododendron wiltonii*** Hemsley and Wilson

ILLUSTRATION *Curtis's Botanical Magazine*, 9388 (1935); Fang, *Icones Plantarum Omeiensium*, t. 25 (1942); *Iconographia Cormophytorum Sinicorum* 3, t. 4230 (1974); Feng, *Rhododendrons of China* 2, pl. 45: 1–7 (1992); Cox and Cox, *The Encyclopedia of Rhododendron Species*, 184 (1997)

HABIT shrub to 4.5 m

LEAVES oblanceolate to broadly elliptic, 5–12 cm, 2.5–6 × as long as broad; upper surface hairless, with deeply impressed veins; lower surface with a dense, brown or rusty red indumentum of fasciculate to ramiform hairs

CALYX to 1 mm, hairy at first

COROLLA campanulate, 3–4 cm, white to pink, with red spots

OVARY densely covered with rust-red, woolly hairs, eglandular

STYLE hairless or hairy at the base

CAPSULE 2.2–2.5 cm, curved

DISTRIBUTION western China (western Sichuan)

FLOWERING spring
HARDINESS ZONE 6

Recent nonauthenticated material from Sichuan is in cultivation.

90. ***Rhododendron wasonii*** Hemsley and Wilson

ILLUSTRATION *Curtis's Botanical Magazine,* 9190 (1927), reprinted in Halliday, *The Illustrated Rhododendron,* pl. 88 (2001); *Iconographia Cormophytorum Sinicorum* 3, t. 4232 (1974); Fang, *Sichuan Rhododendron of China,* 169–171 (1986); Davidian, *The Rhododendron Species* 3, pl. 71 (1992); Feng, *Rhododendrons of China* 2, pl. 44: 1–7 (1992); Cox and Cox, *The Encyclopedia of Rhododendron Species,* 183 (1997)
HABIT small shrub to 1.5 m
LEAVES ovate-lanceolate, 7–8 cm, 1.6–3 × as long as broad, hairless above when mature, with a sparse to dense reddish brown indumentum beneath composed of long-rayed hairs intermixed with a few glands
CALYX minute, hairy
COROLLA openly campanulate, 3.5–4 cm, yellow or white to pink, with purple spots
OVARY densely reddish-hairy, eglandular
STYLE hairless
DISTRIBUTION western China (central Sichuan)
FLOWERING spring
HARDINESS ZONE 7

Classic wild-collected material is available under *Wilson 1876*. Recent nonauthenticated material from Sichuan and Gansu is also in cultivation.

Plants with pink corollas are known as forma *rhododactylum* Hort.; their status is uncertain. For an illustration, see Davidian, *The Rhododendron Species* 3, pl. 72 (1992).

91. ***Rhododendron lacteum*** Franchet

ILLUSTRATION *Revue Horticole,* 375–376 (1912); *Curtis's Botanical Magazine,* 8988 (1923), reprinted in Halliday, *The Illustrated Rhododendron,* pl. 89 (2001); Stevenson, *The Species of Rhododendron,* 380 (1930); *Iconographia Cormophytorum Sinicorum* 3, t. 4201 (1974); Feng, *Rhododendrons of China* 1, pl. 31: 1–6 (1988); *Rhododendrons with Camellias and Magnolias* 43: f. 21 (1991); Cox and Cox, *The Encyclopedia of Rhododendron Species,* 187 (1997)
HABIT shrub or small tree to 7.5 m; bark brown, breaking into oblong scales
LEAVES elliptic to obovate, 8–17 cm, 2–2.5 × as long as broad; lower surface with a thin indumentum of grey-brown stellate hairs

Inflorescence buds spherical or somewhat spherical-elongate; scales very broad, slightly cuspidate or notched at the tip, conspicuously fringed, hairy all over the surface

Calyx to 1 mm; lobes rounded, hairless

Corolla widely campanulate, 4–5 cm, pure yellow, without spots though sometimes with a purplish basal blotch

Stamens anthers pale brown

Ovary densely hairy

Style hairless

Capsule to 2 cm, curved

Distribution western China (western Yunnan)

Flowering spring

Hardiness zone 7

Classic wild-collected material is available under *Forrest 6778*. Recent nonauthenticated material from Yunnan is also in cultivation.

92. *Rhododendron beesianum* Diels

Illustration *Curtis's Botanical Magazine*, n.s., 125 (1950); *Rhododendron and Camellia Yearbook* 10: f. 47 (1955); *Iconographia Cormophytorum Sinicorum* 3, t. 4203 (1974); Feng, *Rhododendrons of China* 1, pl. 30: 1–2 (1988); Cox and Cox, *The Encyclopedia of Rhododendron Species*, 185 (1997)

Habit shrub or tree to 9 m

Leaves oblanceolate to elliptic, 9–19 cm, 2.6–2.8 × as long as broad; lower surface with a thin, compacted, fawn to brown indumentum

Calyx 0.5–1 mm; lobes rounded, hairless

Corolla broadly campanulate, 3.5–4.5(–5.5) cm, white flushed with pink or red, sometimes with purple spots and a purple basal blotch

Ovary densely hairy with white or brown hairs

Style hairless

Capsule 2–4.5 cm, curved

Distribution western China (southeastern Xizang, northwestern Yunnan, southwestern Sichuan)

Flowering spring

Hardiness zone 7

Classic wild-collected material is available under *Forrest 10195, 30526*, and *Rock 176, 10896, 23308*. Recent nonauthenticated material from Yunnan is also in cultivation.

93. *Rhododendron wightii* Hooker

ILLUSTRATION Hooker, *Rhododendrons of the Sikkim Himalaya,* t. 27 (1851); *Curtis's Botanical Magazine,* 8492 (1913); Cox and Cox, *The Encyclopedia of Rhododendron Species,* 188 (1997); Feng, *Rhododendrons of China* 3, pl. 40: 1–3 (1999)

HABIT shrub to 4.5 m; bark brown, breaking into oblong flakes

LEAVES broadly elliptic to obovate, 5–14 cm, 2–2.5 × as long as broad, hairless above when mature, with a dense, rusty red indumentum beneath composed of ramiform hairs

INFLORESCENCE BUDS large, narrowly ovoid, greenish at the base, brownish above; lower scales densely brown-hairy; upper scales densely white-hairy

CALYX minute, hairless

COROLLA 5- to sometimes 7-lobed, more or less campanulate, 3.5–4.5 cm, pale yellow, with brown or purple spots

OVARY densely red-brown-hairy

STYLE hairless

CAPSULE 2–3 cm, straight or curved

DISTRIBUTION Himalaya, western China (southern Xizang)

FLOWERING spring

HARDINESS ZONE 7

Recent nonauthenticated material from India (Sikkim), Nepal, and Bhutan is in cultivation.

Less commonly cultivated are:

Rhododendron bhutanense Long and Bowes-Lyon

ILLUSTRATION *Notes from the Royal Botanic Garden Edinburgh* 45: 328 (1989)

Keying out to *R. phaeochrysum* but rather similar to *R. wightii.*

LEAVES smaller, tapered to the base, less acute at the apex; midrib hairy above; petioles 1.5–2 cm

STAMENS filaments pubescent towards the base

DISTRIBUTION Bhutan

Recently described and introduced, not yet widely distributed in cultivation.

Rhododendron dignabile Cowan

ILLUSTRATION *The Rhododendron Handbook,* f. 3 (1997)

Similar to *R. aganniphum,* but:

LEAVES 4–6.5 cm wide, almost hairless beneath
DISTRIBUTION western China (eastern Xizang)

Rhododendron principis Bureau and Franchet
SYNONYM *R. vellereum* Hutchinson
ILLUSTRATION *Curtis's Botanical Magazine*, n.s., 147 (1951); *Iconographia Cormophytorum Sinicorum* 3, t. 4228 (1974)
Keying out to *R. aganniphum*, but:
LEAVES generally 2.7–3.6 × as long as broad, indumentum silvery to fawn
DISTRIBUTION western China (eastern Xizang)

Rhododendron pronum Tagg and Forrest
Very similar to *R. principis*, but:
HABIT distinctive, dwarf, creeping shrub; vegetative bud scales persistent
DISTRIBUTION western China (western Yunnan)

Rarely flowers in cultivation.

Rhododendron coeloneuron Diels
ILLUSTRATION *Iconographia Cormophytorum Sinicorum* 3, t. 4231 (1974)
Most similar to *R. wiltonii*, probably keying out to *R. rufum* (or something near it), but:
HABIT proper tree to 8 m
LEAVES acuminate
COROLLA 4–4.5 cm, pink or purplish
DISTRIBUTION western China (southeastern Sichuan)

Rhododendron mimetes Tagg and Forrest
Keying out to *R. rufum*, but:
CALYX 3–6 cm
DISTRIBUTION western China (southwestern Sichuan)

Rhododendron elegantulum Tagg and Forrest
Similar to and keying out to R. bureavii, but:
LEAVES c. 3 × as long as broad, with rounded bases
DISTRIBUTION western China (northwestern Yunnan, southwestern Sichuan)

Possibly a hybrid between *R. bureavii* and *R. adenogynum*.

Rhododendron faberi Hemsley

ILLUSTRATION *Iconographia Cormophytorum Sinicorum* 3, t. 4237 (1974)

A rather distinctive species perhaps keying out to *R. adenogynum.*

YOUNG SHOOTS AND PETIOLES densely tomentose, with a 2-layered indumentum, the upper layer falling irregularly

CALYX 5–15 mm

OVARY densely stipitate-glandular, sometimes hairy as well

DISTRIBUTION western China (central Sichuan)

There are 2 subspecies, both of which are occasionally grown. Subspecies *faberi* has leaves 6–11 × 2.8–4.5 cm, with a dense upper indumentum layer when young. Subspecies *prattii* (Franchet) Chamberlain (*R. prattii* Franchet) has leaves 10–17 × 5–8 cm, with a sparse upper layer of indumentum when young, and is illustrated in *Curtis's Botanical Magazine,* 9414 (1935), and *Iconographia Cormophytorum Sinicorum* 3, t. 4236 (1974).

Rhododendron sphaeroblastum Balfour and Forrest

Keying out to *R. taliense,* but:

LEAVES 1.7–2.3 × as long as broad

DISTRIBUTION western China (northern Yunnan, southwestern Sichuan)

Subgenus *Hymenanthes*

Section *Pontica*

Subsection **Fulva** Sleumer (*Fulvum* series)

HABIT shrubs or small trees to 10 m; young shoots hairy

LEAVES lower surface with a dense one- or 2-layered indumentum, the lower layer composed of dendroid hairs, the upper (when present) brownish and composed of capitellate hairs

RACEME dense, 6- to 30-flowered; rachis 5–15 mm

CALYX minute

COROLLA 5-lobed, campanulate, without nectar sacs

STAMENS 10

OVARY AND STYLE hairless

SEEDS elongate, narrowly winged and with appendages at each end

There are 2 species, both of which are cultivated. The leaves have a 2- or 3-layered upper epidermis, the cells of all layers equal in size, the cuticle half as thick to as thick as the cells are deep; water tissue is present, and the cells of the lower epidermis are not prolonged into papillae. Sclereids occur only occasionally.

1 a Leaf indumentum 2-layered, the upper layer brownish, with capitellate hairs . . . . **94. *R. fulvum***
b Leaf indumentum one- or 2-layered, white or silvery, with dendroid hairs . . . . **95. *R. uvarifolium***

94. *Rhododendron fulvum* Balfour and W. W. Smith

ILLUSTRATION *Curtis's Botanical Magazine*, 9587 (1939), reprinted in Halliday, *The Illustrated Rhododendron*, pl. 90 (2001); *Iconographia Cormophytorum Sinicorum* 3, t. 4221 (1974); Feng, *Rhododendrons of China* 1, pl. 44: 1–3 (1988); Davidian, *The Rhododendron Species* 2, pl. 56 (1992); Kneller, *The Book of Rhododendrons*, 29 (1995); Cox and Cox, *The Encyclopedia of Rhododendron Species*, 64–65 (1997)

HABIT shrub or small tree to 8 m; young shoots brownish-hairy; bark brown or greyish brown, breaking into oblong flakes or long shreds

LEAVES oblanceolate to elliptic, 8–22 cm, 2.2–3.5 × as long as broad, hairless above when mature, with a 2-layered indumentum beneath, the lower layer velvety, with stellate hairs, the upper brownish, composed largely of capitellate hairs, which give the surface a granular appearance

INFLORESCENCE BUDS spherical or slightly ovoid; scales brown or the inner mostly green and reddish where exposed, cuspidate, generally sparsely hairy though densely fringed

CALYX very small, hairless

COROLLA campanulate, 2.5–4.5 cm, white to pink, usually with a dark basal blotch, with or without crimson spots

STAMENS anthers mid brown to dark reddish brown

OVARY AND STYLE hairless

CAPSULE 2.5–4 cm, strongly curved

R. fulvum flower

R. fulvum detail

R. fulvum leaf surface

Distribution western China (southeastern Xizang, western Yunnan), northeastern Myanmar
Flowering spring
Hardiness zone 7

Classic wild-collected material is available under *Farrer 874, Forrest 8989, 14988, 18310, 20075, 21897, 24110, 24314, 25944, Rock 9, 26, 50, 143, 180, 25468,* and *Yü 20750.* Recent nonauthenticated material from Yunnan is also in cultivation.

Very variable in leaf shape and the degree of development of the indumentum.

95. ***Rhododendron uvarifolium*** Diels

Synonym *R. niphargum* Balfour and Kingdon-Ward
Illustration *Curtis's Botanical Magazine,* 9480 (1927); *Iconographia Cormophytorum Sinicorum* 3, t. 4222 (1974); Feng, *Rhododendrons of China* 1, pl. 45: 1–4 (1988); Davidian, *The Rhododendron Species* 2, pl. 58–60 (1992); Cox and Cox, *The Encyclopedia of Rhododendron Species,* 66 (1997)
Habit small shrub to small tree, 2–10 m; bark brownish, splitting into oblong flakes or striate
Leaves oblanceolate to elliptic or oblong, 10–22 cm, 2.3–4.6 × as long as broad, hairless above when mature, with a one- or 2-layered silvery indumentum beneath, the lower layer compacted and containing shortly stalked glands, the upper (when present) rather loose, composed of dendroid hairs
Inflorescence buds oblong- or ovoid-spherical; scales densely hairy with usually a mixture of brown and white hairs; lower scales brown or greenish; inner scales green
Calyx to 1 mm, hairless
Corolla campanulate, 3–3.5 cm, white to pale pink, with crimson spots and usually a purplish basal blotch
Stamens anthers pale brown to brown
Ovary hairless
Capsule 2.5–4.5 cm, strongly curved
Distribution western China (northwestern Yunnan, southeastern Xizang, southwestern Sichuan)
Flowering spring
Hardiness zone 7

Classic wild-collected material is available under *Forrest 10292, 10639, Ludlow, Sherriff, and Elliott 15817, Rock 73, 158, 173, 11045, 11075, 11391,* and *Yü 14952.* Recent nonauthenticated material from Yunnan is also in cultivation.

Subgenus *Hymenanthes*

Section *Pontica*

Subsection *Lanata* Chamberlain (*Campanulatum* series, in part)

HABIT shrubs or small trees to 7.5 m; young shoots densely woolly
LEAVES lower surface with a dense, pale brown to rusty or rarely whitish indumentum composed of dendroid hairs
RACEME loose or dense, 3- to 15-flowered
CALYX minute
COROLLA 5-lobed, campanulate or openly campanulate, without nectar sacs
STAMENS 10
OVARY densely hairy
SEEDS elongate, unwinged but with appendages at each end

There are 4 species, of which *R. lanatum* is the only one widely cultivated. The leaves have a 3-layered upper epidermis, the cells of all 3 layers more or less equal, the cuticle about half as thick as the cells are deep; water tissue and lower epidermal papillae are absent.

96. *Rhododendron lanatum* Hooker
ILLUSTRATION Hooker, *Rhododendrons of the Sikkim Himalaya,* t. 16 (1851); *Flore des Serres,* ser. 1, 7: t. 684 (1851–1852); *Revue Horticole,* ser. 4, 4: 161 (1855); *Rhododendron and Camellia Yearbook* 21: frontispiece (1966) and 38, opposite 82 (1984); Davidian, *The Rhododendron Species* 2, pl. 28 (1992); Kneller, *The Book of Rhododendrons,* 39 (1995); Cox and Cox, *The Encyclopedia of Rhododendron Species,* 97 (1997); Halliday, *The Illustrated Rhododendron,* pl. 91 (2001)
HABIT shrub usually to 4 m (rarely more); young shoots densely red- or white-hairy; bark brown, flaking
LEAVES elliptic to obovate, 6.5–11 cm, 2–3.5 × as long as broad; upper surface ultimately more or less hairless except for flock-like hairs persisting along the midrib; lower surface with dense, thick, more or less crisped dendroid hairs, whitish when young, later deep red-brown or brown
CALYX to 1 mm, hairy
COROLLA campanulate, 3.2–5 cm, cream-yellow with crimson spots
STAMENS anthers brown
CAPSULE 1.5–2.5 cm, curved
DISTRIBUTION Himalaya, western China (southern Xizang)

R. lanatum flower

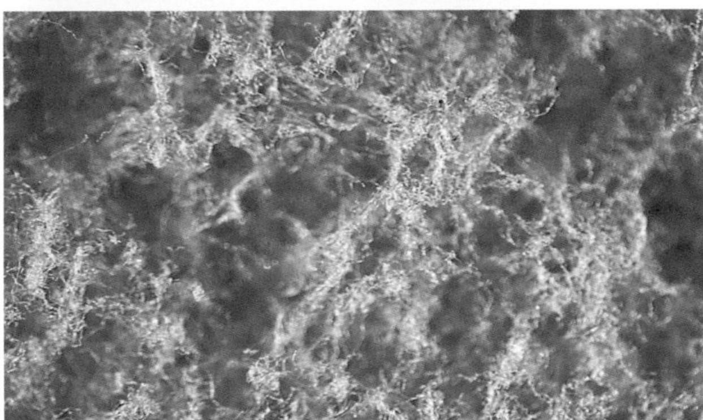

R. lanatum leaf surface

FLOWERING spring
HARDINESS ZONE 7

Classic wild-collected material is available under *Cooper 2148*. Recent nonauthenticated material from India (Sikkim) and Bhutan is also in cultivation.

Rhododendron flinckii Davidian is sometimes recognised as a separate species; it has thinner, reddish leaf indumentum and sometimes rather pinkish flowers. The type is from Bhutan.

Less commonly cultivated is:
Rhododendron tsariense Cowan
LEAVES generally smaller than those of *R. lanatum*
DISTRIBUTION western China (Xizang) and adjacent eastern India

Subgenus *Hymenanthes*

Section *Pontica*

Subsection *Campanulata* Sleumer (*Campanulatum* series, in part)

HABIT shrubs or small trees to 4.5 m; young shoots with a whitish indumentum or hairless

LEAVES lower surface covered with a dense, brownish, woolly indumentum

RACEME 2- to 15-flowered; rachis 1–2.5 cm

COROLLA 5-lobed, openly campanulate to funnel-campanulate, without nectar sacs

STAMENS 10

OVARY AND STYLE hairless

SEEDS elongate, narrowly winged and with appendages at each end (the appendages sometimes very unequal in size)

There are 2 species, both cultivated. The group (as *Campanulatum* series) used to include species here treated as subsections *Venatora* and *Lanata*. The leaves are anatomically similar to those of subsection *Lanata*, with a 3-layered upper epidermis, the cells of all the layers more or less equal in size, the cuticle thin to about half as thick as the cells are deep; water tissue and lower epidermal papillae are absent. Sclereids occur in the leaves of *R. campanulatum*.

1 a Leaves with a dense brown indumentum beneath, composed of capitellate to ramiform hairs .... **97. *R. campanulatum***

b Leaves with sparse dark brown indumentum beneath, composed of fasciculate hairs .... **98. *R. wallichii***

97. *Rhododendron campanulatum* D. Don

HABIT shrub or small tree to 4.5 m; young shoots hairless; bark greyish brown, striate or breaking into oblong flakes

LEAVES ovate to broadly elliptic, 7–14 cm, 2–2.5 × as long as broad; upper surface hairless when mature; lower surface with a dense, brown, woolly indumentum composed of ramiform and capitellate hairs

INFLORESCENCE BUDS spherical to fusiform, green or reddish; scales broad, cuspidate or pointed, fringed with either white or white and brown hairs, sparsely white-hairy on the surface

CALYX to 1 mm, hairless

COROLLA openly campanulate, 3–5 cm, white to pale mauve or pink, usually with purple spots

STAMENS anthers brown to very dark brown or almost black
OVARY hairless
CAPSULE 2–3 cm, usually curved
DISTRIBUTION Himalaya
FLOWERING spring
HARDINESS ZONE 5

R. *campanulatum* subsp. ***campanulatum***

ILLUSTRATION *Curtis's Botanical Magazine,* 3759 (1840); *Iconographia Cormophytorum Sinicorum* 3, t. 4224 (1974); *Rhododendron and Camellia Yearbook* 40: f. 10 (1987); Davidian, *The Rhododendron Species* 2, pl. 25–26 (1992); Kneller, *The Book of Rhododendrons,* 19 (1995); Cox and Cox, *The Encyclopedia of Rhododendron Species,* 30 (1997)
LEAVES 9.5–14 cm, without a blue, metallic bloom when young

Wild-collected material is available under *Beer 643, Beer, Lancaster, and Morris 283, 344, Cooper 5926, Halliwell 124, Hruby 3, 14, Spring-Smythe 6, 7, 8, 11, 14, 41, 44,* and *Stainton, Sykes, and Williams 9107.* Recent nonauthenticated material from northern India and Nepal is also in cultivation.

R. campanulatum subsp. *campanulatum* flower

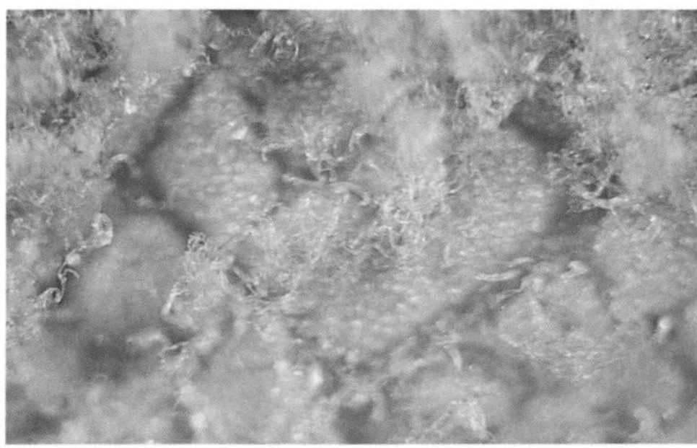

R. campanulatum subsp. *campanulatum* leaf surface

R. campanulatum subsp. *campanulatum* detail

R. campanulatum subsp. ***aeruginosum*** (Hooker) Chamberlain
SYNONYM *R. aeruginosum* Hooker
ILLUSTRATION Davidian, *The Rhododendron Species* 2, pl. 27 (1992); Cox and Cox, *The Encyclopedia of Rhododendron Species,* 30–31 (1997)
LEAVES 7–10 cm, with a remarkable bluish metallic bloom when young

Wild-collected material is available under *Cooper 3480* and *Gould 2A*. Recent nonauthenticated material from Bhutan is also in cultivation.

98. *Rhododendron wallichii* Hooker
ILLUSTRATION *Curtis's Botanical Magazine,* 4928 (1856), reprinted in Halliday, *The Illustrated Rhododendron,* pl. 92 (2001); *Iconographia Cormophytorum Sinicorum* 3, t. 4223 (1974); Cox and Cox, *The Encyclopedia of Rhododendron Species,* 31 (1997); Feng, *Rhododendrons of China* 3, pl. 42: 1–2 (1999)
HABIT shrub to 4.5 m; young shoots with a white, loose indumentum; bark greyish brown, cracking into oblong plates
LEAVES elliptic to ovate, 7–12 cm, 2–2.5 × as long as broad, hairless above, with a sparse, dark brown indumentum of fasciculate hairs beneath
INFLORESCENCE BUDS fusiform or elongate-fusiform; outer scales brownish; inner scales mostly green or whitish green, cuspidate, hairy with brown hairs on the surface and whitish hairs near the tip
CALYX lobes 1–3 mm, irregular, sparsely and shortly hairy to hairless
COROLLA funnel-campanulate, 2.5–5 cm, white to pale mauve or lilac, with or without darker spots
STAMENS anthers brown
OVARY more or less hairless
CAPSULE 1.5–3 cm
DISTRIBUTION Himalaya, western China (southern Xizang)
FLOWERING spring
HARDINESS ZONE 7

Wild-collected material is available under *Chamberlain* (without number), *Hruby 16, Ludlow and Sherriff 2895, 3578, Ludlow, Sherriff, and Hicks 17448, 17527, Ludlow, Sherriff, and Taylor 6424, 6659,* and *Spring-Smythe 17.* Recent nonauthenticated material from India (Sikkim), Nepal, and Bhutan is also in cultivation.

Subgenus *Hymenanthes*

Section *Pontica*

Subsection *Griersoniana* Chamberlain (*Griersonianum* series)

HABIT shrubs to 3 m; young shoots with small glandular bristles and also woolly
VEGETATIVE BUD SCALES long and tapering
LEAVES lower surface with a dense, whitish indumentum of dendroid hairs
RACEME loose, 5- to 12-flowered
CALYX minute
COROLLA 5-lobed, tubular-campanulate to funnel-campanulate, without nectar sacs, densely hairy outside
STAMENS 10
OVARY with dendroid hairs and a few glands
STYLE hairless
SEEDS elongate, narrowly winged and with appendages at each end

Rhododendron griersonianum is the only species. It has leaves with a 2-layered upper epidermis, the cells of both layers similar in size, the cuticle about half as thick as the cells are deep; water tissue and lower epidermal papillae are absent. Sclereids are present in the leaf tissue.

99. *Rhododendron griersonianum* Balfour and Forrest
ILLUSTRATION *Curtis's Botanical Magazine*, 9195 (1930), reprinted in Halliday, *The Illustrated Rhododendron*, pl. 93 (2001); Stevenson, *The Species of Rhododendron*, 41 (1930); *Iconographia Cormophytorum Sinicorum* 3, t. 4118 (1974); *Rhododendron and Camellia Yearbook* 41: f. 7 (1988); Kneller, *The Book of Rhododendrons*, 31 (1995); Cox and Cox, *The Encyclopedia of Rhododendron Species*, 86 (1997)
HABIT shrub to 3 m; young shoots densely covered with a woolly indumentum and short, gland-tipped bristles
LEAVES elliptic, 10–20 cm, 3–4(–7) × as long as broad; upper surface hairless at maturity; lower surface densely woolly, whitish to pale brown
CALYX to 1 mm
COROLLA tubular-campanulate to funnel-campanulate, 5.5–8 cm, densely hairy on the outer surface of the tube, deep pink to crimson or scarlet
STAMENS anthers reddish brown
OVARY densely covered with dendroid hairs and with scattered, shortly stalked glands

Capsule to 2 cm
Distribution western China (western Yunnan), northeastern Myanmar
Flowering late spring
Hardiness zone 8

Classic wild-collected material is available under *Forrest 24116, 30392.*

Very commonly used as a parent of hybrids. Among the most notable of these are 'Elizabeth' (× *R. forrestii*), 'May Day' (× *R. haematodes*), and 'Fabia' (× *R. dichroanthum*).

R. griersonianum flower and leaf

R. griersonianum detail

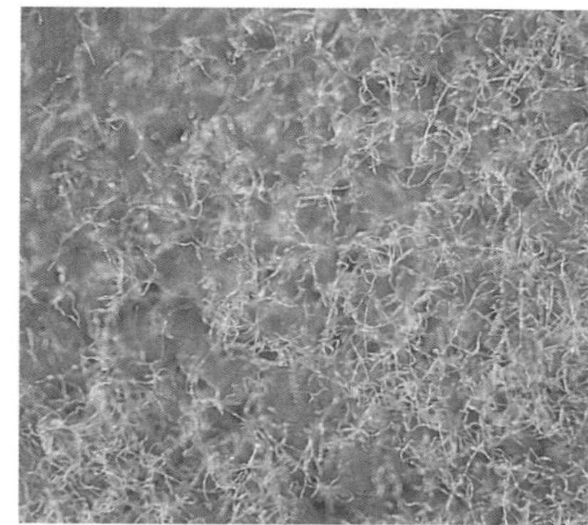

R. griersonianum leaf surface

Subgenus *Hymenanthes*

Section *Pontica*

Subsection *Parishia* Sleumer (*Irroratum* series *Parishii* subseries)

HABIT shrubs or small trees to 10 m; young shoots rusty stellate-hairy, sometimes with glandular bristles

LEAVES lower surface usually becoming hairless when mature, or with a thin indumentum of stellate hairs occasionally mixed with a few glands (mainly on the midrib)

RACEME loose, 5- to 15-flowered; rachis 5–40 mm

CALYX usually small

COROLLA fleshy, 5-lobed, tubular-campanulate to funnel-campanulate, with pronounced nectar sacs

STAMENS 10

OVARY densely hairy and usually with some shortly stalked glands

STYLE hairless or glandular throughout

SEEDS elongate, winged and with appendages at each end

A group of 6 species, characterised by the presence of stellate hairs on the leaves. The leaves have a 2-layered upper epidermis, the cells all more or less equal in size, the cuticle half as thick to as thick as the cells are deep; water tissue is present, but the cells of the lower epidermis are without papillae. Sclereids are present in the leaf tissue of all species.

1a Leaf stalks and shoots with glandular bristles, at least when young . . . . **100. *R. kyawi***
b Leaf stalks and shoots without glandular bristles 2
2a Leaves 8.5–10 cm; corolla funnel-campanulate . . . . **102. *R. elliottii***
b Leaves 10–19 cm; corolla tubular-campanulate . . . . **101. *R. facetum***

100. *Rhododendron kyawi* Lace and W. W. Smith

SYNONYM *R. agapetum* Balfour and Kingdon-Ward

ILLUSTRATION *Curtis's Botanical Magazine*, 9271 (1929), reprinted in Halliday, *The Illustrated Rhododendron*, pl. 94 (2001); Stevenson, *The Species of Rhododendron*, 367 (1930); Cox and Cox, *The Encyclopedia of Rhododendron Species*, 135 (1997)

HABIT shrub to 9 m; young shoots densely stellate-hairy and with glandular bristles

LEAVES elliptic to oblong, 9–22(–30) cm, 2.2–3 × as long as broad; upper surface hairless; lower surface with a cinnamon-brown indumentum of stellate hairs mixed with some shortly stalked glands

Calyx 1–2 mm, glandular-bristly, usually also sparsely floccose
Corolla tubular-campanulate, 4.5–6 cm, bright crimson to scarlet, without spots
Ovary with dense stellate hairs intermixed with shortly stalked glands
Style similarly hairy in the lower part
Capsule 2.5–4 cm, slightly curved
Distribution western China (northern Yunnan), northeastern Myanmar
Flowering spring
Hardiness zone 9

Classic wild-collected material is available under *Forrest 24542, 24680.*

101. ***Rhododendron facetum*** Balfour and Kingdon-Ward

Synonym *R. eriogynum* Balfour and W. W. Smith
Illustration Cox, *The Plant Introductions of Reginald Farrer,* 92 (1930); *Curtis's Botanical Magazine,* 9337 (1934); Cox, *The Larger Species of Rhododendron,* f. 36 (1979); Feng, *Rhododendrons of China* 1, pl. 24 (1988); Davidian, *The Rhododendron Species* 3, pl. 36 (1992); Cox and Cox, *The Encyclopedia of Rhododendron Species,* 134 (1997)
Habit shrub or tree to 10 m; young shoots reddish with stellate hairs
Leaves oblanceolate to elliptic, 10–18.5 cm, 2.3–3.2 × as long as broad, hairless when mature or with vestiges of indumentum beneath, especially towards the base and the midrib
Calyx 3–5 mm, stellate-hairy; lobes broad and rounded
Corolla tubular-campanulate, 4–5 cm, sparingly hairy or hairless outside, deep pink to scarlet
Stamens anthers dark brown
Ovary densely reddish stellate-hairy
Style stellate-hairy and with some glands
Capsule 1.5–2 cm, slightly curved
Distribution western China (Yunnan), northeastern Myanmar
Flowering spring
Hardiness zone 8

Recent nonauthenticated material from Yunnan is in cultivation.

102. ***Rhododendron elliottii*** Watt

Illustration *Notes from the Royal Botanic Garden Edinburgh* 8, t. 140 (1914); *Curtis's Botanical Magazine,* 9546 (1938); Cox and Cox, *The Encyclopedia of Rhododendron Species,* 133–134 (1997)

Habit small shrub; young shoots with stellate hairs and shortly stalked glands
Leaves lanceolate to elliptic, 8.5–10 cm, about 2.5 × as long as broad, hairless when mature
Calyx 3–4 mm; lobes rounded, glandular and glandular-ciliate
Corolla funnel-campanulate, 4–5 cm, purple with darker spots
Ovary reddish-hairy with stellate hairs mixed with shortly stalked glands
Style hairy and glandular to the apex
Capsule to 1.5 cm
Distribution northeastern India
Flowering spring
Hardiness zone 9

R. elliottii flower and leaf. PHOTO BY RAY COX

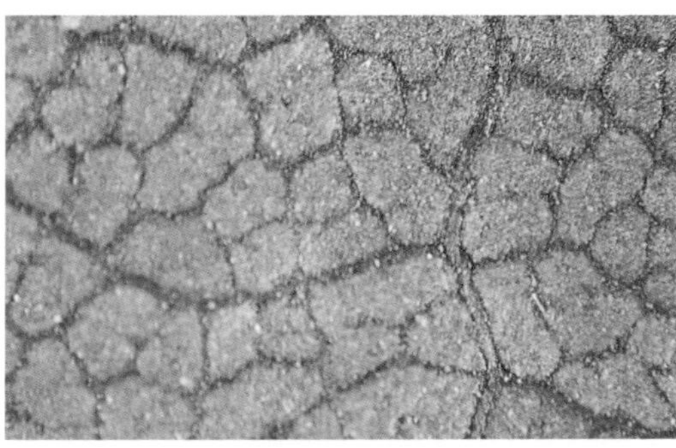

R. elliottii leaf surface

Subgenus *Hymenanthes*

Section *Pontica*

Subsection *Barbata* Sleumer (*Barbatum* series *Barbatum* subseries)

HABIT shrubs or small trees; young shoots usually with bristles; bark smooth, peeling

LEAVES hairless or bristly or with shortly stalked glands, sometimes with a thin covering of dendroid hairs beneath

RACEME dense and congested, 10- to 25-flowered; rachis 5–7 mm

CALYX minute to large and cup-like

COROLLA 5-lobed, fleshy, tubular-campanulate, with nectar sacs, usually crimson to deep red, rarely pink

STAMENS 10

OVARY hairless or with a dense covering of shortly stalked glands, or with a rusty red indumentum of dendroid hairs

STYLE hairless

SEEDS elongate, narrowly winged and with appendages at each end

A group of 4 species, characterised by the presence of bristles on the leaf stalks and the occurrence of nectar sacs in the corolla bases. Only 2 of the species are in cultivation. The leaves have a 3-layered upper epidermis, the cells similar in size, the cuticle thin to about half as thick as the cells are deep; water tissue is present, and the cells of the lower epidermis are prolonged into papillae. Sclereids are present in the leaf tissue.

1a Lower surface of leaves with scattered dendroid hairs and shortly stalked glands . . **103. *R. barbatum***

b Lower surface of leaves with a continuous layer of pale brown hairs which slowly fade to whitish . . . . **104. *R. smithii***

103. *Rhododendron barbatum* G. Don

ILLUSTRATION Hooker, *Rhododendrons of the Sikkim Himalaya,* t. 4 (1849); Stevenson, *The Species of Rhododendron,* 129 (1930); *Iconographia Cormophytorum Sinicorum* 3, t. 4119 (1974); Davidian, *The Rhododendron Species* 2, pl. 12–13 (1992); Kneller, *The Book of Rhododendrons,* 17 (1995); Cox and Cox, *The Encyclopedia of Rhododendron Species,* 26 (1997)

HABIT shrub or tree to 6 m; young shoots with long, stiff bristles; bark purplish brown to plum-red, usually smooth, peeling in large sheets

LEAVES elliptic to obovate, 9–19 cm, about 3 × as long as broad; upper surface hair-

R. barbatum flower

R. barbatum detail

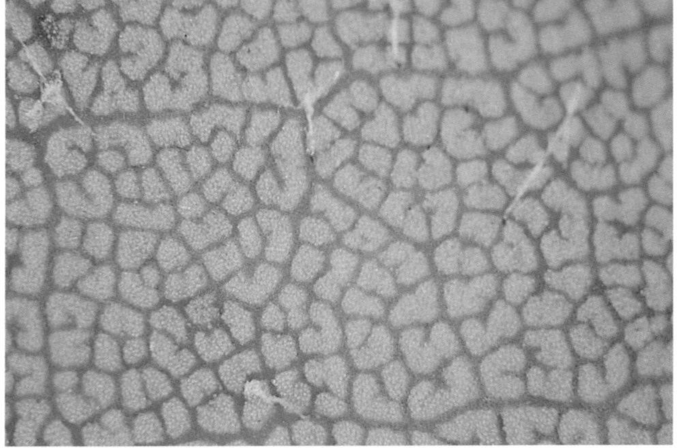

R. barbatum leaf surface

less; lower surface with scattered dendroid hairs and shortly stalked glands, with or without bristles on the midrib; leaf stalks with or without bristles

INFLORESCENCE BUDS fusiform or ovoid, sticky; scales mostly green, pointed, sparsely hairy

RACEME dense

CALYX 1–1.5 cm, cup-like, often reddish, hairless or with a few hairs at the base; lobes well developed, rounded, fringed

COROLLA fleshy, tubular-campanulate, 3–3.5 cm, crimson to blood-red or rarely pure white; nectar sacs dark

STAMENS anthers brown to dark brown or almost black

OVARY densely glandular and with some dendroid hairs

STYLE hairless

CAPSULE 1.5–2 cm, curved

DISTRIBUTION Himalaya

FLOWERING spring

HARDINESS ZONE 7

Wild-collected material is available under *Bartholomew 147, 259, Beer 655, Beer, Lancaster, and Morris 325, Chamberlain* (without number), *Cooper 3507, Gould 37, Ludlow, Sherriff, and Hicks 17512,* and *Spring-Smythe 21, 30.* Recent nonauthenticated collections from Nepal, Bhutan, and Yunnan are also in cultivation.

104. *Rhododendron smithii* Hooker

ILLUSTRATION *Curtis's Botanical Magazine,* 5120 (1859), reprinted in Halliday, *The Illustrated Rhododendron,* pl. 95 (2001)

HABIT shrub or small tree to 7.5 m; young shoots with long, stiff bristles

LEAVES elliptic to obovate-lanceolate, 8–13 cm, 2–3.2 × as long as broad, hairless above, with a thin, continuous layer of pale brown dendroid hairs beneath, usually also with a few bristles on the midrib towards the base

RACEME dense, 15- to 20-flowered; rachis short

CALYX 5–10 mm, fleshy, reddish, 5-lobed; lobes glandular-ciliate

COROLLA tubular-campanulate, 3–4.5 cm, scarlet to crimson, with darker nectar sacs

OVARY with dense, rusty indumentum containing some glandular hairs

STYLE hairless

CAPSULE to 1.5 cm

DISTRIBUTION northeastern India (Sikkim, Arunachal Pradesh), Bhutan, western China (southern Xizang)

FLOWERING spring
HARDINESS ZONE 8

Less commonly cultivated are:

Rhododendron exasperatum Tagg
Similar to *R. barbatum,* but:
LEAVES with gland-tipped bristles on the lower surface
DISTRIBUTION northeastern India (Arunachal Pradesh), northeastern Upper Burma (Myanmar), western China (southeastern Xizang)

Rhododendron succothii Davidian
Similar to *R. barbatum* in flower structure, but:
LEAVES with very reduced, almost nonexistent petioles, without the bristles characteristic of the group
DISTRIBUTION Bhutan, northeastern India

Subgenus *Hymenanthes*

Section *Pontica*

Subsection *Neriiflora* Sleumer (*Neriiflorum* series)

HABIT shrubs, sometimes dwarf and creeping, to small trees; young shoots with a thick or thin, whitish or rusty indumentum composed of rosulate, dendroid, or ramiform hairs

LEAVES hairless or with an indumentum beneath; indumentum sometimes discontinuous

RACEME one- to 20-flowered, loose or dense

CALYX minute or well developed and cup-like

COROLLA 5-lobed, tubular-campanulate or rarely campanulate, usually fleshy and with nectar sacs

STAMENS 10

OVARY hairy, with or without shortly stalked glands, or hairless

STYLE hairless

SEEDS elongate, winged (sometimes narrowly) and with appendages at each end (appendages sometimes small)

There are about 26 species of this subsection; they are particularly difficult to distinguish. Anatomically the leaves of the species of this group are variable. They consistently have a 2- or 3-layered upper epidermis, the cells all more or less equal in size (those of the lower layer larger in *R. catacosmum*), the cuticle half as thick to as thick as the cells are deep; water tissue is absent, and the cells of the lower epidermis are usually not prolonged into papillae, though where papillae are present (*R. aperantum, R. neriiflorum* and its allies) they are large and conspicuous.

1 a Ovary more or less tapering into the style (it may be necessary to scrape off hairs to see this clearly) 2

b Style inserted into a shouldered depression on top of the ovary (it may be necessary to scrape off hairs to see this clearly) 5

2 a Mature leaves hairless beneath . . . . **119. *R. neriiflorum***

b Mature leaves with an evident indumentum beneath 3

3 a Ovary and usually young shoots with shortly stalked glands; leaves with a dense, continuous indumentum beneath . . . . **121. *R. sperabile***

b Ovary and young shoots eglandular; leaves with a sparse, discontinuous indumentum beneath . . . 4

4 a Leaves 3.3 or more × as long as broad; lower leaf surface whitish . . . . **120. *R. floccigerum***

b Leaves up to 3 × as long as broad; lower leaf surface greenish . . . . **122. *R. sperabiloides***

5 a Leaves with a thick, one- or 2-layered, reddish to brown indumentum beneath 6
b Leaves hairless or with a thin, adpressed or felted, whitish or pale brown indumentum beneath .. 13
6 a Leaves strongly wrinkled (rugulose) above 7
b Leaves not wrinkled or only slightly wrinkled above 8
7 a Young shoots and leaf stalks densely hairy, eglandular; usually a small tree with a well-developed trunk .... **105. *R. mallotum***
b Young shoots and leaf stalks glandular-bristly as well as hairy; usually a sprawling shrub without a trunk .... **106. *R. beanianum***
8 a Young shoots sparsely to densely glandular; ovary glandular 9
b Young shoots eglandular; ovary hairy, usually without glands 10
9 a Leaves 2–3 × as long as broad; leaf stalks hairy and glandular ....**107. *R. pocophorum***
b Leaves 1.6–2 × as long as broad; leaf stalks more or less hairless ....**108. *R. coelicum***
10 a Young shoots and leaf stalks densely covered with small bristles ....**110. *R. haematodes***
b Young shoots hairy or hairless, without small bristles 11
11 a Corolla yellow to red; flower stalks with at least a few glands ....**111. *R. citriniflorum***
b Corolla scarlet to crimson; flower stalks eglandular 12
12 a Flower stalks 2.5–3.5 cm; calyx 1.5–2 cm ....**109. *R. catacosmum***
b Flower stalks 1–2.5 cm; calyx 5–15 mm ....**110. *R. haematodes***
13 a Leaves with a more or less continuous, whitish to fawn, adpressed indumentum beneath 14
b Leaves hairless or with a sparse, discontinuous indumentum beneath 16
14 a Corolla 3.5–5 cm, orange-red or yellow flushed with red, rarely pink ....**112. *R. dichroanthum***
b Corolla 2.5–3.5 cm, pink to crimson 15
15 a Leaf indumentum spongy and felted, buff to pale brown ....**113. *R. microgynum***
b Leaf indumentum compacted, whitish to fawn ....**114. *R. sanguineum***
16 a Flowers solitary; dwarf, creeping shrub, usually not more than 10 cm high ....**118. *R. forrestii***
b Racemes 2- to 6-flowered; upright shrub, usually more than 30 cm high 17
17 a Leaves at least 2.5 × as long as broad ....**116. *R. eudoxum***
b Leaves 1.5–2.5 × as long as broad 18
18 a Flower stalks hairy, eglandular; leaf stalks broad, eglandular ....**115. *R. aperantum***
b Flower stalks sparsely covered with shortly stalked glands; leaf stalks narrow, sometimes glandular ....**117. *R. chamaethomsonii***

105. *Rhododendron mallotum* Balfour and Kingdon-Ward

ILLUSTRATION *Curtis's Botanical Magazine,* 9419 (1935); *Iconographia Cormophytorum Sinicorum* 3, t. 4142 (1974); Davidian, *The Rhododendron Species* 3, pl. 14 (1992); Cox and Cox, *The Encyclopedia of Rhododendron Species,* 113–114 (1997)

HABIT shrub or small tree to 6.5 m, usually with a well-defined trunk; young shoots densely reddish-hairy; bark brown or reddish brown, usually scaling in long flakes

LEAVES broadly oblanceolate to obovate, 10–13 cm, 1.8–2.3 × as long as broad, hairless above except for some hairs along the midrib, with a dense, reddish, woolly indumentum of dendroid hairs beneath

INFLORESCENCE BUDS spherical or slightly elongate-spherical; scales brown where exposed, otherwise greenish white, pointed, densely hairy where exposed

CALYX 2–3 mm, hairy

COROLLA fleshy, tubular-campanulate, 4–4.5 cm, crimson

STAMENS anthers dark red to dark brown

OVARY densely reddish-hairy

CAPSULE to 1.2 cm, persistently hairy

DISTRIBUTION western China (western Yunnan), northeastern Myanmar

FLOWERING spring

HARDINESS ZONE 7

Classic wild-collected material is available under *Farrer 815*.

106. *Rhododendron beanianum* Cowan

ILLUSTRATION *Curtis's Botanical Magazine*, n.s., 219 (1953); *Iconographia Cormophytorum Sinicorum* 3, t. 4144 (1974); Cox and Cox, *The Encyclopedia of Rhododendron Species*, 108 (1997)

HABIT to 3 m; young shoots with stellate hairs and shortly stalked glands; bark greyish brown, striate or scaling into oblong flakes

LEAVES obovate to elliptic, 6–9 cm, 2–2.4 × as long as broad; upper surface finely wrinkled; lower surface with a dense, brownish indumentum of dendroid hairs

INFLORESCENCE BUDS spherical to fusiform; scales brown or brown with greenish tips, cuspidate or not, the outer scales densely fringed with brown hairs, sparsely hairy on the surface, the inner scales densely hairy all over the surface

CALYX 5 mm, cup-like, sparsely hairy

COROLLA fleshy, tubular-campanulate, to 3.5 cm, carmine to blood-red

STAMENS anthers black

OVARY with stellate hairs

STYLE hairless

CAPSULE 1.2 cm or more, persistently hairy

DISTRIBUTION northeastern India, northern Myanmar

FLOWERING spring

HARDINESS ZONE 8

Classic wild-collected material is available under *Kingdon-Ward 6805* (the type collection).

107. *Rhododendron pocophorum* Tagg

ILLUSTRATION Davidian, *The Rhododendron Species* 3, pl. 12 (1992); Feng, *Rhododendrons of China* 2, pl. 47: 1–2 (1992); Cox and Cox, *The Encyclopedia of Rhododendron Species,* 112–113 (1997)

HABIT shrub to 3 m; young shoots with dense, shortly stalked glands; bark yellowish brown, striate, ultimately cracking into oblong plates

LEAVES oblong to obovate, 8–15 cm, 2–3 × as long as broad, hairless above, with a thick, continuous or patchy, red-brown indumentum beneath

INFLORESCENCE BUDS almost spherical; scales cuspidate or pointed, sticky with brown-headed glands on the surface; lower scales brownish or green

CALYX 5–10 mm, with irregular, glandular-ciliate, hairless lobes

COROLLA fleshy, tubular-campanulate, 4–5 cm, pale to deep crimson

STAMENS anthers reddish brown or brown

OVARY densely covered with shortly stalked glands

CAPSULE 2–2.5 cm

DISTRIBUTION northeastern India (Arunachal Pradesh), western China (southern Xizang, northwestern Yunnan)

FLOWERING spring

HARDINESS ZONE 7

Classic wild-collected material is available under *Forrest 19977, 21709,* and *Kingdon-Ward 8289.*

Two varieties occur in the wild, and both may be cultivated. Variety *pocophorum* has leaves with a continuous indumentum beneath, while var. *hemidartum* (Tagg) Chamberlain has a patchy, discontinuous indumentum.

108. *Rhododendron coelicum* Balfour and Farrer

ILLUSTRATION *Rhododendron and Camellia Yearbook* 10: f. 19 (1958); Cox and Cox, *The Encyclopedia of Rhododendron Species,* 109 (1997)

HABIT to 2 m; young shoots with sparse, shortly stalked glands

LEAVES obovate, 6–8.5 cm, 1.6–2 × as long as broad, hairless above, with a thick, brownish indumentum of dendroid hairs beneath

CALYX 5–7 mm; lobes rounded, glandular-ciliate

COROLLA fleshy, tubular-campanulate, 3.8–4.5 cm, crimson

Ovary with shortly stalked glands, hairy
Capsule 1.5–1.8 cm, curved
Distribution western China (western Yunnan), northeastern Myanmar
Flowering spring
Hardiness zone 8

Classic wild-collected material is available under *Forrest 25625* and *Kingdon-Ward 10134.*

109. *Rhododendron catacosmum* Tagg

Illustration Davidian, *The Rhododendron Species* 3, pl. 11 (1992); Cox and Cox, *The Encyclopedia of Rhododendron Species,* 109 (1997); Feng, *Rhododendrons of China* 3, pl. 44 (1999)
Habit shrub to 3 m; young shoots brownish-hairy
Leaves obovate, 8–10 cm, 1.6–2 × as long as broad, hairless above, with a brownish-hairy, 2-layered indumentum beneath, the lower layer compacted, the upper loose
Calyx 1.5–2 cm, cup-like, with shallow lobes, hairless
Corolla tubular-campanulate, to 4.5 cm, crimson
Ovary densely hairy
Capsule 2–2.5 cm
Distribution western China (southeastern Xizang, northwestern Yunnan)
Flowering spring
Hardiness zone 7

Classic wild-collected material is available under *Forrest 20078.*

110. *Rhododendron haematodes* Franchet

Habit shrub to 1.8 m; young shoots densely hairy or bristly
Leaves ovate to oblong, 4.5–10 cm, 1.5–2.6 × as long as broad, hairless or with a few scattered hairs above, with a densely matted, 2-layered indumentum beneath, the lower layer whitish and compacted, the upper fawn to red-brown and composed of dendroid hairs
Calyx minute to cup-like; when well developed usually irregular and with lobes 3–15 mm, unequal, hairless
Corolla fleshy, tubular-campanulate, 3.5–4.5 cm, scarlet to deep crimson
Ovary reddish-hairy
Capsule 1–1.5 cm

DISTRIBUTION western China (western and northwestern Yunnan, southeastern Xizang), northeastern Myanmar
FLOWERING spring
HARDINESS ZONE 7

R. *haematodes* subsp. ***haematodes***
ILLUSTRATION *Curtis's Botanical Magazine,* 9165 (1927); *Iconographia Cormophytorum Sinicorum* 3, t. 4141 (1974); Davidian, *The Rhododendron Species* 3, pl. 6 (1992); Cox and Cox, *The Encyclopedia of Rhododendron Species,* 110–111 (1997); Feng, *Rhododendrons of China* 3, pl. 48 (1999)
LEAF STALKS AND YOUNG SHOOTS hairy; bristles few or absent

Classic wild-collected material is available under *Forrest 28351* and *McLaren S124A.* Recent nonauthenticated material from Yunnan is also in cultivation.

Widely used in hybridisation. The most notable hybrids are 'Elizabeth' (× *R. griersonianum*) and 'Humming Bird' (× *R. williamsianum*).

R. *haematodes* subsp. ***chaetomallum*** (Balfour and Forrest) Chamberlain
SYNONYM *R. chaetomallum* Balfour and Forrest
ILLUSTRATION *Curtis's Botanical Magazine,* n.s., 25 (1948); *Iconographia Cormophytorum Sinicorum* 3, t. 4143 (1974); Feng, *Rhododendrons of China* 1, pl. 13: 1–3 (1988); Davidian, *The Rhododendron Species* 3, pl. 9 (1992); Cox and Cox, *The Encyclopedia of Rhododendron Species,* 111 (1997)
HABIT bark cinnamon-brown to pale brown, scaling in large flakes or sheets
INFLORESCENCE BUDS spherical or ovoid; lower scales mostly brown and cuspidate; inner scales dull brown, densely white-hairy, with some brown hairs on the margins or the surface
LEAF STALKS AND YOUNG SHOOTS with stout bristles
STAMENS anthers black or almost so

Classic wild-collected material is available under *Forrest 19911, 25601, Kingdon-Ward 21077,* and *Rock 41, 18359.*

111. *Rhododendron citriniflorum* Balfour and Forrest
HABIT to 1.5 m; young shoots hairless or with a white, fluffy indumentum
LEAVES obovate to elliptic, 4–7.5 cm, 2.2–3.3 × as long as broad; upper surface hairless when mature; lower surface with a dense, thick, grey-brown indumentum of ramiform hairs

CALYX 2–12 mm, cupular when well developed; lobes ciliate or glandular-ciliate
COROLLA thin, tubular-campanulate, 3.2–4.5 cm, yellow, orange, or carmine
OVARY with shortly stalked glands and/or reddish hairs
CAPSULE 8–12 mm
DISTRIBUTION western China (southeastern Xizang, northwestern Yunnan)
FLOWERING spring
HARDINESS ZONE 8

R. *citriniflorum* var. ***citriniflorum***

ILLUSTRATION Davidian, *The Rhododendron Species* 3, pl. 27 (1992); Cox and Cox, *The Encyclopedia of Rhododendron Species,* 115–116 (1997)
CALYX rarely more than 5 mm
COROLLA yellow
FLOWER STALKS with shortly stalked glands
OVARY with shortly stalked glands

Classic wild-collected material is available under *Rock 128, 10905.* Recent nonauthenticated material from Yunnan is also in cultivation.

R. *citriniflorum* var. ***horaeum*** (Balfour and Forrest) Chamberlain

SYNONYM *R. horaeum* Balfour and Forrest
ILLUSTRATION *Iconographia Cormophytorum Sinicorum* 3, t. 4151 (1974); Cox and Cox, *The Encyclopedia of Rhododendron Species,* 116 (1997)
CALYX rarely less than 7 mm
COROLLA yellowish to reddish
FLOWER STALKS without glands
OVARY without glands

Classic wild-collected material is available under *Forrest 25901, 21850, 25564.*

112. *Rhododendron dichroanthum* Diels

HABIT dwarf shrub to 2 m; young shoots white-hairy, sometimes with bristles, which are sometimes gland-tipped; vegetative bud scales deciduous; bark pale brown, shredding in long flakes; underbark striate, brown
LEAVES oblanceolate to elliptic, 4–9.5 cm, 2–3 × as long as broad, hairless above, with a continuous, loose to compacted, silvery to fawn indumentum of rosulate hairs beneath

CALYX 3–15 mm, usually cupular, coloured, hairless except for glandular cilia on the irregular lobes
COROLLA fleshy, tubular-campanulate, 3.5–5 cm, orange-red or occasionally yellow flushed with red
OVARY reddish-hairy, sometimes glandular
CAPSULE 1–1.5 cm
DISTRIBUTION western China (northern and northwestern Yunnan), northeastern Myanmar
FLOWERING spring
HARDINESS ZONE 8

R. dichroanthum subsp. ***apodectum*** (Balfour and W. W. Smith) Cowan
SYNONYM *R. apodectum* Balfour and W. W. Smith
ILLUSTRATION *Curtis's Botanical Magazine*, 9014 (1924); *Iconographia Cormophytorum Sinicorum* 3, t. 4145 (1974); Davidian, *The Rhododendron Species* 3, pl. 33 (1992); Cox and Cox, *The Encyclopedia of Rhododendron Species*, 118 (1997)
YOUNG SHOOTS without glands
OVARY without glands

Classic wild-collected material is available under *Forrest 8987* (the type collection), *18167, 24331*, and *Kingdon-Ward 4486*.

R. dichroanthum subsp. ***scyphocalyx*** (Balfour and Forrest) Cowan
SYNONYMS *R. scyphocalyx* Balfour and Forrest; *R. herpesticum* Balfour and Kingdon-Ward
ILLUSTRATION Davidian, *The Rhododendron Species* 3, pl. 25 (1992); Cox and Cox, *The Encyclopedia of Rhododendron Species*, 118 (1997)
YOUNG SHOOTS glandular
OVARY glandular

Classic wild-collected material is available under *Farrer 1024* and *Forrest 24546, 24603, 25065, 26965, 27003, 27051, 27052, 27059, 27061, 27063, 27087, 27089, 27093, 27099, 27116, 27137, 27657*.

Subspecies *dichroanthum* is not in general cultivation but is illustrated in *Curtis's Botanical Magazine*, 8815 (1919); *Iconographia Cormophytorum Sinicorum* 3, t. 4146 (1974); Davidian, *The Rhododendron Species* 3, pl. 32 (1992); Cox and Cox, *The Encyclopedia of Rhododendron Species*, 117 (1997); and Feng, *Rhododendrons of China* 3, pl. 45: 1–3 (1999).

113. *Rhododendron microgynum* Balfour and Forrest

SYNONYM *R. gymnocarpum* Tagg

ILLUSTRATION Cox and Cox, *The Encyclopedia of Rhododendron Species,* 120 (1997); Feng, *Rhododendrons of China* 3, pl. 49 (1999)

HABIT small shrub to 1.6 m; young shoots whitish-hairy; vegetative bud scales persistent or deciduous; bark grey-brown, cracking

LEAVES elliptic, 5.5–7.5 cm, 2.5–4 × as long as broad, hairless above, densely hairy beneath with a felted, cinnamon-brown to buff indumentum of rosulate hairs

INFLORESCENCE BUDS spherical-cylindric; scales white-hairy on the surface and fringed with brown hairs; outer scales reddish brown; inner scales green, cuspidate

CALYX 2–10 mm, with fleshy, sparsely hairy, glandular lobes

COROLLA more or less fleshy, 3–3.5 cm, pale pink to deep crimson, sometimes with faint spots

OVARY with brown hairs, some of which are glandular

CAPSULE 1–1.2 cm

DISTRIBUTION western China (northwestern Yunnan, southeastern Xizang)

FLOWERING spring

HARDINESS ZONE 8

Classic wild-collected material is available under *Forrest 14242* (the type collection).

114. *Rhododendron sanguineum* Franchet

HABIT small shrub to 1.5 m; young shoots sparsely white-hairy, occasionally also with glandular bristles; vegetative bud scales persistent or deciduous; bark smooth, pale brown, ultimately breaking off in irregular oblong flakes

LEAVES elliptic to obovate, 3–8 cm, 2–3 × as long as broad, hairless above, with a silvery to greyish compacted indumentum of rosulate hairs beneath

INFLORESCENCE BUDS fusiform; scales reddish or brownish green covered with white hairs; outer scales very narrow, the median cuspidate; inner scales slightly cuspidate

CALYX 3–10 mm, usually cup-like, coloured; lobes rounded, glandular-ciliate

COROLLA fleshy, shortly tubular-campanulate, 2.5–3.5 cm, yellow to pink or crimson or blackish crimson, rarely white

STAMENS anthers very dark brown to almost black

OVARY hairy or with shortly stalked glands

CAPSULE 1–1.5 cm

DISTRIBUTION western China (southeastern Xizang, northwestern Yunnan)

FLOWERING spring
HARDINESS ZONE 8

A very variable species, divided into 2 subspecies, one of which is further divided into several varieties. A number of these are grown.

R. *sanguineum* subsp. ***sanguineum*** var. ***sanguineum***

ILLUSTRATION *Iconographia Cormophytorum Sinicorum* 3, t. 4149 (1974); Feng, *Rhododendrons of China* 2, pl. 48: 1–4 (1992); Davidian, *The Rhododendron Species* 3, pl. 20 (1992); Cox and Cox, *The Encyclopedia of Rhododendron Species*, 122 (1997)
VEGETATIVE BUD SCALES usually deciduous
COROLLA bright crimson
OVARY hairy and eglandular

Classic wild-collected material is available under *Rock 106, 126, 136, 150, 10893, 10897, 23650*.

R. *sanguineum* subsp. ***sanguineum*** var. ***haemaleum*** (Balfour and Forrest) Chamberlain

SYNONYM *R. haemaleum* Balfour and Forrest
ILLUSTRATION *Curtis's Botanical Magazine*, 9263 (1929), reprinted in Halliday, *The Illustrated Rhododendron*, pl. 96 (2001); *Iconographia Cormophytorum Sinicorum* 3, t. 4150 (1974); Feng, *Rhododendrons of China* 1, pl. 17 (1988), and 2, pl. 49: 2–4 (1992); Davidian, *The Rhododendron Species* 3, pl. 29–30 (1992); Cox and Cox, *The Encyclopedia of Rhododendron Species*, 123 (1997)
VEGETATIVE BUD SCALES usually deciduous
COROLLA deep blackish crimson
OVARY hairy, eglandular

Classic wild-collected material is available under *Forrest 19958, 20253, 21735, 21740*, and *Rock 31, 65, 10276, 10947, 11049, 22236*.

R. *sanguineum* subsp. ***sanguineum*** var. ***didymoides*** Tagg and Forrest

SYNONYM *R. roseotinctum* Balfour and Forrest
VEGETATIVE BUD SCALES always persistent
COROLLA yellow
OVARY with some glands as well as normal hairs

Classic wild-collected material is available under *Kingdon-Ward 6831* and *Rock 10903, 10904, 11052*.

R. *sanguineum* subsp. ***didymum*** (Balfour and Forrest) Cowan
SYNONYM *R. didymum* Balfour and Forrest
ILLUSTRATION *Curtis's Botanical Magazine,* 9217 (1928); *Iconographia Cormophytorum Sinicorum* 3, t. 4148 (1974); Cox and Cox, *The Encyclopedia of Rhododendron Species,* 123 (1997)
VEGETATIVE BUD SCALES persistent
COROLLA deep blackish crimson
OVARY glandular

Classic wild-collected material is available under *Forrest 20239* and *Rock 53.* There is recent, nonauthenticated, wild-collected material in cultivation which has been identified as *R. sanguineum* but has not yet been identified as far as subspecies or variety.

115. *Rhododendron aperantum* Balfour and Kingdon-Ward
ILLUSTRATION *Curtis's Botanical Magazine,* 9507 (1937); Davidian, *The Rhododendron Species* 3, pl. 34–35 (1992); Cox and Cox, *The Encyclopedia of Rhododendron Species,* 114–115 (1997); Feng, *Rhododendrons of China* 3, pl. 43 (1999)
HABIT dwarf matted shrub to 1.5 m; vegetative bud scales persistent
LEAVES obovate to oblanceolate, 1.4–2.4 cm, as long as broad, hairless when mature; lower surface usually glaucous
CALYX 3–6 mm, cup-like; lobes glandular-ciliate or not
COROLLA tubular-campanulate, 3–4.5 cm, white or yellow flushed with pink to orange or reddish
OVARY coarsely hairy with a few reddish bristles
CAPSULE 8–15 mm
DISTRIBUTION western China (western Yunnan), northeastern Myanmar
FLOWERING spring
HARDINESS ZONE 8

Classic wild-collected material is available under *Forrest 25563, 27020, 27022, 27025, 27079.*

Rhododendron parmulatum Cowan from western China (Xizang) is broadly similar, but the upper lobes and tube of the corolla bear red flecks. It is rarely grown but is illustrated in *Iconographia Cormophytorum Sinicorum* 3, t. 4147 (1974); *The Rhododendron Handbook,* f. 8 and 9 (1997); and Davidian, *The Rhododendron Species* 3, pl. 31 (1992).

116. *Rhododendron eudoxum* Balfour and Forrest

ILLUSTRATION Davidian, *The Rhododendron Species* 3, pl. 21–22 (1992); Cox and Cox, *The Encyclopedia of Rhododendron Species,* 119 (1997)

HABIT small shrub to 1.2 m; young shoots hairy and usually with a few weak bristles, rarely densely bristly; bark red-brown or grey-brown, shredding

LEAVES elliptic, 3.5–9 cm, 2.8–3.5 × as long as broad; upper surface hairless; lower surface with a thin, discontinuous indumentum of whitish to brownish hairs

INFLORESCENCE BUDS more or less spherical, slightly pointed; outer scales reddish brown, cuspidate; inner scales greenish, with brown tips, abruptly cuspidate, fringed with a few hairs

CALYX 2–7 mm, usually cupular, with rounded lobes, very sparsely hairy or glandular

COROLLA not fleshy, tubular-campanulate to campanulate, 2.5–4 cm, pink to carmine

STAMENS anthers dark brown

OVARY hairy or glandular

CAPSULE 1.5–2 cm

DISTRIBUTION western China (southeastern Xizang and adjacent northwestern Yunnan)

FLOWERING spring

HARDINESS ZONE 7

Classic wild-collected material is available under *Forrest 21738* and *Rock 6B, 10950.*

Variable and divided into 3 varieties, only one of which (var. *eudoxum*) is generally cultivated.

117. *Rhododendron chamaethomsonii* (Tagg and Forrest) Cowan and Davidian

HABIT dwarf shrub, rarely to 1 m; young shoots glandular or hairy; vegetative bud scales persistent or not; bark pale grey to whitish

LEAVES broadly obovate to elliptic, 2–6 cm, 1.5–2 × as long as broad, hairless above, hairless or sparsely adpressed and whitish-hairy beneath; leaf stalk hairy, sometimes glandular

INFLORESCENCE BUDS ovoid, yellowish, slightly sticky; scales greenish yellow, covered sparsely with ginger-brown and white hairs, especially on the margins

CALYX 1–7 mm, rarely to 15 mm, minute or with well-developed, sometimes coloured, glandular-ciliate lobes

COROLLA fleshy, campanulate, 2.5–4.5 cm, pink to deep crimson

STAMENS anthers black

Ovary densely to sparsely reddish-hairy, usually with some glands
Capsule to 1.5 cm
Distribution western China (southern and southeastern Xizang, northwestern Yunnan)
Flowering spring
Hardiness zone 7

R. *chamaethomsonii* var. ***chamaethomsonii***
Synonym *R. repens* Balfour and Forrest
Illustration Feng, *Rhododendrons of China* 1, pl. 11: 1–2 (1988); Davidian, *The Rhododendron Species* 3, pl. 4 (1992); Cox and Cox, *The Encyclopedia of Rhododendron Species,* 126 (1997)
Young shoots and leaf stalks glandular
Leaves hairless
Calyx lobes 7 mm or more
Corolla carmine to crimson
Ovary sparsely hairy, sometimes glandular

Classic wild-collected material is available under *Forrest 21900* and *Kingdon-Ward 5846A*.

R. *chamaethomsonii* var. ***chamaedoron*** (Tagg and Forrest) Chamberlain
Synonym *R. repens* Balfour and Forrest var. *chamaedoron* Tagg and Forrest
Young shoots and leaf stalks without glands
Leaves lower surface with a thin, discontinuous indumentum when mature
Calyx lobes 7 mm or more
Corolla carmine to crimson
Ovary sparsely hairy, sometimes glandular

R. *chamaethomsonii* var. ***chamaethauma*** (Tagg) Cowan and Davidian
Synonym *R. repens* Balfour and Forrest var. *chamaethauma* Tagg
Illustration Davidian, *The Rhododendron Species* 3, pl. 5 (1992); Cox and Cox, *The Encyclopedia of Rhododendron Species,* 126 (1997)
Calyx lobes up to 1 mm
Corolla pale to deep pink
Ovary densely hairy

Classic wild-collected material is available under *Kingdon-Ward 5847* (the type collection).

The following collections belong to *R. chamaethomsonii*, but their varietal status is uncertain: *Forrest 21768, Kingdon-Ward 5846, Ludlow, Sherriff, and Elliott 13278*, and *Rock 92, 11169A*.

118. *Rhododendron forrestii* Diels

SYNONYM *R. repens* Balfour and Forrest

ILLUSTRATION *Curtis's Botanical Magazine*, 9186 (1929), reprinted in Halliday, *The Illustrated Rhododendron*, pl. 97 (2001); *Iconographia Cormophytorum Sinicorum* 3, t. 4138 (1974); *The Rhododendron Handbook*, f. 20 (1977); Feng, *Rhododendrons of China* 1, pl. 12: 1–3 (1988); Davidian, *The Rhododendron Species* 2, pl. 1–3 (1992); Cox and Cox, *The Encyclopedia of Rhododendron Species*, 127–128 (1997)

HABIT dwarf, creeping shrub, with stems to 60 cm long, though plant is rarely more than 10 cm high; vegetative bud scales persistent; bark greyish to dark brown

LEAVES obovate to circular, 1–2.8 cm, 1–3 × as long as broad; upper surface hairless; lower surface purple or green, hairless or with a few shortly stalked glands and branched hairs towards the base

INFLORESCENCE BUDS scales mostly yellowish, cuspidate, the inner fragile and hairy

CALYX to 1 mm; lobes fleshy

COROLLA fleshy, tubular-campanulate, 3–3.5 cm, crimson

STAMENS anthers very dark, almost black

OVARY with stalked glands and reddish hairs

CAPSULE 1.5–2 cm

DISTRIBUTION western China (northwestern Yunnan, southeastern Xizang), northeastern Myanmar

FLOWERING spring

HARDINESS ZONE 8

Classic wild-collected material is available under *Forrest 13259, 19515, 21723, 25524, Kingdon-Ward 5846* (see also *R. chamaethomsonii*), *5874A, 6935, Ludlow, Sherriff, and Elliott 13278, Ludlow, Sherriff, and Taylor 5582*, and *Rock 11003, 11169*. Recent nonauthenticated material from Yunnan is also in cultivation.

The above description refers to subsp. *forrestii*. Subspecies *papillatum* Chamberlain, from southern Xizang, is not in general cultivation; it is illustrated in Cox and Cox, *The Encyclopedia of Rhododendron Species*, 128 (1997); and Feng, *Rhododendrons of China* 3, pl. 47: 1–3 (1999).

119. *Rhododendron neriiflorum* Franchet

SYNONYM *R. euchaites* Balfour and Forrest

ILLUSTRATION *Curtis's Botanical Magazine,* 8727 (1917); *Iconographia Cormophytorum Sinicorum* 3, t. 4139 (1974); Davidian, *The Rhododendron Species* 2, pl. 15 (1992); Feng, *Rhododendrons of China* 2, pl. 46: 1–6 (1992); Kneller, *The Book of Rhododendrons,* 43 (1995); Cox and Cox, *The Encyclopedia of Rhododendron Species,* 130–131 (1997)

HABIT shrub or small tree to 6 m; young shoots sparsely hairy, eglandular or rarely with glandular bristles; bark pale or cinnamon-brown, smooth, scaling off in long sheets; underbark smooth, greenish brown

LEAVES elliptic to oblong or oblanceolate, 4–11 cm, 1.7–5 × as long as broad, usually hairless on both surfaces; lower surface glaucous

INFLORESCENCE BUDS spherical to ovoid; scales mostly green, sometimes reddish at the tips, some pointed or cuspidate, others rounded, white-hairy on the surface, with sparse brown glands on the margins

CALYX 2–15 mm, cup-like when well developed; lobes hairy, sometimes glandular

COROLLA fleshy, tubular-campanulate, 3.5–4.5 cm, usually bright red, occasionally pale yellow

STAMENS anthers black or red with black markings around the pores

OVARY densely hairy, the hairs intermixed with a variable number of shortly stalked glands; tapering into the hairless style

CAPSULE 2–2.5 cm, usually strongly curved

DISTRIBUTION western China (western Yunnan, southeastern Xizang), northeastern Myanmar

FLOWERING spring

HARDINESS ZONE 7

Classic wild-collected material is available under *Farrer 877, Forrest 8939,* and *Ludlow and Sherriff 1352.* Recent nonauthenticated material from Yunnan is also in cultivation.

A variable species, but only subsp. *neriiflorum* appears to be grown. Subspecies *phaedropum* (Balfour and Farrer) Tagg (*R. phaedropum* Balfour and Farrer) has leaves with marked reticulations beneath. It is rarely grown but is illustrated in Davidian, *The Rhododendron Species* 2, pl. 16 (1992); *The Rhododendron Handbook,* f. 10 (1997); and Cox and Cox, *The Encyclopedia of Rhododendron Species,* 131 (1997).

R. neriiflorum flower and leaf

R. neriiflorum detail

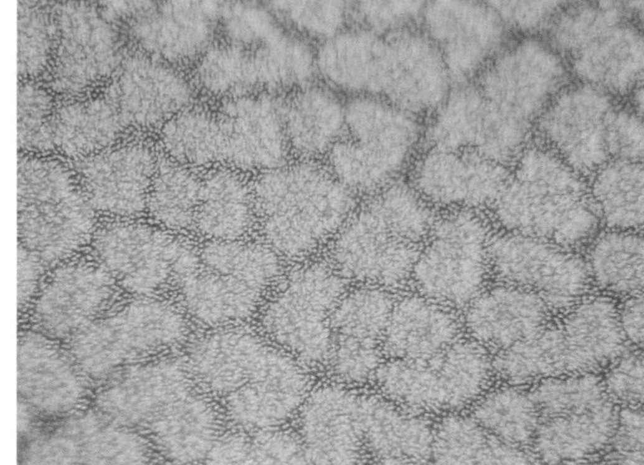

R. neriiflorum leaf surface

120. *Rhododendron floccigerum* Franchet

ILLUSTRATION *Curtis's Botanical Magazine,* 9290 (1929), reprinted in Halliday, *The Illustrated Rhododendron,* pl. 98 (2001); *Iconographia Cormophytorum Sinicorum* 3, t. 4140 (1974); Feng, *Rhododendrons of China* 1, pl. 14: 1–3 (1988); Cox and Cox, *The Encyclopedia of Rhododendron Species,* 129–130 (1997)

HABIT shrub to 3 m; young shoots hairy, sometimes also glandular-bristly; bark cinnamon-brown, scaling off in flakes or rarely large sheets; underbark smooth, greenish brown

LEAVES narrowly elliptic to oblong or elliptic, 3.5–11 cm, 3.3–6 × as long as broad; upper surface hairless; lower surface with a loose, reddish, usually patchy indumentum of ramiform hairs, the surface glaucous

INFLORESCENCE BUDS spherical, fusiform, or ovoid; scales green, white, yellowish, or brown, with reddish or brownish tips, cuspidate, mostly with white hairs, occasionally the surface hairless and only the margins hairy

CALYX 1–4 mm; lobes rounded, hairless or sparsely hairy

COROLLA tubular-campanulate, 3–4 cm, usually crimson to scarlet, rarely yellowish or pink

STAMENS anthers black or almost so

OVARY eglandular, densely stellate-hairy, tapering into the hairless style

CAPSULE 1–2.5 cm

DISTRIBUTION western China (southeastern Xizang and adjacent northwestern Yunnan)

FLOWERING spring

HARDINESS ZONE 6

Classic wild-collected material is available under *Forrest 20305, 21703, 25581,* and *Rock 10, 19, 46, 49, 144, 10959, 10999, 18465, 18467.*

121. *Rhododendron sperabile* Balfour and Farrer

ILLUSTRATION *Curtis's Botanical Magazine,* 9301 (1933); Cox and Cox, *The Encyclopedia of Rhododendron Species,* 132 (1997)

HABIT shrub to 2 m; young shoots with a dense indumentum of stellate hairs intermixed with long-stalked glands; bark brownish, striate

LEAVES elliptic, 5–10 cm, 2.5–4 or more × as long as broad; upper surface hairless; lower surface with a loose, continuous, whitish to brown indumentum of ramiform hairs, with some glandular bristles on the midrib

INFLORESCENCE BUDS ovoid; outer scales bright yellowish green, cuspidate, hairless; inner scales hairy with some brown hairs, especially on the margins

CALYX 2–3 mm with broad, coloured, rounded, glandular-ciliate lobes
COROLLA fleshy, tubular-campanulate, 3.5–4 cm, crimson
STAMENS anthers black
OVARY with dense reddish hairs and shortly stalked glands, tapering into the hairless style
CAPSULE to 1.5 cm, curved
DISTRIBUTION western China (northwestern Yunnan), northwestern Myanmar
FLOWERING spring
HARDINESS ZONE 8

Classic wild-collected material is available under *Forrest 25569, 26478, 30912, Kingdon-Ward 7124, 19405,* and *Rock 18469.*

Two varieties are known, and both have been in general cultivation. Variety *sperabile* has leaves up to 3.5 × as long as broad, with a cinnamon-brown indumentum when mature. Variety *weihsiense* Tagg and Forrest has leaves relatively longer and with a whitish indumentum when mature. The latter is illustrated in Feng, *Rhododendrons of China* 1, pl. 15: 1–2 (1988); Davidian, *The Rhododendron Species* 2, pl. 19 (1992); and Cox and Cox, *The Encyclopedia of Rhododendron Species,* 132 (1997).

122. ***Rhododendron sperabiloides*** Tagg and Forrest

ILLUSTRATION Feng, *Rhododendrons of China* 1, pl. 16: 1–2 (1988); Cox and Cox, *The Encyclopedia of Rhododendron Species,* 133 (1997)
HABIT dwarf shrub to 1.5 m; young shoots stellate-hairy, without glands
LEAVES elliptic, 5.5–6.5 cm, 1.6–3 × as long as broad, hairless above, with a thin, patchy indumentum beneath of ramiform to almost rosulate hairs
CALYX 4–7 mm, cup-like, with ciliate, rounded lobes
COROLLA fleshy, tubular-campanulate, 2.5–3.5 cm, deep red
OVARY densely brown-hairy, the top truncate or somewhat tapering into the hairless style
CAPSULE to 1.3 cm
DISTRIBUTION western China (northwestern Yunnan)
FLOWERING spring
HARDINESS ZONE 8

Classic wild-collected material is available under *Rock 125.*

Less commonly cultivated are:

Rhododendron pearcei Davidian
SYNONYM *R. beanianum* var. *compactum* Cowan
Similar to *R. beanianum,* but:
LEAVES with a 2-layered indumentum beneath, the upper layer reddish and tomentose, the lower whitish and adpressed
DISTRIBUTION western China (southern Xizang)

Rhododendron temenium Balfour and Forrest
Similar to *R. sanguineum* and *R. eudoxum,* but:
LEAVES lower surface glabrous, shining, and glaucous
DISTRIBUTION western China (southeastern Xizang, northwestern Yunnan)

There are 3 varieties: var. *temenium,* with the young shoots and pedicels bristly, the inflorescence dense, and the corolla carmine to crimson; var. *gilvum* (Cowan) Chamberlain (*R. gilvum* Cowan), like var. *temenium* but with the corolla yellow; and var. *dealbatum* (Cowan) Chamberlain (*R. temenium* subsp. *dealbatum* Cowan), with the leaves and pedicels weakly or not bristly, the inflorescence loose, and the corolla white to rose-pink.

Rhododendron albertsenianum Forrest
Similar to *R. sperabiloides,* but:
LEAF INDUMENTUM 2-layered
DISTRIBUTION western China (northwestern Yunnan)

Subgenus *Hymenanthes*

Section *Pontica*

Subsection *Fulgensia* Chamberlain

HABIT shrubs or small trees to 6 m; young shoots glandular and hairy or hairless; bark smooth, peeling

LEAVES lower surface with a dense, woolly indumentum composed of fasciculate hairs

RACEME loose or dense, 4- to 14-flowered

CALYX minute to well developed and cup-like

COROLLA 5-lobed, fleshy, funnel-campanulate to tubular-campanulate, with nectar sacs

STAMENS 10

OVARY AND STYLE hairless

A group of 3 species, of which 2 are in cultivation. The leaves have a 3-layered upper epidermis, the cells all similar in size, the cuticle about half as thick as the cells are deep; water tissue is present, and the cells of the lower epidermis are not prolonged into papillae. Sclereids have not been reported.

1a Inflorescence dense, with 8–14 flowers; corolla 2–3.5 cm . . . . **123. *R. fulgens***

b Inflorescence loose, with 4–5 flowers; corolla 3.5–4 cm . . . . **124. *R. sherriffii***

123. *Rhododendron fulgens* Hooker

ILLUSTRATION Hooker, *Rhododendrons of the Sikkim Himalaya*, t. 25 (1851); *Flore des Serres*, ser. 1, 8: t. 789 (1852–1853); *Curtis's Botanical Magazine*, 5317 (1862), reprinted in Halliday, *The Illustrated Rhododendron*, pl. 99 (2001); Kneller, *The Book of Rhododendrons*, 27 (1995); Cox and Cox, *The Encyclopedia of Rhododendron Species*, 63 (1997)

HABIT shrub to 4.5 m; young shoots hairless; bark deep reddish brown, peeling and scaling like that of a *Platanus*, in large flakes

LEAVES broadly ovate to obovate, 7–11 cm, 1.5–1.8 × as long as broad; upper surface hairless; lower surface with a dense, woolly indumentum of brownish, fasciculate hairs

INFLORESCENCE BUDS fusiform, rather blunt; lower scales greenish, cuspidate, with brownish tips, hairy on the margins only; inner scales densely covered with white, silky hairs

R. fulgens flower and leaf

R. fulgens detail

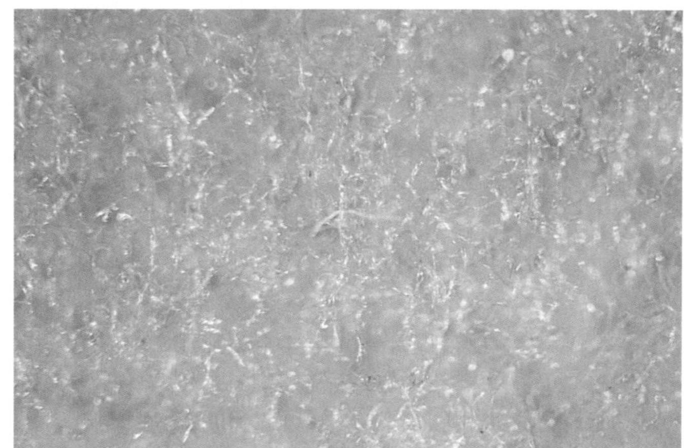

R. fulgens leaf surface

Calyx 1–2 mm, hairless
Corolla tubular-campanulate, 2–3.5 cm, scarlet to blood-red, with darker nectar sacs
Stamens anthers brown to dark brown
Ovary and style hairless
Capsule 1.3–3 cm, curved
Distribution Himalaya, western China (southern Xizang)
Flowering spring
Hardiness zone 7

Classic wild-collected material is available under *Ludlow and Sherriff 1084, 2846.* Recent nonauthenticated material from India (Sikkim), Nepal, and Bhutan is also in cultivation.

124. *Rhododendron sherriffii* Cowan

Illustration *Curtis's Botanical Magazine,* n.s., 337 (1959), reprinted in Halliday, *The Illustrated Rhododendron,* pl. 100 (2001); *Iconographia Cormophytorum Sinicorum* 3, t. 4225 (1974); Cox and Cox, *The Encyclopedia of Rhododendron Species,* 196 (1997)
Habit shrub or small tree to 6 m; young shoots with shortly stalked glands and a mealy indumentum
Leaves obovate, around 7.5 cm, almost twice as long as broad, hairless above, densely brown-hairy beneath
Calyx 3–5 mm, hairless; lobes broad, rounded
Corolla funnel-campanulate, 3.5–4 cm, deep carmine, with darker nectar sacs
Ovary hairless
Capsule to 1.5 cm
Distribution western China (southern Xizang)
Flowering spring
Hardiness zone 8

Classic wild-collected material is available under *Ludlow and Sherriff 2751.*

Subgenus *Hymenanthes*

Section *Pontica*

Subsection **Thomsonia** Sleumer (*Thomsonii* series *Thomsonii* and *Cerasinum* subseries)

HABIT shrubs or small trees; bark smooth, peeling; young shoots hairless or with sparse, shortly stalked glands

LEAVES hairless at maturity, or with a thin dendroid indumentum, or with punctate-based fasciculate hairs on the main veins

RACEME loose, one- to 5-flowered; rachis 1–30 mm

CALYX 2–15 mm, usually well developed and cup-like, often coloured

COROLLA 5-lobed, often fleshy, funnel-campanulate to tubular-campanulate, with nectar sacs

STAMENS 10

OVARY hairless, hairy, or glandular

STYLE hairless or glandular throughout

SEEDS elongate, narrowly winged to almost unwinged, with appendages at each end (these sometimes small)

A group of 13 species. The leaves are rather variable anatomically, with a 2- or 3-layered upper epidermis, the cells of more or less the same size, the cuticle thin to as thick as the cells are deep; water tissue is absent, and the cells of the lower epidermis are prolonged as papillae. Sclereids are few or absent.

1 a Style glandular throughout .... **125. *R. cerasinum***
b Style hairless or glandular only at the extreme base 2
2 a Leaf with a thin, discontinuous indumentum beneath .... **131. *R. stewartianum***
b Leaf hairless beneath, or with fasciculate hairs on the veins 3
3 a Leaf glaucous beneath, 1–1.8 × as long as broad 4
b Leaf greenish beneath, 1.8–3.5 × as long as broad 5
4 a Corolla deep coppery red or purplish crimson .... **126. *R. thomsonii***
b Corolla white or yellow to clear pink .... **129. *R. cyanocarpum***
5 a Ovary hairless .... **130. *R. eclecteum***
b Ovary variously hairy or glandular 6
6 a Large fasciculate hairs present on the main veins of the leaf beneath; leaf stalks 1.5–3 cm .... **127. *R. hookeri***
b Fasciculate hairs absent; leaf stalks 1–1.5 cm .... **128. *R. meddianum***

125. ***Rhododendron cerasinum*** Tagg

ILLUSTRATION *Curtis's Botanical Magazine,* 9538 (1938); *Rhododendron and Camellia Yearbook* 18, t. 4 (1963); *Iconographia Cormophytorum Sinicorum* 3, t. 4179 (1974); *Rhododendrons with Camellias and Magnolias* 41: f. 6 (1988); Davidian, *The Rhododendron Species* 3, pl. 74 (1992); Cox and Cox, *The Encyclopedia of Rhododendron Species,* 189 (1997)

HABIT shrub to 3.5 m; shoots soon become hairless

LEAVES narrowly obovate to elliptic, 4.5–7 cm, 1.7–2.5 × as long as broad, hairless except for a few hair bases beneath and sparse, well-developed dendroid hairs on the leaf stalk which extend onto the upper surface of the midrib

CALYX to 1.5 mm, with shortly stalked glands, at least on the margins

COROLLA campanulate, 3.5–4.5 cm, crimson, scarlet, or white with a deep pink border and darker nectar sacs

OVARY glandular

STYLE glandular to the apex

CAPSULE to 2 cm

DISTRIBUTION western China (southeastern Xizang), northeastern Myanmar

FLOWERING spring

HARDINESS ZONE 7

126. ***Rhododendron thomsonii*** Hooker

SYNONYM *R. lopsangianum* Cowan

ILLUSTRATION Hooker, *Rhododendrons of the Sikkim Himalaya,* t. 12 (1851); *Flore des Serres,* ser. 1, 7: t. 688–690 (1851–1852); *Curtis's Botanical Magazine,* 4997 (1857), reprinted in Halliday, *The Illustrated Rhododendron,* pl. 101 (2001); Davidian, *The Rhododendron Species* 3, pl. 76–77 (1992); Kneller, *The Book of Rhododendrons,* 53 (1995); Cox and Cox, *The Encyclopedia of Rhododendron Species,* 198–199 (1997); Feng, *Rhododendrons of China* 3, pl. 56: 1–4 (1999)

HABIT shrub or small tree to 3.5 m (rarely more); young shoots hairless or sparsely glandular; bark smooth, pale orange-brown, scaling

LEAVES circular to obovate or elliptic, 3–11 cm, 1.1–2 × as long as broad, hairless, glaucous beneath, sometimes with red shortly stalked glands

INFLORESCENCE BUDS ovoid, brownish purple, bloomed; scales slightly sticky, with brown-headed glands

CALYX 2–20 mm, irregular to cup-like, usually hairless, rarely glandular, often coloured

COROLLA campanulate, fleshy, 3.5–5 cm, deep crimson, usually without darker spots

R. thomsonii flower and leaf

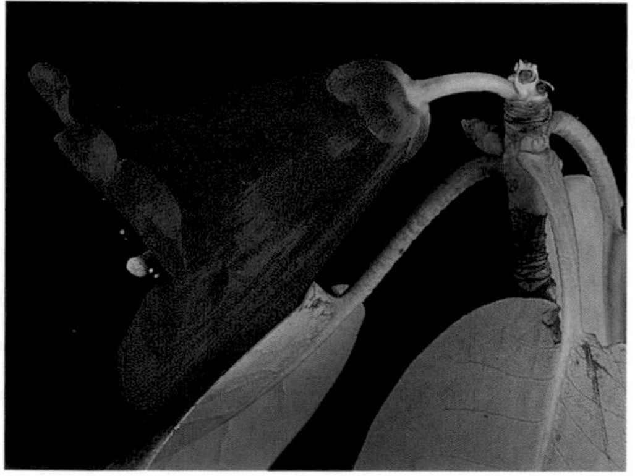

R. thomsonii detail

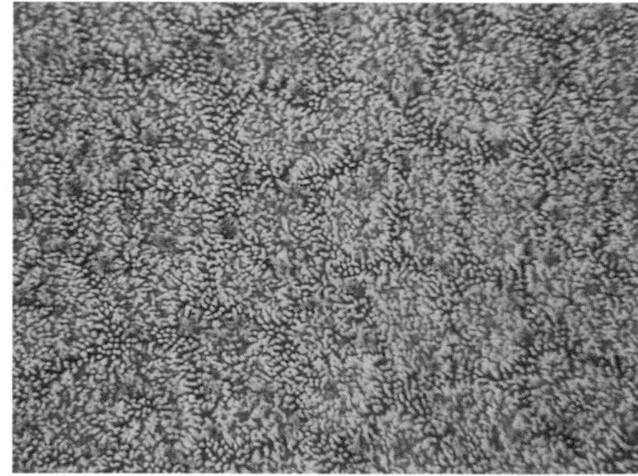

R. thomsonii leaf surface

STAMENS anthers dark brown
OVARY hairless or glandular
STYLE hairless
CAPSULE 1.5–2.5 cm
DISTRIBUTION Himalaya, western China (southeastern Xizang)
FLOWERING spring
HARDINESS ZONE 6

Wild-collected material is available under *Beer, Lancaster, and Morris 228, Binns, Mason, and Wright 153, Kingdon-Ward 6869, Ludlow and Sherriff 2847, Ludlow, Sherriff, and Hicks 21285,* and *Polunin* (without number). Recent nonauthenticated material from India (Sikkim), Nepal, and Bhutan is also in cultivation.

A variable species and the parent of numerous hybrids, such as 'Red Admiral' (× *R. arboreum*) and 'Cornish Cross' (× *R. griffithianum*).

127. ***Rhododendron hookeri*** Nuttall

ILLUSTRATION *Curtis's Botanical Magazine,* 4926 (1856); *Gartenflora* 12, t. 395 (1863); *Iconographia Cormophytorum Sinicorum* 3, t. 4133 (1974); Davidian, *The Rhododendron Species* 3, pl. 81–82 (1992); Cox and Cox, *The Encyclopedia of Rhododendron Species,* 194 (1997)
HABIT shrub or small tree to 4 m; bark smooth
LEAVES broadly oblanceolate, to 13 cm, about 2.5 × as long as broad; upper surface hairless; lower surface hairless except for a few large fasciculate hairs along the veins
CALYX usually 1–2 cm, cup-like, greenish to yellowish, hairless; lobes rounded, erose
COROLLA tubular-campanulate, 3.5–4.5 cm, deep pink to crimson, with darker nectar sacs and a few spots
OVARY AND STYLE hairless
DISTRIBUTION northeastern India (Arunachal Pradesh)
FLOWERING spring
HARDINESS ZONE 8

Classic wild-collected material is available under *Kingdon-Ward 8238, 13650.*

128. *Rhododendron meddianum* Forrest

HABIT shrub to 2.3 m; young shoots hairless; bark slightly rough, greyish cinnamon-brown, striate

LEAVES obovate to broadly elliptic, 8–15 cm, 1.8–2.4 × as long as broad, entirely hairless, green beneath

INFLORESCENCE BUDS fusiform but rather flattened, brownish green; scales broad with small points, fringed with white or white and brown hairs

CALYX 3–18 mm, fleshy, cup-like; lobes broad, rounded, hairless, reddish

COROLLA fleshy, tubular-campanulate, 4.5–6 cm, deep pink to deep blackish crimson

STAMENS anthers almost black

OVARY hairless to densely glandular and sticky

CAPSULE 1.5–2 cm

DISTRIBUTION western China (western Yunnan), northeastern Myanmar

FLOWERING spring

HARDINESS ZONE 7

R. meddianum var. ***meddianum***

ILLUSTRATION *Curtis's Botanical Magazine,* 9636 (1942); *Iconographia Cormophytorum Sinicorum* 3, t. 4134 (1974); Davidian, *The Rhododendron Species* 3, pl. 84 (1992); Cox and Cox, *The Encyclopedia of Rhododendron Species,* 195 (1997)

OVARY more or less hairless

R. meddianum var. ***atrokermesinum*** Tagg

ILLUSTRATION Feng, *Rhododendrons of China* 1, pl. 9: 1–2 (1988); Cox and Cox, *The Encyclopedia of Rhododendron Species,* 195 (1997)

OVARY densely glandular and sticky

Classic wild-collected material is available under *Forrest 26476* and *Kingdon-Ward 21006A.*

129. *Rhododendron cyanocarpum* (Franchet) W. W. Smith

ILLUSTRATION *Iconographia Cormophytorum Sinicorum* 3, t. 4135 (1974); Davidian, *The Rhododendron Species* 3, pl. 85 (1992); Feng, *Rhododendrons of China* 2, pl. 50: 1–4 (1992); Cox and Cox, *The Encyclopedia of Rhododendron Species,* 190 (1997)

HABIT shrub or small tree to 4 m; young shoots hairless; bark brown, breaking into long, oblong flakes

R. cyanocarpum flower

R. cyanocarpum detail

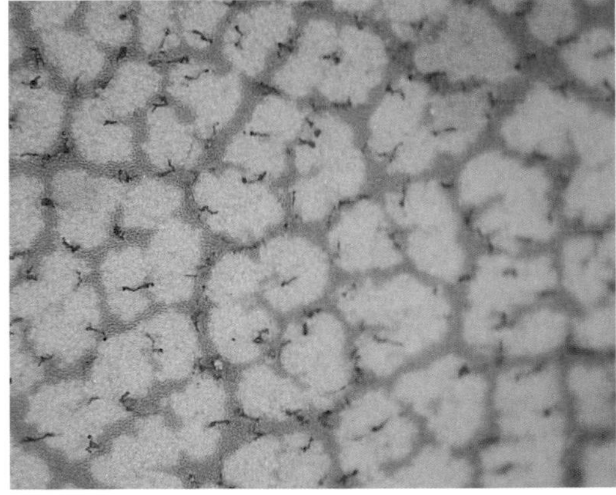

R. cyanocarpum leaf surface

LEAVES broadly elliptic to circular, 6.5–12.5 cm, 1–1.6 × as long as broad, hairless above, hairless and more or less glaucous beneath, rarely with a few hairs on the midrib towards the base

INFLORESCENCE BUDS broadly fusiform, usually somewhat bloomed, brownish though green towards the tip

CALYX 7–15 mm (rarely less), cup-like, greenish, hairless; lobes truncate

COROLLA campanulate to funnel-campanulate, 4–6 cm, white or cream to clear pink, with dark nectar sacs but without other spots

STAMENS anthers dark brown to almost black

OVARY hairless or rarely with a few glands

STYLE hairless

CAPSULE 1.5–2 cm, usually glaucous

DISTRIBUTION western China (western Yunnan)

FLOWERING spring

HARDINESS ZONE 6

Classic wild-collected material is available under *Forrest 15570*. Recent nonauthenticated material from Yunnan is also in cultivation.

130. *Rhododendron eclecteum* Balfour and Forrest

ILLUSTRATION *Iconographia Cormophytorum Sinicorum* 3, t. 4136 (1974); Davidian, *The Rhododendron Species* 3, pl. 89–90 (1992); Cox and Cox, *The Encyclopedia of Rhododendron Species,* 191 (1997); Feng, *Rhododendrons of China* 3, pl. 53 (1999)

HABIT shrub to 4.5 m; young shoots usually sparsely glandular; bark brown or greyish brown, rather smooth, shredding in long strips

LEAVES obovate-lanceolate to elliptic, 4–14.5 cm, 2–2.3 × as long as broad, hairless except for a few hairs near the midrib beneath; veins conspicuous

INFLORESCENCE BUDS spherical but slightly pointed or fusiform, sometimes sticky; outer scales rather narrow; inner scales broader, blunt or cuspidate; at least the inner scales with white or sometimes brownish hairs

CALYX 2–15 mm, usually cupular, with rounded lobes, hairless

COROLLA campanulate to widely funnel-campanulate, 3–5 cm, usually deep crimson, sometimes white or cream, with or without purple spots

STAMENS anthers brown, dark brown, or almost black

OVARY densely covered with shortly stalked glands

STYLE hairless

CAPSULE 1.5–2.5 cm, often glaucous

DISTRIBUTION western China (southeastern Xizang, northwestern Yunnan, southwestern Sichuan), northeastern Myanmar

FLOWERING spring

HARDINESS ZONE 8

Divided into 2 varieties in the wild, but only one of these, var. *eclecteum,* is generally grown.

Classic wild-collected material is available under *Forrest 18943, 21887, Kingdon-Ward 9413,* and *Rock 33, 23512.*

131. *Rhododendron stewartianum* Diels

SYNONYM *R. aiolosalpinx* Balfour and Farrer

ILLUSTRATION *Iconographia Cormophytorum Sinicorum* 3, t. 4137 (1974); Feng, *Rhododendrons of China* 1, pl. 10: 1–7 (1988); Davidian, *The Rhododendron Species* 3, pl. 87–88 (1992); Cox and Cox, *The Encyclopedia of Rhododendron Species,* 196–197 (1997); Halliday, *The Illustrated Rhododendron,* pl. 102 (2001)

HABIT shrub to 2.5 m; young shoots often glandular; bark brown, smooth or rough, peeling on younger branches, shredding into oblong plates

LEAVES obovate to elliptic, 4–12 cm, 1.8–2.5 × as long as broad; upper surface hairless; lower surface with a thin, persistent or quickly falling indumentum containing stalkless glands, especially towards the base

INFLORESCENCE BUDS obovoid, mostly brown; scales rather broad, with small, pointed tips, densely covered with white hairs

CALYX 5–15 mm (rarely less), cup-like; lobes broadly ovate, glandular-ciliate or hairless

COROLLA campanulate to tubular-campanulate, 3.5–5.5 cm, white or cream to pale pink, with or without purple spots

STAMENS anthers brown

OVARY usually densely glandular

STYLE hairless

CAPSULE 1.5–3 cm

DISTRIBUTION western China (southeastern Xizang, northwestern Yunnan), northeastern Myanmar

FLOWERING spring

HARDINESS ZONE 9

Classic wild-collected material is available under *Forrest 26921.* Recent nonauthenticated material from Yunnan is also in cultivation.

Less commonly cultivated are:

Rhododendron eurysiphon Tagg and Forrest
Similar to *R. cerasinum*, but:
INFLORESCENCES one- to 3-flowered
COROLLA creamy white flushed with pale rose
DISTRIBUTION China (southeastern Xizang)

Rhododendron viscidifolium Davidian
Similar to *R. thomsonii*, but:
COROLLA coppery red
OVARY tomentose
DISTRIBUTION western China (southeastern Xizang)

Rhododendron hylaeum Balfour and Farrer
Similar to *R. meddianum* in its hairless ovary, but:
LEAVES 2.5–3.2 × as long as broad
COROLLA whitish to pink
DISTRIBUTION northeastern Upper Burma (Myanmar), western China (southeastern Xizang)

Rhododendron faucium Chamberlain
Similar to *R. eclecteum* and *R. meddianum* in its glandular ovary, but:
INFLORESCENCES rachis 8–20 mm
COROLLA white to yellow or pink
DISTRIBUTION western China (southeastern Xizang)

Rhododendron subansiriense Chamberlain
Similar to *R. faucium*, but:
INFLORESCENCES rachis c. 5 mm
COROLLA scarlet
OVARY hairy but eglandular
DISTRIBUTION northeastern India (Arunachal Pradesh)

Subgenus *Tsutsusi* (Sweet) Pojarkova

HABIT shrubs
INDUMENTUM flattened bristles usually present on young shoots and/or leaves
SEEDS elongate, unwinged and without appendages at each end (or appendages, if present, very short)

The subgenus is divided into 2 sections, species from both of which are in cultivation.

Subgenus *Tsutsusi*

Section ***Tsutsusi*** (*Azalea* series *Obtusum* subseries)

HABIT generally small shrubs with flattened hairs

LEAVES without scales, dimorphic; those borne in spring larger and deciduous; those borne in summer smaller and generally some of them persisting through winter (rarely monomorphic and all deciduous, but then very small)

NEW VEGETATIVE SHOOTS from the same terminal bud as the inflorescence

CALYX 5-lobed

COROLLA generally funnel-shaped, 5-lobed

STAMENS 5–10, declinate

OVARY hairy

STYLE declinate

CAPSULE generally hairy

A difficult group of an uncertain number of species, generally known as evergreen azaleas.

1a Shoots with spreading hairs as well as adpressed, flattened hairs 2
 b Shoots without spreading hairs 3
2a Flowers 2.5–3.5 cm, funnel-shaped; stamens 8–10 . . . . **133. *R. oldhamii***
 b Flowers 3.5–5 cm, broadly funnel-shaped; stamens 5–7; leaves very narrow and corolla divided into linear-lanceolate segments in the commonly cultivated variant . . . . **135. *R. stenopetalum***
3a Stamens 7 or more 4
 b Stamens 6 or fewer 8
4a Young shoots with flattened hairs and also adpressed-hairy . . . . **138. *R. mucronatum***
 b Young shoots with flattened hairs only, not adpressed-hairy 5
5a Bud scales viscid-sticky on their inner surfaces . . . . **137. *R. simsii***
 b Bud scales not viscid-sticky 6
6a Corolla reddish purple spotted with darker purple . . . . **140. *R. ×pulchrum***
 b Corolla not as above 7
7a Corolla red to scarlet . . . . **134. *R. scabrum***
 b Corolla pink . . . . **136. *R. yedoense***
8a Most mature leaves more than 3 cm long 9
 b Most mature leaves less than 3 cm long 11
9a Corolla tubular-campanulate . . . . **132. *R. mariae***
 b Corolla funnel-shaped to funnel-campanulate 10

10 a Leaves 3.5–4 × as long as broad . . . . **144. *R. tosaense***
b Leaves 1.7–3 × as long as broad . . . . **141. *R. kaempferi***
11 a Corolla 5–10 mm, 4- or 5-lobed . . . . **146. *R. tschonoskii***
b Corolla 1–5 cm, 5-lobed 12
12 a Leaves 2–6 mm broad, to 1.4 cm long 13
b Leaves 6–25 mm broad, to 3 cm long 14
13 a Flowers mostly solitary; flower stalks c. 3 mm . . . . **145. *R. serpyllifolium***
b Flowers 3–12 in each raceme; flower stalks 5–10 mm . . . . **142. *R. kiusianum***
14 a Leaves narrowly lanceolate to oblanceolate . . . . **139. *R. indicum***
b Leaves ovate to elliptic-ovate, oblong-lanceolate, or obovate . . . . **143. *R.* ×*obtusum***

132. *Rhododendron mariae* Hance

ILLUSTRATION *Iconographia Cormophytorum Sinicorum* 3, t. 4251 (1974); Feng, *Rhododendrons of China* 2, pl. 97 (1992)

HABIT shrub to 3 m; young shoots with adpressed, flattened, reddish hairs which rapidly turn grey and persist

LEAVES elliptic-lanceolate to elliptic or obovate, 1–9 cm, almost hairless

CALYX minute, with shining, reddish brown hairs

COROLLA tubular-campanulate, 1–2 cm, lilac, hairless

STAMENS 5; filaments hairless

OVARY densely covered with shining, reddish brown hairs

STYLE hairless

CAPSULE 6–8 mm

DISTRIBUTION eastern China (Guizhou, Guangxi, Hunan, Guangdong)

FLOWERING late spring

HARDINESS ZONE 9

133. *Rhododendron oldhamii* Maximowicz

ILLUSTRATION Komatsu, *Icones Plantarum Koisikavenses* 2, t. 119 (1914); *Curtis's Botanical Magazine,* 9059 (1924); *Iconographia Cormophytorum Sinicorum* 3, t. 4261 (1974); Lee, *Flora of Taiwan* 4: 34 (1978); Feng, *Rhododendrons of China* 2, pl. 100: 1–3 (1992)

HABIT shrub to 3 m or more; young shoots with spreading, red-brown, glandular hairs mixed with spreading, flattened hairs; bark greenish brown, striate

LEAVES elliptic or elliptic-oblong to elliptic-ovate or lanceolate, 1.5–8 cm × 8–25 mm, covered on both surfaces with hairs similar to those on the shoots when young; upper surface becoming more or less hairless

CALYX c. 2 mm, variable; lobes rounded or somewhat acute, with long, red-brown, glandular hairs
COROLLA funnel-shaped, orange-red to pink, 2.5–3.5 cm, hairless
STAMENS (8–)10; filaments hairless
OVARY densely glandular-bristly
STYLE papillose below the middle
CAPSULE 8–10 mm, glandular-bristly
DISTRIBUTION Taiwan
FLOWERING late spring
HARDINESS ZONE 9

Wild-collected material is available under *Patrick* (without number).

134. *Rhododendron scabrum* G. Don
ILLUSTRATION *Curtis's Botanical Magazine,* 8478 (1913); Togashi et al., *Species Rhododendron Japan,* 130–132 (1982)
HABIT shrub to 2 m; young shoots with adpressed, flattened, grey-brown hairs which gradually fall
LEAVES elliptic-lanceolate or lanceolate or oblanceolate, 3–10 cm, ciliate and slightly crenulate, at first with scattered greyish hairs, these falling, except from the midrib and veins
CALYX to 6 mm (rarely more); lobes rounded or acuminate, glandular, ciliate, with adpressed, straight, grey hairs
COROLLA broadly funnel-shaped, to 6.5 cm, pinkish red to scarlet, with dark dots on the upper lobes, lobed to about half
STAMENS 10; filaments hairy towards the base
OVARY glandular and bristly
STYLE hairless
CAPSULE to 1.3 cm, sparsely hairy
DISTRIBUTION Japan (Ryukyu Islands)
FLOWERING late spring
HARDINESS ZONE 9

135. *Rhododendron stenopetalum* (Hogg) Mabberley
SYNONYM *R. linearifolium* Siebold and Zuccarini
ILLUSTRATION *Curtis's Botanical Magazine,* 5769 (1869)
HABIT to 1 m (rarely more); young shoots with spreading, greyish hairs, some of them glandular, and a few flattened, spreading hairs

LEAVES in cultivated plants, linear to linear-lanceolate, 3.5–8 cm, sparsely glandular hairy above, more densely so beneath
CALYX greenish, 5-lobed; lobes lanceolate, 1.2–3 cm
COROLLA divided into linear-lanceolate segments, pinkish or purple
STAMENS 5 (rarely more in some cultivars); filaments pubescent below
OVARY glandular-bristly
STYLE hairless
DISTRIBUTION central and southern Japan
FLOWERING late spring
HARDINESS ZONE 6

The cultivated plant, which bears the species name, is a monstrous cultivar long grown in Japan, mainly under the name *R. linearifolium*. The wild type was formerly known as var. *macrosepalum* (Maximowicz) Makino (*R. macrosepalum* Maximowicz); this has a broadly funnel-shaped corolla, 3.5–5 cm across, and is rarely cultivated.

136. *Rhododendron yedoense* Maximowicz
HABIT compact, densely branched shrub to 2 m; shoots with adpressed, grey hairs which fall after the first year
LEAVES elliptic-lanceolate to oblanceolate, 3–8 × 1–2.5 cm, ciliate, with adpressed, shining, grey or brown hairs
CALYX 5–10 mm, green; lobes lanceolate, with long, straight hairs
COROLLA broadly funnel-shaped, to 3.5–4 cm, pink to pale lilac, spotted with purple-brown, fragrant
STAMENS 10; filaments papillose below the middle
OVARY with adpressed hairs
STYLE hairless or pilose towards the base
CAPSULE 5–10 mm, bristly
DISTRIBUTION southern and central Korean Peninsula
FLOWERING late spring
HARDINESS ZONE 5

The description above also covers:

R. yedoense var. ***poukhanense*** Nakai
SYNONYM *R. coreanum* Rehder
ILLUSTRATION *Curtis's Botanical Magazine*, n.s., 455 (1964), reprinted in Halliday, *The*

Illustrated Rhododendron, pl. 106 (2001); Togashi et al., *Species Rhododendron Japan*, 182–184 (1982); Davidian, *The Rhododendron Species* 4, pl. 75 (1995)

Variety *yedoense* was described from cultivated material and has double rose-purple flowers.

Wild-collected material of var. *poukhanense* is available under *Kwanak Arboretum, Seoul* (without number) and *Forest Research Institute, Maisala* (without number).

R. yedoense var. *poukhanense* flower

R. yedoense var. *poukhanense* detail

R. yedoense var. *poukhanense* leaf surface

137. *Rhododendron simsii* Planchon

SYNONYM *R. indicum* misapplied

ILLUSTRATION *Curtis's Botanical Magazine,* 1480 (1812), reprinted in Halliday, *The Illustrated Rhododendron,* pl. 107 (2001); Sweet, *The British Flower Garden,* ser. 2, 2: t. 128 (1833); *Iconographia Cormophytorum Sinicorum* 3, t. 4247 (1974); Fang, *Sichuan Rhododendron of China,* 331–333 (1986); Feng, *Rhododendrons of China* 2, pl. 105: 1–47 (1992); Davidian, *The Rhododendron Species* 4, pl. 81–82 (1995)

HABIT shrub to 3 m; shoots densely covered with shining brown, flattened, adpressed hairs

LEAVES elliptic, oblong-elliptic, ovate to obovate or oblanceolate, 1–7 cm × 5–12 mm, sparsely bristly above, more densely bristly beneath, especially on the midrib and veins

CALYX 3–7 mm; lobes bristly, ciliate

COROLLA broadly funnel-shaped, 2.5–5 cm, red, pink, or white, spotted

STAMENS (8–)10; filaments hairy towards the base

OVARY bristly

STYLE hairless

CAPSULE to 8 mm, bristly

DISTRIBUTION northeastern Myanmar, China, Taiwan, northern Thailand

FLOWERING late spring

HARDINESS ZONE 7

R. simsii var. ***simsii***

COROLLA rich red to carmine, 3.5–6 cm

Wild-collected material is available under *Ejder* (without number) and *Valder 21.* Recent nonauthenticated material from Guizhou is also in cultivation.

R. simsii var. ***mesembrinum*** Balfour and Forrest ex Rehder

COROLLA white to rose-pink, 2.5–4 cm

The origin of the widely cultivated "Indian azalea," usually found with flowers of varying degrees of doubling.

138. *Rhododendron mucronatum* G. Don

SYNONYM *R. ledifolium* G. Don

ILLUSTRATION *Curtis's Botanical Magazine,* 2901 (1829); *Iconographia Cormophytorum*

Sinicorum 3, t. 4262 (1974); Fang, *Sichuan Rhododendron of China*, 340–342 (1986); Feng, *Rhododendrons of China* 2, pl. 98: 1–2 (1992)

HABIT shrub to 2 m (rarely more); young shoots with spreading, grey-brown hairs intermixed with few or many flattened, occasionally glandular, adpressed hairs

LEAVES lanceolate to ovate-lanceolate or oblong-lanceolate, 3–5.5 cm, with adpressed hairs (usually some glandular) on both surfaces

CALYX 5-lobed, to 1.2 cm; lobes glandular-pubescent

COROLLA widely funnel-shaped, 3.5–5 cm, white or rarely pink, fragrant, hairless

STAMENS 8–10; filaments hairless

OVARY densely bristly, without glands

STYLE hairless

CAPSULE to 1 cm, enclosed between the calyx lobes

DISTRIBUTION origin uncertain, long cultivated in China and Japan

FLOWERING late spring

HARDINESS ZONE 5

There are 2 varieties, both cultivated. Variety *mucronatum* has white corollas and is known only in cultivation; var. *ripense* (Makino) Wilson (*R. ripense* Makino) has rose-pink corollas and is from southern Japan.

'Narcissiflorum' has double white flowers, and 'Plenum' has double reddish flowers.

139. ***Rhododendron indicum*** (Linnaeus) Sweet

ILLUSTRATION Togashi et al., *Species Rhododendron Japan*, 146, 151–153 (1982)

HABIT low shrub, at most to 2 m, sometimes prostrate; young shoots with adpressed, flattened, brown bristles

LEAVES crowded, persistent, narrowly lanceolate to oblanceolate, 1.8–3.5 cm × 8–10 mm, usually distantly crenate-serrulate, ciliate, with scattered, adpressed, brownish hairs on both surfaces

CALYX 5-lobed; lobes ovate, obtuse, bristly, ciliate

COROLLA broadly funnel-shaped, 3–5 cm, bright red to scarlet or rarely pinkish red

STAMENS 5; filaments hairless

OVARY densely covered with adpressed, shining, brown hairs

STYLE hairless

CAPSULE to 1 cm

DISTRIBUTION Japan

FLOWERING spring

HARDINESS ZONE 6

Recent nonauthenticated material from Japan is in cultivation.

A very variable species, widely cultivated in Japan, where E. H. Wilson was told there were more than 200 forms (cultivars); some of these have been introduced to Europe and North America. The "Indian azalea" of nurseries is *R. simsii*.

140. *Rhododendron* ×*pulchrum* Sweet

ILLUSTRATION *Iconographia Cormophytorum Sinicorum* 3, t. 4259 (1974); Feng, *Rhododendrons of China* 2, pl. 101: 1–2 (1992)

HABIT shrub to 2 m; shoots with adpressed, flattened, grey-brown hairs

LEAVES elliptic to elliptic-lanceolate or oblong-lanceolate, 2.5–6 cm; both surfaces at first with brownish hairs, the upper surface later hairless

CALYX to 8 mm; lobes ciliate, with adpressed, long, straight hairs, finely toothed

COROLLA broadly funnel-shaped, to 6.5 cm, reddish purple spotted with dark purple

STAMENS 10; filaments pubescent towards the base

OVARY densely bristly

STYLE hairless

CAPSULE to 8 mm

DISTRIBUTION known only from long cultivation in Japan, and of hybrid origin (*R. indicum* × *R. mucronatum*)

FLOWERING late spring

HARDINESS ZONE 7

Rather variable and available in several "varieties," which are probably little more than selections from the total range of variation. Variety *pulchrum* is described above and is less commonly cultivated than var. *maxwellii* (Millais) Rehder (*R. maxwellii* Millais), which has carmine-red flowers.

141. *Rhododendron kaempferi* Planchon

ILLUSTRATION Millais, *Rhododendrons*, 20 (1917); Togashi et al., *Species Rhododendron Japan*, 154–156 (1982); Davidian, *The Rhododendron Species* 4, pl. 93–96 (1995)

HABIT shrub to 3 m; young shoots with adpressed, flattened, red-brown bristles; bark grey-brown, finely striate

LEAVES 1–5 × 1–2.5 cm, entire, bristly above and beneath, especially on the midrib

INFLORESCENCE BUDS borne among the leaves, fusiform, yellow tipped with red, covered with long brown bristles

CALYX 3–5 mm, deeply lobed, bristly

COROLLA funnel-shaped, 2–3 cm, pink or red

STAMENS 5; filaments papillose below the middle; anthers without apiculi at their bases
OVARY densely covered in red-brown bristles
STYLE hairless
CAPSULE c. 5 mm, bristly
DISTRIBUTION Japan
HARDINESS ZONE 5

Very similar to *R. indicum* but with broader leaves.

Wild-collected material is available under *Rokujo* (without number) and *Koishikawa Botanic Garden, Tokyo* (without number). Recent nonauthenticated material from Japan is also in cultivation.

142. *Rhododendron kiusianum* Makino
ILLUSTRATION Togashi et al., *Species Rhododendron Japan,* 162–165 (1982); Davidian, *The Rhododendron Species* 4, pl. 87–92 (1995)
HABIT dwarf shrub to 1 m; young shoots with adpressed, flattened, red-brown bristles
LEAVES deciduous, obovate, 5–20 × 2–15 mm, both surfaces bristly with red-brown hairs
CALYX 5-lobed, 2–3 mm, with red-brown hairs
COROLLA funnel-shaped, 1.5–2 cm, usually rose-pink, occasionally purplish
STAMENS 5; filaments pubescent below the middle
OVARY densely covered with red-brown hairs
STYLE hairless
CAPSULE 5–6 mm, bristly
DISTRIBUTION Japan
FLOWERING late spring
HARDINESS ZONE 6

Wild-collected material is available under *Suzuki* (without number), *Wilson 11250,* and *Wisley* (without number). Recent nonauthenticated material from Japan is also in cultivation.

Long cultivated and taxonomically much confused. The Obtusum Group of cultivars (see *R.* ×*obtusum*) and the Kurume azaleas had their origin in this species and its hybrids with *R. kaempferi.*

143. *Rhododendron ×obtusum* Planchon

ILLUSTRATION Davidian, *The Rhododendron Species* 4, pl. 79–80 (1995)

HABIT small shrub to 1 m; young shoots densely covered with adpressed, flattened bristles

LEAVES ovate to elliptic-ovate or oblong-lanceolate to obovate, 1–3.5 cm, with scattered, adpressed, pale hairs on both surfaces, especially along the midrib

CALYX 1–4 mm, with green, ovate, ciliate lobes

COROLLA funnel-shaped, to 2.5 cm, varying in colour from white through pink and reddish to purplish

STAMENS 5; filaments hairless

OVARY with adpressed, brownish hairs

STYLE hairless

CAPSULE to 7 mm, adpressed-bristly

DISTRIBUTION of garden origin

FLOWERING late spring

HARDINESS ZONE 6

A "species" (really a collection of cultivars of similar origins) known only in cultivation, long cultivated in Japan and thought to have been derived from *R. kiusianum, R. kaempferi,* and hybrids between them, perhaps involving some hybridisation with other species. Many variants are in cultivation and have been given names at the level of (botanical) variety or form, though they are really selections (cultivars) from the range of variation. The most important of these is 'Amoenum' (*R. amoenum* (Lindley) Planchon; *R. ×obtusum* f. *amoenum* (Lindley) Wilson), which has thin, elliptic leaves, 1–2.5 cm, and usually double magenta corollas.

144. *Rhododendron tosaense* Makino

SYNONYM *R. komiyamae* Makino

ILLUSTRATION *Curtis's Botanical Magazine,* n.s., 52 (1949); Togashi et al., *Species Rhododendron Japan,* 166–173 (1982); Davidian, *The Rhododendron Species* 4, pl. 79–80 (1995)

HABIT shrub to 2 m; shoots with greyish brown, flattened hairs

LEAVES lanceolate or oblanceolate or elliptic-lanceolate, 7–40 × 2–10 mm, with scattered, adpressed, greyish hairs on both surfaces

CALYX to 2 mm, bristly and ciliate

COROLLA funnel-shaped, to 1.8–2.5 cm, lilac-purple

STAMENS 5(–10); filaments papillose below the middle

OVARY bristly
STYLE hairless
DISTRIBUTION southern Japan
FLOWERING late spring
HARDINESS ZONE 7

145. *Rhododendron serpyllifolium* Miquel

ILLUSTRATION *Curtis's Botanical Magazine,* 7503 (1896); Togashi et al., *Species Rhododendron Japan,* 179–180 (1982)
HABIT low shrub; young shoots with flattened, brown hairs
LEAVES monomorphic, deciduous, obovate or elliptic or obovate-oblong, 3–10 mm, with scattered, bristly hairs above and a few flattened brown hairs on the midrib beneath
CALYX short, with 5 bristly lobes
COROLLA funnel-shaped, to 2.5 cm, pink
STAMENS 5; filaments papillose for most of their length
OVARY with pale, flattened hairs
STYLE hairless
CAPSULE hairy
DISTRIBUTION central and southern Japan
FLOWERING late spring
HARDINESS ZONE 6

146. *Rhododendron tschonoskii* Maximowicz

ILLUSTRATION Miyoshi and Makino, *Pocket Atlas of Alpine Plants of Japan* 2, t. 43, f. 247 (1907); Nakai, *Flora Sylvatica Koreana* 8, t. 17 (1919); Togashi et al., *Species Rhododendron Japan,* 190–192 (1982)
HABIT shrub to 2 m (rarely more); shoots with adpressed, flattened, red-brown hairs
LEAVES narrowly lanceolate to elliptic-lanceolate or oblanceolate, 1–3.5 cm × 3–10 mm, with adpressed, whitish or red-brown hairs on both surfaces, sometimes conspicuously 3-veined
CALYX very small, densely brown-hairy
COROLLA funnel-shaped, sometimes 4-lobed, to 9 mm, white
STAMENS 4–5; filaments downy below the middle
OVARY brown-hairy
STYLE hairless
CAPSULE to 6 mm, bristly

DISTRIBUTION Japan, South Korea, eastern Russia
FLOWERING late spring
HARDINESS ZONE 6

Wild-collected material is available under *Koishigawa Botanic Garden, Tokyo* (without number). Recent nonauthenticated material from Japan is also in cultivation.

Remarkable for its small flowers, with corollas sometimes 4-lobed. Variants with the leaves strongly 3-veined are referred to as var. *trinerve* (Franchet) Makino (*R. trinerve* Franchet).

Less commonly cultivated are:

Rhododendron eriocarpum (Hayata) Nakai
Probably keying out to *R. yedoense,* but:
CALYX 1–5 mm
COROLLA purplish pink
DISTRIBUTION southernmost Japan

Rhododendron lasiostylum Hayata
Similar to *R. eriocarpum,* keying out to *R. yedoense,* but:
LEAVES hairy beneath
PEDICELS with whitish, flattened hairs
DISTRIBUTION Taiwan

Rhododendron rubropilosum Hayata
Very similar to *R. lasiostylum* and *R. eriocarpum,* but:
PEDICELS concealed among the bud scales
STYLE scarcely hairy
DISTRIBUTION Taiwan

Rhododendron kanehirae Wilson
ILLUSTRATION *Iconographia Cormophytorum Sinicorum* 3, t. 4245 (1974)
Probably keying out near *R. simsii,* but:
CALYX with minute lobes up to 1 mm
DISTRIBUTION southernmost Japan

Perhaps not significantly different from *R. tashiroi.*

Rhododendron tashiroi Maximowicz
See *R. kanehirae.*

Rhododendron breviperulatum Hayata
Similar to *R. kaempferi,* but:
COROLLA pink
ANTHERS each with an apiculus at the base
DISTRIBUTION Taiwan

Rhododendron microphyton Franchet
ILLUSTRATION *Iconographia Cormophytorum Sinicorum* 3, t. 4248 (1974)
Keying out near *R. kaempferi,* but:
INFLORESCENCES 3- to 10-flowered
COROLLA 1.2–1.6 cm; tube 2–3 mm wide at the base
STYLE hairless
DISTRIBUTION western China (Yunnan, southwestern Sichuan)

Rhododendron saxicolum Sleumer
Similar to *R. microphyton,* but:
COROLLA lobes 1.5 or more × longer than the tube
DISTRIBUTION Vietnam

Probably not hardy anywhere in Britain.

Rhododendron tsusiophyllum Sugimoto
Keying out to *R. serpyllifolium* or *R. kiusianum,* but:
COROLLA tubular-campanulate
DISTRIBUTION central Japan

Rhododendron nakaharai Hayata
Similar to *R. serpyllifolium,* but:
STAMENS more than 5
Perhaps keying out near *R. yedoense,* but:
CALYX 1–5 mm
COROLLA 2–2.5 cm
DISTRIBUTION Taiwan

Rhododendron noriakianum Suzuki
Very similar to *R. nakaharai,* but:
COROLLA at most 1.5 cm
DISTRIBUTION northern Taiwan

Rhododendron subsessile Rendle
Very similar to *R. noriakianum* and *R. nakaharai,* but:
LEAVES more than 1.5 cm; upper surface persistently hairy
DISTRIBUTION Philippines

Probably not hardy anywhere in Britain.

Subgenus *Tsutsusi*

Section ***Brachycalyx*** Sweet (*Azalea* series *Schlippenbachii* subseries, in part)

HABIT shrubs with flattened hairs

LEAVES deciduous, without scales, often borne in false whorls of 3 at the ends of the twigs

NEW VEGETATIVE SHOOTS from lower buds within the inflorescence bud

CALYX minute, 5-lobed

COROLLA funnel-shaped to very openly funnel-shaped, not hairy outside

STAMENS 5–10

OVARY generally hairy

STYLE often hairy at the base

CAPSULE hairy

A group of 15 rather similar and easily confused species, of which only 5 are generally cultivated.

1 a Leaves ovate to oblong-lanceolate, broadest below the middle; stamens 10 .... **147. *R. mariesii***
  b Leaves usually ovate-rhombic, broadest at about the middle; stamens 5–10 2
2 a Corolla red to rose-pink 3
  b Corolla magenta to pinkish purple 4
3 a Flowers deep rose-pink .... **150. *R. sanctum***
  b Flowers red .... **151. *R. amagianum***
4 a Corolla 3–4 cm; racemes 2- to 4-flowered .... **149. *R. weyrichii***
  b Corolla 2–3 cm; racemes one- to 2-flowered .... **148. *R. reticulatum***

147. *Rhododendron mariesii* Hemsley and Wilson

ILLUSTRATION *Curtis's Botanical Magazine,* 8206 (1908); *Iconographia Cormophytorum Sinicorum* 3: 4243 (1974); Fang, *Sichuan Rhododendron of China,* 337–339 (1986); Feng, *Rhododendrons of China* 2, pl. 106: 1–3 (1992); Davidian, *The Rhododendron Species* 4, pl. 99–101 (1995)

HABIT upright shrub to 3 m; young shoots with adpressed, silky hairs which soon fall

LEAVES deciduous, ovate-lanceolate to broadly elliptic, 3–9 × 2.5–4 cm, hairless when mature, with yellowish silky hairs when young

CALYX very small, 5-lobed, with grey or yellowish brown hairs

Corolla openly funnel-shaped, 2.5–3 cm, rose-purple with red-purple spots, hairless
Stamens 10; filaments hairless
Ovary densely covered with grey or yellowish brown hairs
Style hairless
Capsule 1.2–1.5 cm, villous
Distribution southeastern and central China, Taiwan
Flowering late spring
Hardiness zone 8

148. *Rhododendron reticulatum* D. Don
Synonyms *R. rhombicum* Miquel; *R. dilatatum* Miquel
Illustration *Curtis's Botanical Magazine*, 6972 (1887), reprinted in Halliday, *The Illustrated Rhododendron*, pl. 108 (2001); Stevenson, *The Species of Rhododendron*, 116 (1930); Moser, *Rhododendron: Wildarten und Hybriden*, 65 (1991); Davidian, *The Rhododendron Species* 4, pl. 102–105 (1995); Kneller, *The Book of Rhododendrons*, 117 (1995)
Habit shrub to 8 m; shoots usually at least sparsely hairy when young, soon hairless; bark brown, finely striate
Leaves broadly ovate or rhombic, 3–6 cm, at first with greyish or yellowish hairs, soon hairless above, the indumentum usually persisting on the midrib and veins beneath
Inflorescence buds scales opening widely like a calyx, green, translucent, each with a band of hairs along the middle; inflorescences one-flowered
Calyx minute, villous; lobes ciliate
Corolla funnel-campanulate, 3.5–5 cm, with a short white tube and spreading lobes, reddish purple to magenta, usually unspotted, somewhat 2-lipped
Stamens usually 10; filaments hairless
Ovary velvety and/or glandular
Style hairless or hairy towards the base
Capsule to 1.2 cm, curved, glandular, sometimes also downy
Distribution Japan
Flowering late spring
Hardiness zone 6

Recent nonauthenticated material from Japan is in cultivation.

R. reticulatum flower

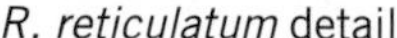

R. reticulatum detail

R. reticulatum leaf surface

149. *Rhododendron weyrichii* Maximowicz

ILLUSTRATION *Curtis's Botanical Magazine,* 9475 (1937); Togashi et al., *Species Rhododendron Japan,* 98–101 (1982)

HABIT shrub to 5 m, sometimes tree-like; young shoots with reddish hairs which soon fall

LEAVES almost orbicular to broadly ovate or rhombic-ovate, 3.5–8 × 1.5–6 cm, with red-brown hairs when young, these soon falling

CALYX minute, toothed, reddish-hairy

COROLLA funnel-campanulate, 3–4 cm, pink, with a short, narrow tube

STAMENS 10; filaments hairless

OVARY reddish pilose

STYLE hairless or downy towards the base

CAPSULE 1–2 cm, adpressed-villous

DISTRIBUTION southern Japan and South Korea (Cheju)

FLOWERING late spring

HARDINESS ZONE 5

Recent nonauthenticated material from Japan is in cultivation.

150. *Rhododendron sanctum* Nakai

ILLUSTRATION Togashi et al., *Species Rhododendron Japan,* 102–105 (1982)

HABIT shrub to 5 m; young shoots reddish brown, downy, soon hairless

LEAVES broadly rhombic to rhombic-ovate, 3–8 × 2.5–6 cm; upper surface with long reddish brown hairs; lower surface with similar hairs restricted to the midrib and veins

FLOWERS usually appearing after leaves expand

CALYX minute

COROLLA funnel-campanulate, 2.5–3.5 cm, hairless, deep pink

STAMENS 10; filaments hairless

OVARY densely brown-downy

STYLE pilose in the lower half

CAPSULE 1–1.5 cm, densely downy

DISTRIBUTION Japan

FLOWERING late spring

HARDINESS ZONE 7

Recent nonauthenticated material from Japan is in cultivation.

151. *Rhododendron amagianum* Makino

ILLUSTRATION *Curtis's Botanical Magazine,* n.s., 379 (1962); Togashi et al., *Species Rhododendron Japan,* 106–109 (1982)

HABIT to 5 m; young shoots densely downy

LEAVES rhomboid to ovate, 4.5–11.5 × 3–9 cm; margins ciliate and minutely toothed; upper surface with long, slender hairs; lower surface pale green, sparsely strigose, with pilose midrib and veins

CALYX minute, 5-lobed

COROLLA openly campanulate, 2.5–4 cm, red or orange-red

STAMENS 10; filaments hairless

OVARY densely brown-hairy

STYLE hairy in the lower part

CAPSULE 1.4–1.8 cm, pilose

DISTRIBUTION Japan

FLOWERING late spring

HARDINESS ZONE 7

Recent nonauthenticated material from Japan is in cultivation.

Less commonly cultivated are:

Rhododendron farrerae Tate apud Sweet

ILLUSTRATION *Iconographia Cormophytorum Sinicorum* 3, t. 4242 (1974)

Very similar to *R. mariesii,* but:

LEAVES 1.5–3 cm; petioles villous

COROLLA pale purple to lilac

DISTRIBUTION China (Guangxi, Guangdong, Fujian, Jiangxi, Hunan)

Rhododendron kiyosumense (Makino) Makino

Similar to *R. reticulatum,* but:

LEAVES with acuminate apices and lamina covered with brown hairs when young

DISTRIBUTION Japan (Honshū)

Rhododendron nudipes Nakai

Similar to *R. reticulatum,* but:

LEAVES petioles and lower part of lamina densely woolly or velvety

DISTRIBUTION Japan

At least 2 of the many subspecies and varieties described in this species—var. *nudipes* and var. *lagopus* (Nakai) Yamazaki (*R. lagopus* Nakai)—are thought to be in cultivation, but their status is doubtful.

Rhododendron decandrum (Makino) Makino
Keying out near *R. weyrichii* and *R. reticulatum*, but:
OVARY glandular
DISTRIBUTION Japan (Honshū, Shikoku)

Rhododendron hidakanum Hara
Similar to *R. decandrum*, but:
LEAVES less hairy
CALYX longer
DISTRIBUTION Japan (southern Hokkaidō)

Rhododendron wadanum Makino
Similar to *R. decandrum* and *R. hidakanum*, but:
STYLE with stipitate glands below
DISTRIBUTION Japan (Honshū)

Subgenus *Pentanthera* G. Don

HABIT shrubs, variously hairy, but without flattened bristles
LEAVES often deciduous

The subgenus is divided into 4 sections.

Subgenus *Pentanthera*

Section ***Rhodora*** (Linnaeus) G. Don (*Azalea* series *Canadense* subseries, in part)

HABIT shrubs

COROLLA 2-lipped, with the upper 3 lobes fused higher than the lower 2, hairless inside and outside

STAMENS usually 7–10

SEEDS winged or not, with appendages at each end; wings, if present, and the appendages at each end of the seed are made up of unique bladder-like cells

1a Corolla divided to the base between the 2 lower lobes and these 2 together and the rest of the corolla; stamens 10 . . . . **152. *R. canadense***

b Corolla with a distinct, though short, tube; stamens usually 7 (rarely fewer) . . . . **153. *R. vaseyi***

152. *Rhododendron canadense* (Linnaeus) Torrey

SYNONYM *R. rhodora* Gmelin

ILLUSTRATION *Curtis's Botanical Magazine,* 474 (1800), reprinted in Halliday, *The Illustrated Rhododendron,* pl. 113 (2001); Gleason, *New Britton and Brown Illustrated Flora of the Northeastern United States and Canada* 3: 12 (1952); Davidian, *The Rhododendron Species* 4, pl. 1–3 (1995); Cox and Cox, *The Encyclopedia of Rhododendron Species,* 219 (1997); Holmgren, *The Illustrated Companion to Gleason and Cronquist's Manual,* 186 (1998)

HABIT slender shrub to 1 m; shoots upright, slender, hairy when young; bark dark brown, striate

LEAVES elliptic to oblong, 1.5–6 cm; margins revolute and ciliate; upper surface dull bluish green and sparsely adpressed-bristly; lower surface thinly hairy, with some glands

INFLORESCENCE BUDS of irregular shape, pinkish green; scales white-hairy on the surfaces and margins

CALYX minute; lobes unequal, bristly

COROLLA very openly campanulate, 2-lipped, the tube on the lower side divided to the base, to 2 cm, rose-purple or rarely white

STAMENS 10

OVARY downy, with a few glands and bristles

STYLE hairless or minutely hairy towards the base

CAPSULE to 1.2 cm, bristly, downy

DISTRIBUTION eastern North America from Labrador to Pennsylvania

FLOWERING spring
HARDINESS ZONE 3

Recent nonauthenticated collections from the United States and Canada are in cultivation.

153. *Rhododendron vaseyi* A. Gray

ILLUSTRATION *Garden* 54: 282 (1898), 76: 332 (1912), 84: 239 (1920); *Curtis's Botanical Magazine,* 8081 (1906); *Addisonia* 16, pl. 525 (1931), as *Biltia vaseyi;* Moser, *Rhododendron: Wildarten und Hybriden,* 256 (1991); Davidian, *The Rhododendron Species* 4, pl. 6–11 (1995); Kneller, *The Book of Rhododendrons,* 113 (1995); Cox and Cox, *The Encyclopedia of Rhododendron Species,* 220 (1997)
HABIT upright shrub to 5 m; shoots downy or sparingly hairy at first, soon hairless; bark grey-brown, striate
LEAVES elliptic to elliptic-oblong, 5–12 cm; upper surface dark green and hairless except for short hairs along the midrib; lower surface pale green and hairless or sparsely hairy on the midrib
INFLORESCENCE BUDS ovoid, greenish pink; scales covered with brown-headed glands
FLOWERS appearing before leaves expand
CALYX small, oblique, with glandular lobes
COROLLA very openly campanulate, deeply lobed with spreading lobes, 2.5–3 cm, somewhat 2-lipped, pink or rarely white, with orange or orange-red spots, hairless
STAMENS (5–)7; filaments hairless; anthers brown
OVARY glandular-downy
STYLE hairless or with a few shortly stalked glands near the base
CAPSULE to 1.3 cm
DISTRIBUTION eastern United States (North Carolina)
FLOWERING late spring
HARDINESS ZONE 4

R. vaseyi flower

R. vaseyi detail

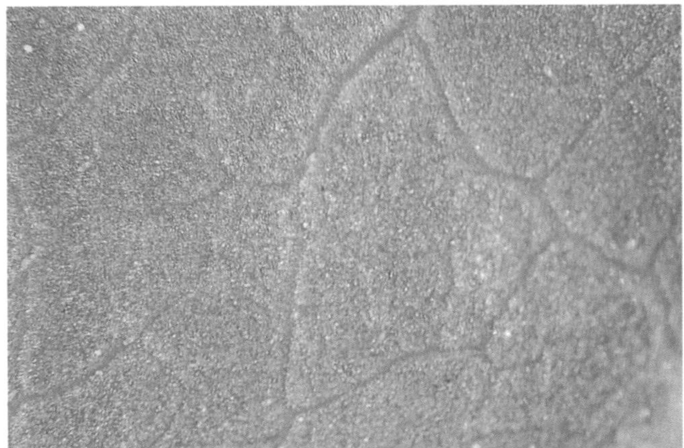

R. vaseyi leaf surface

Subgenus *Pentanthera*

Section ***Sciadorhodion*** Rehder and Wilson (*Azalea* series *Canadense* and *Schlippenbachii* subseries, both in part)

Similar to section *Rhodora,* but:

HABIT shrubs

NEW VEGETATIVE SHOOTS from buds below the terminal (inflorescence) bud or from within the inflorescence bud

LEAVES often in false whorls of 5

COROLLA not 2-lipped

SEEDS elongate, unwinged and without appendages at each end (or appendages, if present, very short)

1 a Leaves obviously alternate, not in false whorls of 5 leaves .... **154. *R. albrechtii***

b Leaves mostly in false whorls of 5 (rarely 3 or up to 9) at the tips of the shoots 2

2 a New shoots from lateral buds below the terminal bud; leaf stalk with a fringe of hairs .... **155. *R. pentaphyllum***

b New shoots from within the terminal bud; leaf stalk hairy or not, but hairs never forming a conspicuous fringe 3

3 a Corolla white; style and ovary hairless or with eglandular hairs .... **157. *R. quinquefolium***

b Corolla pink; style and ovary covered with glandular hairs .... **156. *R. schlippenbachii***

154. *Rhododendron albrechtii* Maximowicz

ILLUSTRATION *Curtis's Botanical Magazine,* 9207 (1928), reprinted in Halliday, *The Illustrated Rhododendron,* pl. 115 (2001); *Rhododendron and Camellia Yearbook* 36: f. 10 (1982); Moser, *Rhododendron: Wildarten und Hybriden,* 123 (1991); Davidian, *The Rhododendron Species* 4, pl. 12–15 (1995); Cox and Cox, *The Encyclopedia of Rhododendron Species,* 221 (1997)

HABIT to 2 m; shoots with curled hairs at first, later hairless and purple-brown; bark greenish brown, striate

LEAVES mostly obovate, rarely narrower, 4–12 cm; margins ciliate and very finely toothed; upper surface with sparse, adpressed hairs; lower surface densely grey-hairy

INFLORESCENCE BUDS ovoid, pale green; scales hairless

FLOWERS appearing before or as leaves expand

CALYX with small, ciliate, purple lobes

Corolla openly campanulate, c. 5 cm, with a short, wide tube, red-purple, hairless outside
Stamens 10; filaments sometimes hairy below the middle; anthers reddish purple
Ovary hairy and glandular
Style hairless
Capsule to 1.2 cm, with yellowish, sticky hairs
Distribution Japan
Flowering late spring
Hardiness zone 5

Recent nonauthenticated material from Japan is in cultivation.

155. *Rhododendron pentaphyllum* Maximowicz
Synonym *R. nikoense* Nakai
Illustration Davidian, *The Rhododendron Species* 4, pl. 4–5 (1995); Cox and Cox, *The Encyclopedia of Rhododendron Species,* 222 (1997)
Habit shrub to 8 m, but usually less in cultivation; shoots at first sparingly hairy, later hairless
Leaves elliptic to elliptic-lanceolate, 2.5–6 cm, ciliate and finely toothed; midrib velvety on both surfaces, especially towards the base
Calyx 2–5 mm, hairless, with triangular lobes
Corolla very widely campanulate, with a short tube and spreading lobes, 4.5–5 cm, rose-pink, unspotted, hairless
Stamens 10; filaments hairy towards the base
Ovary and style hairless
Capsule to 1.5 cm
Distribution central and southern Japan
Flowering late spring
Hardiness zone 7

Recent nonauthenticated material from Korea and Japan is in cultivation.

156. *Rhododendron schlippenbachii* Maximowicz
Illustration *Curtis's Botanical Magazine,* 7373 (1894); *Garden* 46: 80 (1894), 76: 136 (1913); *Iconographia Cormophytorum Sinicorum* 3, t. 4244 (1974); *Rhododendrons with Camellias and Magnolias* 42: f. 6 (1990); Moser, *Rhododendron: Wildarten und Hybriden,* 230 (1991); Feng, *Rhododendrons of China* 2, pl. 107 (1992); Davidian, *The Rhododen-*

dron Species 4, pl. 106–111 (1995); Kneller, *The Book of Rhododendrons,* 115 (1995); Cox and Cox, *The Encyclopedia of Rhododendron Species,* 223 (1997)

HABIT shrub to 5 m, but often less and rather spreading; young shoots glandular-downy, later hairless; bark grey, striate

LEAVES obovate to broadly ovate, 2.5–11 cm × 9–72 mm, truncate, rounded or notched at the apex; both surfaces sparsely downy at first, with hairs persisting only on the main veins of lower surface

R. schlippenbachii flower

R. schlippenbachii detail

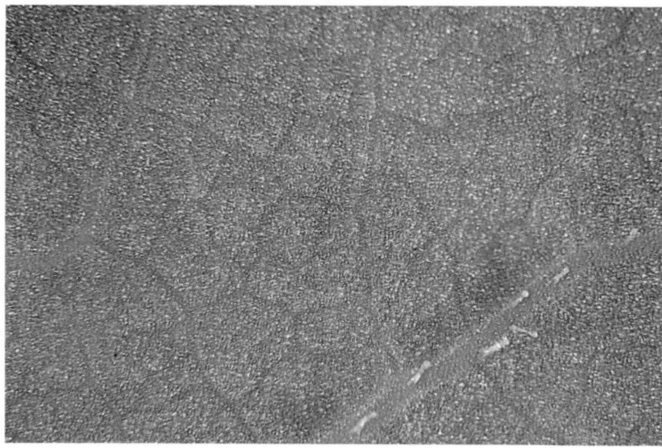

R. schlippenbachii leaf surface

Inflorescence buds ovoid, pointed, green or brown; scales with long white hairs
Flowers appearing as or immediately before leaves expand
Calyx to 5 mm; lobes ovate, green, glandular-hairy
Corolla very openly funnel-shaped, 3–6 cm, pale pink, the upper lobes spotted with red-brown
Stamens 10; filaments hairy towards the base; anthers yellow
Ovary glandular
Style glandular-hairy below the middle
Capsule to 1.8 cm, glandular
Distribution Korea, eastern Russia
Flowering late spring
Hardiness zone 4

Recent nonauthenticated material from Korea is in cultivation.

157. *Rhododendron quinquefolium* Bisset and Moore

Illustration Cox and Cox, *The Encyclopedia of Rhododendron Species,* 222–223 (1997)
Habit shrub or small tree to 8 m; young shoots hairless
Leaves broadly elliptic to obovate, 3–6 cm; margins ciliate and often red-purple; upper surface hairless except along the midrib; lower surface velvety towards the base, with small bristles on the midrib
Calyx 1–3 mm; lobes glandular-ciliate
Corolla very openly campanulate, to 2 cm, white with green spots above; lobes longer than the tube
Stamens 10; filaments dilated and hairy towards the base
Ovary and style hairless
Capsule to 1.2 cm
Distribution central Japan
Flowering late spring
Hardiness zone 6

Recent nonauthenticated material from Japan is in cultivation.

Subgenus *Pentanthera*

Section ***Viscidula*** Matsumura and Nakai (*Azalea* series *Nipponicum* subseries)

HABIT shrub
COROLLA almost regular, tubular-campanulate, white, unspotted
STAMENS 10
SEEDS unwinged but with conspicuous appendages at each end

Rhododendron nipponicum is the only species.

158. *Rhododendron nipponicum* Matsumura

ILLUSTRATION *Curtis's Botanical Magazine,* n.s., 491 (1966), reprinted in Halliday, *The Illustrated Rhododendron,* pl. 114 (2001)
HABIT upright shrub to 2 m; young shoots hairy and with some glands
LEAVES obovate to obovate-oblong, 5–18 cm, adpressed-hairy on both surfaces
CALYX small, with short, unequal lobes, glandular-downy
COROLLA tubular to tubular-campanulate, to 1.8 cm, white, hairless, with 5 rounded, short, slightly spreading lobes
STAMENS 10; filaments hairy below the middle; anthers yellow-brown
OVARY glandular-hairy
STYLE hairless
CAPSULE to 1.2 cm
DISTRIBUTION central Japan
FLOWERING late spring
HARDINESS ZONE 7

Recent nonauthenticated material from Japan is in cultivation.

Very distinctive, and without close allies.

R. nipponicum flower and leaf. PHOTO BY RAY COX

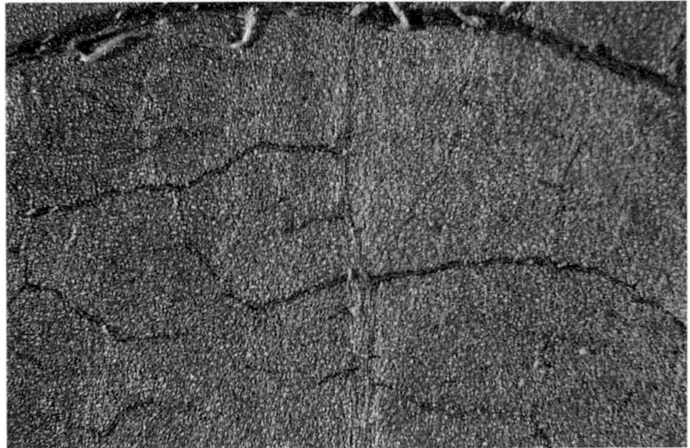

R. nipponicum leaf surface

Subgenus *Pentanthera*

Section ***Pentanthera*** G. Don (*Azalea* series *Luteum* subseries)

HABIT shrubs without scales

LEAVES deciduous, variously hairy

NEW SHOOTS from buds below the terminal inflorescence, or rarely from within the same bud as the inflorescence

FLOWERS appearing before, as, or after leaves expand

CALYX small

COROLLA basically funnel-shaped, strongly bilaterally symmetric, hairy and usually sticky outside

STAMENS 5

SEEDS usually winged (sometimes very broadly so) and with appendages at each end, rarely (*R. arborescens*) unwinged

The species of this section are difficult to distinguish, both in the wild and in gardens, due to the frequent occurrence of hybridisation. The cultivated, deciduous azalea hybrids (Ghent, Exbury, Knaphill, and so forth) are largely derived from species belonging to this section.

1 a Flowers appearing before leaves are fully expanded 2
b Flowers mostly appearing after leaves are fully expanded 11
2 a Upper corolla lobe with a blotch or spots of a contrasting colour 3
b Upper corolla lobe uniform in colour, not spotted or blotched 9
3 a Corolla broadly funnel-shaped; stamens not or scarcely projecting beyond the corolla lobes 4
b Corolla narrowly funnel-shaped; stamens projecting well beyond the corolla lobes 5
4 a Corolla yellow . . . . **164. *R. molle***
b Corolla orange-red . . . . **165. *R. japonicum***
5 a Corolla lobes longer than the tube; tube abruptly widened above . . . . **170. *R. calendulaceum***
b Corolla lobes shorter than the tube; tube gradually widened above 6
6 a Flowers white, though blotch on upper corolla lobe yellow 7
b Flowers yellow to orange or pink 8
7 a Flower bud scales hairless or almost so, eglandular . . . . **166. *R. alabamense***
b Flower bud scales hairy (rarely sparsely so), usually with some glands, at least on the margin . . . . **167. *R. occidentale***
8 a Flower bud scales with their outer surfaces densely downy . . . . **168. *R. austrinum***
b Flower bud scales with their outer surfaces hairless or rarely very sparsely downy . . . . **169. *R. luteum***

9 a Glandular hairs forming lines on the outside of the corolla; plant strongly stoloniferous .... **163. *R. atlanticum***

b Glandular hairs scattered on the outside of the corolla; plant not stoloniferous 10

10 a Flower bud scales hairless; leaves hairless or sparsely hairy beneath ..... **161. *R. periclymenoides***

b Flower bud scales densely hairy; leaves hairy beneath, usually densely so .... **162. *R. canescens***

11 a Shoots hairless; lower surface of leaves hairless or almost so 12

b Shoots hairy, sometimes glandular; lower surface of leaves usually hairy 13

12 a Corolla yellow to red .... **160. *R. prunifolium***

b Corolla white .... **172. *R. arborescens***

13 a Corolla yellow to orange or red, with a darker blotch on the upper lobe .... **171. *R. cumberlandense***

b Corolla white, unblotched .... **159. *R. viscosum***

159. *Rhododendron viscosum* (Linnaeus) Torrey

SYNONYMS *R. serrulatum* (Small) Millais; *R. oblongifolium* (Small) Millais

ILLUSTRATION *Addisonia* 11, pl. 370 (1926); Gleason, *New Britton and Brown Illustrated Flora of the Northeastern United States and Canada* 3: 11 (1952); Davidian, *The Rhododendron Species* 4, pl. 56–58 and 74 (1995); Cox and Cox, *The Encyclopedia of Rhododendron Species,* 216–217 (1997); Holmgren, *The Illustrated Companion to Gleason and Cronquist's Manual,* 185 (1998)

HABIT shrub to 3 m; young shoots with loosely adpressed hairs, later hairless

LEAVES ovate or elliptic-obovate to oblong-lanceolate, 1.8–3 cm; upper surface hairless except for short hairs along the midrib; lower surface adpressed-bristly and pale to almost glaucous

CALYX to 1 mm, with unequal, adpressed-bristly lobes

COROLLA funnel-shaped, 2–3 cm, white or white flushed with pink, rarely deep pink, velvety and finely glandular-hairy outside; tube longer than the lobes

STAMENS filaments hairy in the lower two-thirds

OVARY usually glandular-bristly

STYLE finely downy towards the base

CAPSULE 1.2–2 cm, usually glandular-bristly

DISTRIBUTION eastern United States (from Maine to Florida)

FLOWERING late spring

HARDINESS ZONE 3

Recent nonauthenticated material from the United States is in cultivation.

160. *Rhododendron prunifolium* (Small) Millais

ILLUSTRATION Cox and Cox, *The Encyclopedia of Rhododendron Species,* 216 (1997)

HABIT shrub to 2 m; young shoots hairless

LEAVES elliptic or obovate to oblong, 3–12 cm, ciliate, hairless or appearing adpressed-bristly above, sparingly adpressed-bristly on the midrib and veins beneath

CALYX to 1 mm; lobes unequal, ciliate

COROLLA funnel-shaped, 3.5–5 cm, crimson, finely velvety and sometimes glandular outside, hairy inside; tube gradually widened above the middle

STAMENS filaments velvety towards the base

OVARY bristly, without glands

STYLE hairless

CAPSULE to 2 cm, adpressed-bristly, downy

DISTRIBUTION southeastern United States (southwestern Georgia, eastern Alabama)

FLOWERING late spring

HARDINESS ZONE 6

161. *Rhododendron periclymenoides* (Michaux) Shinners

SYNONYM *R. nudiflorum* Torrey

ILLUSTRATION *Curtis's Botanical Magazine,* 3667 (1839), as *R. nudiflorum scintillans;* Gleason, *New Britton and Brown Illustrated Flora of the Northeastern United States and Canada* 3: 10 (1952); Braun, *The Woody Plants of Ohio,* 288 (1961); Moser, *Rhododendron: Wildarten und Hybriden,* 22, 211 (1991); Davidian, *The Rhododendron Species* 4:, pl. 54–55 (1995); Cox and Cox, *The Encyclopedia of Rhododendron Species,* 214 (1997); Holmgren, *The Illustrated Companion to Gleason and Cronquist's Manual,* 185 (1998)

HABIT shrub to 2 m; young shoots sparsely downy, slightly adpressed-bristly, ultimately more or less hairless

LEAVES elliptic to oblong or oblong-obovate or obovate, 3–8 cm, hairless above except for some hairs along the midrib, adpressed-bristly beneath and somewhat downy along the midrib

CALYX 1–2 mm, long-ciliate; lobes unequal

COROLLA funnel-shaped, 2.5–4 cm, pink or whitish, usually downy outside; tube longer than the lobes

STAMENS filaments downy below the middle

OVARY with bristles or fine white hairs interspersed with bristles

CAPSULE 1.2–2 cm, finely downy, usually adpressed-bristly

DISTRIBUTION eastern United States (from Massachusetts to North Carolina)

Flowering late spring
Hardiness zone 3

Recent nonauthenticated material from the United States is in cultivation.

162. *Rhododendron canescens* (Michaux) Sweet

Illustration Gleason, *New Britton and Brown Illustrated Flora of the Northeastern United States and Canada* 3: 10 (1952); Cox and Cox, *The Encyclopedia of Rhododendron Species*, 209–210 (1997); Holmgren, *The Illustrated Companion to Gleason and Cronquist's Manual*, 185 (1998)
Habit slender shrub to 5 m, usually much less in cultivation; young shoots velvety and sparsely adpressed-bristly
Leaves oblong-obovate to oblanceolate, 2–8 cm; upper surface sparsely downy; lower surface densely downy especially on the veins, somewhat adpressed-bristly on the midrib; margins ciliate, with the cilia inconspicuous, adpressed to the leaf
Calyx to 1 mm, with unequal lobes, ciliate, sometimes glandular
Corolla funnel-shaped, 3–4 cm, velvety outside, pink or pink with white lobes; tube cylindric, widening abruptly
Ovary densely white-downy, sparsely bristly
Style hairy in the lower part
Capsule 1.8–2 cm, downy, bristly
Distribution southeastern United States (from North Carolina to Florida and Texas)
Flowering spring
Hardiness zone 7

Recent nonauthenticated material from the United States is in cultivation.

163. *Rhododendron atlanticum* Rehder

Illustration Gleason, *New Britton and Brown Illustrated Flora of the Northeastern United States and Canada* 3: 10 (1952); Moser, *Rhododendron: Wildarten und Hybriden*, 128 (1991); Davidian, *The Rhododendron Species* 4, pl. 25–28 (1995); Cox and Cox, *The Encyclopedia of Rhododendron Species*, 206–207 (1997); Holmgren, *The Illustrated Companion to Gleason and Cronquist's Manual*, 185 (1998)
Habit low stoloniferous shrub to 60 cm; young shoots sparingly hairy and glandular; bark greyish, striate
Leaves obovate or oblong-obovate; upper surface bright blue-green and hairless except for the velvety midrib; lower surface sparingly adpressed-bristly, sometimes also downy along the midrib

Inflorescence buds ovoid, reddish brown; scales margined with fine white hairs
Flowers appearing as or just before leaves expand, very fragrant
Calyx 2–4 mm, usually glandular-ciliate
Corolla funnel-shaped, 3–4 cm, with a cylindric tube, white or flushed with pink or purple, with short, glandular bristles outside
Ovary bristly, with or without glands
Style hairy below the middle
Capsule c. 2 cm, bristly, glandular or not
Distribution eastern United States (from Delaware to southern Georgia)
Flowering late spring
Hardiness zone 6

Recent nonauthenticated material from the United States is in cultivation.

164. *Rhododendron molle* (Blume) G. Don

Illustration *Iconographia Cormophytorum Sinicorum* 3, t. 4241 (1974); Fang, *Sichuan Rhododendron of China*, 328–329 (1986); Feng, *Rhododendrons of China* 2, pl. 90, 2–3 (1992); Cox and Cox, *The Encyclopedia of Rhododendron Species*, 218 (1997)
Habit small shrub to 2 m; young shoots velvety, often bristly
Leaves oblong to oblong-lanceolate, 4–13 × 1.8–3 cm; upper surface softly downy when young; lower surface with more persistent, greyish white hairs which are sometimes restricted to the veins
Calyx minute, unequally lobed, downy, with a few bristles
Corolla broadly funnel-shaped, 5–7 cm, yellow, golden yellow, or orange, with a large basal greenish blotch composed of contiguous spots on the upper petals, hairy outside; tube shorter than the lobes
Stamens filaments hairy in the lower half
Ovary hairy
Style hairless
Capsule 1.8–2.5 cm, finely downy, somewhat bristly
Distribution eastern and central China
Flowering late spring
Hardiness zone 7

165. *Rhododendron japonicum* (A. Gray) Suringar

Illustration *Curtis's Botanical Magazine*, 5905 (1871), reprinted in Halliday, *The Illustrated Rhododendron*, pl. 112 (2001); Davidian, *The Rhododendron Species* 4, pl. 34–36 (1995); Cox and Cox, *The Encyclopedia of Rhododendron Species*, 218 (1997)

HABIT shrub to 2 m; young shoots sparingly bristly or hairless
LEAVES obovate to obovate-oblong or oblanceolate, 5–10 cm, ciliate, with scattered bristles above and on the veins beneath
CALYX with small, obtuse lobes margined with grey hairs
COROLLA broadly funnel-shaped, 5–6 cm across, orange or salmon to brick-red, with a large orange blotch made up of small dots; tube shorter than the lobes
STAMENS filaments hairy below
OVARY hairy
STYLE hairless
CAPSULE 2–2.5 cm, with scattered hairs
DISTRIBUTION central and eastern Japan
FLOWERING late spring
HARDINESS ZONE 5

Very similar to *R. molle* and perhaps not distinct.

166. ***Rhododendron alabamense*** Rehder

ILLUSTRATION Cox and Cox, *The Encyclopedia of Rhododendron Species,* 205 (1997)
HABIT shrub to 5 m; shoots adpressed-bristly
LEAVES oblong-elliptic or obovate or elliptic, 3–7.5 × 2–2.5 cm, ciliate, usually hairy above, pale or greyish green beneath with usually dense hairs
FLOWERS appearing as leaves expand, fragrant
CALYX to 1 mm; lobes rounded, unequal
COROLLA funnel-shaped, with a cylindric tube which gradually widens towards the top, 3–3.5 cm, white with a yellow blotch; tube longer than the lobes
OVARY densely bristly, glandular or not
STYLE finely hairy and bristly, with or without glands
CAPSULE around 1 cm
DISTRIBUTION eastern United States (Alabama, Tennessee, Georgia, Florida)
FLOWERING late spring
HARDINESS ZONE 7

167. ***Rhododendron occidentale*** A. Gray

ILLUSTRATION *Curtis's Botanical Magazine,* 5005 (1857), reprinted in Halliday, *The Illustrated Rhododendron,* pl. 111 (2001); Abrams and Ferris, *Illustrated Flora of the Pacific Northwest* 3: f. 3675 (1944); Moser, *Rhododendron: Wildarten und Hybriden,* 205 (1991); Davidian, *The Rhododendron Species* 4, pl. 38–53 (1995); Cox and Cox, *The Encyclopedia of Rhododendron Species,* 213 (1997)

HABIT shrub to 3 m; young shoots softly downy or hairless

LEAVES elliptic to oblong-lanceolate, 3–9 cm, ciliate, thinly downy above and beneath (occasionally almost hairless above and/or adpressed-bristly on the midrib beneath)

CALYX 2–5 mm, with broadly oblong, ciliate lobes

COROLLA funnel-shaped, the tube widening gradually upwards, 3.5–5 cm, white or sometimes pink, with a yellow blotch, velvety and glandular-hairy outside

STAMENS filaments hairy below the middle

OVARY glandular-hairy

STYLE variably hairy

CAPSULE 1.2–1.8 cm, bristly, sometimes glandular

DISTRIBUTION western United States (from Oregon to southern California)

FLOWERING late spring

HARDINESS ZONE 6

Recent nonauthenticated material from the United States is in cultivation.

A very variable species, which has contributed much to the modern hybrid deciduous azaleas.

168. *Rhododendron austrinum* Rehder

SYNONYMS *R. roseum* Rehder; *R. prinophyllum* Millais

ILLUSTRATION Gleason, *New Britton and Brown Illustrated Flora of the Northeastern United States and Canada* 3: 10 (1952); Davidian, *The Rhododendron Species* 4, pl. 59–69 (1995); Cox and Cox, *The Encyclopedia of Rhododendron Species,* 207 and 214–215 (1997)

HABIT to 3 m; young shoots with soft hairs intermixed with glands, somewhat adpressed-bristly towards the apex

LEAVES elliptic to oblong-obovate, 3–9 cm, finely downy on both surfaces, more densely so beneath

FLOWERS appearing before or as leaves expand

CALYX 2 mm, with unequal lobes

COROLLA funnel-shaped, to 3.5 cm; tube cylindric, abruptly expanded at the apex, usually purplish or with 5 purple stripes; lobes shorter than the tube, yellow and orange

OVARY hairy, with some glands

STYLE shortly hairy towards the base

CAPSULE 2–2.5 cm, with fine hairs, some of them glandular

DISTRIBUTION southern United States (northern Florida, Georgia, Alabama, Mississippi)

FLOWERING late spring
HARDINESS ZONE 6

Recent nonauthenticated material from the United States is in cultivation.

169. *Rhododendron luteum* (Linnaeus) Sweet

SYNONYM *R. flavum* G. Don
ILLUSTRATION *Curtis's Botanical Magazine,* 433 (1799); Davidian, *The Rhododendron Species* 4, pl. 16–19 (1995); Kneller, *The Book of Rhododendrons,* 111 (1995); Cox and Cox, *The Encyclopedia of Rhododendron Species,* 212 (1997)

R. luteum flower

R. luteum detail

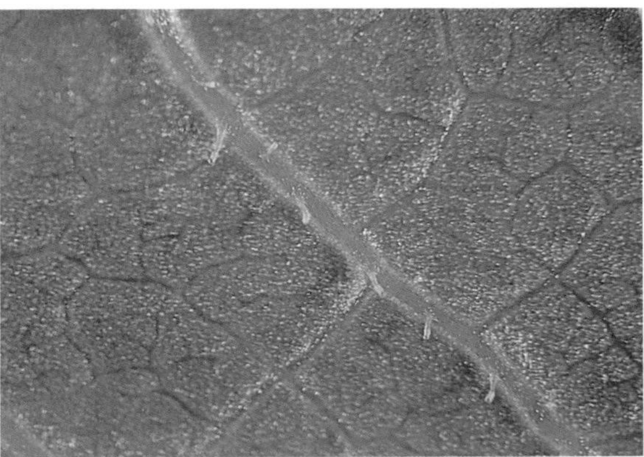

R. luteum leaf surface

Habit shrub to 4 m, usually much less; young shoots glandular-hairy, sticky
Leaves oblong to oblong-lanceolate, 5–10 cm; both surfaces sticky with adpressed, glandular bristles; young leaves with much shorter, eglandular hairs which soon fall
Calyx 2–6 mm, unequally 5-lobed, both glandular-downy and glandular-ciliate
Corolla funnel-shaped, to 3.5 cm; tube cylindric; lobes about as long as the tube, densely glandular-sticky outside
Stamens filaments hairy below the middle
Ovary glandular-hairy
Style somewhat hairy towards the base or hairless
Capsule 2–2.5 cm, soon becoming hairless
Distribution from eastern Europe to the Caucasus
Flowering late spring
Hardiness zone 5

Recent nonauthenticated material from Greece and the Caucasus is in cultivation.

A widely grown species which has been involved in hybridisation to produce the modern range of deciduous azaleas; many cultivars are grafted onto stocks of *R. luteum*.

170. *Rhododendron calendulaceum* (Michaux) Torrey

Synonyms *R. bakeri* Lemmon and McKay; *R. speciosum* (Willdenow) Sweet
Illustration *Curtis's Botanical Magazine,* 1721 (1815), reprinted in Halliday, *The Illustrated Rhododendron,* pl. 109 (2001), 2143 (1820), and 3439 (1835), as different colour variants; Gleason, *New Britton and Brown Illustrated Flora of the Northeastern United States and Canada* 3: 12 (1952); Braun, *The Woody Plants of Ohio,* 288 (1961); Moser, *Rhododendron: Wildarten und Hybriden,* 133, 137 (1991); Davidian, *The Rhododendron Species* 4, pl. 29–33 (1995); Cox and Cox, *The Encyclopedia of Rhododendron Species,* 210 (1997); Holmgren, *The Illustrated Companion to Gleason and Cronquist's Manual,* 186 (1998)
Habit much-branched shrub to 3 m; shoots downy, adpressed-bristly
Leaves elliptic to broadly elliptic or ovate-oblong, 3.5–9 cm, finely downy above, more densely so beneath
Flowers appearing as leaves expand, scarcely fragrant; flower stalks usually with glandular hairs
Calyx 1–4 mm, slightly bristly and glandular-ciliate
Corolla funnel-shaped, to 5 cm, glandular and downy outside, orange, red, or yellow, more rarely pink; tube cylindric at the base, gradually widening; lobes equalling or slightly longer than the tube

OVARY with bristles, some gland-tipped
STYLE usually hairy towards the base
CAPSULE to 2 cm, bristly, downy
DISTRIBUTION eastern United States (Virginia, North Carolina, Tennessee, Georgia)
FLOWERING late spring
HARDINESS ZONE 5

Recent nonauthenticated material from the United States is in cultivation.

Widely used in the production of azalea hybrids, contributing a particularly bright flower colour.

171. ***Rhododendron cumberlandense*** Braun

ILLUSTRATION Gleason, *New Britton and Brown Illustrated Flora of the Northeastern United States and Canada* 3: 11 (1952); Cox and Cox, *The Encyclopedia of Rhododendron Species,* 210 (1997)
Very similar to and difficult to distinguish from *R. calendulaceum,* but:
LEAVES lower surface often hairless
FLOWERS appearing after leaves expand; flower stalks usually eglandular
CALYX margins usually eglandular
DISTRIBUTION eastern United States (western Virginia, eastern Kentucky, Tennessee, northern Alabama, North Carolina, northern Georgia)
FLOWERING late spring
HARDINESS ZONE 6

172. ***Rhododendron arborescens*** Torrey

ILLUSTRATION *Addisonia* 19, pl. 617 (1935); Gleason, *New Britton and Brown Illustrated Flora of the Northeastern United States and Canada* 3: 11 (1952); Davidian, *The Rhododendron Species* 4, pl. 22–24 (1995); Cox and Cox, *The Encyclopedia of Rhododendron Species,* 206 (1997)
HABIT shrub to 3 m, rarely tree-like and then to 6 m; young shoots hairless or with a few scattered hairs; bark grey, striate
LEAVES obovate or rarely elliptic to oblong-lanceolate, 3–8 × 1.5–2.5 cm; upper surface bright green, hairless; lower surface glaucous, sparing adpressed-bristly or hairless
INFLORESCENCE BUDS narrowly ovoid, reddish brown; scales margined with fine white hairs
FLOWERS appearing as or after leaves expand, fragrant

CALYX 3–8 mm, with unequal lobes, glandular-ciliate, sometimes velvety
COROLLA funnel-shaped, 4–5 cm, white or pink, glandular-hairy outside, downy inside; lobes shorter than the tube
OVARY glandular-bristly
STYLE hairless or hairy towards the base
CAPSULE 8–18 mm, glandular-bristly
DISTRIBUTION eastern United States (from West Virginia to Tennessee, North Carolina, Georgia, and Alabama)
FLOWERING late spring
HARDINESS ZONE 4

Recent nonauthenticated material from the United States is in cultivation.

Less commonly cultivated is:
Rhododendron prinophyllum (Small) Millais
ILLUSTRATION Holmgren, *The Illustrated Companion to Gleason and Cronquist's Manual,* 185 (1998)
Similar to *R. canescens,* but:
LEAVES conspicuously ciliate, with cilia diverging from the leaf margin
PEDICELS usually glandular and relatively long
COROLLA tube relatively broad and gradually widening into limb
CAPSULE glabrous or almost so
DISTRIBUTION eastern United States

Subgenus *Therorhodion* (Maximowicz) A. Gray (*Therorhodion* (Maximowicz) Small—as genus; section *Therorhodion* Maximowicz; *Camtschaticum* series)

HABIT small, creeping shrublets
LEAVES deciduous, not scaly; margins ciliate, with small bristles which are at first gland-tipped
RACEME terminal, one- to 2-flowered; bracts borne on the flower stalks, green and leaf-like, though different in shape from the foliage leaves
CALYX 5-lobed
COROLLA very widely campanulate to almost rotate, deeply lobed, divided almost to the base between the 2 lower lobes, downy outside
STAMENS 10, declinate
OVARY downy
STYLE declinate, hairy towards the base
CAPSULE hairy
SEEDS elongate, unwinged and without appendages

There are 2 or 3 species, *R. camtschaticum* the only one commonly in cultivation. The leaves have a one-layered upper epidermis, the cuticle thin; water tissue is absent, and the lower epidermis is not papillose. Sclereids are absent.

173. *Rhododendron camtschaticum* Pallas

SYNONYM *Therorhodion camtschaticum* (Pallas) Maximowicz
ILLUSTRATION *Curtis's Botanical Magazine,* 8210 (1908), reprinted in Halliday, *The Illustrated Rhododendron,* pl. 118 (2001); Moser, *Rhododendron: Wildarten und Hybriden,* 144 (1991); Davidian, *The Rhododendron Species* 3, pl. 110 (1995); Kneller, *The Book of Rhododendrons,* 125 (1995); Robertson and McKelvie, *Scottish Rock Gardening in the 20th Century,* f. 209 (2000)
HABIT creeping shrublet to 20 cm; young shoots with long glandular hairs
LEAVES more or less obovate, 2–5 cm; midrib and margins with gland-tipped hairs which lose their glands as they age
FLOWERS solitary or in pairs; terminal bracts green, leaf-like
CALYX divided almost to the base into 5 oblong lobes to 1.8 cm, bearing glandular hairs
COROLLA very openly campanulate, to 2.5 cm, the tube divided almost to the base on the lower side, pinkish purple, hairy outside
STAMENS 10; anthers purplish brown

R. camtschaticum detail

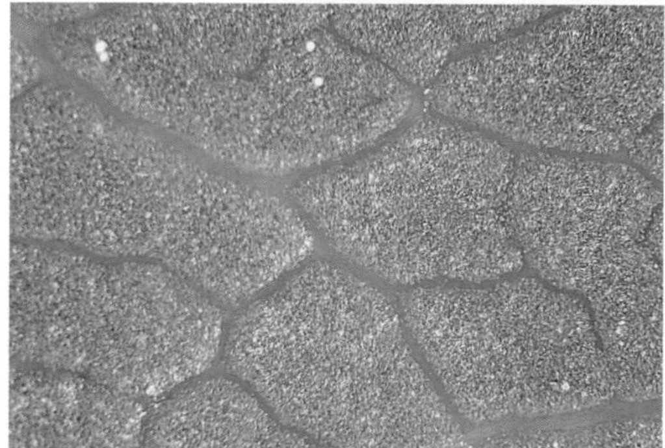

R. camtschaticum leaf surface

R. camtschaticum flower and leaf

OVARY shortly hairy
STYLE hairy towards the base
CAPSULE to 1 cm, shortly hairy
DISTRIBUTION United States (Alaska) and the adjacent parts of Russia
FLOWERING late spring
HARDINESS ZONE 5

Recent nonauthenticated material is in cultivation.

Less commonly cultivated is:
Rhododendron redowskianum Maximowicz
ILLUSTRATION *Iconographia Cormophytorum Sinicorum* 3, t. 4002 (1974)
Similar to *R. camtschaticum*, but:
CALYX c. 5 mm
COROLLA to 1.5 cm
DISTRIBUTION Russia (eastern Siberia), China (Manchuria), Korea

Subgenus *Azaleastrum* Planchon

LEAVES evergreen
INFLORESCENCES all lateral
STAMENS 5 or 10

The subgenus is divided into 2 sections.

Subgenus *Azaleastrum*

Section **Azaleastrum** (Planchon) Maximowicz (*Ovatum* series)

HABIT shrubs without scales
LEAVES evergreen
INFLORESCENCES lateral, always one-flowered; vegetative growth continued by the terminal buds of the main shoots above the inflorescences
OVARY with the style borne in a shouldered depression
STAMENS 5

There are several species, but only 2 are commonly cultivated. The whole group is characterised by the leaves, which have a 2-layered upper epidermis, the cells of the lower layer much larger than those of the upper, the cuticle about as thick as the cells of the upper layer are deep; water tissue is absent, and the cells of the lower epidermis are not papillose.

1 a Leaves rounded-ovate to broadly elliptic .... **174. *R. ovatum***
b Leaves narrowly elliptic to lanceolate .... **175. *R. leptothrium***

174. *Rhododendron ovatum* (Lindley) Maximowicz
SYNONYM *R. bachii* Léveillé
ILLUSTRATION *Curtis's Botanical Magazine,* 5064 (1858), reprinted in Halliday, *The Illustrated Rhododendron,* pl. 104 (2001); *Iconographia Cormophytorum Sinicorum* 3, t. 4263–4264 (1974); Feng, *Rhododendrons of China* 2, pl. 108, 1–2 (1992)
HABIT shrub to 4 m; young shoots minutely downy, sometimes slightly glandular
LEAVES broadly ovate or ovate-elliptic, about 2 × as long as broad, hairless except for a few hairs along the midrib above
RACEME lateral, one-flowered
CALYX 4–7 mm, 5-lobed, hairless or ciliate, and/or glandular
COROLLA very openly campanulate, with a very short tube, 4–5 cm, white, pink, or pale purple, spotted above, hairless or the tube finely downy outside
STAMENS 5; filaments hairy towards the base
OVARY bristly and glandular
STYLE hairless
CAPSULE to 7 mm
DISTRIBUTION central and southern China, Taiwan
FLOWERING spring

HARDINESS ZONE 7

Classic wild-collected material is available under *Kingdon-Ward 6335.*

175. *Rhododendron leptothrium* Balfour and Forrest

ILLUSTRATION *Curtis's Botanical Magazine,* n.s., 502 (1967); *Iconographia Cormophytorum Sinicorum* 3, t. 4265 (1974); Feng, *Rhododendrons of China,* 1, pl. 91, 1–4 (1988); *Rhododendrons with Camellias and Magnolias* 43: f. 10 (1991); Davidian, *The Rhododendron Species* 3, pl. 107 (1992); *The Rhododendron Handbook,* f. 13 (1997); Cox and Cox, *The Encyclopedia of Rhododendron Species,* 2 (1997)

HABIT shrub to 8 m; young shoots finely downy

LEAVES narrowly elliptic to lanceolate, 3.5–12 cm, 2–4 × as long as broad

INFLORESCENCE BUDS lateral, one-flowered, clustered near the ends of the leafy shoots

CALYX 5-lobed; lobes 6–8 mm (rarely less), hairless or fringed with fine, sometimes glandular hairs

COROLLA very openly campanulate, to 5 cm across, pink to magenta-purple with darker spots, the tube sometimes finely downy outside

STAMENS filaments hairy towards the base

OVARY bristly with glandular hairs

STYLE hairless

CAPSULE 6–8 mm

DISTRIBUTION western China (northwestern Yunnan, adjacent Sichuan, and Xizang), northeastern Myanmar

FLOWERING spring

HARDINESS ZONE 7

Recent nonauthenticated material from China (Yunnan) is in cultivation.

Less commonly cultivated are:

Rhododendron hongkongense Hutchinson

ILLUSTRATION *Iconographia Cormophytorum Sinicorum* 3, t. 4266 (1974)

Keying out to *R. leptothrium,* but:

COROLLA ground colour white

DISTRIBUTION China (Guangdong, Hong Kong)

Probably not hardy anywhere in Britain.

Rhododendron vialii Delavay and Franchet
ILLUSTRATION *Iconographia Cormophytorum Sinicorum* 3, t. 4267 (1974)
Unlike other species of the section, as below:
COROLLA tube much longer than the lobes, cylindric and widening only slightly
DISTRIBUTION China (southern Yunnan), Laos, Vietnam

Probably not hardy anywhere in Britain.

Subgenus *Azaleastrum*

Section ***Choniastrum*** Franchet (*Stamineum* series)

HABIT shrubs without scales
LEAVES evergreen
INFLORESCENCES lateral, one- or more-flowered; vegetative growth continued by the terminal bud above the inflorescences
STAMENS 10
OVARY tapering into the style
SEEDS elongate, unwinged and without appendages

Another small group, with 3 species in cultivation. The leaves have a one-layered upper epidermis, the cuticle as thick as the cells are deep; water tissue is absent, and the cells of the lower epidermis are not papillose.

1 a Corolla tube about a third the total length of the corolla .... **178. *R. latoucheae***
b Corolla tube about half the total length of the corolla 2
2 a Corolla 4.5–6 cm; stamens only slightly projecting beyond the corolla lobes . . **177. *R. moulmainense***
b Corolla 2.5–3.5 cm; stamens projecting well beyond the corolla lobes .... **176. *R. stamineum***

176. *Rhododendron stamineum* Franchet

ILLUSTRATION *Curtis's Botanical Magazine,* 8601 (1915); *Iconographia Cormophytorum Sinicorum* 3, t. 4268 (1974); Fang, *Sichuan Rhododendron of China,* 322–324 (1986); Feng, *Rhododendrons of China* 2, pl. 115: 1–6 (1992); Cox and Cox, *The Encyclopedia of Rhododendron Species,* 7 (1997)
HABIT shrub or small tree to 13 m; young shoots hairless
LEAVES elliptic to oblanceolate, 6–14 cm, 3–3.5 × as long as broad, completely hairless
INFLORESCENCES lateral, 3- to 5-flowered (rarely to 8-flowered) at the ends of leafy branches
CALYX hairless, with 5 minute lobes
COROLLA funnel-shaped, 2.5–3.5 cm, with a narrow tube and spreading or reflexed lobes, white or pink, with a yellow blotch, hairless
STAMENS filaments slightly hairy towards the base
OVARY hairless or slightly hairy
STYLE hairless
CAPSULE 2.5–4 cm, tapered at each end, often curved

DISTRIBUTION western China (Yunnan, Sichuan, Guizhou, Hunan, Hubei, Guangxi, Anhui)

FLOWERING spring

HARDINESS ZONE 9

177. ***Rhododendron moulmainense*** Hooker

SYNONYMS *R. mackenzieanum* Forrest; *R. oxyphyllum* Franchet; *R. stenaulum* Balfour and Forrest

ILLUSTRATION *Curtis's Botanical Magazine,* 4904 (1856), reprinted in Halliday, *The Illustrated Rhododendron,* 105 (2001) and 9656 (1944); *Rhododendrons with Camellias and Magnolias* 43: f. 10 (1991); Feng, *Rhododendrons of China* 2, pl. 117: 1–5 (1992); Cox and Cox, *The Encyclopedia of Rhododendron Species,* 6 (1997)

HABIT shrub or small tree to 15 m; young shoots hairless; bark greenish brown, very finely striate

LEAVES 6–17 cm, 3–3.5 × as long as broad, hairless or rarely with a few marginal bristles

CALYX minute, 5-lobed, hairless

COROLLA 4.6–6.2 cm, white, pink, violet, or magenta, with a yellow basal blotch, hairless; tube narrow and broad; lobes spreading and much longer than the tube

STAMENS filaments hairy below

OVARY AND STYLE hairless

CAPSULE to 7 cm

DISTRIBUTION eastern and southeastern Asia (widespread from India and Thailand to China and Malaysia)

FLOWERING spring

HARDINESS ZONE 10

Classic wild-origin material is available under *Kingdon-Ward 20679, Lauener* (without number), and *Page 10230, 10273, 10276.* Recent nonauthenticated material from Hong Kong, Taiwan, and Malaysia is in cultivation.

A very variable species, but not clearly divisible into segregate species.

178. ***Rhododendron latoucheae*** Franchet

SYNONYM *R. wilsonae* Hemsley and Wilson

ILLUSTRATION *Iconographia Cormophytorum Sinicorum* 3, t. 4271 (1974); Cox and Cox, *The Encyclopedia of Rhododendron Species,* 5–6 (1997)

HABIT shrub to 7 m; young shoots hairless

Leaves elliptic or obovate to elliptic-lanceolate, 5–10 × 1.8–5 cm, hairless
Calyx hairless, with 5 minute lobes
Corolla 3.5–4 cm, the tube forming about a third of the total length, pink with darker spots
Stamens filaments hairy below the middle
Ovary and style hairless
Capsule 3–4 cm, curved
Distribution China (Hubei, Guizhou, Hunan, Guangdong, Fujian, Jiangxi, Zhejiang), Japan (Ryukyu Islands)
Flowering spring
Hardiness zone 9

Very similar to *R. moulmainense* but with a shorter corolla tube.

Less commonly cultivated are:

Rhododendron championae Hooker
Illustration *Iconographia Cormophytorum Sinicorum* 3, t. 4275 (1974)
Unlike other species of the section, as below:
Mature leaves ciliate and with hairs on the midribs
Distribution China (Guangxi, Guangdong, Fujian, Zhejiang, Hunan, Jiangxi, Hong Kong)

Rhododendron hancockii Hemsley
Illustration *Hooker's Icones Plantarum* 24, t. 2381 (1895); *Iconographia Cormophytorum Sinicorum* 3, t. 4273 (1974)
Keying out to *R. latoucheae,* with which it is broadly similar, but:
Inflorescences generally one-flowered
Ovary with silky hairs
Distribution China (Yunnan, Guangxi)

Subgenus *Candidastrum* (Sleumer) Philipson and Philipson (*Albiflorum* series)

HABIT shrubs without scales
LEAVES deciduous
INFLORESCENCES lateral, one- to 2-flowered, scattered along the shoots; vegetative growth continued by the terminal bud above the inflorescences
STAMENS 10
SEEDS elongate, unwinged, with very short appendages at each end

Rhododendron albiflorum is the only species. The leaves have a one-layered upper epidermis, the cuticle thin; water tissue is absent, and the cells of the lower epidermis are not prolonged into papillae.

179. *Rhododendron albiflorum* Hooker

ILLUSTRATION *Curtis's Botanical Magazine,* 3670 (1839), reprinted in Halliday, *The Illustrated Rhododendron,* pl. 117 (2001); Abrams and Ferris, *Illustrated Flora of the Pacific Northwest* 3, t. 3674 (1944); Cox and Cox, *The Encyclopedia of Rhododendron Species,* 8 (1997)
HABIT to 2 m; shoots hairy and glandular when young
LEAVES oblong-elliptic or oblong or obovate, 2.5–7 cm, hairy above when young, hairless beneath except for long, adpressed hairs on the midrib
RACEME one- to 2-flowered, axillary
FLOWERS appearing after leaves expand, almost completely regular
CALYX 1–1.2 cm, with triangular lobes, glandular-downy, with scattered long brown hairs
COROLLA openly campanulate, to 2 cm, white, rarely spotted with yellow or orange
STAMENS 10
OVARY glandular-hairy
STYLE hairy in the lower half
CAPSULE up to 8 mm
DISTRIBUTION western North America (from British Columbia to Oregon and Colorado)
FLOWERING late spring
HARDINESS ZONE 4

Recent nonauthenticated material from the United States is in cultivation.

R. albiflorum
flower and leaf

R. albiflorum detail

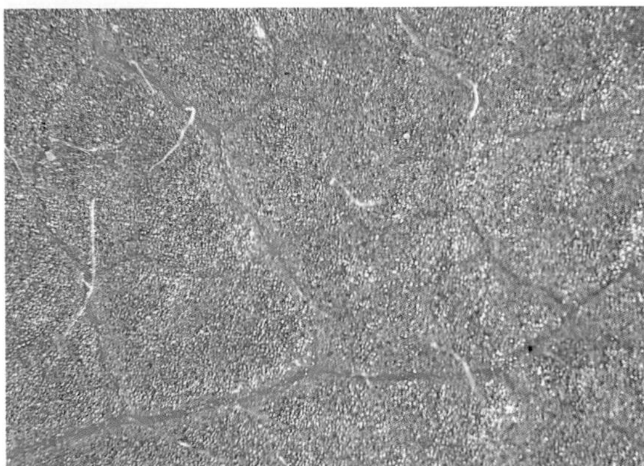

R. albiflorum leaf surface

Subgenus *Mumeazalea* (Makino) Philipson and Philipson (*Semibarbatum* series)

HABIT shrubs
LEAVES deciduous, hairless except for a few bristles on the main veins
RACEME lateral, one-flowered
CALYX short
COROLLA 5-lobed, very openly campanulate
STAMENS 5 (3 with long, hairless filaments and oblong anthers, the other 2 shorter with hairy filaments and almost spherical anthers)
SEEDS unwinged, with a small appendage at the apex and a larger one at the other end

Rhododendron semibarbatum is the only species. The leaves have a one-layered upper epidermis, the cuticle thin; water tissue is absent, and the cells of the lower epidermis are not prolonged into papillae.

180. *Rhododendron semibarbatum* Maximowicz

ILLUSTRATION *Curtis's Botanical Magazine,* 9147 (1926), reprinted in Halliday, *The Illustrated Rhododendron,* 117 (2001); Kneller, *The Book of Rhododendrons,* 121 (1995)
HABIT shrub to 3 m; young shoots downy, glandular-hairy, ultimately hairless
LEAVES elliptic to elliptic-oblong or elliptic-ovate, 1.8–5 cm, minutely scolloped, dark green and hairless above except for short hairs along the midrib, pale green and hairless beneath except for sparse bristles on the midrib and on a few of the main veins
FLOWERS appearing after leaves expand
CALYX to 2 mm; lobes downy, glandular-bristly
COROLLA widely campanulate, to 2 cm, yellowish or white flushed with pink, with red dots
STAMENS 5 (3 with long, hairless filaments and oblong anthers, the other 2 shorter with hairy filaments and almost spherical anthers)
OVARY glandular-bristly
STYLE hairless
CAPSULE to 4 mm, glandular-bristly
DISTRIBUTION central and southern Japan
FLOWERING late spring
HARDINESS ZONE 6

Recent nonauthenticated material from Japan is in cultivation.

R. semibarbatum flower and leaf

R. semibarbatum detail

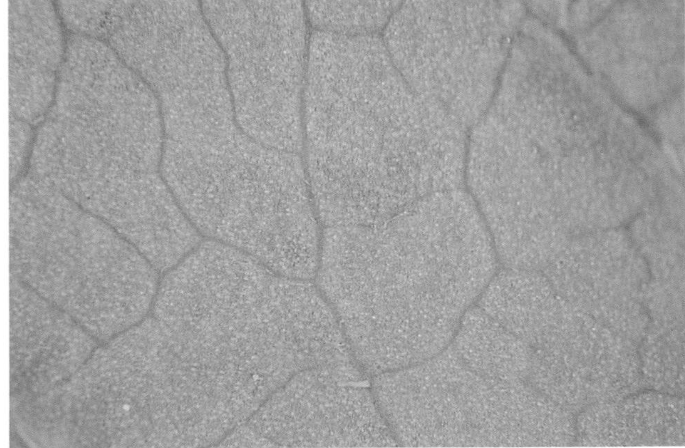

R. semibarbatum leaf surface

Subgenus ***Rhododendron*** (subgenus *Maddenodendron* Spethmann 1980a, 163)

HABIT shrubs with scales on at least some of the leaves, young shoots, flower stalks, calyces, or corollas

The subgenus is divided into 3 sections, one of which, section *Vireya* (Blume) Copeland/subgenus *Vireya* Blume, contains no species widely cultivated in northwestern Europe.

Subgenus *Rhododendron*

Section *Rhododendron*

HABIT small to large shrubs or small trees

SCALES present on at least some parts, usually entire, more rarely undulate, crenulate, or vesicular

RACEME usually terminal, occasionally lateral as well, very rarely all lateral, with few to many flowers

CALYX minute to large and well developed

COROLLA variously shaped, usually 5-lobed, more rarely 6- to 10-lobed

STAMENS 10–27, rarely fewer

OVARY usually scaly

STYLE hairless or hairy and/or scaly

SEEDS elongate, winged or unwinged, with or without appendages at each end, very rarely these appendages both narrow and tail-like

1a Leaves very densely hairy beneath, the hairs completely obscuring the small, golden scales .... Subsection ***Edgeworthia*** (p. 264)

b Leaves hairless or variously hairy beneath, but the hairs never obscuring the scales 2

2a Style thin, declinate or straight, never markedly deflexed, usually longer than the generally declinate stamens 3

b Style thick, markedly deflexed from the apex of the ovary (occasionally straightening after pollination), usually shorter than the radially arranged stamens 24

3a Lateral inflorescences present; terminal inflorescences present or not 4

b All inflorescences terminal 10

4a Corolla lobes shorter than the tube 5

b Corolla lobes longer than the tube (sometimes only slightly so) 7

5a Corolla funnel-shaped, downy outside; calyx clearly lobed, the lobes 2–3 mm .... Subsection ***Virgata*** (p. 368)

b Corolla tubular, hairless outside; calyx a mere rim 6

6a Flowers erect; stamens and style projecting beyond the corolla lobes; leaves downy and bristly above .... Subsection ***Scabrifolia*** (p. 306)

b Flowers pendulous; stamens and style not projecting beyond the corolla lobes; leaves hairless .... Subsection ***Cinnabarina*** (p. 358)

7a Terminal inflorescences usually present as well as lateral inflorescences; corolla very openly funnel-shaped, very bilaterally symmetric .... Subsection ***Triflora*** (p. 289)

b All inflorescences lateral; corolla funnel-shaped, usually less bilaterally symmetric 8

8 a Corolla yellow; leaves with prominent drip tips .... Subsection ***Triflora*** (p. 289)
b Corolla white to pink; leaves without prominent drip tips 9
9 a Corolla hairy outside, at least near the base; each inflorescence one-flowered
.... Subsection ***Rhodorastra*** (p. 343)
b Corolla hairless outside; each inflorescence 2- or more-flowered .... Subsection ***Scabrifolia*** (p. 306)
10 a Corolla lobes longer than the tube 11
b Corolla lobes shorter than or rarely almost as long as the tube 13
11 a Corolla to 10 mm, white, unspotted and unblotched, glabrous within . . Subsection ***Micrantha*** (p. 371)
b Corolla larger, variously coloured (if white, then spotted or blotched), downy to hairy within 12
12 a Flower stalks in line with the ovary and style; scales undulate ...... Subsection ***Lapponica*** (p. 320)
b Flower stalks making an angle with the ovary and style; scales crenulate
.... Subsection ***Saluenensia*** (p. 347)
13 a Corolla 4 cm or more .... Subsection ***Maddenia*** (p. 267)
b Corolla 6–35 mm 14
14 a Corolla campanulate to tubular-campanulate, the sides of the tube parallel or almost so 15
b Corolla funnel-shaped, flaring from the base, the sides of the tube diverging 21
15 a Scales of 2 colours, golden and dark brown, standing out clearly against the whitish lower leaf surface .... Subsection ***Glauca*** (p. 379)
b Scales not generally of 2 colours, not as above 16
16 a Calyx reduced to a rim, sometimes slightly undulate, less than 2 mm 17
b Calyx conspicuously 5-lobed; lobes more than 2 mm 19
17 a Corolla fleshy; nectar copious, forming 5 large drops within the base of the corolla tube
.... Subsection ***Cinnabarina*** (p. 358)
b Corolla not fleshy; nectar a mere sticky smear around the base of the ovary 18
18 a Inflorescences one- to 3-flowered; stamens and style projecting beyond the corolla lobes
.... Subsection ***Monantha*** (p. 287)
b Inflorescences many-flowered; stamens and style not projecting beyond the corolla lobes
.... Subsection ***Rhododendron*** (p. 340)
19 a Leaf margins, leaf stalks, and young shoots without bristle-like hairs
.... Subsection ***Tephropepla*** (p. 363)
b Leaf margins, leaf stalks, and young shoots with bristle-like hairs 20
20 a Ovary tapering smoothly into the style .... Subsection ***Moupinensia*** (p. 285)
b Ovary with a shouldered depression at the apex, into which the style is set
.... Subsection ***Maddenia*** (p. 267)
21 a Corolla downy outside; small shrublets .... Subsection ***Uniflora*** (p. 353)
b Corolla scaly outside; tall shrubs 22

22 a Calyx rim-like, not lobed, or, if slightly lobed, not margined with bristle-like hairs
. . . . Subsection ***Heliolepida*** (p. 313)

b Calyx well developed, clearly lobed; lobes margined with bristle-like hairs 23

23 a Style downy; corolla white to pink with deeper pink or dark red spots . Subsection ***Lapponica*** (p. 320)

b Style hairless or scaly; corolla white to pink with greenish or yellowish spots
. . . . Subsection ***Caroliniana*** (p. 318)

24 a Stamens 12–16 . . . . Subsection ***Camelliiflora*** (p. 377)

b Stamens (5–)10 25

25 a Inflorescence a raceme with a long, conspicuous axis, not at all umbel-like; corolla greenish white . . . . Subsection ***Afghanica*** (p. 400)

b Inflorescence an umbel-like raceme with a short axis, or flowers solitary; corolla usually coloured, rarely greenish white 26

26 a Scales of 2 colours, golden and dark brown, standing out clearly against the whitish lower leaf surface . . . . Subsection ***Glauca*** (p. 379)

b Scales and lower leaf surface not as above 27

27 a Scales vesicular 28

b Scales clearly rimmed, the rims sometimes upturned 30

28 a Corolla whitish-bloomed, pink to purple . . . . Subsection ***Campylogyna*** (p. 386)

b Corolla not whitish-bloomed, yellow to white, sometimes flushed with pink 29

29 a Ovary tapering smoothly into the style; flower stalks shorter than the corollas
. . . . Subsection ***Boothia*** (p. 373)

b Ovary with a shouldered depression at the top, into which the style is inserted; flower stalks longer than the corollas . . . . Subsection ***Trichoclada*** (p. 395)

30 a Scales crenulate . . . . Subsection ***Baileya*** (p. 393)

b Scales entire 31

31 a Ovary tapering smoothly into the style . . . . Subsection ***Boothia*** (p. 373)

b Ovary with a shouldered depression at the top, into which the style is inserted 32

32 a Tall shrubs, usually more than 1 m; lower surface of leaves and corolla whitish-bloomed; racemes with 4 or more flowers . . . . Subsection ***Genestieriana*** (p. 389)

b Small shrubs, usually much less than 1 m; lower surface of leaves and corolla not whitish-bloomed; racemes with 1–3 flowers . . . . Subsection ***Lepidota*** (p. 390)

Subgenus *Rhododendron*

Section *Rhododendron*

Subsection *Edgeworthia* (Hutchinson) Sleumer (*Edgeworthii* series; section *Bullatorhodion* Spethmann 1980a, 166)

LEAVES densely hairy, the hairs completely obscuring the small, golden scales (though scales generally visible on flower stalk and calyx)
STAMENS 10, declinate or rather radially arranged
STYLE declinate or abruptly deflexed at the base
CAPSULE hairy
SEEDS elongate, winged and with appendages at each end

The subsection contains 3 species, 2 of which are cultivated. All have a very dense hair covering on the lower surface of the leaves, and this tends to completely obscure the small, golden scales; the latter are more easily seen on the flower stalk, calyx, and corolla. *Rhododendron pendulum* is an unusual species in that its leaves are revolute in bud (a feature not found otherwise in subgenus *Rhododendron*), and it has a sharply deflexed style, similar to those found in subsections *Boothia* and *Afghanica*. However, in general appearance and the balance of characteristics, it is related to *R. edgeworthii*. The other species of the subsection, *R. seinghkuense* Kingdon-Ward, has been in cultivation but is very difficult to grow and propagate; it is similar to *R. pendulum*, but the leaves are shortly acuminate and the corolla is bright yellow.

The leaves have a 2- or 3-layered upper epidermis, the cells all similar in size, the cuticle thin to half as thick as the cells are deep; water tissue is absent, and the cells of the lower epidermis are prolonged into papillae. Sclereids are present in the leaf tissue.

1 a Corolla 3.5–6 cm; style declinate, exceeding the declinate stamens .... **181. *R. edgeworthii***
b Corolla 1.5–2 cm; style sharply deflexed, shorter than the nondeclinate stamens . **182. *R. pendulum***

181. *Rhododendron edgeworthii* Hooker
SYNONYM *R. bullatum* Franchet
ILLUSTRATION Hooker, *Rhododendrons of the Sikkim Himalaya*, t. 21 (1851); *Flore des Serres*, ser. 1, 8: t. 797–798 (1851–1852); *Curtis's Botanical Magazine*, 4936 (1856), reprinted in Halliday, *The Illustrated Rhododendron*, pl. 21 (2001); *Gartenflora* 5, t. 170 (1956); Hara, *Photo-Album of Plants of Eastern Himalaya*, t. 164 (1968); Cox, *Dwarf Rhododendrons*, t. 14 (1973); *Iconographia Cormophytorum Sinicorum* 3, t. 4017 (1974); *Notes from the Royal Botanic Garden Edinburgh* 39: 19 (1980); Davidian, *The Rhododendron Species* 1, pl. 20 (1982); Feng, *Rhododendrons of China* 1, pl. 56: 1–2 (1988);

R. edgeworthii flower and leaf

R. edgeworthii detail

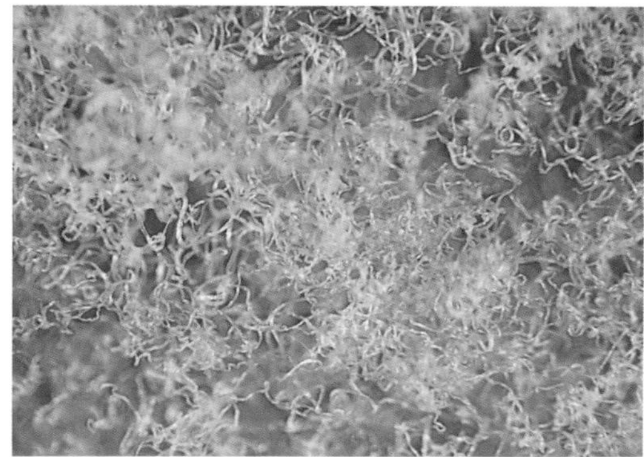

R. edgeworthii leaf surface

Kneller, *The Book of Rhododendrons,* 71 (1995); Cox and Cox, *The Encyclopedia of Rhododendron Species,* 247–248 (1997)

HABIT epiphytic shrub to 2.5 m; young shoots and leaves with orange to pale beige hairs

LEAVES flat or curved in bud; upper surface wrinkled when mature

RACEME with 2–3 fragrant flowers

CALYX 1.1–1.4 cm, clearly 5-lobed

COROLLA broadly funnel-shaped, 3.5–6.5 cm, white, sometimes flushed with pink, usually with a yellowish blotch at the base, scaly outside

STAMENS 10

STYLE declinate, exceeding the stamens, hairy and/or scaly towards the base

SEEDS winged

DISTRIBUTION Himalaya, southwestern China

FLOWERING late spring

HARDINESS ZONE 9

Wild-collected material is available under *Sino-British Expedition to Cangshan 207, 607.* Recent nonauthenticated material from Bhutan and Yunnan is also in cultivation.

Material grown under *Kingdon-Ward 6793* is probably *R. edgeworthii,* but the herbarium material under this number is *R. seinghkuense,* a species not available in general cultivation.

182. *Rhododendron pendulum* Hooker

ILLUSTRATION Hooker, *Rhododendrons of the Sikkim Himalaya,* t. 14 (1851); *Flore des Serres,* ser. 1, 7: t. 662 (1851–1852); Cox, *Dwarf Rhododendrons,* t. 15 (1973); *Notes from the Royal Botanic Garden Edinburgh* 39: 19 (1980); Davidian, *The Rhododendron Species* 1, pl. 21 (1982); Cox and Cox, *The Encyclopedia of Rhododendron Species,* 248 (1997)

Similar to *R. edgeworthii,* but:

HABIT smaller, with whitish to beige hairs

LEAVES revolute in bud; upper surface smooth and shining

COROLLA almost radially symmetric, 1.5–2.2 cm

STYLE sharply deflexed from the base, shorter than the stamens, usually with a few hairs and scales at the base

DISTRIBUTION Himalaya

FLOWERING spring

HARDINESS ZONE 8

Classic wild-collected material is available under *Ludlow, Sherriff, and Taylor 6660.* Recent nonauthenticated material from India (Sikkim) and Nepal is also in cultivation.

Subgenus *Rhododendron*

Section *Rhododendron*

Subsection *Maddenia* (Hutchinson) Sleumer (*Maddenii* series)

HABIT shrubs or small trees, often epiphytic in the wild
LEAVES evergreen, scaly
RACEME terminal, with 1–11 usually fragrant flowers
CALYX very variable, from rim-like to conspicuously 5-lobed
COROLLA mostly large, 5- or more-lobed, usually funnel-campanulate, more rarely campanulate, the tube often compressed and fluted with 5 grooves
STAMENS (8–)10–27, declinate
OVARY 5- to 12-celled, scaly, either tapering smoothly into the style or with the style inserted in a shouldered depression at the apex
CAPSULE scaly
SEEDS elongate, winged and with appendages at each end

A large and rather variable subsection, which might with advantage be divided into 4 subsections: a) *R. maddenii* itself; b) *R. megacalyx;* c) species with very large flowers and the midrib raised on the upper surface of the leaf, as with *R. lindleyi* and *R. dalhousiae;* and d) the rest of the species. Even this last group is somewhat variable, containing a number of rather small-flowered species (for example, *R. ciliatum*) as well as many larger-flowered species. However, they are kept together here because the groups are similar in overall morphology as well as in terms of their cultivation requirements. Most are from low elevations in the Himalayan and Chinese valleys, or from areas to the south of the Himalaya, and so are either not hardy or are marginally hardy in Britain. Because of their epiphytic habit, they tend to be rather gawky shrubs with long stems and a few leaves and flowers; they are usually cultivated in conservatories behind other vegetation.

Anatomically the leaves of this group are rather uniform. They have a 2-, 3-, or rarely 4-layered upper epidermis, the cells of the lower layers larger than those of the upper layer, the cuticle half as thick to as thick as the cells of the upper layer are deep; water tissue is absent, and the cells of the lower epidermis are prolonged into papillae. Sclereids are present in the leaf tissue of all species.

1a Stamens 15 or more; ovary 10- to 12-celled . . . . **183. *R. maddenii***
b Stamens 10; ovary 5- to 7-celled 2
2a Flower stalks and calyx whitish-bloomed, the flower stalks recurved and spreading in fruit; capsule not exceeding the persistent calyx . . . . **184. *R. megacalyx***

b Flower stalks and calyx not bloomed, the flower stalks not recurved in fruit; capsule clearly exceeding whatever persists of the calyx 3

3 a Leaf with the main vein raised towards the base on the upper surface; calyx conspicuous, deeply lobed 4

b Leaf with the main vein not at all raised on the upper surface; calyx inconspicuous or conspicuous . . 7

4 a Leaves with the secondary and tertiary veins forming a conspicuous network over the whole surface beneath; scales very unequal, the smaller more or less rimless, the larger with broad, usually ascending, irregular rims . . . . **185. *R. nuttallii***

b Leaves and their scales not as above 5

5 a Flower stalks and calyx lobes downy (scales may also be present) . . . . **186. *R. dalhousiae***

b Flower stalks scaly but not downy; calyx lobes sometimes ciliate, otherwise hairless 6

6 a Calyx lobes ciliate with fine hairs . . . . **187. *R. lindleyi***

b Calyx lobes margined with scales . . . . **188. *R. taggianum***

7 a Style inserted into a shouldered depression on top of the ovary 8

b Ovary smoothly tapering into the style 14

8 a Corolla yellow 9

b Corolla white, often flushed with pink, often with a yellow blotch on the upper lobes towards the base 11

9 a Calyx small and disc-like, at most 2 mm; corolla with scales all over the outer surface . . . . **192. *R. burmanicum***

b Calyx conspicuous, clearly lobed, 5–9 mm; corolla not or very sparsely scaly 10

10 a Leaves scolloped in the upper half; lower surface green, with distant scales . . **191. *R. fletcherianum***

b Leaves entire; lower surface brown, with contiguous to overlapping scales . . . **190. *R. valentinianum***

11 a Calyx more than 5 mm; lobes more or less equal, leaf-like; corolla to 4 cm; style completely scaleless . . . . **189. *R. ciliatum***

b Calyx less than 4 mm, or, if longer, the lobes markedly unequal and not herbaceous; corolla usually longer than 5 cm; style scaly at least near the base 12

12 a Leaves not more than 2 cm wide; margins and leaf stalk usually persistently bristly . . . . **193. *R. formosum***

b Leaves more than 2 cm wide; margins and leaf stalks not bristly when mature (though often so when young) 13

13 a Calyx without a persistent fringe of bristles . . . . **195. *R. dendricola***

b Calyx with a persistent fringe of bristles . . . . **194. *R. johnstoneanum***

14 a Corolla scaly outside only along the upper part of the tube; lobes with crisped margins . . . . **200. *R. veitchianum***

b Corolla tube scaly all over the outside; lobes not crisped 15

15 a Leaves persistently scaly above; corolla pink throughout . . . . **197. *R. carneum***

b Leaves not scaly above when mature; corolla white or white flushed with pink, though often completely pink in bud 16

16 a Corolla downy but not scaly outside at the base of the tube .... **196. *R. ciliicalyx***
b Corolla both downy and scaly outside at the base of the tube 17
17 a Leaves mostly obovate .... **198. *R. roseatum***
b Leaves mostly elliptic .... **199. *R. pachypodum***

183. *Rhododendron maddenii* Hooker

HABIT shrub to 2 m, often epiphytic; bark greenish brown, shredding in long strips
LEAVES elliptic to broadly obovate, 6–18 cm, densely scaly beneath, the surface often brownish
RACEME with 1–7 fragrant flowers
CALYX 5–16 mm, 5-lobed
COROLLA white, often flushed with pink or purplish, rarely wholly pink, usually with a yellow blotch at the base, at first narrowly funnel-shaped, later wider, often with more than 5 lobes, usually 6–10 cm; outside of the tube and bases of the lobes scaly
STAMENS 15–27
OVARY 8- to 12-celled
CAPSULE 1–2 cm
DISTRIBUTION Himalaya, Myanmar, southwestern China, Vietnam
FLOWERING late spring
HARDINESS ZONES 9–10

A widespread species, divisible into 2 rather overlapping subspecies.

R. maddenii subsp. ***maddenii***

SYNONYMS *R. brachysiphon* Hutchinson; *R. polyandrum* Hutchinson
ILLUSTRATION Hooker, *Rhododendrons of the Sikkim Himalaya,* t. 18 (1851); *Flore des Serres,* ser. 1, 9: t. 912 (1853–1854); *Revue Horticole,* ser. 4, 4: t. 16 (1855); *Curtis's Botanical Magazine,* 4805 (1854) and 5002 (1857); *Iconographia Cormophytorum Sinicorum* 3, t. 4020 (1974); Cox and Cox, *The Encyclopedia of Rhododendron Species,* 288 (1997)
LEAVES often obovate, less than 5.5 cm broad, usually 6–15 × 2.8–5.5 cm
STAMENS filaments often hairless
CAPSULE ovoid-spherical, rounded to the apex
DISTRIBUTION Himalaya

Wild-collected material is available under *Bailey 2, Cooper 3601, Cox and Hutchison 438, Ludlow, Sherriff, and Taylor 6754, Ludlow, Sherriff, and Elliott 12248,* and *Nishioka* (without number). Recent nonauthenticated material from India (Sikkim) and Bhutan is also in cultivation.

Somewhat less hardy than subsp. *crassum* and usually requiring glasshouse protection in Europe. A parent of a few hybrids, most hardier than subsp. *maddenii* itself, including 'Royal Flush' and 'Rose Mangles' (both × *R. cinnabarinum* subsp. *cinnabarinum*) and 'Nonesuch' (× *R. cinnabarinum* subsp. *cinnabarinum* 'Roylei').

R. maddenii subsp. ***crassum*** (Franchet) Cullen

SYNONYMS *R. crassum* Franchet; *R. odoriferum* Hutchinson

ILLUSTRATION *Curtis's Botanical Magazine,* 8212 (1908) and 9673 (1946); *Notes from the Royal Botanic Garden Edinburgh* 39: 19 (1980); Feng, *Rhododendrons of China* 2, pl. 57: 1–3 (1992); Cox and Cox, *The Encyclopedia of Rhododendron Species,* 288–289 (1997)

LEAVES usually more or less elliptic, usually 9–18 × 5.5–8 cm wide

STAMENS filaments often hairy

CAPSULE oblong-cylindric, abruptly rounded to almost truncate at the apex

DISTRIBUTION northeastern India (Manipur), Myanmar, western and southwestern China, Vietnam

Mostly classic wild-collected material is available under *Forrest 15887, 24496, 24747, 25586, 25574, 25629, 28312, Gothenburg Botanic Garden* (without number), *Kingdon-Ward 8400, 7136, Ludlow, Sherriff, and Taylor 6676,* and *Yü 16694, 21031.* Recent nonauthenticated material from Yunnan and Vietnam is also in cultivation.

Some plants of this subspecies (mainly from Yunnan) are rather more hardy and survive out of doors in the British Isles as far north as Edinburgh. Not much used in hybridisation, but a cross with a scaleless species, *R. griersonianum,* is known as 'Pan'.

184. *Rhododendron megacalyx* Balfour and Kingdon-Ward

ILLUSTRATION *Curtis's Botanical Magazine,* 9326 (1933); *Iconographia Cormophytorum Sinicorum* 3: 4022 (1974); *Notes from the Royal Botanic Garden Edinburgh* 39: 19 (1980); Cox and Cox, *The Encyclopedia of Rhododendron Species,* 295 (1997)

HABIT shrub to 5 m; young shoots glaucous

LEAVES elliptic to obovate, 10–16 cm; upper surface hairless; lower surface with dense, golden or brownish scales of 2 kinds, the smaller rimless and sunk in pits, the larger with rims and less deeply sunk

CALYX 2.2–3 cm, cup-like, lobed for half to almost its complete length, hairless, scaleless, glaucous, enlarging and becoming papery in fruit

Corolla funnel-campanulate, 6.5–9.5 cm, white or cream, rarely flushed with pink or purplish; tube very sparsely scaly outside
Stamens 10; filaments hairy below
Ovary densely scaly, tapering into the style, which is scaly in the lower part
Capsule 2–2.5 cm, scaly, shorter to longer than the persistent calyx; fruit stalks spreading or reflexed
Distribution northeastern India, western China (northwestern and western Yunnan, southeastern Xizang), northeastern Myanmar
Flowering late spring
Hardiness zone 9

Classic wild-collected material is available under *Kingdon-Ward 20836.*

A very distinctive species, not generally available in cultivation.

185. *Rhododendron nuttallii* Booth
Synonyms *R. sinonuttallii* Balfour and Forrest; *R. goreri* Davidian
Illustration *Flore des Serres,* ser. 2, 3: t. 1326–1327 (1858); *Curtis's Botanical Magazine,* 5146 (1859); *Illustration Horticole* 6, t. 208 (1859); *Revue Horticole,* 348 (1917); *Iconographia Cormophytorum Sinicorum* 3, t. 4025 (1974); *Notes from the Royal Botanic Garden Edinburgh* 39: 19 (1980); Davidian, *The Rhododendron Species* 1, pl. 49 (1982); Cox and Cox, *The Encyclopedia of Rhododendron Species,* 293–294 (1997); Feng, *Rhododendrons of China* 1: pl. 62: 1–3 (1988), 3: pl. 62: 1–2 (1999)
Habit shrub or small tree to 10 m
Leaves oblong-elliptic or oblong-obovate, 17–26 cm; upper surface somewhat wrinkled; lower surface with a conspicuous network of secondary and tertiary veins; midrib raised on the upper surface towards the base; scales on lower surface very unequal, the larger with irregular, ascending to almost cup-shaped rims
Raceme with 2–5 fragrant flowers
Calyx deeply 5-lobed
Corolla funnel-campanulate, white with a yellow blotch at the base, 7.5–12.5 cm
Stamens 10; filaments hairy at the base
Style scaly towards the base
Capsule 5–7 cm
Distribution northeastern India, western China, Indochina
Flowering late spring
Hardiness zone 10

Recent nonauthenticated material from Vietnam is in cultivation, and some material in cultivation under the name *R. excellens* Hemsley and Wilson is actually *R. nuttallii.*

A parent of a few hybrids, including 'Victorianum' and 'Cream Trumpet' (both × *R. dalhousiae* var. *dalhousiae*), 'Tyermannii' (× *R. formosum*), 'Leonardslee Yellow' (× *R. lindleyi*), and 'William Wright Smith' (× *R. veitchianum*).

186. *Rhododendron dalhousiae* Hooker

HABIT large epiphytic or free-growing shrub; young shoots bristly; bark chestnut-brown, scaling in long shreds

LEAVES narrowly elliptic, 7.5–17 × 3.5–7 cm; lower surface greyish or brownish green with small, rather distant, slightly unequal, reddish scales; midrib raised on upper surface

INFLORESCENCE BUDS fusiform; scales mostly green and pointed, hairless and scaleless except for a fine, marginal fringe of hairs

RACEME 2- to 3-flowered; flower stalks scaly, finely hairy

FLOWERS fragrant

CALYX deeply 5-lobed, 1–1.5 cm; lobes scaly at the base and with fine hairs on the surface

COROLLA narrowly funnel-shaped, white or cream, often yellowish inside, sometimes with 5 red lines running from lobes to base, 8.5–10.5 cm; tube without scales or sparsely scaly outside

STAMENS 10

STYLE scaly towards the base

CAPSULE 4–5 cm, scaly

DISTRIBUTION Himalaya

FLOWERING late spring

HARDINESS ZONE 9

R. dalhousiae var. ***dalhousiae***

ILLUSTRATION Hooker, *Rhododendrons of the Sikkim Himalaya,* pl. 1, not pl. 2 (1849), reprinted in Halliday, *The Illustrated Rhododendron,* frontispiece (2001); *Flore des Serres,* ser. 1, 5: t. 460–468 (1849); *Curtis's Botanical Magazine,* 4718 (1853), reprinted in Halliday, *The Illustrated Rhododendron,* pl. 22 (2001); *Garden* 18: 437 (1880), 28: opposite 318 (1885), 48: 108 (1895); Davidian, *The Rhododendron Species* 1, pl. 50 (1982); *Kew Magazine* 4, pl. 73 (1987); Cox and Cox, *The Encyclopedia of Rhododendron Species,* 289–290 (1997)

COROLLA without red lines

Wild-collected material is available under *Beer, Lancaster, and Morris 12288, Sain* (without number), and *Spring-Smythe 28, 31.* Recent nonauthenticated material from India (Sikkim) and Bhutan is also in cultivation.

A parent of a few hybrids, including 'Countess of Haddington' (× *R. ciliatum*). See *R. nuttallii* for hybrids with that species.

R. dalhousiae var. ***rhabdotum*** (Balfour and Cooper) Cullen

SYNONYM *R. rhabdotum* Balfour and Cooper

ILLUSTRATION *Gardeners' Chronicle* 90: 235 (1931) and 96: 34 (1934); *Curtis's Botanical Magazine*, 9447 (1936), reprinted in Halliday, *The Illustrated Rhododendron*, pl. 23 (2001); *Notes from the Royal Botanic Garden Edinburgh* 39: 19 (1980); Davidian, *The Rhododendron Species* 1, pl. 46 (1982); Cox and Cox, *The Encyclopedia of Rhododendron Species*, 290 (1997)

COROLLA with 5 red lines running from the lobes to the base

Recent nonauthenticated material from Bhutan is in cultivation.

187. *Rhododendron lindleyi* T. Moore

SYNONYM *Rhododendron grothausii* Davidian

ILLUSTRATION *Notes from the Royal Botanic Garden Edinburgh* 12: 40 (1919); Urquhart, *The Rhododendron* 1, t. 8 (1958); *Curtis's Botanical Magazine*, n.s., 363 (1960); Hara, *Photo-Album of Plants of Eastern Himalaya*, t. 163 (1968); *Iconographia Cormophytorum Sinicorum* 3, t. 4030 (1974); Davidian, *The Rhododendron Species* 1, pl. 48 (1982); Kneller, *The Book of Rhododendrons*, 79 (1995); Feng, *Rhododendrons of China* 3, pl. 61: 1–2 (1999); Cox and Cox, *The Encyclopedia of Rhododendron Species*, 292–293 (1997)

HABIT epiphytic shrub to 4 m

LEAVES narrowly elliptic to oblong-elliptic, 8.5–13 × 2.5–4.5 cm; lower surface greyish green with rather distant, somewhat unequal, reddish scales; midrib raised on upper surface

RACEME 2- to 5-flowered; flower stalks somewhat scaly

CALYX conspicuous, deeply 5-lobed, 1–1.8 cm; lobes rounded at the apex, rather prominently veined, fringed with fine short hairs, becoming papery in fruit

COROLLA openly funnel-campanulate, 6.5–9.5 cm, white or cream with an orange-yellow blotch at the base, scaly or not and finely hairy or not at the base

STAMENS 10

STYLE scaly in the lower part

CAPSULE c. 4 cm

DISTRIBUTION Himalaya

FLOWERING late spring

HARDINESS ZONE 9

Recent nonauthenticated material from India and Bhutan is in cultivation.

A parent of several hybrids, including 'Leonardslee Yellow' (× *R. nuttallii*).

188. *Rhododendron taggianum* Hutchinson

SYNONYM *R. headfortianum* Hutchinson

ILLUSTRATION *Curtis's Botanical Magazine,* 9612 (1942) and 9614 (1942); *Iconographia Cormophytorum Sinicorum* 3, t. 4027 (1974); Feng, *Rhododendrons of China* 3, pl. 65: 1–2 (1999); Cox and Cox, *The Encyclopedia of Rhododendron Species,* 294 (1997)

Similar to *R. lindleyi,* but:

CALYX lobes 1.7–1.9 mm and margined with quickly deciduous scales rather than fine hairs

DISTRIBUTION western China (northwestern Yunnan), northeastern Myanmar

FLOWERING spring

HARDINESS ZONE 10

189. *Rhododendron ciliatum* Hooker

ILLUSTRATION *Curtis's Botanical Magazine,* 4648 (1852) and 7686 (1899), as *R. modestum;* Hara, *Photo-Album of Plants of Eastern Himalaya,* t. 166 (1968); Stainton, *Forests of Nepal,* t. 102 (1972); *Iconographia Cormophytorum Sinicorum* 3, t. 4031 (1974); *Notes from the Royal Botanic Garden Edinburgh* 39: 19 (1980); Davidian, *The Rhododendron Species* 1, pl. 9 (1982); Cox and Cox, *The Encyclopedia of Rhododendron Species,* 297 (1997); Feng, *Rhododendrons of China* 3, pl. 59: 1–2 (1999); Robertson and McKelvie, *Scottish Rock Gardening in the 20th Century,* f. 29 (2000)

HABIT shrub to 2 m; young shoots bristly, old shoots with the bases of the bristles persistent; bark brown or chestnut-brown, peeling off in large flakes and whorls; underbark smooth, cinnamon-brown

LEAVES elliptic to narrowly elliptic, 4.5–9 × 2–3.5 cm; upper surface bristly, particularly along the lower part of the midrib; lower surface with scattered, rather unequal scales

INFLORESCENCE BUDS ovoid to spherical or fusiform, green below, reddish above; scales slightly cuspidate, sometimes shouldered, fringed with fine white hairs and some scales

RACEME 2- to 5-flowered; flower stalks scaly, densely bristly

CALYX somewhat unequally 5-lobed, 6–9 mm; lobes scaly near the base, fringed with bristles

COROLLA campanulate to funnel-campanulate, white or white flushed with pink, 3–4 cm, hairless and scaleless outside

STAMENS 10; anthers yellowish brown to brown
OVARY scaly
STYLE hairless and scaleless
CAPSULE oblong-spherical, 1–1.6 cm, scaly
DISTRIBUTION Himalaya
FLOWERING spring
HARDINESS ZONE 7

Wild-collected material is available under *Beer, Lancaster, and Morris 314, 324, Ludlow, Sherriff, and Hicks 16019, 17498, 18683,* and *Pradhan and Lachungpa 13.* Recent nonauthenticated material from India (Sikkim), Nepal, and Bhutan is also in cultivation.

Widely used in hybridisation to produce a range of mostly hardier hybrids, including 'Dora Amateis' (× *R. minus*), 'Countess of Haddington' (× *R. dalhousiae* var. *dalhousiae*), 'Praecox' (× *R. dauricum*), 'Princess Alice' (× *R. edgeworthii*), 'Rosy Bell' (× *R. glaucophyllum* var. *glaucophyllum*), 'Cilpinense' (× *R. moupinense*), and 'Racil' (× *R. racemosum*).

190. *Rhododendron valentinianum* Hutchinson

ILLUSTRATION Urquhart, *The Rhododendron* 1, t. 7 (1958); *Curtis's Botanical Magazine*, n.s., 623 (1972); Davidian, *The Rhododendron Species* 1, pl. 10 (1982); Cox and Cox, *The Encyclopedia of Rhododendron Species*, 301 (1997)
HABIT small shrub to 1.3 m; young growth densely bristly, older shoots smooth with scaling bark
LEAVES elliptic, 2.5–5 × 1.6–2.2 cm, bristly-ciliate; upper surface bristly along the midrib; lower surface brown with dense, overlapping, unequal scales
RACEME 2- to 6-flowered; flower stalks sparsely scaly, densely bristly
CALYX deeply 5-lobed, 5–7 mm, scaly; margins bristly
COROLLA 2–3.2 cm, funnel-campanulate, bright yellow; tube downy outside; lobes scaly outside
STAMENS 10
OVARY scaly, rarely with a few bristles towards the apex
STYLE variably scaly towards the base
CAPSULE ovoid-spherical, scaly, 6–9 mm
DISTRIBUTION western China (Yunnan), northeastern Myanmar
FLOWERING spring
HARDINESS ZONE 9

Classic wild-collected material is available under *Forrest 24347* (the type collection).

A parent of a few hybrids, such as 'Goldfinger' (× *R. burmanicum*).

191. *Rhododendron fletcherianum* Davidian

ILLUSTRATION *Curtis's Botanical Magazine,* n.s., t. 508 (1967), reprinted in Halliday, *The Illustrated Rhododendron,* pl. 24 (2001); Davidian, *The Rhododendron Species* 1, pl. 8 (1982); Cox and Cox, *The Encyclopedia of Rhododendron Species,* 298 (1997)

Similar to *R. valentinianum,* but:

BARK greyish, irregularly striate

LEAVES margins finely scolloped in the upper half; scales on lower surface distant; both surfaces green; midrib usually not bristly on upper surface

INFLORESCENCE BUDS fusiform, somewhat sunk in upper leaves; outer scales reddish, pointed; inner scales white or yellowish with reddish tips, pointed, scaly on the surface and with a fringe of hairs

STAMENS anthers brown

OVARY conspicuously bristly towards the apex, the bristles persisting on the capsule

DISTRIBUTION western China (southeastern Xizang)

FLOWERING spring

HARDINESS ZONE 7

Classic wild-collected material is available under *Rock 22302* (the type collection).

192. *Rhododendron burmanicum* Hutchinson

ILLUSTRATION *Curtis's Botanical Magazine,* 9031 (1924); Cox and Cox, *The Encyclopedia of Rhododendron Species,* 296 (1997)

HABIT to 2 m; young shoots with numerous, quickly falling bristles

LEAVES obovate, 5–5.5 cm; upper surface dark green, densely scaly; lower surface with dense, overlapping to contiguous scales; margins bristly

CALYX disc-like, scarcely lobed

COROLLA funnel-campanulate, greenish yellow, 3–3.5 cm, scaly outside; tube hairy at the base outside

OVARY scaly; style scaly at the base

DISTRIBUTION central Myanmar (Mt. Victoria)

FLOWERING late spring

HARDINESS ZONE 9

Classic wild-collected material is available under *Kingdon-Ward 21921.*

Generally uncommon in cultivation.

193. *Rhododendron formosum* Wallich

HABIT erect shrub to 2 m; young shoots bristly; bark scaling; underbark smooth, greenish brown

LEAVES narrowly elliptic to linear-elliptic or linear-obovate, long-tapering to the base, 4–7.5 × 1–2.1 cm; blade narrowly decurrent on the bristly stalk; margin bristly, at least when young; scales on lower surface about their own diameter apart, unequal

RACEME 2- to 3-flowered; flower stalks scaly

CALYX rim-like, scaly, weakly bristly

COROLLA funnel-campanulate, 4–5.5 cm, white or white flushed with pink, usually with a yellow blotch at the base

STAMENS 10

OVARY scaly

STYLE impressed in a depression on top of the ovary, scaly to well above the base

CAPSULE to 1.6 cm, scaly

DISTRIBUTION Himalaya

FLOWERING spring

HARDINESS ZONE 8

R. formosum var. ***formosum***

ILLUSTRATION Wallich, *Plantae Asiaticae Rariores* 3, t. 207 (1832); *Gartenflora* 9, t. 277 (1860); *Curtis's Botanical Magazine,* 4457 (1849), reprinted in Halliday, *The Illustrated Rhododendron,* pl. 25 (2001), n.s., 563 (1970); Cox and Cox, *The Encyclopedia of Rhododendron Species,* 299 (1997)

LEAVES 1–1.6 cm wide, rather willow-like

Wild-collected material is available under *Chamberlain 109* and *Kingdon-Ward 12585.*

A parent of several widely grown hybrids, such as 'Fragrantissimum' and 'Sesterianum' (both × *R. edgeworthii*) and 'Tyermannii' (× *R. nuttallii*).

R. formosum var. ***inaequale*** (Hutchinson) Cullen

SYNONYM *R. inaequale* Hutchinson

ILLUSTRATION *Curtis's Botanical Magazine,* n.s., 171 (1957); Cox and Cox, *The Encyclopedia of Rhododendron Species,* 299 (1997)

LEAVES 1.5–2.1 cm broad, not willow-like

Wild-collected material is available under *Chamberlain 103* (from the type locality) and *Cox and Hutchison 302.*

194. *Rhododendron johnstoneanum* Hutchinson

ILLUSTRATION *Gardeners' Chronicle* 95: 327 (1934); Davidian, *The Rhododendron Species* 1, pl. 51 (1982); Cox and Cox, *The Encyclopedia of Rhododendron Species,* 302–303 (1997)

HABIT variably sized shrub; young shoots bristly

LEAVES elliptic to broadly elliptic, 5.5–7.5 cm; margins variably bristly; lower surface brownish, with dense, contiguous or overlapping scales

CALYX disc-like, bristly

COROLLA white, usually with a yellow blotch at the base, often with a pink or purplish flush, 4.5–5.5 cm, loosely scaly over most of the outer surface

STAMENS 10

STYLE impressed into a depression on top of the ovary

CAPSULE 1.6–2.2 cm, scaly

DISTRIBUTION northeastern India (Manipur, Mizoram)

FLOWERING spring

HARDINESS ZONE 7

Classic wild-collected material is available under *Kingdon-Ward 7732.*

Rhododendron parryae Hutchinson is synonymous with this; however, the name has been used in cultivation for a hybrid of this species with some other, unknown species of subsection *Maddenia. Cox and Hutchison 373,* from India, was distributed in cultivation as *R. parryae* but seems to be a naturally occurring hybrid.

Little used in hybridisation, though 'Laerdal' (× *R. dalhousiae* var. *dalhousiae*) is still grown.

195. *Rhododendron dendricola* Hutchinson

SYNONYM *R. taronense* Hutchinson

ILLUSTRATION *Notes from the Royal Botanic Garden Edinburgh* 12: 61 (1919); *Curtis's Botanical Magazine,* n.s., 1 (1948); *Iconographia Cormophytorum Sinicorum* 3, t. 4038 (1974); *Notes from the Royal Botanic Garden Edinburgh* 39: 19 (1980); Feng, *Rhododendrons of China* 1, pl. 58 (1988); Cox and Cox, *The Encyclopedia of Rhododendron Species,* 302 (1997)

HABIT tall epiphytic or free-growing shrub; young shoots usually not bristly; bark brown, striate

LEAVES midgreen, narrowly elliptic to narrowly obovate, 7–12 × 3–5 cm; lower surface with a covering of scales of variable density

CALYX disc-like or very obscurely lobed, not bristly

Corolla white, often with a yellow, greenish, or orange blotch, often flushed with pink, funnel-shaped, to 7 cm, hairy at the base of the tube outside
Stamens 10; anthers dark brown
Style impressed into a depression on top of the ovary
Capsule scaly, to 2 cm
Distribution Himalaya, western China, eastern Myanmar
Flowering spring
Hardiness zone 8

Classic wild-collected material is available under *Forrest 17227* and *Kingdon-Ward 280, 20981.*

A variable and widespread species cultivated under a variety of names, including *R. ciliicalyx.*

R. dendricola flower and leaf

R. dendricola detail

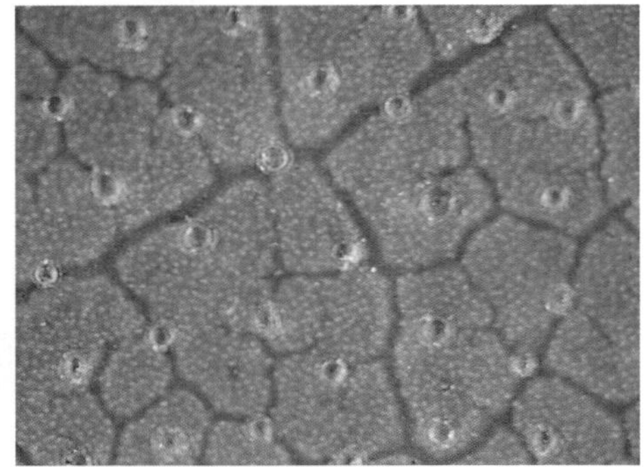

R. dendricola leaf surface

196. *Rhododendron ciliicalyx* Franchet

ILLUSTRATION *Revue Horticole,* 36 (1899); *Curtis's Botanical Magazine,* 7782 (1901); *Iconographia Cormophytorum Sinicorum* 3, t. 4033 (1974)

Very similar to *R. dendricola,* but:

LEAVES lower surface with rather dense but not overlapping scales

CALYX wavy, persistently ciliate, with fine hairs

COROLLA white or pink, 5–6 cm

OVARY tapering smoothly and gradually into the style

DISTRIBUTION western China (Yunnan)

FLOWERING spring

HARDINESS ZONE 10

A much-confused species, probably no longer in cultivation, very similar to *R. dendricola* and most easily distinguished from it by the ovary tapering into the style. *Rhododendron ciliicalyx* is reputedly the parent of several hybrids, but it seems likely that this is the result of misidentification, several of these hybrids involving *R. dendricola,* or even other species, rather than *R. ciliicalyx.*

197. *Rhododendron carneum* Hutchinson

ILLUSTRATION *Curtis's Botanical Magazine,* 8634 (1915); *Iconographia Cormophytorum Sinicorum* 3, t. 4037 (1974); Cox and Cox, *The Encyclopedia of Rhododendron Species,* 304 (1997)

HABIT small shrub to 1 m; young shoots not bristly

LEAVES narrowly elliptic or rarely obovate, 5–11 × 3–4 cm; upper surface dark green, persistently scaly; lower surface brownish or greyish, with scales about their own diameter apart

RACEME 2- to 4-flowered

CALYX shortly and unequally 5-lobed; margins bristly

COROLLA pink all over (sometimes only faintly so), funnel-shaped, 4–5 cm, moderately scaly all over the outer surface; base of the tube hairy

STAMENS 10

OVARY very densely scaly, tapering smoothly and gradually into the scaly style

CAPSULE scaly, to 2 cm

DISTRIBUTION known only in cultivation

FLOWERING late spring

HARDINESS ZONE 9

198. *Rhododendron roseatum* Hutchinson

ILLUSTRATION Feng, *Rhododendrons of China* 1, pl. 60 (1988); Cox and Cox, *The Encyclopedia of Rhododendron Species,* 307 (1997)

HABIT shrub to 4 m; young shoots bristly, the bristles deciduous; bark shredding in long, coppery strips; underbark coppery

LEAVES more or less obovate, tapered to the base, abruptly acute at the apex, 7–12 cm; lower surface with sparse to dense scales

INFLORESCENCE BUDS ovoid, pointed, greenish pink; scales slightly cuspidate, scaly, margined with fine white hairs

CALYX obscurely lobed

COROLLA funnel-campanulate, white or more commonly white flushed with pink with a yellow blotch at the base, 5–7.5 cm, hairy at the base outside and sparsely scaly over the whole surface

OVARY tapering into the style

CAPSULE to 2 cm, scaly

DISTRIBUTION western China (western and southwestern Yunnan)

FLOWERING late spring

HARDINESS ZONE 9

199. *Rhododendron pachypodum* Balfour and W. W. Smith

SYNONYMS *R. supranubium* Hutchinson; *R. scottianum* Hutchinson

ILLUSTRATION *Curtis's Botanical Magazine,* 9238 (1928); *Iconographia Cormophytorum Sinicorum* 3, t. 4036 (1974); Feng, *Rhododendrons of China* 1, pl. 59: 1–4 (1988); Cox and Cox, *The Encyclopedia of Rhododendron Species,* 306 (1997)

HABIT shrub to 4 m; young shoots sparsely bristly, the bristles quickly deciduous

LEAVES more or less elliptic, 7–12 cm, brownish beneath with rather distant scales

CALYX very small, obscurely lobed, bristly-ciliate

COROLLA funnel-campanulate, 5.5–7.5 cm, white or rarely flushed with pink, with a yellow blotch at the base, sparsely scaly, downy at the base of the tube outside

OVARY tapering into the style

CAPSULE to 2 cm, scaly

DISTRIBUTION western China (western and southwestern Yunnan)

FLOWERING late spring

HARDINESS ZONE 8

Classic wild-collected material is available under *Forrest 7516.* Recent nonauthenticated material from Yunnan is also in cultivation.

It is extremely doubtful if this species exists in cultivation outside botanic gardens. The name *R. supranubium*, which, judging by the type specimen, is strictly a synonym of *R. pachypodum*, was widely and wrongly used by gardeners in the 1930s and perhaps later; plants cultivated under this name are usually *R. dendricola*.

200. *Rhododendron veitchianum* Hooker

SYNONYM *R. cubitii* Hutchinson

ILLUSTRATION *Curtis's Botanical Magazine*, 4992 (1857), reprinted in Halliday, *The Illustrated Rhododendron*, pl. 26 (2001); *Flore des Serres*, ser. 2, 4: t. 1416 and 1519–1520 (1861); *Garden* 18: 280 (1880), 35: 237 (1889); Davidian, *The Rhododendron Species* 1, pl. 45 (1982); Cox and Cox, *The Encyclopedia of Rhododendron Species*, 308 (1997)

HABIT epiphytic or free-growing shrub to 2 m; young shoots sparsely bristly, the bristles quickly deciduous

LEAVES obovate or narrowly elliptic, 6.5–10 × 2.5–4 cm; upper surface dark green, scaleless; lower surface pale, with distant, unequal, golden scales

RACEME 2- to 5-flowered

CALYX disc-like; margins bristly

COROLLA white, usually with a yellow blotch at the base, openly funnel-campanulate, 5–6.5 cm, sparsely downy outside at the base, the upper part somewhat scaly; margins of the lobes very wavy

STAMENS 10

OVARY scaly, tapering smoothly and gradually into the scaly style

CAPSULE scaly, to 3 cm

DISTRIBUTION Myanmar, Laos, Thailand

FLOWERING spring

HARDINESS ZONE 9

Wild-collected material is available under *Valder 29, 30, 42.*

Material cultivated as *R. cubitii* is generally a hybrid between *R. dendricola* and some other unknown species. For an illustration, see Davidian, *The Rhododendron Species* 1, pl. 44 (1982). *Rhododendron veitchianum* is the parent of a few widely grown hybrids, such as 'Forsterianum' (× *R. edgeworthii*) and 'William Wright Smith' (× *R. nuttallii*).

Less commonly cultivated are:

Rhododendron levinei Merrill

ILLUSTRATION *Iconographia Cormophytorum Sinicorum* 3, t. 4023 (1974)

Similar to *R. lindleyi* and keying out to it, but:

PETIOLES AND MARGINS OF YOUNG LEAVES loriform-setose with variably deciduous bristles

MATURE LEAVES 6–6.5 × 2.8–3 cm

COROLLA to 4.5 cm

DISTRIBUTION China (Guangdong)

Probably not hardy in most of Britain.

Rhododendron liliiflorum Léveillé

ILLUSTRATION *Iconographia Cormophytorum Sinicorum* 3, t. 4024 (1974); *Notes from the Royal Botanic Garden Edinburgh* 39: 19 (1980)

Very similar to *R. levinei,* but:

MATURE LEAVES 10–13 × 3–5 cm

COROLLA 6–8 cm

DISTRIBUTION China (Guizhou, Guangxi)

Probably not hardy in most of Britain.

Rhododendron ciliipes Hutchinson

Keying out to *R. johnstoneanum,* but:

LEAVES scales on the lower surface not contiguous

CALYX clearly lobed

DISTRIBUTION China (northern and northwestern Yunnan)

A rather obscure species which may not be genuinely in cultivation anywhere, though the name appears in some lists.

Rhododendron scopulorum Hutchinson

ILLUSTRATION *Iconographia Cormophytorum Sinicorum* 3, t. 4032 (1974)

Similar to *R. dendricola,* but:

MATURE LEAVES pale greyish green

STYLE scaly only at the extreme base

DISTRIBUTION western China (southeastern Xizang)

Rhododendron walongense Kingdon-Ward
Similar to *R. dendricola* and *R. ciliipes,* but:
CALYX with a persistent fringe of loriform-setose hairs
COROLLA densely pubescent over the whole outer surface
DISTRIBUTION western China (southeastern Xizang)

Rhododendron horlickianum Davidian
ILLUSTRATION Davidian, *The Rhododendron Species* 1, pl. 47 (1982)
Similar to *R. veitchianum,* but:
CALYX lobes fringed with fine filiform-acicular hairs
COROLLA hairy outside over most of its surface
DISTRIBUTION northern Myanmar

Very rare in cultivation.

Rhododendron ludwigianum Hosseus
Similar to *R. veitchianum,* but:
COROLLA lobes lepidote and hairy over most of the surface
STYLE pubescent, lepidote
DISTRIBUTION northern Thailand

Probably not hardy anywhere in Britain.

Rhododendron surasianum Balfour and Craib
Similar to *R. veitchianum,* but:
LEAVES scales on the lower surface conspicuously flaky and overlapping
DISTRIBUTION Thailand (Chiang Mai province)

Subgenus *Rhododendron*

Section *Rhododendron*

Subsection *Moupinensia* Sleumer (*Moupinense* series; section *Moupinensiorhodion* Spethmann 1980a, 165)

HABIT shrubs, frequently epiphytic
COROLLA openly funnel-campanulate
STAMENS 10, declinate
OVARY tapering smoothly and gradually into the style
SEEDS elongate, winged and with a conspicuous appendage at each end

This subsection is very similar to parts of subsection *Maddenia*, but the plants are smaller, not epiphytic, and have smaller flowers. There are 3 known species, but only one has maintained a place in cultivation; it is prized for its very early flowers, though they are often damaged by late frosts.

The leaves have a 2-layered upper epidermis, the cells of both layers more or less equal in size, the cuticle as thick as the cells are deep; water tissue is absent, and the cells of the lower epidermis are prolonged into papillae. Sclereids are present in the leaf tissue.

201. *Rhododendron moupinense* Franchet

ILLUSTRATION *The Garden* 78: 96 (1914); *Revue Horticole*, 155 (1914); *Curtis's Botanical Magazine*, 8598 (1915), reprinted in Halliday, *The Illustrated Rhododendron*, pl. 27 (2001); Cox, *Dwarf Rhododendrons*, pl. 4 (1973); *Iconographia Cormophytorum Sinicorum* 3, t. 4044 (1974); *Notes from the Royal Botanic Garden Edinburgh* 39: 19 (1980); Davidian, *The Rhododendron Species* 1, pl. 52 (1982); Fang, *Sichuan Rhododendron of China*, 191–193 (1986); Feng, *Rhododendrons of China* 2, pl. 60: 1–2 (1992); Kneller, *The Book of Rhododendrons*, 83 (1995); Cox and Cox, *The Encyclopedia of Rhododendron Species*, 311 (1997)

HABIT shrub to 1 m; young shoots bristly, the bristles variably deciduous; bark cinnamon-brown, smooth but not shining

LEAVES narrowly ovate or elliptic or obovate, 3–4 × 1.6–2.2 cm, rounded to cordate at the base; upper surface green, scaleless, with a few fine short hairs at the base of the midrib; lower surface pale green or brownish, with rather dense scales; margins bristly

INFLORESCENCE BUDS scales pale green, reddish at the tips, sparsely scaly towards the tips

RACEME one- to 2-flowered; flower stalks scaly, finely hairy

CALYX 5-lobed, to 2 mm; lobes scaly, finely hairy
COROLLA 3–4 cm, white, often flushed with pink and with dark red spots on the upper part of the tube inside, hairless and scaleless outside
STAMENS anthers brown
STYLE scaleless, slightly hairy towards the base
CAPSULE tapering, scaly, 2–2.5 cm
DISTRIBUTION western China (Sichuan)
FLOWERING from winter to early spring
HARDINESS ZONE 7

Classic wild-collected material is available under *Wilson 879*. Recent nonauthenticated material from Sichuan is also in cultivation.

An early-flowering species whose flowers are often damaged by late frosts. A parent of several widely grown hybrids, including 'Cilpinense' (× *R. ciliatum*), 'Bo-peep' (× *R. lutescens*), 'Tessa' and 'Tessa Rosa' (× *R.* 'Praecox', itself *R. ciliatum* × *R. dauricum*), 'Seta' (× *R. spinuliferum*), and 'Golden Oriole' (× *R. sulfureum*).

R. moupinense flower and leaf

R. moupinense detail

R. moupinense leaf surface

Subgenus *Rhododendron*

Section *Rhododendron*

Subsection *Monantha* Cullen

HABIT small shrubs, epiphytic or free-growing in the wild
LEAVES evergreen, with large, flat, often unequal, broadly rimmed scales on lower surface
INFLORESCENCES terminal, one- to 3-flowered
CALYX obscure or 5-lobed
COROLLA funnel-tubular to tubular-campanulate, scaly outside
STAMENS 10, declinate
OVARY scaly
STYLE inserted in a shouldered depression on top of the ovary, declinate
CAPSULE scaly
SEEDS elongate, winged and with a conspicuous appendage at each end

A subsection known from one widespread species and 3 other species which are extremely poorly known. It is doubtful if any of them is in cultivation, but *R. flavantherum* (one of the very poorly known species) is mentioned in some garden lists and so is included here.

The leaves are anatomically rather like those of subsection *Maddenia*. They have a 3-layered upper epidermis, the cells of the lower layers larger than those of the upper layer, the cuticle about half as thick as the cells of the upper layer are deep; water tissue is absent, and the cells of the lower epidermis are prolonged into papillae. Sclereids are present in the leaf tissue.

202. *Rhododendron flavantherum* Balfour and W. W. Smith
HABIT shrub to 1 m, usually epiphytic
LEAVES ovate-elliptic to elliptic, 3–4.5 cm; upper surface dark green, with dried-out scales; lower surface somewhat papillose, with rather distant, pale, unequal scales
CALYX to 2.5 mm, 5-lobed; lobes triangular, obtuse
COROLLA funnel-tubular to tubular-campanulate, 1.4–2 cm, bright yellow
OVARY scaly
STYLE impressed, hairless
CAPSULE scaly, 1.4–1.6 cm
DISTRIBUTION western China (southeastern Xizang)

FLOWERING spring
HARDINESS ZONE 9

It is extremely doubtful if any material of this species, which has been found only once in the wild, is now or has ever been in cultivation. Plants identified as *R. kasoense* Hutchinson and Kingdon-Ward have been collected recently and may well find their way into collections; their identification remains uncertain.

Subgenus **Rhododendron**

Section **Rhododendron**

Subsection **Triflora** (Hutchinson) Sleumer (*Triflorum* series)

HABIT small to large shrubs
LEAVES evergreen or variably deciduous
RACEME terminal and lateral
COROLLA very bilaterally symmetric; lobes longer than the tube
STAMENS 10, declinate
STYLE declinate, inserted into a depression on top of the ovary
SEEDS elongate, unwinged and without appendages

A large subsection containing about 20 species, most of which are well established in cultivation. It is linked with subsection *Maddenia* through *R. zaleucum*, which has some characteristics in common with subsection *Maddenia*. The main characteristic of subsection *Triflora* is the presence of 2- to 3-flowered inflorescences, many of which are lateral, so that lateral and terminal inflorescences usually occur on the same shoot. The flowers tend to be very strongly bilaterally symmetric and butterfly-like.

Anatomically the leaves are rather variable. They have a one-, 2-, or 3-layered upper epidermis; when 2- or 3-layered, the cells of the lower layers may be similar in size to those of the upper layer or much larger than them, generally with a thin cuticle. Water tissue is absent, and the cells of the lower epidermis are either not prolonged or are prolonged slightly into small papillae. Sclereids are rare.

1a Corolla basically yellow, sometimes suffused with reddish brown or green 2
b Corolla basically white, pink, lilac, purple, or almost blue, without any yellow except in the form of yellow spots 5
2a Scales small, less than 0.1 mm in diameter, almost rimless; corolla hairy at the sinuses between the lobes outside .... **217. *R. triflorum***
b Scales larger, at least 0.2 mm; corolla hairless or downy all over outside 3
3a Corolla densely downy outside with backwardly pointing hairs; leaves with conspicuous, acuminate drip tips .... **220. *R. lutescens***
b Corolla hairless or minutely downy outside; leaves without drip tips 4
4a Scales on the lower leaf surface close to contiguous; upper surface with short hairs at the base of the midrib .... **218. *R. ambiguum***
b Scales on the lower leaf surface distant; upper surface with short hairs along the length of the midrib and on the blade on either side of it .... **219. *R. keiskei***
5a Midrib of the leaves hairy beneath with long, straight or somewhat twisted bristles 6
b Midrib of the leaves hairless beneath, or downy with minute hairs 7

6 a Corolla, calyx, flower stalks, leaf stalks, and midrib on the lower leaf surface (also often the upper leaf surface) with a dense indumentum of somewhat twisted, fine bristles .... **212. *R. trichanthum***

b Fine bristles absent from corolla, flower stalks, and leaf upper surface; leaf midrib with more or less straight, narrow bristles beneath .... **211. *R. augustinii***

7 a Leaves white beneath, with large, flat, more or less rimless scales; corolla tube downy outside at the base .... **203. *R. zaleucum***

b Leaves not white beneath; scales various but not as above; corolla tube hairless at the base 8

8 a Scales more or less rimless, vesicular, small, and reddish, purplish, or almost grey; young leaves, flower stalks, and calyx whitish-bloomed .... **210. *R. oreotrephes***

b Scales flat, rimmed, and brown, golden, or yellow; flower stalks and calyx not whitish-bloomed 9

9 a Corolla purple; tube scaly outside 10

b Corolla white, pink, or lavender; tube scaleless outside 12

10 a Scales on the lower leaf surface dense, overlapping, flaky; leaves 3 or more × as long as broad .... **216. *R. polylepis***

b Scales on the lower leaf surface dense but not overlapping or flaky; leaves 2–3 × as long as broad 11

11 a Leaf stalks bearing long, somewhat twisted hairs .... **214. *R. amesiae***

b Leaf stalks hairless .... **213. *R. concinnum***

12 a Scales contiguous, in 3 size classes; leaves silvery grey beneath .... **215. *R. searsiae***

b Scales close to distant but never contiguous, not in 3 size classes; leaves brownish or green beneath 13

13 a Scales 1–2 × their own diameter apart 14

b Scales 3–8 × their own diameter apart 16

14 a Scales very broadly rimmed, the central part forming at most half the diameter; outer flower stalks recurving in fruit .... **206. *R. siderophyllum***

b Scales narrowly rimmed, the central part forming more than half the total diameter; flower stalks not recurving in fruit 15

15 a Leaves 2 or more × as long as broad; corolla 1.8–2.6 cm; young shoots brownish or green .... **205. *R. davidsonianum***

b Leaves up to 2 × as long as broad; corolla 1.6–2 cm; young shoots usually reddish crimson .... **204. *R. tatsienense***

16 a Bristles present on the margins and upper surfaces of the leaves and on the leaf stalks, the bristles variably deciduous .... **207. *R. yunnanense***

b Bristles completely absent from the leaves 17

17 a Leaf stalks hairless, usually whitish-bloomed beneath; scales 5–8 × their own diameter apart .... **209. *R. rigidum***

b Leaf stalks downy, not whitish-bloomed; scales 3–5 × their own diameter apart .... **208. *R. pleistanthum***

203. *Rhododendron zaleucum* Balfour and W. W. Smith

ILLUSTRATION *Curtis's Botanical Magazine,* 8878 (1921); Millais, *Rhododendrons,* opposite 244 (1924); *Iconographia Cormophytorum Sinicorum* 3, t. 4079 (1974); *Notes from the Royal Botanic Garden Edinburgh* 39: 19 (1980); Feng, *Rhododendrons of China* 1, pl. 79: 1–3 (1988); Cox and Cox, *The Encyclopedia of Rhododendron Species,* 347 (1997)

HABIT shrub to 8 m or more

LEAVES lanceolate to oblong-lanceolate, 4–6.5 × 2–2.8 cm; upper surface scaleless; midrib finely hairy; lower surface shining, white-papillose, with distant, flat, large, rimless, golden scales; margins bristly, at least when young

RACEME one- to 4-flowered

CALYX very small, scarcely lobed; margins often with fine hairs and/or bristles

COROLLA white, sometimes flushed with pink or lavender, finely hairy at the base of the tube outside

CAPSULE scaly, 1 cm or more

DISTRIBUTION northern Myanmar, western China (Yunnan)

FLOWERING spring

HARDINESS ZONE 9

Classic wild-collected material is available under *Forrest 15688, 24562, 25576, and Kingdon-Ward 20937.* The species has also been cultivated under *Forrest 20537,* but the herbarium specimen of this number is not a rhododendron. Related plants with yellowish flowers have been described as var. *flavantherum* Davidian, but these are almost certainly hybrids.

204. *Rhododendron tatsienense* Franchet

SYNONYM *R. stereophyllum* Hutchinson

ILLUSTRATION *Iconographia Cormophytorum Sinicorum* 3, t. 4092 (1974); *Notes from the Royal Botanic Garden Edinburgh* 39: 21 (1980); Fang, *Sichuan Rhododendron of China,* 228 (1986); Feng, *Rhododendrons of China* 2, pl. 67: 1–6 (1992); Cox and Cox, *The Encyclopedia of Rhododendron Species,* 351 (1997)

HABIT shrub to 5 m, usually much less in cultivation; young shoots deep reddish crimson, not bristly; bark brown, striate

LEAVES up to 2 × as long as broad, 2–5 × 1.2–2.5 cm, broadly elliptic to elliptic; base rounded or almost cordate, usually scaly above with dried-out scales; lower surface with a dense covering of small, slightly unequal, narrowly rimmed scales 1–2 × their own diameter apart

INFLORESCENCE BUDS fusiform, pointed, mainly brown; scales broad but not mucronate, with lepidote scales and a fine fringe of white hairs

Raceme few-flowered
Calyx disc-like or somewhat wavy; margins often with fine hairs
Corolla 1.6–2.1 cm, whitish, rose-pink or lavender, scaleless outside
Stamens anthers pale purple
Capsule 7–12 mm
Distribution western China (northern Yunnan, southwestern Sichuan)
Flowering spring
Hardiness zone 7

Classic wild-collected material is available under *Forrest 15263, 29331*. Recent nonauthenticated material from Yunnan and Sichuan is also in cultivation.

205. *Rhododendron davidsonianum* Rehder and Wilson

Illustration *Revue Horticole,* opposite 324 (1914); *Curtis's Botanical Magazine,* 8605 (1915), 8665 (1916), and 8759 (1918); *Iconographia Cormophytorum Sinicorum* 3, t. 4093 (1974); *Notes from the Royal Botanic Garden Edinburgh* 39: 21 (1980); Fang, *Sichuan Rhododendron of China,* 217–220 (1986); Davidian, *The Rhododendron Species* 1, pl. 65 (1982); Cox and Cox, *The Encyclopedia of Rhododendron Species,* 348 (1997); Feng, *Rhododendrons of China* 3, pl. 67: 1–3 (1999)
Habit shrub to 5 m; young shoots greenish or brownish
Leaves 3–6.5 × 1–2 cm, 3 or more × as long as broad, tapering to the base, often V-shaped in section; lower surface densely scaly, with small brown scales which have narrow rims, 1–2 × their own diameter apart
Raceme few-flowered
Calyx disc-like or slightly wavy
Corolla 2.3–2.7 cm, usually pink, more rarely pinkish lavender or lavender, hairless and scaleless outside
Capsule 1–1.3 cm
Distribution western China (southwestern and central Sichuan)
Flowering spring
Hardiness zone 7

Classic wild-collected material is available under *Wilson 1274, 1352*.

206. *Rhododendron siderophyllum* Franchet

Illustration *Curtis's Botanical Magazine,* 8759 (1918); *Iconographia Cormophytorum Sinicorum* 3, t. 4091 (1974); *Notes from the Royal Botanic Garden Edinburgh* 39: 21 (1980); Fang, *Sichuan Rhododendron of China,* 221–222 (1986); Feng, *Rhododendrons* *of China* 1, pl. 77: 1–8 (1988); Cox and Cox, *The Encyclopedia of Rhododendron Species,* 350 (1997)

HABIT shrub to 7 m; young shoots brownish

LEAVES broadly elliptic to elliptic, 4.6–8.5 × 2–3.2 cm, tapering to the base, scaleless above, with a dense covering beneath of large, flat, broadly rimmed scales 1–2 × their own diameter apart

RACEME many-flowered, dense, the laterals and terminal coalescing, the outer flower stalks recurved, particularly in fruit

COROLLA white or pale pinkish violet, 1.8–2.5 cm, scaleless and hairless outside

CAPSULE 1–1.4 cm

DISTRIBUTION western China (central and southern Yunnan)

FLOWERING spring

HARDINESS ZONE 8

Classic wild-collected material is available under *McLaren AA16*. Recent nonauthenticated material from Yunnan is also in cultivation.

Not common in cultivation. Much material found under this name belongs to other species (*R. tatsienense, R. davidsonianum,* and *R. yunnanense*).

207. *Rhododendron yunnanense* Franchet

SYNONYMS *R. chartophyllum* Franchet; *R. hormophorum* Balfour and Forrest; *R. suberosum* Balfour and Forrest; *R. aechmophyllum* Balfour and Forrest

ILLUSTRATION *Curtis's Botanical Magazine,* 7614 (1898); *Flora and Sylva* 2: 360 (1904); *Iconographia Cormophytorum Sinicorum* 3, t. 4088 and 4097–4098 (1974); *Notes from the Royal Botanic Garden Edinburgh* 39: 21 (1980); Davidian, *The Rhododendron Species* 1, pl. 60, 62, and 68 (1982); Fang, *Sichuan Rhododendron of China,* 207–209 (1986); Feng, *Rhododendrons of China* 1, pl. 78: 1–6 (1988); Kneller, *The Book of Rhododendrons,* 97 (1995); Cox and Cox, *The Encyclopedia of Rhododendron Species,* 351–352 (1997); Halliday, *The Illustrated Rhododendron,* pl. 29 (2001)

HABIT shrub to 6 m; young shoots scaly and sometimes bristly, the bristles quickly deciduous; bark brown, striate

LEAVES evergreen or some or all deciduous, narrowly elliptic to elliptic, 3–7 × 1.2–2 cm, tapering to the base, usually scaleless above, scaly beneath with flat scales 2–3 × their own diameter apart; margins and upper surface with bristles, at least when young

INFLORESCENCE BUDS small, ellipsoid, yellow overlaid with pink; scales sparsely scaly on the back, fringed with dense white hairs

RACEME loose

R. yunnanense flower

R. yunnanense detail

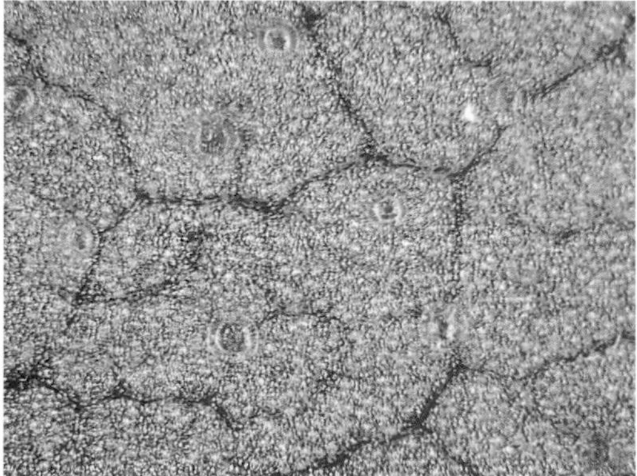

R. yunnanense leaf surface

CALYX minute, disc-like, scaly; margins with fine short hairs or sometimes bristles
COROLLA 2–3 cm, white, pink, or lavender, usually densely spotted above with red or yellow, scaleless outside
STAMENS pinkish brown
CAPSULE to 1.7 cm
DISTRIBUTION northeastern Myanmar, western China (Yunnan, Sichuan, Guizhou)
FLOWERING spring
HARDINESS ZONE 7

Classic wild-collected material is available under *Forrest 16790, 20430, 20485, 20930, 21358, 24618, 26463, 26486, 26596, 27745, Kingdon-Ward 4974,* and *Yü 15014.* Recent nonauthenticated material from Yunnan and Sichuan is also in cultivation. Material grown as *Forrest 11299* is usually labelled correctly as this, but the herbarium specimen of this number is *R. tatsienense.*

A variable and widespread species. Especially variable in the persistence of the leaves; plants with most of the leaves regularly deciduous have been called *R. hormophorum* but differ in no other essential way from *R. yunnanense.* A parent of a few hybrids, notably 'Yunncinn' (× *R. cinnabarinum* subsp. *cinnabarinum*).

208. ***Rhododendron pleistanthum*** Wilding

ILLUSTRATION Cox and Cox, *The Encyclopedia of Rhododendron Species,* 353 (1997)
Very similar to *R. yunnanense,* but:
LEAVES bristles completely absent, even on young leaves
DISTRIBUTION western China (Yunnan, Sichuan)
FLOWERING spring
HARDINESS ZONE 7

Classic wild-collected material is available under *Forrest 15002.* Some material cultivated as *R. yunnanense* is this species.

209. ***Rhododendron rigidum*** Franchet

SYNONYM *R. caeruleum* Léveillé
ILLUSTRATION *Iconographia Cormophytorum Sinicorum* 3, t. 4087 (1974); *Notes from the Royal Botanic Garden Edinburgh* 39: 21 (1980); Davidian, *The Rhododendron Species* 1, pl. 64 (1982); Fang, *Sichuan Rhododendron of China,* 223–225 (1986); Cox and Cox, *The Encyclopedia of Rhododendron Species,* 349 (1997)

HABIT shrub to 10 m; young shoots sparsely scaly, usually with a grey bloom; bark grey-brown, finely striate

LEAVES elliptic to narrowly elliptic, 3–6.5 × 1.3–2.5 cm, thick and hard, scaleless above, sparsely scaly beneath with distant scales 5–8 × their own diameter apart; leaf stalk and upper part of midrib usually bloomed

INFLORESCENCE BUDS ovoid, yellow tinged reddish; scales scaly on the back and with a dense fringe of fine white hairs

RACEME loose

CALYX minute, disc-like or wavy, sparsely scaly, usually hairless

COROLLA usually white, sometimes rose-pink or lilac, unspotted or spotted with red, 2.4–3 cm, scaleless outside

CAPSULE to 1.6 cm

DISTRIBUTION western China (Yunnan, southwestern Sichuan)

FLOWERING spring

HARDINESS ZONE 7

Classic wild-collected material is available under *Rock 59207* (equivalent herbarium specimen *Rock 11288*). A parent of a few hybrids, such as 'Lemon Bill' (× *R. cinnabarinum* subsp. *xanthocodon*).

210. *Rhododendron oreotrephes* W. W. Smith

SYNONYMS *R. timeteum* Balfour and Forrest; *R. artosquameum* Balfour and Forrest; *R. exquisetum* Hutchinson

ILLUSTRATION *Curtis's Botanical Magazine,* 8784 (1918) and 9597 (1939–1940); *Gardeners' Chronicle* 84: supplementary pl. opposite 440, and 493 (1928); *Iconographia Cormophytorum Sinicorum* 3, t. 4085–4086 and 4095 (1974); *Notes from the Royal Botanic Garden Edinburgh* 39: 21 (1980); Davidian, *The Rhododendron Species* 1, pl. 70 (1982); Fang, *Sichuan Rhododendron of China,* 210–213 (1986); Feng, *Rhododendrons of China* 1, pl. 76: 1–2 (1988); Cox and Cox, *The Encyclopedia of Rhododendron Species,* 353–354 (1997)

HABIT shrub to 8 m; young shoots scaly, usually whitish- or greyish-bloomed; bark grey-brown, striate

LEAVES mostly evergreen (sometimes semi-deciduous), circular to elliptic or oblong, 2–8 × 1.8–4 cm, rounded at the base and apex; upper surface scaleless, sometimes slightly, finely hairy along the midrib; lower surface with dense but not contiguous purplish, reddish brown, or greyish, opaque, narrowly rimmed scales

INFLORESCENCE BUDS more or less spherical but slightly pointed, yellow overlaid with pink; scales densely scaly on the back, fringed with dense white hairs

RACEME one- to 4-flowered
CALYX a mere rim, sparsely scaly, sometimes fringed with short fine hairs
COROLLA rose or rose-lavender, 2.5–3.4 cm, scaleless and hairless outside
CAPSULE cylindric, to 1.6 cm
DISTRIBUTION western China (Yunnan, Xizang, southwestern Sichuan)
FLOWERING spring
HARDINESS ZONE 6

Classic wild-collected material is available under *Forrest 5873* (the type collection), *16584, 20629,* and *Rock 96, 165, 59593* (equivalent herbarium specimens *9511* and *11300*). Recent nonauthenticated material from Yunnan is also in cultivation.

Plants cultivated under *Rock 59542* are generally correctly identified as this species, but the equivalent herbarium specimens (*10131, 11184*) are of a different, elepidote species, and so this number should not be used.

211. *Rhododendron augustinii* Hemsley

HABIT shrub or small tree to 10 m or more; young shoots finely hairy or rarely hairless; bark grey-brown, scaling in oblong flakes
LEAVES usually evergreen, narrowly elliptic to elliptic, 4–11 × 1.5–4 cm; upper surface scaleless and hairless or with fine short hairs along the midrib; lower surface scaly, with distant golden or brown scales, the midrib covered with long, straight hairs, at least near the base; leaf stalk hairy or hairless
INFLORESCENCE BUDS ovoid-fusiform, pointed; scales mostly yellowish tinged with brownish red, with some scales on the back; margins with white hairs
RACEME 2- to 5-flowered
CALYX disc-like or obscurely lobed, often finely hairy, especially on the margins
COROLLA openly funnel-shaped, 2.8–4 cm, purple, lavender, or almost blue, rarely white, with greenish or brownish spots inside, the outside of the tube scaly or sparsely hairy
STAMENS anthers dark brown
OVARY variably hairy towards the apex, scaly all over
DISTRIBUTION western China (Hubei, Sichuan, Yunnan, Xizang)
FLOWERING spring
HARDINESS ZONE 6

A variable species, divisible into 4 subspecies, all of which occur in cultivation.

R. *augustinii* subsp. ***augustinii***

SYNONYM *R. vilmorinianum* Balfour

ILLUSTRATION *Flora and Sylva* 3: 162 (1905); *Gardeners' Chronicle* 52: 4 (1912); *Curtis's Botanical Magazine,* 8497 (1913); Millais, *Rhododendrons,* opposite 24 (1917); Urquhart, *The Rhododendron* 1, t. 6 (1958); *Iconographia Cormophytorum Sinicorum* 3, t. 4075 (1974); Fang, *Sichuan Rhododendron of China,* 240–242 (1986); Moser, *Rhododendron: Wildarten und Hybriden,* 130 (1991); Feng, *Rhododendrons of China* 2, pl. 63: 1–4 (1992); Cox and Cox, *The Encyclopedia of Rhododendron Species,* 337–338 (1997)

LEAVES mostly evergreen; hairs on the midrib beneath and extending onto the leaf stalk

COROLLA lavender to blue; tube scaly outside

DISTRIBUTION western China (eastern Sichuan, Hubei)

Classic wild-collected material is available under *Wilson 1207, 4238.*

R. *augustinii* subsp. ***chasmanthum*** (Diels) Cullen

SYNONYMS *R. chasmanthum* Diels; *R. hirsuticostatum* Handel-Mazzetti

ILLUSTRATION *Curtis's Botanical Magazine,* n.s., 79 (1949); *Iconographia Cormophytorum Sinicorum* 3, t. 4077 (1974); *Notes from the Royal Botanic Garden Edinburgh* 39: 21 (1980); Feng, *Rhododendrons of China* 1, pl. 75: 3 (1988)—pl. 75: 1 and pl. 75: 2 are doubtful; Cox and Cox, *The Encyclopedia of Rhododendron Species,* 338 (1997)

LEAVES mostly evergreen; hairs only on the midrib beneath, not extending onto the leaf stalk

COROLLA lavender to blue; tube hairy, not scaly, outside

DISTRIBUTION western China (northern Yunnan, northwestern Sichuan, Xizang)

Classic wild-collected material is available under *Forrest 16360, 19814, 20064.* Recent nonauthenticated material from Yunnan is also in cultivation.

R. *augustinii* subsp. ***rubrum*** (Davidian) Cullen

SYNONYMS *R. augustinii* var. *rubrum* Davidian; *R. bergii* Davidian

ILLUSTRATION Davidian, *The Rhododendron Species* 1, pl. 63 (1982); Cox and Cox, *The Encyclopedia of Rhododendron Species,* 339 (1997)

LEAVES mostly evergreen; leaf stalk with bristles; hairs beneath only on the midrib

COROLLA purple

DISTRIBUTION western China (northwestern Yunnan)

Classic wild-collected material is available under *Forrest 25914* (the type collection).

R. augustinii subsp. ***hardyi*** (Davidian) Cullen

SYNONYM *R. hardyi* Davidian

ILLUSTRATION *The Rhododendron Handbook,* f. 19 (1997); Cox and Cox, *The Encyclopedia of Rhododendron Species,* 339 (1997)

LEAVES deciduous

COROLLA white with brownish spots

DISTRIBUTION western China (northern Yunnan)

Classic wild-collected material is available under *Rock 199* (the type collection).

Most material in cultivation is apparently subsp. *chasmanthum,* though specimens of subsp. *augustinii* are also found; subspp. *rubrum* and *hardyi* are much less common. *Rhododendron augustinii* is a parent of many hybrids (especially with dwarf species in an attempt to combine the "blue" flowers with a dwarf habit); which of the subspecies are involved in which of the hybrids is uncertain. The hybrids include 'Bluebird' (× *R. intricatum*), 'Blue Stone' (× R. 'Bluebird'), 'Blue Tit' (× *R. impeditum*), and 'Blue Diamond' (× R. 'Intrifast', itself *R. fastigiatum* × *R. intricatum*).

212. *Rhododendron trichanthum* Rehder

SYNONYM *R. villosum* Hemsley and Wilson

ILLUSTRATION *Curtis's Botanical Magazine,* 8880 (1921), reprinted in Halliday, *The Illustrated Rhododendron,* pl. 30 (2001); *Iconographia Cormophytorum Sinicorum* 3, t. 4076 (1974); Fang, *Sichuan Rhododendron of China,* 231–232 (1986); Feng, *Rhododendrons of China* 2, pl. 68: 1–2 (1992); Cox and Cox, *The Encyclopedia of Rhododendron Species,* 343 (1997)

HABIT shrub to 6 m, but usually much less; young shoots densely bristly, the bristles persisting for more than a year; bark brown, striate

LEAVES evergreen, ovate-elliptic, 5.5–8 × 2.5–3.5 cm; upper surface hairless or bristly; lower surface hairy at least on the midrib with hairs of varying length; scales brown, distant; leaf stalk bristly, with shorter hairs

INFLORESCENCE BUDS ellipsoid-fusiform, pointed; scales yellow with dark margins, with a few dark scales on the back and fringed with white hairs

RACEME 2- to 3-flowered

CALYX weakly 5-lobed; lobes to 2 mm, scaly and bristly on the margins

COROLLA 3–3.6 cm, light to dark purple, funnel-shaped, with somewhat flattened bristles on the outer surface

OVARY scaly, variably finely hairy

CAPSULE to 2 cm, scaly, variably hairy

DISTRIBUTION western China (northwestern Sichuan)

FLOWERING spring
HARDINESS ZONE 7

Classic wild-collected material is available under *Wilson 1342.* Recent nonauthenticated material from Sichuan is also in cultivation.

213. *Rhododendron concinnum* Hemsley

SYNONYMS *R. yanthinum* Bureau and Franchet; *R. benthamianum* Hemsley; *R. coombense* Hemsley; *R. apiculatum* Rehder and Wilson; *R. laetevirens* Hutchinson
ILLUSTRATION *Curtis's Botanical Magazine,* 8280 (1909), 8620 (1915), and 8912 (1921); Urquhart, *The Rhododendron* 2, t. 27 (1962); *Iconographia Cormophytorum Sinicorum* 3, t. 4082–4083 (1974); Fang, *Sichuan Rhododendron of China,* 236–239 (1986); Feng, *Rhododendrons of China* 2, pl. 64: 1–5 (1992); Cox and Cox, *The Encyclopedia of Rhododendron Species,* 340–341 (1997)
HABIT shrub to 2 m; young shoots not bristly
LEAVES ovate or elliptic, 3.5–6 × 1.8–3.5 cm, rounded or cordate at the base; upper surface scaly, the scales somewhat deciduous; lower surface grey or brownish with numerous contiguous or overlapping, large, flat, broadly rimmed scales
RACEME 2- to 4-flowered
CALYX minute, variably lobed; margins with bristles and fine short hairs
COROLLA purple or reddish purple, 2–3 cm; tube scaly outside
OVARY scaly and minutely hairy at the apex
CAPSULE 8–14 mm
DISTRIBUTION western China (Sichuan, Hubei)
FLOWERING spring
HARDINESS ZONE 7

Classic wild-collected material is available under *H. Smith 17920* and *Wilson 4233A.* Recent nonauthenticated material from Sichuan is also in cultivation.

A variable species and the parent of a few hybrids.

214. *Rhododendron amesiae* Rehder and Wilson

ILLUSTRATION *Curtis's Botanical Magazine,* 9221 (1928); *Iconographia Cormophytorum Sinicorum* 3, t. 4081 (1974); Fang, *Sichuan Rhododendron of China,* 214–216 (1986)
Very similar to *R. concinnum,* but:
LEAF STALKS AND YOUNG SHOOTS with dense bristles
COROLLA c. 2.4 cm
DISTRIBUTION western China (northwestern Sichuan)

FLOWERING spring
HARDINESS ZONE 7

Classic wild-collected material is available under *Wilson 4233* (the type collection).

215. *Rhododendron searsiae* Rehder and Wilson

ILLUSTRATION *Curtis's Botanical Magazine,* 8993 (1923); *Iconographia Cormophytorum Sinicorum* 3, t. 4089 (1974); Fang, *Sichuan Rhododendron of China,* 229–230 (1986); Moser, *Rhododendron: Wildarten und Hybriden,* 231 (1991); Cox and Cox, *The Encyclopedia of Rhododendron Species,* 343 (1997)

Very similar to *R. concinnum,* but:

LEAVES narrowly elliptic or very narrowly elliptic, c. 7 × 2 cm, much longer than broad; lower surface greyish or silver, with scales which are trimorphic as to size and colour, some small, golden, and milky, others larger, golden, and milky, others larger still and clear gold

COROLLA white or pale purple, scaleless outside, c. 2.2 cm

DISTRIBUTION western China (southwestern Sichuan)

FLOWERING spring

HARDINESS ZONE 6

Classic wild-collected material is available under *Wilson 1343* (the type collection).

216. *Rhododendron polylepis* Franchet

SYNONYM *R. harrovianum* Hemsley

ILLUSTRATION *Curtis's Botanical Magazine,* 8309 (1910); *Iconographia Cormophytorum Sinicorum* 3, t. 4080 (1974); Fang, *Sichuan Rhododendron of China,* 233–235 (1986); Cox and Cox, *The Encyclopedia of Rhododendron Species,* 343 (1997); Feng, *Rhododendrons of China* 3, pl. 68: 1–2 (1999)

HABIT shrub to 6 m, but usually less; young shoots densely scaly

LEAVES narrowly to very narrowly elliptic, 5–10 × 1.5–3 cm, tapered to the base; upper surface dark green, scaleless or somewhat scaly; lower surface very densely covered with overlapping, flaky, yellowish or dark brown scales

RACEME 3- to 4-flowered

CALYX minute, wavy, scaly

COROLLA purple, 2.5–3 cm, scaly outside

OVARY scaly, somewhat hairy towards the apex

CAPSULE c. 1.5 cm

DISTRIBUTION western China (Sichuan)

FLOWERING spring
HARDINESS ZONE 6

Recent, nonauthenticated, wild-collected material from Sichuan is in cultivation.

217. *Rhododendron triflorum* Hooker

HABIT straggling shrub to 7 m, but often much less; bark of mature shoots usually smooth, reddish brown, peeling, more rarely greyish brown and striate
LEAVES usually evergreen, ovate or lanceolate, 4–6.5 × 2–3.2 cm; upper surface dark green, scaleless; lower surface greyish brown, with close, small scales (less than 0.1 mm in diameter) which are almost rimless
INFLORESCENCE BUDS pointed, yellowish brown; scales scaly on the back and fringed with short, fine, white hairs
RACEME 2- to 4-flowered
CALYX inconspicuous, usually wavy, scaly
COROLLA variable in shape, pale yellow or yellow suffused with reddish brown, or with dark red spots, 2–3 cm, densely scaly, downy at the sinuses between the lobes outside
OVARY scaly; style sometimes hairy at the base
CAPSULE scaly, 1–1.3 cm
DISTRIBUTION Himalaya
FLOWERING spring

Two varieties occur in the wild, and both are cultivated, though the 2nd much less so than the first.

R. triflorum var. *triflorum*

ILLUSTRATION Hooker, *Rhododendrons of the Sikkim Himalaya*, t. 19 (1851); *Flore des Serres*, ser. 1, 7: t. 673 (1851–1852); *Gardeners' Chronicle* 18: 45 (1882); Hara, *Photo-Album of Plants of Eastern Himalaya*, t. 162 (1968); Stainton, *Forests of Nepal*, t. 101 (1972); *Iconographia Cormophytorum Sinicorum* 3, t. 4070 (1974); *Notes from the Royal Botanic Garden Edinburgh* 39: 21 (1980); Cox and Cox, *The Encyclopedia of Rhododendron Species*, 346 (1997); Feng, *Rhododendrons of China* 3, pl. 69: 1–3 (1999)
COROLLA widely funnel-shaped
DISTRIBUTION Himalaya, northeastern India
HARDINESS ZONE 6

Wild-collected material is available under *Beer, Lancaster, and Morris 239, Chamberlain* (without number), *Kingdon-Ward 5687, 6263, 6409, Ludlow and Sherriff 1353, Ludlow, Sher-*

riff, and Elliott 15819, Ludlow, Sherriff, and Taylor 3795, and *Schilling 2295.* Recent nonauthenticated material from Nepal and Bhutan is also in cultivation.

Variants with the corolla suffused with reddish brown have been called var. *mahogani* Hutchinson. There is also some variation in the bark colour, some specimens having very smooth, coppery bark, others more striate and brownish; the significance of this is not understood.

R. triflorum var. ***bauhiniiflorum*** (Hutchinson) Cullen

SYNONYM *R. bauhiniiflorum* Hutchinson

ILLUSTRATION Cox and Cox, *The Encyclopedia of Rhododendron Species,* 346 (1997)

COROLLA very widely open, almost flat

DISTRIBUTION northeastern India (Manipur)

HARDINESS ZONE 9

Classic wild-collected material is available under *Kingdon-Ward 7731.*

218. *Rhododendron ambiguum* Hemsley

ILLUSTRATION *Curtis's Botanical Magazine,* 8400 (1911); Millais, *Rhododendrons,* 21, 234 (1917); Bartels, *Gartengehölze,* 194 (1973); *Iconographia Cormophytorum Sinicorum* 3, t. 4071 (1974); *Notes from the Royal Botanic Garden Edinburgh* 39: 21 (1980); Davidian, *The Rhododendron Species* 1, pl. 69 (1982); Fang, *Sichuan Rhododendron of China,* 203 (1986); Moser, *Rhododendron: Wildarten und Hybriden,* 125 (1991); Feng, *Rhododendrons of China* 2, pl. 61: 1–6 (1992); Cox and Cox, *The Encyclopedia of Rhododendron Species,* 336–337 (1997)

HABIT shrub to 5 m; young shoots scaly; bark greyish brown, shredding

LEAVES narrowly ovate or obovate or narrowly elliptic, 3–8 × 1.5–3.2 cm; upper surface dark green, persistently scaly; lower surface densely scaly, with contiguous or overlapping, dark brown, somewhat unequal, large, broadly rimmed scales; leaf stalk and midrib downy towards the base

RACEME 3- to 5-flowered

CALYX wavy or very slightly 5-lobed, scaly, sometimes with fine short hairs

COROLLA funnel-shaped, 2–2.6 cm, yellow, often with darker yellow or greenish spots on the upper side of the tube, variably scaly but not hairy outside

OVARY scaly

STYLE usually hairless

CAPSULE 9–13 mm

DISTRIBUTION western China (central Sichuan)

FLOWERING spring
HARDINESS ZONE 7

Classic wild-collected material is available under *Wilson 4252*.

Little used in hybridisation but a parent of 'Mozari' (× *R. cinnabarinum* subsp. *xanthocodon*).

219. *Rhododendron keiskei* Miquel

ILLUSTRATION Miyoshi and Makino, *Pocket Atlas of Alpine Plants of Japan* 2, t. 65, f. 375 (1907); *Curtis's Botanical Magazine,* 8300 (1910); Moser, *Rhododendron: Wildarten und Hybriden,* 184 (1911); Davidian, *The Rhododendron Species* 1, pl. 34–35 (1982); Cox and Cox, *The Encyclopedia of Rhododendron Species,* 341–342 (1997); Robertson and McKelvie, *Scottish Rock Gardening in the 20th Century,* f. 211 (2000)
HABIT small shrub, 30–300 cm, often creeping or almost so; bark brown striped with greyish brown
LEAVES lanceolate or oblong-lanceolate to narrowly elliptic, 2.5–7.5 cm × 8–28 mm; upper surface dark green, variably scaly; both surfaces with fine hairs along the whole length of the midrib and blade towards the base; lower surface greenish with distant, large scales, rarely bristly on margin and stalk
INFLORESCENCE BUDS fusiform; scales few, pointed, the exposed parts yellowish green, fringed with white hairs and with a few scales on the surface
RACEME 2- to 4-flowered
CALYX minute or 5-lobed; lobes to 2.5 mm, often bristly
COROLLA pale yellow, unspotted, 1.8–2.5 cm, funnel-shaped, variably scaly outside and sometimes sparsely downy with short, straight hairs
STAMENS anthers yellowish brown
STYLE hairless
CAPSULE 6–13 mm
DISTRIBUTION Japan
FLOWERING spring
HARDINESS ZONE 5

Wild-collected material of American and Japanese origin is available. Recent nonauthenticated material from Japan is also in cultivation.

A very variable species; some specimens from high altitudes are very dwarf, and these have been given various species or cultivar names. *Rhododendron keiskei* is a parent of a few hybrids, including 'Chink' (× *R. trichocladum*).

220. *Rhododendron lutescens* Franchet

ILLUSTRATION *Revue Horticole,* 324 (1914); *Curtis's Botanical Magazine,* 8851 (1920); Millais, *Rhododendrons,* opposite 244 (1924); Fang, *Icones Plantarum Omeiensium,* t. 35 (1942); *Iconographia Cormophytorum Sinicorum* 3, t. 4073 (1974); Fang, *Sichuan Rhododendron of China,* 204–206 (1986); Feng, *Rhododendrons of China* 2, pl. 65: 1–5 (1992); Cox and Cox, *The Encyclopedia of Rhododendron Species,* 342–343 (1997)

HABIT straggling shrub to 6 m; bark grey, very finely striate or almost smooth

LEAVES mostly evergreen, lanceolate to oblong, 5–9 × 1.3–3.5 cm, acuminate with a long drip tip at the apex; upper surface variably scaly; lower surface with large, distant, broadly rimmed, golden scales

INFLORESCENCE BUDS fusiform; bud scales with a few scales on the surface and fringed with white hairs; lower scales brownish and upper scales greenish, or all scales greenish

RACEME mostly axillary, with terminal racemes often lacking

CALYX wavy or obscurely lobed, scaly, sometimes bristly

COROLLA pale yellow with greenish spots on the inside of the upper lobes, funnel-shaped, 1.8–2.5 cm, downy outside with backwardly pointing hairs

STAMENS anthers brown

OVARY scaly, often downy at the apex

STYLE hairless or slightly hairy at the base

CAPSULE 9–11 mm

DISTRIBUTION western China (central Sichuan)

FLOWERING from winter to early spring

HARDINESS ZONE 7

Classic wild-collected material is available under *Wilson 4277.* Recent nonauthenticated material from Sichuan is also in cultivation.

A parent of a few hybrids, such as 'Kittiwake' (× *R. edgeworthii*) and 'Bo-peep' (× *R. moupinense*).

Subgenus *Rhododendron*

Section *Rhododendron*

Subsection *Scabrifolia* (Hutchinson) Cullen (*Scabrifolium* series; section *Trachyrhodion* Sleumer)

HABIT small shrubs; scales more or less vesicular
RACEME all axillary
STYLE impressed into a depression on top of the ovary, declinate or straight
SEEDS elongate, unwinged and without appendages

A group of 5 species, related to subsection *Triflora* but with the inflorescences all lateral. The leaves are somewhat different. They have a 2-layered upper epidermis, the cells of the lower layer larger than those of the upper layer, the cuticle about half as thick as the cells of the upper layer are deep; water tissue is absent, and the cells of the lower epidermis are prolonged into papillae. Sclereids are present in the leaf tissue of all species.

This group was treated as a section of subgenus *Rhododendron* by Sleumer (1949), because of the fact that all its inflorescences are lateral. However, the plants so much resemble those of subsections *Triflora* (in which the inflorescences are both terminal and lateral), *Heliolepida*, and *Lapponica* that treatment at the subsectional level seems more appropriate.

1a Leaves hairless above except for a few hairs along the midrib; ovary hairless . . .**221. *R. racemosum***
b Leaves persistently hairy on the upper surface; ovary hairy 2
2a Leaves with a monomorphic indumentum of small hairs above 3
b Leaves with a dimorphic indumentum of small hairs and longer bristles above 4
3a Corolla 9.5–14.5 mm; leaves whitish and hairless beneath except for a few hairs along the midrib . . . . **222. *R. hemitrichotum***
b Corolla 1.9–3 cm; leaves with a dense indumentum beneath, not whitish . . . . . **223. *R. mollicomum***
4a Corolla 6–8 mm, shortly hairy inside; bristles on the leaf upper surface flexuous, without swollen bases . . . . **224. *R. pubescens***
b Corolla 9–30 mm, hairless inside; bristles on leaf upper surface stiff, with swollen bases 5
5a Corolla horizontal to pendulous; nectar a sticky smear around the base of the ovary; filaments hairy towards the base . . . . **225. *R. scabrifolium***
b Corolla erect; nectar copious, watery; filaments entirely hairless . . . . **226. *R. spinuliferum***

221. *Rhododendron racemosum* Franchet

ILLUSTRATION *Curtis's Botanical Magazine,* 8301 (1893), reprinted in Halliday, *The Illustrated Rhododendron,* pl. 31 (2001); *Gartenflora* 57, t. 1577 (1908); *Revue Horticole,* 134 (1912); Urquhart, *The Rhododendron* 1, t. 2 (1958); *Iconographia Cormophytorum Sinicorum* 3, t. 4280 (1974); *Notes from the Royal Botanic Garden Edinburgh* 39: 21 (1980); Davidian, *The Rhododendron Species* 1, pl. 56 (1982); Fang, *Sichuan Rhododendron of China,* 244–246 (1986); Feng, *Rhododendrons of China* 1, pl. 82: 1–6 (1988); Moser, *Rhododendron: Wildarten und Hybriden,* 220 (1991); Cox and Cox, *The Encyclopedia of Rhododendron Species,* 324 (1997); Robertson and McKelvie, *Scottish Rock Gardening in the 20th Century,* f. 31 (2000)

HABIT shrub to 3 m, but often much less; young shoots scaly, variably downy; bark chestnut-brown, scaling off in shreds and flakes

LEAVES broadly obovate to oblong-elliptic, 1.5–5 cm × 7–30 mm; upper surface hairless except for a few small fine hairs on the base of the midrib; lower surface shining white-papillose, with dense scales

INFLORESCENCE BUDS fusiform, pointed; scales yellowish brown, scaly, with white hairs on the margins

RACEME 2- to 3-flowered

CALYX rim-like, densely scaly

COROLLA openly funnel-shaped, white to pale or deep pink, 7–17 mm

STAMENS anthers greyish pink to brownish

OVARY densely scaly, hairless

CAPSULE scaly, 7–10 mm

DISTRIBUTION western China (Yunnan, southwestern Sichuan)

FLOWERING spring

HARDINESS ZONE 5

Classic wild-collected material is available under *Forrest 19404* (this collection has strongly pink flowers), *21549, Rock 11403, 59578* (equivalent herbarium specimens *8404, 11265*), *59638* (equivalent herbarium specimen *11476*), and *Yü 10925, 10993, 15011, 15012.* Recent nonauthenticated material from Yunnan is also in cultivation. Material is also grown as *Forrest 10,* but this is not a genuine Forrest collecting number.

A quite variable but easily recognised species, it is the parent of several widely cultivated hybrids, such as 'Racil' (× *R. ciliatum*), 'Fittra' (× *R. dauricum*), and 'Radmosum' (× *R. calostrotum* subsp. *keleticum*).

R. racemosum flower and leaf

R. racemosum detail

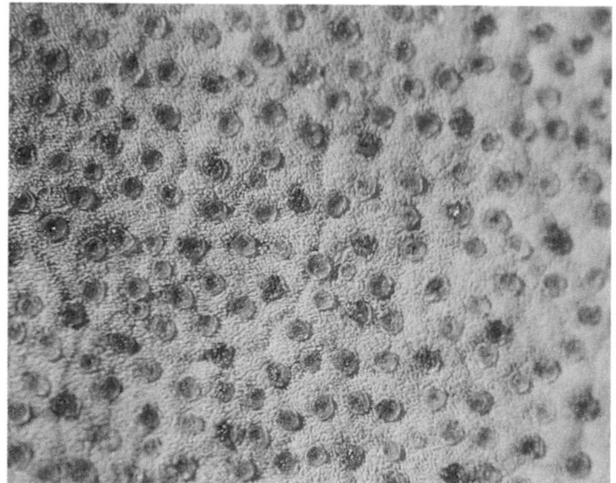

R. racemosum leaf surface

222. *Rhododendron hemitrichotum* Balfour and Forrest

ILLUSTRATION Fang, *Sichuan Rhododendron of China,* 247–248 (1986); Cox and Cox, *The Encyclopedia of Rhododendron Species,* 322 (1997)

HABIT shrub to 2 m; young shoots scaly, downy with short, fine hairs; bark brown to greyish brown, striate

LEAVES narrowly elliptic, 2.5–4 cm × 7–13 mm; upper surface hairy, the hairs short and fine; lower surface white-papillose, hairless except for a few hairs along the midrib, scaly

INFLORESCENCE BUDS ovoid or fusiform, rather blunt, mostly brownish; scales scaly on the back and fringed with longer and shorter white hairs

RACEME 2- to 3-flowered

CALYX rim-like, scaly, fringed with short fine hairs and longer bristles

COROLLA openly funnel-shaped, 9–15 mm, pink or white edged with pink

STAMENS anthers pale pink to brown

OVARY densely scaly, sparsely hairy

STYLE often sparsely hairy at the base

CAPSULE scaly, sparsely hairy, 5–7 mm

DISTRIBUTION western China (northern Yunnan, southwestern Sichuan)

FLOWERING spring

HARDINESS ZONE 8

Classic wild-collected material is available under *Kingdon-Ward 4050* and *Yü 14843.*

223. *Rhododendron mollicomum* Balfour and W. W. Smith

ILLUSTRATION Cox and Cox, *The Encyclopedia of Rhododendron Species,* 323 (1997)

Similar to *R. hemitrichotum,* but:

LEAVES lower surface greenish and covered with fine hairs

COROLLA pale to deep pink, rather narrowly funnel-shaped, 2–3 cm

DISTRIBUTION western China (northern Yunnan, southwestern Sichuan)

FLOWERING spring

HARDINESS ZONE 8

Classic wild-collected material is available under *Forrest 10347.*

224. *Rhododendron pubescens* Balfour and Forrest

ILLUSTRATION *Curtis's Botanical Magazine,* 9319 (1933); *Iconographia Cormophytorum Sinicorum* 3, t. 4277 (1974); Fang, *Sichuan Rhododendron of China,* 249–250 (1986); Cox and Cox, *The Encyclopedia of Rhododendron Species,* 323 (1997)

HABIT small shrub to c. 1 m; young shoots scaly, downy; bark brown, faintly striate

LEAVES very narrowly elliptic to very narrowly lanceolate, strongly revolute, 1.8–2.5 cm × 3–6 mm; upper surface with persistent, short hairs and longer, eventually deciduous bristles; lower surface scaly, with a covering of short hairs

INFLORESCENCE BUDS fusiform; scales greenish white, not cuspidate, hairy and scaly

RACEME 2- to 3-flowered

CALYX rim-like, fringed with bristles

COROLLA funnel-shaped, 6–11 mm, rose-pink, hairy inside

STAMENS occasionally fewer than 10; anthers yellowish pink

OVARY scaly, hairy

CAPSULE scaly, hairy, 5–6 mm

DISTRIBUTION western China (northern Yunnan, southwestern Sichuan)

FLOWERING spring

HARDINESS ZONE 6

Classic wild-collected material is available under *Kingdon-Ward 3953*.

225. *Rhododendron scabrifolium* Franchet

HABIT shrub to 3 m; young shoots scaly, with short, fine hairs and longer, swollen-based bristles

LEAVES narrowly elliptic to oblanceolate, 1.5–9 cm × 4–15 mm; upper surface with hairs like those on the young shoots; lower surface scaly, with a dense covering of bristles

RACEME 2- to 5-flowered

CALYX rim-like or 5-lobed; lobes 2–3 mm, fringed with bristles

COROLLA variable in shape and size, white to deep pink, hairless inside

STAMENS filaments hairy at the base

OVARY scaly, densely hairy

CAPSULE scaly, densely hairy, 6–9 mm

DISTRIBUTION western China (Yunnan, Sichuan)

FLOWERING spring

Three intergrading varieties are found in the wild, and all 3 have been cultivated.

R. scabrifolium var. *scabrifolium*

ILLUSTRATION *Iconographia Cormophytorum Sinicorum* 3, t. 4276 (1974); *Notes from the Royal Botanic Garden Edinburgh* 39: 21 (1980); Fang, *Sichuan Rhododendron of China*,

251–253 (1986); Feng, *Rhododendrons of China* 2, pl. 70: 1–6 (1992); Kneller, *The Book of Rhododendrons,* 91 (1995); Cox and Cox, *The Encyclopedia of Rhododendron Species,* 325 (1997)
COROLLA openly funnel-shaped, 9–15 mm; tube 3–7 mm
DISTRIBUTION western China (northern Yunnan, southern Sichuan)
HARDINESS ZONE 8

R. *scabrifolium* var. ***spiciferum*** (Franchet) Cullen
SYNONYM *R. spiciferum* Franchet
ILLUSTRATION *Iconographia Cormophytorum Sinicorum* 3, t. 4278 (1974); *Notes from the Royal Botanic Garden Edinburgh* 39: 21 (1980); Feng, *Rhododendrons of China* 1, pl. 83: 1–2 (1988); Kneller, *The Book of Rhododendrons,* 91 (1995); Cox and Cox, *The Encyclopedia of Rhododendron Species,* 326 (1997)
LEAVES mostly 1.5–3 cm × 4–10 mm
COROLLA narrowly funnel-shaped, 1.2–1.5 cm
DISTRIBUTION western China (central and southern Yunnan)
HARDINESS ZONE 8

R. *scabrifolium* var. ***pauciflorum*** Franchet
ILLUSTRATION Cox and Cox, *The Encyclopedia of Rhododendron Species,* 326 (1997)
LEAVES mostly 2.5–9 cm × 8–25 mm
COROLLA narrowly funnel-shaped, 1.6–2.3 cm
DISTRIBUTION western China (central and southern Yunnan)
HARDINESS ZONE 9

Classic wild-collected material is available under *McLaren AA17, 33.*

Variety *pauciflorum* is somewhat intermediate between *R. scabrifolium* var. *scabrifolium* and *R. spinuliferum,* and may be a natural hybrid between them.

226. *Rhododendron spinuliferum* Franchet
ILLUSTRATION *Curtis's Botanical Magazine,* 8408 (1911); Millais, *Rhododendrons,* opposite 246 (1917); *Gardeners' Chronicle* 63: 248 (1918); *Iconographia Cormophytorum Sinicorum* 3, t. 4279 (1974); *Notes from the Royal Botanic Garden Edinburgh* 39: 21 (1980); Fang, *Sichuan Rhododendron of China,* 254–255 (1986); Feng, *Rhododendrons of China* 1, pl. 84: 1–2 (1988); Cox and Cox, *The Encyclopedia of Rhododendron Species,* 326 (1997); Halliday, *The Illustrated Rhododendron,* pl. 32 (2001)
HABIT shrub to 3 m, very similar vegetatively to *R. scabrifolium,* differing as below

Leaves larger than *R. scabrifolium*, ultimately hairless above, though with short fine hairs persisting along the midrib, and the bases of the bristles always evident
Calyx disc-like, not lobed, finely hairy
Corolla erect, tubular to very narrowly funnel-shaped, filled with watery nectar, 1.7–2.3 cm, bright, deep red; filaments and style projecting beyond the very short corolla lobes
Stamens filaments hairless
Capsule 1.1–1.7 cm
Distribution western China (southern Yunnan, Sichuan)
Flowering spring
Hardiness zone 8

Classic wild-collected material is available under *McLaren AA22*. Recent nonauthenticated material from Yunnan is also in cultivation.

A remarkable species, easily identified within the scaly rhododendrons as the only one with upright, tubular flowers filled with watery nectar. It has been used as a parent of several widely grown hybrids, such as 'Seta' (× *R. moupinense*).

Subgenus *Rhododendron*

Section *Rhododendron*

Subsection *Heliolepida* (Hutchinson) Sleumer (*Heliolepis* series)

HABIT shrubs or small trees; young shoots scaly, often purple or reddish
LEAVES evergreen, often very aromatic when crushed, densely scaly beneath with large, conspicuous, rather variable, broadly rimmed scales
RACEME all terminal
STAMENS 10, declinate
STYLE straight and shorter than the stamens, or declinate and longer than them, impressed into a depression on top of the ovary
SEEDS elongate, unwinged and without appendages

This subsection is allied to subsection *Triflora* (though the plants are generally much more obviously scaly) and subsection *Lapponica* (through *R. cuneatum*). There are 4 species altogether, of which 3 are found in cultivation. The leaves have either a one-layered upper epidermis or, in *R. rubiginosum*, a 2-layered epidermis, the cells of the lower layer larger than those of the upper layer, the cuticle half as thick to as thick as the cells of the epidermis are deep; water tissue is absent, and the cells of the lower epidermis are generally not prolonged into papillae. Sclereids are few.

1a Style longer than the longest stamens, declinate, hairless; calyx and corolla hairless .... **229. *R. rubiginosum***
b Style shorter than the longest stamens, straight, usually hairy at the base (where impressed into the ovary); calyx fringed with minute hairs; corolla sparsely downy outside, at least near the bases of the sinuses between the lobes 2
2a Flower stalks downy at the base; corolla 1.5–2.2 cm; old leaf bud scales persistent .... **227. *R. bracteatum***
b Flower stalks hairless; corolla 2.4–3.4 cm; old leaf bud scales deciduous .... **228. *R. heliolepis***

227. *Rhododendron bracteatum* Rehder and Wilson
ILLUSTRATION *Curtis's Botanical Magazine,* 9031 (1924); *Iconographia Cormophytorum Sinicorum* 3, t. 4078 (1974); Fang, *Sichuan Rhododendron of China,* 261–263 (1986); Cox and Cox, *The Encyclopedia of Rhododendron Species,* 257 (1997)
HABIT shrub to 2 m, with thin, scaly branches; young shoots purplish, scaly
LEAVES ovate to elliptic, to 3.5 × 1.5 cm, scaleless above, scaly beneath with somewhat distant, golden scales

Bud scales of the leaf buds persistent
Raceme 4- to 6-flowered
Calyx weakly 5-lobed; lobes 1–2 mm, sparsely scaly; margins finely hairy
Corolla openly funnel-shaped, 1.5–2.5 cm, white with many red-purple spots, sparsely scaly and hairy towards the bases of the sinuses between the lobes outside
Ovary scaly and sparsely fine-hairy towards the apex
Style shorter than the longest stamens at maturity, hairless or sparsely hairy at the base
Capsule scaly, 1–1.5 cm
Distribution western China (central Sichuan)
Flowering spring
Hardiness zone 7

Classic wild-collected material is available under *Wilson 4253* (the type collection). Recent, nonauthenticated, wild-collected material, presumably from Sichuan, is also in cultivation.

228. *Rhododendron heliolepis* Franchet

Habit shrub to 3 m; young shoots scaly, purplish
Leaves oblong-ovate to oblong-elliptic, 5–11 × 2–4 cm; upper surface with whitish, scurfy, deciduous scales; lower surface with close, but not contiguous, golden or brownish scales
Raceme 4- to 10-flowered
Calyx rim-like or variably lobed; lobes at most 3 mm (often one about this length while others much shorter), sparsely scaly, fringed with fine hairs
Corolla funnel-shaped, white to pink, more rarely purplish, with reddish, greenish, or brownish spots on the upper lobes, downy outside towards the base of the tube and at the sinuses between the lobes, 2.2–3.4 cm
Ovary scaly, usually hairy at the base of the style
Style straight, shorter than the longest stamens, variably downy towards the base
Capsule scaly, 1–1.4 cm
Distribution western China (Yunnan, Sichuan, Xizang), northeastern Myanmar
Flowering from late spring to early summer
Hardiness zone 7

A variable species. Two varieties occur in the wild, with intermediates between them; both varieties, and some of the intermediates, have been introduced into cultivation.

R. heliolepis var. **heliolepis**

SYNONYMS *R. fumidum* Balfour and W. W. Smith; *R. oporinum* Balfour and Kingdon-Ward; *R. plebeium* Balfour and W. W. Smith

ILLUSTRATION *Iconographia Cormophytorum Sinicorum* 3, t. 4068 (1974); *Notes from the Royal Botanic Garden Edinburgh* 39: 21 (1980); Feng, *Rhododendrons of China* 1, pl. 73 (1988); Cox and Cox, *The Encyclopedia of Rhododendron Species*, 258 (1997)

LEAVES truncate or rounded at the base, 2.2–2.8(–3.3) × as long as broad

RACEME 4- to 8-flowered

DISTRIBUTION western China (Yunnan, Xizang), northeastern Myanmar

Classic wild-collected material is available under *Farrer 878, 1065, Forrest 6762,* and *Rock 129, 148, 4007.*

R. heliolepis var. **brevistylum** (Franchet) Cullen

SYNONYMS *R. brevistylum* Franchet; *R. pholidotum* Balfour and W. W. Smith

ILLUSTRATION *Curtis's Botanical Magazine,* 8898 (1921); *Iconographia Cormophytorum Sinicorum* 3, t. 4068–4069 (1974); *Notes from the Royal Botanic Garden Edinburgh* 39: 21 (1980); Feng, *Rhododendrons of China* 2, pl. 72: 1–3 (1992); Cox and Cox, *The Encyclopedia of Rhododendron Species,* 258 (1997)

LEAVES tapered to the base, 2.7–3.6 × as long as broad

RACEME 6- to 10-flowered

DISTRIBUTION western China (Yunnan, southeastern Xizang, southwestern Sichuan)

Classic wild-collected material is available under *Forrest 10438, 27489, Kingdon-Ward 7108,* and *Rock 145.*

Recent, nonauthenticated, wild-collected material belonging to *R. heliolepis* but not, as yet, identified to variety, is also in cultivation.

229. *Rhododendron rubiginosum* Franchet

SYNONYM *R. desquamatum* Balfour and Forrest

ILLUSTRATION *Curtis's Botanical Magazine,* 7621 (1898) and 9497 (1937), reprinted in Halliday, *The Illustrated Rhododendron,* pl. 33 (2001); Millais, *Rhododendrons,* opposite 236 (1917); *Iconographia Cormophytorum Sinicorum* 3, t. 4065–4066 (1974); *Notes from the Royal Botanic Garden Edinburgh* 39: 21 (1980); Fang, *Sichuan Rhododendron of China,* 257–260 (1986); Feng, *Rhododendrons of China* 1, pl. 74: 1–2 (1988); Cox and Cox, *The Encyclopedia of Rhododendron Species,* 259 (1997)

Habit shrubs or small trees to 10 m or more; young shoots scaly, purplish; bark brown or greyish brown, striate, breaking into oblong plates

Leaves narrowly elliptic to elliptic or almost lanceolate, 5–11.5 × 1.2–4.5 cm, hairless and scaleless above, with overlapping or contiguous, unequal scales beneath, the larger scales often somewhat darker than the others and distributed all over the surface or restricted to the area adjoining the midrib

Inflorescence buds fusiform to almost spherical but slightly pointed, brownish outside, white or greenish yellow inside, covered with scales and fringed with white hairs

Raceme with up to 10 flowers

Calyx usually rim-like, rarely wavy, sparsely scaly

Corolla openly funnel-shaped, 1.7–3.8 cm, pink, mauve-pink, or rarely white flushed with pinkish purple, scaly outside

Stamens anthers brownish to reddish purple

Ovary densely scaly

Style hairless, declinate, longer than the longest stamens

Capsule scaly, 1.1–1.6 cm

Distribution western China (Yunnan, southwestern Sichuan, southeastern Xizang), northeastern Myanmar

Flowering spring

Hardiness zone 6

Classic wild-collected material is available under *Forrest 10057, 14372, 20625, 21348, 26482, Kingdon-Ward 4308, Rock 28, 182, 184, 187, 189, 190, 3892* (equivalent herbarium specimen *18384*), *11071, 11271,* and *Yü 10961, 13886, 14703, 14755, 14990.* Recent nonauthenticated material from Yunnan and Sichuan is also in cultivation.

A widespread and rather variable species.

R. rubiginosum flower and leaf

R. rubiginosum detail

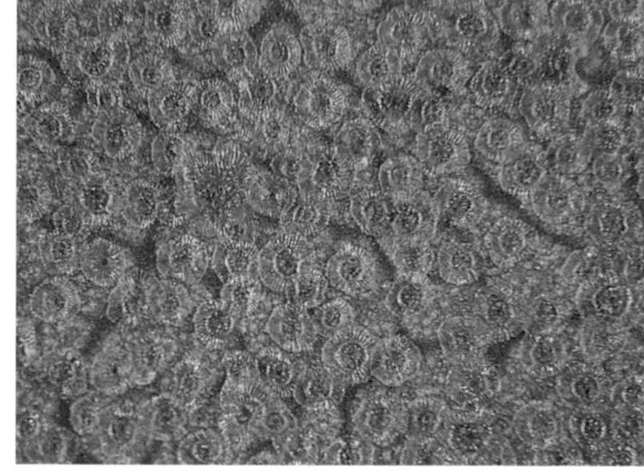

R. rubiginosum leaf surface

Subgenus *Rhododendron*

Section *Rhododendron*

Subsection *Caroliniana* (Hutchinson) Sleumer (*Carolinianum* series)

HABIT shrubs; young shoots scaly
RACEME all terminal
COROLLA densely scaly outside
STAMENS 10, declinate
STYLE impressed into a depression on top of the ovary, usually declinate
SEEDS elongate, unwinged and without appendages

A North American subsection closely allied to subsection *Heliolepida*. *Rhododendron minus* is the only widely cultivated species. The leaves have a one-layered upper epidermis, the cuticle as thick as the cells are deep; water tissue is absent, and the cells of the lower epidermis are not prolonged into papillae. Sclereids are absent.

230. *Rhododendron minus* Michaux
SYNONYM *R. carolinianum* Rehder
ILLUSTRATION *Curtis's Botanical Magazine*, 2285 (1821), reprinted in Halliday, *The Illustrated Rhododendron*, pl. 34 (2001); *Addisonia* 1, t. 1 (1916); Millais, *Rhododendrons*, 232 (1917); *Notes from the Royal Botanic Garden Edinburgh* 39: 21 (1980); Kneller, *The Book of Rhododendrons*, 67 (1995); Cox and Cox, *The Encyclopedia of Rhododendron Species*, 243 (1997)
HABIT shrub to 5 m, usually much less; young shoots green or purplish, sparsely scaly; bark ginger-brown, shredding
LEAVES elliptic to broadly elliptic, 5–11 × 2–4 cm; upper surface dark green, with dried-out scales, and short, fine hairs along the midrib; lower surface densely scaly, with narrowly rimmed, brownish scales
RACEME dense, 5- to 8-flowered
CALYX 5-lobed; lobes 1–2 mm, scaly and sparsely bristly on the margins
COROLLA funnel-shaped, 2–3.5 cm, sparsely scaly outside (sometimes with sparse hairs as well)
STYLE hairless or sparsely hairy at the base, declinate at first, smoothly curved downwards following the shedding of the pollen
CAPSULE cylindric, scaly, c. 1.5 cm

Distribution southeastern United States (Tennessee, Carolinas, Georgia, Alabama)
Flowering spring
Hardiness zone 4

Much material has been gathered by American collectors over recent years and introduced into cultivation.

Introduced early, and widely hybridised in gardens, especially in North America. The hybrids, generally found under the parentage name of *R. carolinianum*, include 'Louis Amateis' and 'Mildred Amateis' (both × *R. edgeworthii*), as well as 'Dora Amateis' (× *R. ciliatum*).

R. minus flower and leaf

R. minus detail

R. minus leaf surface

Subgenus *Rhododendron*

Section *Rhododendron*

Subsection *Lapponica* (Balfour) Sleumer (*Lapponicum* series)

HABIT mostly dwarf shrubs; scales usually with wavy rims
RACEME terminal
CALYX usually conspicuously 5-lobed
FLOWERS small; style straight or declinate; axis continues the line of the flower stalk (except in *R. cuneatum*)
STAMENS 5–10, declinate or radially arranged
STYLE inserted into a depression on top of the ovary
SEEDS elongate, unwinged and without appendages

A subsection in which identification is difficult and based to a considerable degree on the scales on the lower surface of the leaves. Many hybrids exist in gardens, which makes identification of specimens of unknown origin extremely difficult. There are some 28 species altogether. The subsection is characterised by the fact that, unlike all other rhododendrons, the ovary and style form a continuation of the line of the flower stalk (in others there is always a distinct angle between the top of the flower stalk and the axis of the ovary and style).

Anatomically the leaves are rather uniform. They have a one-layered upper epidermis, the cuticle occasionally thin but generally about half as thick as the cells are deep; water tissue is absent, and the cells of the lower epidermis are prolonged into papillae (except in *R. setosum*). Sclereids are absent.

1a Corolla 1.5–3 cm . . . . **231. *R. cuneatum***
b Corolla up to 1.5 cm, often much less 2
2a Shoots of the current year covered with long bristles . . . . **250. *R. setosum***
b Shoots of the current year hairless or with fine short hairs 3
3a Scales on the lower leaf surface opaque, white or pinkish . . . . **239. *R. fastigiatum***
b Scales not as above 4
4a Scales on the lower leaf surface all of the same colour 5
b Scales on the lower leaf surface of 2 colours or shades (usually pale golden brown and darker brown) 18
5a Corolla yellow or white 6
b Corolla neither yellow nor white 7
6a Scales on the lower leaf surface widely spaced . . . . **240. *R. flavidum***
b Scales on the lower leaf surface contiguous or almost so . . . . **243. *R. orthocladum***

7 a All scales on the lower leaf surface pale, yellowish to fawn or almost translucent 8
b All scales on the lower leaf surface reddish brown to dark brown 10
8 a Racemes with 2 or more flowers . . . . **233. *R. hippophaeoides***
b Racemes with 1–2 flowers 9
9 a Stamens and style included in the corolla tube . . . . **232. *R. intricatum***
b Stamens and style projecting beyond the corolla tube . . . . **234. *R. thymifolium***
10 a Style shorter than or the same length as the stamens 11
b Style distinctly longer than the stamens 13
11 a Stamens 5–6 . . . . **235. *R. complexum***
b Stamens usually 10 12
12 a Leaves lanceolate or narrowly elliptic . . . . **243. *R. orthocladum***
b Leaves elliptic to broadly elliptic . . . . **236. *R. yungningense***
13 a Scales on the lower leaf surface distant 14
b Scales on the lower leaf surface contiguous or almost so 15
14 a Calyx lobes 2.5 mm or more . . . . **241. *R. impeditum***
b Calyx lobes up to 2.5 mm . . . . **242. *R. polycladum***
15 a Calyx lobes up to 2 mm 16
b Calyx lobes 2 mm or more 17
16 a Leaves broadly elliptic to almost circular, reddish brown beneath . . . . **237. *R. tapetiforme***
b Leaves lanceolate to narrowly elliptic, brown beneath . . . . **243. *R. orthocladum***
17 a Corolla densely hairy outside . . . . **238. *R. dasypetalum***
b Corolla hairless or occasionally minutely downy near the base outside . . . . . . **236. *R. yungningense***
18 a Darker scales on the lower leaf surface few and scattered 19
b Darker scales on the lower leaf surface numerous and evenly dispersed 21
19 a Background scales of the lower leaf surface brown . . . . **243. *R. orthocladum***
b Background scales of the lower leaf surface yellowish or buff 20
20 a Corolla purplish, scaly outside . . . . **244. *R. telmateium***
b Corolla yellow, not scaly outside . . . . **240. *R. flavidum***
21 a Leaf usually less than 9 mm, without a thickened apex, the scales beneath sharply contrasted, pale and dark . . . . **245. *R. nivale***
b Leaf not with the above combination of characters 22
22 a Calyx to 2.5 mm 23
b Calyx 2.5 mm or more 24
23 a Leaves lanceolate or narrowly elliptic . . . . **243. *R. orthocladum***
b Leaves elliptic or broader . . . . **246. *R. lapponicum***
24 a Leaf without a thickened apex . . . . **247. *R. capitatum***
b Leaf with a thickened apex 25
25 a Calyx lobes with a central band of scales . . . . **249. *R. rupicola***
b Calyx lobes without a central band of scales . . . . **248. *R. russatum***

231. *Rhododendron cuneatum* W. W. Smith

SYNONYM *R. ravum* Balfour and W. W. Smith

ILLUSTRATION *Curtis's Botanical Magazine,* 9561 (1939); *Iconographia Cormophytorum Sinicorum* 3, t. 4051 (1974); Davidian, *The Rhododendron Species* 1, pl. 30 (1982); Cox and Cox, *The Encyclopedia of Rhododendron Species,* 262–263 (1997)

HABIT shrub 1–2 m or more; bark greyish, finely striate

LEAVES narrowly to broadly elliptic, 1–7 cm × 5–26 mm; upper surface somewhat scaly; lower surface fawn to deep reddish brown, with dense, contiguous or overlapping scales

INFLORESCENCE BUDS spherical or slightly pointed, yellowish to brownish purple; scales broad, especially towards the base, with small abrupt points; inner scales whitish, fringed with long white hairs, covered with scales

RACEME with up to 6 flowers

CALYX 5–10 mm; lobes usually oblong; apex rounded or acute, somewhat scaly; margins ciliate

COROLLA 1.5–3 cm, funnel-shaped, often downy and/or scaly outside, deep purple to rose-lavender, often with darker purple spots, rarely almost white

STAMENS declinate; anthers whitish to very pale brown

STYLE declinate, longer than or equalling the stamens, downy towards the base

CAPSULE scaly, to 1.4 cm

DISTRIBUTION western China (northern and western Yunnan, southwestern Sichuan)

FLOWERING spring

HARDINESS ZONE 5

Classic wild-collected material is available under *Forrest 10435, Kingdon-Ward 4486,* and *Rock 59253* (equivalent herbarium specimens *8362* and *11392*), *18462.* Recent nonauthenticated material from Yunnan is also in cultivation.

The largest species of this subsection, similar in many ways to *R. rubiginosum.*

232. *Rhododendron intricatum* Franchet

SYNONYM *R. peramabile* Hutchinson

ILLUSTRATION *Curtis's Botanical Magazine,* 8163 (1907); *Garden* 78: 294 (1914), 80: 524 (1916), 83: 224 (1919); *Iconographia Cormophytorum Sinicorum* 3, t. 4054 (1974); Fang, *Sichuan Rhododendron of China,* 302–303 (1986); Feng, *Rhododendrons of China* 2, pl. 78: 1–3 (1992); Cox and Cox, *The Encyclopedia of Rhododendron Species,* 268 (1997)

HABIT compact and intricately branched shrub to 1.5 m

LEAVES oblong to elliptic or almost circular, 5–12 × 3–7 mm; upper surface somewhat scaly; lower surface buff to pale yellow, with dense, contiguous to overlapping scales

RACEME 2- to 7-flowered

CALYX 5-lobed, 0.5–2 mm; lobes narrowly triangular to oblong; margins scaly or with long hairs

COROLLA with a short, parallel-sided tube and spreading lobes, pale lavender to dark purplish blue, 8–14 mm

STAMENS included in the corolla tube

OVARY scaly

STYLE shorter than the stamens

CAPSULE ovoid, scaly, to 5 mm

DISTRIBUTION western China (northern Yunnan, southwestern and central Sichuan)

FLOWERING spring

HARDINESS ZONE 5

Classic wild-collected material is available under *Forrest 29266.* Recent nonauthenticated material from Sichuan is also in cultivation. Material of this species is also cultivated under *Forrest 20,* but this number is not a genuine collecting number. Material cultivated under this name as *Rock 24446* is usually a hybrid (*R. intricatum* × *R. russatum*).

Readily identifiable by the unusual flower shape and very short stamens. A parent of a few hybrids, including 'Bluebird' (× *R. augustinii*) and 'Intrifast' (× *R. fastigiatum*).

233. *Rhododendron hippophaeoides* Balfour and W. W. Smith

SYNONYM *R. fimbriatum* Hutchinson

ILLUSTRATION *Curtis's Botanical Magazine,* 9156 (1926), reprinted in Halliday, *The Illustrated Rhododendron,* pl. 35 (2001); *Iconographia Cormophytorum Sinicorum* 3, t. 4057 (1974); Davidian, *The Rhododendron Species* 1, pl. 37 (1982); Fang, *Sichuan Rhododendron of China,* 300–301 (1986); Feng, *Rhododendrons of China* 1, pl. 67: 2–5 (1988); Cox and Cox, *The Encyclopedia of Rhododendron Species,* 266 (1997)

HABIT erect, openly branched shrub to 1.2 m; bark brown to greyish brown, striate

LEAVES elliptic or oblong or narrowly obovate, 5–12 × 2–6 mm; upper surface greyish; lower surface yellowish or greyish, with numerous contiguous to overlapping scales

INFLORESCENCE BUDS ovoid or ovoid-fusiform, brownish or yellowish; scales mostly yellowish, some with reddish markings, scaly all over the surface and with a weak fringe of hairs around the margins

RACEME one- to 2-flowered

CALYX 0.5–1.2 mm, or rim-like; lobes rounded or triangular, margined with hairs or scales or both

COROLLA broadly funnel-shaped, pale lavender to deep purplish, rarely white, 1–1.5 cm, downy outside

STAMENS anthers pale brown to reddish brown

OVARY scaly

STYLE straight, slightly shorter than the stamens, occasionally with a few hairs towards the base

CAPSULE 5–6 mm, scaly

DISTRIBUTION western China (Yunnan, southwestern Sichuan)

FLOWERING spring

HARDINESS ZONE 6

Classic wild-collected material is available under *Forrest 12461, 21462, Rock 59241* (equivalent herbarium specimen *11364*), *59615* (equivalent herbarium specimens *8527, 11363*), and *Yü 13845, 13937.* Recent nonauthenticated material from Yunnan is also in cultivation. Correctly named material is also grown under *Forrest 21,* but this is not a genuine collector's number. *Yü 15010* is grown as this species, but all material I have seen under this number is a hybrid. *Forrest 22197* is also this species in cultivation, but the herbarium specimen is *R. cuneatum,* and therefore this number is suspect.

The plants described above are all var. *hippophaeoides;* var. *occidentale* Philipson and Philipson is not cultivated but is illustrated in Cox and Cox, *The Encyclopedia of Rhododendron Species,* 266 (1997).

234. ***Rhododendron thymifolium*** Maximowicz

SYNONYM *R. polifolium* Franchet

ILLUSTRATION *Iconographia Cormophytorum Sinicorum* 3, t. 4053 (1974); Fang, *Sichuan Rhododendron of China,* 280–281 (1986); Feng, *Rhododendrons of China* 2, pl. 80: 1–3 (1992); Cox and Cox, *The Encyclopedia of Rhododendron Species,* 279 (1997)

HABIT openly or tightly branched shrub to 1.25 m

LEAVES elliptic or oblong or narrowly obovate, 4–12 × 2–6 mm; lower surface yellowish brown, with contiguous or overlapping scales

RACEME one- or rarely 2-flowered

CALYX rim-like or 5-lobed; lobes 0.5–1.2 mm, rounded or triangular, scaly and/or fringed with hairs

Corolla broadly funnel-shaped, pale lavender-blue to deep purple, 7–11 mm
Stamens projecting beyond the corolla
Ovary scaly
Style short (3–6 mm) or long (1–1.6 cm), hairless or with a few hairs or scales towards the base
Capsule 3–3.5 mm, hairless
Distribution central China (northern Sichuan, Qinghai, Gansu)
Flowering spring
Hardiness zone 5

Classic wild-collected material is available under *Rock 24320*.

235. *Rhododendron complexum* Balfour and W. W. Smith
Illustration Davidian, *The Rhododendron Species* 1, pl. 32 (1982); Feng, *Rhododendrons of China* 2, pl. 74: 1–3 (1992); *The Rhododendron Handbook*, f. 5 (1997); Cox and Cox, *The Encyclopedia of Rhododendron Species*, 261–262 (1997)
Habit much-branched shrub to 60 cm; bark greyish brown, striate
Leaves broadly or narrowly elliptic to ovate, 3.5–11 × 1.8–6 mm; lower surface reddish brown, with contiguous scales
Inflorescence buds oblong, blunt, with few scales; scales brownish and densely scaly on the surface, densely hairy on the margins
Raceme 3- to 5-flowered
Calyx rim-like or 5-lobed; lobes to 1.5 mm, rounded or triangular; margins scaly or hairy
Corolla narrowly funnel-shaped, 9–13 mm, pale lilac to rosy purple, occasionally downy outside
Stamens 5 or 6, rarely to 8; anthers pale brown to whitish
Ovary scaly
Style usually short (to 3 mm), rarely longer (6–8 mm), hairless or slightly hairy towards the base
Capsule c. 5 mm, scaly
Distribution western China (northern Yunnan)
Flowering spring
Hardiness zone 7

Classic wild-collected material is available under *Forrest 15392*. Recent nonauthenticated material from Yunnan is also in cultivation.

236. *Rhododendron yungningense* Balfour

SYNONYM *R. glomerulatum* Hutchinson

ILLUSTRATION Cox and Cox, *The Encyclopedia of Rhododendron Species,* 280–281 (1997)

HABIT erect shrub to c. 1 m; bark brown to greyish brown, striate

LEAVES elliptic to broadly elliptic or oblong, 7–20 × 3–8 mm; lower surface brownish to reddish brown, with more or less contiguous scales

INFLORESCENCE BUDS ovoid and blunt to fusiform; outer scales brownish; inner scales pale yellow, densely scaly on the margins, densely fringed with fine white hairs

RACEME 3- to 6-flowered

CALYX irregularly lobed; lobes usually 2–3 mm, triangular to strap-shaped, variably scaly, margined with hairs

COROLLA broadly funnel-shaped, deep purplish blue, rose-lavender, or whitish, 1.1–1.4 cm, rarely downy outside

STAMENS 8–10; anthers brown to reddish brown

OVARY scaly

STYLE short (3.5–6 mm) or longer (1–1.5 cm), hairless

CAPSULE scaly, c. 5 mm

DISTRIBUTION western China (northern and northwestern Yunnan, southwestern Sichuan)

FLOWERING spring

HARDINESS ZONE 8

Classic wild-collected material is available under *Forrest 16282, 21304, 29259, 29260* (the herbarium specimen of *29259* contains a mixture of *R. yungningense* and *R. rupicola* var. *rupicola*).

237. *Rhododendron tapetiforme* Balfour and Kingdon-Ward

ILLUSTRATION Cox and Cox, *The Encyclopedia of Rhododendron Species,* 277–278 (1997); Feng, *Rhododendrons of China* 3, pl. 77: 1–2 (1999)

HABIT low, matted or densely rounded, much-branched shrub, prostrate or to 90 cm; bark greyish brown, striate

LEAVES broadly elliptic to almost circular, 4–15 × 2–8 mm; lower surface dark reddish brown, with contiguous scales

INFLORESCENCE BUDS ovoid; scales few, densely scaly on the surface and fringed with white hairs

RACEME one- to 4-flowered

CALYX rim-like or 5-lobed; lobes to 2 mm, rounded or triangular, variably scaly and/or hairy
COROLLA broadly funnel-shaped, 9–16 mm, usually purplish or purplish blue, occasionally violet or lavender, exceptionally yellow, sometimes downy outside
STAMENS usually 10, rarely 5 or 6; anthers brown
OVARY scaly
STYLE exceeding the stamens, sometimes hairy towards the base
CAPSULE scaly, 5–7 mm
DISTRIBUTION western China (southeastern Xizang, northwestern Yunnan), northeastern Myanmar
FLOWERING spring
HARDINESS ZONE 5

Classic wild-collected material is available under *Forrest 16450.* Recent nonauthenticated material from Yunnan is also in cultivation. Plants grown under *Forrest 16577* as *R. edgarianum* (a little-used synonym of *R. tapetiforme*) are generally *R. yungningense.*

238. *Rhododendron dasypetalum* Balfour and Forrest
ILLUSTRATION Cox and Cox, *The Encyclopedia of Rhododendron Species,* 263 (1997)
HABIT much-branched shrub to 75 cm
LEAVES elliptic or oblong-elliptic, 8–15 × 3–7.5 mm; lower surface uniformly tawny brown, with contiguous scales; bases of margins and sometimes the leaf stalk with short hairs
RACEME 2-flowered
CALYX 5-lobed; lobes to 3 mm, broadly strap-shaped, downy, scaly
COROLLA broadly funnel-shaped, 1.2–1.6 cm, bright purplish rose, hairy outside with conspicuous hairs
STAMENS 10
OVARY scaly
STYLE exceeding the stamens, hairy at the base
CAPSULE c. 5 mm, scaly
DISTRIBUTION western China (northwestern Yunnan)
FLOWERING spring
HARDINESS ZONE 7

Classic wild-collected material is available under *Forrest 13905* (the type collection).

Known only from one wild collection, but well established in cultivation, though much material grown as *Forrest 13905* is incorrectly named.

239. *Rhododendron fastigiatum* Franchet

ILLUSTRATION *Iconographia Cormophytorum Sinicorum* 3, t. 4058 (1974); Davidian, *The Rhododendron Species* 1, pl. 41 (1982); Fang, *Sichuan Rhododendron of China,* 298–299 (1986); Feng, *Rhododendrons of China* 2, pl. 75: 1–4 (1992); Cox and Cox, *The Encyclopedia of Rhododendron Species,* 263–264 (1997)

HABIT prostrate or cushion-forming shrub to 1.5 m

LEAVES broadly elliptic to ovate, 5–16 × 3–8 mm; lower surface fawn to greyish, with opaque, pink or greyish, scattered to contiguous scales

RACEME one- to 4-flowered

CALYX 2.5–5.5 mm, 5-lobed; lobes oblong or bluntly triangular, variably scaly; margins usually hairy

COROLLA funnel-shaped, 1–1.8 cm, bright lavender-blue to pinkish purple or rich purple, scaleless outside, but sometimes finely hairy

STAMENS usually 10, rarely as few as 6

OVARY scaly, occasionally with an apical tuft of hairs

STYLE exceeding the stamens, usually scaleless and hairless

CAPSULE scaly, 5–6 mm

DISTRIBUTION western China (northern and central Yunnan)

FLOWERING spring

HARDINESS ZONE 6

Classic wild-collected material is available under *Forrest 5847* and *Rock 188.* Recent nonauthenticated material from Yunnan is also in cultivation.

A parent of many hybrids; its influence can generally be detected by the presence of opaque, pinkish or greyish scales on the lower surface of the leaf, as with *R.* 'Intrifast' (× *R. intricatum*).

240. *Rhododendron flavidum* Franchet

SYNONYM *R. primulinum* Hemsley

ILLUSTRATION *Curtis's Botanical Magazine,* 8326 (1910); *Iconographia Cormophytorum Sinicorum* 3, t. 4047 (1974); Fang, *Sichuan Rhododendron of China,* 275–276 (1986); Feng, *Rhododendrons of China* 2, pl. 76: 1–4 (1992); Cox and Cox, *The Encyclopedia of Rhododendron Species,* 265 (1997)

HABIT erect shrub to 2.5 m; bark pale brown, somewhat scaling

LEAVES broadly elliptic to oblong, 7–15 × 3–7 mm; lower surface pale grey-green, with well-spaced scales

INFLORESCENCE BUDS fusiform, pointed, yellowish brown; scales scaly where exposed and with a fringe of hairs; lower scales cuspidate

Raceme one- to 3-flowered
Calyx 2–5 mm, minutely downy at the base; lobes strap-shaped or triangular, sometimes unequal, sparsely scaly to scaleless; margins hairy
Corolla broadly funnel-shaped, 1.2–1.8 mm, yellow, downy outside
Stamens 8–10, about as long as the corolla; anthers pale yellow-brown
Ovary densely scaly
Style exceeding the stamens, downy at the base
Capsule scaly, c. 6 mm
Distribution western China (northwestern Sichuan)
Flowering spring
Hardiness zone 6

Recent, nonauthenticated, wild-collected material from Sichuan is in cultivation. A parent of the widely grown 'Yellowhammer' (× *R. sulfureum*).

241. *Rhododendron impeditum* Franchet

Illustration *Curtis's Botanical Magazine*, n.s., 489 (1966); Cox and Cox, *The Encyclopedia of Rhododendron Species*, 267 (1997)
Habit compact, much-branched shrub to 1 m, usually much less; bark brown to yellowish brown, striate
Leaves 4–14 × 2.5–7 mm; lower surface pale grey-green speckled with brown, or more uniformly brown, with scales spaced to almost contiguous
Inflorescence buds ovoid to obovoid, pointed or blunt; scales mostly brown or the inner paler, all covered with orange scales and fringed with white hairs
Raceme one- to 4-flowered
Calyx 2.5–4 mm; lobes strap-shaped, usually with a few scales forming a central band; margins hairy
Corolla broadly funnel-shaped, 8–15 mm, violet to purple, rarely lavender, occasionally downy outside
Stamens usually 10 but somewhat variable in number; anthers brown
Ovary scaly
Style very variable in length, shorter to longer than the stamens, hairless or downy at the base
Capsule scaly, 4–6 mm
Distribution western China (northern Yunnan, southwestern Sichuan)
Flowering spring
Hardiness zone 5

Classic wild-collected material is available under *Forrest 20454* and *Rock 3839* (equivalent herbarium specimen *18223*), *24278*, *59263* (equivalent herbarium specimen *11460*). Material cultivated as this species under *Forrest 29268* is generally *R. yungningense*.

Among the most popular small rhododendrons, often with a very compact, ground-covering habit. An important species in hybridisation, contributing its low growth habit to a series of bluish-flowered hybrids, such as 'Blue Tit' (× *R. augustinii*).

242. *Rhododendron polycladum* Franchet

SYNONYM *R. scintillans* Balfour and W. W. Smith

ILLUSTRATION Feng, *Rhododendrons of China* 1, pl. 69: 1–2 (1988); Cox and Cox, *The Encyclopedia of Rhododendron Species*, 273 (1997)

HABIT erect shrub to 1.25 m; bark brownish, striate

LEAVES narrowly elliptic to elliptic, 6–18 × 2–8 mm; lower surface greyish with brownish dots or more uniformly reddish brown; scales almost contiguous, or contiguous in groups

INFLORESCENCE BUDS fusiform, slightly pointed; scales mostly brown, though a few of the innermost paler, densely scaly, fringed with white hairs

RACEME one- to 5-flowered

CALYX rim-like or 5-lobed, to 2.5 mm; lobes somewhat unequal, triangular or rounded; margins hairy and/or scaly

COROLLA broadly funnel-shaped, 7.5–13 mm, lavender to purplish blue, rarely whitish, occasionally hairy outside

STAMENS 10; anthers reddish brown

OVARY scaly

STYLE exceeding the stamens, hairless or rarely with a few hairs at the base

CAPSULE scaly, to 6 mm

DISTRIBUTION western China (Yunnan)

FLOWERING spring

HARDINESS ZONE 8

Classic wild-collected material is available under *Forrest 10014, 19450, 22299, 25555.*

Material grown as *Forrest 17165, R. scintillans,* is incorrectly numbered, as the herbarium specimen of this number is *R. trichocladum.*

Widely known under the name *R. scintillans.*

243. *Rhododendron orthocladum* Balfour and Forrest

HABIT much-branched, erect shrub to 1.3 m; bark brown, striate

LEAVES narrowly elliptic to lanceolate, 8–16 × 2.5–6 mm; lower surface yellowish brown to fawn, usually with darker speckling; scales contiguous or almost so, mostly golden with a few to many dark brown

INFLORESCENCE BUDS ovoid; bud scales covered with scales and fringed with long, white hairs; outer scales brownish; inner scales white

RACEME one- to 5-flowered

CALYX 0.5–1.5 mm; lobes rounded to triangular, with scales on tube and middles of lobes; margins of lobes usually hairy

COROLLA funnel-shaped, 7–13.5 mm, pale to deep lavender-blue to purple or white, sometimes sparsely scaly outside

STAMENS 8–10, shorter than or equalling the corolla; anthers brown

OVARY scaly

STYLE 3–5.5 mm or 1.5–1.6 cm, scaleless or sparsely scaly at the base

CAPSULE scaly, c. 5 mm

DISTRIBUTION western China (northern Yunnan, southwestern Sichuan)

FLOWERING spring

HARDINESS ZONE 6

Three varieties occur, 2 of them known in the wild.

R. orthocladum var. ***orthocladum***

ILLUSTRATION Feng, *Rhododendrons of China* 1, pl. 68: 1–3 (1988); Cox and Cox, *The Encyclopedia of Rhododendron Species*, 272–273 (1997)

COROLLA blue to purple

STYLE 3.5–5 mm

DISTRIBUTION western China (northern Yunnan, southwestern Sichuan)

Classic wild-collected material is available under *Forrest 20488, 20493, 21274*. Plants grown under this name as *Forrest 10284* are incorrectly numbered, as the herbarium specimen of this collection is *R. fastigiatum*.

R. orthocladum var. ***longistylum*** Philipson and Philipson

COROLLA blue to purple

STYLE 1.5–1.6 cm

DISTRIBUTION western China (northern and northwestern Yunnan)

R. orthocladum var. ***microleucum*** (Hutchinson) Philipson and Philipson

SYNONYM *R. microleucum* Hutchinson

ILLUSTRATION *Curtis's Botanical Magazine,* n.s., 171a (1951); Cox and Cox, *The Encyclopedia of Rhododendron Species,* 273 (1997)

COROLLA white

DISTRIBUTION known only in cultivation

A parent of the popular 'Ptarmigan' (× *R. leucaspis*).

244. *Rhododendron telmateium* Balfour and W. W. Smith

SYNONYM *R. drumonium* Balfour and W. W. Smith

ILLUSTRATION Fang, *Sichuan Rhododendron of China,* 290–291 (1986); Feng, *Rhododendrons of China* 1, pl. 72: 1–2 (1988); Cox and Cox, *The Encyclopedia of Rhododendron Species,* 278–279 (1997)

HABIT much-branched shrub forming dense cushions or mats, or erect and up to 1 m

LEAVES narrowly elliptic or lanceolate, 3–14 × 1.5–6 mm; lower surface golden fawn to orange-brown or reddish brown with densely overlapping scales, the majority pale gold to reddish brown, mixed with few to many dark brown scales

RACEME one- to 3-flowered

CALYX 0.5–2.5 mm, 5-lobed; lobes often unequal, rounded or triangular, scaly; margins with scales and long hairs

COROLLA broadly funnel-shaped, 7–14 mm, lavender-pink to purple, often downy outside, always scaly there

STAMENS 10, varying in length, the longest usually as long as the corolla

OVARY scaly

STYLE 3–17 mm, shorter to longer than the stamens, hairless or hairy, sometimes somewhat scaly towards the base

CAPSULE c. 3 mm, scaly

DISTRIBUTION western China (northern and central Yunnan, southwestern Sichuan)

FLOWERING spring

HARDINESS ZONE 8

Classic wild-collected material is available under *Forrest 20477, 21250.* Recent non-authenticated material from Yunnan is also in cultivation.

245. *Rhododendron nivale* Hooker

HABIT low, compact, much-branched shrub, prostrate or up to 1 m; bark brown to pale brown, striate

LEAVES broadly elliptic or ovate or almost circular, 3.5–12 × 1.5–6 mm; lower surface yellowish to fawn, often with dark brown speckling; scales contiguous or almost so, the majority pale gold, mixed with fewer, scattered, darker brown scales

INFLORESCENCE BUDS spherical to oblong or ovoid; bud scales with sparse scales on the surface and fringed with sparse hairs; outer scales brownish, slightly pointed; inner scales paler, not pointed

RACEME one- to 3-flowered

CALYX rim-like or 5-lobed, 2–4.5 mm; lobes oblong or narrowly triangular, scaly and sometimes downy at the base; margins of lobes scaly, sometimes hairy

COROLLA broadly funnel-shaped, 7–16 mm, pinkish magenta to purple, often somewhat downy outside

STAMENS 10, shorter than the corolla; anthers brown to pale orange-brown

OVARY scaly

STYLE 3.5–18 mm, longer or shorter than the stamens, sometimes slightly hairy at the base

CAPSULE 3–5 mm, scaly

DISTRIBUTION Himalaya, western China

FLOWERING spring

HARDINESS ZONE 5

R. nivale subsp. ***nivale***

SYNONYM *R. paludosum* Hutchinson and Kingdon-Ward

ILLUSTRATION Hooker, *Rhododendrons of the Sikkim Himalaya,* t. 26 (1851); *Iconographia Cormophytorum Sinicorum* 3, t. 4063 (1974); *The Rhododendron Handbook,* f. 23 (1997); Cox and Cox, *The Encyclopedia of Rhododendron Species,* 271 (1997); Feng, *Rhododendrons of China* 3, pl. 75: 1–2 (1999)

LEAF APEX rounded

CALYX lobes 2–4.5 mm; margins scaly

DISTRIBUTION from the Himalaya to western China (Xizang)

Wild-collected material is available under *Cooper 3483, Hruby 10, Kingdon-Ward 5777,* and *Schilling 2269.* Recent nonauthenticated material from Nepal and Bhutan is also in cultivation.

R. nivale subsp. ***boreale*** Philipson and Philipson

SYNONYMS *R. nigropunctatum* Franchet; *R. stictophyllum* Balfour; *R. yaragongense* Balfour

ILLUSTRATION *Curtis's Botanical Magazine,* 8529 (1913); *Iconographia Cormophytorum Sinicorum* 3, t. 4059 (1974); Davidian, *The Rhododendron Species* 1, pl. 33 (1982); Fang, *Sichuan Rhododendron of China,* 282–283 (1986); Cox and Cox, *The Encyclopedia of Rhododendron Species,* 271–272 (1997)

CALYX rim-like

DISTRIBUTION western China (southeastern Xizang, northwestern Yunnan, western Sichuan)

Classic wild-collected material is available under *Rock 23310, 24385.* Plants cultivated as this variety under *Forrest 15370* and *Rock 25377* are incorrectly named.

R. nivale subsp. ***australe*** Philipson and Philipson

ILLUSTRATION Fang, *Sichuan Rhododendron of China,* 284–285 (1986)

LEAF APEX more or less acute

CALYX lobes 2–4.5 mm; margins hairy

DISTRIBUTION western China (northwestern and central Yunnan)

Recent, nonauthenticated, wild-collected material identified as *R. nivale,* but not yet identified to subspecies, is also in cultivation.

246. *Rhododendron lapponicum* (Linnaeus) Wahlenberg

SYNONYMS *Azalea lapponica* Linnaeus; *R. parvifolium* Adams

ILLUSTRATION *Curtis's Botanical Magazine,* 3106 (1831) and 9229 (1928); Davidian, *The Rhododendron Species* 1, pl. 39 (1982); Moser, *Rhododendron: Wildarten und Hybriden,* 187 (1991); Cox and Cox, *The Encyclopedia of Rhododendron Species,* 269 (1997)

HABIT much-branched, prostrate or erect shrub to 1 m

LEAVES oblong-elliptic to elliptic-ovate, 4–25 × 2–9 mm; lower surface fawn to reddish brown; scales contiguous, some pale yellowish brown and others reddish brown

RACEME 3- to 6-flowered

CALYX 1–2 mm; lobes triangular, variably scaly; margins hairy

COROLLA broadly funnel-shaped, 6.5–15 mm, violet-rose to purple, rarely whitish

STAMENS 5–10

OVARY scaly

STYLE 1–1.5 cm, exceeding the stamens, scaleless, hairless

CAPSULE scaly, 4–6 mm

DISTRIBUTION scattered around the northern hemisphere
FLOWERING spring
HARDINESS ZONE 2

Much material of this species has been collected in recent years, though not a great deal of it has been spread widely in cultivation.

247. *Rhododendron capitatum* Maximowicz

ILLUSTRATION *Iconographia Cormophytorum Sinicorum* 3, t. 4060 (1974); Fang, *Sichuan Rhododendron of China*, 294–297 (1986); Cox and Cox, *The Encyclopedia of Rhododendron Species*, 261 (1997)
HABIT compact or rounded shrub to 1.5 m; bark greyish brown, ridged
LEAVES elliptic or oblong-elliptic, 1–2.2 cm × 3–9 mm; lower surface pale brown with darker speckling; scales spaced or almost contiguous, mostly colourless to yellowish with pale golden centres, the rest brown to dark orange with dark centres
INFLORESCENCE BUDS fusiform, greenish at the base, brownish at the tip; scales with a patch or stripe of hairs down the midline
RACEME 3- to 5-flowered
CALYX variably lobed; lobes often unequal, to 6 mm, downy or scaly at the base; margins hairy
COROLLA broadly funnel-shaped, 1–1.5 cm, pale lavender to bluish purple or deep purple
STAMENS 10; anthers brown
OVARY scaly; style 6–13 mm, usually slightly exceeding the stamens, hairless or slightly hairy towards the base
CAPSULE 5–6 mm, scaly
DISTRIBUTION China (northern Sichuan, Qinghai, Gansu, Shaanxi)
FLOWERING spring
HARDINESS ZONE 8

Classic wild-collected material is available under *Rock 13605*.

248. *Rhododendron russatum* Balfour and Forrest

SYNONYM *R. cantabile* Hutchinson
ILLUSTRATION *Curtis's Botanical Magazine*, 8963 (1923); *Kew Magazine* 7, pl. 161 (1990), reprinted in Halliday, *The Illustrated Rhododendron*, pl. 36 (2001); *Iconographia Cormophytorum Sinicorum* 3, t. 4050 (1974); Cox and Cox, *The Encyclopedia of Rhododendron Species*, 276 (1997)

R. russatum flower and leaf

R. russatum detail

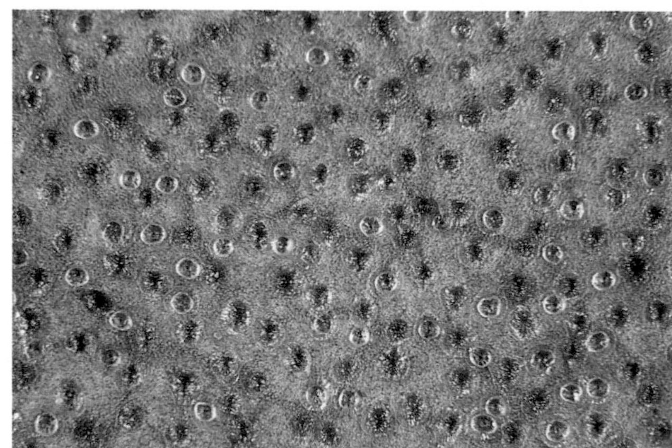

R. russatum leaf surface

HABIT shrub to 1.5 m; bark greyish brown, striate

LEAVES narrowly to broadly elliptic or oblong, 1.6–4 cm × 6–17 mm; lower surface heavily speckled with brown or reddish brown, or almost uniformly reddish brown; scales contiguous or almost so, varying in colour from pale gold to deep brown

INFLORESCENCE BUDS ovoid to spherical, yellow or brownish, scaly on the surface, fringed with long brown or white hairs; outer scales brownish; inner scales white or yellow sometimes tipped with red

RACEME with up to 6 flowers

CALYX 5-lobed; lobes to 6 mm, broadly oblong, with a few scales at the base and in central bands on the lobes; margins hairy and sometimes with a few scales

COROLLA broadly funnel-shaped, 1–2 cm, purple, pink, or rose, often downy outside

STAMENS 10; anthers pinkish brown to dark purple

OVARY scaly and sometimes with a tuft of hairs at the apex

STYLE 1.4–2 cm, downy for about the lower half of its length

CAPSULE to 6 mm, scaly, hairy at the apex

DISTRIBUTION western China (northern Yunnan, southwestern Sichuan)

FLOWERING spring

HARDINESS ZONE 5

Classic wild-collected material is available under *Forrest 13915, 19440, 19458, 25500,* and *Rock 3963* (equivalent herbarium specimen *18462*), *11243, 11296, 11284, 59597* from China (Yunnan, Li-ti-ping, 3650 m; equivalent herbarium specimen *11318*). Recent nonauthenticated material from Yunnan is also in cultivation. Material named as *R. russatum* and grown as *Forrest 21932* is either wrongly named, wrongly numbered, or both, as the herbarium specimen of this collection is *R. telmateium.*

249. ***Rhododendron rupicola*** W. W. Smith

HABIT much-branched shrub to 1.2 m

LEAVES broadly elliptic to elliptic or oblong or almost ovate, 6.5–20 × 3–13 mm; lower surface fawn, heavily stippled with reddish brown; scales overlapping or almost so, mostly dark brown, but some golden or amber

RACEME with up to 6 flowers

CALYX lobes 2.5–6 mm, broadly ovate, occasionally downy, with a broad central band of scales; margins hairy

COROLLA broadly funnel-shaped, 8–18 mm, usually intense purple or yellow, occasionally reddish or almost white

STAMENS 5–10, the number varying within one inflorescence
OVARY either entirely downy or bearing scales in the upper half, occasionally with an apical tuft of hairs as well
STYLE 1–2 cm, usually downy towards the base
CAPSULE 4–6 mm, usually downy, scaly above
DISTRIBUTION northeastern Myanmar, western China
FLOWERING spring
HARDINESS ZONE 5

R. *rupicola* var. ***rupicola***
SYNONYM *R. achroanthum* Balfour and W. W. Smith
ILLUSTRATION Feng, *Rhododendrons of China* 1, pl. 70 (1988); Cox and Cox, *The Encyclopedia of Rhododendron Species*, 274 (1997)
COROLLA purple or reddish, rarely whitish
DISTRIBUTION northeastern Myanmar, western China (southeastern Xizang, northern Yunnan, southwestern Sichuan)

Classic wild-collected material is available under *Forrest 15367, 16579* (herbarium specimen in part also var. *chryseum*), *21975*, and *Kingdon-Ward 7048*. Recent nonauthenticated material from Yunnan is also in cultivation. Plants cultivated as this variety under *Forrest 20464* are either wrongly named, wrongly numbered, or both.

R. *rupicola* var. ***chryseum*** (Balfour and Kingdon-Ward) Philipson and Philipson
SYNONYM *R. chryseum* Balfour and Kingdon-Ward
ILLUSTRATION *Curtis's Botanical Magazine*, 9246 (1928); Davidian, *The Rhododendron Species* 1, pl. 38 (1982); Feng, *Rhododendrons of China* 1, pl. 71: 1–2 (1988); Cox and Cox, *The Encyclopedia of Rhododendron Species*, 274–275 (1997)
CALYX lobes margined with hairs only
COROLLA yellow
DISTRIBUTION northeastern Myanmar, western China (southeastern Xizang, northwestern Yunnan)

Classic wild-collected material is available under *Kingdon-Ward 9609, Rock 7, 59189* (equivalent herbarium specimens *10126, 11198*), and *Yü 19741* (herbarium specimen also includes some material of var. *rupicola*). Recent nonauthenticated material from Yunnan is also in cultivation.

R. rupicola var. ***muliense*** (Balfour and Forrest) Philipson and Philipson
SYNONYM *R. muliense* Balfour and Forrest
ILLUSTRATION *Iconographia Cormophytorum Sinicorum* 3, t. 4048 (1974); Fang, *Sichuan Rhododendron of China*, 277–279 (1986); Cox and Cox, *The Encyclopedia of Rhododendron Species*, 275 (1997)
CALYX lobes margined with hairs and scales
COROLLA yellow
DISTRIBUTION western China (southwestern Sichuan)

Classic wild-collected material is available under *Forrest 29249* and *Yü 14641*.

250. *Rhododendron setosum* D. Don
ILLUSTRATION Hooker, *Rhododendrons of the Sikkim Himalaya*, t. 20 (1851); *Curtis's Botanical Magazine*, 8523 (1913); *Iconographia Cormophytorum Sinicorum* 3, t. 4055 (1974); Cox and Cox, *The Encyclopedia of Rhododendron Species*, 277 (1997)
HABIT small, intricate shrub to 30 cm; young shoots densely scaly, densely bristly; bark grey-brown, striate
LEAVES elliptic or oblong or obovate, 1–1.5 cm × 6–8 mm; upper surface with bristly margins, dark green, persistently scaly, with golden scales; lower surface pale green, densely scaly, with golden, vesicular scales mixed with flat, broadly rimmed, pale to dark brown scales
INFLORESCENCE BUDS ovoid, pointed, reddish brown; scales with white hairs on the surface and on the margins
RACEME one- to 3-flowered
CALYX 5-lobed; lobes 5–8 mm, oblong or rounded, scaly, sometimes bristly
COROLLA openly funnel-shaped, 1.5–1.8 cm, purple or pinkish
STAMENS 10, projecting beyond the corolla
OVARY scaly and downy towards the apex
STYLE exceeding the stamens, hairless, scaleless
CAPSULE to 5 mm, scaly
DISTRIBUTION Himalaya
FLOWERING spring
HARDINESS ZONE 6

Wild-collected material is available under *Bartholomew 193, Beer 633, Hruby 10, Polunin 106*, and *Schilling 2260*. Recent nonauthenticated material from India (Sikkim), Nepal, and Bhutan is also in cultivation.

Easily recognised, as it is the only species in this subsection to have bristles on the young shoots and leaf margins.

Subgenus *Rhododendron*
Section *Rhododendron*
Subsection *Rhododendron* (*Ferrugineum* series)

HABIT small shrubs
RACEME terminal, with a conspicuous axis
CALYX small but clearly lobed
COROLLA tubular-campanulate, scaly and usually downy outside
STAMENS 10
STYLE short or long, straight or declinate, inserted into a depression on top of the ovary
SEEDS elongate, unwinged and without appendages

This subsection contains the only European members of subgenus *Rhododendron*. The plants of all 3 species tend to be small, forming dense clumps, and the flowers have rather long, parallel-sided corolla tubes. The leaves have a one-layered upper epidermis, the cuticle as thick as the cells are deep; water tissue is absent, and the cells of the lower epidermis are slightly prolonged into papillae. Sclereids are absent.

1 a Leaves ciliate with bristle-like hairs; style downy at the base . . . . **252. *R. hirsutum***
b Leaves not ciliate; style hairless . . . . **251. *R. ferrugineum***

251. *Rhododendron ferrugineum* Linnaeus
ILLUSTRATION Reichenbach, *Icones Florae Germanicae* 17, t. 1158 (1855); Hegi, *Illustrierte Flora von Mitteleuropa* 5 (3), t. 206 (1926); Hess et al., *Flora der Schweiz* 2: 912 (1970); Davidian, *The Rhododendron Species* 1, pl. 90 (1982); Moser, *Rhododendron: Wildarten und Hybriden,* 165 (1991); Kneller, *The Book of Rhododendrons,* 85 (1995); Cox and Cox, *The Encyclopedia of Rhododendron Species,* 312 (1997)
HABIT small shrub with erect or ascending branches, to 1.5 m; young shoots densely scaly, sometimes with a few bristles; bark grey-brown, striate
LEAVES narrowly elliptic to elliptic, slightly revolute, 2.8–4 cm × 8–16 mm; upper surface dark green; lower surface reddish brown, with dense, overlapping scales
INFLORESCENCE BUDS ovoid, rounded, yellowish green; scales with a few scales near the midrib, and with a fringe of fine white hairs
RACEME many-flowered
CALYX lobes to 1.5 mm, scaly and bristly on the margins
COROLLA 1.2–1.7 cm, deep pink, rarely pale or whitish, scaly and downy outside
STAMENS anthers yellow

OVARY scaly; style hairless and scaleless, about twice as long as the ovary
CAPSULE sparsely scaly, 5–7 mm
DISTRIBUTION central Europe (Alps, Pyrenees)
FLOWERING late spring
HARDINESS ZONE 4

Much wild-origin material of this species has been collected in Europe.

R. ferrugineum flower and leaf

R. ferrugineum detail

R. ferrugineum leaf surface

252. *Rhododendron hirsutum* Linnaeus

ILLUSTRATION *Curtis's Botanical Magazine,* 1853 (1816), reprinted in Halliday, *The Illustrated Rhododendron,* pl. 37 (2001); Reichenbach, *Icones Florae Germanicae* 17, t. 1158 (1855); Hegi, *Illustrierte Flora von Mitteleuropa* 5 (3), t. 206 (1926); Hess et al., *Flora der Schweiz* 2: 912 (1970); Urquhart, *The Rhododendron* 2, t. 24 (1972); Davidian, *The Rhododendron Species* 1, pl. 22 (1982); Moser, *Rhododendron: Wildarten und Hybriden,* 176 (1991); Cox and Cox, *The Encyclopedia of Rhododendron Species,* 313 (1997)

HABIT small shrub to 1 m; young shoots sparsely scaly, downy, bristly

LEAVES flat, narrowly obovate to obovate or almost circular, 1.3–3.3 cm × 7–14 mm; upper surface scaleless; lower surface with well-separated golden scales and margins with long bristles

RACEME many-flowered

CALYX lobes 2–4 mm, narrowly triangular, scaly; margins with bristles

COROLLA pink, sparsely scaly and hairy outside, 1.2–1.8 cm

OVARY scaly

STYLE as long as the ovary or a little longer, sparsely hairy at the base

CAPSULE sparsely scaly, 5–6 mm

DISTRIBUTION central Europe (Alps)

FLOWERING spring

HARDINESS ZONE 4

Many wild-origin collections have been made in recent years. One of the few rhododendrons that can be cultivated in a calcareous soil.

Less commonly cultivated is:

Rhododendron myrtifolium Schott and Kotschy

SYNONYM *R. kotschyi* Simonkai

ILLUSTRATION Reichenbach, *Icones Florae Germanicae* 17, t. 1157 (1855); *Curtis's Botanical Magazine,* 9132 (1927); Cox and Cox, *The Encyclopedia of Rhododendron Species,* 313–314 (1997)

Very similar to *R. ferrugineum,* but:

HABIT smaller, rarely exceeding 50 cm

LEAVES narrowly obovate; lower surface less densely scaly; margins obscurely scolloped

COROLLA more densely hairy and less scaly outside

STYLE shorter than or as long as the ovary

DISTRIBUTION eastern Europe (Bulgaria, former Yugoslavia, Romania, western European part of Russia)

FLOWERING late spring

HARDINESS ZONE 4

Subgenus *Rhododendron*

Section *Rhododendron*

Subsection *Rhodorastra* (Maximowicz) Cullen (section *Rhodorastra* Maximowicz; subgenus *Rhodorastra* (Maximowicz) C. B. Clarke; *Dauricum* series)

HABIT small to medium shrubs
LEAVES partially or entirely deciduous
NEW VEGETATIVE GROWTH from buds borne below those which produce the inflorescences
RACEME one-flowered, axillary, clustered at the ends of the branches
CALYX small, rim-like
COROLLA openly funnel-shaped, densely hairy outside near the base
STAMENS 10, declinate
STYLE declinate, impressed into a depression on top of the ovary
SEEDS elongate, unwinged and without appendages

This is a small subsection of 2 (or more) species from eastern Asia, characterised by having generally at least some of the leaves deciduous, and by the corolla being hairy outside. The leaves have a one-layered upper epidermis, the cuticle thin; water tissue is absent, and the cells of the lower epidermis are not prolonged into papillae. Sclereids are absent.

Because of the one-flowered, lateral inflorescences, this group has been variously treated as a subgenus or a section; however, it is so similar to the subsections around it in this account, that treatment at the subsectional level seems most appropriate.

1a Leaves usually thick, usually at least some persisting through winter, obtuse or notched at the apex, 1–3.6 cm; corolla to 3.5 cm in diameter . . . . **253. *R. dauricum***
b Leaves thin, deciduous, acute to acuminate at the apex, 4–6 cm; corolla 3.3–4 cm in diameter . . . . **254. *R. mucronulatum***

253. *Rhododendron dauricum* Linnaeus

ILLUSTRATION *Curtis's Botanical Magazine,* 636 (1803) and 1888 (1817), reprinted in Halliday, *The Illustrated Rhododendron,* pl. 38 (2001) and 8930 (1921); *Loddiges' Botanical Cabinet* 15, t. 1446 (1828); *Gardeners' Chronicle* 53: 51 (1913); *Iconographia Cormophytorum Sinicorum* 3, t. 4238 (1974); Feng, *Rhododendrons of China* 2, pl. 81: 1–2 (1992); Cox and Cox, *The Encyclopedia of Rhododendron Species,* 314–315 (1997); Robertson and McKelvie, *Scottish Rock Gardening in the 20th Century,* f. 211 (2000)
HABIT straggling shrubs to 1.5 m; young shoots scaly, downy; bark greyish brown, striate

LEAVES at least some overwintering, leathery, elliptic, 1–3.5 cm × 5–20 mm, minutely downy along the base of the midrib above, densely scaly beneath

INFLORESCENCE BUDS scales few, small, brownish or whitish, the exposed parts with lepidote scales

FLOWER STALKS very short and obscure

CALYX rim-like, densely scaly

COROLLA 1.4–2 cm, 2–3.5 cm in diameter, pink or violet-pink

STAMENS projecting beyond the corolla; anthers grey

OVARY scaly

STYLE scaleless

CAPSULE scaly

DISTRIBUTION Russia (eastern Siberia), Mongolia, northern China, Japan

FLOWERING late winter

HARDINESS ZONE 5

Many wild-origin collections of this species have been made in recent years, generally in Japan and eastern Asia.

A very variable species, especially with regard to the persistence of the leaves and their shape and size. Russian authors (see Pojarkova 1952) recognise 3 species: in this sense, genuine *R. dauricum* has leaves which are dark green above, rusty brown beneath, and mostly overwintering, the plant flowering in spring while covered in last year's leaves. *Rhododendron ledebourii* Pojarkova has leaves pale above and beneath, mostly falling in late autumn, with a few scales on the upper surface, whereas *R. sichotense* Pojarkova is similar but has no scales on the upper leaf surface. These 2 names are used in gardens, but it is still uncertain what they really represent.

Rhododendron dauricum (in the general sense) is a parent of several hybrids, including 'Praecox' (× *R. ciliatum*) and 'Fittra' (× *R. racemosum*).

254. *Rhododendron mucronulatum* Turczaninow

ILLUSTRATION *Curtis's Botanical Magazine,* 8304 (1910); Nakai, *Flora Sylvatica Koreana* 8, t. 10 (1919); Komarov (ed.), *Flora SSSR* 18, t. 2 (1952); *Iconographia Cormophytorum Sinicorum* 3, t. 4284 (1974); Feng, *Rhododendrons of China* 2, pl. 82: 1–3 (1992); Kneller, *The Book of Rhododendrons,* 87 (1995); Cox and Cox, *The Encyclopedia of Rhododendron Species,* 316 (1997)

HABIT straggling, open shrub to 2 m; young shoots scaly, downy

LEAVES completely deciduous, thin, 4–6 × 1.5–3 cm; upper surface with bristles parallel to the surface towards the margins, at least when young; lower surface sparsely scaly

R. mucronulatum flower

R. mucronulatum detail

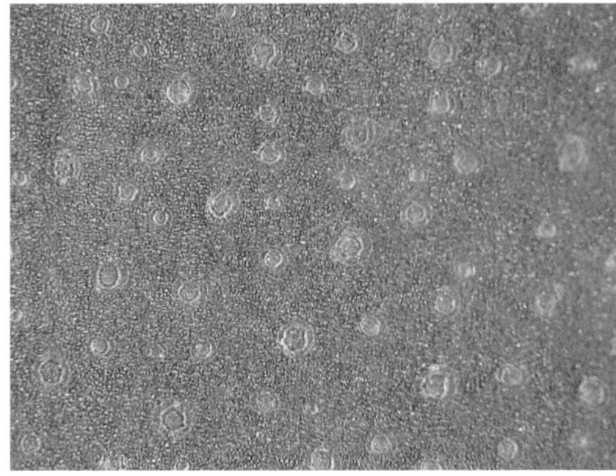

R. mucronulatum leaf surface

Flowers appearing before leaves expand; flower stalks very short, obscure
Calyx rim-like, scaly
Corolla very openly funnel-shaped, 2–2.6 cm, 3.3–4.2 cm in diameter, bright mauve-pink, rarely white, hairy outside towards the base
Stamens projecting beyond the corolla; anthers blue or magenta, sometimes black at the tip
Ovary scaly
Style scaleless
Capsule scaly
Distribution eastern Russia, northern and central China, Mongolia, Korea, Japan
Flowering late winter
Hardiness zone 4

Wild-collected material is available under *Beyer, Erskine, and Cowley 45, Kalmthout Arboretum* (without number), *Kwanak Arboretum, Seoul* (without number), *Maisala Arboretum* (without number), *Suzuki* (without number), and *Waimea Arboretum* (without number).

'Cornell Pink' has large, clear pink flowers.

Subgenus *Rhododendron*

Section *Rhododendron*

Subsection *Saluenensia* (Hutchinson) Sleumer (*Saluenense* series)

HABIT small shrubs; young shoots densely scaly and variably bristly, the bristles variably deciduous

LEAVES evergreen; lower surface very densely scaly, the scales often in 2 or more tiers; margins of the rims finely scolloped (at a magnification of 15× or 20×)

RACEME terminal, several-flowered

CALYX deeply 5-lobed

COROLLA very openly funnel-shaped to almost flat, downy and scaly outside

STAMENS 10, declinate

STYLE declinate, inserted into a depression on top of the ovary

SEEDS elongate, unwinged and without appendages (or appendages minute)

A subsection of 2 closely related and variable species. The plants are small and form dense clumps or mats. The subsection is characterised by the inflorescences being rather sunk in a depression in the centre of the whorl of leaves, and the uppermost leaves themselves are bract-like, with rather small blades and very broad stalks. The leaves have a one-layered upper epidermis, the cuticle half as thick to as thick as the cells are deep; water tissue is absent, and the cells of the lower epidermis are not prolonged as papillae. Sclereids are absent.

Subsection *Fragariflora* Cullen, which consists of a single species, *R. fragariflorum* Kingdon-Ward, from Bhutan and western China (Xizang), is very similar but has leaves with crenulate margins and scales that are vesicular. The species has been in cultivation but is now very rare; it is illustrated in *The Rhododendron Handbook*, f. 11 and 14 (1997).

1 a Shoots, leaf stalks, leaf midribs beneath, leaf margins, and usually flower stalks bristly-hairy; ovary downy, at least at the apex . . . . **256. *R. saluenense***

b Shoots, leaf stalks, and leaf midribs beneath not bristly-hairy; leaf margins and flower stalks bristly-hairy or not; ovary completely hairless . . . . **255. *R. calostrotum***

255. *Rhododendron calostrotum* Balfour and Kingdon-Ward

HABIT prostrate, matted, or erect intricate shrub, 5–150 cm high; young shoots scaly, bristly only at first, then rather sparsely so; bark brownish, gradually scaling

LEAVES oblong-ovate to almost circular, 1–3.3 cm × 4–20 mm; upper surface usually matt, with persistent, dried-out scales and bristly margins; lower surface with dense, overlapping scales arranged in 3 or 4 tiers, those of the uppermost tier with long stalks and cup-shaped rims

INFLORESCENCE BUDS spherical, reddish brown; scales scaly, with white hairs on exposed surfaces and brown hairs on the margin

RACEME one- to 5-flowered

CALYX lobes ovate to oblong, often unequal, variably scaly and downy on the outer surface; margins bristly; inner surface finely downy

COROLLA magenta or more rarely pink or purple, often with darker spots on the upper lobes, 1.8–2.8 cm, hairy and occasionally somewhat scaly outside

STAMENS anthers very dark brown

OVARY scaly but hairless

CAPSULE 6–9 mm, scaly

DISTRIBUTION northeastern India (Arunachal Pradesh), northeastern Myanmar, western China (southeastern Xizang, northern Yunnan)

FLOWERING spring

HARDINESS ZONE 6

A variable species. Four subspecies occur in the wild, and all have been grown.

R. *calostrotum* subsp. ***calostrotum***

ILLUSTRATION *Curtis's Botanical Magazine,* 9001 (1923), reprinted in Halliday, *The Illustrated Rhododendron,* pl. 39 (2001); *The Garden* 88: 268 (1924); *Gardeners' Chronicle* 87: 511 (1930); Urquhart, *The Rhododendron* 1, t. 9 (1958); *Iconographia Cormophytorum Sinicorum* 3, t. 4041 (1974); Davidian, *The Rhododendron Species* 1, pl. 53 (1982); Feng, *Rhododendrons of China* 1, pl. 63: 1–2 (1988); Cox and Cox, *The Encyclopedia of Rhododendron Species,* 317 (1997)

LEAVES 1.2–2.2 cm × 7–20 mm, persistently scaly above, obtuse, scales on the lower surface clearly borne in 3 or 4 tiers

FLOWERS 1–2 in each raceme; flower stalks 1.6–2.7 cm

DISTRIBUTION northeastern Myanmar, western China (northern Yunnan)

Classic wild-collected material is available under *Farrer 1045, Rock 18453,* and *Yü 19757.*

Material grown as this subspecies under *Rock 3954* is incorrectly numbered, as the herbarium specimen equivalent to this seed number (*18453*) is subsp. *riparioides.* Further material grown as this subspecies under *Forrest 29666* is also incorrect, as the herbarium material of this number is *R. saluenense.*

R. calostrotum subsp. ***riparium*** (Kingdon-Ward) Cullen

SYNONYMS *R. riparium* Kingdon-Ward; *R. calciphilum* Hutchinson; *R. nitens* Hutchinson; *R. calostrotum* var. *calciphilum* (Hutchinson and Kingdon-Ward) Davidian

ILLUSTRATION Davidian, *The Rhododendron Species* 1, pl. 54 (1982); Cox and Cox, *The Encyclopedia of Rhododendron Species,* 317 (1997)

Similar to subsp. *calostrotum,* but:

FLOWERS 2–5 in each raceme; flower stalks 1–1.5 cm

DISTRIBUTION northern India (Arunachal Pradesh), northeastern Myanmar, western China (northwestern Yunnan, southern and southeastern Xizang)

Classic wild-collected material is available under *Kingdon-Ward 5482, 6903, 6984, 7061, 7062, 8229, 9394,* and *Ludlow, Sherriff, and Taylor 6588.*

R. calostrotum subsp. ***riparioides*** Cullen

LEAVES 2.2–3.3 cm; lower surface with scales flattened together, not clearly arranged in 3 or 4 tiers; upper surface scaly, with obtuse apex

DISTRIBUTION western China (northwestern Yunnan)

Classic wild-collected material is available under *Forrest 25542, 30540.*

R. calostrotum subsp. ***keleticum*** (Balfour and Forrest) Cullen

SYNONYMS *R. keleticum* Balfour and Forrest; *R. radicans* Balfour and Forrest

ILLUSTRATION *Gardeners' Chronicle* 83: 333 (1928); Davidian, *The Rhododendron Species* 1, pl. 55 (1982); Feng, *Rhododendrons of China* 1, pl. 64: 1–3 (1988); Moser, *Rhododendron: Wildarten und Hybriden,* 140 (1991); Cox and Cox, *The Encyclopedia of Rhododendron Species,* 318 (1997)

HABIT prostrate shrublet

LEAVES 2–9 mm wide, acute, without scales and shining dark green above

DISTRIBUTION northeastern Myanmar, western China (southeastern Xizang, northwestern Yunnan)

Classic wild-collected material is available under *Forrest 19915, 19919, 20255, 21756, 21757,* and *Rock 58, 59182* (equivalent herbarium specimens *10122, 11188*). Recent nonauthenticated material belonging to *R. calostrotum,* but not identified to subspecies, is also in cultivation.

The last of these subspecies, a high-alpine variant, is probably the most widely grown; some variants of it are completely prostrate, and these are the plants that have been called *R. radicans;* one of these is a parent of 'Radmosum' (× *R. racemosum*).

256. *Rhododendron saluenense* Franchet

HABIT prostrate to upright shrub, 5–150 cm; young shoots persistently bristly; bark yellowish brown, striate or scaling

LEAVES oblong-circular to oblong-elliptic or rarely oblong-obovate, 8–30 × 5–15 mm; upper surface scaleless (rarely scaly), dark glossy green, often with a few bristles on the midrib near the base, with persistently bristly margins; lower surface fawn to brown, with dense, overlapping scales borne in several tiers, and midrib with some bristles

INFLORESCENCE BUDS fusiform, closely surrounded by the upper, bract-like leaves; scales yellowish or reddish to white, densely hairy all over the surface, especially towards the margins

RACEME one- to 3-flowered

CALYX lobes oblong-circular, 4.5–8 mm, variably scaly, downy and bristly outside, downy within

COROLLA widely spreading, 1.7–2.8 cm, magenta to purple, rarely bluish purple, hairy and with a few scales outside

OVARY scaly, usually also downy, especially within the depression at the apex

CAPSULE scaly, 6–8 mm

DISTRIBUTION northeastern Myanmar, western China (northern Yunnan, southeastern Xizang, southwestern Sichuan)

FLOWERING spring

HARDINESS ZONE 6

R. saluenense subsp. ***saluenense***

ILLUSTRATION *Curtis's Botanical Magazine,* 9095 (1925); *Iconographia Cormophytorum Sinicorum* 3, t. 4040 (1974); *Notes from the Royal Botanic Garden Edinburgh* 39: 21 (1980); Feng, *Rhododendrons of China* 1, pl. 65: 1–3 (1988); Kneller, *The Book of Rhododendrons,* 89 (1995); Cox and Cox, *The Encyclopedia of Rhododendron Species,* 319–320 (1997)

HABIT erect shrub to 1.5 m

LEAVES upper surface persistently scaly and usually with bristles

DISTRIBUTION northeastern Myanmar, western China (northwestern Yunnan, southeastern Xizang)

Classic wild-collected material is available under *Forrest 19479, 21760, 21772, Kingdon-Ward 6991, 7012, 9633, 10582, Rock 110, 23634, 59194* (equivalent herbarium specimen *11238*), *59478* (equivalent herbarium specimens *8822, 11005*), *59484* (equivalent herbarium specimens *9282, 11012*), and *Yü 7860.*

R. saluenense subsp. *saluenense* flower and leaf

R. saluenense subsp. *saluenense* detail

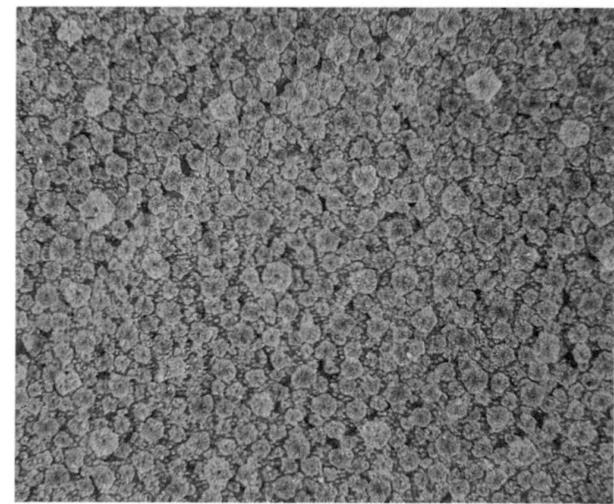

R. saluenense subsp. *saluenense* leaf surface

R. saluenense subsp. ***chameunum*** (Balfour and Forrest) Cullen

SYNONYMS *R. chameunum* Balfour and Forrest; *R. prostratum* W. W. Smith

ILLUSTRATION *Curtis's Botanical Magazine*, 8747 (1918); *Iconographia Cormophytorum Sinicorum* 3, t. 4042 (1974); Cox and Cox, *The Encyclopedia of Rhododendron Species*, 321 (1997)

HABIT prostrate or mat-forming shrub, rarely as much as 1 m high

LEAVES upper surface usually glossy green and without scales or bristles

DISTRIBUTION western China (northwestern Yunnan, southeastern Xizang, southwestern Sichuan)

Classic wild-collected material is available under *Forrest 5862, 12968, 13904, 19437, 25508, 25560, Rock 56, 23330, 25303*, and *Yü 8611, 8654*. Recent nonauthenticated material from Yunnan is also in cultivation, as is some recent material not yet identified to subspecies.

Subgenus *Rhododendron*

Section *Rhododendron*

Subsection *Uniflora* (Cowan and Davidian) Sleumer (*Uniflorum* series)

HABIT small shrubs, often prostrate or mat-forming
LEAVES evergreen, revolute or scolloped
RACEME terminal, one- to 3-flowered; flower stalks increasing in length and becoming rigid and erect in fruit
COROLLA funnel-campanulate, densely hairy outside
STAMENS 10, declinate
OVARY scaly
STYLE straight or declinate, impressed in a depression on top of the ovary
SEEDS elongate, unwinged and without appendages (or appendages minute)

There are 4 species in this subsection, and all of them are cultivated, though 3 of them are known from very little material in the wild. The plants form low, creeping or spreading clumps, and the flower stalks harden and become erect as the fruit develops. The leaves usually have a one-layered upper epidermis (in *R. ludlowii* it is 2-layered, the cells of both layers equal in size), the cuticle thin to thick; water tissue is absent, and the cells of the lower epidermis are generally prolonged into papillae. Sclereids are absent.

1a Corolla yellow; leaves slightly scolloped . . . . **260. *R. ludlowii***
b Corolla pink to purple; leaves not scolloped 2
2a Corolla 1.1–2.1 cm; tube 7–14 mm; style shorter than the stamens . . . . **257. *R. pumilum***
b Corolla 2.1–3 cm; tube 1.2–1.8 cm; style exceeding the stamens 3
3a Leaves obovate, the scales beneath close, markedly unequal; corolla 2.4–3 cm . . . . **258. *R. pemakoense***
b Leaves oblong-elliptic or narrowly elliptic, the scales beneath distant, more or less equal; corolla 2.1–2.5 cm . . . . **259. *R. uniflorum***

257. *Rhododendron pumilum* Hooker

ILLUSTRATION Hooker, *Rhododendrons of the Sikkim Himalaya,* t. 14 (1851); *Flore des Serres,* ser. 1, 7: t. 667 (1851–1852); *Iconographia Cormophytorum Sinicorum* 3, t. 4014 (1974); Cox and Cox, *The Encyclopedia of Rhododendron Species,* 357 (1997)
HABIT creeping small shrub to 10 cm high; young shoots scaly, downy
LEAVES elliptic to broadly elliptic, 9–19 × 4.5–12 mm; upper surface dark green,

more or less scaleless, revolute; lower surface pale greyish green, with distant, small, more or less equal, golden scales

RACEME one- to 3-flowered

CALYX reddish, deeply 5-lobed; lobes 2–3.5 mm, ovate-oblong or oblong, scaly

COROLLA campanulate, with slightly oblique mouth, 1–2 cm, pink or purple, densely hairy all over the outer surface; scales few, mostly on the lobes

STAMENS anthers brown

R. pumilum flower

R. pumilum detail

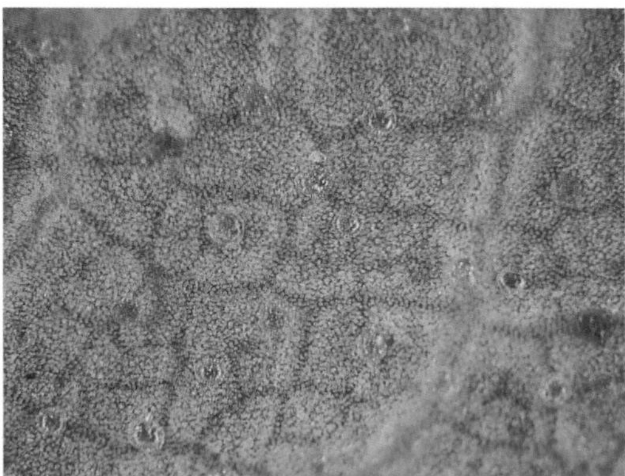

R. pumilum leaf surface

OVARY densely scaly
STYLE straight, somewhat club-shaped, shorter than the stamens
CAPSULE 7–10 mm, scaly
DISTRIBUTION Himalaya
FLOWERING spring
HARDINESS ZONE 6

Wild-collected material is available under *Ludlow, Sherriff, and Hicks 21184* and *McBeath 1120.* Recent nonauthenticated material from Nepal is also in cultivation.

258. *Rhododendron pemakoense* Kingdon-Ward
SYNONYM *R. patulum* Kingdon-Ward
ILLUSTRATION *Gardeners' Chronicle* 92: 480 (1932); Urquhart, *The Rhododendron* 2, t. 21 (1967); *Iconographia Cormophytorum Sinicorum* 3, t. 4016 (1974); Cox, *Dwarf Rhododendrons,* 181 (1979); Kneller, *The Book of Rhododendrons,* 99 (1995)—poor; Cox and Cox, *The Encyclopedia of Rhododendron Species,* 356 (1997)
HABIT prostrate or erect dwarf shrub; young shoots scaly, downy; bark pale shining brown, gradually scaling
LEAVES obovate or obovate-elliptic, 1.7–2.6 × 6–13 mm; upper surface more or less persistently scaly; lower surface with rather dense, unequal scales, the larger with somewhat wavy margins, all golden when young and often becoming dark brown
INFLORESCENCE BUDS ellipsoid, reddish; scales margined with white hairs; outer scales with few lepidote scales; inner scales more densely lepidote
RACEME one- to 2-flowered; flower stalks 9–10 mm in flower, to 2.5 cm in fruit
CALYX 5-lobed; lobes oblong, 2.5–4 mm, scaly, reddish
COROLLA campanulate, 2.4–3 cm, pink to pale purplish mauve, densely hairy and sparsely scaly outside
OVARY scaly, sometimes downy towards the apex; style exceeding the stamens, downy towards the base
CAPSULE scaly, to 1 cm
DISTRIBUTION eastern Himalaya
FLOWERING spring
HARDINESS ZONE 6

Classic wild-collected material is available under *Kingdon-Ward 6301* (the type collection).

Plants with pale purplish mauve corollas have been called *R. patulum,* but there seems no other significant difference.

259. *Rhododendron uniflorum* Kingdon-Ward

HABIT dwarf, more or less prostrate shrub, the ends of the branches ascending to c. 5 cm high; young shoots scaly

LEAVES oblong-elliptic, 1.3–2.5 cm × 5–10 mm; upper surface scaleless, revolute; lower surface with very distant, small, equal scales with very narrow rims, at first golden but rapidly becoming dark brown to almost black

RACEME one- to 2-flowered; flower stalks 1–1.2 cm in flower, to 2.5 cm in fruit

CALYX lobes 1.5–2.5 mm, oblong, scaly

COROLLA campanulate, purple, densely hairy and sparsely scaly outside, 2–2.5 cm

OVARY scaly; style longer than the stamens

CAPSULE scaly, to 1 cm

DISTRIBUTION northeastern Myanmar, western China (southeastern Xizang)

FLOWERING spring

HARDINESS ZONE 8

R. uniflorum var. ***uniflorum***

ILLUSTRATION Urquhart, *The Rhododendron* 2, t. 21 (1962); Davidian, *The Rhododendron Species* 1, pl. 72 (1982); Cox and Cox, *The Encyclopedia of Rhododendron Species,* 357–358 (1997)

LEAVES rounded at the apex

DISTRIBUTION western China (southeastern Xizang)

Classic wild-collected material is available under *Kingdon-Ward 5876* (the type collection).

R. uniflorum var. ***imperator*** (Kingdon-Ward) Cullen

SYNONYM *R. imperator* Kingdon-Ward

ILLUSTRATION *Curtis's Botanical Magazine,* n.s., 514 (1966), reprinted in Halliday, *The Illustrated Rhododendron,* pl. 41 (2001); Davidian, *The Rhododendron Species* 1, pl. 74 (1982); *The Rhododendron Handbook,* f. 16 (1997); Cox and Cox, *The Encyclopedia of Rhododendron Species,* 355 (1997)

LEAVES acute at the apex

DISTRIBUTION northeastern Myanmar

Classic wild-collected material is available under *Kingdon-Ward 6884* (the type collection).

Each variety is known from only a single wild collection, and from material in cultivation.

260. *Rhododendron ludlowii* Cowan

ILLUSTRATION *Curtis's Botanical Magazine,* n.s., t. 412 (1962), reprinted in Halliday, *The Illustrated Rhododendron,* pl. 42 (2001); Cox, *Dwarf Rhododendrons,* t. 35 (1973); Davidian, *The Rhododendron Species* 1, pl. 73 (1982); Cox and Cox, *The Encyclopedia of Rhododendron Species,* 355 (1997)

HABIT small, spreading shrub to 30 cm; young shoots scaly, with somewhat stalked scales

LEAVES broadly obovate or oblong-obovate, 1.5–1.6 cm × 9–10 mm, obtuse at the apex; margins somewhat scolloped; lower surface pale green with prominent veins and distant, brown, flat, rather narrowly rimmed scales

RACEME one-flowered

CALYX lobes to 7 mm, oblong, rounded, scaly, sparsely downy

COROLLA broadly funnel-campanulate, 2–2.3 cm, yellow drying greenish yellow, sometimes with red spots on the inside of the tube, densely downy and scaly on the outer surface

OVARY scaly

STYLE hairless, exceeding the stamens

DISTRIBUTION western China (southern Xizang)

FLOWERING spring

HARDINESS ZONE 6

Known only from a single wild collection, *Ludlow and Sherriff 1895* from China, and from material in cultivation which is probably derived from it.

Subgenus *Rhododendron*

Section *Rhododendron*

Subsection *Cinnabarina* (Hutchinson) Sleumer (*Cinnabarinum* series; section *Keysia* Spethmann 1980a, 165)

HABIT shrubs to 7 m; young shoots scaly, often glaucous
LEAVES evergreen or partly deciduous; lower surface scaly, with unequal, narrowly rimmed, close but not contiguous scales
RACEME terminal or axillary; flowers usually pendent
CALYX small, disc-like, sometimes wavy
COROLLA fleshy, waxy, tubular to campanulate; lobes not greatly spreading, often bloomed
STAMENS 10, declinate
OVARY scaly
STYLE declinate, impressed into a depression on top of the ovary
NECTAR copious, forming 5 droplets in the base of the corolla tube
CAPSULE scaly
SEEDS elongate, unwinged and without appendages (or appendages very small)

This is a subsection of 3 or 4 species, all characterised by tubular, tubular-campanulate, or campanulate flowers which contain rather copious amounts of watery nectar, either in the form of 5 droplets or in a single large drop; this combined with the bright reddish, yellowish, or magenta coloration of the corollas suggests that these species may be pollinated by birds. The leaves have a 2-layered upper epidermis, the cells of both layers more or less similar in size, the cuticle thin to about half as thick as the cells are deep; water tissue is absent, and the cells of the lower epidermis are prolonged into papillae. Sclereids are absent.

1a Inflorescences all terminal; corolla 2.5–3.6 cm; scales very narrowly rimmed . . **261. *R. cinnabarinum***
b Inflorescences mostly lateral; corolla to 2 cm; scales broadly rimmed . . . . **262. *R. keysii***

261. *Rhododendron cinnabarinum* Hooker
HABIT straggling shrub to 7 m; young shoots scaly, glaucous; bark grey-brown, striate
LEAVES usually evergreen but sometimes many deciduous, broadly to narrowly elliptic, 3–9 × 2.5–5 cm; upper surface scaly or scaleless; lower surface with rather fleshy, very narrowly rimmed, equal or unequal scales which are often reddish or purplish

INFLORESCENCE BUDS ovoid to obovoid, yellow-brown; scales bloomed, lepidote, fringed with white hairs
RACEME 2- to 7-flowered, all terminal
CALYX disc-like, wavy, scaly
COROLLA tubular-campanulate to campanulate, very variable in colour (yellow, orange [sometimes with a purple flush], red, red and yellow, or purplish), usually with a waxy bloom, 2.5–3.5 cm, scaly or scaleless outside
OVARY scaly and sometimes downy at the top
STYLE hairless or sparsely downy at the base, rarely somewhat scaly there
CAPSULE scaly, to 1 cm
DISTRIBUTION from the Himalaya to northern Myanmar
FLOWERING spring
HARDINESS ZONE 6

A variable species, divided into 3 intergrading subspecies, the extreme examples of which look very different from each other but which are connected (in the wild at least) by numerous intermediates.

R. *cinnabarinum* subsp. ***cinnabarinum***
SYNONYMS *R. roylei* Hooker; *R. blandfordiiflorum* Hooker
ILLUSTRATION Hooker, *Rhododendrons of the Sikkim Himalaya*, t. 8 (1849); *The Garden* 15, pl. 169 (1879) and 44, t. 940 (1893); *Curtis's Botanical Magazine*, 4930 (1856), reprinted in Halliday, *The Illustrated Rhododendron*, pl. 43 (2001); Urquhart, *The Rhododendron* 2, t. 25 (1962); Stainton, *Forests of Nepal*, t. 109 (1972); *Iconographia Cormophytorum Sinicorum* 3, t. 4045 (1974); Davidian, *The Rhododendron Species* 1, pl. 11–14 (1982); Moser, *Rhododendron: Wildarten und Hybriden*, 153 (1991); Cox and Cox, *The Encyclopedia of Rhododendron Species*, 244–245 (1997); Feng, *Rhododendrons of China* 3, pl. 78: 1 (1999)
LEAVES mostly evergreen, 2.2 or more × as long as broad, usually without scales above
COROLLA tubular-campanulate, not scaly outside, usually with some red, never purple
DISTRIBUTION from the Himalaya to western China (southeastern Xizang)

Wild-collected material is available under *Beer 652, Beer, Lancaster, and Morris 234, Cooper 3493, Ludlow and Sherriff 2850,* and *Swiss Expedition 1820.* Recent nonauthenticated material from India (Sikkim) and Bhutan is also in cultivation.

R. *cinnabarinum* subsp. ***xanthocodon*** (Hutchinson) Cullen
SYNONYMS *R. xanthocodon* Hutchinson; *R. concatenans* Hutchinson; *R. cinnabarinum* var. *purpurellum* Cowan

Illustration Urquhart, *The Rhododendron* 1, t. 13 (1958); Hara, *Photo-Album of Plants of Eastern Himalaya*, t. 165 (1968); *Curtis's Botanical Magazine*, n.s., 634 (1972); Davidian, *The Rhododendron Species* 1, pl. 15–16 (1982); Moser, *Rhododendron: Wildarten und Hybriden*, 154 (1991); *The Rhododendron Handbook*, f. 22 (1997); Cox and Cox, *The Encyclopedia of Rhododendron Species*, 245–246 (1997); Feng, *Rhododendrons of China* 3, pl. 78: 2 (1999)

R. cinnabarinum subsp. *xanthocodon* flower and leaf

R. cinnabarinum subsp. *xanthocodon* detail

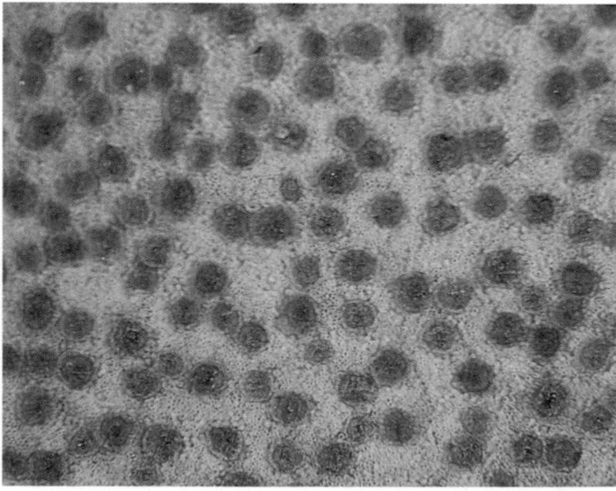

R. cinnabarinum subsp. *xanthocodon* leaf surface

LEAVES mostly evergreen, less than 2.2 × as long as broad, without scales above
COROLLA campanulate, not scaly outside, yellow, orange, orange with a purplish flush, or purple
STAMENS anthers usually brown
DISTRIBUTION northeastern India (Arunachal Pradesh), Bhutan, China (southern Xizang)

Classic wild-collected material is available under *Kingdon-Ward 5874, 6026, Ludlow, Sherriff, and Hicks 17521, Ludlow, Sherriff, and Taylor 6349, 6349A, 6560,* and *Sherriff 6/38.* Recent nonauthenticated material from Bhutan is also in cultivation.

R. cinnabarinum subsp. ***tamaense*** (Davidian) Cullen
SYNONYM *R. tamaense* Davidian
ILLUSTRATION Cox and Cox, *The Encyclopedia of Rhododendron Species,* 246 (1997)
LEAVES mostly deciduous, narrow, scaly above
COROLLA purple; lobes scaly outside
DISTRIBUTION northeastern Myanmar

Classic wild-collected material is available under *Kingdon-Ward 21003, 21021, 20837.* Cultivated material named as *R. cinnabarinum* subsp. *tamaense* is often the rather similar *R. oreotrephes.* There are recent, nonauthenticated, wild collections identified as *R. cinnabarinum* but not as yet identified to the subspecies.

Though often appearing quite distinct in gardens, where conscious selection has given rise to stable, widely distributed variants, the 3 subspecies intergrade considerably in the wild. Many selections have been given names and are best dealt with as cultivars. The most notable are subsp. *cinnabarinum* 'Roylei' (flowers rather campanulate, red, very bloomed), subsp. *cinnabarinum* 'Blandfordiiflorum' (corolla rather tubular, coppery red, the tips of the lobes yellow), subsp. *xanthocodon* 'Concatenans' (corolla orange-yellow or apricot, sometimes flushed with purple), and subsp. *xanthocodon* 'Purpurellum' (corolla purple).

The species has been widely used in hybridisation. Some of the hybrids, previously thought to be interspecific, are now within the species, such as 'Conroy' (*R. cinnabarinum* subsp. *cinnabarinum* 'Roylei' × subsp. *xanthocodon*); others involve other species, such as 'Cinnkeys' (× *R. keysii*), 'Royal Flush' and 'Rose Mangles' (both × *R. maddenii* subsp. *maddenii*), and 'Yunncinn' (× *R. yunnanense*).

262. *Rhododendron keysii* Nuttall

SYNONYM *R. igneum* Cowan

ILLUSTRATION *Curtis's Botanical Magazine,* 4875 (1855); *Flore des Serres,* ser. 2: t. 1110 (1856); *Gartenflora* 12, t. 415 (1863); Hara, *Photo-Album of Plants of Eastern Himalaya,* t. 168 (1968); *Iconographia Cormophytorum Sinicorum* 3, t. 4046 (1974); *Notes from the Royal Botanic Garden Edinburgh* 39: 21 (1980); Davidian, *The Rhododendron Species* 1, pl. 17 (1982); Cox and Cox, *The Encyclopedia of Rhododendron Species,* 246–247 (1997); Feng, *Rhododendrons of China* 3, pl. 79 (1999)

HABIT straggling shrub to 6 m

LEAVES elliptic, 6–15 × 2–3.5 cm; upper surface persistently scaly; lower surface densely so, with close to distant, flat, broadly rimmed scales

RACEME all axillary, each 2- to 5-flowered, with individual racemes often coalescing

CALYX rim-like, wavy, scaly, rarely fringed with hairs

COROLLA tubular, 1.5–2.5 cm, deep red to salmon-pink, usually with yellow lobes, rarely the whole corolla yellow; lobes slightly flaring

OVARY scaly, slightly hairy at the top

STYLE downy towards the base

CAPSULE scaly, to 1 cm

DISTRIBUTION Himalaya

FLOWERING spring

HARDINESS ZONE 7

Classic wild-collected material is available under *Kingdon-Ward 6437A*. Recent non-authenticated material from Bhutan is also in cultivation.

Not widely used in hybridisation, but a parent of 'Cinnkeys' (× *R. cinnabarinum* subsp. *cinnabarinum*).

Subgenus **Rhododendron**

Section **Rhododendron**

Subsection ***Tephropepla*** (Cowan and Davidian) Sleumer (*Tephropeplum* series)

HABIT small to medium shrubs

LEAVES evergreen, papillose beneath

RACEME usually terminal, but axillary inflorescences very occasionally present

CALYX deeply 5-lobed; lobes conspicuous, erect or reflexed

COROLLA campanulate to funnel-campanulate, occasionally downy outside

STAMENS 10, declinate

OVARY tapering smoothly and gradually into the style or style impressed in a depression on top of the ovary

SEEDS elongate, unwinged and with a minute appendage at each end

A group of 7 species, rather variable. The leaves are anatomically also rather variable. They have a 2- or 3-layered upper epidermis, the cells of the lower layer usually larger than those of the upper layer (cells of both layers more or less equal in *R. hanceanum*), the cuticle half as thick to as thick as the cells of the upper layer are deep; water tissue is absent, and the cells of the lower epidermis are prolonged into papillae or not. Sclereids are generally present in the leaf tissue.

1 a Style inserted into a shouldered depression on top of the ovary; corolla white, red, or pink 2
b Ovary tapering smoothly into the style; corolla cream or yellow 4
2 a Corolla red or pink; style scaly for about half its length; scales on the lower leaf surface contiguous or up to their own diameter apart . . . . **265. *R. tephropeplum***
b Corolla white; style completely scaleless; scales on the lower leaf surface very distant 3
3 a Raceme 5- to 15-flowered, with a conspicuous rachis; leaves with a conspicuous, acuminate drip tip . . . . **266. *R. hanceanum***
b Racemes up to 3-flowered; rachis very short; leaves acute but without a drip tip .**267. *R. longistylum***
4 a Calyx lobes reflexed; leaves brown beneath, with contiguous or overlapping scales . .**264. *R. auritum***
b Calyx lobes spreading or erect; leaves silvery brown beneath with close but not contiguous scales . . . . **263. *R. xanthostephanum***

263. *Rhododendron xanthostephanum* Merrill

SYNONYM *R. aureum* Franchet not Georgi

ILLUSTRATION *Curtis's Botanical Magazine*, 8882 (1921); Millais, *Rhododendrons*, opposite 244 (1924); *Iconographia Cormophytorum Sinicorum* 3, t. 4018 (1974); *Notes from the Royal Botanic Garden Edinburgh* 39: 21 (1980); Feng, *Rhododendrons of China* 1, pl. 54: 1–3 (1988); Cox and Cox, *The Encyclopedia of Rhododendron Species,* 331 (1997)

HABIT shrub to 2 m; mature bark smooth, reddish brown, somewhat bloomed

LEAVES oblong-elliptic to elliptic, 5–10 × 1.5–3 cm; upper surface brownish green; lower surface silvery brown, with unequal scales about their own diameter apart, the smaller and more numerous deeply sunk in pits, scarcely reaching the surface, the larger borne on the surface, though with their stalks in pits

RACEME usually terminal, 3- to 5-flowered

CALYX lobes semi-circular to ovate or oblong, 5–7 mm, variably scaly, not hairy, erect or spreading

COROLLA narrowly campanulate, 1.8–2.8 cm, deep yellow, lemon-yellow, or yellow-orange, variably scaly and sometimes slightly downy outside

OVARY scaly, tapering smoothly and gradually into the style, which is scaly towards the base

CAPSULE scaly, 8–11 mm

DISTRIBUTION northeastern India (Arunachal Pradesh), northeastern Myanmar, western China (northwestern and central Yunnan)

FLOWERING spring

HARDINESS ZONE 8

Classic wild-collected material is available under *Kingdon-Ward 5446.* Recent nonauthenticated material from Yunnan is also in cultivation.

264. *Rhododendron auritum* Tagg

ILLUSTRATION Cox and Cox, *The Encyclopedia of Rhododendron Species,* 328 (1997)

Very similar to *R. xanthostephanum,* but:

HABIT taller; bark not as smooth

LEAVES lower surface brown, with unequal, more or less contiguous scales, the smaller in pits but reaching the leaf surface

CALYX lobes reflexed

COROLLA very pale yellow or cream, occasionally with a faint pink flush

DISTRIBUTION western China (southeastern Xizang)

FLOWERING spring

HARDINESS ZONE 8

Classic wild-collected material is available under *Kingdon-Ward 6278.*

265. *Rhododendron tephropeplum* Balfour and Farrer

ILLUSTRATION *Curtis's Botanical Magazine,* 9343 (1934), reprinted in Halliday, *The Illustrated Rhododendron,* pl. 44 (2001); *Gardeners' Chronicle* 96: t. 69 (1934); Cox, *Dwarf Rhododendrons,* 87 (1973); *Iconographia Cormophytorum Sinicorum* 3, t. 4019 (1974); *Notes from the Royal Botanic Garden Edinburgh* 39: 21 (1980); Davidian, *The Rhododendron Species* 1, pl. 57 (1982); Kneller, *The Book of Rhododendrons,* 93 (1995); Cox and Cox, *The Encyclopedia of Rhododendron Species,* 330 (1997)

R. tephropeplum flower and leaf

R. tephropeplum detail

R. tephropeplum leaf surface

Habit to 1.3 m; bark scaling, brownish

Leaves narrowly oblanceolate to narrowly elliptic (rarely oblanceolate), 4–10 × 1–4 cm; upper surface dark green; lower surface brownish grey, papillose, with unequal scales slightly sunk in pits in the surface, contiguous to their own diameter apart, rapidly becoming blackish brown

Raceme 3- to 9-flowered

Calyx lobes spreading, 5–8 mm, circular to oblong, scaly at the base and on the margins; margins bristly

Corolla campanulate, 2–2.5 cm, pink to red, variably scaly outside, hairless

Stamens anthers yellow-brown

Ovary scaly

Style impressed in a depression on top of the ovary, scaly for about half its length from the base

Capsule 7–10 mm

Distribution northeastern India (Arunachal Pradesh), northeastern Myanmar, western China (northwestern Yunnan, southwestern Xizang)

Flowering spring

Hardiness zone 8

Classic wild-collected material is available under *Forrest 25714, 26431,* and *Kingdon-Ward 6303, 8165.*

266. *Rhododendron hanceanum* Hemsley

Illustration *Kew Bulletin,* 202 (1914); Millais, *Rhododendrons,* opposite 10 (1917); Fang, *Icones Plantarum Omeiensium* 1, t. 34 (1942); *Iconographia Cormophytorum Sinicorum* 3, t. 4074 (1974); Davidian, *The Rhododendron Species* 1, pl. 67 (1982); Fang, *Sichuan Rhododendron of China,* 265 (1986); Cox and Cox, *The Encyclopedia of Rhododendron Species,* 328 (1997)

Habit shrub to 2 m; young shoots scaly; bark pale brown, scaling, smooth

Leaves narrowly ovate or oblong-elliptic, 7–11 × 3–5.5 cm, acuminate with a conspicuous drip tip at the apex; lower surface pale green, with rather distant, flat or slightly sunken, golden brown scales; upper surface slightly downy along the main vein near the base

Inflorescence buds spherical, green to reddish brown; scales with a few lepidote scales on the surface, fringed with a few white hairs

Raceme 5- to 15-flowered, with a long, conspicuous axis

CALYX lobes to 5 mm, narrowly triangular, sparsely fringed with scales
COROLLA narrowly funnel-campanulate, white, c. 2 cm, hairless and scaleless outside
OVARY scaly
STYLE impressed into a depression on top of the ovary, scaleless, exceeding the stamens
CAPSULE scaly, to 1 cm
DISTRIBUTION western China (central Sichuan)
FLOWERING spring
HARDINESS ZONE 8

A very distinctive species with a long raceme axis. Most of the material in cultivation under this name is a low-growing selection ('Nanum'), and it is doubtful if the pure species is to be found in gardens.

267. *Rhododendron longistylum* Rehder and Wilson
ILLUSTRATION *Revue Horticole,* 232–233 (1914); Fang, *Sichuan Rhododendron of China,* 266–269 (1986); Cox and Cox, *The Encyclopedia of Rhododendron Species,* 329 (1997)
HABIT shrub to 2 m; young shoots sparsely scaly, usually finely downy
LEAVES obovate or oblong-obovate, 3.5–5.5 cm × 9–15 mm; lower surface pale green, with distant, unequal, golden and brown scales with broad rims; upper surface sparsely but persistently scaly, downy along the main vein
RACEME 2- to 3-flowered
CALYX lobes to 3.5 mm, narrowly triangular, fringed with scales; tube scaly, slightly downy
COROLLA narrowly funnel-shaped, to 2 cm, hairless and scaleless outside, white or pale pink
STAMENS projecting well beyond the corolla
OVARY scaly and downy at the apex
STYLE impressed into a depression on top of the ovary, as long as or longer than the stamens
CAPSULE scaly, to 6 mm
DISTRIBUTION western China (central Sichuan)
FLOWERING spring
HARDINESS ZONE 8

Classic wild-collected material is available under *Wilson 4726.*

Doubtfully placed in this subsection, but fitting better here than in any other.

Subgenus *Rhododendron*

Section *Rhododendron*

Subsection *Virgata* (Hutchinson) Cullen (subgenus *Pseudorhodorastrum* Sleumer section *Rhabdorhodion* Sleumer; section *Pseudorhodorastrum* Spethmann 1980a, 165; *Virgatum* series)

HABIT small shrubs; young shoots scaly

LEAVES evergreen, scaly on both surfaces

RACEME one-flowered (very rarely 2-flowered), axillary, borne in the axils of the upper leaves, the terminal bud vegetative and continuing growth of the shoot

CALYX 5-lobed

COROLLA funnel-shaped

STAMENS 10, declinate

OVARY scaly

STYLE impressed into a depression at the apex of the ovary

SEEDS unwinged but with a short, tail-like appendage at each end

Rhododendron virgatum is the only species. The leaves have a 2-layered epidermis, the cells of the lower layer larger than those of the upper layer, the cuticle about half as thick as the cells of the upper layer are deep; water tissue is absent, and the cells of the lower epidermis are slightly prolonged into papillae.

This group, like other scaly groups with lateral inflorescences, has been treated as a subgenus or section in earlier classifications of the genus; however, its similarity to subsections *Tephropepla, Cinnabarina,* and *Uniflora* is striking, and it seems better treated at the same level.

268. *Rhododendron virgatum* Hooker

HABIT shrub to 1.5 m; young shoots scaly; bark greyish white, scaling in long shreds; underbark chestnut-brown

LEAVES narrowly oblong or oblong-elliptic, to 5 cm; upper surface loosely scaly, especially along the midrib; lower surface papillose, densely scaly, with unequal scales

INFLORESCENCE BUDS fusiform, long, tapering; scales densely hairy; lower scales brown, the inner scales whitish

CALYX 2–3 mm, scaly on the tube; lobes sometimes ringed with fine short hairs

COROLLA 1.5–3.7 cm, white, pink, or mauve; tube downy, sparsely scaly outside; lobes scaly only

OVARY scaly

STYLE scaly and or hairy towards the base

CAPSULE scaly, 9–13 mm
DISTRIBUTION Himalaya, western China
FLOWERING spring
HARDINESS ZONE 8

Two subspecies occur in the wild, and both have been introduced into cultivation.

R. virgatum subsp. **virgatum**

ILLUSTRATION Hooker, *Rhododendrons of the Sikkim Himalaya*, t. 26 (1851); *Curtis's Botanical Magazine*, 5060 (1858), reprinted in Halliday, *The Illustrated Rhododendron*, pl. 45 (2001); *Flore des Serres*, ser. 2, 4: t. 1408 (1861); Hara, *Photo-Album of Plants of Eastern Himalaya*, t. 167 (1968); *Iconographia Cormophytorum Sinicorum* 3, t. 4281 (1974); *Notes from the Royal Botanic Garden Edinburgh* 39: 21 (1980); Feng, *Rhododendrons of China* 1, pl. 81: 1–2 (1988); Cox and Cox, *The Encyclopedia of Rhododendron Species*, 358–359 (1997)
COROLLA 2.5–3.7 cm, pale to deep pink or mauve; tube 1.1–2 cm
DISTRIBUTION Himalaya, western China (southeastern Xizang)

Recent, nonauthenticated, wild-collected material from India (Sikkim) and Bhutan is in cultivation.

R. virgatum subsp. *virgatum* flower and leaf.
PHOTO BY RAY COX

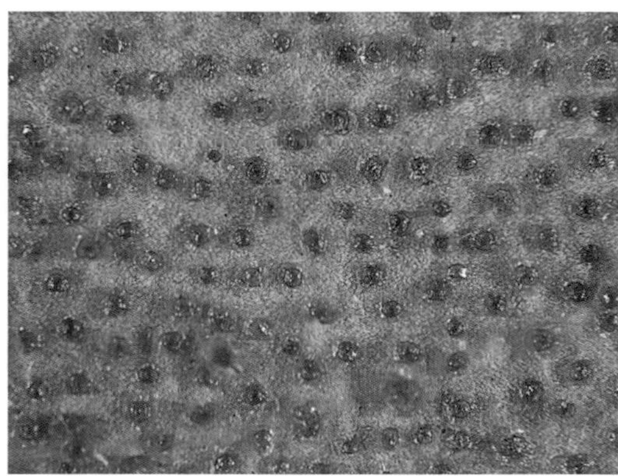

R. virgatum subsp. *virgatum* leaf surface

R. *virgatum* subsp. ***oleifolium*** (Franchet) Cullen

SYNONYMS *R. oleifolium* Franchet; *R. sinovirgatum* Hort.

ILLUSTRATION *Revue Horticole,* 348 (1917); *Gardeners' Chronicle* 65: 317 (1919); *Curtis's Botanical Magazine,* 8802 (1919); *Iconographia Cormophytorum Sinicorum* 3, t. 4282 (1974); Cox and Cox, *The Encyclopedia of Rhododendron Species,* 359 (1997)

COROLLA 1.5–2.5 cm, white or pink; tube 8–15 mm

DISTRIBUTION western China (southeastern Xizang, northern and western Yunnan)

Recent, nonauthenticated, wild-collected material from Yunnan is in cultivation.

Subgenus *Rhododendron*

Section *Rhododendron*

Subsection *Micrantha* (Hutchinson) Sleumer (*Micranthum* series)

HABIT shrubs to 2 m; young shoots scaly, finely downy
LEAVES evergreen, densely scaly beneath
RACEME terminal, very many-flowered, with a conspicuous axis
COROLLA funnel-campanulate, very deeply lobed
STAMENS 10, not or scarcely declinate
OVARY scaly
STYLE straight, impressed into a depression on top of the ovary
SEEDS elongate, conspicuously winged and with an appendage at each end

Rhododendron micranthum is the only species. The leaves have a one-layered upper epidermis, the cuticle thin; water tissue is absent, and the cells of the lower epidermis are slightly prolonged into papillae.

269. *Rhododendron micranthum* Turczaninow
ILLUSTRATION *Curtis's Botanical Magazine,* 8198 (1908), reprinted in Halliday, *The Illustrated Rhododendron,* pl. 46 (2001); *Iconographia Cormophytorum Sinicorum* 3, t. 4039 (1974); Fang, *Sichuan Rhododendron of China,* 271–272 (1986); Feng, *Rhododendrons of China* 2, pl. 83: 1–2 (1992); Kneller, *The Book of Rhododendrons,* 81 (1995); Cox and Cox, *The Encyclopedia of Rhododendron Species,* 309 (1997)
HABIT shrub to 2 m
LEAVES oblong-elliptic to narrowly oblong-elliptic, 1.6–5 cm × 8–25 mm; upper surface sparsely scaly, downy along the midrib; lower surface densely to moderately scaly, with brownish, broadly rimmed scales which are contiguous to overlapping
RACEME with usually more than 20 flowers
CALYX lobes 1–2 mm, triangular, scaly, fringed with short bristles
COROLLA 5–8 mm, white, unspotted, densely scaly outside
STAMENS 10, projecting beyond the corolla; anthers light brown
OVARY scaly
STYLE shorter than the stamens
CAPSULE scaly, 5–6 mm
DISTRIBUTION northern China, Korea

FLOWERING late spring
HARDINESS ZONE 3

Classic wild-collected material is available under *Wilson 1320.*

A very distinctive species, looking superficially like a very large *Ledum* (this genus is sunk into *Rhododendron* by some authors).

R. micranthum flower and leaf

R. micranthum detail

R. micranthum leaf surface

Subgenus *Rhododendron*

Section *Rhododendron*

Subsection *Boothia* (Hutchinson) Sleumer (*Boothii* series)

HABIT free-growing or epiphytic shrubs; young shoots bristly, the bristles variably persistent

LEAVES evergreen; lower surface whitish-papillose, with rimmed or vesicular scales deeply sunk in pits on the surface

RACEME terminal, one- to many-flowered; flower stalks often very short

COROLLA broadly campanulate or almost disc-shaped

STAMENS 10, radially arranged

OVARY scaly, tapering into the style, which is scaly and sharply deflexed at the base

CAPSULE scaly

SEEDS elongate, prominently winged and with an appendage at each end

A subsection of 6 species. The leaves are often very hard and have a 2-, 3-, or 4-layered upper epidermis, the cells of the lower layer larger than those of the upper layer, the cuticle thin to very thick; water tissue is absent, and the cells of the lower epidermis are prolonged into papillae. Sclereids are present in the leaf tissue of all species.

Rhododendron leptocarpum Nuttall (*R. micromeres* Tagg), which is from northeastern India, northeastern Myanmar, and southwestern China, was at one time in cultivation; it has long flower stalks (2.5–5 cm), small corollas (9–13 mm), and glabrous stems and leaf margins.

1a Scales with rims (which are sometimes upturned); calyx lobes ovate or oblong; racemes with 3 or more flowers .... **270. *R. sulfureum***

b Scales vesicular; calyx lobes obovate; racemes one- to 3-flowered 2

2a Corolla almost rotate, white (sometimes tinged with pink); leaves bristly above ... **272. *R. leucaspis***

b Corolla broadly campanulate, yellow or rarely cream; leaves hairless above except for a few bristles on the base of the midrib and on the margin .... **271. *R. megeratum***

270. *Rhododendron sulfureum* Franchet

ILLUSTRATION *Curtis's Botanical Magazine,* 8946 (1922); Millais, *Rhododendrons,* opposite 244 (1924); *Iconographia Cormophytorum Sinicorum* 3, t. 4008 (1974); *Notes from the Royal Botanic Garden Edinburgh* 39: 21 (1980); Feng, *Rhododendrons of China* 1, pl. 53: 1–2 (1988); Kneller, *The Book of Rhododendrons,* 61 (1995); Cox and Cox, *The Encyclopedia of Rhododendron Species,* 239 (1997)

HABIT epiphytic or free-growing shrub to 1.6 m; young shoots bristly, the bristles usually quickly deciduous

LEAVES mostly obovate, sometimes broadly so, 3.5–7.5 × 2–4.5 cm; upper surface scaleless, with bristly margins, at least when young; lower surface with close, unequal scales sunk in pits, usually with rims upturned

RACEME 3- to 6-flowered

CALYX lobes ovate to oblong, 5–6 mm, scaly, sometimes bristly or finely downy along the margins

COROLLA greenish to bright yellow, unspotted, 1.5–2 cm, sparsely to densely scaly outside, sometimes downy on the tube

CAPSULE scaly, 1–1.3 cm

DISTRIBUTION northeastern Myanmar, western China (western Yunnan, southeastern Xizang)

FLOWERING late spring

HARDINESS ZONE 9

Classic wild-collected material is available under *Forrest 13512, 24235*. Recent non-authenticated material from Yunnan is also in cultivation.

A parent of a few widely grown hybrids, notably 'Yellow Hammer' (× *R. flavidum*) and 'Golden Oriole' (× *R. moupinense*).

271. *Rhododendron megeratum* Balfour and Forrest

ILLUSTRATION *Curtis's Botanical Magazine*, 9120 (1926); *Gardeners' Chronicle* 89: 431 (1931); Cox, *Dwarf Rhododendrons*, t. 11 (1973); *Iconographia Cormophytorum Sinicorum* 3, t. 4006 (1974); *Notes from the Royal Botanic Garden Edinburgh* 39: 21 (1980); Feng, *Rhododendrons of China* 1, pl. 52 (1988); Cox and Cox, *The Encyclopedia of Rhododendron Species*, 238 (1997)

HABIT usually a free-growing shrub to 1 m; shoots bristly, the bristles persisting for at least a year

LEAVES elliptic or elliptic-obovate to almost circular, 2–3.6 × 1.2–2 cm; upper surface hairless, except for a few bristles at the base of the midrib, and with bristly margins; lower surface whitish-papillose, with vesicular scales sunk in pits; leaf stalk bristly

RACEME one- to 3-flowered

CALYX lobes green, obovate, 6–10 mm, sparsely scaly outside, sparsely to densely bristly

COROLLA broadly campanulate, yellow or rarely cream, sometimes with darker spots, scaly outside, 1.6–2.3 cm

CAPSULE scaly, 8–11 mm
DISTRIBUTION northeastern India (Arunachal Pradesh), northeastern Myanmar, western China (northwestern Yunnan, southern and southeastern Xizang)
FLOWERING spring
HARDINESS ZONE 7

Classic wild-collected material is available under *Kingdon-Ward 6819* and *Rock 3857* (equivalent herbarium specimen *18341*). The species has been grown as *Forrest 13350*, but the herbarium specimen of this number is not a rhododendron.

272. *Rhododendron leucaspis* Tagg

ILLUSTRATION *Curtis's Botanical Magazine*, 9665 (1944), reprinted in Halliday, *The Illustrated Rhododendron*, pl. 47 (2001); Urquhart, *The Rhododendron* 1, t. 11 (1958); Cox, *Dwarf Rhododendrons*, 85, t. 10 (1973); Davidian, *The Rhododendron Species* 1, pl. 5 (1982); Cox and Cox, *The Encyclopedia of Rhododendron Species*, 237–238 (1997)
HABIT shrub to 1 m; young shoots densely covered with straight bristles; bark smooth, silver-brown, scaling
LEAVES broadly elliptic, 3–4.5 × 1.8–2.2 cm; upper surface and margins bristly; lower surface with vesicular scales sunk in pits

R. leucaspis flower and leaf

R. leucaspis detail

R. leucaspis leaf surface

INFLORESCENCE BUDS ovoid, yellow-brown; scales with dark brown lepidote scales; margins fringed with white hairs
RACEME one- to 2-flowered; flower stalks scaly, sometimes hairy
CALYX 5-lobed, 7–8 mm, greenish or often reddish; margins bristly
COROLLA very broadly campanulate to almost disc-like, white, often tinged with pink, 2.5–3 cm, scaly outside, especially on the lobes
OVARY scaly
CAPSULE scaly, to 1 cm
DISTRIBUTION western China (Xizang)
FLOWERING spring
HARDINESS ZONE 7

Classic wild-collected material is available under *Kingdon-Ward 6273* (the type collection), *7171*.

A parent of a number of popular hybrids, notably 'Ptarmigan' (× *R. orthocladum* var. *microleucum*).

Subgenus *Rhododendron*

Section *Rhododendron*

Subsection *Camelliiflora* (Hutchinson) Sleumer (*Camelliiflorum* series)

HABIT shrubs to 2 m, often epiphytic
LEAVES evergreen
CALYX conspicuously 5-lobed, scaly but hairless
COROLLA openly campanulate, with a short tube; lobes scaly outside
STAMENS 12–16, more or less radially arranged
OVARY 5- to 10-celled, the cells tapering into the short, deflexed style
SEEDS elongate, conspicuously winged and with an appendage at each end

Rhododendron camelliiflorum is the only species. The leaves are similar to those of subsection *Boothia*. They have a 2-layered upper epidermis, the cells of the lower layer larger than those of the upper layer, the cuticle about half as thick as the cells of the upper layer are deep; water tissue is absent, and the cells of the lower epidermis are prolonged into papillae.

273. *Rhododendron camelliiflorum* Hooker
ILLUSTRATION Hooker, *Rhododendrons of the Sikkim Himalaya*, t. 28 (1851); *Curtis's Botanical Magazine*, 4932 (1856), reprinted in Halliday, *The Illustrated Rhododendron*, pl. 48 (2001); *Gartenflora* 14, t. 400 (1865); *Notes from the Royal Botanic Garden Edinburgh* 39: 21 (1980); Kneller, *The Book of Rhododendrons*, 63 (1995)—poor; Cox and Cox, *The Encyclopedia of Rhododendron Species*, 240 (1997)
HABIT shrub with scaly young shoots
LEAVES narrowly elliptic to oblong-elliptic, 6–10 × 2–3.5 cm; upper surface shining dark green, with a few dried-out scales; lower surface pale green to brownish, with dense, almost contiguous, broadly rimmed scales, a few larger and darker than the rest
RACEME one- to 2-flowered
CALYX lobes 5–8 mm, fringed with scales, scaly or not on the surface
COROLLA waxy, with a short, broad tube, white to deep pink, scaly outside, 1.4–2 cm
STAMENS anthers brown
STYLE shorter than the stamens
CAPSULE ovoid, scaly, 7–13 mm
DISTRIBUTION Himalaya

Flowering late spring
Hardiness zone 9

Wild-collected material is available under *Beer 662, 10637, Sinclair and Long 5696,* and *Spring Smythe 33A*. Recent nonauthenticated material from Bhutan is also in cultivation.

Marginally hardy in most of Europe.

R. camelliiflorum flower and leaf

R. camelliiflorum detail

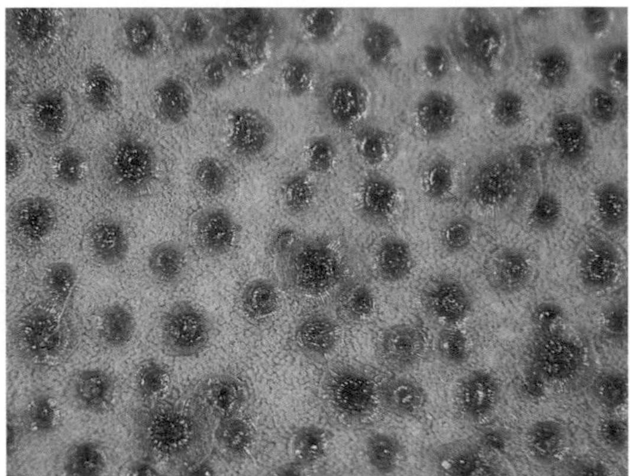

R. camelliiflorum leaf surface

Subgenus *Rhododendron*

Section *Rhododendron*

Subsection *Glauca* (Hutchinson) Sleumer (Glaucum series; *Glaucophyllum* series)

HABIT generally small shrubs; bark often coppery, smooth, scaling
LEAVES small, evergreen; lower surface white- or greyish-papillose, with scales of 2 kinds, the smaller scales golden, flat, and more numerous than the larger, longer-stalked, funnel-shaped, dark brown scales
CALYX deeply 5-lobed
COROLLA campanulate or rarely tubular-campanulate, pink, red, purple, or yellow, sometimes spotted
STAMENS 10, unequal but radially arranged, rarely declinate
OVARY 5-celled, scaly
STYLE impressed in a depression on top of the ovary, usually sharply deflexed from the base, more rarely declinate
SEEDS elongate, unwinged and with a small appendage at each end

There are 6 species altogether. The leaves have a 2-layered upper epidermis, the cells of both layers similar in size (those of the lower layer larger in *R. glaucophyllum*), the cuticle thin; water tissue is absent, and the cells of the lower epidermis are conspicuously prolonged into papillae. Sclereids are generally absent.

1a Calyx lobes acuminate, with a tuft of hairs inside at the apex; margins ciliate with bristle-like hairs; leaves usually acute . . . . . **274. *R. glaucophyllum***
b Calyx lobes obtuse or rounded, without a tuft of hairs inside at the apex, not ciliate; leaves usually obtuse or rounded 2
2a Corolla 1–1.8 cm; raceme axis developed, though short, hairless or very sparsely hairy 3
b Corolla 1.8–2.5 cm; raceme axis extremely short, completely covered in bristle-like hairs 4
3a Corolla dull red to purple; all scales on the lower leaf surface clouded or milky . . **277. *R. pruniflorum***
b Corolla yellow; at least some scales on the lower leaf surface clear, golden . . **278. *R. brachyanthum***
4a Corolla yellow; flower stalk 1.3–2 cm . . . . . **275. *R. luteiflorum***
b Corolla pink to purplish; flower stalks 2–3 cm . . . . . **276. *R. charitopes***

274. *Rhododendron glaucophyllum* Rehder
HABIT shrub to 1.5 m; bark coppery, scaling in long flakes; underbark smooth, coppery

LEAVES narrowly elliptic to elliptic, 3.5–6 × 1.3–2.5 cm; upper surface dark brownish green

INFLORESCENCE BUDS spherical, reddish brown; scales densely lepidote and fringed with fine white hairs

RACEME 3- to 6-flowered; axis very short, scaly

CALYX lobes ovate, acuminate, 6–11 mm, often somewhat glaucous, scaly at the base and on the margins; margins usually slightly bristly and with a tuft of hairs inside at the apex

COROLLA campanulate to tubular-campanulate, 1.8–3.2 cm, pink or white flushed with pink, rather densely scaly outside

STYLE sharply deflexed from the base or declinate

CAPSULE scaly, to 1 cm

DISTRIBUTION Himalaya, western China (southern Xizang)

FLOWERING spring

HARDINESS ZONE 8

Two varieties occur in the wild, and both are in cultivation.

R. *glaucophyllum* var. ***glaucophyllum***

SYNONYM *R. glaucum* Hooker not Sweet

ILLUSTRATION Hooker, *Rhododendrons of the Sikkim Himalaya,* t. 17 (1851); *Flore des Serres,* ser. 1, 7: t. 672 (1851–1852); *Curtis's Botanical Magazine,* 4721 (1853), reprinted in Halliday, *The Illustrated Rhododendron,* pl. 49 (2001); *Gardeners' Chronicle* 67: 275 (1920); Davidian, *The Rhododendron Species* 1, pl. 23 (1982); Kneller, *The Book of Rhododendrons,* 73 (1995); Cox and Cox, *The Encyclopedia of Rhododendron Species,* 254 (1997)

COROLLA campanulate

STYLE sharply deflexed from the base

DISTRIBUTION Himalaya

Wild-collected material is available under *Beer, Lancaster, and Morris 315* and *Ludlow and Sherriff 2764.* Material in cultivation as *Forrest 25414, R. shweliense,* is usually this; genuine *R. shweliense* Balfour and Forrest, of which *Forrest 25414* is a herbarium specimen, is apparently no longer in cultivation (it is doubtful if it ever was).

Variety *glaucophyllum* is a parent of the popular 'Rosy Bell' (× *R. ciliatum*).

R. glaucophyllum var. *glaucophyllum* flower and leaf

R. glaucophyllum var. *glaucophyllum* detail

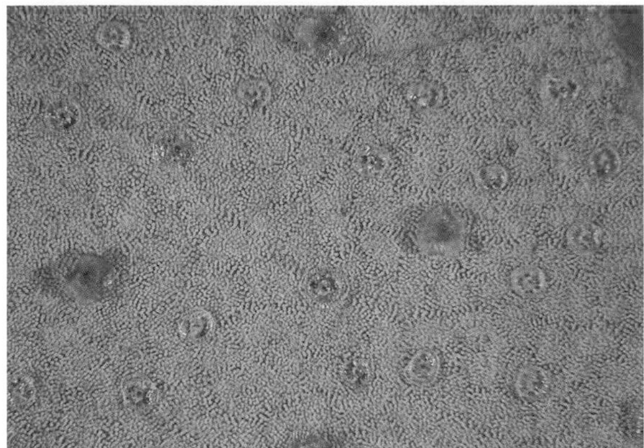

R. glaucophyllum var. *glaucophyllum* leaf surface

R. glaucophyllum var. ***tubiforme*** Cowan and Davidian
SYNONYM *R. tubiforme* (Cowan and Davidian) Davidian
ILLUSTRATION Davidian, *The Rhododendron Species* 1, pl. 26 (1982); Cox and Cox, *The Encyclopedia of Rhododendron Species,* 254 (1997)
COROLLA tubular-campanulate
STYLE declinate, not deflexed
DISTRIBUTION eastern Himalaya, western China (southern Xizang)

Classic wild-collected material is available under *Ludlow and Sherriff 2856.* Recent nonauthenticated material from Bhutan is also in cultivation.

Variety *tubiforme* is somewhat aberrant within the subsection in possessing a declinate, long style and a more tubular corolla; it may well be a naturally occurring hybrid with some other species (such as *R. ciliatum*).

Recent, nonauthenticated, wild-collected material identified as *R. glaucophyllum,* but without indication of variety, is available.

275. *Rhododendron luteiflorum* (Davidian) Cullen
SYNONYM *R. glaucophyllum* var. *luteiflorum* Davidian
ILLUSTRATION *Rhododendron Yearbook,* t. 4 (1967); Kneller, *The Book of Rhododendrons,* 73 (1995); Cox and Cox, *The Encyclopedia of Rhododendron Species,* 255 (1997)
Very similar to *R. glaucophyllum* var. *glaucophyllum,* but:
LEAVES more sparsely scaly beneath
CALYX lobes rounded at the apex and without a tuft of hairs inside there
COROLLA bright clear yellow, 2–2.2 cm
DISTRIBUTION northeastern Myanmar
FLOWERING spring
HARDINESS ZONE 8

Classic wild-collected material is available under *Kingdon-Ward 21040.*

276. *Rhododendron charitopes* Balfour and Farrer
HABIT shrub to 1.5 m
LEAVES elliptic to obovate, 3–5.5 × 1.5–3 cm; upper surface dark green, scaleless or almost so; lower surface variably scaly, with marked veins
RACEME 3- to 5-flowered; axis very short, downy, with some bristles
CALYX lobes ovate, rounded at the apex, 3–9 mm, somewhat glaucous, scaly at the base and on the margins
COROLLA campanulate, 1.5–2.5 cm, pink to purplish, scaleless or almost so outside

CAPSULE ovoid, to 1 cm
DISTRIBUTION northeastern Myanmar, western China (northwestern Yunnan, southern Xizang)
FLOWERING spring
HARDINESS ZONE 7

Two subspecies occur in the wild, and both have been in cultivation.

R. *charitopes* subsp. ***charitopes***
ILLUSTRATION Cox, *The Plant Introductions of Reginald Farrer,* 84 (1930); *Curtis's Botanical Magazine,* 9358 (1934); *Iconographia Cormophytorum Sinicorum* 3, t. 4005 (1974); Cox and Cox, *The Encyclopedia of Rhododendron Species,* 253 (1997)
CALYX lobes 6–9 mm
COROLLA pinkish
DISTRIBUTION northeastern Myanmar, western China (northwestern Yunnan)

Classic wild-collected material is available under *Forrest 25570.*

R. *charitopes* subsp. ***tsangpoense*** (Kingdon-Ward) Cullen
SYNONYMS *R. tsangpoense* Kingdon-Ward; *R. curvistylum* Kingdon-Ward; *R. tsangpoense* var. *curvistylum* (Kingdon-Ward) Cowan and Davidian
ILLUSTRATION *The Rhododendron Handbook,* f. 12 (1997); Kneller, *The Book of Rhododendrons,* 73 (1995); Cox and Cox, *The Encyclopedia of Rhododendron Species,* 253 (1997)
CALYX lobes 3–6 mm
COROLLA pinkish to purplish
DISTRIBUTION western China (southern Xizang)

Classic wild-collected material is available under *Kingdon-Ward 5844.* Material in cultivation under *Kingdon-Ward 5843* is a natural hybrid between *R. charitopes* subsp. *tsangpoense* and *R. campylogynum.*

277. *Rhododendron pruniflorum* Hutchinson
SYNONYM *R. tsangpoense* var. *pruniflorum* (Hutchinson) Cowan and Davidian
ILLUSTRATION Cox and Cox, *The Encyclopedia of Rhododendron Species,* 255 (1997)
HABIT shrub to 1 m; bark grey-brown, shredding; underbark mahogany-red
LEAVES obovate or narrowly obovate, 3–4.5 × 1.5–2.5 cm; upper surface dark green, more or less scaleless; lower surface densely scaly, the smaller scales often contiguous, pale yellow, and clouded or milky

INFLORESCENCE BUDS spherical-ovoid, slightly pointed, reddish brown; scales lepidote along the middle, margined with fine white hairs

RACEME 4- to 6-flowered; axis obvious, scaly, not hairy

CALYX lobes 3.5–5 mm, rounded at the apex, scaly at the base and on the margins

COROLLA 1–1.3 cm, campanulate, dull crimson to plum-purple, scaleless outside

CAPSULE 4–6 mm

DISTRIBUTION northeastern India (Arunachal Pradesh), northeastern Myanmar

FLOWERING spring

HARDINESS ZONE 7

Classic wild-collected material is available under *Kingdon-Ward 7038, 7188, 8257, 9735, 10500.*

Not to be confused with *R. prunifolium*, which is a totally distinct species.

278. *Rhododendron brachyanthum* Franchet

HABIT shrub to 2 m; bark coppery, scaling in long flakes; underbark smooth, coppery

LEAVES narrowly elliptic to narrowly obovate, 3.5–5.5 × 1.2–2.5 cm; upper surface dark green, scaleless; lower surface with scales more than twice their own diameter apart, the smaller scales clear or milky

RACEME 3- to 10-flowered; axis distinct, scaly or rarely minutely downy

CALYX lobes short, rounded at the apex, slightly glaucous, scaly at the base and sometimes around the margins, persistent into fruit

COROLLA campanulate, pale or greenish yellow, 1–2 cm, more or less scaleless outside

CAPSULE almost spherical, to 8 mm

DISTRIBUTION northeastern Myanmar, western China (central and northwestern Yunnan, southeastern Xizang)

FLOWERING spring

HARDINESS ZONE 6

Two subspecies occur in the wild, and both have been introduced into cultivation.

R. brachyanthum subsp. *brachyanthum*

ILLUSTRATION *Gardeners' Chronicle* 70: 7 (1921); Millais, *Rhododendrons,* opposite 168 (1924); *Iconographia Cormophytorum Sinicorum* 3, t. 4003 (1974); Davidian, *The Rhododendron Species* 1, pl. 27 (1982); Cox and Cox, *The Encyclopedia of Rhododendron Species,* 251–252 (1997); Feng, *Rhododendrons of China* 3, pl. 83: 1–4 (1999)

LEAVES scales on the lower surface very sparse and distant, sometimes almost entirely deciduous
DISTRIBUTION western China (central Yunnan)

Recent nonauthenticated material from Yunnan is in cultivation.

R. brachyanthum subsp. ***hypolepidotum*** (Franchet) Cullen
SYNONYMS *R. brachyanthum* var. *hypolepidotum* Franchet; *R. hypolepidotum* (Franchet) Balfour and Forrest
ILLUSTRATION *Iconographia Cormophytorum Sinicorum* 3, t. 4004 (1974); Cox and Cox, *The Encyclopedia of Rhododendron Species,* 252 (1997)
LEAVES scales on the lower surface much closer, 1–3 × their own diameter apart
DISTRIBUTION northeastern Myanmar, western China (northwestern Yunnan)

Classic wild-collected material is available under *Forrest 13302* (some cultivated material under this number is *R. pruniflorum,* clearly the result of confused labelling), *Kingdon-Ward 3302, 7046,* and *Rock 12, 93, 23553, 59076* (equivalent herbarium specimens *10068, 10991*). Recent nonauthenticated material from Yunnan is also in cultivation.

Subgenus *Rhododendron*

Section *Rhododendron*

Subsection *Campylogyna* (Hutchinson) Sleumer (*Campylogynum* series)

HABIT small shrubs, often forming cushions; young shoots scaly, rarely slightly downy

LEAVES evergreen, small, papillose, often silvery or whitish beneath with distant, small, vesicular scales which are often deciduous (except around the margin)

RACEME terminal; flower stalks rigid and increasing in length in fruit

CALYX 5-lobed or wavy

COROLLA campanulate, bloomed, pink to purple

STAMENS 10, radially arranged

STYLE impressed into a depression on top of the ovary, sharply deflexed at the base, thickening upwards

FLOWER STALKS erect and hardened in fruit

SEEDS elongate, unwinged and with a minute appendage at each end

Rhododendron campylogynum is the only species. The leaves have a one- or 2-layered upper epidermis; when 2-layered, the cells of the lower layer are larger than those of the upper layer, the cuticle about half as thick as the cells of the upper layer are deep; water tissue is present, and the cells of the lower epidermis are not prolonged into papillae. Sclereids are absent.

279. *Rhododendron campylogynum* Franchet

ILLUSTRATION *Curtis's Botanical Magazine,* 9407a (1935), reprinted in Halliday, *The Illustrated Rhododendron,* pl. 50 (2001); Cox, *Dwarf Rhododendrons,* 93, t. 12 (1973); *Iconographia Cormophytorum Sinicorum* 3, t. 4009 (1974); *Notes from the Royal Botanic Garden Edinburgh* 39: 21 (1980); Davidian, *The Rhododendron Species* 1, pl. 6–7 (1982); Feng, *Rhododendrons of China* 1, pl. 55: 1–4 (1988); Kneller, *The Book of Rhododendrons,* 65 (1995)—poor; Cox and Cox, *The Encyclopedia of Rhododendron Species,* 241–242 (1997)

HABIT creeping, prostrate, or decumbent shrub to 60 cm, more rarely rather erect and to 1 m; young shoots sparsely scaly, sometimes downy

LEAVES obovate or narrowly elliptic, 1–3.5 cm × 4–12 mm; upper surface dark green, sparsely downy along the midrib; lower surface papillose, often whitish or silver, hairless, with distant or very distant scales

RACEME 1–3 flowered; flower stalks hardening and lengthening in fruit

Calyx lobes rarely obscure, usually 4–7 mm, hairless, usually scaleless
Corolla pink to red or purple, 1–2.3 cm, bloomed and scaleless outside
Stamens anthers yellow-brown
Capsule sparsely scaly, 7–9 mm
Distribution northeastern India, northeastern Myanmar, western China (Yunnan, southern and southeastern Xizang)
Flowering spring
Hardiness zone 7

Classic wild-collected material is available under *Farrer 1046, 1046A,* and *Forrest 18030, 27357, 30967.* Recent nonauthenticated material from Yunnan is also in cultivation.

A variable species; some selections from the range of variation have been given specific or varietal names, but these are merely cultivars. The species is similar to *R. genestierianum* and *R. pumilum.*

R. campylogynum flower and leaf

R. campylogynum detail

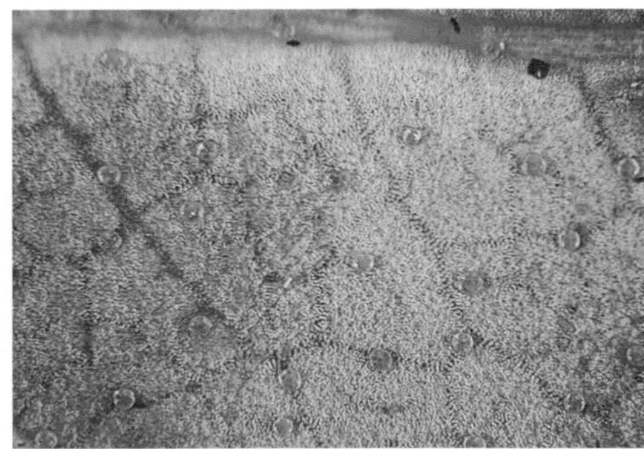

R. campylogynum leaf surface

Subgenus *Rhododendron*

Section *Rhododendron*

Subsection *Genestieriana* (Cowan and Davidian) Sleumer (*Glaucum* series *Genestierianum* subseries)

Very similar to subsection *Campylogyna*, but:

HABIT much taller

RACEME many-flowered

CALYX scarcely lobed

FLOWER STALKS not hardened and erect in fruit

SEEDS elongate, unwinged and without appendages

Rhododendron genestierianum is the only species. The leaves are similar anatomically to those of subsection *Campylogyna*, but the upper epidermis is strictly one-layered, the cuticle thin; the cells of the lower epidermis are prolonged into papillae.

280. *Rhododendron genestierianum* Forrest

ILLUSTRATION *Curtis's Botanical Magazine*, 9310 (1933), reprinted in Halliday, *The Illustrated Rhododendron*, pl. 51 (2001); *Notes from the Royal Botanic Garden Edinburgh* 39: 21 (1980); *Iconographia Cormophytorum Sinicorum* 3, t. 4012 (1974); Kneller, *The Book of Rhododendrons*, 105 (1995); Cox and Cox, *The Encyclopedia of Rhododendron Species*, 250–251 (1997); Feng, *Rhododendrons of China* 3, pl. 84: 1–2 (1999)

HABIT shrub to 5 m; young shoots hairless, scaleless; bark of older shoots smooth, purplish

LEAVES narrowly elliptic to narrowly elliptic-oblanceolate, 6.5–12 × 2.5–4 cm, dark green above, whitish-papillose beneath, with distant, golden yellow to brown scales

RACEME many-flowered

CALYX a mere rim or rarely slightly lobed (lobes 1–2 mm), bloomed, hairless and scaleless or rarely sparsely scaly

COROLLA fleshy, 1.2–1.7 cm, reddish purple, bloomed, scaleless and hairless outside

CAPSULE scaly, 6–9 mm

Distribution northeastern Myanmar, western China (western Yunnan, southeastern Xizang)
Flowering late spring
Hardiness zone 9

Classic wild-collected material is available under *Kingdon-Ward 9415, 20682.*

R. genestierianum flower and leaf.
PHOTO BY RAY COX

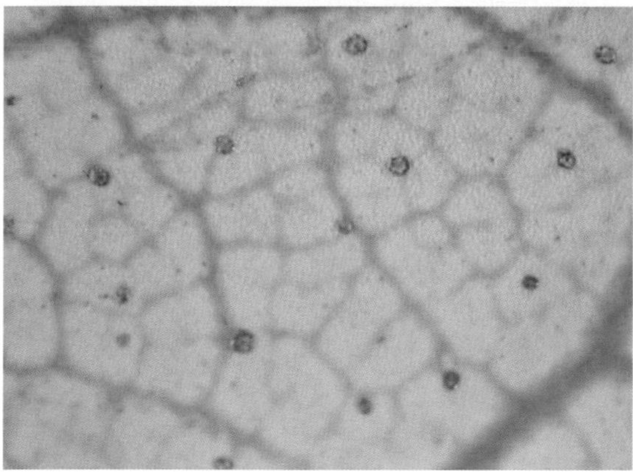

R. genestierianum leaf surface

Subgenus *Rhododendron*

Section *Rhododendron*

Subsection *Lepidota* (Hutchinson) Sleumer (*Lepidotum* series)

HABIT small shrubs

LEAVES evergreen or deciduous; scales on lower surface with flat, broad, translucent rims

RACEME terminal, one- to 5-flowered

CALYX conspicuously 5-lobed

COROLLA campanulate, usually scaly outside

STAMENS radially arranged

OVARY scaly

STYLE impressed in a depression in its apex, short, sharply deflexed at the base

SEEDS elongate, unwinged and with a minute appendage at each end

A small and rather variable subsection. The leaves have a one-layered upper epidermis (but, at least in *R. lepidotum,* the cells may be divided horizontally), the cuticle about half as thick as the cells are deep; water tissue is absent, and the cells of the lower epidermis are prolonged into papillae. Sclereids are absent.

1 a Leaves evergreen, not ciliate . . . . **281. *R. lepidotum***
 b Leaves deciduous, ciliate . . . . **282. *R. lowndesii***

281. *Rhododendron lepidotum* G. Don

SYNONYMS *R. elaeagnoides* Hooker; *R. obovatum* Hooker; *R. salignum* Hooker

ILLUSTRATION Royle, *Illustrations of the Botany of the Himalaya,* t. 64 (1839); *Curtis's Botanical Magazine,* 4657 (1852), 4802 (1854), and 6450 (1879); Millais, *Rhododendrons,* opposite 146 (1917); *Iconographia Cormophytorum Sinicorum* 3, t. 4010 (1974); *Notes from the Royal Botanic Garden Edinburgh* 39: 21 (1980); Davidian, *The Rhododendron Species* 1, pl. 43 (1982); Feng, *Rhododendrons of China* 2, pl. 84: 1–3 (1992); Kneller, *The Book of Rhododendrons,* 106 (1995); *The Rhododendron Handbook,* f. 7 (1997); Cox and Cox, *The Encyclopedia of Rhododendron Species,* 285 (1997); Robertson and McKelvie, *Scottish Rock Gardening in the 20th Century,* f. 30 (2000)

HABIT small evergreen shrub to 2 m; young shoots densely scaly; bark grey

LEAVES narrowly elliptic or obovate or rarely lanceolate, 6–30 × 3–16 mm; upper surface dark green, usually densely scaly, with scales of varying persistence; lower surface pale greyish green, with distant to overlapping, large, brownish scales with translucent rims

INFLORESCENCE BUDS small, ovoid, brownish; scales densely lepidote, with a weak fringe of white hairs
RACEME one- to 2-flowered
CALYX lobes greenish or reddish, scaly, 2–4 mm
COROLLA white, yellow, pink, or reddish, usually densely scaly outside, 1–1.7 cm
STAMENS anthers brown

R. lepidotum flower and leaf

R. lepidotum detail

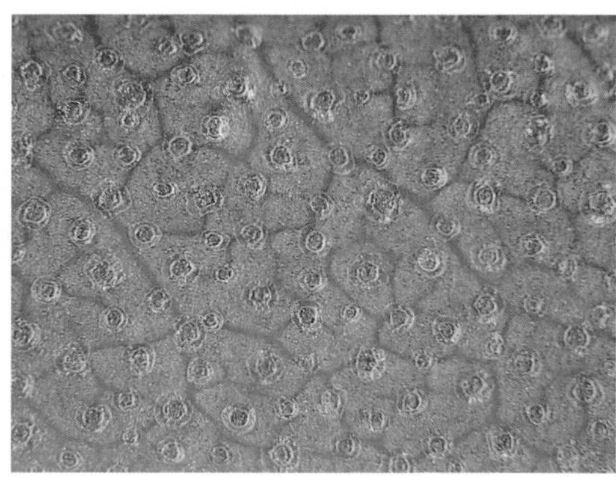

R. lepidotum leaf surface

STYLE very short
CAPSULE scaly, 4–6 mm
DISTRIBUTION Himalaya, northeastern Myanmar, western China (Yunnan, southern and southeastern Xizang)
FLOWERING spring
HARDINESS ZONE 6

Wild-collected material is available under *Bailey 28, Chamberlain* (without number), *Beer 620, Beer, Lancaster, and Morris 279, Gould 18, Hruby 4, 15, Ludlow, Sherriff, and Hicks 17552, 21292, McBeath 1110, Milde Arboretum* (without number), *Schilling 2264,* and *Spring-Smythe 35A, 46, 51, 52.* Recent nonauthenticated material from India (Sikkim), Nepal, Bhutan, and China (Yunnan) is also in cultivation.

A very widespread and variable species. The species described by Hooker (which have been treated as varieties by some later authors) are merely selections from the range of variation.

282. ***Rhododendron lowndesii*** Davidian

ILLUSTRATION Stainton, *Forests of Nepal,* t. 100 (1972); Cox, *Dwarf Rhododendrons,* t. 18 (1973); *Notes from the Royal Botanic Garden Edinburgh* 39: 21 (1980); *The Rhododendron Handbook,* f. 15 (1997); Cox and Cox, *The Encyclopedia of Rhododendron Species,* 286 (1997); Halliday, *The Illustrated Rhododendron,* pl. 52 (2001)
HABIT small creeping shrub to 25 cm; shoots bristly, downy
LEAVES deciduous, thin, narrowly elliptic to oblanceolate, 1.5–2.5 cm × 6–11 mm; margins scolloped, bristly; upper surface bristly, dark green, very sparsely scaly; lower surface pale green, with distant yellow scales with broad translucent margins
RACEME one- to 2-flowered; flower stalks lengthening and hardening in fruit
CALYX lobes greenish or reddish, 2.5–3.5 mm, sparsely scaly, bristly and downy on the margins
COROLLA yellow, sometimes spotted or streaked with red, 1.3–1.5 cm, sparsely to densely scaly outside
CAPSULE to 5 mm, scaly
DISTRIBUTION Nepal
FLOWERING spring
HARDINESS ZONE 6

Wild-collected material is available under *Lowndes* (without number). Recent nonauthenticated material from Nepal is also in cultivation.

Subgenus *Rhododendron*

Section *Rhododendron*

Subsection *Baileya* Sleumer (*Lepidotum* series, in part)

HABIT small shrubs; young shoots scaly

LEAVES evergreen; lower surface densely covered with overlapping, flaky scales which have finely scolloped margins

RACEME terminal, several-flowered

CALYX 5-lobed

COROLLA campanulate

STAMENS radially arranged

OVARY scaly, the short, deflexed style impressed into a depression at its apex

SEEDS elongate, unwinged and without appendages (or appendages minute)

Rhododendron baileyi is the only species. The leaves have a one-layered upper epidermis, the cuticle thick; water tissue is absent, and the cells of the lower epidermis are prolonged into papillae. Sclereids are absent.

283. *Rhododendron baileyi* Balfour

ILLUSTRATION *Curtis's Botanical Magazine*, 9842 (1922), reprinted in Halliday, *The Illustrated Rhododendron*, pl. 53 (2001); *Gardeners' Chronicle* 89: 385 (1933); Kneller, *The Book of Rhododendrons*, 61 (1995); *Iconographia Cormophytorum Sinicorum* 3, t. 4011 (1974); Cox and Cox, *The Encyclopedia of Rhododendron Species*, 235 (1997); Feng, *Rhododendrons of China* 3, pl. 85: 1–2 (1999)

HABIT shrub to 2 m

LEAVES very narrowly elliptic to elliptic (rarely obovate or ovate), 2–5 × 1–2.6 cm; upper surface densely scaly when young, the scales soon deciduous; lower surface usually dark brown, with overlapping scales

RACEME 4- to 8-flowered

CALYX lobes 1.5–4 mm, scaly, often fringed with bristles

COROLLA magenta to purple, 1.2–1.5 cm, usually densely scaly outside, especially on the tube

CAPSULE 5–7.5 mm, scaly

DISTRIBUTION Himalaya, western China (southern Xizang)

FLOWERING spring

HARDINESS ZONE 7

Classic wild-collected material is available under *Ludlow, Sherriff, and Taylor 6656* and *Ludlow, Sherriff, and Hicks 17359*. Recent nonauthenticated material from Bhutan is also in cultivation.

R. baileyi flower and leaf

R. baileyi detail

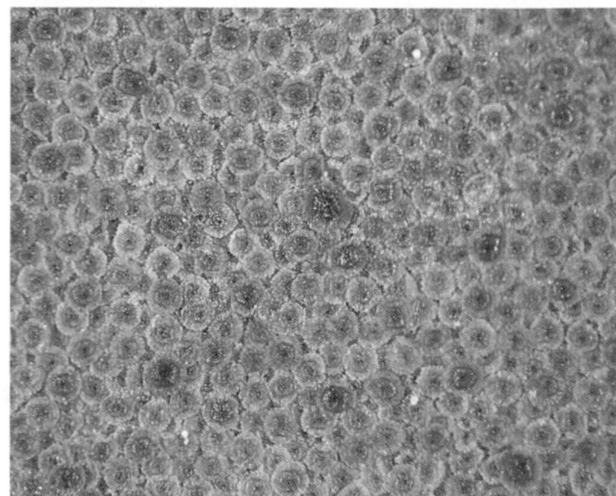

R. baileyi leaf surface

Subgenus *Rhododendron*

Section *Rhododendron*

Subsection *Trichoclada* (Balfour) Cullen (subgenus *Pseudazalea* Sleumer; *Trichocladum* series)

HABIT shrubs to 2 m; young shoots often bristly and scaly
LEAVES mostly deciduous, more rarely evergreen, hairless or with bristles and/or short, fine hairs, and with variously coloured, vesicular scales
CALYX variably developed, rim-like to clearly and often unequally lobed, usually bristly at the margin
COROLLA funnel-campanulate, yellow, sometimes tinged with red, variably spotted, scaly and sometimes bristly outside
OVARY scaly
STYLE impressed in a depression in its apex, sharply deflexed
SEEDS elongate, unwinged and with a minute appendage at each end

A group of 4 or 5 species, 2 or 3 of them with deciduous leaves. The 4th species, *R. caesium* Hutchinson, is similar to *R. trichocladum* but with straight hairs on the lower surface of the leaf, which is shining white-papillose; it may be found in a few specialist collections.

The leaves have a one- or 2-layered upper epidermis; when 2 layers are present, the cells of both layers are similar in size (*R. lepidostylum, R. caesium*), the cuticle thin. Water tissue is absent, and the cells of the lower epidermis are prolonged into small papillae. Sclereids are absent.

1a Most leaves evergreen, leathery, with a bluish bloom, revolute; ovary scaly, densely bristly .... **284. *R. lepidostylum***
b Most leaves deciduous, thin, flat, without bloom; ovary scaly, hairless or with a few hairs at the insertion of the style 2
2a Scales on the lower leaf surface markedly unequal, close, and brownish, greyish, or red-purple when mature .... **286. *R. mekongense***
b Scales on the lower leaf surface more or less equal, very distant, golden ..... **285. *R. trichocladum***

284. *Rhododendron lepidostylum* Balfour and Forrest
ILLUSTRATION *Rhododendron Yearbook*, t. 7 (1963); Cox, *Dwarf Rhododendrons*, t. 33 (1973); Davidian, *The Rhododendron Species* 1, pl. 58 (1982); Kneller, *The Book of Rhododendrons*, 95 (1995); Cox and Cox, *The Encyclopedia of Rhododendron Species*, 332 (1997)

HABIT shrub to 1.5 m; young shoots scaly, bristly

LEAVES evergreen, leathery, somewhat revolute, with long-persistent bluish grey bloom, obovate or obovate-elliptic, 3–3.5 × 1.5–2 cm; upper surface hairless and scaleless; lower surface with straight bristles and equal, distant, golden scales

RACEME 2- to 3-flowered

CALYX 5-lobed

COROLLA 2–3.3 cm, clear yellow, sometimes with orange spots, scaly and sparsely bristly outside

OVARY bristly, scaly

STYLE not scaly (less often scaly at the base)

CAPSULE to 1 cm, bristly towards the apex

DISTRIBUTION western China (southwestern Yunnan)

FLOWERING spring

HARDINESS ZONE 6

Classic wild-collected material is available under *Forrest 24633*.

Rhododendron viridescens Hutchinson, a species recently revived on the basis of observations in the field in China, may occasionally be cultivated. It has more or less evergreen leaves, somewhat glaucous, though less so than in *R. lepidostylum*, and close, unequal, reddish or blackish scales, like those of *R. mekongense*. It is generally rather low-growing and flowers in summer.

285. *Rhododendron trichocladum* Franchet

SYNONYM *R. oulotrichum* Balfour and Forrest

ILLUSTRATION *Curtis's Botanical Magazine*, 9073 (1925), reprinted in Halliday, *The Illustrated Rhododendron*, pl. 54 (2001); *Iconographia Cormophytorum Sinicorum* 3, t. 4111 and 4113 (1974); *Notes from the Royal Botanic Garden Edinburgh* 39: 21 (1980); Feng, *Rhododendrons of China* 1, pl. 87 (1988); Cox and Cox, *The Encyclopedia of Rhododendron Species*, 334–335 (1997)

HABIT shrub to 1.5 m, usually flowering before the leaves are developed; young shoots scaly, with twisted or curled bristles; bark greyish brown, striate

LEAVES deciduous, flat, thin, obovate or obovate-elliptic, 2.4–4 × 1–2 cm; lower surface greenish, with dense, curled or twisted bristles and very distant, equal, golden scales; upper surface with straight bristles and/or fine short hairs

INFLORESCENCE BUDS ovoid, yellowish brown; scales bearing large, yellow, lepidote scales and a dense fringe of white hairs

RACEME one- to 3-flowered

CALYX lobes often unequal, 2–5 mm, scaly, bristly

COROLLA yellow or greenish yellow, occasionally somewhat orange, 1.8–2.3 cm, scaly and variably bristly outside
OVARY usually without hairs
CAPSULE 8–10 mm
DISTRIBUTION northeastern Myanmar, western China (central and southwestern Yunnan)
FLOWERING late spring
HARDINESS ZONE 6

Classic wild-collected material is available under *Farrer 876, Kingdon-Ward 3097, 9519, 10490, 21072, 21079,* and *McLaren 112A*. Recent nonauthenticated material from Yunnan is also in cultivation.

Rather variable; a number of variants have been given species names in the past, but these names are not widely used among gardeners and so are not listed. A parent of 'Chink' (× *R. keiskei*).

286. *Rhododendron mekongense* Franchet

HABIT shrubs to 2 m, usually flowering before the leaves develop; young shoots scaly, variably bristly with straight or curled bristles; bark grey-brown, striate
LEAVES mostly deciduous, flat, thin, obovate or more rarely obovate-elliptic, 2.5–6 × 1.4–2.5 cm; upper surface downy along the midrib, rarely scaly; lower surface variably bristly, usually with at least some bristles on the base of the midrib and on margins, and with dense, very unequal scales, the smaller soon becoming reddish or purplish
INFLORESCENCE BUDS ovoid, yellow-brown; scales with dark brown lepidote scales and a fringe of white hairs
RACEME 2- to 4-flowered
CALYX usually obscure, or with lobes to 2.5 mm (rarely one lobe much longer), scaly, bristly or not
COROLLA yellow to greenish yellow, sometimes flushed with red, 1.7–2.3 cm, scaly but hairless outside
CAPSULE 9–11 mm
DISTRIBUTION Himalaya, northeastern Myanmar, western China (Yunnan, Xizang)
FLOWERING from late spring to early summer
HARDINESS ZONE 7

A very variable species. Four varieties occur in the wild, of which 3 have been cultivated.

R. mekongense var. **mekongense**

ILLUSTRATION *Notes from the Royal Botanic Garden Edinburgh* 39: 21 (1980); Davidian, *The Rhododendron Species* 1, pl. 59 (1982); Cox and Cox, *The Encyclopedia of Rhododendron Species,* 333 (1997); Feng, *Rhododendrons of China* 3, pl. 86: 1–2 (1999)

LEAVES not bristly above, rather densely so beneath

CALYX bristly

FLOWER STALKS usually bristly over their whole length

DISTRIBUTION Himalaya, northeastern Myanmar, western China (northwestern Yunnan, southeastern Xizang)

Classic wild-collected material is available under *Kingdon-Ward 5489, 21079, Ludlow, Sherriff, and Elliott 12505,* and *Rock 122, 146.*

R. mekongense var. *mekongense* flower

R. mekongense var. *mekongense* detail

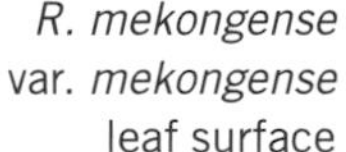

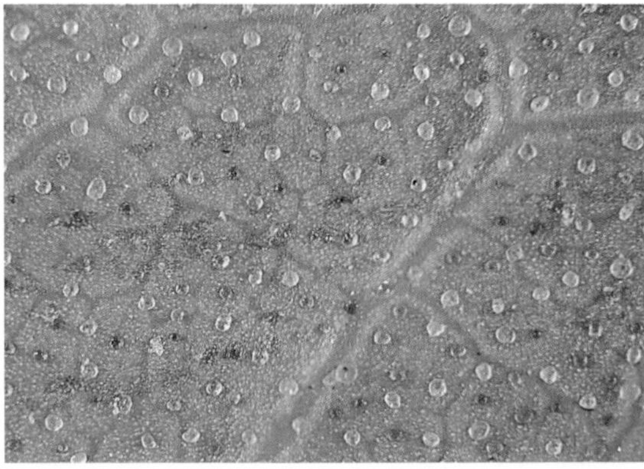

R. mekongense var. *mekongense* leaf surface

R. mekongense var. ***melinanthum*** (Balfour and Kingdon-Ward) Cullen

SYNONYM *R. melinanthum* Balfour and Kingdon-Ward; *R. chloranthum* Balfour and Forrest; *R. semilunatum* Balfour and Forrest

ILLUSTRATION *Curtis's Botanical Magazine,* 8903 (1921), reprinted in Halliday, *The Illustrated Rhododendron,* pl. 55 (2001); *Iconographia Cormophytorum Sinicorum* 3, t. 4112 and 4114–4115 (1974); *Notes from the Royal Botanic Garden Edinburgh* 39: 21 (1980); Feng, *Rhododendrons of China* 1, pl. 85: 1–2 (1988); Cox and Cox, *The Encyclopedia of Rhododendron Species,* 333 (1997)

LEAVES not bristly above, rather densely so beneath

CALYX hairless

FLOWER STALKS not bristly or bristly only at the extreme base

DISTRIBUTION northeastern Myanmar, western China (northwestern Yunnan, southeastern Xizang)

Classic wild-collected material is available under *Forrest 13900.*

R. mekongense var. ***rubrolineatum*** (Balfour and Forrest) Cullen

SYNONYM *R. rubrolineatum* Balfour and Forrest

ILLUSTRATION *Iconographia Cormophytorum Sinicorum* 3, t. 4115 (1974); Cox and Cox, *The Encyclopedia of Rhododendron Species,* 334 (1997)

LEAVES upper surface without bristles; lower surface with very sparse bristles restricted to the margins and midrib

DISTRIBUTION northeastern India (Arunachal Pradesh), western China (northwestern Yunnan, southern and southeastern Xizang)

The 4th variety, *longipilosum* (Cowan) Cullen, has long bristles on the upper surface of the leaves and is from Yunnan and Xizang. It has not been in cultivation.

Recent, nonauthenticated, wild collections of *R. mekongense* not yet identified to variety are also in cultivation: *Chungtien, Lijiang, and Dali Expedition 1514, Sino-British Expedition to Cangshan 351, Sino-Scottish Expedition to NW Yunnan 372, Chungtien, Lijiang, and Dali Expedition 1347,* and *Cox 6055.*

Subgenus *Rhododendron*

Section *Rhododendron*

Subsection *Afghanica* Cullen

HABIT small shrub
LEAVES evergreen; lower surface with spaced, pale, translucent or yellowish scales
RACEME terminal, distinct, many-flowered and with a long axis
CALYX 5-lobed
COROLLA campanulate
STAMENS radially arranged
STYLE impressed in a depression at the apex of the ovary, sharply deflexed at the base
SEEDS elongate, unwinged and without appendages

Rhododendron afghanicum is the only species. The leaves have a 2-layered upper epidermis, the cells of both layers similar in size, the cuticle about as thick as the cells are deep; water tissue is absent, and the cells of the lower epidermis are slightly prolonged into papillae.

287. *Rhododendron afghanicum* Aitchison and Hemsley
ILLUSTRATION *Journal of the Linnean Society* 19, t. 21 (1882); *Curtis's Botanical Magazine,* 8907 (1921), reprinted in Halliday, *The Illustrated Rhododendron,* pl. 56 (2001); Davidian, *The Rhododendron Species* 1, pl. 66 (1982); Kneller, *The Book of Rhododendrons,* 104 (1995); Cox and Cox, *The Encyclopedia of Rhododendron Species,* 234 (1997)
HABIT shrub to 50 cm; young shoots scaly, sometimes downy
LEAVES narrowly elliptic to elliptic, 4.5–8 × 1.3–2.5 cm, thick; upper surface dark green, scaleless, downy along the midrib; lower surface pale green, with scales 1–2 × their own diameter apart
RACEME 12- to 16-flowered, with an axis 2–5 cm
CALYX lobes 4–6 mm, scaly and often margined with scales
COROLLA white or greenish white, with a tubular base and a widely spreading limb, 1–1.4 cm, scaleless and hairless outside
STAMENS anthers white
CAPSULE scaly, to 7 mm
DISTRIBUTION Afghanistan-Pakistan border area (Kurram Valley)
FLOWERING late spring
HARDINESS ZONE 8

Wild-collected material is available under *Hedge and Wendelbo 9706.*

Introduced on several occasions but difficult to maintain in cultivation and now perhaps lost. A very distinct species, unlike others in its long racemes.

R. afghanicum flower and leaf

R. afghanicum leaf surface

Subgenus *Rhododendron*

Section ***Pogonanthum*** G. Don (*Anthopogon* series; *Cephalanthum* series)

HABIT small shrubs (at most to 2 m) with characteristic, pineapple-like odour

LEAVES evergreen, small, densely scaly, the scales characteristically with lacerate margins and frequently arranged in several tiers on the lower leaf surface; leaf bud scales sometimes persistent

INFLORESCENCE BUDS scales margined with branched hairs

RACEME terminal, condensed, often head-like, many-flowered

CALYX somewhat bilaterally symmetric, 5-lobed

COROLLA with a parallel- or flared-sided tube and usually widely spreading limb, always with a conspicuous ring of hairs in the throat

STAMENS 5–10, radially arranged, not projecting from the corolla tube

OVARY small, scaly, sometimes downy

STYLE very short, straight, club-shaped, not projecting from the corolla tube

CAPSULE scaly

SEEDS elongate, unwinged and without appendages (or appendages minute)

A group of 12 species, all difficult to identify. The group as a whole is identifiable by its fragrance, its lacerate scales arranged in several tiers on the lower surface of the leaf, its floral bracts margined with branched hairs, and its corollas with a cylindric tube and spreading lobes. The leaves have a one-layered upper epidermis, the cuticle thick; water tissue is absent, and the cells of the lower epidermis are prolonged into papillae. Sclereids are few or absent.

1a Scales of the lowermost tiers on the lower leaf surface as dark as or darker than those of the upper tiers; all scales brown to dark brown 2

b Scales of the lowermost tiers golden yellow, paler than those of the upper tiers 3

2a Corolla tube densely hairy outside . . . . **290. *R. laudandum***

b Corolla tube not hairy outside . . . . **289. *R. anthopogon***

3a Calyx lobes 1–2.5 mm; leaves linear, linear-oblong, or narrowly oblanceolate, 4 or more × as long as broad . . . . **295. *R. trichostomum***

b Calyx lobes 2.5 mm or more; leaves up to 3 × as long as broad, variously shaped 4

4a Leaf bud scales persistent and conspicuous 5

b Leaf bud scales quickly deciduous 6

5a Corolla yellow; tube densely scaly outside; leaves 9–15 mm . . . . **292. *R. sargentianum***

b Corolla white or pink, rarely yellowish; tube not scaly outside; leaves 1.5–5 cm . . . . **291. *R. cephalanthum***

6a Stamens 8–10; corolla tube with flaring sides .... **288. *R. collettianum***
b Stamens 5–6; corolla tube with parallel sides 7
7a Scales clearly in several tiers, very few or none of them with domed, shining centres; corolla usually white, rarely flushed with pink .... **294. *R. primuliflorum***
b Scales rather plastered together and to the surface, not so obviously in several tiers, most of them with domed, shining centres; corolla usually red, rarely pink .... **293. *R. kongboense***

288. *Rhododendron collettianum* Aitchison and Hemsley

ILLUSTRATION *Journal of the Linnean Society* 19, t. 20 (1882); *Curtis's Botanical Magazine*, 7019 (1888); Davidian, *The Rhododendron Species* 1, pl. 92 (1982); Cox and Cox, *The Encyclopedia of Rhododendron Species*, 228–229 (1997)

HABIT shrub to 1 m; leaf bud scales deciduous; bark pale grey-brown, scaling

LEAVES more or less elliptic, 3–4 × 1.3–1.7 cm; upper surface pale green, scaleless; lower surface pale greenish brown to brown, with dense, overlapping, plastered scales, all uniformly golden brown

INFLORESCENCE BUDS oblong-ovoid; scales densely lepidote, fringed with fine white hairs

RACEME rather elongate, 16- to 20-flowered

CALYX lobes 5–5.5 mm, sparsely scaly outside; margins bristly; inner surface downy

COROLLA with a tube with flaring sides, 1.6–2 cm, white (often pink in bud), hairless and scaleless outside

STAMENS 8–10

CAPSULE scaly, to 5 mm

DISTRIBUTION Afghanistan-Pakistan border area

FLOWERING late spring

HARDINESS ZONE 8

Wild-collected material is available under *Hedge and Wendelbo 8975*.

From the same general area as *R. afghanicum* and, like it, with an unusual, elongate raceme.

289. *Rhododendron anthopogon* D. Don

HABIT small, often closely and intricately branched shrub to 1 m; leaf bud scales persistent or not; bark reddish brown to grey, striate or breaking into oblong flakes

LEAVES ovate or elliptic, rarely almost circular, 1–3.5 cm × 8–16 mm; upper surface dark green, scaly or scaleless; lower surface dark brown, with dense, overlapping scales in 2 or 3 tiers, those of the lower tier as dark as or darker than those of the upper tiers

INFLORESCENCE BUDS more or less spherical, dark brown; scales pointed, sticky, fringed with branched white hairs
RACEME head-like, many-flowered
CALYX lobes oblong, 3.5–4.5 mm, usually scaly outside; margins bristly; inner surface variably downy
COROLLA usually white or pink, rarely cream or yellowish, 1–2 cm, hairless and scaleless outside
STAMENS anthers brown
CAPSULE scaly, 4–5 mm, scarcely exceeding the calyx
DISTRIBUTION Himalaya, western China (southern Xizang)
FLOWERING spring
HARDINESS ZONE 7

Two varieties occur in the wild, and both are in cultivation in Europe.

R. *anthopogon* var. ***anthopogon***
ILLUSTRATION Royle, *Illustrations of the Botany of the Himalaya,* t. 64 (1839); *Iconographia Cormophytorum Sinicorum* 3, t. 4099 (1974); *Notes from the Royal Botanic Garden Edinburgh* 39: 21 (1980); Davidian, *The Rhododendron Species* 1, pl. 2 (1982); Cox and Cox, *The Encyclopedia of Rhododendron Species,* 226 (1997); Feng, *Rhododendrons of China* 3, pl. 89 (1999)
LEAF BUD SCALES quickly deciduous
DISTRIBUTION Himalaya, western China

Wild-collected material is available under *Bartholomew 192, Beer, Lancaster, and Morris 332,* and *Kingdon-Ward 10542.*

R. *anthopogon* var. ***hypenanthum*** (Balfour) Cullen
SYNONYM *R. hypenanthum* Balfour
ILLUSTRATION Royle, *Illustrations of the Botany of the Himalaya,* t. 64 (1839); *Iconographia Cormophytorum Sinicorum* 3, t. 4100 (1974); *Notes from the Royal Botanic Garden Edinburgh* 39: 21 (1980); Cox and Cox, *The Encyclopedia of Rhododendron Species,* 226 (1997)
LEAF BUD SCALES persistent
DISTRIBUTION northern India, Nepal, Bhutan, possibly Pakistan

Wild-collected material is available under *McBeath 1183, Ludlow and Sherriff 1091,* and

R. anthopogon
var. *hypenanthum*
leaf surface

Stainton, Sykes, and Williams 9090. Recent nonauthenticated material from Pakistan is also in cultivation.

Recent, nonauthenticated, wild-collected material which is *R. anthopogon,* but which has not yet been identified to the variety, is also in cultivation.

290. *Rhododendron laudandum* Cowan

HABIT small shrub to 60 cm; leaf bud scales persistent but not very conspicuous

LEAVES oblong to ovate or almost circular, 1–1.7 cm × 6–9 mm; upper surface dark green or brownish, scaleless; lower surface dark chocolate-brown, with dense, overlapping scales in 2 or 3 tiers, those of the lowest tier as dark as or darker than the others

RACEME dense, head-like, many-flowered

CALYX lobes 5–6 mm, oblong to obovate, densely scaly outside, bristly on the margins

COROLLA white or pink, rarely yellowish, 8–17 mm; tube densely to loosely hairy outside

STAMENS 5–6

OVARY scaly or sparsely scaly, downy

CAPSULE very small

DISTRIBUTION western China (southeastern Xizang)

FLOWERING spring

HARDINESS ZONE 8

Two varieties occur in the wild, and both are reputed to be in cultivation, though most cultivated material under the name *R. laudandum* (of either variety) appears to be hybrid—see, for an example, *The Rhododendron Handbook,* f. 17 (1997).

R. *laudandum* var. ***laudandum***

ILLUSTRATION *Iconographia Cormophytorum Sinicorum* 3, t. 4102 (1974)

LEAVES 2 or more × as long as broad

COROLLA tube densely hairy outside; limb usually pink

R. *laudandum* var. ***temoense*** Cowan and Davidian

LEAVES less than 2 × as long as broad

COROLLA tube loosely hairy outside; limb usually white

291. *Rhododendron cephalanthum* Franchet

ILLUSTRATION *Gardeners' Chronicle* 91: 133 (1932); Cox, *Dwarf Rhododendrons,* 76 (1973); *Iconographia Cormophytorum Sinicorum* 3, t. 4101 (1974); *Notes from the Royal Botanic Garden Edinburgh* 39: 21 (1980); Fang, *Sichuan Rhododendron of China,* 309–310 (1986); Feng, *Rhododendrons of China* 1, pl. 88: 1–4 (1988); Cox and Cox, *The Encyclopedia of Rhododendron Species,* 227 (1997)

HABIT variably sized, often contorted, sometimes prostrate shrub, 10–120 cm high, often with thick lower stem; leaf bud scales persistent, conspicuous

LEAVES broadly elliptic to almost circular, 1.5–4.5 cm × 7–23 mm; upper surface dark glossy green, usually scaleless; lower surface fawn to brown or rusty, with dense scales in 2 or 3 tiers, those of the lower tier golden and paler than the others

RACEME dense

CALYX lobes 3–7 mm, scaly or scaleless outside; margins usually ciliate; inner surface hairless or finely downy

COROLLA white or pink, rarely yellowish, 1–2.2 cm; tube scaleless and hairless outside; lobes often with a few scales outside

STAMENS 5–7; anthers yellow

OVARY scaly

CAPSULE scarcely exceeding the calyx

DISTRIBUTION northeastern India (Arunachal Pradesh), northeastern Myanmar, western China (north, northwestern, and central Yunnan)

FLOWERING spring

HARDINESS ZONE 7

Classic wild-collected material is available under *Kingdon-Ward 6914, 8337,* and *Yü 20817.* Recent nonauthenticated material from Yunnan is also in cultivation.

Variety *platyphyllum* (Balfour and Forrest) Cullen is not in general cultivation but is illustrated in Cox and Cox, *The Encyclopedia of Rhododendron Species,* 228 (1997).

R. cephalanthum flower and leaf. PHOTO BY KEN HULME

292. *Rhododendron sargentianum* Rehder and Wilson

ILLUSTRATION *The Garden* 84: 324 (1920); *Curtis's Botanical Magazine,* 8871 (1920); *Gardeners' Chronicle* 91: 57 (1932); *Iconographia Cormophytorum Sinicorum* 3, t. 4105 (1974); Davidian, *The Rhododendron Species* 1, pl. 1 (1982); Fang, *Sichuan Rhododendron of China,* 311–313 (1986); Cox and Cox, *The Encyclopedia of Rhododendron Species,* 232 (1997)

HABIT small shrub to 60 cm; leaf bud scales persistent

LEAVES elliptic, 9–15 × 3–8 mm; upper surface dark green, scaleless; lower surface brown or pale brown, with scales in 2 or 3 tiers, those of the lower tier golden and paler than the others

RACEME 5- to 12-flowered

CALYX lobes to 3 mm, sparsely scaly outside; margins conspicuously bristly; inner surface downy

COROLLA whitish to yellowish, to 1.2 cm; tube and bases of lobes scaly outside and somewhat downy

STAMENS 5

Capsule sparsely scaly, to 4 mm
Distribution western China (central Sichuan)
Flowering spring
Hardiness zone 8

Classic wild-collected material is available under *Wilson 1208* (the type collection).

293. *Rhododendron kongboense* Hutchinson

Illustration *Curtis's Botanical Magazine,* 9492 (1937); Kneller, *The Book of Rhododendrons,* 101 (1995); Cox and Cox, *The Encyclopedia of Rhododendron Species,* 229 (1997)
Habit spindly, branched shrub to 1 m; leaf bud scales deciduous; bark pale grey, shining, striate
Leaves oblong or elliptic-oblong, 1.3–2.8 cm × 6–12 mm; upper surface usually persistently scaly; lower surface fawn to pale brown, with dense, plastered scales, all similar and pale brown, most with well-developed, domed centres
Inflorescence buds oblong; scales narrow, brownish, with a few scales on the surface, fringed with branched hairs
Raceme many-flowered
Calyx lobes 3–4 mm, scaly or not outside; margins bristly, occasionally scaly as well; inner surface hairless
Corolla pink to red, rarely pinkish white, 8.5–12 mm; tube variably hairy outside
Stamens 5; anthers pale to mid brown
Capsule scaly, scarcely exceeding the calyx
Distribution western China (southern Xizang)
Flowering spring
Hardiness zone 8

Classic wild-collected material is available under *Kingdon-Ward 5700, 6020.*

294. *Rhododendron primuliflorum* Bureau and Franchet

Synonyms *R. cephalanthoides* Balfour and W. W. Smith; *R. lepidanthum* Balfour and W. W. Smith
Illustration *Gardeners' Chronicle* 87: 453 (1930); *Iconographia Cormophytorum Sinicorum* 3, t. 4107 (1974); *Notes from the Royal Botanic Garden Edinburgh* 39: 21 (1980); Fang, *Sichuan Rhododendron of China,* 319–320 (1986); Feng, *Rhododendrons of China* 1, pl. 89: 1–7 (1988); *The Rhododendron Handbook,* f. 26 (1997); Cox and Cox, *The Encyclopedia of Rhododendron Species,* 231 (1997); Robertson and McKelvie, *Scottish Rock Gardening in the 20th Century,* f. 28 (2000)

HABIT small shrub to 1.5 m; leaf bud scales quickly deciduous; bark pale yellowish brown, peeling in long flakes

LEAVES narrowly elliptic or somewhat oblong, more rarely elliptic, 1–3.5 cm × 5–15 mm; upper surface dark glossy green, scaly or scaleless; lower surface pale brown to brown, with scales in 2 or 3 often very clearly distinguished tiers, those of the lower tier golden and paler than the others

INFLORESCENCE BUDS fusiform, pointed; scales few, mostly dark brown, paler green in some parts, densely hairy with branched hairs

RACEME several-flowered

CALYX lobes 2.5–6 mm, usually scaly outside; margins variably scaly and/or bristly; inner surface variably downy

COROLLA white, rarely flushed with pink, often yellowish orange towards the base, 9–18 mm; tube usually hairless outside, more rarely sparsely hairy or somewhat scaly

STAMENS 5–7; anthers brown

CAPSULE scaly, to 5 mm

DISTRIBUTION western China (northern and northwestern Yunnan, southern and southeastern Xizang, southwestern Sichuan)

FLOWERING spring

HARDINESS ZONE 6

Classic wild-collected material is available under *Forrest 15245, 16306, Kingdon-Ward 4160, Rock 23322,* and *Yü 14647, 15629.* Recent nonauthenticated material from Yunnan is also in cultivation.

Plants cultivated as this species under *Yü 15139* are incorrectly numbered, as the herbarium specimen is *R. trichostomum.*

A very variable species in the wild, with several variants introduced into cultivation.

295. ***Rhododendron trichostomum*** Franchet

SYNONYMS *R. ledoides* Balfour and W. W. Smith; *R. radinum* Balfour and W. W. Smith; *R. trichostomum* var. *ledoides* (Balfour and W. W. Smith) Cowan and Davidian; *R. trichostomum* var. *radinum* (Balfour and W. W. Smith) Cowan and Davidian

ILLUSTRATION *Curtis's Botanical Magazine,* 8831 (1920) and 9202 (1927); Cox, *Dwarf Rhododendrons,* pl. 2 (1973); *Iconographia Cormophytorum Sinicorum* 3, t. 4104 (1974); *Notes from the Royal Botanic Garden Edinburgh* 39: 21 (1980); Davidian, *The Rhododendron Species* 1, pl. 3 (1982); Fang, *Sichuan Rhododendron of China,* 315 (1986); Kneller, *The Book of Rhododendrons,* 101 (1995); Cox and Cox, *The Encyclopedia of Rhododendron Species,* 233 (1997); Halliday, *The Illustrated Rhododendron,* pl. 57 (2001)

Habit small, intricately branched shrub, 30–150 cm, often forming rounded bushes; leaf bud scales usually deciduous, rarely a few persisting, but not conspicuous

Leaves linear or oblong or oblanceolate, 1.2–3 cm × 3–6 mm; upper surface green, scaly or not, usually revolute; lower surface pale brown, with scales in 2 or 3 tiers, those of the lower tier golden and paler than the others

Raceme many-flowered, almost spherical

Calyx lobes 1–2.5 mm, usually scaly outside; margins bristly; inner surface variably downy

Corolla white or pink, 6–15 mm; tube hairless outside; lobes generally with a few scales on their backs

Stamens 5–6

Capsule scaly, 2–4 mm

Distribution western China (northern and northwestern Yunnan, southwestern and central Sichuan)

Flowering spring

Hardiness zone 7

Classic wild-collected material is available under *Forrest 20476, 20480, 21299, Kingdon-Ward 3998, 4465,* and *Rock 59196* (equivalent herbarium specimen *11260*), *59257* (equivalent herbarium specimen *11401*). Recent nonauthenticated material from Yunnan and Sichuan is also in cultivation.

Another variable species; the species and varieties separated from it in the past are merely selected parts of the total range of variation.

Identification Tables

THESE TABLES make use of the same information found in the bracketed, dichotomous keys used throughout "*Rhododendron:* Keys and Descriptions." However, the layout is different and may well prove easier for gardeners to use.

Each table consists of 2 columns of information. The left-hand column includes entries labelled by number (1, 2, 3). The right-hand column includes entries corresponding with some of the entries in the left-hand column; these corresponding entries are subdivided and labelled by letter (A, B, C).

In identifying an unknown plant, start with the first entry in the left-hand column of the first table. If the plant matches the description, read the boldfaced information that follows. This will include either a named group (with an instruction to proceed to another identification table or another section of the same table) or the name of a species.

If no boldfaced information is provided in the left-hand column, continue on to the right-hand column. Compare the entries in the right-hand column serially with the plant. Because of the nature of the table, the plant should agree with one of these entries; if it does not, a mistake has probably been made in deciding that the plant matches the description in the left-hand column. If the plant agrees with one of the entries, read the boldfaced information that follows. Note that the plant must agree *entirely* with the contents of the entry in each case (with the usual caveats of "sometimes," "somewhat," "usually," and so on).

An example may help. Begin with table 1. The first entry in the left-hand column, entry 1, states that, to be included here, the unknown plant must have scales. If this is true, read the corresponding entries in the right-hand column, labelled A and B. If the plant matches A, it is identified as belonging to subgenus *Rhododendron* section *Pogonanthum,* which can be found in table 6; turning to section *Pogonanthum* in table 6, begin with the first entry. If the plant matches B, it belongs to subgenus *Rhododendron* section *Rhododendron,* which can be found in table 3.

If the plant in question has no scales, skip entry 1 and proceed to entry 2, which includes only nonscaly plants with axillary inflorescences. Here again, if the plant has axillary inflorescences, proceed to A, B, C, and D in the right-hand column and, reading them in order, decide which description matches the plant. Each entry leads to a sectional or subgeneric name and another table.

In this way, proceed down the table until an answer is obtained. Note that entries 4–9 do not include corresponding entries in the right-hand column; this is because each of these entries leads directly to a named group.

By working through the various tables, you will eventually reach the name of an individual, numbered species, and this can then be compared with the description in "*Rhododendron:* Keys and Descriptions."

Table 1: Subgenera and Sections

(excluding subgenus *Rhododendron* section *Vireya*)

1. Plant bearing scales on at least the lower leaf surface, usually also on some or all of the following: young shoots, leaf stalks and upper surfaces, flower stalks, calyx, corolla	A. Corolla with a parallel-sided or narrowly flaring tube and spreading limb; stamens and club-shaped style included within the corolla tube; plant with inflorescence bud scales margined with branched hairs **Subgenus *Rhododendron* section *Pogonanthum* (table 6)**
	B. Corolla campanulate to tubular; stamens and styles usually projecting from the corolla; inflorescence bud scales not margined with branched hairs **Subgenus *Rhododendron* section *Rhododendron* (table 3)**
2. Inflorescence and inflorescence buds lateral on the shoots; new vegetative growth continuing the shoot above the inflorescence	A. Leaves evergreen; stamens 5 **Subgenus *Azaleastrum* section *Azaleastrum* (table 5)**
	B. Leaves evergreen; stamens 10 **Subgenus *Azaleastrum* section *Choniastrum* (table 5)**
	C. Leaves deciduous; stamens 5 **Subgenus *Mumeazalea* (table 5)**
	D. Leaves deciduous; stamens 10 **Subgenus *Candidastrum* (table 5)**

3. At least some of the leaves evergreen (or, if all deciduous, none longer than 1 cm)	A. Leaves generally dimorphic (spring and summer leaves), the summer leaves evergreen; new shoots from the same terminal bud as the inflorescence; flattened bristles present **Subgenus *Tsutsusi* section *Tsutsusi* (table 5)**
	B. Leaves not dimorphic, always evergreen; new shoots from separate buds below the inflorescence bud **Subgenus *Hymenanthes* section *Pontica* (table 2)**
4. Plant low and creeping; corolla very deeply split between the 2 lower lobes; bracts green and leaf-like, though differing in size from the foliage leaves **Subgenus *Therorhodion* (table 5)**	
5. Flattened bristles present; leaves usually in false whorls of 3 at the tips of the shoots **Subgenus *Tsutsusi* section *Brachycalyx* (table 5)**	
6. Corolla hairy outside; stamens 5 **Subgenus *Pentanthera* section *Pentanthera* (table 5)**	
7. Corolla more or less regular, white, unspotted, tubular-campanulate **Subgenus *Pentanthera* section *Viscidula* (table 5)**	
8. Corolla 2-lipped, the upper 3 lobes fused higher than the lower 2, hairless inside **Subgenus *Pentanthera* section *Rhodora* (table 5)**	
9. Corolla not 2-lipped, hairy inside **Subgenus *Pentanthera* section *Sciadorhodion* (table 5)**	

Table 2: Subsections of Subgenus *Hymenanthes* Section *Pontica*

1. Stamens more than 10; corolla lobes usually more than 5 **Group 1 (below)**	
2. Corolla with conspicuous black, dark red, or purple nectar sacs at the base, often tubular or tubular-campanulate and red	A. Mature leaves more or less glabrous beneath, occasionally with hair bases or a few scattered hairs or glands near the midrib **Group 2 (below)**
	B. Mature leaves obviously hairy beneath over most of the surface **Group 3 (below)**
3. Young shoots and usually petioles with a covering of often glandular bristles **Group 4 (below)**	
4. Young shoots and petioles without bristles **Group 5 (below)**	

GROUP 1

1. Young shoots and petioles stipitate-glandular-bristly, the bristles conspicuous **Subsection *Auriculata* (table 4)**	
2. Leaf indumentum composed, at least in part, of cup-shaped hairs **Subsection *Falconera* (table 4)**	
3. Mature leaves glabrous beneath, occasionally with persistent hair bases or sparse hairs near the midrib	A. Corolla with obvious, dark nectar sacs **Subsection *Irrorata* (table 4)**
	B. Corolla without dark nectar sacs **Subsection *Fortunea* (table 4)**
4. Corolla lobes 5 **Subsection *Argyrophylla* (table 4)**	
5. Inflorescence more or less spherical, dense; rachis very short or absent **Subsection *Grandia* (table 4)**	
6. Ovary glabrous; leaf indumentum beneath whitish to buff, 2-layered **Subsection *Taliensia* (table 4)**	
7. Ovary white-tomentose; leaf indumentum beneath grey to fawn, one-layered **Subsection *Pontica* (table 4)**	

GROUP 2

1. Style glandular or glandular-hairy over most of its length	A. Young shoots and petioles hairy or not, but not stipitate-glandular **Subsection *Thomsonia* (table 4)**
	B. Ovary tomentose and with glandular hairs **Subsection *Parishia* (table 4)**
	C. Ovary with glandular hairs only, not tomentose **Subsection *Irrorata* (table 4)**
2. Calyx obsolete or to 3 mm, if obvious then disc-like or rarely weakly lobed, never cupular	A. Petioles absent or up to 5 mm; inflorescence dense, spherical; corolla red **Subsection *Barbata* (table 4)**
	B. Petioles more than 5 mm; inflorescence loose, not spherical; corolla usually not red **Subsection *Irrorata* (table 4)**
3. Ovary glabrous or stipitate-glandular, not tomentose **Subsection *Thomsonia* (table 4)**	
4. Young shoots and petioles with glandular bristles **Subsection *Venatora* (table 4)**	
5. Young shoots and petioles without glandular bristles **Subsection *Neriiflora* (table 4)**	

GROUP 3

1. Young shoots and petioles bristly, the bristles sometimes glandular	A. Rachis of inflorescence to 4 cm; style glandular in the lower half **Subsection *Parishia* (table 4)**
	B. Inflorescence dense, spherical; petioles usually with dense, eglandular bristles **Subsection *Barbata* (table 4)**
	C. Leaves with crisped, glandular bristles beneath **Subsection *Maculifera* (table 4)**
	D. Leaves with a dense, 2-layered, nonglandular indumentum beneath **Subsection *Neriiflora* (table 4)**

GROUP 3 (continued)

2. Corolla purplish to violet **Subsection *Argyrophylla* (table 4)**	
3. Leaves densely hairy beneath; ovary glabrous **Subsection *Fulgensia* (table 4)**	
4. Calyx 1–2 mm **Subsection *Arborea* (table 4)**	
5. Ovary glabrous or stipitate-glandular only **Subsection *Thomsonia* (table 4)**	
6. Ovary tomentose, sometimes also stipitate-glandular **Subsection *Neriiflora* (table 4)**	

GROUP 4

1. Corolla densely hairy outside **Subsection *Griersoniana* (table 4)**	
2. Calyx indistinct, rim-like, to 1 mm at most **Subsection *Williamsiana* (table 4)**	
3. Leaves bristly beneath **Subsection *Glischra* (table 4)**	
4. Leaves variously hairy or glabrous but not bristly beneath **Subsection *Selensia* (table 4)**	

GROUP 5

1. Inflorescence usually many-flowered, pyramidal, with well-developed rachis (to 6 cm); corolla lobes usually longer than the tube (sometimes only slightly so) **Subsection *Pontica* (table 4)**	
2. Mature leaf lamina glabrous beneath; midrib hairy or not	A. Midrib of leaf persistently hairy beneath with folioliferous hairs **Subsection *Maculifera* (table 4)**
	B. Corolla 5–6 cm **Subsection *Fortunea* (table 4)**

GROUP 5 (continued)

2. (continued) Mature leaf lamina glabrous beneath; midrib hairy or not	C. Corolla 2.5–4 cm **Subsection *Irrorata* (table 4)**
	D. Leaves relatively broad; bases rounded to cordate **Subsection *Campylocarpa* (table 4)**
3. Leaf indumentum beneath white to fawn (not reddish to brown)	A. Ovary tomentose; leaf hairs radiate **Subsection *Taliensia* (table 4)**
	B. Ovary tomentose; leaf hairs rosulate to ramiform **Subsection *Argyrophylla* (table 4)**
	C. Ovary glabrous; longest leaves at least 14 cm; corolla with a purplish blotch **Subsection *Fulva* (table 4)**
	D. Ovary glabrous; longest leaves up to 14 cm; corolla without a purplish blotch **Subsection *Taliensia* (table 4)**
4. Leaf indumentum beneath 2-layered, the lower layer compacted and whitish, obscured by the reddish brown upper layer	A. Upper layer of indumentum woolly; hairs ramiform **Subsection *Taliensia* (table 4)**
	B. Upper layer of indumentum granular; hairs capitellate **Subsection *Fulva* (table 4)**
5. Leaf hairs dendroid and crisped **Subsection *Lanata* (table 4)**	
6. Leaf indumentum compacted, composed of radiate or long-rayed hairs (if hairs ramiform, then indumentum splitting and becoming patchy) **Subsection *Taliensia* (table 4)**	
7. Leaf indumentum loose, composed of fascic-ulate, capitellate, or very rarely ramiform hairs, when not splitting and becoming patchy **Subsection *Campanulata* (table 4)**	

Table 3: Subsections of Subgenus *Rhododendron* Section *Rhododendron*

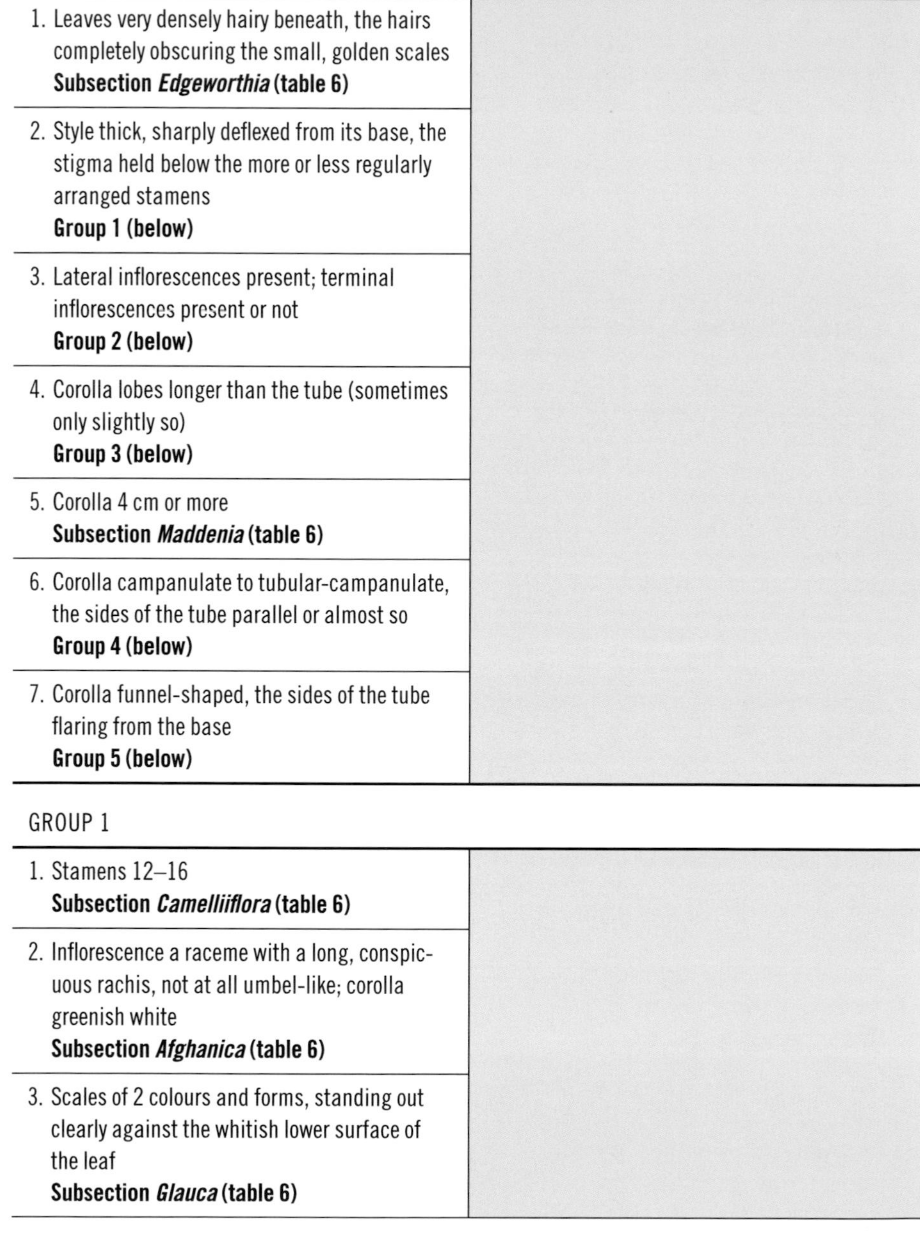

1. Leaves very densely hairy beneath, the hairs completely obscuring the small, golden scales **Subsection *Edgeworthia* (table 6)**	
2. Style thick, sharply deflexed from its base, the stigma held below the more or less regularly arranged stamens **Group 1 (below)**	
3. Lateral inflorescences present; terminal inflorescences present or not **Group 2 (below)**	
4. Corolla lobes longer than the tube (sometimes only slightly so) **Group 3 (below)**	
5. Corolla 4 cm or more **Subsection *Maddenia* (table 6)**	
6. Corolla campanulate to tubular-campanulate, the sides of the tube parallel or almost so **Group 4 (below)**	
7. Corolla funnel-shaped, the sides of the tube flaring from the base **Group 5 (below)**	

GROUP 1

1. Stamens 12–16 **Subsection *Camelliiflora* (table 6)**	
2. Inflorescence a raceme with a long, conspicuous rachis, not at all umbel-like; corolla greenish white **Subsection *Afghanica* (table 6)**	
3. Scales of 2 colours and forms, standing out clearly against the whitish lower surface of the leaf **Subsection *Glauca* (table 6)**	

GROUP 1 (continued)

4. Scales vesicular	A. Corolla whitish-bloomed, pink to purple **Subsection *Campylogyna* (table 6)**
	B. Ovary tapering smoothly into the style; flower stalks shorter than the corollas **Subsection *Boothia* (table 6)**
	C. Style inserted into a depression at the top of the ovary; flower stalks longer than the corollas **Subsection *Trichoclada* (table 6)**
5. Scales crenulate **Subsection *Baileya* (table 6)**	
6. Ovary tapering smoothly into the style **Subsection *Boothia* (table 6)**	
7. Tall shrubs, usually more than 1 m; lower surface of leaves and corolla whitish-bloomed; racemes with 4 or more flowers **Subsection *Genestieriana* (table 6)**	
8. Small shrubs, usually much less than 1 m, lower surface of leaves and corolla not whitish-bloomed; racemes with 1–3 flowers **Subsection *Lepidota* (table 6)**	

GROUP 2

1. Corolla lobes shorter than the tube	A. Corolla funnel-shaped, downy outside; calyx lobes 2–3 mm; racemes one-flowered, themselves arranged in a distinct raceme **Subsection *Virgata* (table 6)**
	B. Flowers erect; stamens and styles projecting beyond the corolla lobes; leaves downy and bristly above **Subsection *Scabrifolia* (table 6)**
	C. Flowers pendulous; stamens and styles not projecting beyond the corolla lobes; leaves hairless **Subsection *Cinnabarina* (table 6)**

GROUP 2 (continued)

2. Terminal inflorescences usually present as well as lateral inflorescences; corolla very openly funnel-shaped, very bilaterally symmetric **Subsection *Triflora* (table 6)**	
3. Corolla yellow, bristly outside **Subsection *Triflora* (table 6)**	
4. Corolla hairy outside, at least near the base; each inflorescence one-flowered **Subsection *Rhodorastra* (table 6)**	
5. Corolla not hairy outside; each inflorescence with 2 or more flowers **Subsection *Scabrifolia* (table 6)**	

GROUP 3

1. Corolla to 10 mm, white, unspotted, unblotched, glabrous within **Subsection *Micrantha* (table 6)**	
2. Flower stalks in line with the axis of the ovary and style; scales undulate **Subsection *Lapponica* (table 6)**	
3. Flower stalks making a sharp angle with the axis of the ovary and style; scales crenulate **Subsection *Saluenensia* (table 6)**	

GROUP 4

1. Scales of 2 forms and colours, standing out sharply against the whitish lower surface of the leaf **Subsection *Glauca* (table 6)**	
2. Calyx reduced to a rim or slightly undulate, not more than 2 mm	A. Corolla fleshy; nectar forming 5 large drops in the base of the corolla **Subsection *Cinnabarina* (table 6)**
	B. Inflorescences one- to 3-flowered; stamens and style projecting beyond the corolla lobes **Subsection *Monantha* (table 6)**
	C. Inflorescences many-flowered; stamens and style not projecting beyond the corolla lobes **Subsection *Rhododendron* (table 6)**

GROUP 4 (continued)

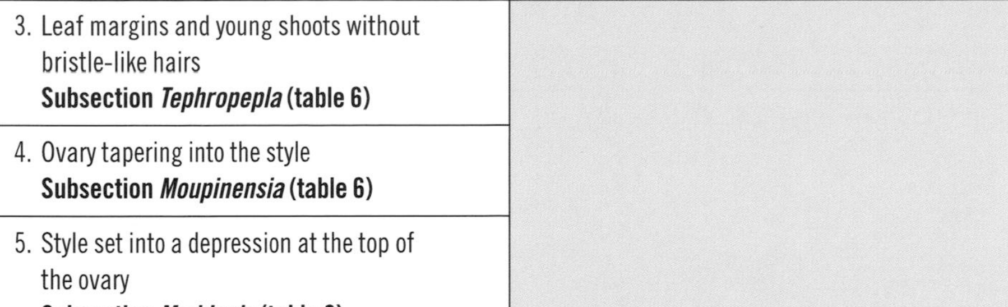

3. Leaf margins and young shoots without bristle-like hairs **Subsection *Tephropepla* (table 6)**	
4. Ovary tapering into the style **Subsection *Moupinensia* (table 6)**	
5. Style set into a depression at the top of the ovary **Subsection *Maddenia* (table 6)**	

GROUP 5

1. Corolla downy outside; small shrublets **Subsection *Uniflora* (table 6)**	
2. Calyx rim-like, or, if slightly lobed, the lobes not margined with bristles **Subsection *Heliolepida* (table 6)**	
3. Style downy; corolla white to pink with deeper pink or dark red spots **Subsection *Lapponica* (table 6)**	
4. Style hairless or scaly; corolla white to pink with greenish or yellowish spots **Subsection *Caroliniana* (table 6)**	

Table 4: Subgenus *Hymenanthes* Section *Pontica*

SUBSECTION *FORTUNEA* (page 48)

1. Style glandular throughout	A. Calyx 1.5–2 cm **8. *R. griffithianum***
	B. Rachis of inflorescence 5–10 mm; glands on style usually red **4. *R. vernicosum***
	C. Leaf base cordate **7. *R. hemsleyanum***
	D. Filaments hairless **6. *R. fortunei***
	E. Filaments hairy below the middle **5. *R. decorum***
2. Leaves circular to ovate-circular, 1.2–1.5 × as long as broad **9. *R. orbiculare***	
3. Stigma a flattened disc; racemes 5- to 30-flowered **3. *R. calophytum***	
4. Corolla up to 4 cm **10. *R. oreodoxa***	
5. Corolla with a basal blotch; leaves completely hairless beneath **2. *R. praevernum***	
6. Corolla without a basal blotch; leaves with a more or less persistent indumentum along the midrib beneath **1. *R. sutchuenense***	

SUBSECTION *AURICULATA* (page 61): **11. *R. auriculatum*** only

SUBSECTION *GRANDIA* (page 63)

1. Ovary hairless; leaf stalks to 5 mm **20. *R. watsonii***	
2. Leaf stalks strongly flattened and winged **16. *R. praestans***	

SUBSECTION *GRANDIA* (page 63) (continued)

3. Corolla ventricose-campanulate or obliquely campanulate; leaf indumentum silvery, compacted, one-layered	A. Ovary and flower stalks glandular **13. *R. grande***
	B. Leaves 2.2–2.8 × as long as broad; corolla pale cream-white **14. *R. sinogrande***
	C. Leaves 3–5 × as long as broad; corolla pink **15. *R. montroseanum***
4. Corolla lemon-yellow; leaf indumentum 2-layered, the upper layer woolly **19. *R. macabeanum***	
5. Flower stalks 2 cm or more; leaf indumentum buff, sometimes restricted to the margins or absent **17. *R. protistum***	
6. Raceme with about 15 flowers; leaves 11–16 cm **12. *R. wattii***	
7. Raceme with about 30 flowers; leaves 20 cm or more **18. *R. magnificum***	

SUBSECTION *FALCONERA* (page 72)

1. Leaf stalks flattened, winged **21. *R. basilicum***	
2. Ovary and flower stalks eglandular **26. *R. falconeri***	
3. Ovary hairless **23. *R. galactinum***	
4. Leaves 1.5–2.5 × as long as broad, the upper surface wrinkled; corolla pale yellow **22. *R. rex***	
5. Corolla intense pink or rose-purple, without spots **25. *R. hodgsonii***	

SUBSECTION *FALCONERA* (page 72) (continued)

6. Leaves at most 6.2 cm wide; indumentum whitish to fawn or rarely pale brown **24. *R. coriaceum***	
7. Leaves generally more than 6.2 cm wide; indumentum fawn to rusty brown **22. *R. rex***	

SUBSECTION *WILLIAMSIANA* (page 80): **27. *R. williamsianum*** only

SUBSECTION *CAMPYLOCARPA* (page 82)

1. Style hairless; corolla campanulate to funnel-campanulate; calyx 1–5 mm	A. Corolla whitish to pink **28. *R. callimorphum***
	B. Corolla pale yellow to sulphur-yellow **29. *R. campylocarpum***
2. Corolla purplish pink **31. *R. souliei***	
3. Corolla whitish to yellow **30. *R. wardii***	

SUBSECTION *MACULIFERA* (page 88)

1. Corolla tubular-campanulate, usually with nectar sacs; young shoots with shortly stalked glands or glandular bristles which are not matted **33. *R. strigillosum***	
2. Leaf bases more or less tapering; leaf stalks and midrib beneath densely rusty-hairy; calyx 6 mm or more **32. *R. longesquamatum***	
3. Leaves 10 cm or more	A. Flower stalks, ovary, and style base with at least a few glands or hairs **36. *R. morii***
	B. Flower stalks and ovary without glands; style base hairless **34. *R. pachytrichum***

SUBSECTION *MACULIFERA* (page 88) (continued)

4. Flower stalks 2.5 cm or more **37. *R. pseudochrysanthum***	
5. Flower stalks up to 2 cm **35. *R. maculiferum***	

SUBSECTION *SELENSIA* (page 95)

1. Young shoots and leaf stalks with glandular bristles	A. Leaves with a more or less continuous indumentum beneath, generally more than 2.5 × as long as broad **38. *R. bainbridgeanum***
	B. Leaves glabrous or with very sparse indumentum beneath, up to 2.5 × as long as broad **41. *R. hirtipes***
2. Leaves 4.5–5 cm; racemes one- to 4-flowered **40. *R. martinianum***	
3. Leaves 5–12 cm; racemes 3- to 10-flowered **39. *R. selense***	

SUBSECTION *GLISCHRA* (page 100)

1. Lower surface of leaves with a dense covering of loosely matted hairs	A. Leaves 7–17 × 2.3–4.2 cm; apex cuspidate; large shrubs to 5 m **45. *R. crinigerum***
	B. Leaves 3–7 × 1–2 cm; apex blunt; dwarf shrubs to 1.5 m **46. *R. recurvoides***
2. Leaves up to 2.4 × as long as broad **43. *R. habrotrichum***	
3. Calyx fleshy, cup-like, 8–20 mm; corolla rose-crimson **44. *R. diphrocalyx***	
4. Calyx neither fleshy nor cupular, deeply lobed, 7–10 mm; corolla white to pale pink **42. *R. glischrum***	

SUBSECTION *VENATORA* (page 106): **47. *R. venator*** only

SUBSECTION *IRRORATA* (page 108)

1. Leaves with a persistent, continuous indumentum beneath **52. *R. tanastylum***	
2. Leaves up to 6 cm **48. *R. aberconwayi***	
3. Corolla openly campanulate; leaf stalks hairless even when young **49. *R. annae***	
4. Flower stalks, leaf stalks, and ovary covered with shortly stalked glands; corolla yellow, white, pink, or red **51. *R. irroratum***	
5. Corolla 6- to 7-lobed **53. *R. anthosphaerum***	
6. Corolla up to 3.5 cm, white flushed with pink **50. *R. araiophyllum***	
7. Corolla 4 cm or more, crimson **52. *R. tanastylum***	

SUBSECTION *PONTICA* (page 115)

1. Lower leaf surface with reddish, punctate hair bases (sometimes also with scattered dendroid hairs) **54. *R. hyperythrum***	
2. Leaves hairless beneath or with a thin, sparse indumentum at maturity	A. Corolla yellow; dwarf shrub, to 1 m **61. *R. aureum***
	B. Ovary hairless **62. *R. ponticum***
	C. Leaves 3.5 or more × as long as broad; ovary and flower stalks glandular; calyx at least 3 mm **64. *R. maximum***

SUBSECTION *PONTICA* (page 115) (continued)

2. (continued) Leaves hairless beneath or with a thin, sparse indumentum at maturity	D. Corolla lilac-purple; leaves to 2.3 × as long as broad **63. *R. catawbiense***
	E. Leaf apex acute; base cuneate; corolla 3 cm or more **65. *R. macrophyllum***
	F. Leaf apex and base rounded; corolla to 2.5 mm **55. *R. brachycarpum***
3. Dwarf shrub to 1 m; leaves with a compacted indumentum beneath; corolla yellow or creamy white **60. *R. caucasicum***	
4. Leaves to 2.5 × as long as broad; corolla more than 2.5 cm; leaf indumentum usually thick, compacted to woolly	A. Leaf indumentum very thick, covering the midribs beneath; similar indumentum present on one-year-old shoots **57. *R. yakushimanum***
	B. Young shoots eglandular; inflorescence rachis to 2 cm **56. *R. degronianum***
	C. Ovary and leaf stalks with shortly stalked glands; leaves 11–21 cm; calyx 5–9 mm **58. *R. ungernii***
	D. Ovary and leaf stalks eglandular; leaves to 11 cm; calyx 2–3 mm **59. *R. smirnowii***

SUBSECTION *ARGYROPHYLLA* (page 126)

1. Leaf indumentum 2-layered, the upper layer more or less woolly and loose	A. Inflorescence rachis 1 cm or more; leaves at least 4 × as long as broad **67. *R. hunnewellianum***
	B. Inflorescence rachis to 7 mm; leaves to 3.3 × as long as broad **66. *R. floribundum***

SUBSECTION *ARGYROPHYLLA* (page 126) (continued)

2. Inflorescence rachis at most 5 mm	A. Flower stalks to 1 cm; leaf indumentum white; corolla purplish violet, with nectar sacs **71. *R. rirei***
	B. Flower stalks 2 cm or more; leaf indumentum fawn, shining; corolla pink, without nectar sacs **70. *R. insigne***
3. Style glandular throughout **68. *R. thayerianum***	
4. Style hairless or with a few glands at the base only **69. *R. argyrophyllum***	

SUBSECTION *ARBOREA* (page 133)

1. Leaves generally not less than 16 cm; indumentum beneath 2-layered, the upper layer woolly-hairy **73. *R. lanigerum***	
2. Corolla rose-pink to deep carmine, rarely white; usually a tree with a single, defined trunk **72. *R. arboreum***	
3. Corolla lilac to deep magenta; usually a large shrub with several main branches arising from the base **74. *R. niveum***	

SUBSECTION *TALIENSIA* (page 139)

1. Calyx 5 mm or more	A. Leaf indumentum whitish to pale pink **77. *R. balfourianum***
	B. Leaf indumentum olive-brown, containing some glands **76. *R. adenogynum***
	C. Leaf indumentum deep pink to rusty brown, without glands **75. *R. bureavii***

SUBSECTION *NERIIFLORA* (page 174) (continued)

5. Leaves at least 2.5 × as long as broad **116. *R. eudoxum***	
6. Flower stalks hairy, eglandular; leaf stalks broad, eglandular **115. *R. aperantum***	
7. Flower stalks with sparse, shortly stalked glands; leaf stalks narrow, sometimes glandular **117. *R. chamaethomsonii***	

SUBSECTION *FULGENSIA* (page 193)

1. Inflorescence dense, with 8–14 flowers; corolla 2–3.5 cm **123. *R. fulgens***	
2. Inflorescence loose, with 4–5 flowers; corolla 3.5–4 cm **124. *R. sherriffii***	

SUBSECTION *THOMSONIA* (page 196)

1. Style glandular throughout **125. *R. cerasinum***	
2. Leaves with a thin, discontinuous indumentum beneath **131. *R. stewartianum***	
3. Leaf glaucous beneath, 1–1.8 × as long as broad	A. Corolla deep coppery red or purplish crimson **126. *R. thomsonii***
	B. Corolla white, yellow, or clear pink **129. *R. cyanocarpum***
4. Ovary hairless **130. *R. eclecteum***	
5. Large fasciculate hairs present on the main veins of the leaf beneath; leaf stalks 1.5–3 cm **127. *R. hookeri***	
6. Large fasciculate hairs absent; leaf stalks 1–1.5 cm **128. *R. meddianum***	

Table 5: Subgenera *Tsutsusi*, *Pentanthera*, *Therorhodion*, *Azaleastrum*, *Candidastrum*, and *Mumeazalea*

SUBGENUS *TSUTSUSI* SECTION *TSUTSUSI* (page 206)

1. Shoots with spreading hairs as well as adpressed, flattened hairs	A. Flowers 2.5–3.5 cm, funnel-shaped; stamens 8–10 **133. *R. oldhamii***
	B. Flowers 3.5–5 cm, broadly funnel-shaped; stamens 5–7; leaves very narrow and corolla divided into linear-lanceolate segments in the commonly cultivated variant **135. *R. stenopetalum***
2. Stamens 7 or more	A. Young shoots with flattened hairs and also adpressed-hairy **138. *R. mucronatum***
	B. Bud scales viscid-sticky on their inner surfaces **137. *R. simsii***
	C. Corolla reddish purple spotted with darker purple **140. *R. ×pulchrum***
	D. Corolla red to scarlet **134. *R. scabrum***
	E. Corolla pink **136. *R. yedoense***
3. Most mature leaves more than 3 cm long	A. Corolla tubular-campanulate **132. *R. mariae***
	B. Leaves 3.5–4 × as long as broad **144. *R. tosaense***
	C. Leaves up to 3 × as long as broad **141. *R. kaempferi***
4. Corolla 5–10 mm, 4- or 5-lobed **146. *R. tschonoskii***	
5. Leaves 2–6 mm broad, to 1.4 cm long	A. Flowers mostly solitary, their stalks up to 3 mm **145. *R. serpyllifolium***
	B. Flowers 3 or more in racemes, their stalks 5–10 mm **142. *R. kiusianum***

SUBGENUS *TSUTSUSI* SECTION *TSUTSUSI* (page 206) (continued)

6. Leaves narrowly lanceolate to oblanceolate **139. *R. indicum***	
7. Leaves ovate to elliptic-ovate, oblong-lanceolate, or obovate **143. *R. ×obtusum***	

SUBGENUS *TSUTSUSI* SECTION *BRACHYCALYX* (page 220)

1. Leaves ovate to oblong-lanceolate, broadest below the middle; stamens always 10 **147. *R. mariesii***	
2. Corolla red to rose-pink	A. Corolla deep rose-pink **150. *R. sanctum***
	B. Corolla red **151. *R. amagianum***
3. Corolla 3–4 cm; racemes 2- to 4-flowered **149. *R. weyrichii***	
4. Corolla 2–3 cm; racemes one- to 2-flowered **148. *R. reticulatum***	

SUBGENUS *PENTANTHERA* SECTION *RHODORA* (page 227)

1. Corolla divided to the base between the 2 lower lobes and these 2 together and the rest of the corolla; stamens 10 **152. *R. canadense***	
2. Corolla with a distinct, though short, tube; stamens usually 7 **153. *R. vaseyi***	

SUBGENUS *PENTANTHERA* SECTION *SCIADORHODION* (page 230)

1. Leaves clearly alternate, not in false whorls at the tips of the shoots **154. *R. albrechtii***	
2. New shoots from lateral buds below the terminal bud; leaf stalks with a fringe of hairs **155. *R. pentaphyllum***	

SUBGENUS *PENTANTHERA* SECTION *SCIADORHODION* (page 230)

3. Corolla white; style and ovary hairless or with eglandular hairs **157. *R. quinquefolium***	
4. Corolla pink; style and ovary covered with glandular hairs **156. *R. schlippenbachii***	

SUBGENUS *PENTANTHERA* SECTION *VISCIDULA* (page 234): **158. *R. nipponicum*** only

SUBGENUS *PENTANTHERA* SECTION *PENTANTHERA* (page 236)

1. Flowers appearing before leaves are fully expanded	A. Upper corolla lobe with a blotch or spots of contrasting colour **Pentanthera Group A (below)**
	B. Upper corolla lobe uniform in colour, not blotched or spotted **Pentanthera Group B (below)**
2. Flowers appearing after leaves are fully expanded **Pentanthera Group C (below)**	

PENTANTHERA GROUP A

1. Corolla broadly funnel-shaped; stamens not or scarcely projecting beyond the corolla lobes	A. Corolla yellow **164. *R. molle***
	B. Corolla orange-red **165. *R. japonicum***
2. Corolla lobes longer than the tube, which is abruptly widened above **170. *R. calendulaceum***	
3. Corolla lobes shorter than the tube, which is gradually widened above	A. Corolla basically white; flower bud scales hairless or almost so, eglandular **166. *R. alabamense***
	B. Corolla basically white; flower bud scales hairy, usually with some glands **167. *R. occidentale***

PENTANTHERA GROUP A (continued)

3. (continued) Corolla lobes shorter than the tube, which is gradually widened above	C. Corolla tube purplish; lobes reddish; flower bud scales with their outer surface densely downy **168. *R. austrinum***
	D. Corolla yellow; flower bud scales with their outer surface hairless or rarely sparsely downy **169. *R. luteum***

PENTANTHERA GROUP B

1. Glandular hairs forming lines on the outside of the corolla; plant strongly stoloniferous **163. *R. atlanticum***	
2. Flower bud scales hairless; leaves hairless or sparsely hairy beneath **161. *R. periclymenoides***	
3. Flower bud scales densely hairy; leaves hairy beneath, usually densely so **162. *R. canescens***	

PENTANTHERA GROUP C

1. Shoots hairless; lower leaf surface hairless or almost so	A. Corolla yellow to red **160. *R. pruniflorum***
	B. Corolla white **172. *R. arborescens***
2. Corolla yellow to orange or red, with a darker blotch on the upper lobe **171. *R. cumberlandense***	
3. Corolla white, unblotched **159. *R. viscosum***	

SUBGENUS *THERORHODION* (page 247): **173. *R. camtschaticum*** only

SUBGENUS *AZALEASTRUM* SECTION *AZALEASTRUM* (page 250)

1. Leaves rounded-ovate to broadly elliptic **174. *R. ovatum***	
2. Leaves narrowly elliptic to lanceolate **175. *R. leptothrium***	

SUBGENUS *AZALEASTRUM* SECTION *CHONIASTRUM* (page 253)

1. Corolla tube at most a third the total length of the corolla **178. *R. latoucheae***	
2. Corolla 4.5–6 cm; stamens only slightly projecting beyond the corolla lobes **177. *R. moulmainense***	
3. Corolla 2.5–3.5 cm; stamens projecting well beyond the corolla lobes **176. *R. stamineum***	

SUBGENUS CANDIDASTRUM (page 256): **179. *R. albiflorum*** only

SUBGENUS *MUMEAZALEA* (page 258): **180. *R. semibarbatum*** only

Table 6: Subgenus *Rhododendron*

SECTION *RHODODENDRON* SUBSECTION *EDGEWORTHIA* (page 264)

1. Corolla 3.5–6 cm; style declinate **181. *R. edgeworthii***	
2. Corolla 1.5–2 cm; style sharply deflexed from the base **182. *R. pendulum***	

SECTION *RHODODENDRON* SUBSECTION *MADDENIA* (page 267)

1. Stamens 15 or more; ovary 10- to 12-celled **183. *R. maddenii***	
2. Flower stalks and calyx whitish-bloomed, the flower stalks recurved in fruit; capsule not exceeding the persistent calyx **184. *R. megacalyx***	
3. Leaf with the main vein raised towards the base on the upper surface; calyx conspicuous, deeply lobed **Maddenia Group A (below)**	
4. Leaf with the main vein not at all raised; calyx conspicuous or inconspicuous **Maddenia Group B (below)**	

MADDENIA GROUP A

1. Leaves with the secondary and tertiary veins forming a conspicuous network over the whole surface beneath; scales very unequal, the smaller more or less rimless, the larger with broad, usually ascending, irregular rims **185. *R. nuttallii***	
2. Flower stalks and calyx lobes downy (scales may also be present) **186. *R. dalhousiae***	
3. Calyx ciliate with fine hairs **187. *R. lindleyi***	
4. Calyx margined with scales **188. *R. taggianum***	

MADDENIA GROUP B

1. Ovary tapering smoothly into the style	A. Corolla scaly outside only along the upper side of the tube; lobes with crisped margins **200. *R. veitchianum***
	B. Leaves persistently scaly above; corolla pink throughout **197. *R. carneum***
	C. Corolla downy but not scaly at the base of the tube outside **196. *R. ciliicalyx***
	D. Leaves mostly obovate **198. *R. roseatum***
	E. Leaves mostly elliptic **199. *R. pachypodum***
2. Corolla yellow	A. Calyx small and disc-like, at most 2 mm; corolla with scales all over the outer surface **192. *R. burmanicum***
	B. Leaves scolloped in the upper half; lower surface green, with distant scales **191. *R. fletcherianum***
	C. Leaves entire; lower surface brown, with contiguous or overlapping scales **190. *R. valentinianum***
3. Calyx more than 5 mm; lobes more or less equal, herbaceous; corolla to 4 cm; style completely scaleless **189. *R. ciliatum***	
4. Leaves not more than 2 cm wide; margins and leaf stalks usually persistently bristly **193. *R. formosum***	
5. Calyx without a persistent fringe of bristles **195. *R. dendricola***	
6. Calyx with a persistent fringe of bristles **194. *R. johnstoneanum***	

SECTION *RHODODENDRON* SUBSECTION *MOUPINENSIA* (page 285): **201. *R. moupinense*** only

SECTION *RHODODENDRON* SUBSECTION *MONANTHA* (page 287): **202. *R. flavantherum*** only

SECTION *RHODODENDRON* SUBSECTION *TRIFLORA* (page 289)

1. Corolla basically yellow, sometimes suffused with reddish brown or green	A. Scales less than 0.1 mm, almost rimless; corolla hairy only at the sinuses between the lobes outside **217. *R. triflorum***
	B. Corolla densely downy outside with backwardly pointing hairs; leaves with conspicuous drip tips **220. *R. lutescens***
	C. Scales on the lower leaf surface close to contiguous; upper surface with short hairs at the base of the midrib **218. *R. ambiguum***
	D. Scales on the lower leaf surface distant; upper surface with short hairs along the midrib and on the blade on either side of it **219. *R. keiskei***
2. Midrib of the leaves beneath with long, straight or somewhat twisted bristles	A. Corolla, calyx, flower stalks, leaf stalks, and leaf midrib beneath with a dense indumentum of somewhat twisted, fine bristles **212. *R. trichanthum***
	B. Fine bristles absent from corolla, flower stalks, and leaf upper surface; leaf midrib beneath with more or less straight, narrow bristles beneath **211. *R. augustinii***
3. Leaves white beneath with large, flat scales; corolla tube downy outside at the base **203. *R. zaleucum***	
4. Scales more or less rimless, vesicular, small, reddish purple or almost grey when mature; young leaves, flower stalks, and calyx whitish-bloomed **210. *R. oreotrephes***	

SECTION *RHODODENDRON* SUBSECTION *TRIFLORA* (page 289) (continued)

5. Corolla distinctly purple; tube scaly outside	A. Scales on the lower leaf surface dense, overlapping, flaky; leaves 3 or more × as long as broad **216. *R. polylepis***
	B. Leaf stalks bearing long, somewhat twisted bristles **214. *R. amesiae***
	C. Leaf stalks without bristles **213. *R. concinnum***
6. Scales on the silvery grey lower leaf surface contiguous, in 3 size classes **215. *R. searsiae***	
7. Scales at most 2 × their own diameter apart	A. Scales very broadly rimmed, the central part forming at most half the diameter; outer flower stalks recurving in fruit **206. *R. siderophyllum***
	B. Leaves 2 or more × as long as broad; corolla 1.8–2.6 cm; young shoots brownish or green **205. *R. davidsonianum***
	C. Leaves up to 2 × as long as broad; corolla up to 2 cm; young shoots usually reddish crimson **204. *R. tatsienense***
8. Bristles present on the margins and upper surfaces of the leaves and on the leaf stalks, the bristles variably deciduous **207. *R. yunnanense***	
9. Leaf stalks hairless, usually whitish-bloomed beneath; scales 5–8 × their own diameter apart **209. *R. rigidum***	
10. Leaf stalks downy, not whitish-bloomed; scales 3–5 × their own diameter apart **208. *R. pleistanthum***	

SECTION *RHODODENDRON* SUBSECTION *SCABRIFOLIA* (page 306)

1. Flowers erect, tubular, containing copious watery nectar **226. *R. spinuliferum***	
2. Leaves hairless above except for a few hairs on the midrib; ovary hairless **221. *R. racemosum***	
3. Hairs on the leaf above all of the same form and length	A. Corolla 9.5–14.5 mm; leaves whitish and hairless beneath except for a few hairs along the midrib **222. *R. hemitrichotum***
	B. Corolla 1.9–3 cm; leaves with a dense indumentum beneath, not whitish **223. *R. mollicomum***
4. Corolla 6–8 mm, shortly hairy inside; bristles on the upper leaf surface flexuous, without swollen bases **224. *R. pubescens***	
5. Corolla 9–30 mm, hairless inside; bristles on the upper leaf surface stiff, with swollen bases **225. *R. scabrifolium***	

SECTION *RHODODENDRON* SUBSECTION *HELIOLEPIDA* (page 313)

1. Style longer than the longest stamens, declinate, hairless; calyx and corolla completely hairless **229. *R. rubiginosum***	
2. Flower stalks downy at the base; corolla 1.5–2.2 cm; old leaf bud scales persistent **227. *R. bracteatum***	
3. Flower stalks hairless; corolla 2.4–3.4 cm; old leaf bud scales deciduous **228. *R. heliolepis***	

SECTION *RHODODENDRON* SUBSECTION *CAROLINIANA* (page 318): **230. *R. minus*** only

SECTION *RHODODENDRON* SUBSECTION *LAPPONICA* (page 320)

1. Corolla 1.5 cm or more **231. *R. cuneatum***	
2. Shoots of the current year covered with long bristles **250. *R. setosum***	
3. Scales on the lower leaf surface opaque, white or pinkish **239. *R. fastigiatum***	
4. Scales on the lower leaf surface all of the same colour **Lapponica Group A (below)**	
5. Scales on the lower leaf surface of 2 colours or shades (usually pale golden brown and darker brown) **Lapponica Group B (below)**	

LAPPONICA GROUP A

1. Corolla yellow or white	A. Scales on the lower leaf surface widely spaced **240. *R. flavidum***
	B. Scales on the lower leaf surface contiguous or almost so **243. *R. orthocladum***
2. All scales on the lower leaf surface pale yellowish	A. Racemes with 2 or more flowers **233. *R. hippophaeoides***
	B. Racemes with 1–2 flowers; stamens and style included in the corolla tube **232. *R. intricatum***
	C. Racemes with 1–2 flowers; stamens and style projecting beyond the corolla tube **234. *R. thymifolium***

SECTION *RHODODENDRON* SUBSECTION *LAPPONICA* (page 320) (continued)

3. Style shorter than or equalling the stamens	A. Stamens 5–6 **235. *R. complexum***
	B. Leaves lanceolate or narrowly elliptic **243. *R. orthocladum***
	C. Leaves elliptic to broadly elliptic **236. *R. yungningense***
4. Scales on the lower leaf surface distant	A. Calyx lobes 2.5 mm or more **241. *R. impeditum***
	B. Calyx lobes up to 2.5 mm **242. *R. polycladum***
5. Calyx lobes up to 2 mm	A. Leaves broadly elliptic to almost circular, reddish brown beneath **237. *R. tapetiforme***
	B. Leaves lanceolate to narrowly elliptic, brown beneath **243. *R. orthocladum***
6. Corolla densely hairy outside **238. *R. dasypetalum***	
7. Corolla hairless or sparsely and minutely hairy near the base only outside **236. *R. yungningense***	
LAPPONICA GROUP B	
1. Darker coloured scales on the lower leaf surface few and scattered	A. Background scales of the lower leaf surface brown **243. *R. orthocladum***
	B. Corolla purplish, scaly outside **244. *R. telmateium***
	C. Corolla yellow, not scaly outside **240. *R. flavidum***
2. Leaf usually less than 9 mm, without a thickened apex, the scales beneath sharply contrasted, pale and dark **245. *R. nivale***	

LAPPONICA GROUP B (continued)

3. Calyx to 2.5 mm	A. Leaves lanceolate to narrowly elliptic **243. *R. orthocladum***
	B. Leaves elliptic or relatively broader **246. *R. lapponicum***
4. Leaf without a thickened apex **247. *R. capitatum***	
5. Calyx lobes with a central band of scales **249. *R. rupicola***	
6. Calyx lobes without a central band of scales **248. *R. russatum***	

SECTION *RHODODENDRON* SUBSECTION *RHODODENDRON* (page 340)

1. Leaves ciliate with bristle-like hairs; style downy at the base **252. *R. hirsutum***	
2. Leaves not ciliate; style hairless **251. *R. ferrugineum***	

SECTION *RHODODENDRON* SUBSECTION *RHODORASTRA* (page 344)

1. Leaves thick, usually at least some persisting through winter, obtuse or notched at the apex, 1–3.6 cm; corolla to 3.5 cm in diameter **253. *R. dauricum***	
2. Leaves thin, deciduous, acute to acuminate, 4–6 cm; corolla 3.3–4 cm in diameter **254. *R. mucronulatum***	

SECTION *RHODODENDRON* SUBSECTION *SALUENENSIA* (page 347)

1. Shoots, leaf stalks, leaf midribs beneath, leaf margins, and (usually) flower stalks bristly; ovary hairy, at least at the apex **256. *R. saluenense***	
2. Shoots, leaf stalks, and leaf midribs beneath not bristly; leaf margins and flower stalks bristly or not; ovary completely hairless **255. *R. calostrotum***	

SECTION *RHODODENDRON* SUBSECTION *UNIFLORA* (page 353)

1. Corolla yellow; leaves slightly scolloped **260. *R. ludlowii***	
2. Corolla 1.1–2.1 cm; tube 7–14 mm; style shorter than the stamens **257. *R. pumilum***	
3. Leaves obovate, the scales beneath close, markedly unequal; corolla 2.4–3 cm **258. *R. pemakoense***	
4. Leaves oblong-elliptic or narrowly elliptic, the scales beneath distant, more or less equal; corolla 2.1–2.5 cm **259. *R. uniflorum***	

SECTION *RHODODENDRON* SUBSECTION *CINNABARINA* (page 358)

1. Inflorescences all terminal; corolla 2.5–3.6 cm; scales very narrowly rimmed **261. *R. cinnabarinum***	
2. Inflorescences mostly lateral; corolla to 2 cm; scales broadly rimmed **262. *R. keysii***	

SECTION *RHODODENDRON* SUBSECTION *TEPHROPEPLA* (page 363)

1. Style inserted into a shouldered depression on top of the ovary; corolla white, pink, or red	A. Corolla pink or red; style scaly for about half its length; scales on the lower leaf surface contiguous or up to their own diameter apart **265. *R. tephropeplum***
	B. Raceme 5- to 15-flowered, with a conspicuous rachis; leaves with a well-developed drip tip **266. *R. hanceanum***
	C. Racemes with up to 3 flowers; leaves acute but without a drip tip **267. *R. longistylum***

SECTION *RHODODENDRON* SUBSECTION *TEPHROPEPLA* (page 363) (continued

2. Calyx lobes reflexed; leaves brown beneath with contiguous or overlapping scales **264. *R. auritum***	
3. Calyx lobes spreading or erect; leaves silvery brown beneath with close but not contiguous scales **263. *R. xanthostephanum***	

SECTION *RHODODENDRON* SUBSECTION *VIRGATA* (page 368): **268. *R. virgatum*** only

SECTION *RHODODENDRON* SUBSECTION *MICRANTHA* (page 371): **269. *R. micranthum*** only

SECTION *RHODODENDRON* SUBSECTION *BOOTHIA* (page 373)

1. Scales with rims (which are sometimes upturned); calyx lobes ovate or oblong; racemes with 3 or more flowers **270. *R. sulfureum***	
2. Corolla almost flat, white (sometimes tinged pink); leaves bristly above **272. *R. leucaspis***	
3. Corolla broadly campanulate, yellow or rarely cream; leaves hairless above except for a few bristles on the base of the midrib and on the margin **271. *R. megeratum***	

SECTION *RHODODENDRON* SUBSECTION *CAMELLIIFLORA* (page 377): **273. *R. camelliiflorum*** only

SECTION *RHODODENDRON* SUBSECTION *Glauca* (page 379)

1. Calyx lobes acuminate, each with a tuft of hairs inside at the apex; margins ciliate with bristle-like hairs; leaves usually acute **274. *R. glaucophyllum***	
2. Corolla to 1.8 cm; raceme axis short, hairless or sparsely hairy	
3. Corolla yellow; flower stalks to 2 cm **275. *R. luteiflorum***	
4. Corolla pink to purplish; flower stalks 2 cm or more **276. *R. charitopes***	

SECTION *RHODODENDRON* SUBSECTION *CAMPYLOGYNA* (page 356): **279. *R. campylogynum*** only

SECTION *RHODODENDRON* SUBSECTION *GENESTIERIANA* (page 389): **280. *R. genestierianum*** only

SECTION *RHODODENDRON* SUBSECTION *LEPIDOTA* (page 391)

1. Leaves evergreen, not ciliate **281. *R. lepidotum***	
2. Leaves deciduous, ciliate **282. *R. lowndesii***	

SECTION *RHODODENDRON* SUBSECTION *BAILEYA* (page 393): **283. *R. baileyi*** only

SECTION *RHODODENDRON* SUBSECTION *TRICHOCLADA* (page 395)

1. Most leaves evergreen, leathery, with a bluish bloom, revolute; ovary scaly, densely bristly **284. *R. lepidostylum***	
2. Scales on the lower leaf surface markedly unequal, and greyish, red-purple, or brownish when mature **286. *R. mekongense***	
3. Scales on the lower leaf surface more or less equal, very distant, golden **285. *R. trichocladum***	

SECTION *RHODODENDRON* SUBSECTION *AFGHANICA* (page 400): **287. *R. afghanicum*** only

SECTION *POGONANTHUM* (page 402)

1. Scales of the lowermost tiers on the lower leaf surface as dark as or darker than those of the upper tiers; all scales brown to dark brown	A. Corolla tube densely hairy outside **290. *R. laudandum***
	B. Corolla tube not hairy outside **289. *R. anthopogon***
2. Calyx lobes up to 2.5 mm; leaves linear, linear-oblong, or narrowly oblanceolate, 4 or more × as long as broad **295. *R. trichostomum***	
3. Leaf bud scales persistent and conspicuous	A. Corolla yellow; tube densely scaly outside; leaves 9–15 mm **292. *R. sargentianum***
	B. Corolla white or pink, rarely yellowish, tube not scaly outside; leaves 1.5–5 cm **291. *R. cephalanthum***

SECTION *POGONANTHUM* (page 402) (continued)

4. Stamens 8–10, corolla tube with flaring sides **288. *R. collettianum***	
5. Scales clearly in several tiers, very few or none of them with domed, shining centres; corolla usually white, rarely flushed with pink **294. *R. primuliflorum***	
6. Scales rather plastered together and to the surface, not obviously in several tiers, most of them with domed, shining centres; corolla usually red, rarely pink **293. *R. kongboense***	

Character Lists

THIS FINAL identificatory aid consists of lists of individual characters and the groups and species which exhibit them. The lists are divided into 2 parts: nonscaly species (pp. 452–467) and scaly species (pp. 467–476). Each part lists the characters in ascending order of the number of groups in which they occur, so that the lists provide, at least towards their beginnings, indications of those groups or species which show unusual or very distinctive characters.

Once it is known whether the plant in question is nonscaly or scaly, proceed through the appropriate list looking for the earliest occurring character that describes the plant. If this occurs towards the beginning of the list, there will be relatively few groups and species which exhibit this character, so the range of possibilities will be reduced. From this point, proceed to find the next character that describes the plant. By comparing the groups and species listed under the second character with those listed under the first, the range of possibilities is further reduced. Proceed on this basis until a single group or species is reached. By this method it is not always possible to arrive at a single species or group, but the list of "possibles" will be quite small.

A couple of examples may help.

If the unknown plant is nonscaly and has a ventricose-campanulate corolla, find "Corolla ventricose-campanulate" at the beginning of the list of nonscaly species. Immediately following this is "1/35 groups, 3 species," meaning the character occurs in one out of 35 nonscaly groups, and in 3 species. Below this is the name of the group, Grandia, and "3/9," indicating that the character occurs in 3 out of 9 species in the group: *grande, montroseanum,* and *sinogrande.* Knowing that the character belongs to one of these 3 species, you can now use the plant descriptions in "*Rhododendron:* Keys and Descriptions" to come to a conclusion.

Alternatively, if the plant is nonscaly and has bristly leaf stalks, it could be one of 15 species belonging to 5 groups. If it is also true that the corolla is funnel-shaped, the plant could belong to 8 groups and 34 species. However, only one group and one species are common to both lists: Auriculata and *R. auriculatum.*

By proceeding in this way, it should be possible in most cases to obtain a small enough collection of groups and species for simple comparison of descriptions to resolve the issue.

This type of list may well be of help in determining possible parentage (at least as far as the group) for plants which are either known to be hybrid or which won't identify to anything sensible using the other keys and descriptions. By comparing the various characters carefully, and making use of the descriptions of the taxa to which they lead, it should be possible to gain some understanding of the groups or species that may have contributed to the hybrid. Some of the complexities of the whole situation concerning hybrids are described in Leslie (2003).

In these lists, several characters refer to corolla colour. The colour as given in the lists refers to the basic colour of the corolla and not to spots or blotches of a different colour which may occur; it is not possible to distinguish between corollas which are white, white flushed with pink, or pink. Because overall similarities are not important in this context, the groups and the species within them are listed in alphabetical order.

Nonscaly Species

Indumentum containing flagellate hairs (1/35 groups, 1 species). The indumentum referred to is that on the lower leaf surface; it may need to be scraped off and examined in water under a microscope.

Maculifera (1/6): *longesquamatum*

Corolla lobes fewer than 5 (1/35 groups, 1 species)

Tsutsusi (1/5): *tschonoskii*

Corolla tube parallel-sided; lobes spreading at right angles (1/35 groups, 1 species)

Viscidula (1/1): *nipponicum*

Corolla ventricose-campanulate (1/35 groups, 3 species)

Grandia (3/9): *grande, montroseanum, sinogrande*

Indumentum containing capitellate hairs (2/35 groups, 2 species)

Campanulata (1/2): *campanulatum*

Fulva (1/2): *fulvum*

Corolla saucer-shaped (2/35 groups, 3 species)

Campylocarpa (2/4): *souliei, wardii*

Irrorata (1/6): *aberconwayi*

Corolla up to 2 cm long (2/35 groups, 3 species)
Tsutsusi (2/15): *mariae* (occasionally longer), *tschonoskii*
Viscidula (1/1): *nipponicum* (sometimes longer)

Indumentum containing folioliferous hairs (2/35 groups, 5 species). The indumentum referred to is that on the lower leaf surface; it may need to be scraped off and examined in water under a microscope.
Maculifera (4/6): *maculiferum, morii, pachytrichum, pseudochrysanthum*
Venatora (1/1): *venator*

Corolla orange (2/35 groups, 7 species)
Neriiflora (3/18): *aperantum, citriniflorum, dichroanthum*
Pentanthera (4/14): *calendulaceum, cumberlandense, japonicum, molle*

Corolla glandular outside (2/35 groups, 9 species)
Fortunea (3/10): *decorum, fortunei, hemsleyanum*
Pentanthera (6/14): *arborescens, atlanticum, calendulaceum, occidentale, prunifolium, viscosum*

Indumentum made up, at least in part, of flattened, adpressed bristles (2/35 groups, 20 species)
Brachycalyx (5/5): *amagianum, mariesii, reticulatum, sanctum, weyrichii*
Tsutsusi (15/15): *indicum, kaempferi, kiusianum, mariae, mucronatum, ×obtusum, oldhamii, ×pulchrum, scabrum, serpyllifolium, simsii, stenopetalum, tosaense, tschonoskii, yedoense*

Ovary tapering into the style (3/35 groups, 8 species)
Auriculata (1/1): *auriculatum*
Choniastrum (3/3): *latoucheae, moulmainense, stamineum*
Neriiflora (4/18): *floccigerum, neriiflorum, sperabile, sperabiloides*

At least some racemes lateral (4/35 groups, 7 species)
Azaleastrum (2/2): *leptothrium, ovatum*
Candidastrum (1/1): *albiflorum*
Choniastrum (3/3): *latoucheae, moulmainense, stamineum*
Mumeazalea (1/1): *semibarbatum*

Indumentum containing stellate or radiate hairs (4/35 groups, 7 species). The indumentum referred to is that on the lower leaf surface; it may need to be scraped off and examined in water under a microscope.
Fulva (1/2): *fulvum*
Neriiflora (2/18): *beanianum, sperabile*
Parishia (3/3): *elliottii, facetum, kyawi*
Taliensia (1/19): *lacteum*

Leaf stalks bristly with glandular bristles, at least when young (5/35 groups, 15 species). The bristles referred to are long, thick, rather stiff or curled hairs.

Auriculata (1/1): *auriculatum*

Barbata (2/2): *barbatum, smithii*

Glischra (5/5): *crinigerum, diphrocalyx, glischrum, habrotrichum, recurvoides*

Maculifera (6/6): *longesquamatum, maculiferum, morii, pachytrichum, pseudochrysanthum, strigillosum*

Therorhodion (1/1): *camtschaticum*

Indumentum containing ramiform hairs (6/35 groups, 22 species). The indumentum referred to is that on the lower leaf surface; it may need to be scraped off and examined in water under a microscope.

Argyrophylla (2/6): *floribundum, hunnewellianum*

Campanulata (1/2): *campanulatum*

Glischra (2/15): *crinigerum, recurvoides*

Grandia (1/9): *macabeanum*

Neriiflora (4/14): *citriniflorum, floccigerum, sperabile, sperabiloides*

Taliensia (12/19): *adenogynum, aganniphum, balfourianum, bathyphyllum, bureavii, clementinae, phaeochrysum, proteoides, rufum, taliense, wightii, wiltonii*

Stamens fewer than 10 (6/35 groups, 31 species)

Azaleastrum (2/2): *leptothrium, ovatum*

Brachycalyx (1/5): *reticulatum* (stamens sometimes 10)

Mumeazalea (1/1): *semibarbatum*

Pentanthera (14/14): *alabamense, arborescens, atlanticum, austrinum, calendulaceum, canescens, cumberlandense, japonicum, luteum, molle, occidentale, periclymenoides, prunifolium, viscosum*

Rhodora (1/2): *vaseyi*

Tsutsusi (12/15): *indicum, kaempferi, kiusianum, mariae, mucronatum* (stamens sometimes 10), *×obtusum, oldhamii* (stamens sometimes 10), *serpyllifolium, simsii* (stamens sometimes 10), *stenopetalum, tosaense* (stamens sometimes 10), *tschonoskii*

Most mature leaves less than 2.5 cm long (7/35 groups, 19 species)

Argyrophylla (1/6): *argyrophyllum* (mostly longer)

Mumeazalea (1/1): *semibarbatum* (usually longer)

Neriiflora (3/18): *aperantum, chamaethomsonii* (usually longer), *forrestii* (occasionally longer)

Pentanthera (2/14): *canescens* (usually longer), *viscosum* (usually longer)

Rhodora (1/2): *canadense* (usually longer)

Tsutsusi (10/15): *indicum* (sometimes longer), *kaempferi* (also longer), *kiusianum, mariae*

(usually longer), ×*obtusum* (occasionally longer), *oldhamii* (usually longer), *serpyllifolium*, *simsii* (usually longer), *tosaense* (occasionally longer), *tschonoskii*
Williamsiana (1/1): *williamsianum* (mostly longer)

Indumentum on the lower leaf surface 2-layered (7/35 groups, 21 species)
Arborea (1/3): *arboreum*
Argyrophylla (2/6): *floribundum, hunnewellianum*
Falconera (5/6): *basilicum, coriaceum, falconeri, galactinum, hodgsonii*
Fulva (2/2): *fulvum, uvarifolium*
Grandia (2/9): *macabeanum, magnificum*
Neriiflora (2/18): *catacosmum, haematodes*
Taliensia (7/19): *alutaceum, bathyphyllum, clementinae, proteoides, roxieanum, rufum, taliense*

Corolla lobes more than 5 (7/35 groups, 28 species)
Auriculata (1/1): *auriculatum*
Falconera (6/6): *basilicum, coriaceum* (also corolla lobes 5), *falconeri, galactinum, hodgsonii, rex*
Fortunea (8/10): *calophytum* (also corolla lobes 5), *decorum, fortunei, hemsleyanum, orbiculare, oreodoxa, sutchuenense* (also corolla lobes 5), *vernicosum*
Grandia (9/9): *grande, macabeanum, magnificum, montroseanum, praestans, protistum, sinogrande, watsonii, wattii*
Irrorata (1/6): *anthosphaerum*
Pontica (1/12): *degronianum* subsp. *heptamerum*
Taliensia (2/19): *clementinae, wightii* (corolla lobes usually 5)

Stamens more than 10 (7/35 groups, 28 species)
Auriculata (1/1): *auriculatum*
Falconera (6/6): *basilicum, coriaceum* (stamens sometimes 10), *falconeri, galactinum, hodgsonii, rex*
Fortunea (9/10): *calophytum, decorum, fortunei, griffithianum, hemsleyanum, orbiculare, oreodoxa* (stamens sometimes 10), *sutchuenense, vernicosum*
Grandia (9/9): *grande, macabeanum, magnificum, montroseanum, praestans, protistum, sinogrande, watsonii, wattii*
Irrorata (1/6): *anthosphaerum*
Pontica (1/12): *degronianum* subsp. *heptamerum*
Taliensia (1/19): *clementinae*

At least some leaves more than 20 cm long (8/35 groups, 20 species)
Arborea (1/3): *lanigerum*
Auriculata (1/1): *auriculatum*
Falconera (5/6): *basilicum, falconeri, galactinum, hodgsonii, rex*

Fortunea (3/10): *calophytum, griffithianum, sutchuenense*
Fulva (2/2): *fulvum, uvarifolium*
Grandia (6/9): *grande, macabeanum, magnificum, praestans, protistum, sinogrande*
Parishia (1/3): *kyawi*
Pontica (1/12): *ungernii*

Corolla funnel-shaped (8/35 groups, 34 species)
Argyrophylla (1/6): *thayerianum*
Auriculata (1/1): *auriculatum*
Brachycalyx (1/5): *mariesii*
Choniastrum (1/3): *stamineum*
Pentanthera (14/14): *alabamense, arborescens, atlanticum, austrinum, calendulaceum, canescens, cumberlandense, japonicum, luteum, molle, occidentale, periclymenoides, prunifolium, viscosum*
Pontica (1/12): *degronianum*
Sciadorhodion (1/4): *schlippenbachii*
Tsutsusi (14/15): *indicum, kaempferi, kiusianum, mucronatum, ×obtusum, oldhamii, ×pulchrum, scabrum, serpyllifolium, simsii, stenopetalum, tosaense, tschonoskii, yedoense*

Leaves all or mostly deciduous (9/35 groups, 30 species)
Brachycalyx (5/5): *amagianum, mariesii, reticulatum, sanctum, weyrichii*
Candidastrum (1/1): *albiflorum*
Mumeazalea (1/1): *semibarbatum*
Pentanthera (14/14): *alabamense, arborescens, atlanticum, austrinum, calendulaceum, canescens, cumberlandense, japonicum, luteum, molle, occidentale, periclymenoides, prunifolium, viscosum*
Rhodora (2/2): *canadense, vaseyi*
Sciadorhodion (4/4): *albrechtii, pentaphyllum, quinquefolium, schlippenbachii*
Therorhodion (1/1): *camtschaticum*
Tsutsusi (1/15): *serpyllifolium*
Viscidula: (1/1): *nipponicum*

Corolla purple or pale purple (10/35 groups, 11 species)
Arborea (1/3): *niveum*
Argyrophylla (1/6): *rirei*
Azaleastrum (1/2): *ovatum*
Brachycalyx (1/5): *reticulatum*
Falconera (1/7): *hodgsonii*
Parishia (1/3): *elliottii*

Pentanthera (1/14): *austrinum*
Pontica (2/12): *catawbiense, ponticum*
Sciadorhodion (1/4): *albrechtii*
Tsutsusi (1/15): *tosaense*

Corolla scarlet (10/35 groups, 14 species)
Barbata (1/2): *smithii*
Brachycalyx (1/5): *amagianum*
Fulgensia (1/2): *fulgens*
Glischra (1/5): *glischrum*
Griersoniana (1/1): *griersonianum*
Neriiflora (2/18): *floccigerum, haematodes*
Parishia (2/3): *facetum, kyawi*
Pentanthera (1/14): *japonicum*
Thomsonia (1/7): *cerasinum*
Tsutsusi (3/15): *indicum, oldhamii, scabrum*

Style hairy with eglandular hairs; glands present or not (10/35 groups, 23 species)
Brachycalyx (4/5): *amagianum, reticulatum, sanctum, weyrichii*
Candidastrum (1/1): *albiflorum*
Glischra (1/5): *diphrocalyx*
Maculifera (1/6): *morii*
Parishia (3/3): *elliottii, facetum, kyawi*
Pentanthera (9/14): *alabamense, arborescens, atlanticum, austrinum, calendulaceum, canescens, luteum, occidentale, viscosum*
Rhodora (1/2): *canadense*
Taliensia (1/19): *wiltonii*
Therorhodion (1/1): *camtschaticum*
Tsutsusi (1/15): *oldhamii*

Corolla yellow (10/35 groups, 28 species)
Campylocarpa (2/4): *campylocarpum, wardii*
Falconera (2/7): *basilicum, rex*
Grandia (4/9): *grande, macabeanum, praestans, sinogrande*
Lanata (1/1): *lanatum*
Mumeazalea (1/1): *semibarbatum*
Neriiflora (5/18): *aperantum, citriniflorum, floccigerum, neriiflorum, sanguineum*
Pentanthera (4/14): *calendulaceum, cumberlandense, luteum, molle*

Pontica (2/12): *aureum, caucasicum*
Selensia (2/4): *bainbridgeanum, martinianum*
Taliensia (5/19): *lacteum, roxieanum, taliense, wasonii, wightii*

Corolla with distinct, dark nectar sacs at the base (11/35 groups, 45 species)
Arborea (3/3): *arboreum, lanigerum, niveum*
Argyrophylla (1/6): *rirei*
Barbata (2/2): *barbatum, smithii*
Fulgensia (2/2): *fulgens, sherriffii*
Grandia (4/9): *grande, magnificum, protistum, wattii* (perhaps doubtful×)
Irrorata (3/6): *anthosphaerum, irroratum, tanastylum*
Maculifera (1/6): *strigillosum*
Neriiflora (18/18): *aperantum, beanianum, catacosmum, chamaethomsonii, citriniflorum, coelicum, dichroanthum, eudoxum, floccigerum, forrestii, haematodes, mallotum, microgynum, neriiflorum, pocophorum, sanguineum, sperabile, sperabiloides*
Parishia (3/3): *elliottii, facetum, kyawi*
Thomsonia (7/7): *cerasinum, cyanocarpum, eclecteum, hookeri, meddianum, stewartianum, thomsonii*
Venatora (1/1): *venator*

Corolla deep red or crimson (13/35 groups, 40 species)
Arborea (1/3): *arboreum*
Barbata (2/2): *barbatum, smithii*
Brachycalyx (1/5): *amagianum*
Fulgensia (2/2): *fulgens, sherriffii*
Griersoniana (1/1): *griersonianum*
Irrorata (2/6): *anthosphaerum, tanastylum*
Maculifera (1/6): *strigillosum*
Neriiflora (16/18): *beanianum, catacosmum, chamaethomsonii, citriniflorum, coelicum, dichroanthum, floccigerum, forrestii, haematodes, mallotum, microgynum, neriiflorum, pocophorum, sanguineum, sperabile, sperabiloides*
Pentanthera (3/14): *calendulaceum, cumberlandense, prunifolium*
Selense (1/5): *diphrocalyx*
Thomsonia (5/7): *cerasinum, eclecteum, hookeri, meddianum, thomsonii*
Tsutsusi (4/15): *indicum, kaempferi, ×obtusum, simsii*
Venatora (1/1): *venator*

Corolla pinkish purple (14/35 groups, 23 species)
Arborea: (1/3): *lanigerum*

Argyrophylla (2/6): *floribundum, hunnewellianum*
Azaleastrum (1/2): *leptothrium*
Brachycalyx (2/5): *mariesii, reticulatum*
Campanulata (2/2): *campanulatum, wallichii*
Choniastrum: (1/3): *moulmainense*
Falconera (1/7): *hodgsonii*
Fortunea (1/10): *vernicosum*
Grandia (2/9): *magnificum, montroseanum*
Irrorata (1/6): *anthosphaerum*
Pontica (1/12): *maximum*
Rhodora (1/2): *canadense*
Therorhodion (1/1): *camtschaticum*
Tsutsusi (6/15): *kiusianum, mariae, ×obtusum, ×pulchrum, stenopetalum, yedoense*

Corolla funnel-campanulate (14/35 groups, 31 species)
Argyrophylla (1/6): *argyrophyllum*
Brachycalyx (3/5): *reticulatum, sanctum, weyrichii*
Campanulata (1/2): *wallichii*
Falconera (1/6): *coriaceum*
Fortunea (3/10): *decorum, fortunei, vernicosum*
Fulgensia (1/2): *sherriffii*
Glischra (1/5): *diphrocalyx*
Grandia (3/9): *macabeanum, magnificum, protistum*
Griersoniana (1/1): *griersonianum*
Parishia (1/3): *elliottii*
Pontica (7/12): *brachycarpum, catawbiense, degronianum, hyperythrum, smirnowii, ungernii, yakushimanum* subsp. *makinoi*
Selensia (2/4): *martinianum, selense*
Taliensia (4/19): *alutaceum, phaeochrysum, roxieanum, traillianum*
Thomsonia (2/7): *cyanocarpum, eclecteum*

Corolla tubular-campanulate (14/35 groups, 38 species)
Arborea (2/3): *arboreum, niveum*
Barbata (2/2): *barbatum, smithii*
Falconera (1/6): *hodgsonii*
Fulgensia (1/2): *fulgens*
Grandia (2/9): *macabeanum, wattii*
Griersoniana (1/1): *griersonianum*
Irrorata (3/6): *anthosphaerum, irroratum, tanastylum*

Maculifera (1/6): *strigillosum*

Neriiflora (17/18): *aperantum, beanianum, catacosmum, citriniflorum, coelicum, dichroanthum, eudoxum, floccigerum, forrestii, haematodes, mallotum, microgynum, neriiflorum, pocophorum, sanguineum, sperabile, sperabiloides*

Parishia (2/3): *facetum, kyawi*

Thomsonia (3/7): *hookeri, meddianum, stewartianum*

Tsutsusi (1/15): *mariae*

Venatora (1/1): *venator*

Viscidula (1/1): *nipponicum*

Calyx 6 mm or more (14/35 groups, 46 species)

Azaleastrum (2/2): *leptothrium, ovatum* (sometimes shorter)

Barbata (2/2): *barbatum, smithii* (rarely shorter)

Campylocarpa (2/4): *souliei* (sometimes shorter), *wardii* (rarely shorter)

Candidastrum (1/1): *albiflorum*

Fortunea (1/10): *griffithianum*

Glischra (4/5): *crinigerum, diphrocalyx, glischrum* (rarely shorter), *recurvoides*

Maculifera (1/6): *longesquamatum*

Neriiflora (12/18): *catacosmum, chamaethomsonii* (usually shorter), *citriniflorum* (sometimes shorter), *coelicum* (rarely shorter), *dichroanthum* (sometimes shorter), *eudoxum* (usually shorter), *haematodes* (sometimes shorter), *microgynum* (sometimes shorter), *neriiflorum* (sometimes shorter), *pocophorum* (rarely shorter), *sanguineum* (sometimes shorter), *sperabiloides* (sometimes shorter)

Pontica (2/12): *ungernii* (rarely shorter), *yakushimanum* subsp. *makinoi* (rarely shorter)

Selensia (2/4): *hirtipes* (rarely shorter), *selense* (rarely shorter)

Taliensia (3/19): *adenogynum* (rarely shorter), *balfourianum, bureavii* (rarely shorter)

Therorhodion (1/1): *camtschaticum*

Thomsonia (5/7): *cyanocarpum, eclecteum* (rarely shorter), *hookeri, meddianum* (rarely shorter), *thomsonii* (sometimes shorter)

Tsutsusi (8/15): *arborescens* (sometimes shorter), *indicum* (sometimes shorter), *mucronatum, ×pulchrum* (usually shorter), *scabrum* (usually shorter), *simsii* (sometimes shorter), *stenopetalum, yedoense*

Style glandular, at least towards the base (16/35 groups, 33 species)

Argyrophylla (1/6): *thayerianum*

Auriculata (1/1): *auriculatum*

Campylocarpa (4/4): *callimorphum, campylocarpum, souliei, wardii*

Fortunea (5/10): *decorum, fortunei, griffithianum, hemsleyanum, vernicosum*

Glischra (3/5): *crinigerum, diphrocalyx, glischrum*

Irrorata (3/6): *aberconwayi, annae, irroratum*
Maculifera (2/6): *longesquamatum, pachytrichum*
Parishia (2/3): *elliottii, facetum*
Pentanthera (1/14): *alabamense*
Pontica (1/12): *hyperythrum*
Rhodora (1/2): *vaseyi*
Sciadorhodion (1/4): *schlippenbachii*
Selensia (3/4): *bainbridgeanum, hirtipes, martinianum*
Taliensia (3/19): *adenogynum, balfourianum, bureavii*
Thomsonia (1/7): *cerasinum*
Williamsiana (1/1): *williamsianum*

Calyx absent or a mere rim, less than 1 mm long (17/35 groups, 48 species)
Argyrophylla (2/6): *floribundum* (also larger), *hunnewellianum* (also larger)
Auriculata (1/1): *auriculatum*
Campanulata (1/2): *campanulatum* (also larger)
Choniastrum (3/3): *latoucheae, moulmainense, stamineum*
Falconera (2/6): *coriaceum* (also larger), *galactinum* (also larger)
Fortunea (3/10): *hemsleyanum* (also larger), *orbiculare, oreodoxa*
Fulva (2/2): *fulvum, uvarifolium* (also larger)
Grandia (4/9): *grande* (also larger), *macabeanum* (also larger), *magnificum* (also larger), *montroseanum* (also larger)
Griersoniana (1/1): *griersonianum* (also larger)
Lanata (1/1): *lanatum*
Maculifera (2/6): *maculiferum* (also larger), *strigillosum* (also larger)
Neriiflora (1/18): *forrestii* (also larger)
Pentanthera (6/14): *alabamense* (also larger), *canescens* (also larger), *japonicum, molle, prunifolium* (also larger), *viscosum* (also larger)
Pontica (2/12): *catawbiense* (also larger), *macrophyllum* (also larger)
Taliensia (15/19): *aganniphum* (also larger), *alutaceum* (also larger), *bathyphyllum, beesianum, clementinae* (also larger), *lacteum* (also larger), *phaeochrysum* (also larger), *proteoides, przewalskii, roxieanum* (also larger), *rufum, traillianum* (also larger), *wasonii, wightii, wiltonii* (also larger)
Tsutsusi (1/15): *mariae*
Williamsiana (1/1): *williamsianum*

Leaves glandular (18/35 groups, 28 species). The glands are often stalked but may also be stalkless or almost so. They are mostly found on the lower surface of the leaves.

Argyrophylla (1/6): *hunnewellianum*
Auriculata (1/1): *auriculatum*
Barbata (1/2): *barbatum*
Campylocarpa (2/4): *callimorphum, campylocarpum*
Fortunea (1/10): *hemsleyanum*
Fulva (1/2): *uvarifolium*
Glischra (2/5): *crinigerum, recurvoides*
Maculifera (3/6): *longesquamatum, pseudochrysanthum, strigillosum*
Neriiflora (3/18): *chamaethomsonii, forrestii, sperabile*
Parishia (1/3): *kyawi*
Pentanthera (1/14): *luteum*
Rhodora (1/2): *canadense*
Selensia (2/4): *bainbridgeanum, hirtipes*
Taliensia (2/19): *adenogynum, wasonii*
Therorhodion (1/1): *camtschaticum*
Thomsonia (2/7): *stewartianum, thomsonii*
Tsutsusi (2/15): *mucronatum, stenopetalum*
Williamsiana (1/1): *williamsianum*

Young shoots glandular or glandular-bristly (18/35 groups, 41 species). The glands are usually stalked but may occasionally be almost stalkless; they are often deciduous as the shoot matures.
Auriculata (1/1): *auriculatum*
Azaleastrum (1/2): *ovatum*
Campylocarpa (4/4): *callimorphum, campylocarpum, souliei, wardii*
Candidastrum (1/1): *albiflorum*
Fulgensia (1/2): *sherriffii*
Glischra (3/5): *crinigerum, glischrum, recurvoides*
Maculifera (1/6): *strigillosum*
Mumeazalea (1/1): *semibarbatum*
Neriiflora (8/18): *beanianum, chamaethomsonii, coelicum, dichroanthum* subsp. *scyphocalyx, neriiflorum, pocophorum, sanguineum, sperabile*
Parishia (2/3): *elliottii, kyawi*
Pentanthera (3/14): *atlanticum, austrinum, luteum*
Pontica (2/12): *maximum, ungernii*
Sciadorhodion (1/4): *schlippenbachii*
Selensia (4/4): *bainbridgeanum, hirtipes, martinianum, selense*
Therorhodion (1/1): *camtschaticum*

Thomsonia (3/7): *eclecteum, stewartianum, thomsonii*
Tsutsusi (3/15): *mucronatum, oldhamii, stenopetalum*
Viscidula (1/1): *nipponicum*

Corolla more than 5 cm long (18/35 groups, 41 species)
Argyrophylla (1/6): *argyrophyllum* (also shorter)
Auriculata (1/1): *auriculatum*
Barbata (1/2): *smithii* (mostly shorter)
Campanulata (2/2): *campanulatum* (mostly shorter), *wallichii* (mostly shorter)
Choniastrum (1/3): *moulmainense*
Fortunea (8/10): *calophytum* (also shorter), *decorum, fortunei, griffithianum, hemsleyanum, praevernum, sutchuenense, vernicosum* (also shorter)
Grandia (7/9): *grande, magnificum, montroseanum* (mostly shorter), *praestans* (mostly shorter), *protistum, sinogrande* (also shorter), *wattii* (mostly shorter)
Griersoniana (1/1): *griersonianum*
Irrorata (1/6): *tanastylum* (also shorter)
Lanata (1/1): *lanatum* (mostly shorter)
Maculifera (1/6): *strigillosum* (also shorter)
Neriiflora (1/18): *dichroanthum* (mostly shorter)
Parishia (3/3): *elliottii, facetum, kyawi*
Pentanthera (2/14): *japonicum, molle*
Sciadorhodion (2/4): *albrechtii, pentaphyllum* (also shorter)
Taliensia (2/19): *beesianum* (also shorter), *lacteum* (mostly shorter)
Thomsonia (4/7): *cyanocarpum* (also shorter), *eclecteum* (also shorter), *meddianum, stewartianum* (also shorter)
Tsutsusi (2/15): *×pulchrum, scabrum*

Seeds broadly winged and finned (24/35 groups). Because complete information on all species is not available, only the major groups are listed. Groups for which information on the seeds in uncertain are listed in square brackets in the category which seems most likely.
Arborea (most, a few unwinged), Argyrophylla, Auriculata, Barbata, Campanulata, Campylocarpa, Falconera, Fortunea, [Fulgensia], Glischra, Grandia, Griersoniana, Irrorata, Maculifera, Neriiflora (most, a few unwinged), Parishia, Pentanthera, Pontica, Rhodora, Selensia, Taliensia (most, a few unwinged), Thomsonia (most, a few unwinged), Venatora, Williamsiana

Corolla campanulate (25/35 groups, 80 species)
Arborea (1/3): *lanigerum*

Argyrophylla (4/6): *floribundum, hunnewellianum, insigne, rirei*
Azaleastrum (2/2): *leptothrium, ovatum*
Brachycalyx (1/5): *amagianum*
Campanulata (1/2): *campanulatum*
Campylocarpa (2/4): *callimorphum, campylocarpum*
Candidastrum (1/1): *albiflorum*
Falconera (4/6): *basilicum, falconeri, galactinum, rex*
Fortunea (7/10): *calophytum, griffithianum, hemsleyanum, orbiculare, oreodoxa, praevernum, sutchuenense*
Fulva (2/2): *fulvum, uvarifolium*
Glischra (4/5): *crinigerum, glischrum, habrotrichum, recurvoides*
Grandia (2/9): *praestans, watsonii*
Irrorata (3/6): *annae, araiophyllum, irroratum*
Lanata (1/1): *lanatum*
Maculifera (5/6): *longesquamatum, maculiferum, morii, pachytrichum, pseudochrysanthum*
Mumeazalea (1/1): *semibarbatum*
Neriiflora (2/18): *chamaethomsonii, eudoxum*
Pontica (6/12): *aureum, caucasicum, macrophyllum, maximum, ponticum, yakushimanum*
Rhodora (2/2): *canadense, vaseyi*
Sciadorhodion (3/4): *albrechtii, pentaphyllum, quinquefolium*
Selensia (3/4): *bainbridgeanum, hirtipes, martinianum*
Taliensia (16/19): *adenogynum, aganniphum, alutaceum, balfourianum, bathyphyllum, beesianum, bureavii, clementinae, lacteum, proteoides, przewalskii, rufum, taliense, wasonii, wightii, wiltonii*
Therorhodion (1/1): *camtschaticum*
Thomsonia (5/7): *cerasinum, cyanocarpum, eclecteum, stewartianum, thomsonii*
Williamsiana (1/1): *williamsianum*

Calyx glandular (26/35 groups, 50 species)
Arborea (1/3): *arboreum*
Argyrophylla (1/6): *thayerianum*
Auriculata (1/1): *auriculatum*
Azaleastrum (2/2): *leptothrium, ovatum*
Campylocarpa (2/4): *callimorphum, campylocarpum*
Candidastrum (1/1): *albiflorum*
Fortunea (3/10): *decorum, fortunei, hemsleyanum*
Glischra (3/5): *crinigerum, habrotrichum, recurvoides*
Grandia (2/9): *grande, wattii*

Irrorata (3/6): *anthosphaerum, irroratum, tanastylum*
Maculifera (1/6): *longesquamatum*
Mumeazalea (1/1): *semibarbatum*
Neriiflora (4/18): *dichroanthum, eudoxum, microgynum, neriiflorum*
Parishia (2/3): *elliottii, kyawi*
Pentanthera (2/14): *canescens, luteum*
Pontica (3/12): *maximum, smirnowii, ungernii*
Rhodora (1/2): *vaseyi*
Sciadorhodion (1/4): *schlippenbachii*
Selensia (4/4): *bainbridgeanum, hirtipes, martinianum, selense*
Taliensia (4/19): *adenogynum, balfourianum, bureavii, roxieanum*
Therorhodion (1/1): *camtschaticum*
Thomsonia (2/7): *cerasinum, thomsonii*
Tsutsusi (2/15): *oldhamii, scabrum*
Venatora (1/1): *venator*
Viscidula (1/1): *nipponicum*
Williamsiana (1/1): *williamsianum*

Ovary glandular (28/35 groups, 83 species)
Arborea (1/3): *arboreum*
Argyrophylla (1/6): *thayerianum*
Auriculata (1/1): *auriculatum*
Azaleastrum (2/2): *leptothrium, ovatum*
Barbata (2/2): *barbatum, smithii*
Brachycalyx (1/5): *reticulatum*
Campylocarpa (4/4): *callimorphum, campylocarpum, souliei, wardii*
Candidastrum (1/1): *albiflorum*
Fortunea (7/10): *decorum, fortunei, hemsleyanum, griffithianum, orbiculare, oreodoxa, vernicosum*
Glischra (4/5): *crinigerum, diphrocalyx, glischrum, recurvoides*
Grandia (1/9): *grande*
Griersoniana (1/1): *griersonianum*
Irrorata (4/6): *aberconwayi, annae, irroratum, tanastylum*
Maculifera (4/6): *longesquamatum, morii, pseudochrysanthum, strigillosum*
Mumeazalea (1/1): *semibarbatum*
Neriiflora (11/18): *chamaethomsonii, citriniflorum, coelicum, dichroanthum, eudoxum, forrestii, microgynum, neriiflorum, pocophorum, sanguineum, sperabile*
Parishia (2/3):): *elliottii, kyawi*

Pentanthera (7/14): *alabamense, arborescens, atlanticum, austrinum, luteum, occidentale, viscosum*
Pontica (3/12): *hyperythrum, maximum, ungernii*
Rhodora (2/2): *canadense, vaseyi*
Sciadorhodion (2/4): *albrechtii, schlippenbachii*
Selensia (4/4): *bainbridgeanum, hirtipes, martinianum, selense*
Taliensia (5/19): *adenogynum, balfourianum, bureavii, roxieanum, rufum*
Thomsonia (6/7): *cerasinum, cyanocarpum, eclecteum, meddianum, stewartianum, thomsonii*
Tsutsusi (3/15): *oldhamii, scabrum, stenopetalum*
Venatora (1/1): *venator*
Viscidula (1/10): *nipponicum*
Williamsiana (1/1): *williamsianum*

Corolla white, white flushed with pink, or pink (28/35 groups, 121 species)
Arborea (2/3): *arboreum, lanigerum*
Argyrophylla (4/6): *argyrophyllum, hunnewellianum, insigne, thayerianum*
Auriculata (1/1): *auriculatum*
Azaleastrum (2/2): *leptothrium, ovatum*
Barbata (1/2): *barbatum*
Brachycalyx (2/5): *sanctum, weyrichii*
Campanulata (2/2): *campanulatum, wallichii*
Campylocarpa (3/4): *callimorphum, souliei, wardii* (uncommon)
Candidastrum (1/1): *albiflorum*
Choniastrum (3/3): *latoucheae, moulmainense, stamineum*
Falconera (5/7): *coriaceum, falconeri, galactinum, hodgsonii, rex*
Fortunea (10/10): *calophytum, decorum, fortunei, griffithianum, hemsleyanum, orbiculare, oreodoxa, praevernum, sutchuenense, vernicosum*
Fulva (2/2): *fulvum, uvarifolium*
Glischra (5/5): *crinigerum, diphrocalyx, glischrum, habrotrichum, recurvoides*
Grandia (5/9): *montroseanum, praestans, protistum, watsonii, wattii*
Irrorata (6/6): *aberconwayi, annae, anthosphaerum, araiophyllum, irroratum, tanastylum*
Maculifera (5/6): *longesquamatum, maculiferum, morii, pachytrichum, pseudochrysanthum*
Mumeazalea (1/1): *semibarbatum*
Neriiflora (6/18): *aperantum, chamaethomsonii, eudoxum, floccigerum, microgynum, sanguineum*
Pentanthera (7/14): *alabamense, arborescens, calendulaceum, canescens, occidentale, periclymenoides, viscosum*
Pontica (10/12): *brachycarpum, caucasicum, degronianum, hyperythrum, macrophyllum, maximum, ponticum, smirnowii, ungernii, yakushimanum* subsp. *makinoi*

Rhodora (2/2): *canadense, vaseyi*
Sciadorhodion (3/4): *pentaphyllum, quinquefolium, schlippenbachii*
Selensia (4/4): *bainbridgeanum, martinianum, hirtipes, selense*
Taliensia (17/19): *adenogynum, aganniphum, alutaceum, balfourianum, bathyphyllum, beesianum, bureavii, clementinae, phaeochrysum, proteoides, przewalskii, roxieanum, rufum, taliense, traillianum, wasonii, wiltonii*
Thomsonia (3/7): *cyanocarpum, eclecteum, stewartianum*
Tsutsusi (8/15): *kaempferi, kiusianum, mucronatum, ×obtusum, oldhamii, scabrum, serpyllifolium, tschonoskii*
Viscidula (1/1): *nipponicum*

Scaly Species

At least some leaves more than 20 cm long (1/27 groups, 1 species)
Maddenia (1/18): *nuttallii*

Corolla orange (1/27 groups, 1 species)
Cinnabarina (1/2): *cinnabarinum*

Seeds with a narrow tail at each end (1/27 groups, 1 species)
Virgata (1/1): *virgatum*

Scales on the lower leaf surface completely obscured by hairs (1/27 groups, 2 species)
Edgeworthia (2/2): *edgeworthii, pendulum*

Leaves with the midrib raised on the upper surface towards the base (1/27 groups, 4 species)
Maddenia (4/18): *dalhousiae, lindleyi, nuttallii, taggianum*

Scales of 2 different shapes and colours, distant, borne on a white-papillose lower leaf surface (1/27 groups, 5 species). Scales should be examined on the lower leaf surface.
Glauca (5/5): *brachyanthum, charitopes, glaucophyllum, luteiflorum, pruniflorum*

Inflorescence bud scales with branched marginal hairs (1/27 groups, 8 species)
Pogonanthum (8/8): *anthopogon, cephalanthum, collettianum, kongboense, laudandum, primuliflorum, sargentianum, trichostomum*

Whole plant with a characteristic pineapple-like smell (1/27 groups, 8 species)
Pogonanthum (8/8): *anthopogon, cephalanthum, collettianum, kongboense, laudandum, primuliflorum, sargentianum, trichostomum*

Flower stalk, ovary, and style forming a continuous, more or less straight line (1/27 groups, 19 species)

Lapponica (19/20): *capitatum, complexum, dasypetalum, fastigiatum, flavidum, hippophaeoides, impeditum, intricatum, lapponicum, nivale, orthocladum, polycladum, rupicola, russatum, setosum, tapetiforme, telmateium, thymifolium, yungningense*

Corolla lobes more than 5 (2/27 groups, 2 species)

Camelliiflora (1/1): *camelliiflorum*

Maddenia (1/18): *maddenii*

Stamens more than 10 (2/27 groups, 2 species)

Camelliiflora (1/1): *camelliiflorum*

Maddenia (1/18): *maddenii*

Scales with minutely scolloped (crenulate) margins (2/27 groups, 3 species). Scales should be examined on the lower leaf surface; a magnification of at least 10× is needed.

Baileya (1/1): *baileyi*

Saluenensia (2/2): *calostrotum, saluenense*

Nectar watery, either filling the base of the corolla tube or as 5 distinct large drops there (2/27 groups, 3 species)

Cinnabarina (2/2): *cinnabarinum, keysii*

Scabrifolia (1/6): *spinuliferum*

Scales on the lower leaf surface arranged in overlapping tiers (2/27 groups, 10 species)

Saluenensia (2/2): *calostrotum, saluenense*

Pogonanthum (8/8): *anthopogon, cephalanthum, collettianum, kongboense, laudandum, primuliflorum, sargentianum, trichostomum*

Corolla almost blue (2/27 groups, 10 species)

Lapponica (9/20): *capitatum, fastigiatum, impeditum, intricatum, orthocladum, polycladum, tapetiforme, thymifolium, yungningense*

Triflora (1/18): *augustinii*

Corolla more than 5 cm long (2/27 groups, 15 species)

Edgeworthia (1/2): *edgeworthii* (also shorter)

Maddenia (14/18): *carneum, ciliicalyx, dalhousiae, dendricola, formosum* (also shorter), *johnstoneanum* (also shorter), *lindleyi, maddenii, megacalyx, nuttallii, pachypodum, roseatum, taggianum, veitchianum*

Corolla tubular (3/27 groups, 4 species)
Cinnabarina (2/2): *cinnabarinum, keysii*
Glauca (1/5): *glaucophyllum* var. *tubiforme*
Scabrifolia (1/6): *spinuliferum*

Ovary tapering into the style (3/27 groups, 9 species)
Maddenia (6/18): *carneum, ciliicalyx, megacalyx, pachypodum, roseatum, veitchianum*
Moupinensia (1/1): *moupinense*
Tephropepla (2/5): *auritum, xanthostephanum*

Corolla tube parallel-sided or almost so, with lobes spreading widely (3/27 groups, 10 species)
Afghanica (1/1): *afghanicum*
Lapponica (1/20): *intricatum*
Pogonanthum (8/8): *anthopogon, cephalanthum, collettianum, kongboense, laudandum, primuliflorum, sargentianum, trichostomum*

Stamens fewer than 10 (3/27 groups, 18 species)
Lapponica (9/20, most with stamens sometimes 10): *complexum, fastigiatum, flavidum, impeditum, lapponicum, orthocladum, rupicola, tapetiforme, yungningense*
Pogonanthum (8/8): *anthopogon* (stamens sometimes 10), *cephalanthum, collettianum* (stamens sometimes 10), *kongboense, laudandum, primuliflorum, sargentianum, trichostomum*
Scabrifolia (1/6): *pubescens* (stamens rarely 10)

Some or all scales opaque or milky (4/27 groups, 4 species). Scales should be examined on the lower leaf surface. The scales referred to are pinkish, greyish, or dark red to almost black and opaque, or golden and milky, and may be mixed with normal scales.
Glauca (1/5): *pruniflorum*
Lapponica (1/20): *fastigiatum*
Trichoclada (1/3): *mekongense*
Triflora (1/18): *searsiae* (many scales not milky)

Corolla tubular-campanulate (4/27 groups, 5 species)
Cinnabarina (1/2): *cinnabarinum*
Glauca (1/5): *glaucophyllum* var. *tubiforme*
Monantha (1/1): *flavantherum*
Rhododendron (2/2): *ferrugineum, hirsutum*

Corolla deep red or crimson (5/27 groups, 6 species)
Campylogyna (1/1): *campylogynum*
Cinnabarina (2/2): *cinnabarinum, keysii*
Glauca (1/5): *prunifolium*
Pogonanthum (1/8): *kongboense*
Scabrifolia (1/6): *spinuliferum*

Leaves all or mostly deciduous (5/27 groups, 8 species)
Cinnabarina (1/2): *cinnabarinum* subsp. *tamaense*
Lepidota (1/2): *lowndesii*
Rhodorastra (2/2): *dauricum* (some leaves persistent), *mucronulatum*
Trichoclada (2/3): *mekongense, trichocladum*
Triflora (2/18): *augustinii* subsp. *hardyi, yunnanense* (also sometimes evergreen)

At least some racemes lateral (5/27 groups, 28 species)
Cinnabarina (1/2): *keysii*
Rhodorastra (2/2): *dauricum, mucronulatum*
Scabrifolia (6/6): *hemitrichotum, mollicomum, pubescens, racemosum, scabrifolium, spinuliferum*
Triflora (18/18, all also often with terminal racemes): *ambiguum, amesiae, augustinii, concinnum, davidsonianum, keiskei, lutescens, oreotrephes, pleistanthum, polylepis, rigidum, searsiae, siderophyllum, tatsienense, trichanthum, triflorum, yunnanense, zaleucum*
Virgata (1/1): *virgatum*

Scales vesicular (6/27 groups, 13 species). Scales should be examined on the lower leaf surface.
Boothia (2/3): *leucaspis, megeratum*
Cinnabarina (1/2): *cinnabarinum* (usually not vesicular)
Glauca (5/5, some species with nonvesicular scales as well): *brachyanthum, charitopes, glaucophyllum, luteiflorum, pruniflorum*
Lapponica (1/20): *setosum*
Trichoclada (3/3): *lepidostylum, mekongense, trichocladum*
Triflora (1/18): *oreotrephes* (often not vesicular)

Corolla funnel-campanulate (6/27 groups, 22 species)
Maddenia (15/18): *burmanicum, ciliatum, ciliicalyx, dendricola, fletcherianum, formosum, johnstoneanum, lindleyi, megacalyx, nuttallii, pachypodum, roseatum, taggianum, valentinianum, veitchianum*
Micrantha (1/1): *micranthum*
Moupinensia (1/1): *moupinense*
Tephropepla (1/5): *hanceanum*

Trichoclada (3/3): *lepidostylum, mekongense, trichocladum*
Uniflora (1/4): *ludlowii*

Leaf stalks bristly with glandular bristles, at least when young (7/27 groups, 16 species)
Boothia (3/3): *leucaspis, megeratum, sulfureum*
Lapponica (1/20): *setosum*
Maddenia (5/18): *ciliatum, fletcherianum, formosum, johnstoneanum, valentinianum*
Moupinensia (1/1): *moupinense*
Saluenensia (1/2): *saluenense*
Trichoclada (3/3): *lepidostylum, mekongense, trichocladum*
Triflora (2/18): *amesiae, augustinii* subsp. *rubrum*

Style scaly, at least at the base (7/27 groups, 24 species)
Cinnabarina (1/2): *cinnabarinum*
Edgeworthia (2/2): *edgeworthii, pendulum*
Maddenia (14/18): *burmanicum, carneum, ciliicalyx, dalhousiae, dendricola, formosum, johnstoneanum, lindleyi, megacalyx, nuttallii, pachypodum, roseatum, valentinianum, veitchianum*
Lapponica (3/20): *orthocladum, telmateium, thymifolium*
Tephropepla (2/5): *tephropeplum, xanthostephanum*
Trichoclada (1/3): *lepidostylum* (sometimes not scaly)
Virgata (1/1): *virgatum*

Seeds broadly winged and finned (7/27 groups). Because complete information on all species is not available, only the major groups are listed. Groups for which information on the seeds in uncertain are listed in square brackets in the category which seems most likely.
Boothii, Camelliiflora, Edgeworthia, Maddenia, Micrantha, Monantha, Moupinensia

Corolla purple or pale purple (7/27 groups, 31 species)
Baileya (1/1): *baileyi*
Cinnabarina (1/2): *cinnabarinum*
Glauca (2/5): *charitopes, pruniflorum*
Lapponica (17/20): *capitatum, complexum, cuneatum, fastigiatum, hippophaeoides, impeditum, intricatum, lapponicum, nivale, orthocladum, polycladum, rupicola, russatum, setosum, tapetiforme, telmateium, thymifolium*
Saluenensia (2/2): *calostrotum, saluenense*
Triflora (6/18): *amesiae, augustinii, concinnum, polylepis, searsiae, trichanthum*
Uniflora (2/4): *pumilum, uniflorum*

Leaves margined with bristles, at least when young (9/27 groups, 23 species)
Boothia (3/3): *leucaspis, megeratum, sulfureum*
Lapponica (1/20): *setosum*
Lepidota: (1/2): *lowndesii*
Maddenia (8/18): *burmanicum, ciliatum, dalhousiae, fletcherianum, formosum, johnstoneanum, megacalyx, valentinianum*
Moupinensia (1/1): *moupinense*
Rhododendron (1/2): *hirsutum*
Saluenensia (2/2): *calostrotum, saluenense*
Trichoclada (3/3): *lepidostylum, mekongense, trichocladum*
Triflorum (3/18): *keiskei* (usually not bristly), *yunnanense, zaleucum*

Calyx absent or a mere rim, less than 1 mm long (9/27 groups, 46 species)
Cinnabarina (2/2): *cinnabarinum, keysii*
Genestieriana (1/1): *genestierianum* (also larger)
Heliolepida (1/3): *heliolepis* (mostly larger)
Lapponica (9/20, mostly also larger): *complexum, hippophaeoides, intricatum, nivale, orthocladum, polycladum, tapetiforme, telmateium, thymifolium*
Maddenia (7/18): *burmanicum, ciliicalyx, formosum, dendricola, johnstoneanum, pachypodum, veitchianum*
Rhodorastra (2/2): *dauricum, mucronulatum*
Scabrifolia (6/6): *hemitrichotum, mollicomum, pubescens, racemosum, scabrifolium* (mostly larger), *spinuliferum*
Trichoclada (1/3): *mekongense* (also larger)
Triflora (17/18): *ambiguum, amesiae, augustinii, concinnum, davidsonianum, keiskei, lutescens, oreotrephes, pleistanthum, polylepis, rigidum, searsiae, siderophyllum, tatsienense, triflorum, yunnanense, zaleucum*

Style sharply deflexed from the apex of the ovary (10/27 groups, 19 species)
Afghanica (1/1): *afghanicum*
Baileya (1/1): *baileyi*
Boothia (3/3): *leucaspis, megeratum, sulfureum*
Camelliiflora (1/1): *camelliiflorum*
Campylogyna (1/1): *campylogynum*
Edgeworthia (1/2): *pendulum*
Genestieriana (1/1): *genestierianum*
Glauca (5/5): *brachyanthum, charitopes, glaucophyllum* (not var. *tubiforme*), *luteiflorum, pruniflorum*
Lepidota (2/2): *lepidotum, lowndesii*
Trichoclada (3/3): *lepidostylum, mekongense, trichocladum*

Style hairy with eglandular hairs, at least towards the base; scales present or not (10/27 groups, 26 species)

Caroliniana (1/1): *minus*

Cinnabarina (2/2): *cinnabarinum, keysii*

Edgeworthia (1/2): *pendulum*

Heliolepida (2/3): *bracteatum, heliolepis*

Lapponica (14/20): *capitatum, complexum, cuneatum, dasypetalum, flavidum, hippophaeoides, impeditum, nivale, polycladum, rupicola, russatum, tapetiforme, telmateium, thymifolium*

Rhododendron (1/2): *hirsutum*

Scabrifolia (1/6): *hemitrichotum*

Triflora (2/18): *lutescens, triflorum*

Uniflora (1/4): *pemakoense*

Virgata (1/1): *virgatum*

Corolla campanulate (11/27 groups, 22 species)

Baileya (1/1): *baileyi*

Boothia (3/3): *leucaspis, megeratum, sulfureum*

Camelliiflora (1/1): *camelliiflorum*

Campylogyna (1/1): *campylogynum*

Cinnabarina (1/2): *cinnabarinum*

Genestieriana (1/1): *genestierianum*

Glauca (5/5): *brachyanthum, charitopes, glaucophyllum, luteiflorum, pruniflorum*

Lepidota (2/2): *lepidotum, lowndesii*

Maddenia (1/18): *ciliatum*

Tephropepla (3/5): *auritum, tephropeplum, xanthostephanum*

Uniflora (3/4): *pemakoense, pumilum, uniflorum*

Corolla funnel-shaped (11/27 groups, 59 species)

Caroliniana (1/1): *minus*

Edgeworthia (2/2): *edgeworthii, pendulum*

Heliolepida (3/3): *bracteatum, heliolepis, rubiginosum*

Lapponica (19/20): *capitatum, complexum, cuneatum, dasypetalum, fastigiatum, flavidum, hippophaeoides, impeditum, lapponicum, nivale, orthocladum, polycladum, rupicola, russatum, setosum, tapetiforme, telmateium, thymifolium, yungningense*

Maddenia (4/18): *carneum, dalhousiae, dendricola, maddenii*

Rhodorastra (2/2): *dauricum, mucronulatum*

Saluenensia (2/2): *calostrotum, saluenense*

Scabrifolia (6/6): *hemitrichotum, mollicomum, pubescens, racemosum, scabrifolium, spinuliferum*

Tephropepla (1/5): *longistylum*

Triflora (18/18): *ambiguum, amesiae, augustinii, concinnum, davidsonianum, keiskei, lutescens, oreotrephes, pleistanthum, polylepis, rigidum, searsiae, siderophyllum, tatsienense, trichanthum, triflorum, yunnanense, zaleucum*
Virgata (1/1): *virgatum*

Corolla yellow (12/27 groups, 26 species)
Boothia (2/3): *megeratum, sulfureum*
Cinnabarina (1/2): *cinnabarinum*
Glauca (2/5): *brachyanthum, luteiflorum*
Lapponica (3/20): *flavidum, rupicola, tapetiforme*
Lepidota (2/2): *lepidotum, lowndesii*
Maddenia (3/18): *burmanicum, fletcherianum, valentinianum*
Monantha (1/1): *flavantherum*
Pogonanthum (2/8): *anthopogon, sargentianum*
Tephropepla (2/3): *auritum, xanthostephanum*
Trichoclada (3/3): *lepidostylum, mekongense, trichocladum*
Triflora (4/18): *ambiguum, keiskei, lutescens, triflorum*
Uniflora (1/4): *ludlowii*

Calyx 6 mm or more (12/27 groups, 32 species)
Afghanica (1/1): *afghanicum* (usually shorter)
Boothia (3/3): *leucaspis, megeratum, sulfureum* (also shorter)
Camelliiflora (1/1): *camelliiflorum* (rarely shorter)
Campylogyna (1/1): *campylogynum* (also shorter)
Edgeworthia (2/2): *edgeworthii, pendulum* (rarely shorter)
Glauca (3/5): *charitopes* (also shorter), *glaucophyllum, luteiflorum*
Lapponica (2/20): *cuneatum* (rarely shorter), *setosum* (rarely shorter)
Maddenia (9/18): *ciliatum, dalhousiae, fletcherianum* (rarely shorter), *lindleyi, maddenii, megacalyx, nuttallii, taggianum, valentinianum* (rarely shorter)
Pogonanthum (4/8, all also shorter): *cephalanthum, collettianum, laudandum, primuliflorum*
Saluenensia (2/2, both sometimes shorter): *calostrotum, saluenense*
Tephropepla (3/5, all rarely shorter): *auritum, tephropeplum, xanthostephanum*
Uniflora (1/4): *ludlowii* (sometimes shorter)

Corolla pinkish purple (12/27 groups, 32 species)
Baileya (1/1): *baileyi*
Campylogyna (1/1): *campylogynum*
Genestieriana (1/1): *genestierianum*
Glauca (1/5): *charitopes*
Heliolepida (1/3): *rubiginosum*

Lapponica (11/20): *capitatum, complexum, cuneatum, dasypetalum, fastigiatum, lapponicum, nivale, russatum, setosum, telmateium, yungningense*

Lepidota (1/1): *lepidotum*

Rhodorastra (2/2): *dauricum, mucronulatum*

Saluenensia (2/2): *calostrotum, saluenense*

Triflora (8/18): *augustinii, davidsonianum, oreotrephes, pleistanthum, rigidum, siderophyllum, tatsienense, yunnanense*

Uniflora (2/4): *pemakoense, pumilum*

Virgata (1/1): *virgatum*

Most mature leaves less than 2.5 cm long (13/27 groups, 46 species)

Baileya (1/1): *baileyi* (usually longer)

Campylogyna (1/1): *campylogynum* (occasionally longer)

Lapponica (20/20): *capitatum, complexum, cuneatum* (usually longer), *dasypetalum, fastigiatum, flavidum, hippophaeoides, impeditum, intricatum, lapponicum, nivale, orthocladum, polycladum, rupicola, russatum* (sometimes longer), *setosum, tapetiforme, telmateium, thymifolium, yungningense*

Lepidota (2/2): *lepidotum* (rarely longer), *lowndesii*

Micrantha (1/1): *micranthum* (usually longer)

Pogonanthum (7/8): *anthopogon* (sometimes longer), *cephalanthum* (often longer), *kongboense* (rarely longer), *laudandum, primuliflorum* (sometimes longer), *sargentianum, trichostomum*

Rhododendron (1/2): *hirsutum* (also longer)

Rhodorastra (1/2): *dauricum* (also longer)

Saluenensia (2/2): *calostrotum* (sometimes longer), *saluenense* (sometimes longer)

Scabrifolia (4/6): *pubescens* (sometimes longer), *racemosum* (usually longer), *scabrifolium* (usually longer), *spinuliferum* (usually longer)

Triflora (1/18): *oreotrephes* (usually longer)

Uniflora (4/4): *ludlowii, pemakoense, pumilum, uniflorum*

Virgata (1/1): *virgatum* (usually longer)

Corolla up to 2 cm long (14/27 groups, 44 species)

Afghanica (1/1): *afghanicum*

Baileya (1/1): *baileyi*

Campylogyna (1/1): *campylogynum*

Genestieriana (1/1): *genestierianum*

Glauca (2/5): *brachyanthum* (also longer), *pruniflorum*

Lapponica (19/20): *capitatum, complexum, dasypetalum, fastigiatum* (sometimes longer), *flavidum* (sometimes longer), *hippophaeoides, impeditum, intricatum, lapponicum, nivale,*

orthocladum, polycladum, rupicola (occasionally longer), *russatum* (also longer), *setosum* (mostly longer), *tapetiforme, telmateium, thymifolium, yungningense*
Lepidota (2/2): *lepidotum* (occasionally longer), *lowndesii*
Micrantha (1/1): *micranthum*
Monantha (1/1): *flavantherum* (sometimes longer)
Pogonanthum (7/8): *anthopogon* (also longer), *cephalanthum* (also longer), *kongboense, laudandum, primuliflorum, sargentianum, trichostomum*
Rhododendron (2/2, both also longer): *ferrugineum, hirsutum*
Rhodorastra (1/2): *dauricum* (also longer)
Scabrifolia (4/6): *hemitrichotum, pubescens, racemosum, scabrifolium* (also longer)
Uniflora (1/4): *pumilum* (also longer)

Corolla white, white flushed with pink, or pink (22/27 groups, 65 species)
Afghanica (1/1): *afghanicum*
Boothia (1/3): *leucaspis*
Camelliiflora (1/1): *camelliiflorum*
Campylogyna (1/1): *campylogynum*
Caroliniana (1/1): *minus*
Cinnabarina (1/2): *keysii*
Edgeworthia (2/2): *edgeworthii, pendulum*
Glauca (1/5): *glaucophyllum*
Heliolepida (3/3): *bracteatum, heliolepis, rubiginosum*
Lapponica (4/20): *cuneatum, orthocladum, russatum, yungningense*
Lepidota (1/2): *lepidotum*
Maddenia (15/18): *carneum, ciliatum, ciliicalyx, dalhousiae, dendricola, formosum, johnstoneanum, lindleyi, maddenii, megacalyx, nuttallii, pachypodum, roseatum, taggianum, veitchianum*
Micrantha (1/1): *micranthum*
Moupinensia (1/1): *moupinense*
Pogonanthum (8/8): *anthopogon, cephalanthum, collettianum, kongboense, laudandum, primuliflorum, sargentianum, trichostomum*
Rhododendron (2/2): *ferrugineum, hirsutum*
Rhodorastra (2/2): *dauricum, mucronulatum*
Scabrifolia (5/6): *hemitrichotum, mollicomum, pubescens, racemosum, scabrifolium*
Tephropepla (3/5): *hanceanum, longistylum, tephropeplum*
Triflora (9/18): *davidsonianum, oreotrephes, pleistanthum, rigidum, searsiae, siderophyllum, tatsienense, yunnanense, zaleucum*
Uniflora (1/4): *pemakoense*
Virgata (1/1): *virgatum*

Bibliography

This list includes the most important taxonomic works on the genus.

Additions to the International Rhododendron Register. 1971. Wageningen, Holland.

Argent, G. C., J. Bond, D. F. Chamberlain, P. Cox, and A. Hardy. 1997. *The Rhododendron Handbook 1998: Rhododendron Species in Cultivation.* London: Royal Horticultural Society.

Argent, G. C., and M. McFarlane, eds. 2003. *Rhododendrons in Horticulture and Science.* Royal Botanic Garden Edinburgh.

Balfour, I. B. 1916. New species of *Rhododendron. Notes from the Royal Botanic Garden Edinburgh* 9: 207–320.

Balfour, I. B. 1917a. New species of *Rhododendron* II. *Notes from the Royal Botanic Garden Edinburgh* 10: 79–166.

Balfour, I. B. 1917b. A review of the species in the "Irroratum" series. *Transactions of the Botanical Society of Edinburgh* 2: 157–220.

Balfour, I. B. 1919. New species of *Rhododendron* III. *Notes from the Royal Botanic Garden Edinburgh* 11: 19–154.

Balfour, I. B. 1920a. New species of *Rhododendron* IV. *Notes from the Royal Botanic Garden Edinburgh* 12: 85–186.

Balfour, I. B. 1920b. *Rhododendron:* Diagnoses Specierum Novarum. *Notes from the Royal Botanic Garden Edinburgh* 13: 25–65.

Balfour, I. B. 1922. *Rhododendron:* Diagnoses Specierum Novarum II. *Notes from the Royal Botanic Garden Edinburgh* 13: 223–306.

Bean, W. J. 1919. The Fortunea Group of rhododendrons. *Rhododendron Society Notes* 1: 187–194.

Chamberlain, D. F. 1980. The taxonomy of elepidote rhododendrons excluding *Azalea* (subgenus *Hymenanthes*). In *Contributions Towards a Classification of Rhododendron.* Ed. J. Luteyn. Proceedings of the International Rhododendron Conference, New York. 39–52.

Chamberlain, D. F. 1982. A revision of *Rhododendron,* I: subgenus *Hymenanthes. Notes from the Royal Botanic Garden Edinburgh* 39: 209–486.

Chamberlain, D. F., B. J. Coppins, and N. M. Gregory, eds. 1985. Proceedings of the 2nd International Rhododendron Conference. *Notes from the Royal Botanic Garden Edinburgh* 43: 3–182.

Chamberlain, D. F., and F. Doleshy. 1987. Japanese members of *Rhododendron* subsection *Pontica:* distribution and classification. *Journal of Japanese Botany* 62: 225–243.

Chamberlain, D. F., R. Hyam, G. Argent, G. Fairweather, and K. S. Walter. 1996. *The Genus Rhododendron: Its Classification and Synonymy.* Royal Botanic Garden Edinburgh.

Chamberlain, D. F., and S. J. Rae. 1990. A revision of *Rhododendron,* IV: subgenus *Tsutsusi. Edinburgh Botanical Journal* 47: 89–203.

Cooper, R. E., A. O. Curle, and W. S. Fair. 1935. *George Forrest.* Edinburgh: Scottish Rock Garden Club.

Cowan, J. M. 1940. Rhododendrons of the Sanguineum Alliance. *Notes from the Royal Botanic Garden Edinburgh* 20: 55–91.

Cowan, J. M. 1949. A survey of the genus *Rhododendron. Rhododendron Yearbook* (Royal Horticultural Society) 4: 29–58.

Cowan, J. M. 1950. *The Rhododendron Leaf: A Study of the Epidermal Appendages.* Edinburgh: Oliver and Boyd.

Cowan, J. M., ed. 1952. *The Journeys and Plant Introductions of George Forrest.* London: Oxford University Press.

Cowan, J. M., and H. H. Davidian. 1947. The Anthopogon Alliance. *Rhododendron Yearbook* (Royal Horticultural Society) 2: 64–86.

Cowan, J. M., and H. H. Davidian. 1948. A review of rhododendrons in their series, II: the Boothii, Glaucum, Lepidotum Alliance. *Rhododendron Yearbook* (Royal Horticultural Society) 3: 51–111.

Cowan, J. M., and H. H. Davidian. 1949. A review of rhododendrons in their series, III: the *Campanulatum* and *Fulvum* series. *Rhododendron Yearbook* (Royal Horticultural Society) 4: 159–182.

Cowan, J. M., and H. H. Davidian. 1951. A review of rhododendrons in their series, IV: the *Thomsonii* series. *Rhododendron Yearbook* (Royal Horticultural Society) 6: 116–183.

Cowan, J. M., and H. H. Davidian. 1955. A review of rhododendrons in their series, VI: the *Lacteum* series. *Rhododendron and Camellia Yearbook* (Royal Horticultural Society) 10: 122–159.

Cox, E. H. M. 1930. *The Plant Introductions of Reginald Farrer.* London: New Flora and Silva.

Cox, K., K. S. Junior, and I. Baker, eds. 2001. *Frank Kingdon-Ward's* Riddle of the Tsangpo Gorges: *Retracing the Epic Journey of 1924–25 in South-East Tibet.* Woodbridge, Suffolk: Antique Collectors' Club.

Cox, P. A., and K. N. E. Cox. 1997. *The Encyclopedia of Rhododendron Species.* Perth: Glendoick Press.

Cullen, J. 1980a. *Rhododendron* taxonomy and nomenclature. In *Contributions Towards a Classification of Rhododendron.* Ed. J. Luteyn. Proceedings of the International Rhododendron Conference, New York. 27–38.

Cullen, J. 1980b. A revision of *Rhododendron,* I: subgenus *Rhododendron* sections *Rhododendron* and *Pogonanthum. Notes from the Royal Botanic Garden Edinburgh* 39: 1–207.

Cullen, J. 1996. The importance of the herbarium. In *The Rhododendron Story: 200 Years of*

Plant Hunting and Garden Cultivation. Ed. C. Postan. London: Royal Horticultural Society. 38–48.

Davidian, H. H. 1954. A review of rhododendrons in their series, V: the *Campylogynum* and *Saluenense* series. *Rhododendron Yearbook* (Royal Horticultural Society) 8: 75–98.

Davidian, H. H. 1982–1995. *The Rhododendron Species.* 4 vols. Portland, Oregon: Timber Press.

Doleshy, F. 1968. Distribution and ecology of certain Japanese rhododendrons: a progress report. *Quarterly Bulletin of the American Rhododendron Society* 22: 145–159.

Duncan, W. H., and T. M. Pullen. 1962. Lepidote rhododendrons of the southeastern United States. *Brittonia:* 14: 290–298.

Evans, D., K. H. Kane, B. A. Knights, and V. B. Math. 1980. Chemical taxonomy in the genus *Rhododendron.* In *Contributions Towards a Classification of Rhododendron.* Ed. J. Luteyn. Proceedings of the International Rhododendron Conference, New York. 187–246.

Evans, D., B. A. Knights, and V. B. Math. 1975. Steryl acetates in *Rhododendron* waxes. *Phytochemistry* 14: 2453–2454.

Evans, D., B. A. Knights, V. B. Math, and A. L. Ritchie. 1975. Diketones in *Rhododendron* waxes. *Phytochemistry* 14: 2441–2451.

Feng, G., ed. 1988–1999. *Rhododendrons of China.* 3 vols. Beijing: Science Press.

Fletcher, H. R. 1952. *The International Rhododendron Register.* London: Royal Horticultural Society.

Fletcher, H. R. 1975. *A Quest of Flower: The Plant Exploration of Frank Ludlow and Charles Sherriff.* Edinburgh University Press.

Forrest, M. 1996. Hooker's rhododendrons: their distribution and survival. In *The Rhododendron Story: 200 Years of Plant Hunting and Garden Cultivation.* Ed. C. Postan. London: Royal Horticultural Society. 55–70.

Franchet, A. 1883, 1889. *Plantae Davidianae.* 2 parts. Paris.

Franchet, A. 1889–1890. *Plantae Delavayanae.* 2 parts. Paris.

Harborne, J. B. 1980. Flavonoid pigments as both taxonomic and phyletic markers in the genus *Rhododendron.* In *Contributions Towards a Classification of Rhododendron.* Ed. J. Luteyn. Proceedings of the International Rhododendron Conference, New York. 145–162.

Harborne, J. B., and C. A. Williams. 1969. A leaf survey of flavonoids and simple phenols in the genus *Rhododendron. Phytochemistry* 10: 2727–2744.

Hayes, S., J. Keenan, and J. M. Cowan. 1951. A survey of the anatomy of the *Rhododendron* leaf in relation to the taxonomy of the genus. *Notes from the Royal Botanic Garden Edinburgh* 21: 1–34.

Hedegaard, J. 1980a. Morphological studies in the genus *Rhododendron.* In *Contributions Towards a Classification of Rhododendron.* Ed. J. Luteyn. Proceedings of the International Rhododendron Conference, New York. 117–144.

Hedegaard, J. 1980b. *Morphological Studies in the Genus Rhododendron: Dealing with Seeds, Fruits, and Seedlings and Their Associated Hairs.* 2 vols. Copenhagen: GEC Gads.

Hooker, J. D. 1849, 1851. *Rhododendrons of the Sikkim Himalaya.* London.

Hutchinson, J. 1919. A revision of the *Maddenii* series of the genus *Rhododendron*. *Notes from the Royal Botanic Garden Edinburgh* 12: 1–84.

Judd, W. S., and K. Kron. 1995. A revision of *Rhododendron*, VI: subgenus *Pentanthera* (sections *Sciadorhodion*, *Rhodora*, and *Viscidula*). *Edinburgh Botanical Journal* 52: 1–54.

King, B. 1980. The systematic implications of flavonoids in *Rhododendron* subgenus *Pentanthera*. In *Contributions Towards a Classification of Rhododendron*. Ed. J. Luteyn. Proceedings of the International Rhododendron Conference, New York. 163–188.

Kingdon-Ward, F. 1935. *Rhododendron* seeds, with special reference to their classification. *Journal of Botany* 73: 241–247.

Kingdon-Ward, F. 1949. *Rhododendrons*. London: Latimer House.

Kneller, M. 1995. *The Book of Rhododendrons*. Newton Abbot: David and Charles.

Kron, K. A. 1993. A revision of *Rhododendron*, V: section *Pentanthera*. *Edinburgh Botanical Journal* 50: 249–364.

Krüssmann, G. 1984. *Manual of Cultivated Broad-leaved Trees and Shrubs*. 4 vols. Trans. K. Beckett. Newton Abbot: David and Charles.

Leach, D. G. 1962. *Rhododendrons of the World*. London: G. Allen and Unwin.

Lennon, J. M. 1985. J. M. Delavay in Yunnan and his relationship with David, Franchet, and others. *Rhododendrons with Camellias and Magnolias* (Royal Horticultural Society): 20–25.

Leslie, A. c. 2003. *Rhododendron* registration and the preparation of a new register. In *Rhododendrons in Horticulture and Science*. Eds. G. C. Argent and M. McFarlane. Royal Botanic Garden Edinburgh. 61–65.

McLean, B. 1997. *A Pioneering Plantsman: A. K. Bulley and the Great Plant Hunters*. London: HMSO.

McLean, B. 2004a. George Forrest. *The Garden* 129: 260–263.

McLean, B. 2004b. *George Forrest*. Woodbridge, Suffolk: Antique Collectors' Club.

Moser, E. 1991. *Rhododendron: Wildarten und Hybriden*. Radebeul, Germany: Neumann Verlag.

Palser, B. F., Philipson, W. R., and Philipson, M. N. 1985. The ovary, ovule, and megagametophyte in *Rhododendron*. *Notes from the Royal Botanic Garden Edinburgh* 43: 133–160.

Philipson, M. N. 1970. Cotyledons and the taxonomy of *Rhododendron*. *Notes from the Royal Botanic Garden Edinburgh* 30: 55–77.

Philipson, M. N. 1980. Cotyledons and *Rhododendron* classification. In *Contributions Towards a Classification of Rhododendron*. Ed. J. Luteyn. Proceedings of the International Rhododendron Conference, New York. 75–88.

Philipson, M. N. 1985. The *Rhododendron* nectary. *Notes from the Royal Botanic Garden Edinburgh* 43: 117–131.

Philipson, W. R. 1980. Problems in the classification of the *Azalea* complex. In *Contributions Towards a Classification of Rhododendron*. Ed. J. Luteyn. Proceedings of the International Rhododendron Conference, New York. 53–62.

Philipson, W. R. 1985. Shoot morphology in *Rhododendron*. *Notes from the Royal Botanic Garden Edinburgh* 43: 161–171.

Philipson, W. R., and M. N. Philipson. 1968. Diverse nodal types in *Rhododendron*. *Journal of the Arnold Arboretum* 49: 193–217.

Philipson, W. R., and M. N. Philipson. 1974. A history of *Rhododendron* classification. *Notes from the Royal Botanic Garden Edinburgh* 32: 223–238.

Philipson, W. R., and M. N. Philipson. 1975. A revision of *Rhododendron* section *Lapponica*. *Notes from the Royal Botanic Garden Edinburgh* 34: 1–72.

Philipson W. R., and M. N. Philipson. 1986. A revision of *Rhododendron*, III: subgenera *Azaleastrum*, *Mumeazalea*, *Candidastrum*, and *Therorhodion*. *Notes from the Royal Botanic Garden Edinburgh* 44: 1–24.

Philipson, W. R., and M. N. Philipson. 1996. The taxonomy of the genus: a history. In *The Rhododendron Story: 200 Years of Plant Hunting and Garden Cultivation*. Ed. C. Postan. London: Royal Horticultural Society. 22–37.

Pojarkova, A. L. 1952. *Rhododendron*. In *Flora SSSR*, vol. 18. Ed. V. N. Komarov. Moscow. 722.

Reynolds, T., S. M. Smith, and P. A. Thompson. 1969. A chromatographic survey of anthocyanin types in the genus *Rhododendron*. *Kew Bulletin* 23: 413–437.

Rhododendron Society Notes. 1924. *Rhododendron* series. *Rhododendron Society Notes* 2: 215–227.

Rhododendron Society Notes. 1928. List of *Rhododendron* species [in their series]. *Rhododendron Society Notes* 3: 209–219.

Royal Horticultural Society. 1946–1956. *Rhododendron Yearbook* 1–10.

Royal Horticultural Society. 1947–1997. *The Rhododendron Handbook*.

Royal Horticultural Society. 1957–1971. *Rhododendron and Camellia Yearbook* 11–25.

Royal Horticultural Society. 1972–2003. *Rhododendrons with Camellias and Magnolias* 26–54, some unnumbered.

Schweinfurth, U., and H. Schweinfurth-Marby. 1975. *Exploration in the Eastern Himalayas and the River Gorge Country of Southeastern Tibet: Francis (Frank) Kingdon-Ward (1885–1958): an annotated bibliography with a map of the area of his expeditions*. Wiesbaden, Germany: Steiner.

Seithe, A. 1960. Die Haarformen der Gattung *Rhododendron* L. und die Möglichkeit ihrer taxonomische Verwertung. *Botaniche Jahrbücher* 79: 297–393.

Seithe, A. 1980. *Rhododendron* hairs and taxonomy. In *Contributions Towards a Classification of Rhododendron*. Ed. J. Luteyn. Proceedings of the International Rhododendron Conference, New York. 89–116.

Sinclair, J. 1937. The *Rhododendron* bud and its relation to the taxonomy of the genus. *Notes from the Royal Botanic Garden Edinburgh* 19: 267–271.

Sleumer, H. 1949. Ein System der Gattung *Rhododendron* (A system of the genus *Rhododendron*). *Botanische Jahrbücher* 74: 511–553. Trans. H. F. Becker, 1980, in *Contributions Towards a Classification of Rhododendron*. Ed. J. Luteyn. Proceedings of the International Rhododendron Conference, New York. 1–18.

Sleumer, H. 1956. The genus *Rhododendron* in Indochina and Siam. *Blumea* (supplement) 4: 40–47.

Sleumer, H. 1968. *Rhododendron*. *Flora Malesiana* 1, 6: 474–668.

Sleumer, H. 1980. Past and present taxonomic systems of *Rhododendron* based on macromorphological characters. In *Contributions Towards a Classification of Rhododendron*. Ed. J. Luteyn. Proceedings of the International Rhododendron Conference, New York. 19–26.

Spethmann, W. 1979. *Untersuchungen über das Zustandekommen der Blütenfarbe bei Rhododendron Mitteilungen der Deutschen Dendrologischen Gesellschaft* 71: 125–143.

Spethmann, W. 1980a. *Infragenerische Gliederung der Gattung Rhododendron unter Berücksichtigung der flavonoiden und carotinoiden Blüteninhaltsstoffe und der Entstehung der Blütenfarben.* Doctoral dissertation, Hamburg University.

Spethmann, W. 1980b. Flavonoids and carotenoids of *Rhododendron* flowers. In *Contributions Towards a Classification of Rhododendron*. Ed. J. Luteyn. Proceedings of the International Rhododendron Conference, New York. 247–276.

Spethmann, W., M. Oetting, and B. Walter. 1992, 1996. *Rhododendron Bibliography*. German Rhododendron Society. University of Hanover.

Stevenson, J. B., ed. 1930. *The Species of Rhododendron*. London: Rhododendron Society.

Sutton, S. B. 1974. *In China's Border Provinces: The Turbulent Career of Joseph Rock, Botanist-Explorer.* New York: Hastings House.

Tagg, H. F. 1928. Notes on certain changes in the tentative listing of rhododendrons in their series in so far as these changes concern the elepidote series. *Rhododendron Society Notes* 3: 220–224. See also *Rhododendron Society Notes* 1928.

Williams, E. G., J. L. Rouse, and R. B. Knox. 1985. Barriers to sexual compatibility in *Rhododendron*. *Notes from the Royal Botanic Garden Edinburgh* 43: 81–98.

Wilson, E. H. 1913. *A Naturalist in Western China*. 2 vols. London: Methuen.

Wilson, E. H. 1922. Rhododendrons of northeast Asia. *Rhododendron Society Notes* 2: 93–106.

Wilson, E. H. 1923. The rhododendrons of C. Hupeh. *Rhododendron Society Notes* 2: 160–174.

Wilson, E. H. 1925. Rhododendrons of eastern China. *Rhododendron Society Notes* 3: 18–28.

Wilson, E. H., and A. Rehder. 1921. *A Monograph of Azaleas:* Rhododendron *subgenus* Anthodendron. Cambridge, Massachusetts: University Press.

Conversion Tables

INCHES	CM
1/10	0.3
1/6	0.4
1/4	0.6
1/3	0.8
1/2	1.3
3/4	1.9
1	2.5
2	5.1
3	7.6
4	10
5	13
6	15
7	18
8	20
9	23
10	25
20	51
30	76
40	100
50	130
60	150
70	180
80	200
90	230
100	250

FEET	M
1	0.3
2	0.6
3	0.9
4	1.2
5	1.5
6	1.8
7	2.1
8	2.4
9	2.7
10	3
20	6
30	9
40	12
50	15
60	18
70	21
80	24
90	27
100	30
200	60
300	90
400	120
500	150
600	180
700	210

FEET	M
800	240
900	270
1,000	300
2,000	610
3,000	910
4,000	1,200
5,000	1,500
6,000	1,800
7,000	2,100
8,000	2,400
9,000	2,700
10,000	3,000
15,000	4,600

Index to Taxa

Boldfaced numbers are pages with illustrations.